Getting StartED with Google Apps

Paul Darbyshire

Adam Darbyshire

friendsof

an Apress® company

GETTING STARTED with Google Apps

Copyright © 2010 by Paul Darbyshire and Adam Darbyshire

ISBN-13 (pbk): 978-1-4302-2665-9

ISBN-13 (electronic): 978-1-4302-2666-6

Printed and bound in the United States of America 9 8 7 6 5 4 3 2 1

Distributed to the book trade worldwide by Springer-Verlag New York, Inc., 233 Spring Street, 6th Floor, New York, NY 10013. Phone 1-800-SPRINGER, fax 201-348-4505, e-mail orders-ny@springer-sbm.com, or visit www.springeronline.com.

For information on translations, please e-mail rights@apress.com, or visit www.apress.com.

Apress and friends of ED books may be purchased in bulk for academic, corporate, or promotional use. eBook versions and licenses are also available for most titles. For more information, reference our Special Bulk Sales–eBook Licensing web page at www.apress.com/info/bulksales.

The source code for this book is available to readers at www.apress.com. You will need to answer questions pertaining to this book in order to successfully download the code.

Credits

President and Publisher:
Paul Manning

Lead Editor:
Douglas Pundick

Technical Reviewer:
Kunal Mittal

Editorial Board:
Clay Andres, Steve Anglin, Mark Beckner, Ewan Buckingham, Gary Cornell, Jonathan Gennick, Jonathan Hassell, Michelle Lowman, Matthew Moodie, Duncan Parkes, Jeffrey Pepper, Frank Pohlmann, Douglas Pundick, Ben Renow-Clarke, Dominic Shakeshaft, Matt Wade, Tom Welsh

Coordinating Editor:
Laurin Becker

Copy Editor:
Chris Marcheso; Patrick Meader; Andy Rosenthal

Compositors:
MacPS, LLC

Indexers:
Toma Mulligan

Artist:
April Milne

Cover Designer:
Anna Ishchenko

I would like to dedicate this book first to the girls in my life. To my wife Kay, who has yet again put up with another of my projects spanning many months; and who, as always, has given her full support. I can now take you to the movies again. Also, to my beautiful daughter, Mai-Ling, whose bright personality has often been a source of inspiration over the last few years. She has let daddy and her brother work on the book and is quite excited that her name will appear in it. We can now spend more time doing daddy-daughter stuff.

I'd like to also mention my son Adam, my co-author. It's not often that a father and son get to bond all over again after they both grow up, over late-night coffee sessions discussing chapter titles and structures. I suppose, in really ancient times, we might have gone out and hunted a mammoth together. This book is our mammoth.

Paul

To everyone I've annoyed while writing this book... sorry.

Adam

Contents at a Glance

Contents at a Glance iv

Contents v

About the Authors xx

About the Technical Reviewer xxi

Acknowledgments xxii

Introduction xxiii

Chapter 1: Getting Started with Chrome 1

Chapter 2: Gmail 45

Chapter 3: Introduction to Google Docs 109

Chapter 4: Google Docs - Document 139

Chapter 5: Google Docs - Spreadsheets 207

Chapter 6: Google Docs - Presentations 301

Chapter 7: Forms 357

Chapter 8: Calendar 379

Chapter 9: Google Sites 427

Chapter 10: Google Maps 489

Chapter 11: Google Talk 517

Chapter 12: Blogger 541

Chapter 13: Integrating Google Apps 583

Index 617

Contents

Contents at a Glance iv

Contents v

About the Authors xx

About the Technical Reviewer xxi

Acknowledgments xxii

Introduction xxiii

Chapter 1: Getting Started with Chrome 1

    Getting and Installing Chrome 2

    Surfing with Chrome 4

        New Tabs and Windows 6

        Surfing Incognito 8

    Configuring Chrome 9

        Setting the Home Page 9

        Security 10

        Privacy 14

    Controlling What You See 18

        Text Size 18

        Encoding 19

        Fonts and Languages 20

        Developer Viewing 23

        Bookmark Toolbar 24

        Full Screen 25

        Search Field 25

    Managing Bookmarks 26

        Creating a New Bookmark 26

        Selecting a Bookmark 29

Using the Bookmark Manager 31

Themes 33

Chrome Plug-ins 35

Downloading 39

Internet Security 40

Security Certificates 41

Malware sites.. 42

Phishing 42

Best Practices 43

Summary... 44

Chapter 2: Gmail 45

Creating a Gmail Account... 46

Basic E-mail Functions... 49

Composing and Sending Mail... 50

Reading Mail.. 57

Replying to E-mails.. 60

Conversation View... 62

Selecting e-mails 65

Sent Messages 65

Draft Messages 67

Deleting Messages 68

Archiving Mail.. 68

Starred Mail 70

Working with Labels 72

Dealing with Spam 76

Managing Contacts 78

Creating a List of Tasks 84

Your Gmail Preferences 91

General Settings 92

Importing from Other Accounts 94

Using Different E-mail Addresses 97

Using Outlook and Other E-mail Programs with Gmail.....................100

Using Filters to Control Where Your E-mail Goes............................102

Using Themes to Change How Gmail Looks...................................105

Synchronizing Gmail with Your Mobile Phone...........................106

Summary...106

Chapter 3: Introduction to Google Docs 109

Why Use Google Documents? 109

Is My Data Secure? 110

Starting Google Docs...112

Creating Documents 114

Sharing Documents...115

Concurrent Editing 121

Working with Folders 123

Deleting and Renaming Documents.............................127

Using the Trash Folder......................................127

Deleting a Shared File 129

Exporting and Importing Documents 130

Publishing Documents 135

Hiding Documents 136

Changing Owners 137

Summary..137

Chapter 4: Google Docs - Document............................. 139

Elements of the Screen...140

Menu Bar 141

Tool bar 141

Getting Help 142

Working with Documents 143

    Saving and Closing Documents 144

    Renaming a Document 146

    Opening Documents 146

    Uploading Documents 147

    Downloading Your Document to Your Computer 149

    Printing Documents 151

Entering and Manipulating Text 157

    View as You Type 158

    Moving Around and Editing Text 159

    Selecting Text 160

    Cutting and Pasting Text 161

    Moving Text with Drag and Drop 162

Formatting Text 162

    Bold, Italic, and Underline 162

    Styles 163

    Font 164

    Size 165

    Color 165

    Document Settings 167

    Text Alignment 168

    Line Spacing 169

    Modifying the Text Indent and Margin Width 170

Working with Images 171

    Obtaining Images 171

    Inserting Images 172

    Image Options 175

Inserting Page Breaks, Headers, and Footers 178

Page Breaks 178

Headers and Footers 179

Inserting a Table of Contents 181

Working with Lists and Bullets 183

Tables 185

Creating Tables 185

Changing Table Properties 188

Resizing Rows and Columns 189

Borders 191

Formatting Cells 192

Inserting and Deleting Rows and Columns 193

Document Proofing 194

Spell Checking 194

Word Lookup 196

Translating Your Document 197

Footnotes 198

Working with Document Revisions 199

Inserting Comments 199

Document Revisions 200

Comparing Revisions 203

A Work Around 204

Summary 204

Chapter 5: Google Docs – Spreadsheets 207

Elements of the Spreadsheets Space 209

Menubar 209

Toolbar 210

Formula Bar 210

The Sort Bar 211

Getting Help 211

Document Functions 213

    Saving and Closing Documents 213

    Opening Documents 215

    Downloading Your Document 216

    Printing Spreadsheets 218

    Selecting Spreadsheet Settings 219

Basic Spreadsheet Usage 219

    Types of Cells 220

    Entering and Editing Data 221

    Moving Between Cells 222

    Cell References 223

    Cell Ranges 223

    Selecting Cells 224

    Cutting and Pasting Cells 224

    Text Display and Merging Cells 225

    Deleting Cell Contents 227

    Inserting Rows and Columns 228

    Deleting Rows and Columns 230

Formatting Cells 231

    Bold, Italic, and Underline 232

    Font 232

    Size 233

    Text Color and Cell Background 234

    Formatting Numeric and Date Types 236

    Date Picker 242

    Resizing Cells 243

Simple Formulas 244

    Elements of a Formula 245

    Creating and Copying Simple Formulas 246

Building Simple Formulas.. 249

Using Cell Ranges in Formulas 251

Quick Sum 252

Using Percentages 253

Editing a Cell's Formula 254

Using More Complex Functions 254

Building More Complex Spreadsheets 261

Working with Multiple Sheets.. 261

Using Cell References between Worksheets...................... 262

Absolute Cell Referencing.. 263

Using Named Ranges 265

Sheet Protection... 267

Data Validation 269

Conditional Formatting 272

Freezing Rows and Columns 275

Using Gadgets 280

Inserting a Chart 284

Chart Elements 285

Limitations to Spreadsheets' Charting 287

Inserting a Pie Chart 288

Positioning, Resizing and Editing a Chart......................... 291

Sorting a Column 292

Using More Advanced Formulas 294

Using the IF Function for Conditional Calculations............. 294

Using VLOOKUP 296

Using Google Functions 297

Summary.. 300

Chapter 6: Google Docs - Presentations 301

Elements of the Presentations Workspace 302

Menubar 303

Toolbar 304

Getting Help 305

Understanding Basic Presentation Functions 306

Saving and Closing Presentations 306

Renaming a Presentation 308

Opening Presentations 308

Uploading Existing Presentations 309

Downloading Your Presentation to Your Computer 311

Printing Presentations 313

Creating Your First Presentation 314

Inserting and Deleting Slides 316

Using Layouts 317

Adding Text to a Presentation 319

Manipulating the Text Area 321

Manipulating Text 322

Re-ordering Slides 332

Using Advanced Features 334

Using Images 334

Resizing Images 336

Re-ordering Objects 338

Adding Shapes 340

Drawing Objects 340

Using Tables 343

Adding Video 346

Using Speaker Notes 349

Backgrounds and Themes 350

Delivering Your Presentation 353

Presenting Your Slide Show 353

Best Practices for Creating Slides 354

Summary 356

Chapter 7: Forms **357**

Why do I need Forms? 357

Creating a form 358

Types of questions 359

    Text 361

    Paragraph text 362

    Multiple Choice 363

    Check Boxes 364

    List 365

    Scale 366

    Grid 367

Adding Questions 369

Adding Sections and Page Breaks 369

Advanced Use of Multiple Choice Questions 371

Moving Items 372

Publishing Your Form 372

Viewing results 374

Editing forms 376

Deleting forms from Spreadsheets 377

Themes 377

Summary 378

Chapter 8: Calendar **379**

Creating a New Calendar 379

    Elements of the Screen 381

    Calendar Views 383

Creating Events 388

Clicking to Add Events 393

Quick Add 394

Finding, Viewing and Modifying Events 397

Recurring Events 403

Repeating Events with Quick Add 406

Calendar Settings 406

Inviting Other People 413

Receiving Invitations 414

Creating and Deleting Calendars.. 417

Why Use Multiple Calendars? 419

Sharing Calendars 420

Accessing Your Calendar from Outlook and Other Applications 423

Receiving Notifications on Your Mobile Phone............................ 423

Synchronizing Google Calendar with Your Mobile Phone................. 425

Summary... 425

Chapter 9: Google Sites 427

Creating a Site.. 429

Choosing a Theme 430

Site Name and URL 430

Editing a Site... 432

Getting Help... 434

Editing a Page... 435

Changing Text... 438

Adding Links 444

Adding Images... 447

Using Tables 450

Using Layouts.. 452

Inserting Different Objects into Your Web Pages............................ 454

Viewing and Editing the HTML Source... 463

Editing the Side Bar 463

Creating New Pages 466

Deleting Pages 475

Managing Your Site... 476

Changing the Theme 476

Customizing the Site Layout 476

Displaying the Site on Your Own Domain 478

Using Google AdSense... 478

Sharing 480

Revision History 482

Backing up your site... 485

Limitations on Google Sites.. 486

Web Site Tips 487

Summary.. 488

Chapter 10: Google Maps **489**

Panning and Zooming Maps 489

Changing the Default location 492

Searching for a Business or Location 493

Searching Near a Location 495

Reviewing Businesses 496

Filtering Search results 499

Search by Pointing to a Location.. 500

Checking Traffic Conditions 502

Getting Directions.. 504

Viewing the details of a route... 506

Using Overlays to Show Extra Information 507

Using Different Views... 510

Exploring with Street View 512

Summary..515

Chapter 11: Google Talk 517

Getting Talk..517

Getting Started...518

Adding Contacts 519

Responding to a Friend request...521

Warnings...521

Communicating with Contacts via IM 522

Personalizing Google Talk with Display Pictures 524

Further Interaction with your Contacts....................................525

    Sending Files 526

    Receiving Files 526

Communicating with Contacts via Voice...................................527

    Blocking contacts 529

    Unblocking Contacts 530

    Viewing your Chat History..531

    Off the record...532

Setting your Preferences...533

    Logging 535

    Orkut 535

    Notification..536

    Audio 536

    Appearance..538

Summary...540

Chapter 12: Blogger 541

Creating a Blog 542

Dashboard 546

Editing Your Profile 547

Privacy 548

Identity.. 549

Creating a New Post 549

Placing Images in Your Blog Posts...................... 552

Placing Videos in Your Blog Posts 554

Inserting Links into Your Posts 555

Editing Existing and Draft Posts........................... 555

Adding Web Pages to Your Blog 557

Editing, Viewing, and Deleting Your Pages................. 559

Blogging with Caution to Limit Your Liability............. 560

Commenting on Blogs....................................... 560

Making Comments on Other People's Blogs 560

Comments on Your Blog 561

Moderating Comments on Your Blog...................... 562

Viewing the Reading List................................... 563

Following Other Blogs.................................... 563

Blogger Buzz... 565

Blogs of Note 565

Setting Your Preferences................................... 565

Basic Settings 566

Changing the Location of Your Blog 568

Changing the Formatting Settings 569

Changing Your Blog's Comment Settings................. 570

Automatically Archiving Your Older Posts 572

Granting Permissions to Your Blog 572

Changing the Layout of Your Blog 573

Customizing Page Elements.............................. 573

Customizing Fonts and Colors 574

Choosing a New Template for Your Blog................. 575

Making Money from Your Blog 576

    Controlling your ads.. 577

    Amazon Associates 578

Blogging with E-mail 579

Blogging with Your Mobile Phone 580

Creating Multiple Blogs... 581

Using Your Google Account with OpenID 581

Marketing Your Blog 582

Summary.. 582

Chapter 13: Integrating Google Apps............................ 583

Using Sites to Integrate Google Apps.. 584

    Google Document.. 584

    Google Spreadsheets 587

    Google Forms.. 591

    Google Presentations 592

    Google Maps 594

    Google Calendar 594

Using iGoogle to Integrate Google Apps 596

    Adding and Deleting Gadgets 598

    Docs Gadget 600

    Gmail Gadget 601

    Calendar Gadget.. 603

    Maps Gadget.. 605

    Blogger Gadget 606

Cross Integration of Google Apps 608

The Google Dashboard.. 609

Google Apps and Non-Google Software 611

    Google Apps Sync for Microsoft Outlook 612

    Google Apps Widgets for Mac, Vista, and Windows 7 612

Google Apps and Microsoft Office.. 613

Google Apps and WS02... 614

Chrome Extensions 614

Backup utilities 616

Summary..616

Index.. **617**

About the Authors

Paul Darbyshire

Paul has been lecturing, first within the School of Information Systems, then within the School of Management and Information Systems at Victoria University, Melbourne, Australia, for more than 23 years. Paul worked as a software programmer, then as an analyst/programmer for a number of firms, before becoming an academic at Victoria University. Paul graduated with a BSc (Hons) in pure mathematics from Monash University in 1980, then with a Graduate qualification in Computer Science at Melbourne University in 1984. Paul also graduated with a Masters by research in Engineering (software) in 1998, and he is currently working his way towards his PhD. Since becoming an academic, Paul has developed a keen interest in a number of areas, including AI, simulation, techniques, teaching programming, and, in particular, on-line learning. Paul has also been teaching on-line for the Department of Computer Science at University of Liverpool through the school's on-line MSc since 1999. Paul has authored and co-authored a number of academic conference papers, journal articles, and chapters on various topics; he is also a member of the ACM.

When he is not teaching, studying, or writing, Paul enjoys spending time with his family, drinking lattes, and watching the world go by at his favorite cafe in the local shopping mall. Additionally, he likes traveling to warm places.

Adam Darbyshire

Adam is a Licensed Investigator who has enjoyed trying out many different career paths. Adam has a student pilot's license, and he is an experienced computer technician who specializes in computer security. Adam has a BSc from Victoria University, and he is currently studying for a Masters in eForensics and Enterprise Security at Melbourne University. Adam runs a business that provides services to the legal industry and specializes in electronic process service over mediums such as e-mail or Facebook.

About the Technical Reviewer

 **Kunal Mittal** serves as an Executive Director of Technology at Sony Pictures Entertainment, where he is responsible for the SOA, Identity Management, and Content Management programs. He provides a centralized engineering service to different lines of business, and he leads efforts to introduce new platforms and technologies into the Sony Pictures Enterprise IT environment.

Kunal is an entrepreneur who helps startups defining their technology strategy, product roadmap, and development plans. With his strong relations with several development partners worldwide, he is able to help startups and even large companies build appropriate development partnerships. He generally works in an Advisor or Consulting CTO capacity, and he serves actively in the Project Management and Technical Architect functions.

He has authored and edited several books and articles on J2EE, cloud computing, and mobile technologies. He holds a Master's degree in Software Engineering and is an instrument-rated private pilot.

Acknowledgments

There are a number of people we are indebted to and need to thank for the initial ideas and help in getting this book off the ground and to completion.

We would like to begin by thanking Steve Anglin at Apress for steering us from our initial proposal towards the topic of this book. We would also like to thank Douglas Pundick for his encouraging comments and reviews, and the Technical Reviewer, Kunal Mittal, for his excellent feedback, which has helped shaped this book into a much better form. We would also like to thank the numerous copy editors who have provided valuable edits and comments to improve readability. Also, many thanks to Laurin Becker, Coordinating Editor at Apress, for helping to keep it together, especially in the last few weeks of the project. Additionally we would like to thank all the other people at Apress who have helped in getting this project to the stage it is at now.

We cannot of course forget Google for creating the excellent applications—the subject matter of this book.

Lastly, thanks to Kay and Mai-Ling; you know what for.

Paul Darbyshire

Lecturer, Victoria University

Adam Darbyshire

Director, eNinja Pty. Ltd.

Introduction

Just about everyone has heard of Google. Google began life as a search engine, and this probably remains one of the most visible aspects of Google on the Web. The Search Engine Watch still ranks Google at number one, with its search engine accounting for well over 60% of all Internet searches. However, as most people are aware, Google is much more than a search engine. Google also builds web applications. Today we have a much more mobile workforce, and the Internet is blurring the lines between the traditional division of office and home hours. People can increasingly choose when they want to work, and where. This means that they often want to run the same applications on their home computers that they do at the office. Additionally, with a more mobile workforce, people are more likely to want to access their work from remote locations.

Google has developed a number of web-based applications that have collectively become known as Google Apps (short for applications). These applications provide most of the functionality we have associated with the more traditional office suite applications we buy and install on our office or home computer. Google Apps have a number of advantages over the traditional office suite applications—in particular, Google Apps now take us into the realm of *cloud computing*.

Cloud Computing

The term *cloud computing* is a fuzzy thing, as there are almost as many definitions as there are papers on the term. However, cloud computing represents an evolution and a convergence of a number of existing key concepts and technologies[1], such as the Internet, distributed application design, and web services. Simply put, cloud computing essentially involves utilizing the Internet to access software and services that you would traditionally access from your own local computer. While the concept is simple, the advantages and benefits of the cloud computing concept are far reaching.

---

[1] Architectural Strategies for Cloud Computing, Oracle white paper in Enterprise Architecture, Oracle, 2009 http://www.oracle.com/technology/architect/entarch/pdf/architectural_ strategies_for_cloud_computing.pdf

"The rise of the cloud is more than just another platform shift that gets geeks excited. It will undoubtedly transform the IT industry, but it will also profoundly change the way people work and companies operate."

The Economist, *"Let it Rise"* 10/23/2008

Cloud computing is a paradigm shift away from the traditional computing paradigm we are all used to. Figure 0-1 depicts the traditional computing paradigm for most home and office users. In this paradigm, we operate a computer that is connected to the Internet. We access the Internet through a web browser (which browser doesn't matter at this stage), and we load applications such as our word processing, spreadsheet, and other applications from our computer. These applications are purchased and loaded onto our office or home computer; and as we use the applications and create various documents, we save them to our own local hard drive, USB key, or other attached device. In some companies, we may save files on a shared network drive, but we are all familiar with this setup or paradigm.

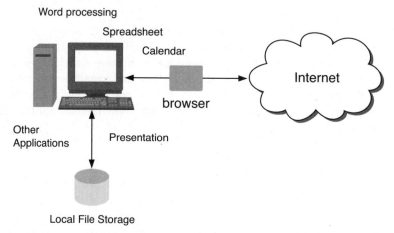

Figure 0-1. The traditional computing paradigm

The cloud computing paradigm is vastly different. Figure 0-2 shows a depiction of the cloud computing paradigm that is available to you via Google Apps. In cloud computing, software (and other traditional services such as file storage and retrieval) is viewed as a service to be accessed from the Internet. That is, instead of running software from your local computer, you run it from the Internet through your web browser. Your documents are also stored in the cloud.

"In this architecture, the data is mostly resident on servers 'somewhere on the Internet' and the application runs on both the 'cloud servers' and the user's browser."

Eric Schmidt in "*Information Factories*" by G. Gilder, *WIRED*, October 2006

The term *cloud* in cloud computing comes from the fact that the Internet is often depicted as a cloud shape in diagrams (see Figures 0-1 and 0-2). In fact, in many ways, the term *cloud computing* can almost be thought of as a metaphor for the Web.

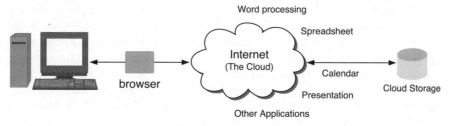

Figure 0-2. The cloud computing paradigm

Many of the advantages of cloud computing are not immediately obvious, but its advantages can include huge costs savings for business cost savings for the home user, as well. You don't need to purchase software any more (Google Apps software is free for the individual user, but access to other cloud-based software may require a subscription). Since you access your software from the Internet, it is not loaded on your local computer. The latest updates can be pushed out to all users without physical distribution. From a business perspective, being able to push the latest version of your app to your clients all at the same time represents a huge advantage.

NotED

Google Apps software is free of charge for individual users.

We mentioned that in cloud computing your files are stored in the cloud and not on your local computer. This is often a difficult thing for people to come to terms with; and at its heart, is often a stumbling block for people making the paradigm switch to cloud computing. The issue is not just the fact that files are stored in the cloud, but that this approach is in essence a "*transfer of control*." When using the traditional paradigm, you control where your files are stored, whether they are backed-up, and so on. You also control the applications, what is installed, what is updated, and when it is updated. When you adopt the cloud-computing paradigm, you are transferring the control of these aspects of computing to the cloud. More specifically, you are transferring them to the service provider in the cloud. It is this fundamental transfer of control that often becomes the stumbling block of adopting the cloud-computing paradigm. The paradigm is relatively new, and this does not help. Yet, if you are willing to accept the transfer of control, there are many benefits.

You don't need to keep updating your software. You don't have to worry about backing up your files. If you work from home as well as an office, your files are there, as is the same software—you just need an Internet connection. If you travel and make presentations at conferences or for business, you don't need to worry about taking copies of the files with you and whether they will be corrupted in transit. All you need at the presentation is an Internet connection, and you have everything you need. There are also benefits for academics and teachers. All your students have access to the same software (provided they have Internet connections, of course). There are additional benefits as well, including the ability to share files and collaborate on projects. Cloud computing is touted to be the way of the future.

Google has been one of the pioneers of cloud computing, and Google Apps allow you make the step into this paradigm as painlessly as possible.

Google Apps

Google Apps can be a little confusing to the newcomer, especially when you factor in the various Google Apps, Google accounts, Gmail accounts, and Google Docs. Where does it all fit in? Figure 0-3 is a depiction of Google Apps and helps to put this in perspective. Collectively, all the applications and services from Google are called Google Apps, which is short for Google Applications. Gmail is the flagship product of Google Apps, and you must set up a Gmail account to gain access to the rest. If you already have an existing email account with another provider, you can use that to create a Google account; but for most people, access will be through their Gmail address. Thus Gmail becomes your point of entry to Google Apps.

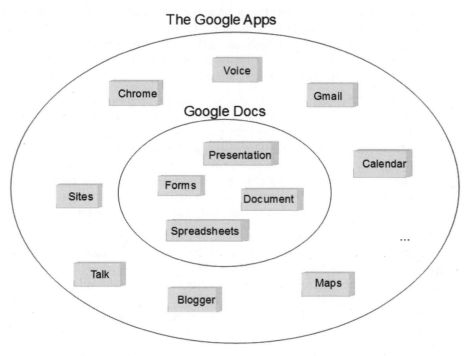

Figure 0-3 Depiction of Google Apps

Google Docs is a subset of Google Apps, and it represents those apps that together form Google's office suite. Google Docs consists of Presentations, Spreadsheets, Documents, Drawings, and Forms, which rival the core elements of other office suite applications, such as Microsoft Office and OpenOffice.

Who This Book Is For

This book is for anyone who wishes to learn how to use Google apps and Chrome. This book is a guide for both the beginner and intermediate user. The level of this book is particularly aimed at the beginner level, but it could be used as a reference guide for intermediate users who wish to make effective use of Google Apps.

Chapter 1 is on Chrome. This is Google's browser software, and it is important as all Google Apps are accessed from a web browser. While you can access Google Apps from any web browser, Chrome has a number of features that make it an excellent front-end to the apps.

Chapter 2 is on Gmail. Again, this is an important chapter, as most people get an account for Google Apps by setting up a Gmail account. Gmail is a very good web-based mail client that gives free storage and POP3 /IMAP access to other accounts. Additionally, it is through Gmail accounts that you can collectively collaborate on projects with shared documents.

The next five chapters are on Google Docs. Google Docs can be thought of as a subset of the Google Apps, and they represent the key elements of office suites available on the market. Google Docs consist of a word processor, spreadsheet application, a presentation application, and forms for collecting information from Web users and collating it within a spreadsheet. The word processor, spreadsheet and presentation chapters have been written in a form, making them suitable for an introductory course on basic computer applications. Thus, these chapters may appeal to teachers and educators on these topics.

Chapter 8 covers in detail the elements of Calendar. Using Calendar, you can effectively keep an electronic diary to document all appointments, receive automatic notification, and schedule future repeating events. Using your Google Apps account, you can also share your calendar with others and allow them to book appointments. Again, as with the other Google Apps, your calendar is available wherever there is Internet access, and it can be synched with your mobile applications.

Chapter 9 discusses Google sites. Google sites allows you to create a website free of charge and maintain it using a sophisticated user interface. It also includes hundreds of web-site templates to choose from. You can incorporate Google AdSense into your site to earn money based on Ad clicks.

Chapter 10 discusses Google Maps in detail. You can use Maps for searching, incorporating its data into other Google Apps, such as Google Sites.

Chapter 11 covers Google Talk. Google Talk is Google's instant messaging tool. This is an extremely useful application for holding real-time or asynchronous chat sessions with another Google talk user anywhere on the Internet. Google talk can also be installed and run on mobile devices, increasing the usefulness of this application.

Chapter 12 discusses Google Blogger. As part of your Google account, you can create and manage your own blog. You can also incorporate AdSense into your blog.

Finally, the last chapter concentrates on the integration aspects of the Google Apps discussed in the previous chapters. Many of the Google Apps are able to work with each other, offering a high degree of integration. This allows us to take advantage of the cloud-computing paradigm as much as possible by utilizing the interoperability features of the various applications. In this chapter, we discuss specifically *what fits with what*!

Features of the book include:

- Easy to read descriptions and examples
- Step-by-step instructions for using many of the more popular Google Apps
- All of the major features for each selected application, covered in detail

Who Google Apps Is For

Google Apps is really for everyone, whether you are an individual or corporate user. Anyone can make use of Google Apps. There are costs associated for corporate or business entities on a per-user basis, but these are minimal. However, within this book, we assume that the user is an individual connecting to Google Apps through a free account. Regardless, the information in this book is the same, and it will suit both an individual or business user.

As an individual user, you can sign up for a free account, which we discuss in Chapter 2. Once you have your Google account, you have a Gmail account, which at the time of writing, gives you 7,426 megabytes of email storage space. That is approximately 7.5 gigabytes. This is more than most people will ever use, allowing you store your email indefinitely.

You also get access to all Google Apps for free, including the word processing, spreadsheet, and presentation software, as well as all the other Apps we discuss (and many others not covered). Google gives you one gigabyte of storage space for all your Google Apps storage needs (except Gmail which is counted separately). Now one Gigabyte doesn't sound much, but the one Gigabyte only counts for documents that are uploaded and stored in their native format. Documents that are uploaded and converted to one of the Google Docs formats don't count towards your storage quota. This allows you plenty of storage space for your needs. If you do need extra storage space, you can purchase it from Google for a nominal fee. At the time of writing, Google support pages quoted a price of 25 cents per gigabyte per year if you're on a plan, with the lowest plan being 20 Gigabytes for $5 per year. This fee is nominal, even if you consider the cheap cost of a USB drive.

Once you are using Google Apps, you will then enjoy the ability to access your files and software from anywhere you have access to the Web. If you are ready to make, or at least explore, the paradigm shift to cloud computing, Google Apps is for you.

What Software Will I need?

Usually when starting out with a new application, you will need to install software before you begin to go through any book. In some respects, this book on Google Apps is no different. However, you only need one application and chances are you already have it. **You need only a Web browser**. As we mentioned previously, Google Apps represents a shift to the cloud-computing paradigm, where software and file storage is regarded as being a service delivered from the cloud to your local computer. Your interface to the cloud (or Internet) is the web browser. If you are connected to the Internet, you will already be familiar with using one or more web browsers.

We recommend the use of Google Chrome, though this is not mandatory; any Web browser will do. However, Google Chrome has many advantages, not the least being a small footprint. This is an advantage if you have a smaller device such as a Netbook or similarly small mobile device. It's on-screen footprint also allows you to see more of your application on the screen. In Chapter 1, we detail how you can download and install Chrome on your computer. Thereafter, we assume you are using Chrome, though there is nothing specific in the remaining Google Apps that requires it, and you can continue to use your browser of choice.

No other software is required, and all Google Apps are run as normal applications using your browser as the window. The one assumption we do make is that **you have an Internet connection**. Without an Internet connection, you cannot access Google Apps or indeed anything else on the Web.

Chapter 1

Getting Started with Chrome

Chrome is a web browser developed by Google Inc. for the Internet as it stands today. Earlier web browsers were developed for older technologies of the Internet where you could not interact with a web site like you can today. Current Internet technologies allow for web pages that dynamically change based on the choices you make. Earlier in the life of the internet, web pages were unchanging only meant to display static pictures and text. Chrome was designed to allow users to experience the web as it should be.

Chrome was built to be as small as possible and require as few of your computer's resources as possible (both memory and processor time). It loads very fast and runs multiple pages in their own protected environments (called sandboxes). In this way, Chrome can protect one web application from another, so if one application fails it won't affect the others running under Chrome at the same time. This also provides the added advantage that one web page running in one tab can't access any information in any other tab. This design can protect your critical data, such as Internet banking details from an attacker who has placed malicious software on a web site that you have open. The screen layout of chrome takes a minimalist approach. The browser menus and components take up as little space as possible on the screen in order to allow Chrome to provide as much of the screen as possible for web applications. Thus, we can focus on the application and not the browser interface.

Chrome is still a full-featured browser which works as well as, or better than, the other popular browsers on the market. As Chrome was designed by Google, the Google Apps run particularly well in this environment.

In this chapter you will learn how to effectively use Google Chrome to access rich Internet content and customize Google Chrome's settings, allowing you to manage how the browser works for you. At the end of the chapter there is general security advice which may help protect you from malicious activity on the Internet.

Getting and Installing Chrome

Chrome is a free, open source browser and can be found online at the following web address [http://www.google.com/chrome] (see Figure 1-1):

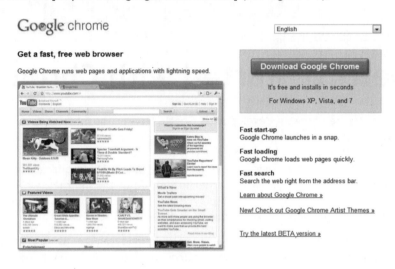

Figure 1-1: Google Chrome browser download page

To download Chrome, click the download button shown on the screen and follow the instructions to complete the download. Choose the option "Accept and Install" to download and install Chrome. Once you choose this option, your current browser will download the ChromeSetup application in your downloads directory. Your browser should automatically proceed to install the Chrome application. If this does not occur, locate where ChromeSetup.exe was saved to and run it. When the installation completes you will have the choice of accepting the default import options and making Chrome your default browser. For those people not wanting to bother with a custom configuration we suggest accepting the default options (see Figure 1-2).

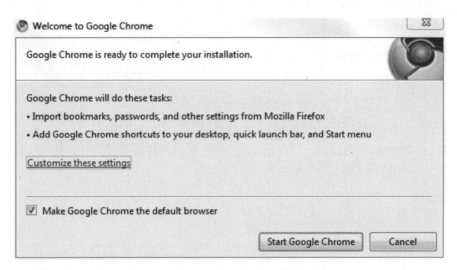

Figure 1-2: Google Chrome complete installation dialog box

The default import options will depend on your current browser, but the Chrome installation will import bookmarks, passwords, and settings from your default browser and add a shortcut to the desktop, quick launch, and start menu. By checking the "Make Google Chrome the default browser" option (see Figure 1-2), Chrome will become the computer system's default browser. You can change these options by selecting the "Customize these settings" link on the dialog box (see Figure 1-2). You will then be presented with the "Customize Your Settings" dialog box (see Figure 1-3).

If you have multiple browsers installed on your computer, choose from the drop-down list from which browser Chrome will import. You can also choose where shortcuts to Chrome will be placed on the desktop, quick launch bar, or both. Again, you can choose whether to make Chrome your default browser by checking the appropriate check box. When you have customized the settings, click the "Start Google Chrome" button.

You are now ready to surf the Web with Chrome.

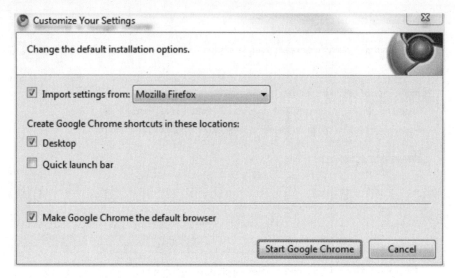

Figure 1-3: Chrome "Customize Your Settings"

Surfing with Chrome

Surfing the Web with Chrome is much like surfing with most other browsers, though the experience will be slightly different. The most immediate notable difference when you first load Chrome is the smaller-than-average footprint the browser leaves on the screen. This leaves more of the window available for applications. Many of the differences to how the browser operates will not be immediately noticeable and these will be discussed later in this chapter. When Chrome is loaded, a screen will appear to the user (see Figure 1-4). The image has been annotated, highlighting all the major components on the screen to help you surf the Web.

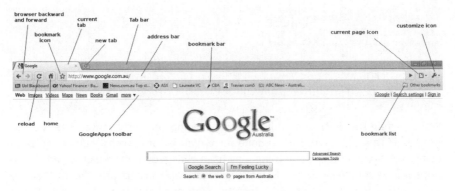

Figure 1-4: Annotated Chrome browser screen

NotED

Many of Chrome's basic functions work similarly to other browsers.

One of the first things you should do when you install Chrome is to set up a home page, which will be loaded every time you load Chrome. This is explained in the next section, and we suggest setting the home page to a good search engine, such as Google (google.com). This should be the default home page in Chrome when it is installed, but if during the installation process you imported your settings from an already installed browser, it may have changed. You can begin surfing by typing in a search term to your search engine and following the links or by typing a known web address directly into the address bar (see Figure 1-4). The web address is also known as a URL (Uniform Resource Locator). No matter where you are in browsing the Web, clicking the "Home" icon in the Google toolbar will load the web page you have set as your Chrome home page.

When surfing, sometimes we need to move backward and forward between web pages already visited. This can be quicker than re-typing in the web address again or searching for it if we only need to move back a few pages. The browser's backward and forward buttons are located toward the top left of the Chrome toolbar (see Figure 1-4) and work the same way as they do in popular browsers such as Firefox and Internet Explorer.

ExplainED

Right clicking on the backward or forward buttons will show a list of web sites that can be revisited using the backward or forward buttons.

While surfing the Web, sometimes the page being currently visited needs to be reloaded. This could need to be done for a number of reasons. For example, in many web applications, something may have changed and the page needs to be reloaded to see the change. Some Web mail applications are like this as are some online learning tools. Additionally, Web pages seem to get "stuck" and not finish loading sometimes. This can happen for a number of reasons including timeouts (exceeding built-in time limits for a response) when the Web is busy, but if this does happen, the page can then be reloaded. You reload the current Web page by clicking the "Reload" button in the Google toolbar (see Figure 1-4).

When browsing the Web, place-holders (or bookmarks) can be set for Web addresses that interest us, and by recalling the bookmark at a later stage the page can be quickly revisited. Bookmarks and managing them in detail is discussed later in this chapter, however, bookmarks can be located in two places within Chrome: the "Bookmark" bar and "Other Bookmarks" (see Figure 1-4).

New Tabs and Windows

When working with a web browser, multiple browser windows might need to be worked with at the same time. For example, if you are researching a particular topic, you might want to load different web pages in different windows and quickly flip between them rather than having to re-load them each time you want to go backward and forward between pages. Open multiple Chrome windows or simply create a new "Tab" in the current Chrome window. There are a number of ways to do this in Chrome. Click the "Customize" button in the Chrome toolbar on the right-hand side. This will activate the "Customize Menu" drop down list (see Figure 1-5).

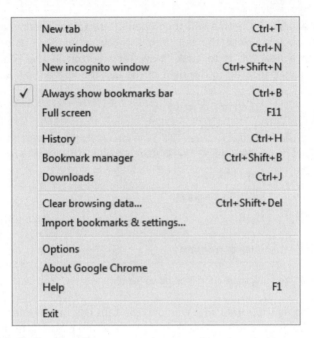

New tab	Ctrl+T
New window	Ctrl+N
New incognito window	Ctrl+Shift+N
✓ Always show bookmarks bar	Ctrl+B
Full screen	F11
History	Ctrl+H
Bookmark manager	Ctrl+Shift+B
Downloads	Ctrl+J
Clear browsing data...	Ctrl+Shift+Del
Import bookmarks & settings...	
Options	
About Google Chrome	
Help	F1
Exit	

Figure 1-5: Customize options

From the drop down customize list, if you choose the "New Window" option, a new Chrome window will open, and the Web can be independently surfed in this window, from the previous window. To switch between the two windows, select the window from the "Operating Systems" window list. A different option is to open a new tab instead of a new window for independent surfing. To open a new tab, choose "New Tab" from the "Customize" drop down list (see Figure 1-5). A new tab will be created and shown on the "Tab" bar, and an associated window will open displaying in large icon format a list of the most commonly visited web sites. From here, you can either choose one of the icons representing a common site you visit, click the home page link to go to your home page, or type in the web address of the new page you wish to load. The page in the new tab is independent of the previous page being working on, and you can easily swap between the different tabs by clicking on the tab of the page you want in the "Tab Bar" (see Figure 1-4). Using tabs instead of windows can save on system resources if they are tight, depending on your computer configuration.

Another way of opening a new tab or window is to right-click a link (or web address) from a Chrome window. A small drop-down list will appear (see Figure 1-6). From this drop down list, choose either "Open link in new tab," or "Open link in new window." Chrome will then open a new tab or window and load the web page associated with the link into the tab or window. Another way to quickly open a new tab is to click "New Tab" button in the "Tab Bar" (see Figure 1-4). This is located to the right of the last tab in the "Tab Bar."

Figure 1-6: Web link right-click drop down menu

When creating multiple tabs in a window, the tabs can be re-ordered simply by clicking a tab with the left mouse button, holding the mouse button down, and then dragging the tab either before or after another tab and releasing the mouse button.

Surfing Incognito

Another feature in Chrome is the ability to surf in stealth mode. To do this, an "incognito window" needs to be opened. Click the "Customize" button in the Chrome toolbar, the same as when creating a new tab or window and select "New incognito window." Alternately, a web link could be right-clicked in a normal Chrome window, "Open link in incognito window" could be selected. When an incognito window is opened, you can surf the Web as you would in any other Chrome tab or window, but there is a difference. In incognito mode, any pages you visit will not be tracked as normal. The pages won't show up in your browser history or search history, and any cookies (small pieces of information that web sites store on your computer) left behind are automatically deleted when you exit the incognito window. This is like searching in stealth mode. However, you do need to be aware that if you make any changes to the Chrome settings while incognito, then those changes will remain, and any files you download or bookmarks that you store will still be saved.

When you open a new window in incognito mode, the incognito icon will appear in the tab bar before the first tab of the window. Any new windows or tabs you create from an incognito window will also be put into incognito mode.

Configuring Chrome

As with other web browsers, there are a variety of changeable settings to alter the way that Chrome behaves and appears to us as we view web pages. Chrome is no different, except that once Chrome is installed, there is usually very little configuration to be done. This is one of the strong features of Chrome. As Chrome is usually installed online, you are usually already connected, and Chrome configures itself by grabbing settings from other browsers. This is an excellent feature for non-technical users. However, as our environment changes these settings sometimes need to be changed.

Setting the Home Page

One of the most common changes is changing our home page (the web page that Chrome loads every time when it is started). Click the "Customize" button in the Chrome toolbar on the right-hand side. This will activate the customize menu drop down list (see Figure 1-5). Select the "Options" menu item and the "Google Chrome Options" dialog will appear (see Figure 1-7). Click the "Basics" tab at the top of the dialog window if it is not already selected. This is where the current home page can be adjusted. In the first part of the dialog window, make sure the "Open the home page" option is selected. In the section underneath that section click the option "Open this page," and type in the URL of the web page you want to become the home page in the field to the right.

This new URL will become the home page and be opened every time Chrome loads. It will also be the page that Chrome loads when you click the "Home" button on the Chrome toolbar. You can now click the "Close" button to save the new changes.

Figure 1-7: Google Chrome Options dialog window

Security

Privacy and security is a critical issue in the current climate. Identity theft, electronic fraud, and scams are only a part of what every user should be aware of while using the Internet. With that in mind, users should understand each component of the privacy and security in Chrome. These can be viewed and changed if necessary through the "Google Chrome Options" dialog window (see Figure 1-7). To begin, select the "Options" menu item from the "Customize" button on the Chrome toolbar (see Figure 1-5), and the "Google Chrome Options" dialog window will appear (see Figure 1-7). Select the "Personal Stuff" tab at the top of dialog window to see the dialog (see Figure 1-8).

Figure 1-8: Google Chrome Options "Personal Stuff" window

Google Chrome has the ability to store passwords which are used on web pages and frequently used text to save you from re-entering information. Chrome will automatically detect passwords and field information when you access various sites. When you enter a password, Chrome will present an information bar which is displayed toward the top of the browser window just underneath the bookmark bar (see Figure 1-9). This bar allows users to either save the password they have just entered, not save the password, or to never save passwords for the current site. You can choose to not save the password for this site by clicking the cross (x) icon on the far right of the bar.

Do you want Chrome to save your password? | Save password | Never for this site | ×

Figure 1-9: Google Chrome password option bar

You can choose to save the password that you have entered by clicking "Save Password" button, or you can choose to never save passwords on the web site by clicking the "Never for this site" button. It is recommended for security reasons that you never save any passwords using this feature, no matter how secure the browser may be.

ExplainED

Passwords are stored in Chrome using simple plain text. Do not use this feature on a public computer.

To control how Chrome behaves with passwords, click "Never save passwords" in the "Google Chrome Options" dialog window (see Figure 1-8) that you have opened. Chrome will not give you the option of saving passwords on new and existing sites and disables all passwords that have been stored. Note that Chrome will not delete your stored passwords unless they are removed manually. By clicking the "Show saved passwords" button, the "Passwords and Exceptions" dialog window will be shown (see Figure 1-10) and will open. This dialog window shows any saved passwords and the web sites they were saved from. To delete existing entries you have to click on the entry and press the "Remove" button. To remove all entries, press the "Remove All" button and confirm in the next dialog window.

ExplainED

Clicking the "Show password" button when an entry is selected will display your password in clear text. Ensure that no one else can see your screen if you click this button.

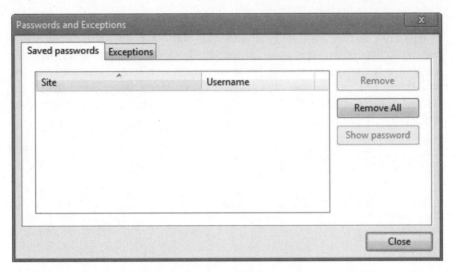

Figure 1-10: Passwords and Exceptions "Saved Passwords" tab

If you click on the "Exceptions" tab of the "Passwords and Exceptions" dialog window, you will see a list of exceptions representing web sites that have been prevented from saving passwords (see Figure 1-11). Much like the "Saved passwords" tab, you can remove exceptions by clicking on the site you wish to remove the exception from and clicking the "Remove" button. You can also remove all listed exceptions.

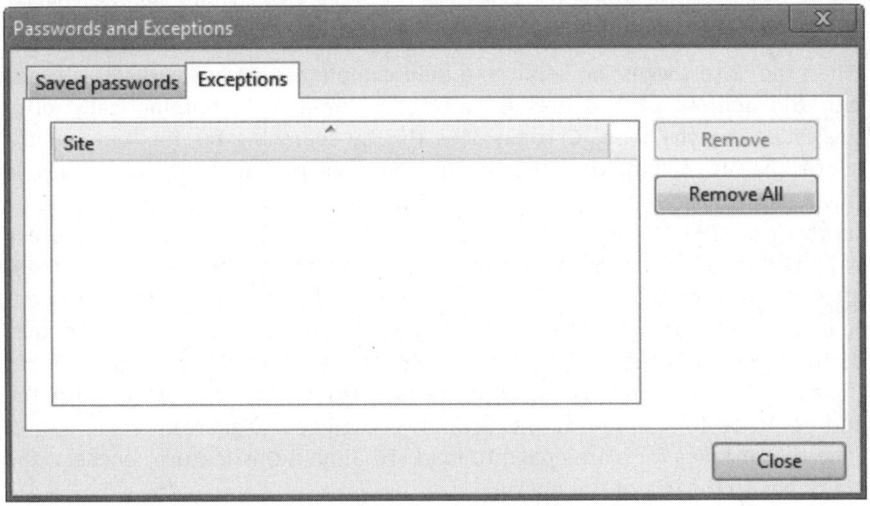

Figure 1-11: Passwords and Exceptions "Exceptions" tab

In the "Google Chrome Options" dialog window (see Figure 1-8) underneath the "Passwords" section are two options for "Autofill." Autofill works by detecting commonly used items such as email addresses, names, and phone numbers for which it will then automatically fill in for you in web forms, ultimately saving you time. You can disable this feature by clicking "Never save text from forms." It is recommended that you disable this feature by choosing the "Never save text from forms" option.

ExplainED

It is recommended to disable the autofill feature on a public computer.

Privacy

In the "Google Chrome Options" dialog window (see Figure 1-8), if you click the "Under the Hood" tab at the top of the window, you will see the dialog window (see Figure 1-12). If you use the scroll bar on the right with the mouse and scroll down, you will see the same data (see Figure 1-12). The settings here help control the privacy settings under Chrome. Chrome will display a suggestion page when it is unable to locate a web page. On a regular browser, if you go to a web page that does not exist, an error page will appear. However, in Chrome you will be presented an information page that has some search suggestions. Unchecking the tick box labeled 'Show suggestions for navigation errors' will disable the suggestion page.

When the "Use suggestion service to help complete searches and URL's typed into the address bar" option is selected, Chrome will automatically offer suggestions as you type. Chrome does this by searching for the term in the address bar as you type each letter. This can be helpful at times, but to disable this feature, uncheck the box to the left. You will no longer be offered suggestions as you type URLs. The option, "Use DNS pre-fetching to improve page performance" helps to shorten the time taken by Chrome to load pages after the address has been entered. To view a web site, your computer needs to locate what computer the web page is stored on. To do this, your computer performs what is called a DNS lookup. DNS pre-fetching automatically fetches the data Chrome needs as you type the address, rather than waiting for the address to be fully entered. This process is designed to shorten the length of time that it takes for a web page to load. To disable this feature, uncheck the check box to the left of the option.

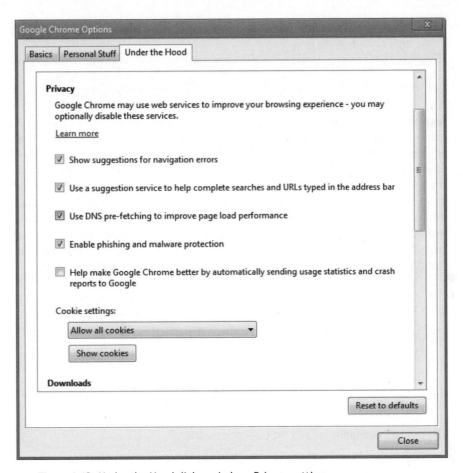

Figure 1-12: Under the Hood dialog window: Privacy settings

Phishing and Malware protection are automated services designed to protect your computer and the information stored on the computer. This is done in Chrome with the option "Enable phishing and malware protection." Chrome automatically downloads a list of web sites that are known to cause damage to your computer. This enables Chrome to keep up to date with new sites being placed on the list. Every time you visit a site, Chrome compares it to entries in the list and will warn you if you visit one of them. Phishing and malware protection is enabled by default for your safety, but if necessary, disable this option by unchecking the box to the left.

ExplainED

Do not disable the malware detector. This is for your protection.

Another option to carefully consider is the use of cookies in Chrome. These can contain information including login details to keep you logged in on a web site or information about sites you have visited so you can be greeted again when you return. Other cookies may contain tracking data so the web site owners can track how a user navigates their site. The original idea behind cookies was good, and tool was designed to help programmers program the web for dynamic interactivity. However, while still useful, some uses of cookies have become suspect and many people disable the use of cookies. To change how cookies are stored, click the drop-down menu at the bottom of the "Google Chrome Options" dialog and select an option from those available (see Figure 1-13).

Cookie settings:

Allow all cookies ▼
Allow all cookies
Restrict how third-party cookies can be used
Block all cookies

Figure 1-13: Cookie settings

The options available for setting the cookies are:

Allow all cookies: This option will allow any cookie to be written to your computer from any web site.

Restrict how third-party cookies can be used: This option will allow all cookies from the site you're accessing, as well as any web sites you have visited previously that are associated with the page you are viewing.

Block all cookies: This will prevent any web site from storing any cookies on your computer.

Many people conscious of security will restrict the use of cookies, but not necessarily block all cookies. This will prevent some web sites from working.

ExplainED

Changing cookie settings may prevent some websites from working properly.

You can inspect which cookies have been stored on your computer by clicking the "Show cookies" button in the "Google Chrome Options" dialog window and inspecting the "Cookies Manager" dialog window that appears (see Figure 1-14). This will list all cookies stored on your computer including specific information about them. If you click a cookie from the list, you get to see all the information about that cookie, including information such as the name of the cookie, information held within the cookie, and when it expires. Much like the password deletion process you can delete entries individually by clicking "Remove," and all of the entries by clicking "Remove all" and confirming this in the next prompt.

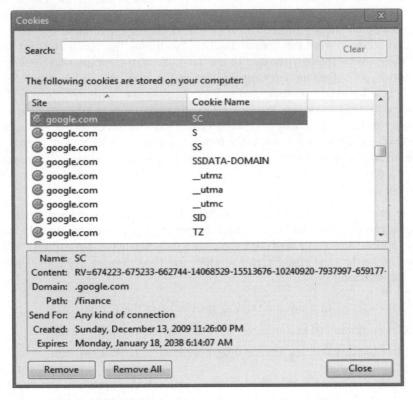

Figure 1-14: Managing cookies

Controlling What You See

As you are browsing the Web looking at different pages, Chrome will read the pages from the server as they are sent and will then display the pages in the current tab. You do not have much control over how the pages are presented to you, but there are settings that are adjustable, and they somewhat alter how the environment looks.

In the following sections, we will address how you can change text size and colors to make it clearer to read, and we will also cover more advanced text handling including letter encoding and using Chrome to help you develop web pages.

Text Size

You can easily control the way a page is displayed through the "Zoom" menu and changing the text size. Difficulty reading small text requiring corrective lenses is one of a number of reasons you may need to adjust the size of the text, or perhaps you need to make it smaller to see more of the page depending on the circumstance. Text size is controlled through the "Zoom" option accessed from the Chrome toolbar. By clicking the "Current page" icon on the Chrome toolbar (located to the far right of the toolbar) and selecting "Zoom" you can either increase the size of the text, reduce the size of the text, or return the text to normal size by choosing the "Larger," "Smaller," or "Normal" menu items (see Figure 1-15). You can continue to make the text size smaller or larger until you get the size you need. Increasing or decreasing the text will change what you see in the browser and how it is displayed. Increasing the size will generally mean you see less in the window, while decreasing means you generally see more. However, it may not display as the web page designer intended.

Once you have finished viewing the web page in either larger or smaller size, it is always a good idea to return it to its original state by selecting the "Normal" size option. There are keyboard short-cuts to achieve the same thing. While the Chrome browser is the active window, use the following key combinations on the keyboard:

Ctrl - + (press Ctrl key and the + key) to increase the text one size

Ctrl - − (press Ctrl key and the - key) to decrease the text one size

Ctrl - 0 (press Ctrl key and the 0 key) to return to normal text size

If you have a mouse with a center wheel, you can also press the Ctrl key and rotate the mouse wheel to increase and decrease the text size.

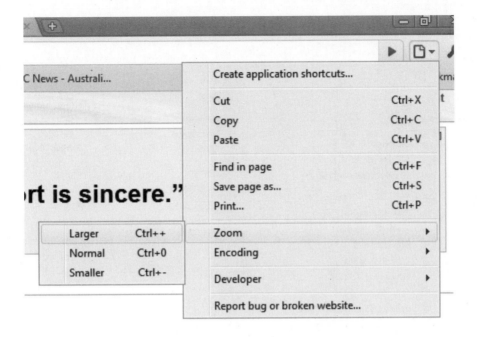

Figure 1-15: Accessing the Zoom menu option

Encoding

Sometimes when you are viewing pages on the Web, the default encoding used by Chrome won't match that of the web site you are viewing. In such cases, the text may not display correctly, or will display using unfamiliar symbols. You can change the encoding used by Chrome if you're familiar with the encoding used within the web page you are viewing. It should be specified in the page if they are not using the default. To change the encoding for the page, select the "Encoding" option from the "Current page" icon on the toolbar. You will see a large drop-down list appear with possible encoding options (see Figure 1-16). For the most part, you should leave the encoding options as they are with "Auto detect" turned on and "Unicode" (UTF-8) selected. Unicode is an industry standard for representing characters. Changing these unnecessarily could result in display problems.

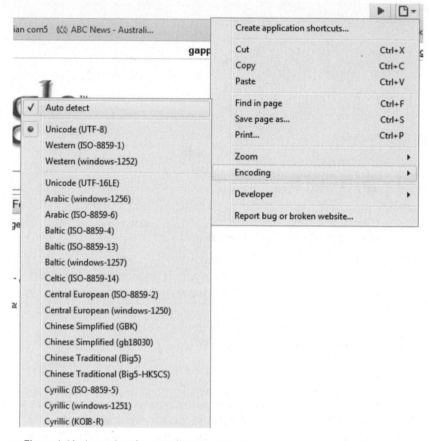

Figure 1-16: Accessing the encoding options

Fonts and Languages

You have some control over the standard fonts used to display the web pages in the browser, and you gain access to these by clicking on the "Customize" button in the Chrome toolbar on the right hand side. This will activate the customize menu drop-down list (see Figure 1-5). Select the "Options" menu item and the "Google Chrome Options" dialog will appear (see Figure 1-7). Click on the "Under the Hood" tab at the top of the dialog window to display it (see Figure 1-12). Use the scroll bar on the left of the window to scroll down until you see the portion of the dialog window (see Figure 1-17). Click the "Change font and language settings" button and you will see the dialog window (see Figure 1-18). Choose the fonts that Google Chrome will use when rendering the browser screen.

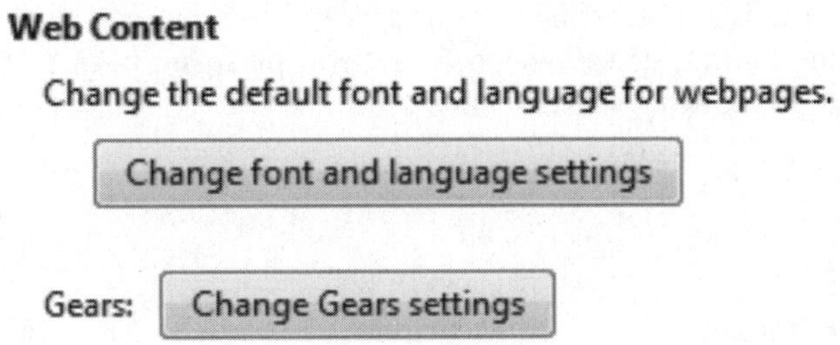

Web Content

Change the default font and language for webpages.

Change font and language settings

Gears: Change Gears settings

Figure 1-17: Google Chrome Options "Web content"

You are able to change three fonts including the Serif Font, Sans-Serif Font, and Fixed-width Font used by Chrome. To change each of the fonts, click the "Change" button to the right of the corresponding font type and choose a new font, font style, and font size from the available options (see Figure 1-19).

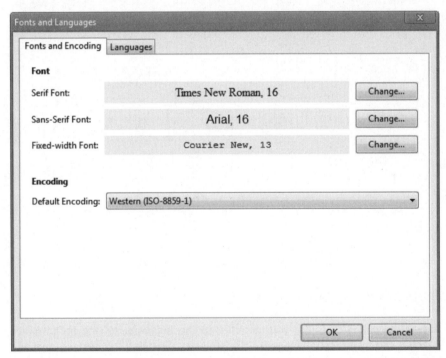

Figure 1-18: Fonts and Encoding

When you have finished selecting the options for the new font, click the "OK" button near the bottom of the window. You will be taken back to the "Fonts and Encoding" dialog window (see Figure 1-18).

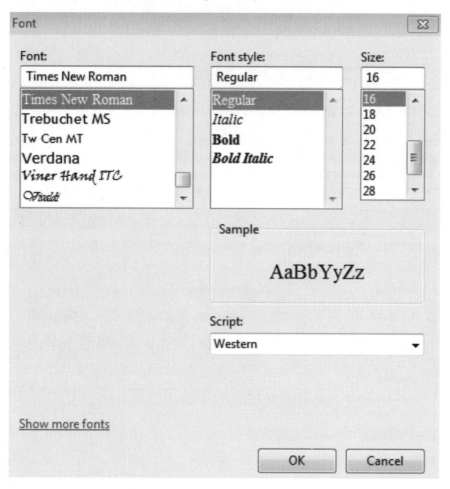

Figure 1-19: Font selection

As well as changing fonts, you can change the language setting for Chrome, which is the interface language for the browser. Changing the default language setting affects the language used for displaying the menus and dialog boxes. The default language used by Chrome will be based on the language you selected when you downloaded Chrome. To access this feature, click the "Languages" tab in the window (see Figure 1-18). The new tab showing the

"Languages" window will then be displayed (see Figure 1-20). From this window, you can add languages, select the current spell-check language, and change the default language by Chrome for the menus and dialog boxes. When you have finished selecting the desired interface language, close the dialog window by clicking the "OK" button on the bottom of the window.

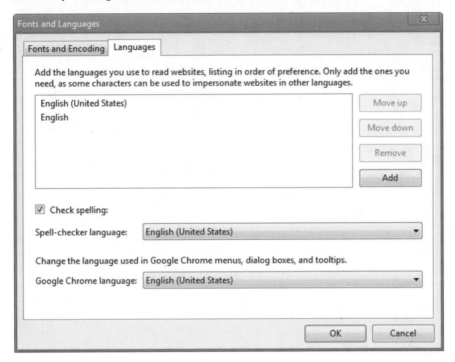

Figure 1-20: Languages

Developer Viewing

If you are a web page developer and are building and viewing your web pages in Chrome, you may need to look at the raw data stream that the browser is receiving. The normal browser page is rendered from the data stream and presented to the reader as a formatted page. But while developing, you occasionally need to see that data stream. To view the current web page as received by the browser, click the "Current page" icon in the Chrome toolbar and select the "Developer" menu option (see Figure 1-21). From here you can select from the options "View source," "JavaScript console," or "Task manager." To view the current web page source, select the "View source" option. A new tab will be opened in Chrome and the source code of the current web page will be displayed in the tab. When you have finished viewing the source, you can simply delete the Chrome tab.

Choosing the "JavaScript console" option will open the JavaScript console in a new dialog window. This will be useful for developers wanting to work with JavaScript in web pages. Additionally, if you select "Task manager," a small window will open displaying all of the process Chrome tasks associated with the current Chrome process and the subsequent memory requirements.

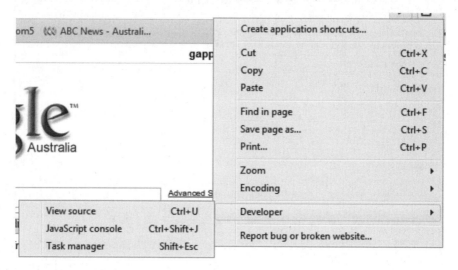

Figure 1-21: Developer options

Bookmark Toolbar

We briefly discussed the bookmarks toolbar in a previous section, and will be discussed again in later on. However, regardless of its functionality, from a viewing perspective we are able to control whether it is displayed in Chrome or whether it is hidden. You can control this option from the "Customize" button on the toolbar. Clicking on the "Customize" button will display the drop-down menu (see Figure 1-5). The option "Always show "Bookmarks bar"" is a toggle option and can be turned on or off by repeatedly selecting it from this menu. When it is unchecked, it will not be displayed in Chrome and will give slightly more screen space for the applications.

Full Screen

In some instances, web applications running in the browser may need more room to display, or you may want to try and see more on a page. Chrome is a minimalist browser, in many respects, and does not take much screen space to begin with. However, you can place the browser in full-screen mode. You can do this by selecting the "Full screen" option from the "Customize" button on the toolbar (see Figure 1-5). This will remove all browser elements except the scroll bar on the right, and possibly the bottom of the screen if it is needed. The entire screen will then be devoted to the web page in the current tab. You can also enter full-screen mode by pressing the F11 (Function 11) key on the keyboard.

To exit from full-screen mode, you can press F11 again, or you can move your mouse cursor to the very top of the screen and a slide-down tab will appear. Clicking on this tab will exit full-screen mode.

Search Field

You can slightly change the Chrome toolbar by causing a drop-down search field to appear just under the "Bookmarks bar," and to the right of the screen. You can activate this in one of two ways: by clicking the "Find in page" option from the "Current page" icon menu on the toolbar or by pressing the Ctrl + F keys. This will cause the drop-down search field to appear (see Figure 1-22). If you need to search the current web page for a combination of letters or words, begin typing them in this field. As you type the letters of a word, the page will move finding the first instance of the combination of letters and highlighting them on the page. If there is more than one instance of the word or letters, you can then use the small up and down arrow keys to the right of the search field to move backward and forward on the page to these other occurrences. You can close the search tab by clicking the small cross (x) icon just to the right of the up and down arrows.

The search tab will automatically close when you load a new web page into the current tab.

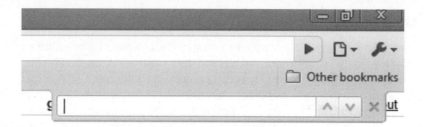

Figure 1-22: Drop-down search field

Managing Bookmarks

Over time, people tend to collect bookmarks as they surf the Web. Collecting bookmarks without any thought on how they might be ordered or grouped can be a recipe for disaster or frustration. Many people collect them and over a period of a year or more the amount of saved bookmarks increases significantly. Chrome provides a Bookmark Manager to help collect out bookmarks into coherent groups or folders. We can even display our most commonly visited bookmarks on the "bookmarks bar," which appears directly under the Chrome toolbar if it is turned on.

To turn on the Chrome bookmark bar, click the "Customize" button at the right of the Chrome toolbar, and from the drop-down menu (see Figure 1-5), choose "Always show Bookmarks bar." This option will then be checked, and the "Bookmarks bar" will appear underneath the Chrome toolbar (see Figure 1-4). On this bar, you can keep your most accessed bookmarks. This can help save you time when you visit these web sites. To visit one of these links, click the link on the "Bookmarks bar," and the page will load into the current window or tab.

Creating a New Bookmark

To bookmark a Web address can be simple using Chrome. When you have the page loaded in the current tab that you wish to bookmark, click the "Bookmark" icon just to the left of the address bar. This icon is the star symbol (see Figure 1-4). This will cause the "Bookmark added" dialog box to appear (see Figure 1-23). This dialog box is used to let the Bookmark Manager know exactly where the bookmark will appear.

Figure 1-23: Bookmark Added! dialog box

In the bookmark dialog box, the name of the bookmark is shown along with the bookmark folder where the new bookmark will be stored. The displayed name in the dialog box is automatically taken from the web page, and the default folder for storage of the bookmark will be the last folder you either created or used for storing a previous bookmark. You can change the name of the bookmark by clicking your mouse in the name field and typing a new name. This new name will then appear when you are searching your bookmark lists. Please be sure to use a name that is obvious and relevant to the bookmark. You can also change the folder that the bookmark will be located in by clicking the drop-down list of folder names. From there, choose the folder you wish to use by clicking it from the available list. Then click the "Close" button in the dialog box and the book will be added to the folder you chose with the name you used.

If during the process of adding a new bookmark you actually decide that you don't want to save the bookmark, click the "Remove" link located in the top right of the dialog box (see Figure 1-23). If you click "Close," the bookmark will still be saved. Additionally, while adding a bookmark, you can access additional editing options by clicking the "Edit" button in the dialog box. The "Edit Bookmark" window then opens (see Figure 1-24).

Figure 1-24: Edit Bookmark window

In this window you can edit the name of the bookmark as before by clicking the "Name" field and typing a new name. You can also edit the URL of the bookmark and edit the bookmark folders. Typically you will not need to edit the actual web address of a bookmark. As you gain more experience in using the Web and identifying different URLs, you may find it beneficial to slightly modify a bookmarked web address by removing or adding parts of the address.

If you want to store the new bookmark into a new folder that doesn't exist, you can create a new bookmark folder in this window. In the lower part of the "Edit Bookmark" window (see Figure 1-24), you will see the structure of the bookmark folders that already exist. The two main folders, the bookmarks bar and the other "Bookmarks bar," are folders created by Chrome and cannot be changed. The bookmarks stored in the bookmarks bar folder are shown directly on the bookmarks bar (see Figure 1-4) for quick access within Chrome. You should limit the number of books in this folder to only your most accessed bookmarks. The other bookmarks folder is where Chrome users can store all "Other bookmarks" and create further sub-folders to help categorize and store bookmarks for ease of access.

If you want to create a new sub-folder to store the new bookmark you are adding, right-click the existing folder that you wish to add the new sub-folder to, and choose the "New Folder" option. Alternatively, you can click the folder and then click the "New folder" button at the bottom of the window. A new sub-folder will be added to the existing bookmarks folder structure, and you can then type the name of the new folder into the highlighted area. Once this is done, if you click the "OK" button on the window (see Figure 1-24), the window is closed and the new bookmark is added to the selected folder. Clicking "Cancel" will close the window and the bookmark and any new folders you created will not be saved.

You can also change the name of an existing folder in this window by right-clicking the existing folder and choosing the "Edit" option. Then type the new name. You cannot change the name of the bookmarks bar or the other bookmarks folder.

ExplainED

You can add folders to the bookmarks bar which will display a drop-down list of bookmarks when clicked.

Selecting a Bookmark

When you wish to recall an existing bookmark and have that page loaded, you can click the "Other bookmarks" link shown on the far right of the "Bookmarks bar" (see Figure 1-4). A drop down list of bookmarks and folders will be displayed (see Figure 1-25). The folders are marked with a windows folder icon and clicking one will open a further drop-down list of folders and bookmarks contained within the selected folder. To load a page, select a bookmark from the list of folders and bookmarks and the selected page will be loaded into the current Chrome tab.

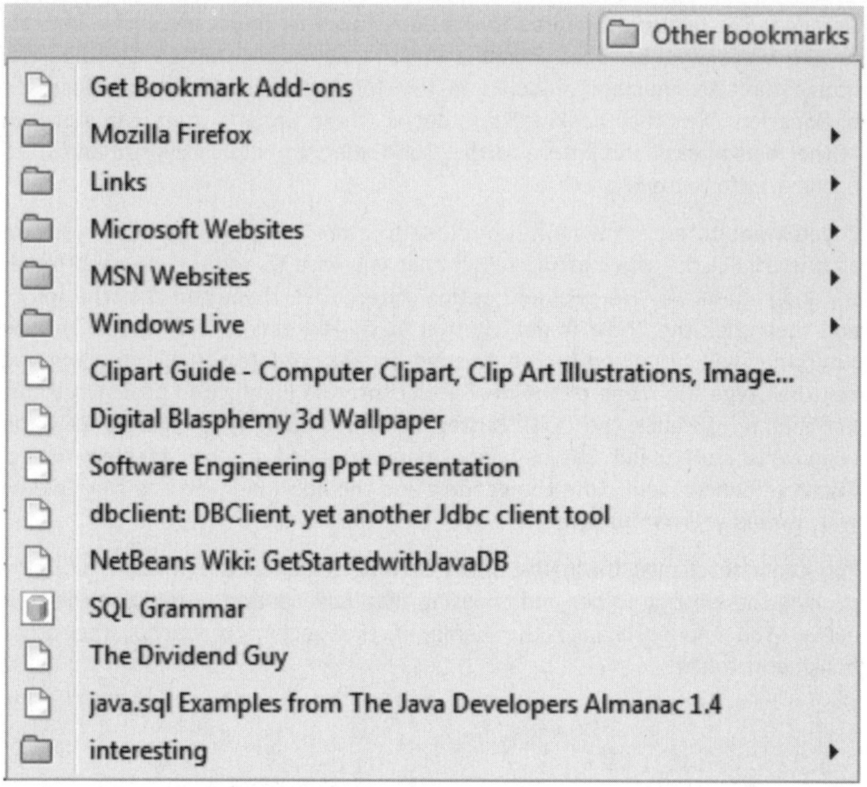

Figure 1-25: Other bookmarks selection window

There are a few other options available when selecting bookmarks to be displayed. If you right-click a bookmark, you can choose where the bookmark is loaded: to a new window, new tab, or a new incognito window. You can choose to delete the bookmark by clicking the "Delete" option or edit the bookmark by choosing the "Edit" option. If you choose to edit the bookmark, the "Edit Bookmark" window is displayed (see Figure 1-24). You can then edit aspects of the bookmark as discussed in the previous section. You can also choose to add a folder, and selecting this option will add a folder to the current folder containing the selected bookmark where you will be able to type the new folder's name. Selecting the "Bookmark Manager" option will load the "Bookmark Manager" discussed in the next section.

If you right click a folder, you have options for editing the current folder similar to options for editing the bookmarks. Additionally, you can choose to open all bookmarks in the current folder. If you choose this option, a new tab will be created for each book in the folder within the current window, and each bookmark will be loaded into one of the tabs. If you choose to open all bookmarks in a new window, all bookmarks are again loaded to separate tabs but within a new window. Similarly, opening all bookmarks in a new incognito window will load all bookmarks into separate tabs in an incognito window.

"Bookmarks bar" bookmarks are selected by clicking the appropriate link on the "Bookmark bar."

Using the Bookmark Manager

As discussed in the previous section, you can get to the Bookmark Manager by right-clicking on a bookmark or folder and choosing the "Bookmark Manager" option. The Bookmark Manager can also be called from the "Customize" menu (see Figure 1-5). When the Bookmark Manager is brought up, you will see the window shown in Figure 1-26. From this window, you can manage all bookmarks and bookmark folders you have created and saved with Chrome.

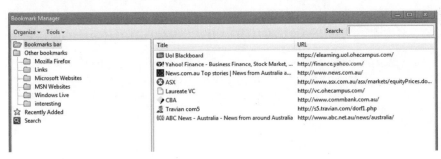

Figure 1-26: Bookmark Manage window

The "Bookmark Manager" window is divided vertically into two sections. The left section contains a hierarchy tree of all the bookmark folders created by Chrome or by you. You will see the "Bookmarks bar" and "Other bookmarks" folders at the top of this list as these are standard folders created by Chrome. Underneath the "Other bookmarks" folders, you will see the other sub-folders that you have created, or that were imported from another browser when you installed Chrome. In the right section of the window, you will see a list of bookmarks and sub-folders contained in the folder that is selected on the left. Similar to the discussion in the previous section, by right clicking a folder on the left, you can open all the bookmarks within a folder into different tabs in the current window, a new window, or an incognito window. You can also choose to rename, add a new folder, or delete an existing folder. Be careful when deleting folders since all the bookmarks contained within a folder are also deleted without warning. Similarly, if you right-click a bookmark in the right section of the window, you can open the bookmark in the current tab, a new window, or an incognito window. Again, you can choose to edit or delete a bookmark as discussed in the previous section.

Within the "Bookmark Manager," you can also move your bookmarks around between folders to sort them in more appropriate groups. The simplest way to do this is dragging and dropping the books into the folder you want. Simply left-click a bookmark in the right of the screen, keep the left mouse button pressed, and drag it to the bookmark folder you want in the left of the screen. The bookmark will be moved. You can also highlight more than one bookmark and drag the group to the folder you want. You can also do this using the cut-and-paste feature. This can be done by highlighting a group of bookmarks, right-clicking over the highlighted bookmarks, and choosing the "Cut" option. Right click the folder you want to place them into and choose the "Paste" option. The bookmarks will be moved.

ExplainED

You should always make a conscious effort to place bookmarks into appropriate folders by categorizing them. After you've collect a significant amount of bookmarks, they can be difficult to find unless placed in some sort of order.

You can also easily re-arrange the bookmark folder's hierarchy structure by moving the folders around. Just as you used drop-and-drag to move bookmarks between folders, you can use drop-and-drag on the folders themselves to move one folder into or out of another folder. This feature quickly allows you to arrange your hierarchy of folders into a meaningful way to reflect your ordered collection of bookmarks. When you drag one folder into another, all the bookmarks in that folder remain in place and can still be accessed from that folder from its new place in the hierarchy.

You can easily alphabetically sort your bookmarks in Chrome. Alphabetically sort a folder of bookmarks by selecting the folder on the left of the screen. From the menu toolbar of the "Bookmark Manager" window select the "Organize" menu option (see Figure 1-26). From the drop-down list choose "Reorder by title" menu option and the bookmarks in that folder will be alphabetically sorted according to the titles in the web pages. You can also alphabetically arrange the bookmark sub-folders in the same way. For example, if you select the "Other bookmarks" folder and choose the "Reorder by title" menu option from the "Organize" menu, the sub-folders of "Other bookmarks" will be alphabetically sorted by folder name.

In order to move your bookmarks from one browser to another, or from Chrome on one computer to another computer, you can export and import your bookmark list. To export your bookmark list, click the "Tools" menu option from the "Bookmark Manager" menu bar and select the "Export bookmarks" option. A "Save-as" dialog window will appear, and you can choose where the bookmark list will be saved. By default, the bookmark list will be saved as a Chrome HTML document (or web page) with the name "Bookmarks." You can change the name by clicking the "File Name" box and typing the new name. You then choose the location of the bookmark list and click the "Save" button. You can then take this bookmark list and import it into another Chrome browser. To import the bookmark list, choose the "Import bookmarks" from the "Tools" menu option. From the "Open" dialog box, select the previously exported bookmark list and click the "Open" button. Your bookmark list will then be loaded into Chrome.

Themes

Google Chrome has an extensive range of built-in themes for you to choose from. The themes allow you to change the appearance of Google Chrome without changing the functionality of the program. There are two ways to access the themes' settings. One method is to open a new tab by clicking on the new tab button (see Figure 1-4). Then in the lower right corner of the new tab, there is a part of the screen that looks like an upturned book page (see Figure 1-27). If you click this you will be taken directly to where you can change the theme for Chrome. The other method for getting to themes is going through the "Google Chrome Options" window. Click the button in the Chrome toolbar and choose the "Options" menu item (see Figure 1-5). This will display the "Google Chrome Options" dialog window (see Figure 1-7). Click in the "Personal Stuff" tab to bring up the dialog screen (see Figure 1-8). If you access themes in this way, you get the option of resetting the default theme by clicking the "Reset to default theme" button in the window.

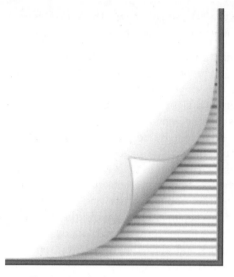

Figure 1-27: Access to Themes method

Either click the "Get themes" button in the window or click into the bottom right-hand corner of the new tab (see Figure 1-28) to load the "Themes gallery" from Google in the new tab window. You can choose from two different classes of themes: select the themes that have been created by artists (which is the default setting), or a set of themes created by Google. Choose from these two classes by clicking the "Themes by Google," or "Themes by Artists" in the link at the top of the current tab's window (see Figure 1-28).

Google chrome

Themes Gallery

Themes by Artists   Themes by Google

Figure 1-28: Theme category tool

At this stage you should look through both the "Themes by Artists" and "Themes by Google" pages and locate a theme you like. If you want to see more information about the theme or how it would look, click the image associated with the theme you are interested in obtaining. By clicking the image, you are taken to a page with a screen-shot of how the theme looks. For example, clicking the picture for the Google theme "Pencil Sketch" will bring up the page (see Figure 1-29).

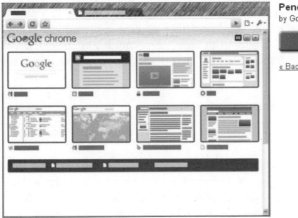

Pencil Sketch
by Google

Apply this theme

« Back to themes

Figure 1-29: Pencil Sketch theme for Chrome

Once you have found a theme that you like, click the "Apply this theme" button, which can be seen when either viewing information about a single theme (see Figure 1-29) or viewing all the themes in the "Themes by Artists" or "Themes by Google" web page. Clicking this button will automatically download and install the theme you have selected. There are no restrictions on changing themes in Chrome, so if you get tired of a theme you can easily change it to a new one.

 NotED

The themes by Google are usually more simplistic than the themes by artists.

Chrome Plug-ins

Some web sites you visit require extra functionality than Chrome supplies by default. Most web browsers are similar in nature, supplying a default functionality with the ability to extend the default functionality by the addition of a "Plug-in." Plug-ins enable developers to extend the functionality of applications. This extra functionality may be for specific content such as video, or for more complexity, so the browser can handle it in its default setting. Regardless of what it's needed for, you will need to have the required plug-in for a web page. Otherwise, you will not be able access all functionality offered by the web page, or some content may not be available. The plug-in system for Google Chrome allows you to enhance Chrome very easily. If you go to a web page that requires a plug-in in order to be displayed correctly, you will be presented with an information bar across the top of the browser (see Figure 1-30).

Figure 1-30: Plug-in required notification

Once this link has appeared, you have to click on the "Install plug-in" button to see what the next step is. One of the most useful plug-ins you can get for Google Chrome is Adobe Flash. Adobe Flash is used for many different types of web pages including online games and YouTube.com. You don't have to wait until you access a web page for it to instruct you to download a plug-in. You can actively seek plug-ins to install them in anticipation of using them. However, most people just wait until a plug-in is needed before installing it.

ExplainED

If you have previously used Mozilla Firefox as a browser, Chrome can automatically use the plug-ins you have installed in Firefox.

The quickest way to install the Adobe Flash plug-in is to visit a site like YouTube.com and clicking on a video to watch (see Figure 1-31).

Once you click on a video you will be taken to the "View video" page. If you see the plug-in information bar (see Figure 1-30) appear at the top of the Chrome window, you are missing the Adobe Flash plug-in. To install the Adobe Flash plug-in, you have to click the "Install plug-in" button on the notification bar on the right-hand side. Once you have clicked the install plug-in button, a dialog box (see Figure 1-32) will appear. Once the plug-in dialog box appears, click "Get Plug-in" and Chrome will automatically download and install the plug-in. Some required plug-ins will be based on your preferences and may involve more complicated steps than the Adobe Flash plug-in. If you encounter a plug-in that you are having difficulty installing, you can always look at the Google help page for plug-ins.

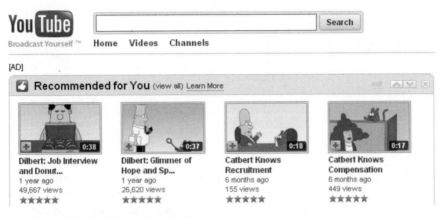

Figure 1-31: YouTube.com web site

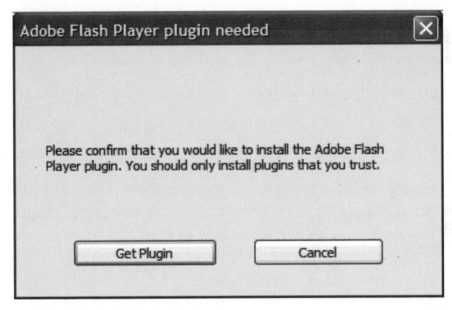

Figure 1-32: Install plug-in dialog box

You can access the help section for plug-ins by pressing the F1 key on your keyboard or selecting the "Help" menu option accessed from the "Customize" icon menu on the Chrome toolbar. This will load the Google help pages into the new tab, and you can get further help on a topic by entering a search term such as plug-ins into the search field (see Figure 1-33).

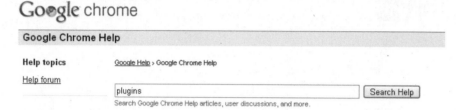

Google Chrome Help

Help topics   <u>Google Help</u> › Google Chrome Help

Help forum

plugins   Search Help

Search Google Chrome Help articles, user discussions, and more.

Figure 1-33: Chrome Help search

Once you enter the search term, click the "Search Help" button on the right of the search field. A search results page will be loaded into the current tab (see Figure 1-34). You can then browse this search page looking for more detailed information about the help topic. The search results to be displayed will be selected from the search term you entered, so you will have to read each search result and click on the links that closely match what you are looking for.

NotED

Your results may differ from what is shown here due to the volatile nature of the web.

Google chrome   plugins   Search Help

Google Chrome Help   Showing: Any source   Results 1 - 10 in Google Chrome Help for **plugins**

<u>Adobe Flash, Windows Media Player, and other **plug-ins** : Webpage ...</u>
Currently, Google Chrome supports most popular **plug-ins**, including Flash,
Acrobat Reader, Java, Windows Media Player, Real Player, QuickTime, ...
Google Chrome Help

<u>Google Chrome webmaster tools : Developers and webmasters</u>
Type any of the following shortcuts in the address bar to see more information:
about: about:dns; about:**plugins**; view-source:[URL]; about:cache ...
Google Chrome Help

<u>I can't update Flash.</u>
Adobe Flash, Java, and other **plug-ins** · Download and install Google Chrome ·
Address bar · Chrome Extensions not enabled yet i believe i enabled them. ...
Google Chrome Help

Figure 1-34: Search results

Downloading

With all browsers, one of the most important features that people make use of is the ability to download material to their own local computer. This may be in the form of a document, graph, charts, a voice recording, newspapers, and music. You get access to down-loadable material on the web by right-clicking links that are made available on web sites that you browse. To download something to your local computer, right-click the link with your mouse and you will see the pop-up dialog appear (see Figure 1-6). To download something, click the "Save link as" menu option. The operating system's standard "Save As" dialog window will then appear. You use this as normal and choose where the file will be downloaded by clicking the "Save" button when finished.

Once you begin the download of a file, a button for each downloaded or currently downloading file will appear in the downloads bar at the bottom of the current active tab (see Figure 1-35). If the file is currently downloading, the button will contain an indication that the download is still in progress. If for some reason during the download process you need to pause the download or cancel it, you can do this in one of two ways:

Figure 1-35: Download files notice button

To pause or cancel the download, click the "Downloads" menu item accessed from the "Customize" icon menu on the Chrome toolbar (see Figure 1-5). A new tab will open in Chrome showing the downloads currently in progress, and those that have been previously downloaded (see Figure 1-36). For the current download, you can pause or cancel it by clicking on the "Pause" or "Cancel" link located to the right of the download information (see Figure 1-36).

Figure 1-36: Downloads tab page

You can also cancel the download by clicking on the small menu arrow that appears on the right-hand side of the download notice button in the downloads bar. This will display the small pop-up menu (see Figure 1-37). Once the file is downloaded, you can access it as any other file on your computer. To access it, go to the directory you downloaded it to via your operating system's file access window. Alternatively, you can click the "Show in folder" menu item from the download notice button (see Figure 1-37). This will open a new access window on your computer system and list all the files in the directory you downloaded the file into. Another alternative is to access the downloads tab page (see Figure 1-36), and click on the link to the downloaded file on your local computer.

Figure 1-37: Download notice button pop-up menu

Internet Security

The Internet can be a dangerous place; however common sense is your best defense against most dangers. There are various tools that you can use to aid you in defense against "attacks." In this section we will cover how to recognize web sites that try to mimic other web sites, malicious web sites, and the best practices for handling these situations.

Security Certificates

The best method of protecting yourself is to look for security certificates. These are encryption keys provided to you by a recognized and trusted third party including Google. Any web site that has "https://" at the front will have a security certificate assigned to it. These certificates can either be issued by a certificate authority or generated by the owner of the web site. Only web sites with security certificates issued by selected authorities are considered trusted. Chrome will protect you by presenting a clear warning if something is wrong (see Figure 1-38).

Figure 1-38: Security Certificate Warning

Figure 1-38 shows an important warning about the web site you are trying to visit. If you see this warning, click the "Back to safety" button, which will take you to the previously visited web page.

You should also note the warning symbol in the upper right-hand corner of the address bar. The icon will either be a warning symbol or a padlock. Whenever you see a warning symbol in the upper-right corner of the address bar, you should always be extra careful.

As well as knowing how Chrome responds to an untrusted web site, you should also know how Chrome behaves with a trusted web site.

Figure 1-39: A trusted, secured website

Figure 1-39 shows the address bar when visiting https://checkout.google.com. The first thing you should check when visiting a web site that you think is secure is the color of the address bar. The address bar turns yellow when the website you visit is presenting appropriate security credentials from a trusted authority. As well as the address bar the letters "https://" will be green and the padlock icon is located in the right corner of the address bar.

Malware sites

Malware is software that is designed to damage your computer and should be avoided at all times. Malware can take many forms such as viruses, trojans, and key loggers, and are frequently created and used by criminals to gain something from you including remote use of your computer, your banking details, or in some cases just to cause havoc.

If you go to a web site that is known to contain malware, Chrome will present you with a warning page (see Figure 1-38).

Warning: Visiting this site may harm your computer!

The website at **malware.testing.google.test** appears to host malware – software that can hurt your computer or otherwise operate without your consent. Just visiting a site that hosts malware can infect your computer.

For detailed information about the problems with this site, visit the Google Safe Browsing diagnostic page for malware.testing.google.test.

Learn more about how to protect yourself from harmful software online.

☐ I understand that visiting this site may harm my computer. [Proceed anyway]
[Back to safety]

Figure 1-40: Malware warning

If you see this page, you should never proceed. If you do continue, your computer may be compromised and used for illegal activates which may draw the attention of your local authorities. You should at very least click "Back to Safety."

Phishing

Phishing is a process where a malicious person creates a web site to mimic an authentic web site. The malicious web site is designed to capture any personal information that is inputted into it. Most phishing web sites are designed to mimic Internet banking web sites. Generally with phishing, you will receive an email saying that there is something wrong with your bank account and asking you to go to a link such as MyBank.com. However, the link actually takes you to a web site that can be along the lines of mybank.secure.banking.example.com. You should always look at the address in the address bar of any web site that you intend to enter any personal details in to ensure that you are where you think you are.

Phishing web sites also do not usually have a valid, if any, security certificate. This is a very easy and quick way to check if a page that you think is your bank's web site is truly your bank's web site.

ExplainED

Phishing sites can be created and distributed to Internet users very quickly so the malware protection may not have caught up.

Best Practices

Best practices for security are designed to keep your computer and your personal information safe. You should always use common sense on the Internet and follow the advice below as a basic guide to keep you safe.

1. Always have a current virus scanner and firewall.

2. Never give out personal details on the Internet.

3. Never trust that information on the Internet is correct only because it is on the Internet.

4. Never give out your credit card details to any insecure web site.

5. Never give out your credit card details to any web site belonging to a company which you can't find and verify a physical address for.

6. Never bypass the malware filter.

7. If you see the malware warning, close the tab as the web site you were on previously may have been changed by an attacker to direct all traffic to the malware web site.

8. Always be aware of the web sites you visit to protect yourself against phishing.

9. If something seems too good to be true, it is.

ExplainED

There are many free virus scanners on the Internet such as Avast (www.avast.com) URL Correct at time of access.

The above is by no means an exhaustive list. There are new threats appearing on the Internet every day. If you notice a significant change in how your computer acts, you should contact a reputable computer technician or service center immediately.

Summary

In this chapter we have covered many parts of Google Chrome. We began by covering how to install Google Chrome, surfing, using tabs, and incognito mode. We then looked at how to configure Chrome, including the privacy and security settings which are vital to protecting users. Following security, we examined how to control what you see by using various menus to adjust how text is displayed, changing the language, using developer features, the bookmarks toolbar, full screen, and the search field. We looked at how to use, create, and manage bookmarks with the Bookmark Manager. We discussed changing the theme for Chrome, how to use plug-ins to change how your browser behaves, as well as downloading files. In the final section we covered security and how you can begin to protect yourself from the many dangers prevalent on the Internet by the use of Chrome's built-in features and external programs such as virus scanners. However, please be aware that in most instances, your common sense and vigilance is the best defense.

Readers who are new to Internet browsers will learn a lot about how Google Chrome works. Readers will also learn how they can change the settings of various components of Google Chrome to suit their individual preferences and needs. Most importantly, the security section will significantly aid readers in protecting their computers and themselves from the dangers of the Internet.

Chapter 2

Gmail

E-mail has become a pervasive technology in society that we all use, and the development and general acceptance has generally mirrored that of the web in recent times. It has become a technology that we use in our daily lives, and indeed for some, it has become a standard way of doing business. E-mail has become a critical business tool and personal communication tool with uses from catching up with your relatives to discussions about contracts. E-mail in some countries has advanced to the same legal status as traditional letters. In Australia, courts can legally serve documents on people and law firms if they provide the court with an appropriate e-mail address. Additionally, some lawyers and process servers in Australia use e-mails to serve notice and legal documents. Because of this, and the dependency of many businesses on e-mail, the reliability, security, and accessibility of an e-mail service is a critical issue.

Gmail is a web-based e-mail application offered by Google. Initially for Google employees only, Gmail was offered to the public in 2004 as an invitation-only service. Since then it has become one of the most popular free e-mail services with a generous storage capacity of over seven GB (gigabytes), equating to approximately 3.5 million pages of text. It is claimed that the average user will never need to delete any e-mail. Gmail has, over the last few years, become the benchmark in reliability, performance, and anti-spam. The spam filtering technique is a community-driven system where individuals can mark e-mail as spam, in turn helping the system to identify possible spam in the future. Additionally, the interface for Gmail is based around a "conversation view" of the e-mails and their response chains, making it easy to follow a chain of e-mail-response messages when tracking issues such as "who-said-what."

If you already have a Gmail account, you can begin using Gmail by going straight to www.gmail.com. If you do not have a Gmail account, the next section describes how to register for one for free.

Creating a Gmail Account

To create your free Gmail account, begin by loading your web browser and navigating to the web page address www.Gmail.com. This web address can be reached by clicking on the "Gmail" link in the GoogleApps toolbar while viewing the Google home page (see Figure 2-1). From here you can log-in to Gmail if you already have an account, or create a new account. To create a new account, begin by clicking on the "Create an account" button located on the bottom right of the web page (see Figure 2-1).

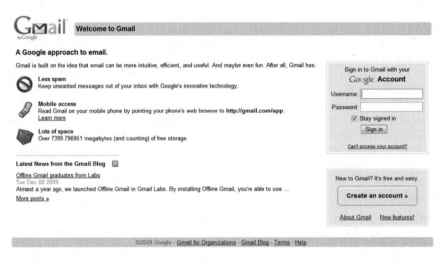

Figure 2-1: Gmail home page

To create a Gmail account, you must fill in all fields on the form displayed on the screen (see Figure 2-2). You need to fill in your first and last name along with a desired login name. The login name is the name that you will use to loginto your Gmail account. It will also be part of your e-mail address. For example, if you choose Fred as your login name, your Gmail e-mail address will be Fred@Gmail.com. Your login name must be unique, and with millions of Gmail users you may not get your first choice.

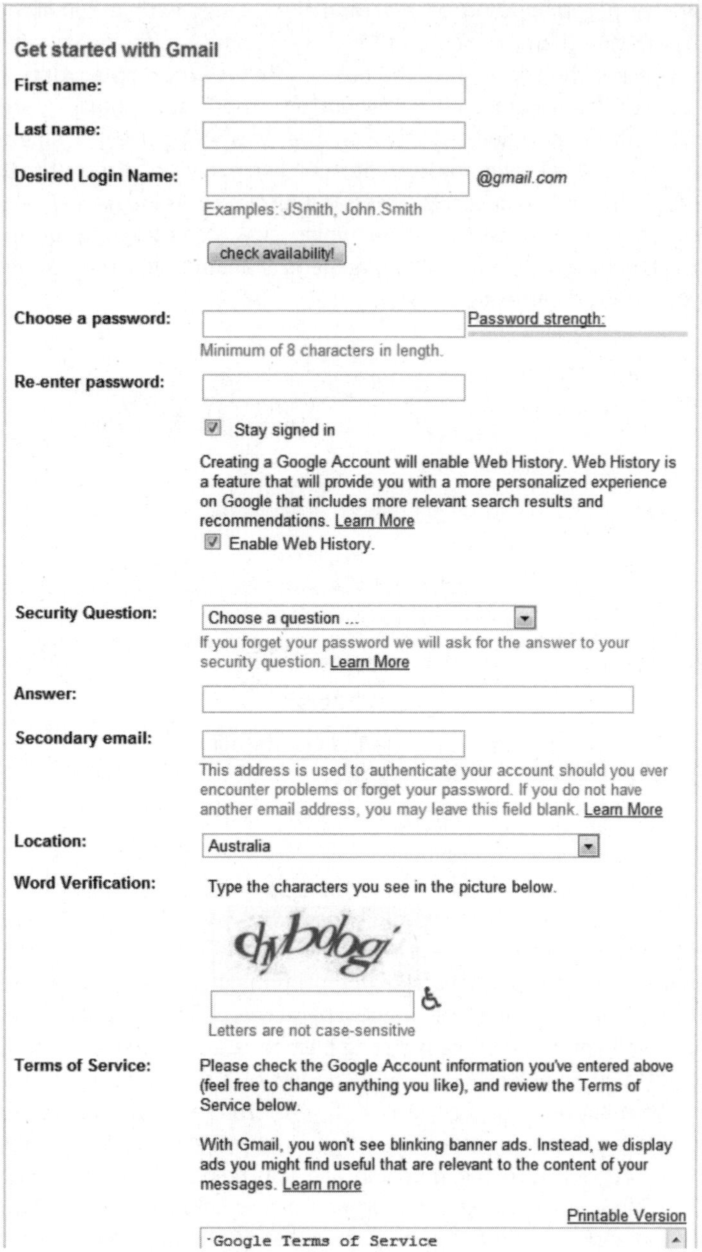

Get started with Gmail

First name:

Last name:

Desired Login Name: @gmail.com

Examples: JSmith, John.Smith

[check availability!]

Choose a password: Password strength:

Minimum of 8 characters in length.

Re-enter password:

☑ Stay signed in

Creating a Google Account will enable Web History. Web History is a feature that will provide you with a more personalized experience on Google that includes more relevant search results and recommendations. Learn More
☑ Enable Web History.

Security Question: Choose a question ...   ▼

If you forget your password we will ask for the answer to your security question. Learn More

Answer:

Secondary email:

This address is used to authenticate your account should you ever encounter problems or forget your password. If you do not have another email address, you may leave this field blank. Learn More

Location: Australia   ▼

Word Verification: Type the characters you see in the picture below.

dybobgi

                                                         &

Letters are not case-sensitive

Terms of Service: Please check the Google Account information you've entered above (feel free to change anything you like), and review the Terms of Service below.

With Gmail, you won't see blinking banner ads. Instead, we display ads you might find useful that are relevant to the content of your messages. Learn more

Printable Version

·Google Terms of Service   ▲

Figure 2-2: Create Gmail account form

47

You could try a combination of first and last names with a full-stop ("." or period) separating them, or some other unique combination. Gmail gives you a means to check if the login name you have chosen is acceptable. After you type in your desired login name, click the button "check availability!" just below the entry. If the login name is not available, you will get a warning message just below the "check availability!" button. For example, if you try the login name *Fred.Smith*, you will see the message displayed in Figure 2-3, along with suggested options. You can keep re-typing new combinations until you no longer see a warning displayed. If the name is available, you will see a message stating your desired name is available.

Figure 2-3: Login name availability warning

You then need to choose and type in a password you will use to login to your Gmail account. You need to enter this twice in the form so the system knows you have not made a typing mistake when filling out the form. Create a strong password with a minimum of eight characters and record the password somewhere and keep it secure. A strong password is considered to be one that would be difficult to guess and usually consists of a combination of characters, digits and special characters such as #, $, etc. You can now choose a security question. This is used in case you forget your password. The Google login process can then ask you the question and you respond with the confidential answer. You should choose a question and answer combination of which only you know the answer. There is a drop-down list of standard questions, and you can choose to create your own question. Enter the answer to the security question in the provided field. Additionally, you can enter a secondary e-mail address if you have one. If you forget your password, Google can send it to this secondary e-mail address. You can leave this field blank if you don't have one. Select your location from the drop-down list of countries. In some countries, when creating an account you may need to supply a mobile phone number that supports text messaging.

Before you can complete the form and accept the terms of service, you will need to read the distorted sequence of red characters (see Figure 2-2) just below the country location. Retype these characters exactly as you see them into the "Word Verification" field, and then accept Google's terms of service by clicking the "I accept, Create my account" button underneath the terms of service. If the word verification is incorrect, you will be given another sequence of characters in which you will need to retype. This is a security measure in place by Google.

If the form is accepted, your Gmail account will be created and you will be logged into Gmail.

Basic E-mail Functions

As with every other e-mail system, Gmail provides you with the basic functionality to read, receive, print, delete, and store e-mails. Additionally, Gmail provides interesting functionality not provided by other systems, particularly a "conversation view" of your e-mail. This makes it simple to identify and recall back and forth conversations on a particular topic. We will discuss these basic functions in the following sections.

When you login to Gmail, you will be presented with the default Gmail view (see Figure 2-4). The default Gmail view consists of a series of links down the left-hand side of the screen to perform basic e-mail functions and to access some of your e-mail boxes such as the inbox, sent mail box, etc. In the middle of the window, and taking up most of the windows readable space, is the box view containing a list of e-mails residing in the current mail box. The default mail box displayed when you first login to Gmail is the inbox. E-mails in the current box are listed in chronological order and conversation view, which we will discuss in a later section.

Figure 2-4: Opening default Gmail screen

Composing and Sending Mail

Sending e-mail is one of the most basic functions you will need to perform in any e-mail software. To send a new e-mail, you must first click on the "Compose Mail" link located in the upper left of the Gmail browser window just under the Gmail logo. You will then be presented with a "Compose e-mail" screen (see Figure 2-5).

The first step you should take when sending an e-mail is to enter the e-mail address of the person you are sending the e-mail to. This is done in the "To" field at the top of the compose e-mail form. You can send the same e-mail to multiple recipients by entering multiple e-mail addresses in the "To" field separated by commas (see Figure 2-6).

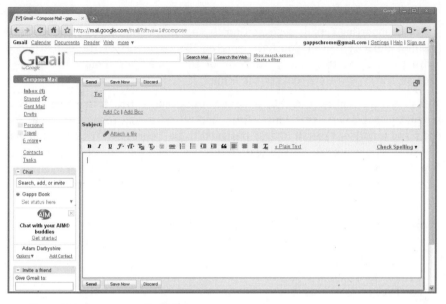

Figure 2-5: Compose mail window

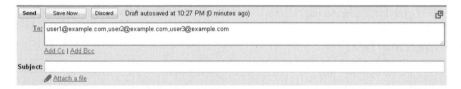

Figure 2-6: Multiple addresses in the "To" field

ExplainED

When addressing e-mails, always ensure you check that e-mail addresses are accurately typed.

The next step when composing an e-mail is to enter an appropriate subject title in the "Subject" field just below the "To" field. An e-mail subject is important as it gives the reader an indication of what the e-mail is about without reading the e-mail itself. This allows people to quickly skim through several e-mail headers deciding what may need urgent attention and what may be dealt with at a later time. When deciding on the subject of an e-mail, always try to make it as concise as possible and not too extensive. The latter point is important as e-mail subject headers may often be read on a mobile device supporting Gmail, such as Google Android mobile devices (which have limited capacity). After you have entered the recipients of the e-mail along with the subject text, click the body of the e-mail just below the subject header and type the contents of the e-mail.

Gmail has the ability to create e-mails with advanced text formatting such as changing text colors, text fonts, sizes, and other textual formatting including lists and emoticons (small images designed to be inserted with text to aid you in expressing yourself). To use text formatting, click the icon corresponding to the formatting option you wish to apply to your text. The icons are located on the "Compose mail" toolbar just above the e-mail body (see Figure 2-7).

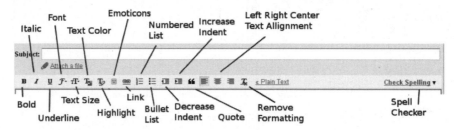

Figure 2-7: Compose mail toolbar

Formatting Text

The "Font," "Text Size," "Text Color," "Highlight," and "Insert emoticon," buttons open a menu to present you with additional options. For example, clicking on the "Font" button opens the drop-down menu (see Figure 2-8). To select a different font, select from the list in the drop-down menu, and from that point on in the message body, the text will be displayed with the new font as you type (unless you change it again). If you only wish the selected font to be applied to a small portion of the selected text in the message, select the text in the message body first before clicking the "Font" button and choosing a new font. The new font will only be applied to the selected text. The "Text Size," "Text Color," and "Highlight" toolbar options behave in exactly the same way, except for the formatting options they apply.

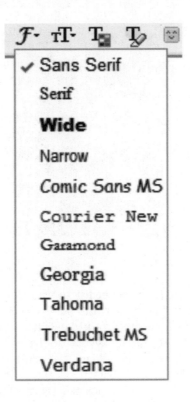

Figure 2-8: Toolbar font options

The "Text Color" and "Text Highlight" toolbar options bring up a color-picked dialog (see Figure 2-9). To use this option, select the new color to apply to either the "Text Color" or "Text Highlight" options by clicking the color. The dialog will then close and the new color option will apply from that point on in the message, or be applied to the selected text as in the "Font" option.

Once you select the option you want in the toolbar options, the drop-down menu or dialog will automatically close in all style menus except for the "Insert Emoticon" option. In this case, a small window permanently opens just below, giving you a number of emoticons to choose from. Clicking an emoticon will place a copy of it in the message text where the cursor currently is. You can keep typing your message and choose any emoticon at any time by clicking it in the window. To close the emoticon window, click the "Insert Emoticon" button on the toolbar again for it to disappear.

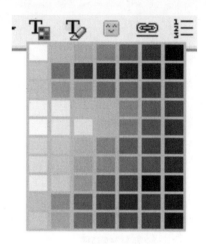

Figure 2-9: Color picker dialog

You can add a numbered list or bullet list to your e-mail message by clicking either the "Numbered list" or "Bullet list" buttons on the toolbar. The current line your cursor is on will be converted to a bullet or numbered point. Type text and press the return key on the keyboard. This will create a new bullet or numbered point on the next line. When you have finished, just click the "Numbered list" or "Bullet list" button on the toolbar again to turn the formatting option off. If when you click the "Numbered list" or "Bullet list" buttons on the toolbar, the cursor is already in a paragraph containing text, the entire paragraph will be converted to a numbered or bullet point. Multiple-level lists can be created by using the "Text indent" buttons to demote parts of the list

Other formatting options available on the toolbar include left, center, or justification of text, along with the standard bold, italic, and underline options. You can clear the formatting of a particular piece of text by selecting the text with the cursor and choosing the "Remove formatting" button in the toolbar. The selected text will have any previously applied formatting removed. You can disable advanced e-mail formatting by clicking on the "Plain text" link in the styles bar. Clicking this button will remove all styles and advanced components that are in the e-mail. This may be necessary when sending e-mail to someone using a much older e-mail system which is not capable of interpreting the advanced formatting options available in Gmail.

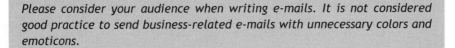

Please consider your audience when writing e-mails. It is not considered good practice to send business-related e-mails with unnecessary colors and emoticons.

Spell checker

Gmail has a built-in spell checker that automatically checks spelling as you type. If Gmail finds words that it does not recognize, it will underline them in red. Additionally, you can easily activate the message spell checker by clicking the "Check spelling" link on the right-hand side of the toolbar. The spell checker will automatically highlight any incorrectly spelled words in yellow (see Figure 2-10). It should be pointed out that words may not actually be incorrect. Gmail and similar programs will only highlight words not contained within its respective dictionary. If you use a technical word, or a word not in the dictionary, it may be correct but still highlighted.

Figure 2-10: Spell checker highlight of incorrect spelling

Once the spell checker has finished checking a document, you can correct misspelled words by left clicking the yellow highlighted words. This will bring up a drop-down menu (see Figure 2-11). As shown, the spell checker will suggest possible corrections for incorrectly spelled words. If the correct spelling of the word is in the list, left click on the correct spelling and Gmail will fix the mistake within the text where you left-clicked. Once you have finished with the spell checker or wish to recheck the spelling of your e-mail, click either the "Done" or "Recheck" link to the right of the toolbar.

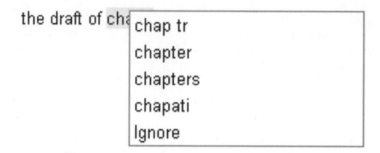

Figure 2-11: Spell checker drop-down menu

At any time during writing the message, you can right-click an underlined word that Gmail believes is spelled incorrectly, or even during the spell-checking phase outlined above. Right-clicking a word displays a drop-down menu (see Figure 2-12). As per the spell checker left-click menu, the right-click menu provides a list of alternative words you can choose from in the upper part of the drop-down menu. If you believe the word is spelled correctly but is not in the dictionary, you can select the "Add to dictionary" option and the word will be added to the Gmail dictionary. Be careful adding words to a dictionary, as adding an incorrectly spelled word to the dictionary will result in Gmail not trying to correct the word again if spelled the way it was when the word was added. By choosing the "Spell-checker options" from the menu, you can modify the language settings for Gmail. This allows you to change the default fonts for all your e-mails and the languages used by Gmail to spell check with, present menus in, and present dialog boxes and interact with you.

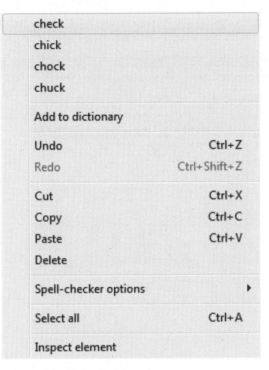

Figure 2-12: Right-click spell checker drop-down menu

Reading Mail

When you receive new e-mail it will be displayed in the main Gmail window (see Figure 2-4) and there will be a number in brackets next to "Inbox" on the left side of the window under the Gmail logo. This is the unread e-mail count. New e-mail will be displayed bold with a white background, and e-mails already read are displayed with a gray background by default (see Figure 2-13).

Figure 2-13: New e-mails

To read an e-mail, click on the e-mail in the list that you wish to read, and it will be displayed in its own read-e-mail box (see Figure 2-14).

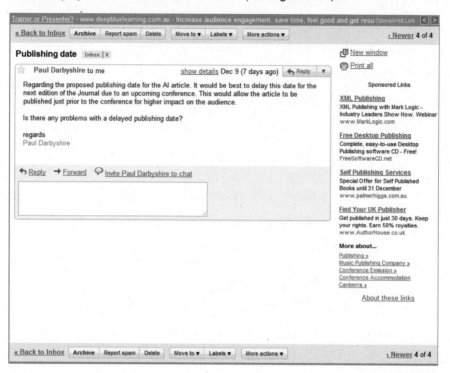

Figure 2-14: Viewing an e-mail

When viewing an e-mail, the screen is split into various sections. Along the top of the message there is an e-mail toolbar containing a number of buttons providing functionality on how to deal with the current e-mail. This same toolbar is also displayed when browsing the various e-mail folders. You can choose to "Archive," "Star," "Delete," or "Move" the current message. Additionally, there are more actions you can perform with the current message, and these can be accessed from the "More actions" drop-down list on the toolbar (see Figure 2-15). We will discuss these various options for dealing with e-mails in following sections. The e-mail toolbar is also repeated at the bottom of the "Read" e-mail window. If the e-mail you are reading is long, you can access the toolbar functionality from either end of the message (or list of messages), possibly saving you time scrolling too far either way. The toolbar is also visible when you are viewing all the mail in the inbox or one of the other folders. In reality, Gmail does not use folders like other e-mail systems, but uses labels. We will discuss labels in detail later in this chapter, but if you are new to Gmail, it can sometimes help at this stage to regard them as folders.

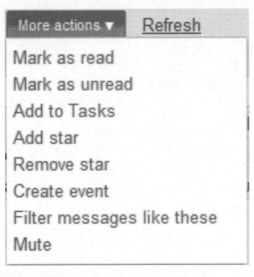

Figure 2-15: Accessing more actions for the current e-mail

When reading a message, just below the toolbar is the header information of the e-mail. This includes the subject, and underneath that in the message box, the sender (who the e-mail is from), and who it was addressed to (labeled as "me" if you are the recipient). To the right of this, the date when the e-mail was sent (with an indication of how many days ago it was sent) and a link you can click if you wish to see more e-mail header information appears. There is also the "Reply" button if you wish to send a response to this message back to the sender. To the left of the e-mail date information is a clickable link labeled "show details." Use this link to see more details of the e-mail header, usually not displayed for brevity. By slicking this, you will expand the header information and it will include the e-mail addresses in full of all recipients except those in the BCC (Blind Carbon Copy) list, the sender and the servers involved in sending and signing the e-mail. Most of the time this information is not needed, but it is available by clicking the link. If the message is a long one, scroll bars will be available on the right of the message window for scrolling through the message window. You can also use the scroll wheel on the mouse if you have one.

NotED

You don't have to be in the "To" field to receive a copy of the e-mail. You could be in the CC or BCC list.

The *"To"* list is used for those people that are directly concerned with the contents of the message. The *"CC"* list is used for people who are not directly concerned with the content, but who will have an interest in the message, for example, project manager, or supervisor receiving *CC's* about project matters between project groups. The *"BCC"* list is used when you want to send a copy of the message to someone, but don't want everyone else on the list to see their inclusion.

Replying to E-mails

Many times we don't need to compose a new e-mail from scratch, but often just want to respond to one we have received. There are a number of ways to do this in Gmail. You can click the "Reply" button located to the right of the e-mail header by the date sent at the top of the message. This will open up an e-mail reply window below the current message you are reading. In the e-mail reply window, you don't need to specify who the e-mail is from or who it is going to unless you want to add more recipients to the list in the "To" field. The "From" and "To" fields will be automatically filled and a copy of the original e-mail will be included in the message body below a blank line where the cursor is placed waiting for you to begin the response (see Figure 2-16).

As this is a response message, the e-mail "Subject" is not typically displayed. However it can be edited and displayed by clicking on the "Edit Subject" link displayed just below the "To" field (see Figure 2-16). You can add "CC" and "BCC" recipients to the reply by clicking on the "Add CC" and "Add BCC" links located near the "Edit Subject" link and adding the e-mail addresses to the appropriate lists. The message you are creating can be formatted in the same way as discussed in "Composing and Sending E-mail."

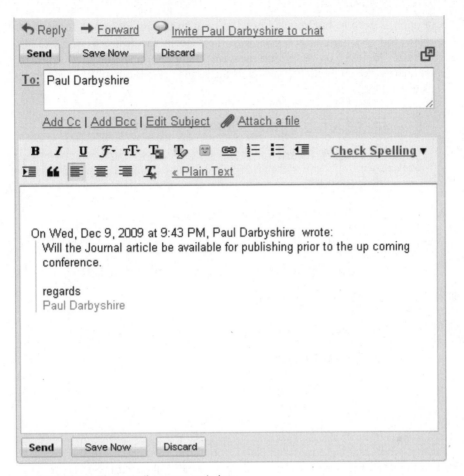

Figure 2-16: The e-mail response window

When choosing to reply to a message, there are also additional options. There is a small down arrow just to the right of the "Reply" button when reading an e-mail. Clicking this will open a drop-down menu (see Figure 2-17). This gives more options for dealing with the current e-mail. Normally, when you click the "Reply" button as discussed before, the return e-mail will be addressed to only the sender of the e-mail. If there were more than one name on the "From," "CC," and "BCC" list in the e-mail, you can choose to return a copy of your response to all people on these lists by choosing the "Reply to all" menu option on the drop-down menu. The e-mail reply window will be opened and you can proceed as before. Alternatively, you could forward a copy of the e-mail to someone by clicking the "Forward" menu option. The e-mail response window will open as before, but you will need to type an e-mail address to forward the e-mail. You can then attach your own message in the forward. You can also choose to "Delete" or "Print the message," and choosing the "Add (insert e-mail address) to contacts list" will add the sender of the e-mail to your current lists of contacts.

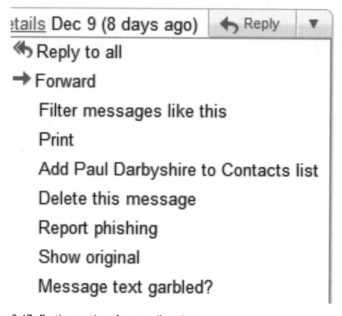

Figure 2-17: Further options for e-mail action

Finally, when reading a message (see Figure 2-16), you could use the mouse to click the small box area below the message, which will additionally open the e-mail response window as if you had clicked the "Reply" button.

After you've finished composing the reply to the e-mail, click the "Send" button located either above or below the message reply window. The response will then be sent to the addresses specified in the response.

Conversation View

One of the unique features of Gmail is the conversation view listings of the messages when viewing the e-mail lists in the Gmail folders. This is designed to group all e-mails by subject regardless of the sender or receiver so that entire conversation tracks can be grouped together. This can be helpful in many situations when trying to track down a sequence of conversations by e-mail and confirming who said what and when. The header of a conversation group can be seen when viewing a list of e-mails in the inbox (see Figure 2-13),. Next to the sender of the e-mail is a number in brackets indicating how many e-mails are in the conversation group. Conversation groups are created automatically based on the subject line of an e-mail. When you send or receive an e-mail if your reply to it this will be saved as part of a conversation. When you open up a conversation group (as you would open any e-mail for reading), the group of messages belonging to the conversation group collectively opens and you can quickly browse through the collection (see Figure 2-18).

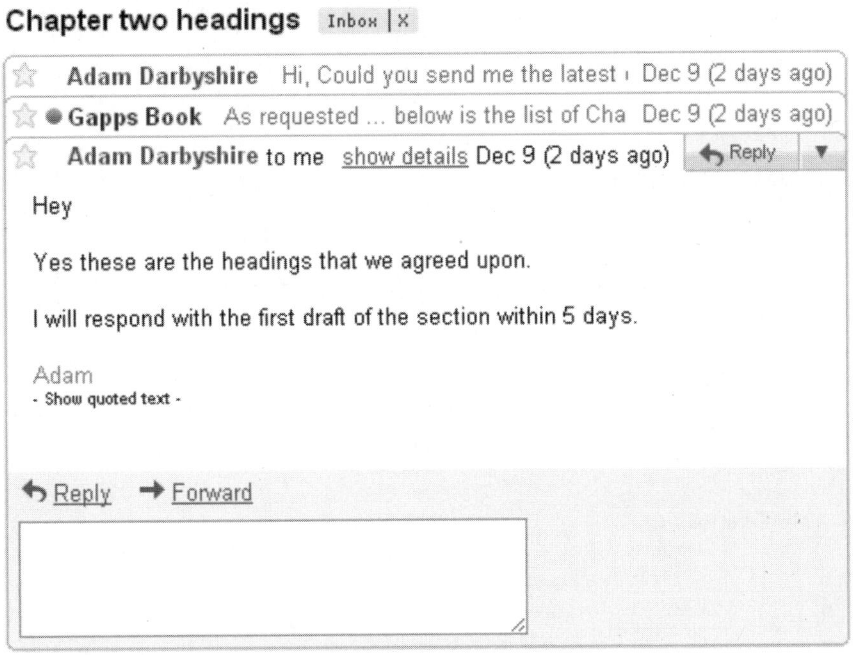

Chapter two headings   Inbox | X

☆	**Adam Darbyshire** Hi, Could you send me the latest ⟨	Dec 9 (2 days ago)
☆ ●	**Gapps Book** As requested ... below is the list of Cha	Dec 9 (2 days ago)
☆	**Adam Darbyshire** to me show details Dec 9 (2 days ago)	↩ Reply ▼

Hey

Yes these are the headings that we agreed upon.

I will respond with the first draft of the section within 5 days.

Adam
- Show quoted text -

↩ Reply   → Forward

Figure 2-18: Conversation view

As you can see, the conversation view groups e-mails by the subject, and the most recent e-mail in the group is displayed. The headers of previously written messages in the conversation can be seen displayed above the most recent in chronological order with the oldest at the top. To see a previous message in a conversation, click the header of that message. The e-mail message will open so it can be read, with any older headers displayed above this message, and new headers in the conversation will be displayed below (see Figure 2-19).

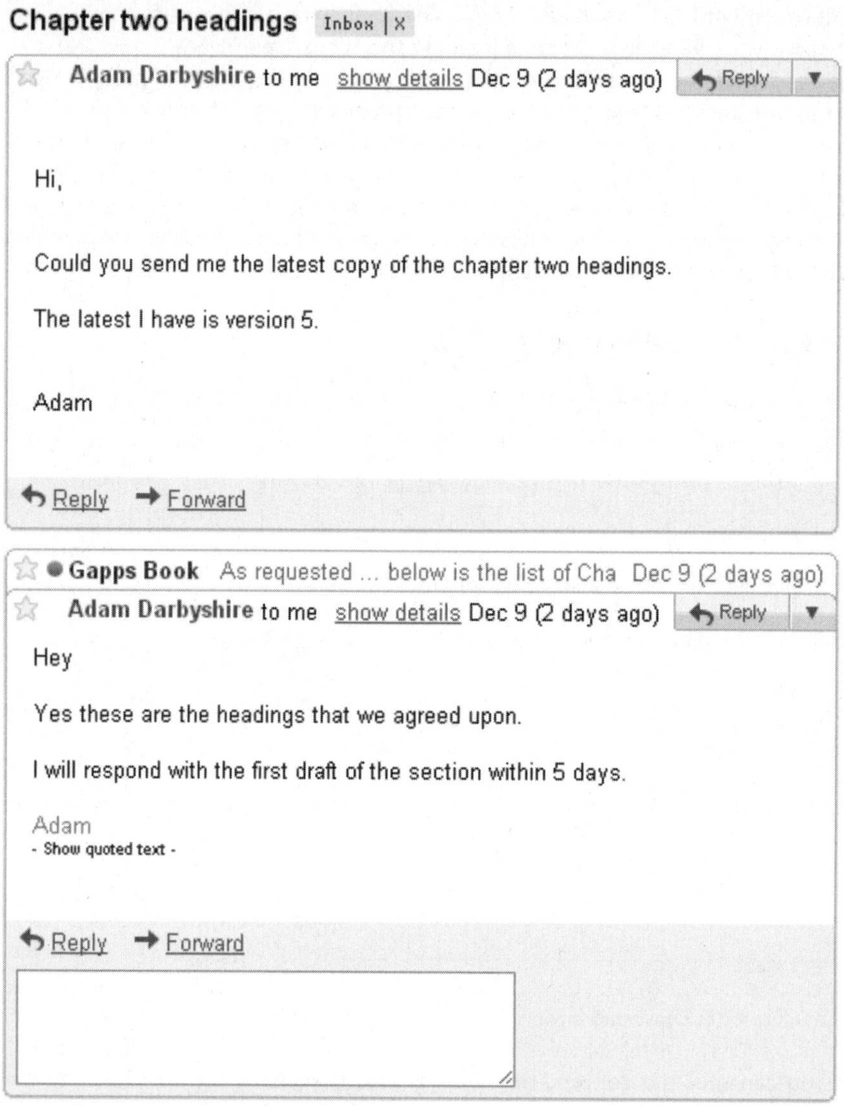

Chapter two headings Inbox | x

☆ **Adam Darbyshire** to me   show details Dec 9 (2 days ago)   ↰ Reply   ▼

Hi,

Could you send me the latest copy of the chapter two headings.

The latest I have is version 5.

Adam

↰ Reply   → Forward

☆ ● **Gapps Book**   As requested ... below is the list of Cha   Dec 9 (2 days ago)

☆ **Adam Darbyshire** to me   show details Dec 9 (2 days ago)   ↰ Reply   ▼

Hey

Yes these are the headings that we agreed upon.

I will respond with the first draft of the section within 5 days.

Adam
- Show quoted text -

↰ Reply   → Forward

Figure 2-19: Expanded conversation view

When viewing any of the messages in a conversation, you have access to all the reply, forwarding, and other features as you would when viewing any single message. After looking at a specific message in the conversation group, click its header again and the message will shrink back to just the header in the conversation group. The last message in the conversation group is always opened, and clicking its header will do nothing. In a conversation, the messages sent by you are marked with a green dot to the left of the header (see Figure 2-18).

Selecting e-mails

The later sections of this chapter will discuss how to manipulate groups of e-mails. In order to do this, you need to know how to select groups of e-mails appropriate to the tasks you wish to perform. When you are viewing a list of e-mails in folder view (see Figure 2-13) you will notice a small check box on the left of each mail message. To select a message or group of messages for processing, use the mouse and click the check boxes of the messages you want to select. When you click a check box, a small "tick" appears in the box and the message header in the list, by default, will be highlighted in yellow (see Figure 2-20). You can check as many boxes corresponding to e-mails as you would like from the list.

Archive	Report spam	Delete	Move to ▼	Labels ▼	More actions ▼	Refresh	1 - 4 of 4

Select: All, None, Read, Unread, Starred, Unstarred

☐ ☆	Paul Darbyshire	Chapter 0 - Please find as an attacl 📎	Dec 9
☐ ☆	Adam, me (3)	Chapter two headings - Hey Yes th	Dec 9
☑ ☆	Paul Darbyshire	Google Conference - Will the Journ:	Dec 9
☑ ☆	Paul Darbyshire	Publishing date - Regarding the pro	Dec 9

Figure 2-20: Selecting multiple e-mails

If you wish to select all e-mails in the list, there is a "Select All" link on the left just above the message list and below the toolbar. Click this to select all messages. If you wish to make sure no messages are selected, click the "Select None" link next to the "Select All" link. Other options for selection include "Read," which will select all read e-mails in the list; "Unread," which will select all the unread messages; "Starred" which will select all starred messages; and "Unstarred" to select all messages that are not starred.

Once a message or group of messages has been selected, the group can then be manipulated as a whole for specific actions.

Sent Messages

Every time you send an e-mail message, Gmail keeps a copy of it in the "Sent Mail" folder. By doing this, you can review older messages you have sent if you can't recall what you have written in past e-mails. If the message was part of a conversation, the entire conversation will be available in the "Sent Mail" folder, not just the messages you have sent. Similarly, when you open a conversation group in the "Sent Mail" folder, the messages sent by you are marked with a green dot to the left of the header.

To access your sent mail folder, click "Sent Mail" (see Figure 2-21). This will open the "Sent Mail" folder and display the message list of all messages in the folder.

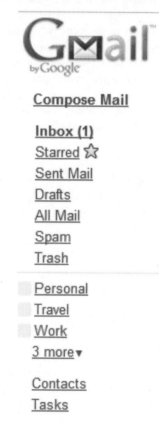

Figure 2-21: Sent mail folder

When viewing sent mail, you can choose to respond to a particular message similar to "Replying to E-mail." The small difference comes when choosing to reply to a message. When you are reading from the inbox, the reply window that opens will automatically have the return address as the sender of the e-mail. However, when you are reading messages in sent mail, the sender of the messages will be you. When you choose to reply to one of these messages, the reply window will open as in "Replying to E-mails," but the return address will be the original "To" address in the sent message. Once the reply window opens, you can edit the message subject and any of the "To," "CC," or "BCC" lists.

Draft Messages

Draft messages are messages you have begun to write but not completed. When you are composing a message by either creating a new e-mail or responding to one through clicking "Reply," instead of canceling the message or sending it, you can click the "Save Now" button next to the "Send" button. By doing this, you save a copy of the message as you left it in the "Drafts" folder. You can go back to this folder at any time by clicking the "Drafts" link just below the "Sent Mail" link (see Figure 2-22). This will display a list of messages you have saved in draft mode. You can open any one of them as you would a normal message from a folder view so you can resume composing the message. Once you have finished the changes, you can send the message as you would when composing a message from scratch, or replying to another message. Then click the "Send" button. The message is sent to the original addressee and automatically removed from the "Drafts" folder. Additionally, a copy is sent to the "Sent Mail" folder.

Figure 2-22: Draft mail

Deleting Messages

There are a number of ways to delete e-mail messages. While reading an individual message, you can click the "Delete" button located in the toolbar, or select the "Delete this message" option from the drop-down menu by clicking the small down arrow near the "Reply" button. No warning will be given and the message will be deleted. Alternatively, when in folder view mode, viewing a list of messages in a folder (such as the inbox), you can select a group of messages by clicking their check boxes as outlined earlier. By clicking the "Delete" button, all selected messages will be deleted.

While no warning is given when a message or group of messages is deleted, this is not a problem. All deleted messages are temporarily put into a "Trash" folder, and they may be retrieved within 30 days, or Gmail will remove it from the "Trash" automatically. If you delete a message and immediately realize that you didn't want to delete it, Gmail will display a yellow bar at the top of the e-mail screen with an "Undo" link. Clicking this will restore it immediately. After retrieving a message in the "Trash" folder, select the "Move to Inbox" from the "Move to" menu button on the toolbar. The message will be moved back to the inbox.

ExplainED

Gmail will automatically remove messages in the "Trash" folder after 30 days.

When you are reading a message as part of a conversation and you delete the message by clicking the "Delete" button on the toolbar, the entire conversation will be deleted. However, by choosing the drop-down menu next to the "Reply" button (see Figure 2-17), only the current message will be deleted.

Archiving Mail

Gmail allows users to archive their e-mail. When you archive your e-mail, it's taken out of your inbox and assigned to a general folder containing all e-mail messages. It is not assigned to any specific folder. To archive an e-mail, you must either have the mail message open or select the e-mail in your folder view of the inbox. Once archived, it can't be accessed from the inbox. It must be located by going to the "All Mail" link in the menu on the left of the screen (see Figure 2-23). Depending on how you set up the display under Gmail, the "All Mail" link may not be immediately visible. In this case, select the "6 more" link in the menu on the left (see Figure 2-23).When further folder options are displayed below, you can select the "All Mail" option from these.

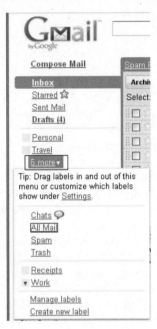

Figure 2-23: All Mail link

Once you are in the "All Mail" folder, you can locate archived mail by looking at the beginning of the subject name. Each e-mail that does not have the word inbox at the front of the subject (or the name of another folder it belongs to) has been archived (see Figure 2-24). If there are many archived e-mails, you may have to search through the "All Mail" folder using a search criteria (discussed later).

Figure 2-24: Locating archived messages

To archive an e-mail or group of e-mails from the inbox, select the group of e-mails to archive by clicking the check box of the e-mails and click the "Archive" button located on the toolbar. When you click "Archive" in a conversation group, or when you are reading a specific message in a conversation, the entire conversation will be archived. To un-archive e-mail, locate the e-mail in the "All mail" folder and either select the message while in folder view or while reading the specific message itself. Then choose the "Move to Inbox" option from the "Move" button menu on the toolbar. This will move the message (or entire conversation) back to the inbox.

Starred Mail

Starred messages are a way of flagging messages to be easily located. Google suggests that you assign stars to special messages or conversations and use them as a visual reminder that something needs to be done with the message. You can star a message by clicking the star icon just to the left of the sender's name just under the subject heading as you are reading the message (see Figure 2-25). The star icon is always there, but if the message has been starred, the star icon shows as a bright yellow icon. Otherwise it remains grayed out.

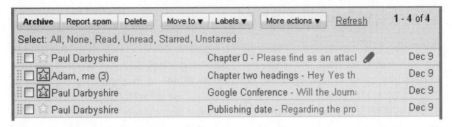

Figure 2-25: Star

You can star a group of messages by selecting the group while in folder view, selecting the "Add star" menu option from the "More actions" pull-down menu on the toolbar. Once you star a message, you can easily find them by going to the "Starred folder" (see Figure 2-26). Access this is via the links on the left just below the inbox folder.

Figure 2-26: Starred mail folder

To unstar a message, click the star on the e-mail while reading it. Additionally, you can unstar a group of e-mails by selecting the group while in folder view and selecting the "Remove star" menu option from the "More actions" pull-down menu on the toolbar.

Working with Labels

Until now we have been referring to various folders including the inbox, starred, trash, all mail, etc. However, as briefly discussed, Gmail does not use folders like other e-mail systems. Gmail uses labels, a method to group various e-mails by their purpose. This is the equivalent of using folders in a traditional e-mail system. However, unlike a traditional e-mail system, multiple labels can be assigned to a single e-mail. There has been discussion on the use of labels on web blogs. But arguably the use of labels is a superior option than that of folders, giving the user the ability to categorize e-mails by several methods.

There are two methods for assigning a label to an e-mail. First, open the e-mail and click the "Labels" menu button in the toolbar. You can assign a label or labels by clicking different available labels you wish to apply to this message. Each label has a check-box on the left, and you can check as many as you would like (see Figure 2-27). After checking the desired labels, select the "Apply" menu option just below the label options and the labels will be applied.

Figure 2-27: Selecting labels

When labels have been assigned to a message, you can see them when either viewing a list of messages in folder view or when reading a particular message (see Figure 2-28). While in folder view, the labels assigned to a message can be seen just before the subject header (see Figure 2-28a), or can be seen just to the right of the subject header while reading an individual message (see Figure 2-28b). You can remove the labels while reading a message by clicking on the small cross icon (x) to the right of the label name (see Figure 2-28b). While in folder view, you can select a message or a group of messages and choose the "Labels" drop-down menu from the toolbar. Uncheck the labels you want to remove and click the "Apply" menu option (see Figure 2-27).

Figure 2-28: Viewing labels

There are two types of labels that Gmail uses: system labels, which are fixed and cannot be modified, and user labels, which can be created and deleted.

The system labels include:

- Inbox: Where new mail goes by default
- Starred: Where starred mail goes
- Sent: Messages that you send are shown here
- Drafts: Messages marked as drafts are shown here
- Spam: Messages automatically detected or marked as spam automatically go here
- Trash: Messages you have deleted go here and are automatically deleted after 30 days
- All mail: All mail except trash and spam are shown here regardless of the label

There are a number of default user labels created for you when your account is created including:

- Personal
- Receipts
- Travel
- Work

The user labels can be modified or deleted, or you can add your own labels in addition to the default ones. To manage labels, click "Manage labels" from the "Labels" drop-down menu on the toolbar. You will be shown a screen (see Figure 2-29) which is the labels section of the Gmail settings options. This will be discussed later. You can create a custom label by entering a name into the "Create a new label" field and then clicking the "Create" button. You can remove existing labels by clicking the "Remove" button next to the label.

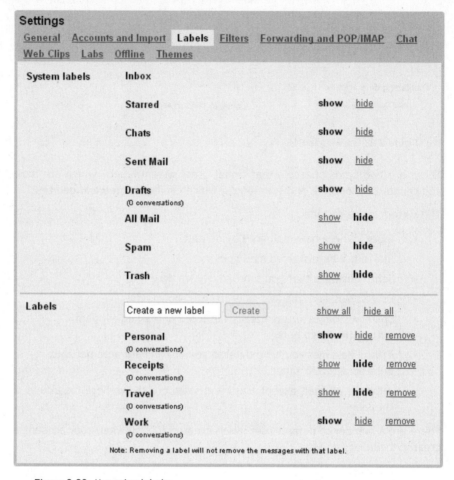

Figure 2-29: Managing labels

Additionally, you can quickly create a label for a message you are reading (or have selected) in folder view. Click the "Labels" menu from the toolbar and select the "Create new" menu option. Enter the new name of the label when prompted (see Figure 2-30). The new label will also show up as a menu option to be checked in the "Labels" drop-down menu, as will a folder option on the menu toward the left of the screen.

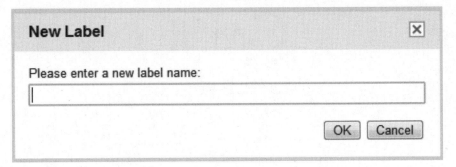

Figure 2-30: New label name

NotED

Removing a label does not delete the e-mails associated with that label.

While managing the labels through the options described earlier, the "Show" and "Hide" buttons next to each label allow users to control whether or not there is a link to the label in the navigation menu on the left side of the screen. If you click "Show" link next to a label, a link to that label will be created in the navigation menu. Similarly, if you click "Hide," the link to the label will be removed (see Figure 2-31).

While we have discussed the use of labels in Gmail, it may still be helpful to consider them as folders. For most users, this will suffice as they won't need to assign multiple labels to messages. We will still continue to talk about message lists in folder view. But as you become more sophisticated in the use of Gmail, you will begin to think in terms of labels rather than folders.

Compose Mail

Inbox
Starred ☆
Chats 💬
Sent Mail
Drafts
All Mail
Spam
Trash

Personal
Receipts
Travel
Work
More ▾

Contacts
Tasks

Figure 2-31: Selecting labels lists

Dealing with Spam

No discussion about e-mail would be complete without a treatment on spam, or unsolicited e-mail. This typically comes in the form of advertising material sent to your e-mail account, but it is not restricted to this. Any unsolicited e-mail can be classed as spam. Over time, spam has become one of the most significant problems on the Internet causing an entire industry to emerge for creating software to detect spam and prevent it from getting into e-mail accounts.

NotED

Some experts are claiming that spam e-mails account for more than 90 percent of all Internet traffic.

Gmail's spam filtration system is well designed and able to filter out most spam messages sent to e-mail accounts. However, like all technology, this process isn't perfect. False positives and negatives will undoubtedly occur. Due to the chance of false positives, you should check the spam folder at least once a week to ensure that no "real" e-mail has accidentally been classified as spam. To do this, click the "Spam" link in the labels menu on the left, or if it is not visible, click the "6 more" link in the navigation menu to see more links, and click the "Spam" link (see Figure 2-32).

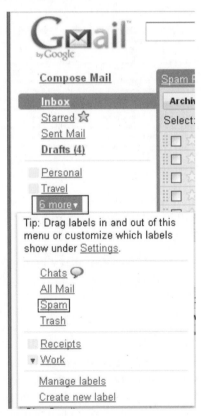

Figure 2-32: Finding the spam folder

ExplainED

E-mail in the spam folder is automatically deleted after 30 days.

Once you are in the spam folder, you will be shown a list of e-mails in folder view having been classified as spam by Gmail (Figure 2-33 shows a selection of spam messages collected over a six-day period). They can accumulate very quickly, but Gmail is efficient in filtering them. If you see an e-mail in the spam folder that you feel should not be there, select the e-mail with either of the methods discussed previously in manipulating e-mail, and click the "Not Spam" button in the toolbar. The message will be moved to the inbox and not marked as spam. Otherwise you can clear all spam e-mails by clicking the "Delete all spam messages now" link. Gmail will also automatically delete these after 30 days.

Grind Master Manuals - Kitchen.ManualsOnline.com - Get User Manuals and How-to Info For Grind Master Products			Sponsored Link
Delete forever Not spam Move to ▼ Labels ▼ More actions ▼ Refresh			1 - 50 of 273 Older › Oldest »
Select: All, None, Read, Unread, Starred, Unstarred			
Delete all spam messages now (messages that have been in Spam more than 30 days will be automatically deleted)			
Ruthie Weston	determinantal - Get stronger down there http://carseed.com Christmas sale		4:12 am
Georgie Yon	_Buy 2 Rep1icaWatches & get 3rd FREE! A.Lange & Sohne, Alain Silberstein, Audemars Pigu... - SwissRep		7:05 pm
Debbi Marsha	Cheap $200 Rep1icaWatches, vRo1exWatches, Specializing in Rep1icaDesignerWatches, Over ... - jRo1exR		Dec 19
Angelic Lorean	Cheap $200 Rep1icaWatches, vRo1exWatches, Specializing in Rep1icaDesignerWatches, Over ... - jRo1exR		Dec 19
Evelina Veronique	Discount Online Pharmacy, Brand & Generic Medication for Less From Your Trusted Canada ... - Your One-S		Dec 19
Shin Crysta	_Buy CheapViagra? $1.05/100mg. Pay 20 Times Less $ Online.. 100% Satisfaction Guarantee... - OrderCializ'		Dec 19
Sharlene Mariann	80% Off LuxuryWatches with 5000+ Styles High Quality Watches. Fast Worldwide Delivery! ... - CheapRo1ex		Dec 18
Mertie Vivian	+Buy ED pills, ED pills on Sale, Shop & Save Deals for you geh g95e - Top SexPills On Sale BuyViagra 100m		Dec 18
Evita Rose	Winter Sale! Codeine, Hydrocodone, Vicodin, XanexValuim & All medications available. Bu... - Codeine, H		Dec 18

Figure 2-33: Spam messages

If a spam message gets through to your inbox, select the message and click the "Report spam" button from your inbox. This will move message to the spam folder and add it to the filter.

Note: Spam derived its name from the Monty Python *comic sketch about Spam.*

Managing Contacts

Like all e-mail systems, Gmail has a built-in contacts list. This lets you manage your lists of contacts and e-mail addresses in an orderly manner. Contacts can be extremely important as they allow you to avoid typing out someone's e-mail address every time. You can also store additional contact information for your contacts including physical addresses and phone numbers. You can access this by clicking "Contacts" on the left side (see Figure 2-34).

Figure 2-34: Contacts list menu selection

The contact list window opens by clicking the "Contacts" link (see Figure 2-35). Contacts can be kept individually or grouped within a contact group. You can create a new contact by clicking the "New Contact" icon on the top left of the contacts window. To create a new contact group, click the "New Group" icon next to it (see Figure 2-35).

When you add a new contact, the new contact form will appear in the right of the contacts window (see Figure 2-36). Here, you can fill in information about this contact. You don't need to fill in all fields of the form as this is information for yourself. The contacts can be as simple as a name and e-mail address, or by using the advanced features, you can use the contacts list to create a complex contact with a larger amount of information.

Figure 2-35: Contacts

Figure 2-36: Adding a new contact

Creating a simple contact is easy, fill in the name and e-mail address and click the "Save" button at the top of the new contact area. Once you have saved the contact, it will be added to the default contact group "All contacts" seen in the "Group list" down the left side of the contacts window (see Figure 2-35). Clicking a contact group will show the contact list belonging to that group in a list to the right of the "Group list" (see Figure 2-35). Clicking a contact in the "Contact list" for a group will display it in the right side of the contact window (see Figure 2-37).

Figure 2-37: A simple contact

ExplainED

While you compose an e-mail, contacts are automatically filled in based on the characters you type into the to field.

When you are adding a contact, the e-mail, telephone, physical address, and website fields have drop down boxes next to them. These allow you to set a tag indicating the type of information in the field next to the box (see Figure 2-38).

81

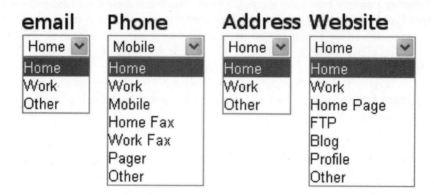

Figure 2-38: Types of information tags

You can add additional fields including secondary e-mails and phone numbers by clicking the small, blue "add" links above the field you wish to duplicate. There is also a drop-down "add" button near the bottom of the page allowing users to add fields including nicknames, dates, web sites, and custom fields. The custom field lets users add a field of their own by allowing the user to set the label of the field and the "Custom value" (see Figure 2-39).

Figure 2-39: The Custom Add button

By using relevant, available fields, you can create a complex contact record (see Figure 2-40).

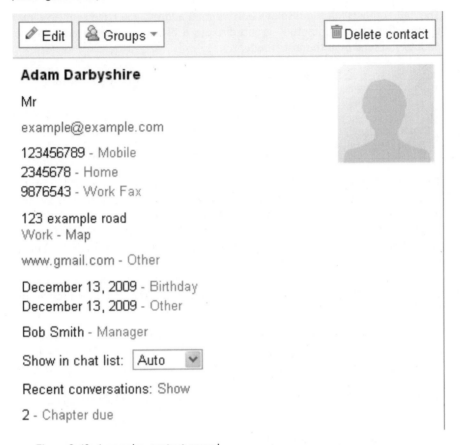

Figure 2-40: A complex contact record

You can edit a contact by selecting the contact record from the contact list and clicking the "Edit" button at the top of the contact details display (see Figure 2-35). To delete a contact, select the contact (or group of contacts by checking the boxes in the contact list) and click the "Delete contact" button appearing at the top of the contact details area on the right. Click the "OK" button in the confirmation dialog box.

As mentioned, contacts can be grouped into relevant categories. You can add or delete groups to sort your contacts, but there are five default groups that you cannot delete or modify. These include "Friends," "Family," "Coworkers,"

"All Contacts," and "Most Contacted." The last two groups are "System" groups.

The "All contacts" group displays every e-mail address you have sent an e-mail to, and the "Most contacted" group displays a list of the e-mail addresses of people you send mail to most frequently.

NotED

E-mail addresses you send e-mail to are automatically added to "All contacts."

To create a group, click the "Add group" button next to the "Add contact" button at top left of the contacts window. This will present you with a dialog box where you can enter the name of the group you wish to create. To delete a group, select the group you wish to delete (which cannot be a system or default group) and in the upper-right corner click the "Delete group" button that will appear. Then click "OK" in the dialog box that asks for confirmation. To rename a group, select the group you wish to rename and click the "Edit" button. From there, enter the new name and click the "Save" button.

To add a contact to a group, first locate and select the contact or group of contacts by either clicking the contact or selecting multiple contacts by clicking the check boxes next to users you wish to add to a group. Select the group you wish to send the contacts to by selecting them from the "Groups" drop-down menu that will become active just above the contact details area.

Creating a List of Tasks

Gmail has a sophisticated, easily accessible task list built into its interface in order to help you keep track of important events or tasks to be accomplished. To access this list, click the "Tasks" link on the left side of the screen (see Figure 2-41).

Compose Mail

Inbox
Starred ☆
Sent Mail
Drafts (4)

Personal
Travel
6 more▾

Contacts
[Tasks]

Figure 2-41: Selecting the task list

Once you have selected the task list, you will see a small window in the lower right hand corner of the screen (see Figure 2-42).

To create the first task, click the empty task white area next to the check box at the top of the task window and type out the text of your task. To create a second or subsequent task, click the "Add new task" button indicated by a plus sign (+) on the bottom of the task window. Once you have clicked the "Create new task" button, start typing what the task is next to the check box of the new task. To complete a task, click the check box next to the task name (this is known as checking a task). You can also mark a completed task as incomplete by clicking the check mark (indicated by a tick sign) next to a completed task. This is known as unchecking a task.

The more advanced features of the task list can be found by clicking a task and clicking the "Actions" drop-down menu (see Figure 2-43).

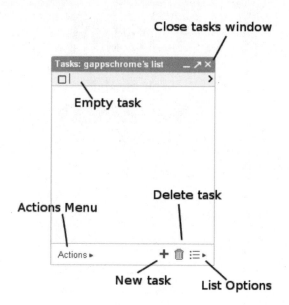

Close tasks window

Empty task

Delete task

Actions Menu

Actions ►

New task

List Options

Figure 2-42: The task list

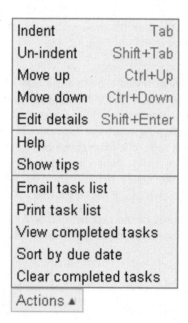

Indent	Tab
Un-indent	Shift+Tab
Move up	Ctrl+Up
Move down	Ctrl+Down
Edit details	Shift+Enter

| Help |
| Show tips |

| Email task list |
| Print task list |
| View completed tasks |
| Sort by due date |
| Clear completed tasks |

Actions ▲

Figure 2-43: Actions menu

With the "Actions" menu, you can indent tasks one level lower than the task above to create sub-tasks. Select the task you wish to indent and click the "Actions" button and select "Indent." This is known as demoting a task. Selecting "Un-Indent" will have the opposite effect called promoting a task. Tasks can be indented one level below their parent task, however there is no restriction on removing indents. Checking a parent task will check all of the parent's child tasks. Unchecking a parent task with checked child tasks will automatically uncheck every child task. Likewise, unchecking a child task of a checked parent will automatically uncheck all parent tasks (see Figure 2-44).

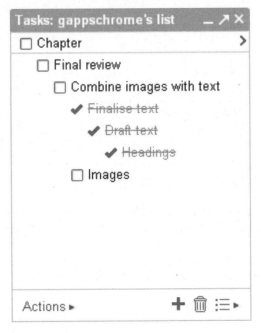

Figure 2-44: Indented task list

Tasks can be edited to add more information including notes and due dates. To edit a task, select the task you wish to edit and click the "Actions" button at the bottom of the task window, and select the "Edit Details" menu option. "Edit task" details will be displayed (see Figure 2-45). You can also click the right arrow symbol to the right of the task (see Figure 2-44) to display "Edit task details" for the task.

Figure 2-45: Editing a task

When editing a task's details, you can assign a due date to a task by clicking the calendar icon to the right of the "Due Date" field. A pop-up calendar will open allowing you to select the date the task is due (see Figure 2-46). To select a date, first locate the correct month by clicking the arrows on the top of the calendar and click the day you wish to set as the due date. The current date will be shown in bold.

Due date:

Note:

Figure 2-46: Due date pop-up calendar

You can also leave notes with a task. To create a note, type it into the "Note" text box below the "Due Date" field. Notes are shown in a condensed version on the main task list. Once you have finished editing a task, click the "Back to list" link at the bottom of "Edit details" to save changes (see Figure 2-47).

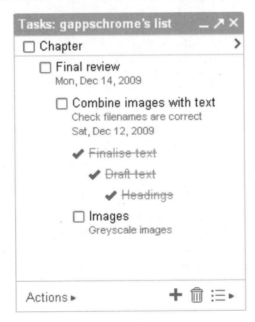

Figure 2-47: Complex task list

You can switch between different task lists or create new lists by going to the "Switch list" drop-down menu on the lower right-hand side of the task window (see Figure 2-48). The lower section of the pop-up menu contains the different task lists. The default list is named after your Gmail account and shown at the bottom of the list of tasks (see Figure 2-48). To create a new list, click the link labeled "New List." A new window will then open where you type the name of the list you want to create. Once the list is created, Gmail tasks will automatically switch to the new list. You can switch between lists by clicking the "Switch list" icon in the lower-left corner and selecting the task list you wish to view. To rename a list, switch to the list you would like to rename and click the rename link on the menu. This will open a box for you to type in the name of the new list.

Figure 2-48: Task list menu

To remove a task within a list, select the task and click the trash bin icon at the bottom of the tasks window. To remove a list, first switch to that list, then select "Remove list" from the "Switch list" menu. Removing a list will delete all tasks associated with the list.

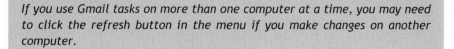

If you use Gmail tasks on more than one computer at a time, you may need to click the refresh button in the menu if you make changes on another computer.

Your Gmail Preferences

Gmail has a large number of settings that users can adjust to suit their own preferences. Some of these settings are familiar to those having previously used e-mail settings while others are not. In this section we will cover many more settings in detail. To get into the setting, click the "Settings" link on the top-right corner of the window (see Figure 2-5). The settings window will open (see Figure 2-49). Based on what features of Gmail they adjust, the different settings for various parts of Gmail are broken down into sections (or groups). Each of these groups of settings can be accessed by clicking the different tabs across the top of the settings window (see Figure 2-49). There are ten tabs that group the settings. We have already seen the "Labels" tab when using labels discussed previously in this chapter. In the following sections, we will look closely at other "Settings" tabs.

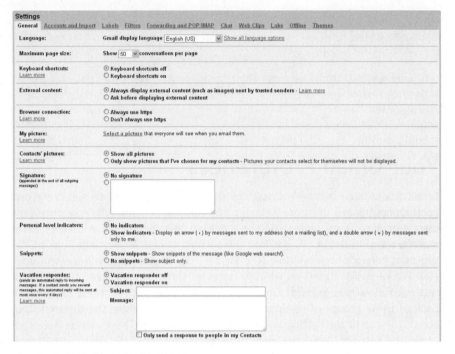

Figure 2-49: The settings menu

General Settings

On this tab, users have the ability to change many facets of how Gmail performs. Below is a list of important adjustable settings. The settings tab is the first (see Figure 2-49).

The settings that could be of use to an average user include:

- Language
- Maximum page size
- My picture
- Browser connection
- Signature
- Vacation responder

The default language used in Gmail for menus, help, and general interfacing with the user can be selected in small drop-down list with a selection of languages. The default is US English.

Maximum page size determines the number of e-mail headers that will be displayed (or conversations) when in folder view. The default is 50. Using the drop-down field, choose from 25, 50 or 100.

My Picture is a function that allows you to upload a small picture of yourself displayed to people that you e-mail or people you chat with in Gmail. When you click the "Select a picture" link, you will be shown an "Upload a picture window." You can browse for pictures in your local file system. The picture should be either in JPG, GIF, or PNG format. Click "Open" to upload the file. You can resize the picture to choose how it will be displayed.

The browser connection setting allows users to toggle the level of security while accessing Gmail. If you click the radio button next to "Always use https." your computer will encrypt all of the information traveling between your computer and Gmail. If you use the default setting, your information can be read by a third party.

ExplainED

If you are using Gmail for anything finance related, you should turn on "Always use https."

A signature is a small message or piece of text attached to the end of e-mails. To create a signature, click the signature box and enter a signature to be used. Signatures are automatically attached to every e-mail. To disable using a signature, click the "No signature" radio button.

A vacation responder is a message automatically sent out to alert the sender of an e-mail that you are away. These messages are typically used when the user will not be regularly checking e-mail for a period of time. To use a vacation responder, click the radio button next to "Vacation responder on," and fill out a subject for the automatically generated e-mail. You can use any subject header, such as "I am on holiday." Below the message box is a checkbox that will allow you to control if vacation messages are only sent to your contacts. By default, Gmail automatically sends a vacation response to any person who e-mails you. If the appropriate checkbox is clicked, Gmail will only send vacation responder e-mails back to the e-mail addresses that are in your contacts list.

ExplainED

Sending vacation responders alerts a sender that you may be away. You should use this with caution if this is a personal e-mail address where people may reasonably know your home address.

Once you have made any changes to the settings, you must click "Save changes" at the bottom of the Gmail window to make them effective.

Importing from Other Accounts

Gmail has the ability to import e-mail and contacts from another e-mail account. To access this functionality, go to "Accounts and Import" tab (see Figure 2-50) and click "Import mail and contacts." This will bring up a window that will guide you through importing all your old e-mails. You will need access to any passwords associated with that account.

ExplainED

This process is not perfect and may not work with other e-mail providers. If the process doesn't work, examine the configuration settings provided by the other e-mail host.

Settings	
General **Accounts and Import** Labels Filters Forwarding and POP/IMAP Chat Web Clips Labs Offline Themes	
Import mail and contacts:	Import from Yahoo!, Hotmail, AOL, or other webmail or POP3 accounts. Import mail and contacts Learn more
Send mail as:	Gapps Book <gappschrome@gmail.com> Send mail from another address Learn more edit info
Check mail using POP3:	Get your mail from other accounts in Gmail using POP3. Add POP3 email account Learn more
Using Gmail for work?	Companies can power their email with Gmail for businesses. Learn more
Add additional storage:	You are currently using 0 MB (0%) of your 7401 MB. Need more space? Upgrade your storage
Google Account settings:	Visit your Google Account settings to reset your password, change your security question, or learn about access to other Google services.

Figure 2-50: Accounts and import settings

To begin the import process, click the "Import mail and contacts" link. This will bring up a window (see Figure 2-51).

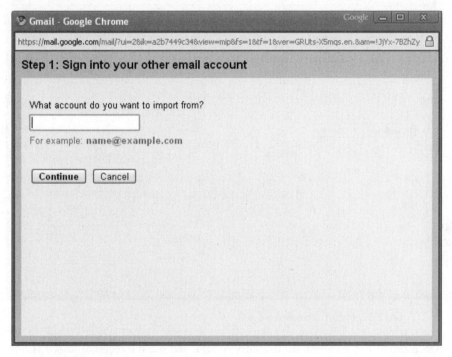

Figure 2-51: The importing process

First, enter your old e-mail address and enter your password (see Figure 2-52). This will enable Gmail to login to your other account and allow you to import old e-mails.

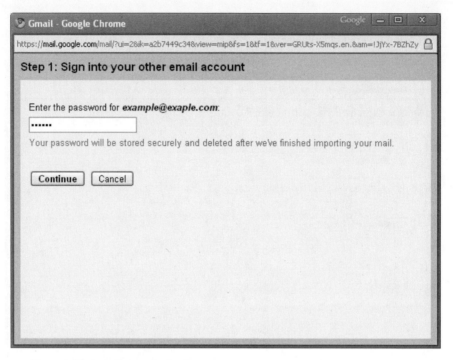

Figure 2-52: Import password entry

Once Gmail has successfully logged into your old e-mail account, there is one more step to complete(see Figure 2-53). This last step allows you to choose how you want to import your e-mail. If you deselect "Import Mail," Gmail will not import your old e-mails. Additionally, you can choose whether or not you would like Gmail to remove the old e-mail messages from the other email provider once it has successfully imported them into Gmail. You also have the option of archiving all imported e-mail messages. The final option is to apply a label to the imported mail.

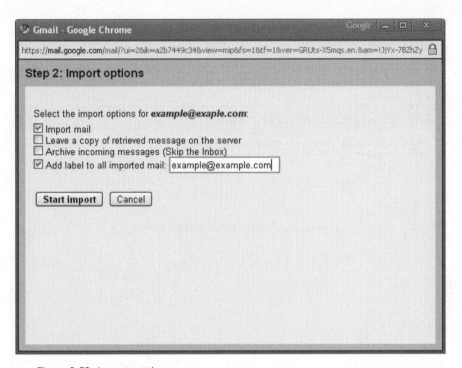

Figure 2-53: Import settings

ExplainED

Once you have successfully imported your e-mail, Gmail will continually check the e-mail account you imported from for new e-mail every hour.

Using Different E-mail Addresses

Gmail allows users to send e-mails from Gmail that appear to come from a different e-mail address. This can be an extremely useful function if you intend to keep other e-mail accounts and use Gmail to consolidate these. You can then use Gmail as your sole e-mail account, importing e-mails from other systems. When sending e-mail, choose who you wish to appear to be to the recipient. For example, a user can send an e-mail from Gmail that appears to come from their work e-mail address. To set this up, click "Send mail from another address" under the "Accounts and Import" tab in settings (see Figure 2-50). This will bring

97

up a new browser window (see Figure 2-54) that will guide you through adding another e-mail address.

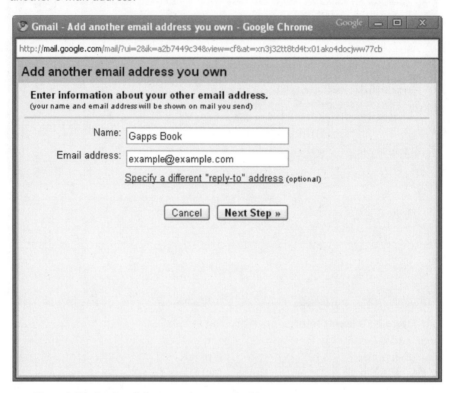

Figure 2-54: Send mail from another e-mail address

To add another e-mail address, first enter the e-mail address you want to be able to send e-mail from. Enter the user name of your Gmail account (this will automatically be filled in) and the e-mail address in the two appropriate fields (see Figure 2-54). Click the "Next Step" button. This will present you with two choices: send mail through Gmail directly, or send e-mail from Gmail through your old e-mail server. Sending through Gmail can be a simpler process, however your e-mail may be marked as spam if it was not sent from your older e-mail provider's server (see Figure 2-55).

Figure 2-55: Choosing SMTP, or Gmail server

To use your existing provider's e-mail server, examine the configuration settings provided by your e-mail host and enter the SMTP (Simple Mail Transfer Protocol) server details in the new text boxes that appear. These will be address details of the computers that host your existing email account. Some domains have special rules on them called SPF (Sender Policy Framework) rules. If your domain has this enabled, any e-mail you send from Gmail from your added address is more likely to be marked as spam. If you are unsure if your domain has SPF setup, contact the person who administers your domain and they can guide you through the appropriate setup. If you select "Send mail through Gmail," you will need to verify that you own the e-mail address you are attempting to send e-mail from (see Figure 2-56).

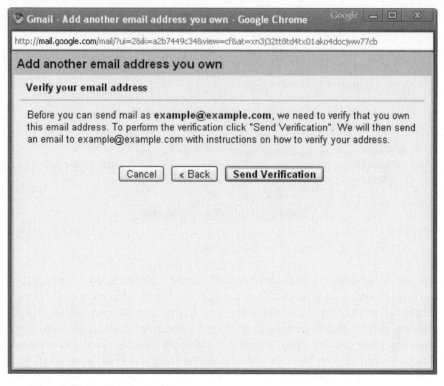

Figure 2-56: Verify e-mail address

Gmail will send an e-mail to the account you want to verify in order to do this. The e-mail will contain a link that you must click for Gmail to allow you to send e-mail from that address. Once you have verified your e-mail address with Gmail, a drop-down box will appear when you compose messages (where the "From" field is). Select which address you want the e-mail to appear to come from.

Using Outlook and Other E-mail Programs with Gmail

Gmail allows users to handle mail externally on another e-mail service or download the e-mail to their preferred e-mail client. These settings can be accessed through the *"Forwarding and POP/IMAP"* tab of the "Gmail settings" (see Figure 2-57).

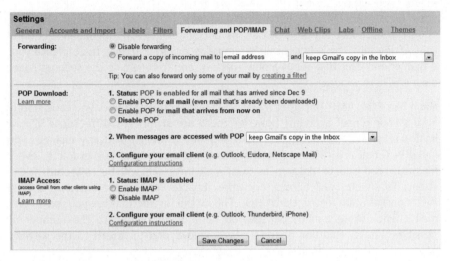

Figure 2-57: Forward/POP/IMAP menu

You can forward your e-mails to another e-mail address by clicking the radio button "Forward a copy of incoming mail." Then place the e-mail address you wish to forward the documents to in the text box on the same line. Choose how the new mail is handled by Gmail by selecting an option from the drop-down. You can choose to:

- Leave the mail in the inbox of your Gmail account
- Flag the new e-mail as archived
- Delete the new e-mail after it has been forwarded

POP (Post Office Protocol) allows a mail client of your choice to download new e-mails to your local computer. POP is one of the two most popular e-mail access protocols to facilitate this function, so you can access your e-mails when you are offline. However, you can only access these on the computer in which you downloaded them. By default, POP access is enabled on your account, and Gmail will keep all new e-mails in your inbox after they have been downloaded. You can change the settings by clicking the radio button. The following options are available:

- Enable POP access for all e-mails in the e-mail account
- Enable POP access for new e-mails that arrive after settings are saved
- Disable POP access for any e-mails

Like e-mail forwarding, you have the option of leaving the e-mail in the inbox, archiving the e-mail, or deleting the e-mail. The default setting is to keep a copy of e-mails in the inbox. To configure your e-mail client, click the "Configuration Instructions" link at the bottom of the POP download section in this setting tab. This will contain the most recent instructions to configure your e-mail client. This link opens a new window, and to return to the settings page, close the help window.

Much like POP, IMAP (Internet Message Access Protocol) allows you to remotely access your e-mail account, however there are significant differences in how IMAP works. Most notably, IMAP is a two-way protocol, and any changes you make in Gmail are reflected in the client and vice-versa. For example, every message read and/or deleted in the Gmail interface will be reflected in the client. To enable IMAP access, click the "Enable IMAP" radio button and click the "Configuration instructions" link. Follow the instructions for your particular mail client. These cannot be covered here in detail due to the number of possible clients. This link opens a new window, and to return to the settings page close the help window.

Using Filters to Control Where Your E-mail Goes

Gmail has filters included allowing users to control the flow of new e-mails. An example would be to filter e-bank notification mail to a specific label so you can easily keep track of it. To create a filter, select the "Filters" tab from the Gmail settings. This will present you with a page that has a list of all existing filters (see Figure 2-58).

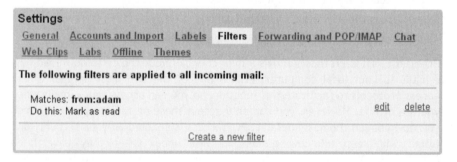

Figure 2-58: The filters tab

To create a new filter, click the "Create a new filter" link at the bottom of the window. Once you have clicked the link, you will be shown a number of blank boxes (see Figure 2-59).

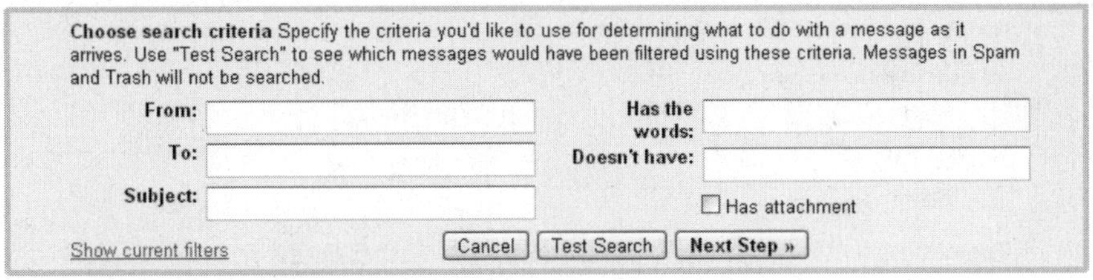

Choose search criteria Specify the criteria you'd like to use for determining what to do with a message as it arrives. Use "Test Search" to see which messages would have been filtered using these criteria. Messages in Spam and Trash will not be searched.

From:		Has the words:	
To:		Doesn't have:	
Subject:		☐ Has attachment	

Show current filters | Cancel | Test Search | Next Step »

Figure 2-59: Setting a new filter

You must fill in the details of the e-mails you wish to match.

Use the "From" field to match the name of the sender. Use this option to search for a name or e-mail address of the person sending the e-mail being received by your account.

Use the "To" field to match the name of the e-mail's recipient. Use this option to search for names or e-mail addresses of the person receiving the e-mail. This can include searching for other people who are also receiving the e-mail.

Use the "Subject" field to match the subject of the e-mail. Use this option to search for words in the subject of the e-mail.

Use the "Has the words" field to search the entire e-mail for the words typed in this text box.

Use the "Doesn't have" field to filter for e-mails that do not have the words typed in the text box.

Check the "Has attachments" checkbox to filter for e-mails that have attachments.

As an example, you can use two text boxes to create advanced filters such as filtering formatting:

Name: Adam

Subject: Invoice

Doesn't contain: "Paid on"

Has attachments

(see Figure 2-60)

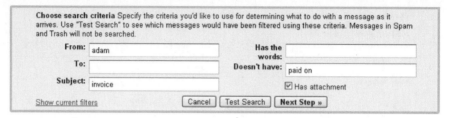

Figure 2-60: An example filter

The filter above can be used to filter for any incoming e-mail from anyone named Adam that has the word invoice in the subject, and does not include the words "Paid on," and has an attachment (presumably an invoice to be paid). After entering the pattern to search for, click the "Test Search" button to check that your filter works correctly, then click the "Next Step" button (see Figure 2-61).

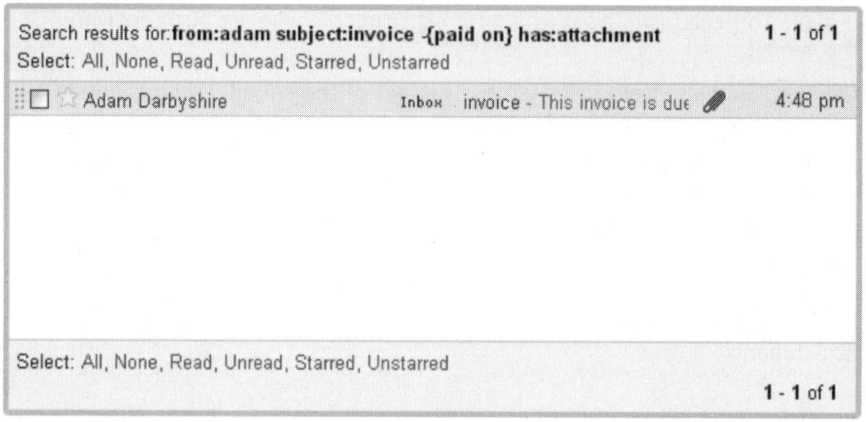

Search results for:**from:adam subject:invoice -{paid on} has:attachment**   **1 - 1 of 1**
Select: All, None, Read, Unread, Starred, Unstarred

☐ ☆ Adam Darbyshire   Inbox   invoice - This invoice is due 📎   4:48 pm

Select: All, None, Read, Unread, Starred, Unstarred

1 - 1 of 1

Figure 2-61: Filtered e-mail heading example

After clicking "Next Step," you are taken to a window (see Figure 2-62) allowing you to dictate what happens to the e-mails once they have been filtered by the filter you have set-up in the previous step.

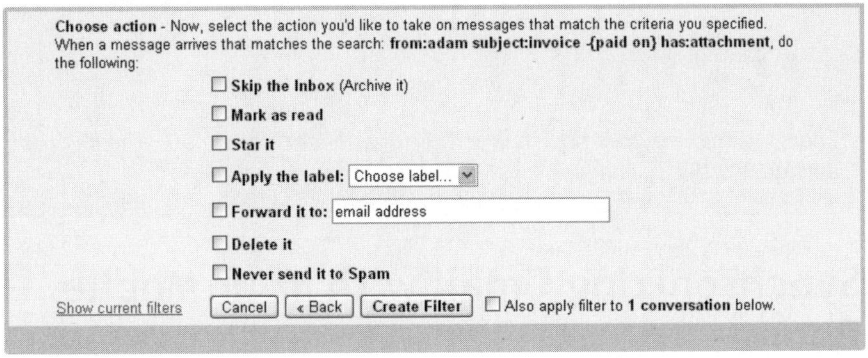

Choose action - Now, select the action you'd like to take on messages that match the criteria you specified.
When a message arrives that matches the search: from:adam subject:invoice {paid on} has:attachment, do
the following:

☐ **Skip the Inbox** (Archive it)

☐ **Mark as read**

☐ **Star it**

☐ **Apply the label:** Choose label... ▼

☐ **Forward it to:** email address

☐ **Delete it**

☐ **Never send it to Spam**

Show current filters   [Cancel] [« Back] [**Create Filter**] ☐ Also apply filter to **1 conversation** below.

Figure 2-62: Filtering actions

Below are options to choose from when filtering a message:

- Archive the e-mail
- Mark the e-mail as read
- Star the e-mail
- Apply a label to the e-mail
- Forward the e-mail to an external e-mail address
- Delete the e-mail
- Prevent the e-mail from being marked as spam

Continuing the example above, the invoice that has been identified as an unpaid invoice can be given the label "Invoice" and "Starred" to make it easy to locate. You can also click the "Also apply filter" check box to run the actions on any e-mail message that was found in the testing of the filter.

To edit an existing filter, click the "Edit" link to the right of the filter in the list. This will take you to the filter creation page with the fields already filled. To delete a filter, click the "Delete" link next to the filter you want to delete.

Using Themes to Change How Gmail Looks

Much like Chrome, a user can change the theme of Gmail by clicking the themes tab in settings. Users are presented with a limited choice of themes to use for Gmail. Most of the themes only change the colors of the page; however some themes such as "Tea House" change images and color schemes depending on the time of day.

NotED

Changing themes does not change the functionality of Gmail. Themes are only an aesthetic change.

Synchronizing Gmail with Your Mobile Phone

NotED

People who own a Google Android-based phone do not need to follow this step. In this case, refer to your user guide about how to display your calendar.

You can install a program on the iPhone, Blackberry, Windows Mobile, or Nokia (S60) mobile phones to automatically synchronize your Gmail and contacts using the Google Sync program for your phone.

ExplainED

This procedure uses mobile Internet. Check with your wireless carrier as to whether you have mobile Internet active. Google Sync can use up to 50 megabytes of mobile traffic each month for a typical user.

To see the installation instructions for your mobile phone, visit (http://www.google.com/mobile/sync/) and follow the instructions for your phone.

Summary

In this chapter we have covered Google's Gmail in great detail. We started off by discussing creating a Gmail account, followed by basic composing of and sending e-mails. We covered reading, replying, and manipulating e-mails. Then we examined how the Google label system works and how you can use it to archive, start, and apply specific labels to e-mails.

We further discussed the significant problem that is spam, followed by managing contacts and using the task list. Finally, we covered the settings for Gmail including importing, filters, alternate e-mail addresses, and using Outlook and other e-mail clients on mobile devices.

Readers new to e-mail in general or Gmail itself may find this chapter a very useful guide on how to use Gmail and its major features. Readers will understand how Google's Gmail and e-mail, when used correctly, can be an extremely useful and powerful productivity and communication tool.

Chapter 3

Introduction to Google Docs

Google Docs (or Google Documents) represent Google's online Office Suite of programs. There are four types of documents you can create, edit, and share with Google Documents. These include Document (the word-processor component of Google Docs), Spreadsheet, Presentation (for making overhead slides for presentations), and Forms. Forms is an interesting component added to Google Docs for the ability to easily design web-based forms and enabling the collection of data from these forms by collecting results into a Google Docs spreadsheet. These can provide online testing or develop and run an online survey. While this type of activity can be done in other Office Suites, the degree of integration of forms into the other components of Google Docs and the other Google Apps make this unique.

The four component applications of Google Docs are covered in detail in following chapters. However, we have covered these applications within the chapters in isolation, as each application is an extensive component of Google Docs in its own right. This chapter covers the interface to the Google Docs components. Each of the four document types have common operations applicable to them including loading, saving, renaming, and sharing. While these operations can be applied to the documents through each of the component applications, we have arranged to cover most of these operations and particularly the sharing aspects through the Google Docs interface.

Why Use Google Documents?

A fair question is "Why should I use Google Docs?" especially if you already have an Office Suite such as Microsoft Office or OpenOffice. Both of these Office Suites are sufficient products and perform similarly, as does Google Docs. In some cases, Google Docs applications, including Document and Spreadsheet, are not as extensive in functionality as other Office Suite counterparts. However, for web-based online applications, they can be powerful tools with functionality rivaling traditional Office products. Most people do not use all available functionality with these products, and for many people, Google Docs applications will accomplish their needs. Moreover, with the introduction of Google Gears (an open source browser extension), you can view Google Docs offline and have limited editing capability. Gears allows you to work offline (without an Internet connection) and sync with your Google Docs when going back online. Currently, you can view Documents, Spreadsheets, and Presentations offline and can only edit Documents offline. Google Docs is free to individuals who register and get a Google account (see Chapter 2).

There are other advantages. They don't need to be installed on any computer, and we can access the applications and all documents wherever we have access to the Internet and a web browser. Consequently, there are no compatibility issues; everyone is on the same version. Documents are stored online and there is no need to carry any media with us when we travel, including USB drives, discs, etc. Because of this, there is no possibility of traveling to a meeting or conference and leaving your notes or presentation behind. Additionally, the collaboration facility is proficient. It can be easy to share your documents and collaborate online with anyone in the world. Documents can be simultaneously edited by collaborators and another person's edits can be viewed almost immediately. A feature often overlooked is the integration of Google Docs and other Google Apps with Google Sites and iGoogle (see the final chapter). By integrating Google Docs with Sites (see Chapter 9), you can develop web sites and easily separate the content management from the format management by sharing integrated Google documents.

One of the basic issues people have, and initially we ourselves did, is relinquishing the control we may have when storing documents locally. For anyone who has experienced computer trouble, this comfort can be an illusion. Google Docs represents an evolution in the way we accomplish tasks, and some have said it will to be the future of computing. We used the term "Cloud Computing" in the introduction. It does represent a paradigm shift, but after using Google Docs the advantages will become apparent.

Is My Data Secure?

Whether or not your data is secure is an important consideration for any computer user wishing to store their document anywhere, and something that should be considered by anyone using a vendor entrusted with data storage requirements. This is not just an issue related to storage of Google Docs. However, it is an issue users are apprehensive about as they relinquish control of where they store their documents when embracing the cloud computing model. Google operates and maintains one of the largest distributed data centers in the world. Consequently, Google takes security seriously and invests billions of dollars in data security, both physical and logical security. The physical security is in place to prevent unauthorized access to the facilities where data is stored, while logical security includes software safeguards preventing access to data over the Internet (passwords, authentication, virus protection, etc.) Access to data centers is audited and tightly controlled, and even the geographical locations have been chosen with care to protect against natural disasters. In many cases, data centers are solely owned by Google therefore access is not shared with third parties, putting to rest many concerns about shared centers.

A source of information on all aspects of Google's security is found in the free white paper from Google itself (named "Comprehensive Review of Security and Vulnerability Protections for Google Apps"). This paper was published by Google in August 2008 and can be accessed for free by visiting http://www.developertutorials.com/white-papers/security/developertutorials.com/white-papers/security/. There are many white papers from developers at this site, so search the page using the browser's search facility. This paper covers in detail the different levels of security layers Google uses to protect data and the built-in redundancy to maximize the uptime for all Google Apps data.

According to the white paper, Google Apps users benefit from the extensive operational experience Google has acquired in securing reliable products. Additionally, Google spends billions of dollars in infrastructure and advanced technology to secure data, and in particular, focuses much of its effort on aspects of security considered critical for business customers. These include:

- *Organizational and operational security*: Google screens all of its employees and has a full-time team consisting of some of the world's experts in security, many from Fortune 500 companies. The operational security team continually audits data center operations and evaluates threat assessments.

- *Data security*: Google regards protecting data as being at the core of its functions and responsibilities and believes this is one of the keys to Google's continued success. The data centers are engineered for efficiency, security, and reliability. Google's servers are protected by multiple levels of firewalls and Google utilizes both industry standards and specific proprietary techniques to secure access to data ultimately eliminating many threats most commercial software is susceptible to. With built-in redundancy, Google maintains data access through machine failure.

- *Threat evasion*: Google uses world-class threat evasion techniques to protect its users from e-mail viruses, phishing attacks, and service attacks. Moreover, Google uses the strongest industry spam and phishing filters to protect its Gmail users, including filters that learn from patterns in messages.

- *Safe access*: Once downloaded to your local computer, data is at risk from malicious software and users attaining access to your computer. Google helps avoid this by providing storage on Google-protected sites. Additionally, if other people normally have access to your data as part of a group arrangement, you can continue to safely share your files through data-sharing functionality built in to Google Apps. You can protect your data while it is being transmitted by using an SSL (secure socket layer) connection through the HTTPS protocol instead of HTTP.

- *Data Privacy*: Google ensures privacy to your data by providing a legally binding policy protecting your data and all services related to Google Apps. This helps Google Apps provide you with a secure framework for storing your data in the cloud.

Given the lengths that Google goes to secure your data, your data is well protected. By using state-of-the-art technology and industry-best practice, in many cases your data is better protected when stored online with Google than it would be traditionally stored on a personal computer connected to the Internet. Couple this with the advantages of the cloud computing model and you have a significantly functional and safe place to store your files. .

Starting Google Docs

To start Google Docs, click the "Documents" option from the "More" menu on the Google Apps tool bar in your browser (see Figure 3-1). If you are not logged in to your Google account, log in or create an account if you don't already have one (see Chapter 2).

Figure 3-1: Accessing Google Docs

Once you have created an account and clicked the "Documents" link (see Figure 3-1), you will see a page similar to the one shown in Figure 3-2 loaded into your browser's current tab. This is the Google Docs interface and provides a common point of access to all documents and applications considered part of Google Docs. The page will vary depending on which document you currently have, if any, already created. The Google Docs screen (see Figure 3-2) shows a listing of your documents in the main part of the screen (which you can sort) and a number of buttons across the top of this area for performing actions on the documents. On the left of the screen is a series of links to help refine the display of the files, and two buttons at the top for creating and uploading new files.

A closer look at the top portion of the screen is shown in Figure 3-3. Links on the left side of the page allow you to choose which type of files will be listed in the file list area. You can choose from all files owned by you, files shared with you, and other options including "Starred" files. Just above the file listing options are two buttons; one to create new types of Google Docs files and the other allowing you to upload existing files and convert them to their Google Docs equivalent. The Google Docs tool bar provides you access to a number of functions that can be performed on selected files including deleting, renaming, publicizing the files, and sharing them. We will cover these options in the following sections.

Figure 3-2: Google Docs main screen

Figure 3-3: Closer look at Google Docs buttons and tool bar

Creating Documents

Google Docs currently has four different types of files you can create. These are a Document (word-processing document): presentation, spreadsheet, and form. Manipulating and editing these files is extensively covered in following chapters. In the Google Docs interface, you can choose to edit an existing file or create a new one. If you choose to create a new file, you can initiate it here and the Google Docs interface will load the appropriate application with a new blank file. To create a file, click the "Create new" button just above the file listing options. A drop-down menu will be displayed (see Figure 3-4).

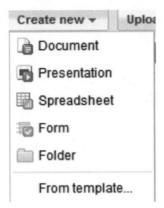

Figure 3-4: Creating a document

Choose the type of file you would like to create by clicking one of the options in Figure 3-4. A new tab will be displayed and a new blank document of the chosen type will be displayed in the new tab becoming the current tab. You can edit and save this document using the Google Docs application that created the document (see appropriate chapter). When you exit the application in this new tab, the new document will be displayed in the Google Docs listing (see Figure 3-2). You may need to reload with browser tab to see the new listed documents. The name of the new document will depend on the name you save it within the Google Docs application. When saving a spreadsheet, you will be asked for the name, but when saving a presentation or a word-processing document, the default name will be the first few words you typed into the document.

You can open several documents at once and each will be created in its own browser tab. You can move between the documents by clicking the appropriate tab in the browser.

Sharing Documents

Once you have created a new document and can see it in the Google Docs listing, you have the ability to share it with other web users. This can be a useful feature in the Google Docs application when sharing documents. This allows academic and business collaboration on documents without the need to create and manage changes within multiple versions on the same document. When you share a document using Google Docs, you are making the same document available to others you choose, and multiple people can simultaneously work on the same document. Changes made by one person to a document are seen almost immediately by the other person depending on the speed of the Internet.

Figure 3-5: Selecting a document in Google Docs

To Share a document, select the document by checking the check box to the left of the document name in the listing (see Figure 3-5). Once you have selected the file to share (you can select more than one file), click the "Share" button in the Google Docs tool bar. This will display a drop-down list (see Figure 3-6). This will display a number of possible sharing options. You can obtain the actual file from Google Docs and share it with people enabling them to edit the file. You can also specifically invite them to share the file. We will discuss both of these options in later sections. Additionally, you can e-mail the file as an attachment, though this is not strictly sharing, but sending a copy.

Figure 3-6: File sharing options

To invite people to share a document, click the "Invite people" option from the "Share" button on the tool bar. This will display the "Share with others" dialog box (see Figure 3-7). This dialog box has three tabs to allow you to accomplish different tasks and inspect options. The first tab "Invite people" allows you to send out invitations to collaborators. To invite someone to share your document, type their e-mail address into the "Invite" box shown in the top left of the dialog box (see Figure 3-7). You can also click the "Choose from contacts" link just below this box. This will display a dialog box of your e-mail contacts (see Gmail chapter). You can choose one or more of your contacts from this list (not shown), and click the "Done" button when finished. The e-mails of the contacts you selected will be shown in the "Invite" box. Select whether these contacts you are sending the invitation to can either edit or just view the file. Select either the "To edit" or "To view" radio button below the "Invite" box. You can then type a subject for the e-mail message and type in a message they will receive with the invite into the boxes on the right (see Figure 3-7). If you want to send a copy of the invite to yourself for your records, check the "Send a copy to myself" check box. To send the invitations, click the "Send" button in the bottom right of the dialog box. Alternatively, you can add these people into the sharing list without sending the invitations by clicking the "Add without sending" link to the right of the "Send" button. The invitations will be sent via email and the contacts will be added to the list of people that can view or edit the file.

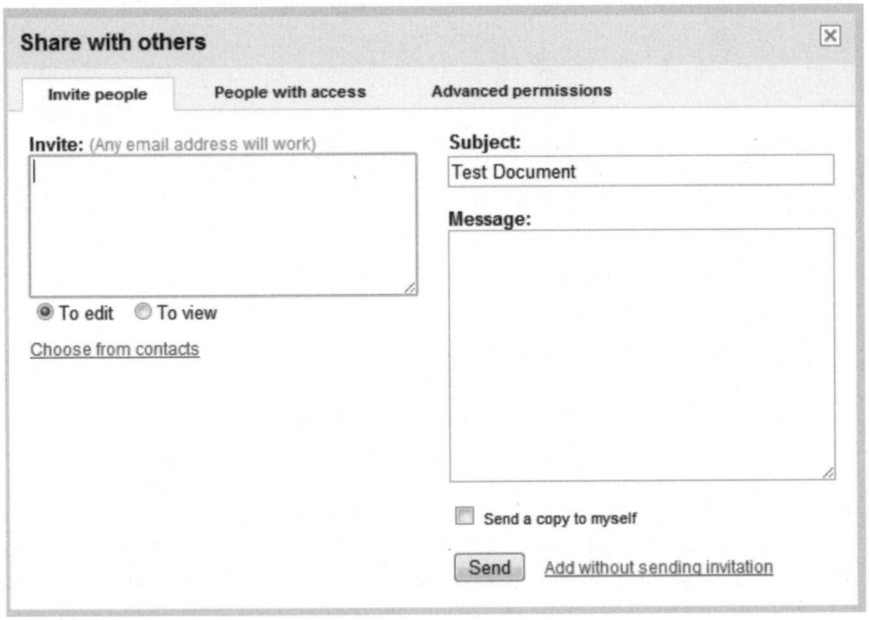

Figure 3-7: Inviting people to share

When people are sent invitations in this way, the recipient will need to log into their own Google Docs account before they can edit or view the file. This will require them to have their own account. This is the recommended way to share files as it requires a login. You can share a file without requiring a user to have his own account by providing a link to the file, but this is a less-secure option and more difficult to control access (we will discuss that later in this section). In the dialog box in Figure 3-7, if you click the "People with access" tab at the top of the dialog, you will see a dialog box (see Figure 3-8.) This allows you to check who has access to the selected file. The dialog box shows two people with access, Gapps Book who is the owner, and Adam who can edit (see Figure 3-8). Using this dialog, you can modify the access a person has.

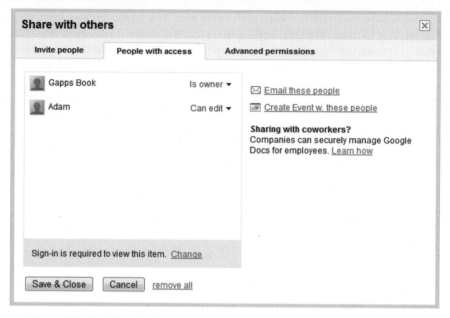

Figure 3-8: Checking who has access

To modify an existing collaborator's access, click the small drop-down arrow to the right of the collaborator's name (see Figure 3-9). In the options, change their access by choosing either "Can edit" or "Can view." This will change their access to viewing only or edit depending on your choice. You can also assign ownership by choosing "Is owner." When collaboration is finished, you can effectively change the ownership. This can be a useful option in an academic environment, as a tutor might get his or her students to give them ownership after a project is finished. If you choose "None" as the option, the person will be removed from the collaborator's list. To save your changes, click the "Save and close" button at the bottom of the dialog box. Alternatively, click the "Cancel" link to exit without making changes, or the "Remove all" link to remove all collaborators.

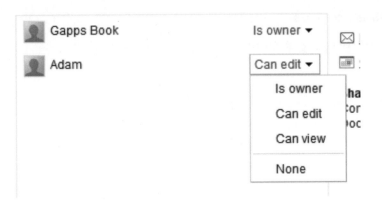

Figure 3-9: Modifying a person's access rights

By clicking the third Tab in the dialog box "Advanced permissions" (see Figure 3-7), you can further set permissions to control what others can do with your invitations. The dialog box shows the advanced two permissions (see Figure 3-10). These are controlled by checking the check boxes against each of the permissions. The first allows other editors to invite users to view or edit the document. The second allows invitations to be forwarded.

ExplainED

If you would like to maintain control over who has access to the document, uncheck both options on the advanced permissions page.

Figure 3-10: Modifying advanced permissions

You can also share you documents with others without requiring them to sign in to a Google Docs account. Choose the "Get link to share" option from the "Share" button on the tool bar. This will bring up a dialog (see Figure 3-11). Check one or both of the check boxes to allow someone to view only or view and edit the document. When you check one of the check boxes, a link to the location on the Web of the document will be shown in the box below the check boxes. Send this link to anyone via e-mail or instant messaging and they can use this link to cut and paste into their browser. This link will be active once you click the "Save & close" button. Choose the "Cancel" button to exit without activating the link. Once someone has the link, they can then paste it into any browser without signing into a Google Docs account. If it was set up for edit, they can begin directly editing the document. The browser will load the corresponding document into the tab where the address was typed and the document will be available for either reading or editing.

ExplainED

To maintain any type of security, it is advisable not to use this option if avoidable.

Figure 3-11: Sharing via a Google Docs link

Concurrent Editing

When sharing your documents, the people you shared with all have access to the one document. Additionally, multiple users can be editing the document at the same time. The number of concurrent users will depend on the document type. Current figures from Google at the time of publishing are:

Documents: You can share the document with up to 200 people and 10 people can concurrently edit the document.

Spreadsheets: You can share the spreadsheet with up to 200 people and 50 people can concurrently edit the spreadsheet.

Presentations: You can share the presentation with up to 200 people and 10 people can concurrently edit the presentation.

The more concurrent editors you have, the slower it will be to edit due to the constant saving and updating of the display. Delay times will vary depending on a number of local factors including the speed of the Internet connection, the capacity of the computer being used, and the speed at which changes are being made by the concurrent users. However, when two and three concurrent users were used in some limited testing, delays of a few seconds were experienced.

When you are collaborating with people on a document (depending on time zones) you may be working asynchronously or concurrently. When you are working concurrently, the names of the people currently working on a document will appear at the top of the screen. To the right of the names is a small, clickable arrow used to open a small chat window and discuss the editing with other collaborators. This can be a useful tool to synchronize editing of the document with collaborators, as problems can possibly occur if two or more people are concurrently working on exactly the same section of the document, spreadsheet, or presentation. There is a simple conflict resolution technique used if a conflict is detected with collaborators working on the same section. If two people change the same sentence in a document or cell in a spreadsheet at approximately the same time, one change will be permitted and the conflicting change will be reversed. The current state of the document will be displayed along with a small message showing the conflicting change. These can be dealt with as they are likely to be small conflicts. There is no way to predict the order of saves as it depends on many factors, timing of saves, frequency of modifications made, speed of the Internet, etc. Perhaps the best way to concurrently collaborate on a document is having collaborators work on different sections of the document or spreadsheet. This makes sense to logically partition the work in this way. The likelihood of conflicts increases with the number of current users. The limitations mentioned above on the number of current users take into account the likelihood of conflicts in the different document types. In spreadsheets, data is stored in specific cells, so it is less likely that you will have conflicts due to people concurrently working on the same cell.

ExplainED

Due to the conflict resolution used, the best way to work concurrently on a document is to partition the work logically so different collaborators work on different sections.

Every time a document is saved, it is saved as a new revision. The number of revisions generated for a document will depend on the number of changes made, the number of collaborators, and how often changes are made. The revisions are similar to versions in other documents, but versions here are assigned consecutive revision numbers and are associated with a last edited date. By scanning through the revision history, you can track the changes made to a document over time with collaborators and see how the document editing has progressed. You can review the revisions and if necessary revert to older revisions. A treatment of working with the document revision history is provided in the Google Document chapter. The process of working with revisions is exactly the same for spreadsheets and presentations as it is for documents. We refer the reader to Chapter 4 for a more extensive treatment on the revisions process.

Working with Folders

To help organize large amounts of files, you can create folders to store documents. This is much like creating directories and sub-directories in your operating system to store all files. The folders help organize documents into coherent groups when you get large numbers of files. While it is convenient to think of folders in Google Docs in this way (as in traditional folders), there is an important difference. Folders in Google Docs act much like the "Labels" in Gmail (see Gmail Chapter). Unlike a traditional file system, files are not assigned to folders, but instead the files independently exist to the folders and folders are assigned to files. A file can exist in multiple folders. Think of it as assigning multiple folders to files. In some respects, this is a superior option to the traditional filing system as sometimes a file might belong to different categories (or folders). For example, an invoice to a client named ABCTraining may be located in a general file named Invoices, but may also be located in a folder named ABCTraining Documents.

Your folders are viewable down the left side of the Google Docs screen (see Figure 3-2). Toward the bottom left you will see an option named "My Folders." Clicking this will display a list of folders you have created. Clicking it again will collapse the list so it will be hidden again. For each folder you create, they in turn may contain other folders and clicking a folder's name will expand the list of sub-folders or collapse it.

To create a new folder, click the "Create new" button just above the file listing options. You will see a drop-down menu (see Figure 3-4). Click the "Folder" option to create a new folder. You will see a screen display (see Figure 3-12). Type in the name of the new folder; otherwise it will default to "New Folder" (it can be changed at a later stage). You can also add descriptive text for the folder.

Figure 3-12: Creating a new folder

You can also display the folder name in the folder tree on the left side of the browser window with a specific color. You can color code your folders to suit your purposes. To choose a display color, click the small drop-down color chooser icon to the right of the folder name (see Figure 3-12). This will show the folder color chooser dialog (see Figure 3-13). Choose the color you would like the folder to be displayed with by clicking the appropriate color patch and the dialog will close. At a later stage when you edit the color, choose another color. Click "Default color", or "Remove color" to remove previous choices. Once you have named the folder and set any other options, click the "Save" button to save the folder or "Cancel" to exit without saving the folder name or color.

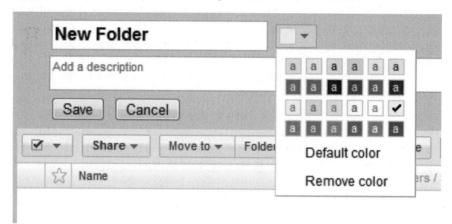

Figure 3-13: Choosing a folder display color

When you create your first folder, it will be directly underneath the "My folders" entry on the left of the screen. When you create further folders, you can create a new folder within an existing folder by first clicking the folder in the folder list tree shown on the left side of the window. Then click the "Create new" button. In this way you can create folders with sub-folders (see Figure 3-14).

Figure 3-14: Folder structure

To add a file to a folder or folders, select a file. You may need to redisplay the list of files by using the file listing options at the left of the file list area (see Figure 3-3). For example, show "All items." Once you have selected your file (see Figure 3-5), click the "Folders" button on the tool bar. This will display a list of your files in their structure tree. You may need to click folders to display the folders beneath (see Figure 3-15). Check the check boxes just to the left of each folder's name that you want to assign your file to (see Figure 3-15). Click the "Apply changes" button when you are done selecting folders. You can select multiple folders.

Figure 3-15: Assigning files to folders

When you have saved changes, the fill will be shown as assigned to multiple folders (see Figure 3-16). Toward the right side of the file listing, you will see a list of folders in which the file has been assigned. When you click on a folder in the left side of the screen, it will replace the list of files in the "File list area" with the files assigned to that folder. In this way you can organize files into folders eliminating long, unstructured lists of files.

Figure 3-16: File assigned to multiple folders

You can manipulate folders by right clicking on a folder in the folder structure on the left side of the window. Doing this will display a drop-down menu (see Figure 3-17). From this menu, you can change the color of a folder, hide it, rename it, delete it, move it (to another folder), or share the folder. To share a folder, click the "Share" option from the drop-down right click menu on a folder. This will give you exactly the same options for sharing a folder as you had when choosing to share a document (see previous section). If you choose to invite people to share, it works exactly the same as inviting people to share a document. The only difference is that all files assigned to a folder will be shared with the people you choose. This makes it easy for people collaborating on a large project that may involve a number of documents. All files concerned with the project can be placed in a folder and the shared folder.

Figure 3-17: Manipulating folders

126

If you choose to delete a folder, the files assigned to a folder will not be deleted. Instead, the folder will be removed and the list of folders assigned to a document will be modified. However, if the folder contains sub-folders, these will also be deleted.

Deleting and Renaming Documents

To delete a file from Google Docs, select the file (or files) by checking the check box against each of the files you would like to delete in the files list area (see Figure 3-5). Click the "Delete" button in the tool bar and the files will be deleted. For a short time in the Google Docs window, an "Undo" link will be displayed at the top of the file list area highlighted with a pale yellow color. To retrieve the file (or files) during the time the link is available, click the "Undo" link and files will be retrieved and placed back into your file list area. You can still retrieve the files, but you will need to do this manually from the "Trash" folder. Using the "Trash" folder will be discussed in a later section. The "Trash" folder is similar to your operating system's trash bin for deleted files.

You can rename an existing file by selecting the file as you previously did and clicking the "Rename" button on the tool bar. The file's name in the file list area will be highlighted and displayed in a small text box, which you can then change (see Figure 3-18). When you have changed the name of the file, press the "Return" (or "Enter") key on the keyboard and the file's name will be changed. Instead of pressing the "Return" key, click the check box beside the file. You can only rename one file at a time.

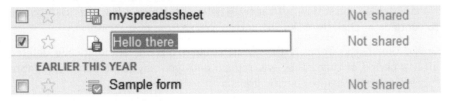

Figure 3-18: Renaming files

Using the Trash Folder

Once you delete a file, it can be retrieved from the "Trash" folder. To retrieve a file, click the "Trash" entry in the file listing options to the left of the screen (see Figure 3-3). This will load the files in the "Trash" folder into the file list area. The listing of files in the "Trash" folder appears exactly the same as a normal listing of files, except that the tool bar is different (see Figure 3-19). You can empty the "Trash" folder to permanently delete these files or you can undelete a file or files. To undelete a file, select the file or files you wish to undelete by checking the check box on the left of each file's entry in the listing. Click the "Undelete" button in the tool bar. The files will be removed from the "Trash" folder and placed back in the normal file area including any associations with folders previously set up.

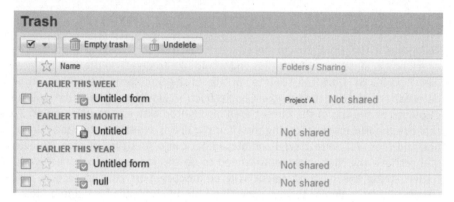

Figure 3-19: The "Trash" folder

You can delete files from the "Trash" folder in one of two ways. To delete individual files or groups of files, select the files in the "Trash" folder by checking the check box on the left of the file entry. Click on the "Empty trash" button in the tool bar. The files will be deleted without warning. To empty the entire "Trash" folder, click the "Empty trash" button in the tool bar without having selected any files. You will receive a warning that you are emptying the "Trash" folder and it will permanently delete all items. Click the "OK" button to continue or click the "Cancel" button to abort the operation.

Unlike Gmail, the items in the "Trash" folder are not automatically deleted after a period of time. They will remain until you physically purge the entire "Trash" folder or delete specific items.

NotED

When you delete an item or the entire contents of the trash, the items are permanently deleted and cannot be recovered.

Additionally, each Google Docs user has a specific amount of free space allocated to them. There is no limit to the size of the "Trash" folder, but files in the "Trash" folder count toward the space limitation. To retrieve this space, permanently delete them.

ExplainED

The files in the "Trash" folder count toward your total file space.

Deleting a Shared File

When you delete a file you have previously shared, the behavior is slightly different. Deleting a shared file will delete the file for everyone you have shared it with making it inaccessible although it is still in the "Trash" folder until purged. When you attempt to delete a shared file for which you are the owner, you will see a dialog box (see Figure 3-20). This is a warning that if you delete the file, it will be moved to the trash for everyone it is shared with. You can choose to assign a new owner for the file or to continue. To continue to delete the file, click the "Trash for everyone" button in the dialog. This will remove the file from the document list for everyone and no one will have access to it. If you choose to assign a new owner, click the "Choose new owner" button in the dialog.

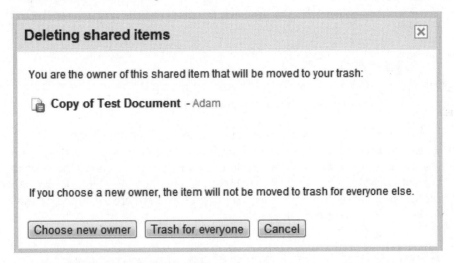

Figure 3-20: Deleting a shared file

This will open a further dialog (see Figure 3-21). Type the e-mail address of the new owner or click the "Choose from contacts" link to the right to choose the

129

new owner from your list of e-mail contacts. Click the "Change owner" button at the bottom of the dialog. This will close the dialog box and the ownership of the file will be transferred to the person you selected.

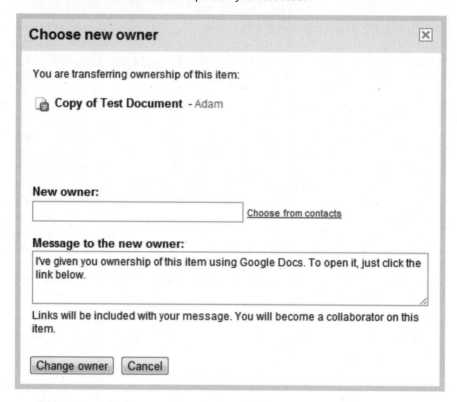

Figure 3-21: Assigning a new owner before deleting

Once the ownership of a file has been transferred, you can delete the file. When you delete a file for which you are not the owner, you will be given a warning message that because you do not own the file, it cannot be trashed but only removed from your document list. If you click the "Yes" button, the file will be removed from your document list. It will not appear in the "Trash" folder since you were not the owner.

Exporting and Importing Documents

The actual exportation of individual documents is covered in detail in the individual applications, however it is important to briefly discuss the process at this point. When you export a Google Docs file, you are saving it to your local computer. You may want to do this for a number of reasons including making a backup copy or taking a copy if you know you will not have access to the Internet from a specific location. When you download (or export) your file, save it in a format to be used on your local computer. The format in which you can save it will depend on the type of file you are downloading, (document, spreadsheet, or presentation). To export a document, select it by checking the check box of the file on the left of the file listing. Choose the "Export" option from the "More actions" drop-down menu on the tool bar. A dialog box will be displayed (see Figure 3-22).

Figure 3-22: Assigning a new owner before deleting

The actual dialog box will be slightly different depending on the type of document you choose to export or whether you selected more than one file to export. Beside the document name in the dialog box will be a drop-down list of options for exporting your document. You can choose which type of file to export your document to based on applications you have on your local computer. The different options for the different Google Docs types include:

Document: HTML, open document (OpenOffice), PDF, rich text format (RTF), plain text, or Word (Microsoft)

Spreadsheet: Microsoft Excel, OpenOffice, spreadsheet, or PDF

Presentation: Microsoft PowerPoint, plain text, or PDF

Choose the format you would like for the file type you are exporting and click the "Download" button at the bottom of the dialog box. Despite a couple exceptions, after you click the "Download" button, a new browser tab will be created and the document will be downloaded within this tab. The documents will be downloaded to your computer's standard download area. From there, you can open the files with appropriate applications as you would open any other file on your computer.

Choosing to export to HTML is slightly different. In this mode, the file created and saved will be a zip file containing one or more other files. Your document may contain other embedded objects including images, drawings, tables, etc. These are stripped out of the document and placed as separate objects together with the HTML file itself into the newly created Zip file. The HTML document will contain links to these objects as any normal HTML file would. The different types of objects stripped out of the original document will be placed into specific directories depending on their type, and when you extract these from the zip file you should preserve the directory structure.

Additionally, you can choose to export more than one document at a time. When you select a number of documents for export, the dialog box (see Figure 3-22) looks like the one in Figure 3-23. There is a small drop-down list for each of the files you choose to export. You need to select the export type for each of the files. Click the "Download" button at the bottom of the dialog box. When you download a group of files, each file is first converted to the chosen type, then the files are placed together in a single Zip file which is downloaded to the computer's download area through a separate browser tab. The Zip file can be accessed as normal from this area.

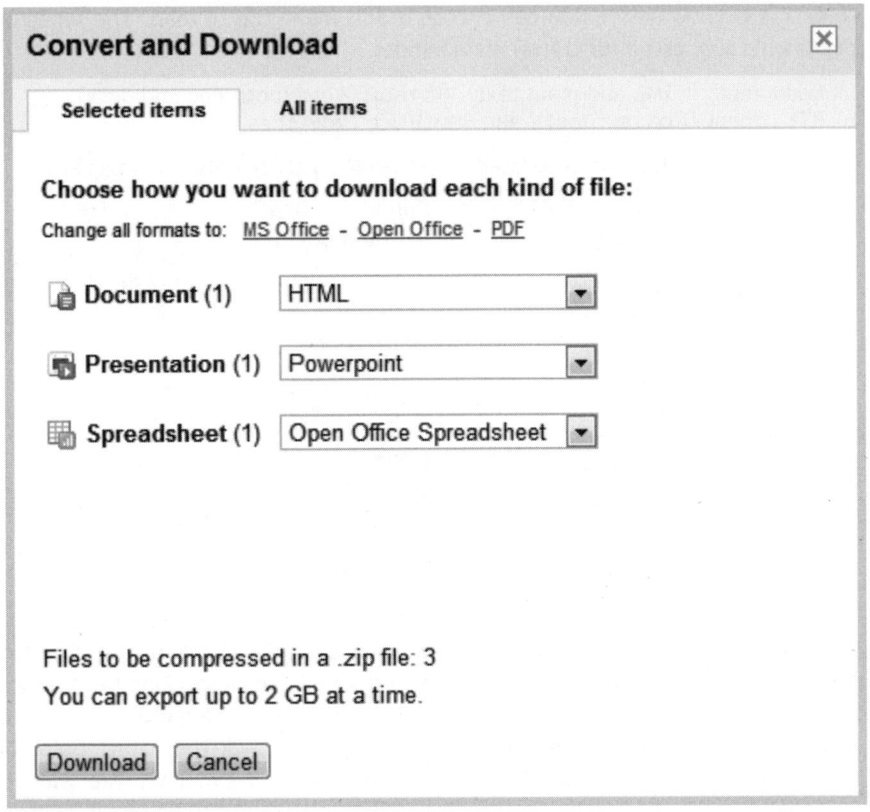

Convert and Download   ☒

Selected items   **All items**

Choose how you want to download each kind of file:

Change all formats to: MS Office - Open Office - PDF

📄 **Document** (1) | HTML | ▼ |

📑 **Presentation** (1) | Powerpoint | ▼ |

📊 **Spreadsheet** (1) | Open Office Spreadsheet | ▼ |

Files to be compressed in a .zip file: 3
You can export up to 2 GB at a time.

[Download] [Cancel]

Figure 3-23: Exporting more than one document

In addition to exporting documents, you can upload them to Google Docs. Google has recently extended this facility. Google allows you to upload documents to Google Docs without converting them to a Google Docs format. You can upload a file of any kind. While you cannot edit it via the Google Docs applications, you can access and download it from anywhere you have Internet access. Alternatively you can upload and convert documents to one of the Google Docs formats. This will allow you to edit the document from anywhere you have Internet access and access to the Google Docs interface.

To upload a document to Google Docs from your local computer, click the "Upload" button just above the file listing options on the top left of the Google Docs window (see Figure 3-3). This will display the file upload facility in the current tab (see Figure 3-24). To begin uploading files, select the "Select files to upload" link (see Figure 3-24). This will take you to your computer's file selection window where you can choose a document file to load. The types of documents supported for conversion include:

Documents: HTML and plain text, Microsoft Word (both doc and docx), RTF, OpenOffice text (odt), and StarOffice (sxw) files

Spreadsheets: Comma separated vale files (csv), Microsoft Excel (xls and xlsx), and OpenOffice Spreadsheet (ods) files

Presentations: Microsoft PowerPoint (ppt and pps) files

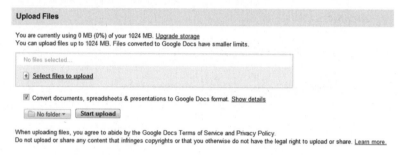

Figure 3-24: File upload option

When you select a file for uploading, you will be taken back to the "Upload files" facility where you can select more files to upload by clicking the "Select more files" link (see Figure 3-25). This allows you to select multiple files and batch upload them. When you are ready to upload, click the "Start Upload" button at the bottom of the list of files (see Figure 3-25). Each file will be uploaded in turn, and when the process is finished, each file you have chosen to upload will have a green tick symbol displayed to the left of the file name. When you are finished, click the "Back to Google Docs" link appearing in the upper left of the browser window.

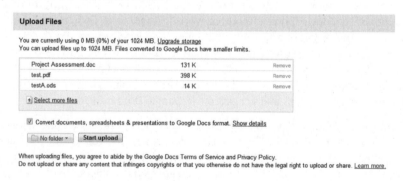

Figure 3-25: Uploading multiple files

If you don't want to convert your documents to a Google Docs format, upload them in their current form. Uncheck the "Convert documents" check box shown just below the list of files to be uploaded (see Figure 3-25) before you start the upload process. This results in the files being uploaded and not converted. When you click one of these files in the Google Docs window, if the file is in a format Google understands, it will be displayed. You will not be able to edit it. You will be given the options for sharing it, downloading it, or printing it (see Figure 3-26).

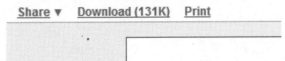

Project Assessment.doc

Share ▼   Download (131K)   Print

Figure 3-26: Uploaded file options

Uploading documents in their native format and not converting them is a convenient way of ensuring you have access to documents where you are (provided you have access to the Internet).

ExplainED

Files that are uploaded and not converted take more space and count toward your file space limits.

Publishing Documents

Google Docs can publish your documents. Essentially, this will make your document available on the Web with a ULR. You can make the URL available to anyone you would like to be able to view the document. It is also possible that people you don't give the ULR to can access your document on the Web. However, they won't be able to make edits. To publish a document on the Web, select the document to be published by checking its check box on the left of the file name. Choose the "Publish" option from the drop-down *"More actions"* list on the tool bar. This opens a new browser tab (see Figure 3-27). To publish the document, click the "Publish document" button on the page (see Figure 3-27). If you want would like the document to be automatically republished every time you modify it, check the check box below the button.

When you click the "Publish document" button, a URL will be displayed on the page. Copy this URL and post it to people you would like to be able to view the web page containing the document. Close the browser tab when finished.

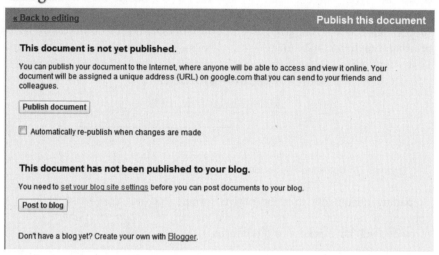

Figure 3-27: Publishing a document

Hiding Documents

"Hiding a file" is another function you can perform on files in Google Docs. This is not meant to literally hide a file from anyone, but can be viewed as more of an archiving-type function. To hide a document, select the document or documents you would like to hide and choose the "Hide" option from the drop-down "More actions" list on the tool bar. This causes the documents to be hidden from all the view list options or "archived." You can access these documents again by clicking the "Hidden" link in the file viewing options on the left of the Google Docs window. This will display a list of all hidden files. To unhide a file or put it back in the view lists, select the file or files from the hidden files list you wish to unhide and choose the "Unhide" option from the drop-down "More actions" list on the tool bar. The file will be placed into the appropriate viewing lists.

Changing Owners

We have previously discussed changing ownership in this chapter. However, it is worthwhile to specifically mention this facility in its own right. This is a feature of Google Docs that is part of the collaboration facility. Quite often in project team groups of people will be assigned a project, the result often becoming a project document. Using the sharing facility discussed previously, there can be a team of people working and collaborating on the same document concurrently. At the end of the lifetime of the project, often the project document is handed over, either to another team or to the project manager. Google Docs easily allows you to achieve this by assigning ownership of the document once it is complete. To assign ownership of a document, select the document you would like to change ownership from the file list area and choose the "Change Owner" option from the drop-down "More actions" list on the tool bar. This will display the same dialog box shown in Figure 3-21. Type the e-mail address of the new owner or click the "Choose from contacts" link to the right to choose the new owner from your list of e-mail contacts. Click the "Change owner" button at the bottom of the dialog. This will close the dialog box and ownership of the file will be transferred to the selected person. This is an efficient way of transferring ownership to the relevant person at some point in a document's lifetime.

Summary

In this chapter we have discussed the Google Docs interface providing a common point of access to the sunset of the Google Apps known as Google Docs. We briefly reviewed the advantages for using Google Docs and discussed the security of your documents when using these applications. We then covered how to create and edit documents with the Google Docs interface, and looked at sharing your documents with other Google users (and non-Google users) over the Internet. We looked at aspects of concurrent editing of documents using the Google Docs applications. An important aspect of the Google Docs interface was working with folders, and we learned how to do this, as well as renaming and deleting files and working with the "Trash" folder. We also learned how to upload and download files in the Google Docs interface, and finally we covered how to publish, hide, and change owners of documents.

Chapter 4

Google Docs—Document

The document component of Google Docs provides you with a very powerful online word-processing application containing most of the features found in other major Microsoft Office suite word-processors. Google Docs Document allows you to create full-featured, rich documents immediately sharable in an online environment. This also saves you from taking copies of your document with you wherever you go. As long as you have access to the Web, you have access to the latest version of your document from any computer with a browser. By default, Google Docs Document · saves its word-processing document online, but they can be saved to local files on your PC for local editing. Your Document files can be loaded from, or downloaded to, your local PC in Word©, OpenOffice, and other standard text formats. They can even be downloaded as PDF files to your computer, however leaving your files online gives you the versatility of being able to write once and edit anywhere.

You can either choose to upload and open an existing document file or create a new one to work with. This is done through the Google Docs interface discussed in Chapter 3 (Google Docs). When a new document is created, a new blank document in your browser window will be shown (see Figure 4-1).

Figure 4-1: New blank Google document

Only the first half of the screen is shown in Figure 4-1, as the bottom half of the screen contains the rest of the blank document, and there are no buttons or icons associated with the Google Document. The blank document appears the same as in other Office Suite word processors, but the menu bar and tool bar is less cluttered. Much of the functionality can be accessed from the extensive context-sensitive right-click menus. Rather than appear as a window in a desktop application, the document appears in the window of a browser tab. You can move backward and forward between the browser tabs as normal.

Elements of the Screen

By expanding the view slightly shown in Figure 4-1, we can see the major elements of the Document working screen. This is shown in Figure 4-2, and is a fairly straightforward working environment consisting of the menu bar, tool bar and the writing area for your document. The menu bar and tool bar are discussed separately later in the chapter, but the main working area is where you type the text of your document. This area can be viewed in a number of ways, but the view shown in Figure 4-1 and Figure 4-2 is a "fixed-width page" view representing the printed page options associated with the document. This will be discussed later in the chapter, but this allows you to see the formatted page as it will be printed. This view is akin to similar view options found in other Office Suite word-processor products. As you keep typing into your document, you can use the scroll bar on the right of your browser window to scroll up and down through the text of your document. One missing piece from the document window is the ruler-guides often seen in other Office Suite word-processors. Unfortunately, at the time of writing, you cannot include either vertical or horizontal rulers in a document when editing. Many people rely on these guides and while they are not necessary, they can be considered useful.

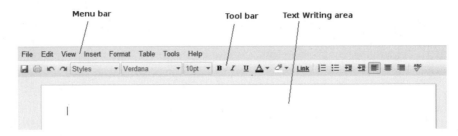

Figure 4-2: Annotated portion of the document environment

Menu Bar

At the top of the document text area is the menu bar which provides a number of pull-down menus allowing you to perform many of the common functions associated with word processing. Menu options include:

- File: Allows you to perform standard file functions and print functions
- Edit: Includes standard edit functions including redo, undo, copy, paste, etc.
- View: Allows control over the text document viewing options
- Insert: Allows you to insert objects including footnotes, images, tables, images, etc.
- Format: Allows you to apply various format and alignment settings to text and paragraphs
- Table: Allows you to insert and manipulate tables in the document
- Tools: Allows you to apply tools including document translation, spell check, etc.
- Help: Provides help with various aspects of Google Docs Document

As we discuss and highlight various features of Google Docs Document throughout this chapter, you will constantly be referred to specific items on the menu bar. We will learn to manipulate and edit a document through most of these menu selections as we go. Additionally, some of the more common tasks associated with document manipulation are also available on the tool bar.

Tool bar

Just below the menu bar is the Document tool bar. This gives you quick access to a number of commonly performed functions by clicking icons on the tool bar. Some of the tool bar icons are grouped according to common functionality (see Figure 4-3).

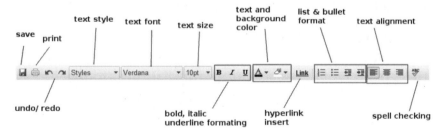

Figure 4-3: Expanded Document tool bar

The first two icons are the "Save" and "Print" icons followed by "Undo" and "Redo." These allow you to undo an operation you have just performed, such as a formatting operation or deletion. Click the "Undo" button to reverse the last operation. If after clicking "Undo" you realize the operation was what you intended, you can click the "Redo" button to automatically restore the operation. The next three buttons allow you to format text, specifically the text style, font, and size. The next grouping of three icons allows you to apply standard formatting of bold, italic, and underline, while the following group lets you control the text and text background colors. You can insert hyperlinks within your document and the "Link" icon allows you to do this as well as control the appearance of the link. The list and bullet format group of icons allow you to format text as either bullet points or lists and control the demotion or promotion of sub-points. The next three icon buttons allow you to control the alignment of selected text, and the final icon on the tool bar lets you initiate spell checking for the document.

As we work through this chapter, we will refer back to these tool bar icons and cover in detail the operations they perform and how they are applied.

Getting Help

You can always get help for Google Docs Document at any time by selecting the "Help" item on the menu bar. This will show the drop-down help menu (see Figure 4-4), and it provides you with various ways to get help with using Google Document. Choosing the "Google Docs Help Center" item will load a web page into another browser tab giving you a number of general links, including specific links for particular Google Document topics. Some of these links can be quite helpful, however, while there are many help topics, help with specific issues or features may be difficult to find. You may sometimes need to persist and use the search facility at the top of the Google Docs "Help" screen. If your issue is very specific, then you may be better off consulting with other Google Docs users. The "Learn From Other Google Users" option on the "Help" menu takes you to a forum where you can scan discussion threads about specific topics and post your own questions. This feature provides for informative and very helpful tips.

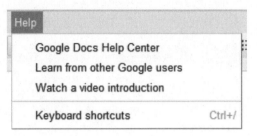

Figure 4-4: Drop-down "Help" menu

If you are new to Google Docs, there is an introduction to Google Docs video on YouTube.com. Selecting the "Watch a Video Introduction" option will load this into a new browser tab. This introductory video is not specifically for Google Document, but Google Docs as a whole. As you become more familiar with Document and wish to speed up your productivity, you can access a list of keyboard shortcuts by choosing the "Keyboard shortcuts" menu option. When you choose this option, a web page will be loaded into another browser tab giving a list of keyboard shortcuts commonly used in Google Docs applications.

Working with Documents

Before you begin to create your documents and undertake the tasks of learning how to do all the things needed to create professional-looking documents, it is worthwhile to quickly review the Google Document, standard document functions. These are functions you will need to be familiar with to load, save, and manipulate your documents. These functions are found through the "File" menu item from the menu bar (see Figure 4-5). Some document functions are available elsewhere within Google Document, and from the Google Docs main interface, but they can all be accessed through this menu item as well.

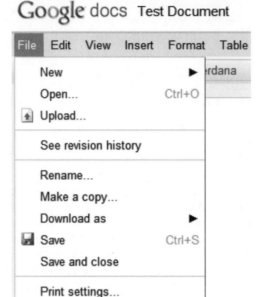

Figure 4-5: Drop-down "File" menu

Saving and Closing Documents

One of the most common things you will need to do with your word-processing document (and most other Google apps documents) is to save it and close it when you are finished. Select the "Save and close" option from the "File" menu. If the document is a new document and has not been saved yet, when you choose the "Save and close" option, the new document is automatically given a name from the first few words you typed in the document. Thus, if the first sentence typed in the document is "Hello world, how are you?," this would become the name of the new document. However, you can change the name of the document at any time. Once the document has been saved, the document tab will close taking you back to the Google Docs interface tab. You should be able to see your new document from the Google Docs tab shortly after, though it may take a little while depending on the server use at the time.

If you wish to save the document but not exit the application and continue editing, you can either select the "Save" menu option from the "File" menu, or click the "Save" icon from the tool bar (see Figure 4-3). This will save the current document and you can then continue editing. However, similar to the "Save and close" menu option, if the file is new and has not been saved previously it will be automatically assigned a name from the first few words in the document. There is no need to periodically save the document as you are working. The document is automatically saved approximately once every minute. This is necessary so that when multiple people are working on the document at the same time, they can see any changes as soon as they are made. The last time the document was autosaved is displayed in grayed lettering in the upper-right corner of the document window. The autosave feature is currently not able to be configured.

If you want to make a copy of a document before you make changes, you can choose the "Make a copy" option from the "File" menu. You will see a dialog box (see Figure 4-6). Click the "OK" button to make a copy of the document. If your document has collaborators (created when you share your document) and you want them to have access to the document, check the box "Also copy document collaborators" before pressing the "OK" button. The new document will be given the same name as the existing document, except it will be preceded with "Copy of." If your document name is "Test," the new document will be called "Copy of Test." You can change the name at a later stage, discussed in the next section. A copy of the current document will be made and loaded into a new browser tab. The tab name will reflect the name of the new copy. Any changes you make will be made to the new copy you have created.

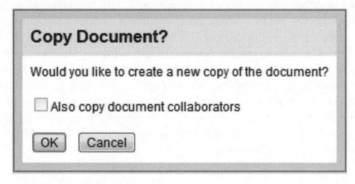

Figure 4-6: Make a copy dialog box

Renaming a Document

While editing a document, you can change the name at any time by choosing the "Rename" menu option from the "File" menu. When choosing this option, a dialog box will appear (see Figure 4-7), and the current name of the document will be highlighted. Type the new name of the document and select "OK." The new name will be reflected in the current browser tab. When you exit from editing the document, the new name should be reflected in the Google Docs interface tab (this could take a short while to change depending on the speed of the Internet and load on the server). You may need to reload the page.

Figure 4-7: Rename dialog box

Opening Documents

You can open a Google Document file from a number of places. It can be opened from the Google Docs interface tab (as discussed in Chapter 3), or you can open another word-processing document while working on an already opened document. When working on a document, rather than closing it and then opening a different document, choose the "Open" option from the "File" menu item. A new tab will be opened in the browser and the Google Docs interface will be loaded showing only the list of document files you have access to (see Figure 4-8). Choose the new document you wish to open from the available list. When you click one of the available documents, it will open in a new tab and that will become the current document. You can move backward and forward between the different documents by clicking the appropriate tab at the top of the browser window.

Figure 4-8: Open a document interface tab

You can also open a new document by simply switching tabs to the Google Docs interface tab, which should still be available after you opened your first document unless you closed it. From this tab, choose the new document to open and it will open in a new tab becoming the current document. Know that when you open a new document while already editing another, this will always create a new tab with the Google Docs interface showing the document files first. Unless you first change to the Google Docs interface tab and choose a new document to open, you will end up with multiple interface tabs in the browser window. You will need to close the documents you don't want open.

You can open a new document from the "File" menu by choosing the "New Document" option from the "File" menu, and a new document tab will be created will become the current working document. When you create a new document in this way, it will initially be untitled. When you save it, it will be given a name consisting of the first few words in the document, which you can simply rename later. As well as creating a new document while editing an existing one, you can create any new Google Docs document.

Uploading Documents

You can upload existing word-processor documents into Google Docs to work with them online and collaborate together with multiple authors. To upload a file from your local computer, select the "Upload" menu option from the "File" menu (see Figure 4-5). The "Upload Files" utility will be opened in a new browser tab (see Figure 4-9). To begin uploading existing files, select the "Select files to upload" link (see Figure 4-9). This will take you to your computer's file selection window where you can choose a document file to load. The types of documents supported are Word documents (.doc, .docx), Open Office Documents (.odt), Star Office (.sxw), and Rich Text Format documents (.rtf). You can also upload standard text (.txt) and HTML files.

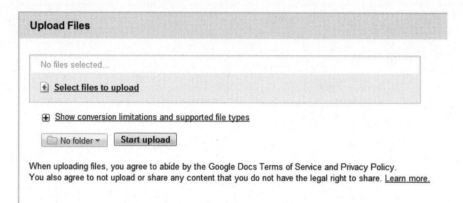

Figure 4-9: File upload option

When you select a file for uploading, you will be taken back to the "Upload Files" utility where you can select more files to upload by clicking the "Select more files" link (see Figure 4-10). This allows you to select multiple files and batch upload them in one hit. When you are ready to upload, click the "Start Upload" button at the bottom of the list of files (see Figure 4-10). Each file will be uploaded in turn, and when the process is complete, each file will have a green tick symbol displayed just to the left of the file name.

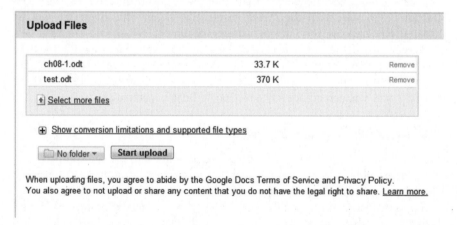

Figure 4-10: Uploading multiple files

The newly uploaded files are not automatically opened in a browser tab, but will be visible from the Google Docs interface tab (you may need to reload the page). Be careful when uploading a document from your local computer because while Google Docs will do the best to translate the document from its existing format to Google Document, sometimes the translation is not perfect. This is the same when translating any file from one format to another. Depending on the complexity of the formatting in the uploaded document, it may not translate perfectly. In particular, there may be minor formatting problems if the uploaded document contains many images. Additionally, Google Document will not contain all the font types present in other word-processing applications, so some translation will occur if your document makes use of some of the more uncommon fonts.

Downloading Your Document to Your Computer

When you save your document, it is saved to your account on a secure Google online storage facility. However, there are times when you might wish to save your document locally on your own computer's local storage, whether a hard drive, USB drive (a small portable data storage device you plug into a USB port) etc. Select the "Download as" option from the "File" menu. You than have a number of options as to what format you can download your document (see Figure 4-11). You can choose between HTML, Text (.txt), RTF, Word, OpenOffice, or PDF formats. Choosing either OpenOffice, PDF, Word, RTF, or Text will create a new local document of the chosen type and download it to your local computer's file download area. Once it is downloaded, you can retrieve the file from your download area as you would any normal file. This will automatically be done, however the behavior may be slightly different depending on your operating system.

Choosing to download as HTML is slightly different. In this mode, the file created and saved will be a Zip file containing one or more other files. Zip files are often used as they compress archive files and reduce the storage requirements. You will need a utility such as WinZip or WinRar to view these on a Windows computer. The reason this type of file is used is that your document may contain other embedded objects such as images, drawings, tables, etc. These are stripped out of the document and placed as separate objects, together with the HTML file itself, into the newly created Zip file. The HTML document will contain links to these objects as any normal HTML file will. The different types of objects stripped out of the original document will be placed into specific directories depending on their type, and when you extract these from the Zip file, you should preserve the directory structure.

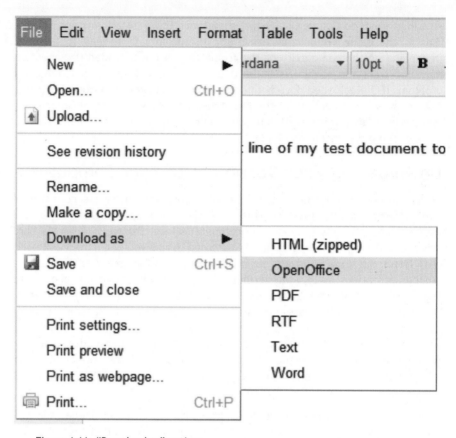

Figure 4-11: "Download as" options

ExplainED

When extracting from a Zip file created by downloading as a HTML file, preserve the directory structure contained within the Zip file.

When you download as a Word document, you cannot save in (.docx) format at this stage, only in the standard (.doc) format.

When you download your document, you must remember that the Google document is being translated into the specific type you have requested. As with any translation, a best effort is made, but in some instances the format may not end up exactly the same as in the original. This is typically caused by complexity surrounding embedded objects. This is not specific to Google Docs. The same is true for any translation from one document format to another.

Printing Documents

Printing your documents is not done directly from Google Document, but is done by transforming the document, similar to the "Downloading the Document" functionality as described in the previous section. You can print the document by selecting the "Print" option from the "File" menu, or by clicking the "Print" icon on the tool bar. The document will first be exported to a PDF version and displayed in a new browser tab via the browser viewer. You can then choose the "Print" icon on the browser PDF viewer icon bar to print the PDF version of the file. This will then show the standard PDF print file dialog box (see Figure 4-12). Using the standard PDF print dialog box, you can select the printer you wish to use, the print range (either all pages, the current page, or a selection of pages), any scaling to be done, and have access to advanced settings. This is the same dialog box you would see when printing any Adobe© PDF file.

Alternatively, instead of choosing the "Print" menu item, you could choose the "Print as webpage" menu option from the "File" menu. This will open a new tab in your browser, and the current document will be transformed into an HTML page and loaded into the new tab. This is the same type of transform that occurs when you download your document in an HTML (zipped) form, although it is opened in the new tab. Your browsers "Print dialog box" will then be automatically opened (see Figure 4-13) waiting for you to make any printer and range selections, and to click the "Print" button. Don't forget to close the browser tab when you have finished. You could also download the document as previously explained and print it locally using your own computer's word-processing software as you would for any other local text document. The recommended method for printing would be using the "Print" icon as described earlier, going through the PDF conversion. But any of the alternatives described will work just as well.

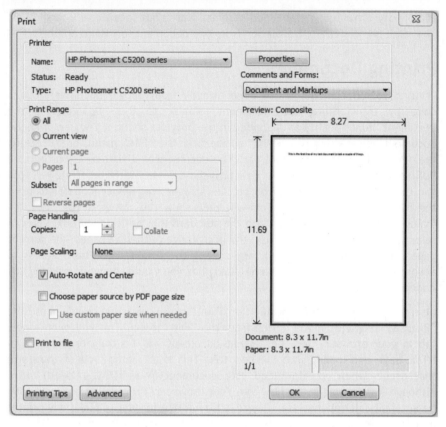

Figure 4-12: PDF print dialog box

The reason the printing is handled this way is because the security restrictions placed on web pages control elements of the local computer. As the Document is an application running in a web browser, it is subject to the security limitations placed on all web-based applications. These limitations are for protection.

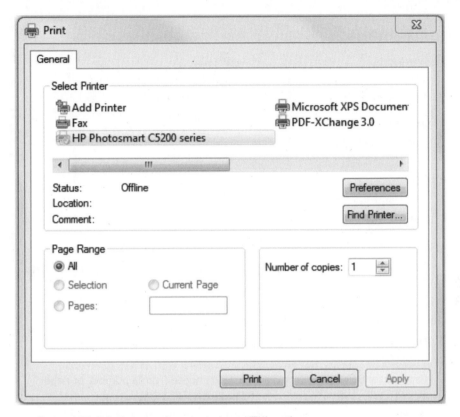

Figure 4-13: Printing your document via an HTML option

Print Settings

There are a number of print settings associated with your document that you can control. These print settings will determine how your document will be exported to other formats (previously discussed) and how it will be formatted when printed to your local printer. To access the print settings in Google Document, choose the "Print Settings" menu option from the "File" menu bringing up a dialog box (see Figure 4-14).

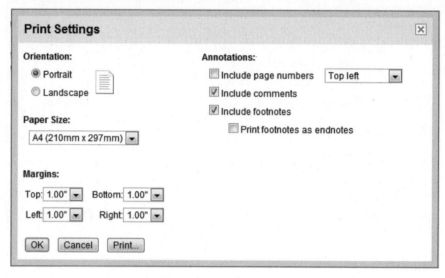

Figure 4-14: Print Settings dialog box

Currently there are four adjustable setting groups including:

Orientation: You can choose between "Standard portrait" or "Landscape mode" for printing.

Paper Size: Select the drop-down box to choose from a number of paper size options. These include A4, legal, and letter sizes.

Margins: Change the top, bottom, left, and right margins by using the drop-down box for each and choose from a number of preset values. (You cannot type a value that does not appear here.) The measurements are currently displayed in Imperial inches.

Annotations: The annotations allow you to control the placement of page numbers, comments, and footnotes by either checking or unchecking the box beside each. When you include page numbers, you can use the drop-down box to choose where to place them. By unchecking the comments box, any comments you insert in the document will not be printed. You can choose to include footnotes when the pages are printed. By default, comments and footnotes are turned on.

ExplainED

While printing, comments are still printed even though the print setting box may have been unchecked. This is a known issue and Google were working on the problem at the time of writing.

Previewing Documents

Before you print your document, you can choose to preview it first. This will give some idea as to how the formatting of your document will look in print before you commit your paper and ink to the task. To preview your document, select the "Print preview" menu option from the "File" menu. Your document will be opened in preview mode inside the same tab (see Figure 4-15). The document, as it will appear printed, is shown in the large window to the left. The "Print settings" discussed in the previous section will affect how this looks. You can access the "Print settings" from the preview mode by clicking the "Print settings" button in the small tool bar appearing just above the formatted document. If you make changes to the print settings, you can save these changes and the document will be re-formatted in preview mode to reflect these new changes.

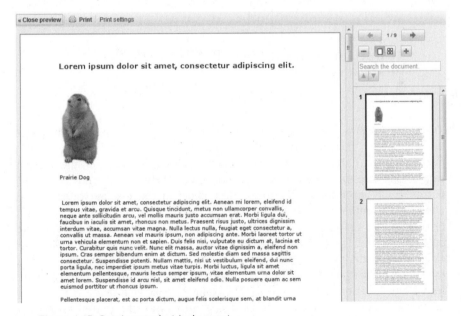

Figure 4-15: Preview mode (single page)

Down the right hand side of the window in preview mode, you will see small versions of the formatted pages according to the print settings. You won't be able to read the text on these small page versions, but you can scroll down using the vertical scroll slider to the right and get an overview for the formatting of the document. Clicking any one of the pages will display that page of the document in the large window on the left. Just above the vertical list of formatted small pages is a set of preview mode control buttons that allows you to scroll through the pages and control other aspects of the display (see Figure 4-16).

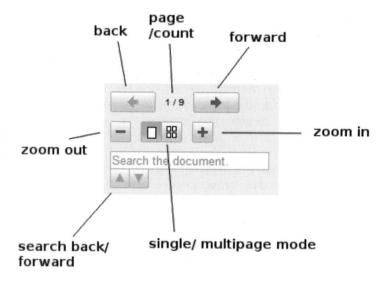

Figure 4-16: Preview mode control buttons

There are backward and forward buttons that can scroll through the pages displaying each page in turn in the display window on the left. Located in between these buttons are the page count and an indication of the current page being displayed. Below these controls is a "zoom out" and "zoom in" button to shrink and magnify the current page in the display window. This allows you to either zoom in to see parts of the formatted document up close, or zoom out to get an overview of the entire page. Located between these two buttons are the "single" and "multiple" page mode buttons. The default is single-page mode, allowing you to see a single page at a time (see Figure 4-15). By clicking the multiple page mode button, you will see a view of your formatted document (see Figure 4-17). Again, this viewing mode is mainly to allow you to quickly scan through the document to view the overall formatting before printing.

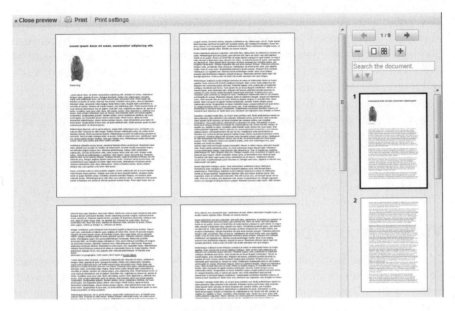

Figure 4-17: Preview mode (multiple page)

At the bottom of the preview mode control buttons is a search facility. Type the term in the document you are looking for within the text box and use the small arrow buttons located below that to search either backward or forward through the document for the term. Matches to the entered search text will be highlighted in the display window.

When you have finished previewing the document in this mode, you can click the "Close preview" button on the tool bar, which will return your document to normal editing mode. You can also click the "Print" button on the tool bar. This will perform the same function as choosing the "Print" menu option from the "File" menu when in editing mode as discussed in the previous section).

Entering and Manipulating Text

As with all word processors, entering text is not difficult. The more difficult parts come in formatting the document after the text is entered (or during the process). The text area directly below the tool bar is where you type in the text of your document. To begin entering text, click the area directly below the tool bar with your mouse cursor and begin typing. As you type, the new text is inserted. This is indicated in your document by a small, flashing vertical bar. You can locate the insertion point anywhere in the document by clicking a new point with the mouse cursor. With Google Document, the document is always in insert mode. Some word processors allow you to switch between overwrite mode and insert mode. Overwrite mode does not insert new text at the insertion point, but rather overwrites existing text, whereas insert mode will insert new text before any text is already there.

ExplainED

With Google Document, you cannot switch between insert and overwrite mode. It is always in insert mode.

View as You Type

As you type your text, you can see in the text window what you have typed. You have a small degree of control over how the text you type is viewed. Selecting the "View" menu option from the menu bar gives you a number of options to choose from for controlling how the text is displayed in the window (see Figure 4-18).

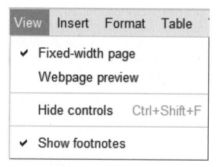

Figure 4-18: View menu options

Your options for viewing control are:

Fixed-width page: If this option is unchecked, the viewing window will become the remainder of the browser window below the tool bar. The text will be displayed without regard to the print settings as previously explained. That is, the text will be displayed with no margins from the left of the browser window to the right. This can be useful if you are either writing text for a web page or if margins won't be applicable at the typing stage and you only wish to view the text. If the menu option is selected, the text area will be formatted with a top, left, and right margin according to the chosen print settings. Thus you will get a good idea of how the text will appear in the printed version.

The print settings include:

Web page preview: This option opens a new tab and displays a preview of the document in a web page format within the tab. This tab is for preview only and cannot be edited. Close this tab when you have finished viewing the web page. This view will be similar to the view given if the fixed-width page option is unchecked, except without any menu bar or tool bar.

Hide controls: This option will hide all the Google Apps control elements in the current tab, including all menu bars and tool bars to give you a full-page view of the document you are currently editing. This can be useful if you wish to view or edit the document without any distraction of the control elements. To return the tab back to normal mode, i.e. with all the control elements, press the escape key (Esc) on the keyboard. This is typically located at the top left of the keyboard.

Show footnotes: This option can be checked or unchecked. If checked, then any footnotes you have included will be shown in small breakout boxes to the right of the text area while editing. If you have unchecked the "Fixed-page width" option, a small right margin will be maintained to enable the display of the footnote boxes. If the "Show footnotes" option is unchecked, then even though you can insert footnotes, they will not be shown. See the section on footnotes below.

NotED

Even when you choose the "Fixed-page width" option to format the pages according to the print settings, no pagination will be displayed. That is, the text will be displayed within the left and right margins but will not be broken into separate pages. You will need to select "Print preview" from the "File" menu to see the page boundaries.

Moving Around and Editing Text

As you continue to type and add to your document, it will become larger, and you may likely need to move around the document, editing, correcting, deleting, and inserting text. There are many ways to move around your document:

- Use the arrow keys to move up and down the lines or left and right within a line.
- Use the "page up" and "page down" keys to scroll the document up or down a page.

- Use the scroll bar to the right of the document window to scroll up and down the document.

- Use the mouse to click anywhere in the document and reposition the insertion point.

- Use the "delete" key to delete characters to the right of the insertion point.

- Use the "backspace" key to backspace over characters to the left of the insertion point.

- Press the "return" (or "enter") key to begin a new line from the insertion point.

- Press the "home" key to move to the beginning of the current line.

- Press the "end" key to move to the end of the current line.

- Press the "ctrl" and "home" keys together to move to the top of the document

- Press the "ctrl" and "end" keys together to move to the bottom of the document.

To edit your existing text, move around the document as described above moving the insertion point and either use the keys above to delete text or insert new next. As discussed, use the return key to begin a new line. This key will end the current paragraph and begin a new one, and will move the insertion point to the beginning of a new line. If you want blank lines between paragraphs, press the return key once for each line you would like in between.

Selecting Text

Often when working with documents, you will need to select a portion of the text to move from one place in the document to another, to delete, edit, or to apply formatting. To select a portion of the text, click with the left mouse button at the point in the document just before the first character of the text you wish to select and, while the button is still pressed, drag the cursor with the mouse until all of the desired text is highlighted and then release the mouse left-button. All the selected text will be highlighted with a light-blue color indicating the selected text (see Figure 4-19). You can also click just before the first character to be selected, press the "Shift" key and click with the mouse just after the last character to be selected and release the shift key. All text in between will be selected. You can also hold down the shift key and use the arrow keys to move from the current insertion point to keep selecting text until finished.

Donec bibendum posuere vulputate. Sed ante felis, elementum et eleifend ut, facilisis vel nulla. Pellentesque quis arcu justo, quis ultrices nisl. Nunc eu tortor sed velit dapibus mollis ac ac quam. Donec sit amet felis id turpis lacinia volutpat in eget massa. In neque nibh, laoreet a bibendum quis, lobortis nec enim. Ut lobortis euismod quam, sed lobortis est placerat et. Class aptent taciti sociosqu ad litora torquent per conubia nostra, per inceptos himenaeos. Integer imperdiet leo sed enim semper tempor. Phasellus pharetra tempor velit, ac lobortis risus cursus ac. Vestibulum sit amet lorem velit, quis sagittis turpis. Duis ut urna nunc. Suspendisse interdum porta semper. Aliquam erat volutpat. Vestibulum vel egestas nisi. Aenean iaculis scelerisque mollis. Nunc risus magna, posuere sed elementum aliquam, aliquet et purus. Maecenas ultricies quam eget nisl suscipit pharetra. Cras a enim sit amet nisl mollis interdum non quis magna.

Figure 4-19: Selected text

ExplainED

To quickly select, double mouse clicking a word will select the word and triple mouse clicking a paragraph will select the paragraph.

Cutting and Pasting Text

As in most Office Suite applications, you can use cut and paste functions to make copies of selected text or to move a selection of text from one place in the document to another. You can use either the standard keyboard short-cuts or do this through the "Edit" menu. To move a selection of text from one place in the document to another, first select the text to be moved as previously discussed. From the keyboard, use the key combination ctrl-X. You can also select the "Cut" option from the "Edit" menu. The selected text will be removed from the document. Choose the point in the document where you want the selected text to appear, and press the keyboard key combination ctrl-V, or you can select the "Paste" option from the "Edit" menu. The selected text that was cut will be inserted at the new location with the insertion point being just after the newly inserted text.

You can copy a selection of text from one location to another as well without moving them. Select the text you wish to copy and from the keyboard, use the key combination ctrl-C, or select the "Copy" option from the "Edit" menu. Then select the point in the document where a copy of the text is to be inserted, and press the keyboard combination ctrl-V, or select the "Paste" option from the "Edit" menu. A copy of the original text selection will be inserted there.

You are not limited to cutting, copying, and pasting within the same document only. If you have another document open in another tab, you can copy or cut the text from one document, select the tab with the other document, and paste the selected text into the new document. If you wish to copy the entire contents of one document, quickly select the entire document by choosing the "Select all" option from the "Edit" menu.

Moving Text with Drag and Drop

As well as moving text with cut and paste, there is a short-hand way to move text around by using only the mouse. First, select the text you wish to move. Then with the mouse, click the selected area with the left mouse button and hold it down. Drag the selected text with the mouse until the insertion point is flashing just at the point where you want the selected text to be moved. Release the left mouse key and the selected text will be moved.

Formatting Text

Apart from being able to type your documents into a computer and retrieve and manipulate them anytime you would like, one of the most important features of a word processor is being able to format your document. By applying different formatting to different areas of your document, you can create professional-looking documents for presentation or printing. Google Document provides a number of options for formatting text. With formatting, you can change the style, font, and color of the text. You control how the text appears including bold, italic, and underline, and you can apply different background colors and text colors. There are not quite as many options available as there are in some of the non-web based word processors, but for a web-based application the options are extensive, and Google continues to enhance these.

Some formatting options are character based, that is, they can be applied to a single character or to a selection of text, while other formatting options can only be applied to entire paragraphs. In this section we will explore the various formatting options available in Google Document.

Bold, Italic, and Underline

The simplest formatting applicable to selected text is the standard bold, italic, underline, or strikethrough. Bold, italic, and underline formatting can be quickly accessed from the icons on the tool bar (see Figure 4-3). First select the text you wish to apply the formatting to and choose the corresponding icon from the tool bar. The selected text will be displayed with the chosen format option. To apply strikethrough formatting, select the text to be formatted and choose the "Strikethrough" option from the "Format" menu. To remove any of the previous formatting from a section of text, select the desired text to remove, and apply the same format option. These format options act like a switch: select them once to turn on and select a second time to turn off.

Styles

There are a number of predefined styles you can apply to your Google document. These styles are found in the "Text Style" icon on the tool bar. Clicking this icon will display a drop-down menu from which you can choose between a number of styles (see Figure 4-20a).

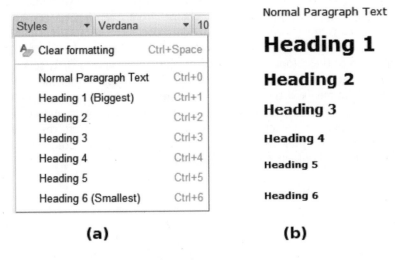

(a)   (b)

Figure 4-20: Style selection and samples

These styles are paragraph styles, as opposed to the bold, italic, underline, and strikethrough formatting. Those are character styles as their formatting could be applied to a single character or a number of characters. The paragraph styles are applied to an entire paragraph. To apply one of these styles (like "Heading 2") click anywhere into a paragraph and from the "Styles" icon on the tool bar, select "Heading 2." The entire paragraph where you clicked will be formatted with the new style (see 4-20b).

All styles shown in Figure 4-20b are based on the standard document font which can be specified in the document settings discussed later in this chapter. The normal paragraph text is what is displayed without any other formatting applied. The heading styles are arranged from the largest ("Heading 1") to the smallest ("Heading 6"). Each has a different font size, but the font face is based on the normal font. To clear a section of text from any applied styles, select the text to be cleared and choose "Clear formatting" from the "Styles" icon drop-down menu on the tool bar. The selected text will be cleared of any applied styles and be displayed in the "Normal" style.

The different styles can also be chosen from the "Paragraph styles" option from the "Format" menu.

Font

The displayed font of a section of a document can be changed by choosing the "Text font" icon from the tool bar. You cannot upload your own fonts at this stage of development, but can only choose from the limited number of available fonts (see Figure 4-21). The standard document default font depends on what has been set in the document settings (discussed later in this chapter). To apply one of these fonts to a section of text, (like "Arial") first, select the text you wish to display in the new font and choose "Arial" from the "Styles" icon drop-down menu on the tool bar. The selected text will be displayed with the new font. To remove this font, select the same text again and choose a new font to apply, or select the "Clear formatting" option from the "Styles" drop-down menu icon on the tool bar. This will cause the selected text to be displayed using the default font for the document.

Figure 4-21: Available fonts

Size

You can resize the text in your document or a portion of the text to suit your purposes. You can do this by selecting the portion of text in the document to be resized and adjusting the size by clicking the "Text size" icon on the tool bar (see Figure 4-3). When you click this icon, you will have the option of changing the size of the selected text to one of the options displayed in the drop-down selection (see Figure 4-22). Font size is usually measured in point (pt) size on a computer screen, where one point is 1/72 of an inch. The default point size for Google Document is 10 pt, unless you change the document settings default.

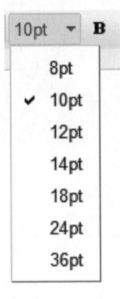

Figure 4-22: Available font sizes

To remove the size selection for a section of text, select the same text and choose a new size to apply, or select the "Clear formatting" option from the "Styles" drop-down menu icon on the tool bar. This will cause the selected text to be displayed using the default point size for the document.

Color

You can change the color of the section of the text displayed in your document by selecting the text to be formatted and choosing the "Text color" icon from the tool bar. You will then see the drop-down color chooser (see Figure 4-23). The current color will show a tick against it, and the default color of documents text is black.

Choose a new text color for the selected text by clicking on the desired color in the color chooser. The selected text will be displayed with the new color.

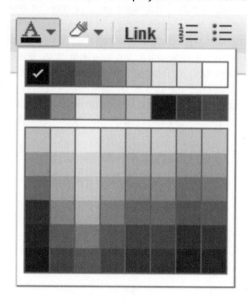

Figure 4-23: Drop-down color chooser

You can also change the background color of section of text in the document by selecting the text and clicking the "Text Background Color" icon in the tool bar. A color chooser similar to the text color chooser in Figure 4-23 will be displayed with the current background color highlighted with a tick. The default background color is white. Choose the new background color to change the background color of the text selection.

ExplainED

Use reasonable colors when choosing text and background colors. Anyone looking at the document for a reasonable length of time may be affected by poor color combinations. Due to different device settings, colors may look different on different computer monitors.

To remove the color selection for a section of text, select the same text again and choose a new color to apply or select the "Clear formatting" option from the "Styles" drop-down menu icon on the tool bar. This will display the selected text using the default color text for the document.

Document Settings

You have the ability to set some default settings for the document. These settings apply to the whole document and will be the default when selections of the document have any other formatting removed. To set the document settings, select the "Document settings" option from the "Format" menu. This will open the document settings dialog box (see Figure 4-24).

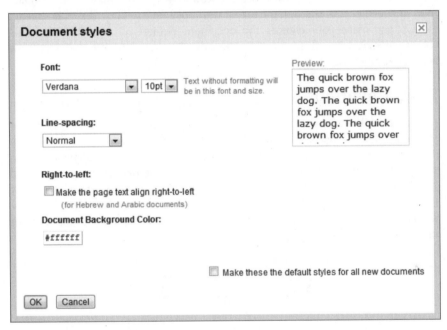

Figure 4-24: Document settings dialog

There are not many settings you have control over. At the time of writing, there were only five settings that are applicable to the document. These include:

Font: Use the drop-down menu to choose from a limited range of fonts. This will become the default for the document and the font shown if formatting is removed (see the sample text to the right of this drop-down selection). The selected font will become the base font for the document "Styles."

Font size: Use the small drop-down menu to choose the default size of your document's font.

Line-spacing: You can choose the default line spacing for the document: normal, single, 1.5-spaced, and double- or triple-spaced.

Right-to-left: This option is mainly for Hebrew and Arabic documents. This will align the text from right to left, and as you type text, it will be inserted at the right pushing other text to the left.

Document background color: The document background color button displays a small drop-down color chooser (see Figure 4-23). Use this to choose the default background color of the document (neutral soft colors are best, and the default is white).

You can check a small box toward the bottom right of the dialog box to make your choices become the default for all new documents. Click the "OK" button to save and make your choices the document default, or click the "Cancel" button to exit without saving any changes. You can change the document settings at any time.

Text Alignment

You can alter the alignment of the text in a paragraph for different sections of your document. This is a paragraph style type formatting option, thus any change you make affects the whole paragraph. To alter the alignment of a paragraph, place the insertion point somewhere in the paragraph to be aligned by clicking it with the left mouse button. You can choose either the "Left Justify," "Center Justify," or "Right Justify" text alignment icons from the tool bar (see Figure 4-3) to left, center, or right justify the text in the current paragraph (see Figure 4-25).

Figure 4-25: Text alignment icons

You can also "Left and Right Justify" paragraphs (known as "Justify"), but there is no icon for this on the tool bar. To "Justify" a paragraph, select the "Justify" option by accessing it from the "Align" option in the "Format" menu (see Figure 4-26). This option will both left and right justify the current paragraph (see Figure 4-26). You can also select the other alignment options from the "Format" menu.

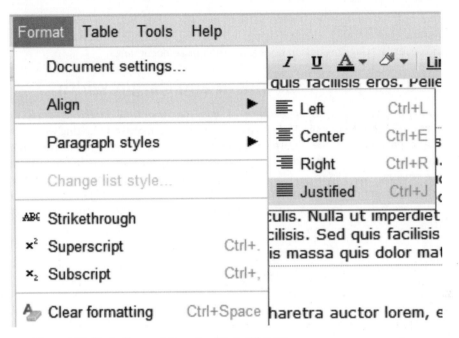

Figure 4-26: Text alignment from the "Format" menu

You can remove the alignment from a paragraph by clicking the paragraph and selecting a new alignment option. You can also select the paragraph and select the "Clear formatting" option from the "Styles" drop-down menu icon on the tool bar.

ExplainED

Currently there seems to be a problem with alignment when a paragraph contains a footnote. It seems to help if the document is saved first, but may need reloading to see the footnote appear again.

Line Spacing

In the current version of Google Document, you can change the spacing of a document but not for a section of a document. Spacing is often used in documents when printing a draft so reviewers can make comments between the lines. It can also be used for effect by increasing the spacing between lines for a small section of a document. In Google Document, you can change the line spacing in the Document Settings as discussed. You can choose either normal (the default), single spacing, 1.5 spacing, and double- or triple-spacing. However, setting this option does alter the entire document.

Modifying the Text Indent and Margin Width

You can also alter the appearance of your document by indenting parts or sections of the document. This is a paragraph style format, so indenting will alter the appearance of the entire paragraph. To indent a paragraph, click the paragraph with the left mouse key, and select the "Increase indent" icon from the tool bar (see Figure 4-3). These are the two right-hand icons in the tool bar grouped under the "list and bullet format" icon group (see Figure 4-27). The "increase indent" icon is the right icon, while the "decrease indent" is the left icon.

Figure 4-27: Indent icons

When you increase the indent of a paragraph, you effectively change the left margin of the paragraph (see Figure 4-28). The right paragraph remains fixed. You can further increase the indent by clicking the paragraph and clicking the "Increase indent" icon. The left margin for the paragraph will move to the right. Indenting text is useful when making points in a document that may contain sub-points. The indent can be used for effect to highlight which are the main points and which are associated sub-points.

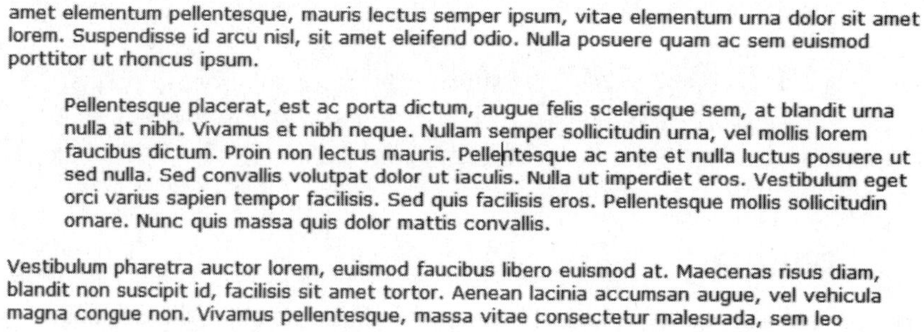

amet elementum pellentesque, mauris lectus semper ipsum, vitae elementum urna dolor sit amet lorem. Suspendisse id arcu nisl, sit amet eleifend odio. Nulla posuere quam ac sem euismod porttitor ut rhoncus ipsum.

Pellentesque placerat, est ac porta dictum, augue felis scelerisque sem, at blandit urna nulla at nibh. Vivamus et nibh neque. Nullam semper sollicitudin urna, vel mollis lorem faucibus dictum. Proin non lectus mauris. Pellentesque ac ante et nulla luctus posuere ut sed nulla. Sed convallis volutpat dolor ut iaculis. Nulla ut imperdiet eros. Vestibulum eget orci varius sapien tempor facilisis. Sed quis facilisis eros. Pellentesque mollis sollicitudin ornare. Nunc quis massa quis dolor mattis convallis.

Vestibulum pharetra auctor lorem, euismod faucibus libero euismod at. Maecenas risus diam, blandit non suscipit id, facilisis sit amet tortor. Aenean lacinia accumsan augue, vel vehicula magna congue non. Vivamus pellentesque, massa vitae consectetur malesuada, sem leo

Figure 4-28: Intending text

You can remove the indent in a paragraph by clicking the paragraph and selecting the decrease indent. This will remove one level of indent. You can also select the paragraph and select the "Clear formatting" option from the "Styles" drop-down menu icon on the tool bar. However, this will remove all formatting from the paragraph including the indenting, and will restore all text to the normal default settings.

In many Office Suites in the word-processing component, you can adjust the left and right margins of a section of the document. In Google Document, you can only set the left and right margins in the Document Settings (previously discussed) which affects the entire document. Using the indent does allow us to alter the left margin for a section of the document, but the right margin remains at the default setting (see Figure 4-28). There is a way around this by using tables. This will be discussed later in this chapter, but by using a table you can adjust the width of the table and place text within the table to simulate different left and right margins.

ExplainED

We can simulate adjusting the left and right margins by using tables.

Working with Images

One of the most striking ways to improve the appearance of a document is to insert images. The old adage "A Picture is Worth a Thousand Words" is certainly true, and can enhance your document's appearance. Working with images in Google Document is relatively easy. There are not as many options for placing and manipulating images in Google Document as in other Office Suites, but there is enough functionality to enable you to create good looking documents with a minimum of fuss.

Obtaining Images

Images can be easily obtained from a variety of sources including personal photographs, Office suite clip-art, and from the web. To obtain an image from the web, right-click on an image and choose the "Save image as" option. This is dependent on the browser you use, but all browsers will provide this functionality in one form or another. You will be able to save the image on your computer, typically in .jpg, .png, .gif, or other Internet formats. Be aware that on most web sites, particularly commercial sites, the right to use and distribute images belongs to the owner of the web site and/or the image owner. You should obtain permission from the owner of an image before using it to include in published documents or web sites. There may be penalties associated with image use without authorization. One source of free images is Free images UK: (www.freeimages.co.uk).

Inserting Images

There are two ways to insert an image in Google Document. You can load the image from your local computer, or you can paste it from the clipboard after originally copying it from another source, like a paint program or from a web browser. To load an image from your computer, place the insertion point in the document at the point where you wish to place the image by clicking the document with the left mouse button. Choose the "Image" option from the "Insert" menu on the menu bar. You will see the small dialog (see Figure 4-29).

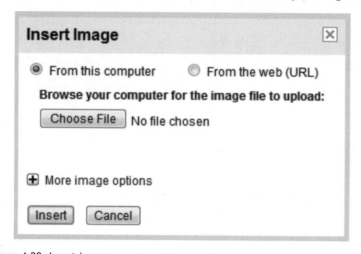

Figure 4-29: Insert image

From the dialog box in Figure 4-29, you can choose to insert an image "From this computer" or "From the web" by clicking the appropriate radio button for the corresponding choice located near the top of the dialog box. If you choose to load an image "From this computer," click the "Choose File" button. You will then be presented with your operating system's file selection utility. Choose where you would like the image to be saved on your computer and select the image. You will be taken back to the dialog box (see Figure 4-29), and the name of the chosen image will be shown just to the left of the "Choose file" button. If you wish to select another image, click the button again and select the new file to load. To insert the image, click the "Insert" button or "Cancel" button to exit without inserting.

facilisis. Sed quis facilisis eros. Pellentesque mollis sollicitudin ornare. Nur mattis convallis.

Vestibulum pharetra a faucibus libero euismo diam, blandit non susc tortor. Aenean lacinia vehicula magna congu pellentesque, massa vi malesuada, sem leo fe tempor tellus erat nec vehicula et pellentesq sapien. Fusce sed urn diam eu mi lobortis aliq nulla id faucibus tristiq urna, tempor dapibus Vivamus varius luctus nunc aliquam sit amet. Nam erat turpis, elementum vel dictum porta, rho Nunc elementum, metus a facilisis luctus, ipsum mauris tempus nisi, non purus.

Fusce commodo nulla eu sem molestie sagittis. Donec sollicitudin est ut tempor lacus pulvinar. Integer quis odio ac lacus feugiat facilisis. Vivamu

Figure 4-30: Inserted image (image: www.freeimages.co.uk)

The image will then be inserted at the point in the document where the insertion point was located (see Figure 4-30). If the image is small enough, the existing text may wrap-around the image (see Figure 4-30). We can further control the appearance of the image by adjusting the image options. You have access to some of these at the time of insertion by clicking the "More image options" link just above the "Insert" button. You can also adjust the image options at any time (as discussed in the following section).

If you want to initially load your image from the web, you need to know the URL (or web address) of the image. From the initial "insert image" dialog box (see Figure 4-29), select the "From the web" radio button. You will be shown the "Insert image" dialog box (see Figure 4-31). Type in and enter the URL of the image you wish to insert into your document, and a small preview will be shown of the image below the URL (see Figure 4-31). Click the "Insert" button at the bottom of the dialog box, or otherwise you can type in a different URL. Click the "Cancel" button to exit without inserting.

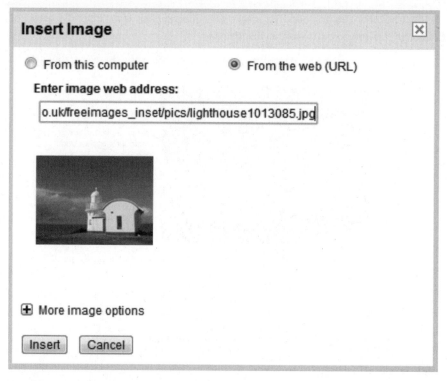

Figure 4-31: Insert image from the web (image: www.freeimages.co.uk)

Another way to insert images quickly is by using the cut-and-paste methods available through your browser and other applications. You can locate an image either within another running application or through your web browser. If the image is on the web and you are viewing it from your browser, right-click the image and choose the option to copy the image. The figure shown in Figure 4-32 shows the right-click pop-up menu for Chrome. The "Copy image" option will copy the image to the clipboard. You can then click into the Google Document in the place where you wish to insert the image and press the key combination ctrl-V. This will copy the image from the clipboard into the document. Use the key combination as the browser doesn't have access to the operating system's clipboard in Chrome.

Figure 4-32: Copying an image from Chrome

Image Options

Once the image is inserted into the document, you can modify its options to control the appearance of the image. Click the image in the document and you will see two links below the image (see Figure 4.33). You can choose the "Remove Image" link to delete the image from the document, or you can choose the "Change Image" link to modify the image options.

When you choose to modify the image options, you will be presented with a dialog box (see Figure 4-34). There are not many options to control the image, but the available options are similar to those for images in a web page. You can control the size of the image, the position, and whether to wrap the text in the document around the image. These options can enable you to create professional-looking documents.

To change the location and size of the image (see Figure 4-30), click the image in the document and click on the "Change Image" link below the image. To adjust the size of the image, click the small arrow to the left of the size drop-down box. You will see a number of preset sizes appear and choose one of these. The sizes only mention the width of the image because in Google Document, the image will always stay in proportion to the original image size, thus adjusting the width will appropriately adjust the height as well. The image measurements are in pixels (picture elements). To enter your own size, select the "Customize size, enter maximum width" option. A small input box will appear to the right of the size drop-down list. In this case, choose the maximum width of 240 pixels.

Figure 4-33: Modifying an image (image: www.freeimages.co.uk)

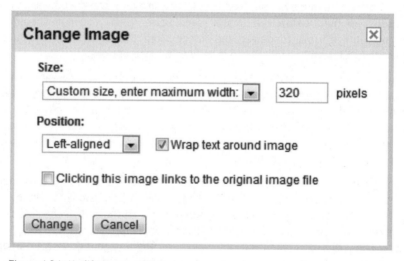

Figure 4-34: Modify image settings

NotED

You can only alter the width of an image, and the height will be adjusted appropriately to keep the image in proportion.

Choose the position you wish the image to occupy in the document by clicking the small drop-down position list. Please choose right-aligned. You can choose from left-aligned, centered, or right-aligned. The small check box to the right of the position list indicates whether you want the text in the document to wrap around the image. If you uncheck this option, the text will appear above and below the image. Checking it will cause the text to wrap down either the left or right side of the image, depending whether it is left- or right-aligned. We will leave this option checked to wrap the text. You cannot choose to center the image and wrap the text around both sides. By default, the text will not wrap around an image. This must be specifically selected at the time of insertion or at a later stage in editing. Additionally, unlike in OpenOffice or Microsoft Office, the image will not "float." The image is fixed in position at the insertion point and is anchored much like the "Anchor as character" in OpenOffice. If you apply document formatting, the image will not move independently of the text around it. Consequently, when inserting an image, it is best to do this in between paragraphs unless you intend to wrap the text around the image. If you wrap the text around the image, it can take a small while before the wrapping adjusts correctly if the image is inserted in the middle of a paragraph.

The small check box underneath the position drop-down list can be checked. If you check this option, the image will become a link in the document and clicking it will display a URL to the image just above the image. Clicking this URL will open another tab in the web browser and the URL will be loaded into that tab. When you click the image, as well as a URL to the image being displayed above the image, there will also be two links labeled "Change" and "Remove." Click the "Remove" link to remove the link associated with the image. Click the "Change" link to change the URL to any URL you would like. You can make your image link to any web page. For this example, leave this option unchecked.

Click the "Change" button at the bottom of the "Change Image" dialog box to save the changes you have made (see Figure 4-35). Compare this to the original inserted image in Figure 4-30. The changed image is smaller aligned on the right of the document with the text wrapped down the left side. You may need to experiment with the size and placement of the image in order to get the document looking exactly how you would like, but this is relatively easy.

volutpat dolor ut iaculis. Nulla ut imperdiet eros. Vestibulum eget orci varius sapien tempor facilisis. Sed quis facilisis eros. Pellentesque mollis sollicitudin ornare. Nunc quis massa quis dolor mattis convallis.

Vestibulum pharetra auctor lorem, euismod faucibus libero euismod at. Maecenas risus diam, blandit non suscipit id, facilisis sit amet tortor. Aenean lacinia accumsan augue, vel vehicula magna congue non. Vivamus pellentesque, massa vitae consectetur malesuada, sem leo fermentum odio, vitae tempor tellus erat nec velit. Nullam nulla tellus, vehicula et pellentesque a, porttitor vitae sapien. Fusce sed urna dui. Praesent lobortis diam eu mi lobortis aliquet. Vivamus tempor, nulla id faucibus tristique, dui est placerat urna, tempor dapibus sapien metus nec enim. Vivamus varius luctus risus, vel condimentum nunc aliquam sit amet. Nam erat turpis, elementum vel dictum porta, rhoncus consectetur eros. Nunc elementum, metus a facilisis luctus, ipsum mauris tempus nisi, non egestas eros ante vitae purus.

Fusce commodo nulla eu sem molestie sagittis. Donec sollicitudin est ut lorem egestas vitae

Figure 4-35: Inserted image after changes (image: www.freeimages.co.uk).

Inserting Page Breaks, Headers, and Footers

In this section, we will look at formatting enabling you to make changes affecting the document and how it prints. Before we go any further, it may be worth mentioning that in Google Document, unlike word processors in the major Office Suites, you cannot turn an option to see the existing paragraph marks. When you view these, they normally show as ¶. However, we cannot see these as yet in Google Document, but there are requests being put forward to change this. To end a paragraph, press the "Return" key on the keyboard. If you need more blank lines (or paragraph marks), press "Return" the desired number of times.

Page Breaks

As previously mentioned, Google Document does not show pagination. Thus, in normal viewing mode, you cannot tell where each page will end. Preview the document using "Print preview" to see this. However, in most cases you will not need to know where the page breaks are, and should let the page breaks occur as they need to. There are occasions when you might want to force a page break at a particular point. Choose the "Page break" option from the "Insert" menu. This will put a page break in your document at the insertion point and will show as a light gray double line in the document (see Figure 4-36). This line won't show in the printing but will be treated as a physical page break.

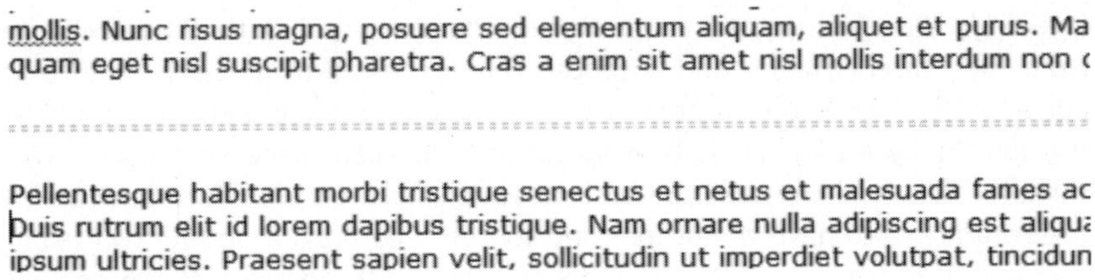

mollis. Nunc risus magna, posuere sed elementum aliquam, aliquet et purus. Ma
quam eget nisl suscipit pharetra. Cras a enim sit amet nisl mollis interdum non (

Pellentesque habitant morbi tristique senectus et netus et malesuada fames ac
Duis rutrum elit id lorem dapibus tristique. Nam ornare nulla adipiscing est aliqua
ipsum ultricies. Praesent sapien velit, sollicitudin ut imperdiet volutpat, tincidun

Figure 4-36: Page break

You can delete page breaks by treating them as any other character by placing
your cursor either before or after the bookmark, and either pressing the delete
or backspace keys.

Headers and Footers

You can add document headers and document footers as you can in other word
processors. However, you do have less control over the placement and
occurrence of them within Google Document. In Word and OpenOffice, you can
control the headers and footers so they do not appear on the first page. In
Google Document, we do not have this granularity of control. Nonetheless, the
features of Document for a web-based application are impressive.

To insert a header in your document, it doesn't matter where you put your
insertion point. Click the "Header" option from the "Insert" menu and a header
will be inserted at the top of the document. Scroll to the top of the document
and you will see a small area surrounded by a light gray, broken outline. You
can place your cursor within this area and type the text you wish to appear as a
page header. Press the return key to have a multiple-line header. The broken
outline will expand (see Figure 4-37). The header will only appear at the top of
your document while in edit mode, but when in "Print preview" mode, or when
you print the document, it will appear at the top of every page.

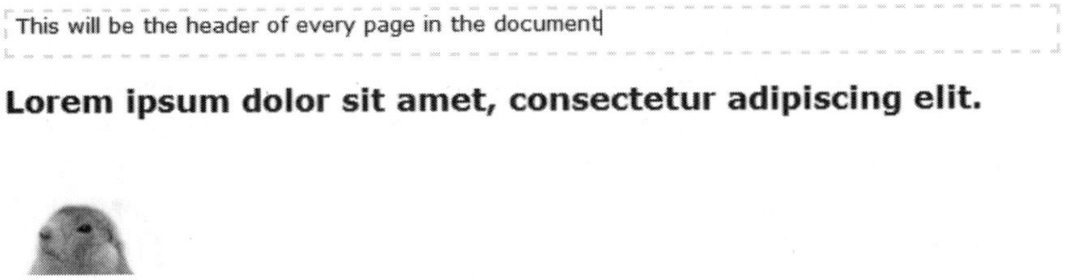

This will be the header of every page in the document

Lorem ipsum dolor sit amet, consectetur adipiscing elit.

Figure 4-37: Page header

Similarly, when you insert a footer in your document, click the "Footer" option from the "Insert" menu and a footer will be inserted at the bottom of the document. Scroll to the bottom of the document and you will see a small area surrounded by a light gray, broken outline. You can place your cursor within this area and type the text you wish to appear as a page footer. You can press the return key to have a multiple-line footer. The broken outline will expand. The footer appears the same as a header only at the bottom of the document (see Figure 4-37). The footer will only appear at the bottom of your document while in edit mode, but when in "Print preview" mode, or when you print the document, it will appear at the bottom of every page.

To delete a header or footer, click the header or footer with your left mouse button and right click with the mouse while in the header or footer area. The drop-down right-click menu will be displayed (see Figure 4-38). You will see either a "Delete Header" or "Delete Footer" menu option in this drop-down menu depending on if you are in the header or footer. Choose this option to delete either the header or footer.

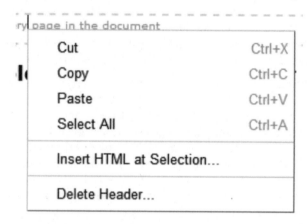

Figure 4-38: Deleting a header or footer

Headers and footers should be unobtrusive and not take too much space in the document. You can format the text within a header or footer as you would format any other text in the document using the techniques previously discussed. Try and limit them to one line and you can choose a smaller font and perhaps a lighter gray color.

Inserting a Table of Contents

You can automatically insert a "Table of Contents" into your document and have it generate page numbers and level numbers when the document is printed or you view the document under "Print Preview" mode. The table of contents is controlled by the use of different styles from the "Styles" icon on the tool bar. In the previous section, we discussed using the different styles for headings within your document. By consistently using the styles for headings and sub-headings, we enable the "Table of contents" generator to automatically recognize these and develop a table of contents for us each time we print or view the document.

As a simple example, in a test document, use the style "Heading 1" from the "Style" icon drop-down menu to place five headings in a document. Each is labeled Heading 1 to Heading 5, and each formatted as a "Heading 1" style through the "Style" icon on the tool bar. Then you can also insert sub-headings under each of the headings. Use the formula of "Heading 1a" and "Heading 1b" as sub-headings for "Heading 1," and "Heading 4a," "Heading 4b," and "Heading 4c" as sub-headings for "Heading 4," etc. Then apply the "Heading 2" style from the "Style" icon on the tool bar to these sub-headings. If there were to be a third level of sub-headings, you would apply the "Heading 3" style from the "Style" icon on the tool bar.

Now you can insert the table of contents, and we will place it at the end of the document in this example. You could place it at the beginning if you like. Go to the end of the document and place a page break after the last line of text in the document. Click the document after the page break and type in a title of the page, (typically "Table of Contents") and format this appropriately. Place the insertion point about three lines down after the title you just typed. Choose the "Table of contents" option from the "Insert" menu. The "Table of Contents" dialog box will appear (see Figure 4-39). The only thing you need to select in the dialog box is the numbering style you wish the table of contents to use when it is printed.

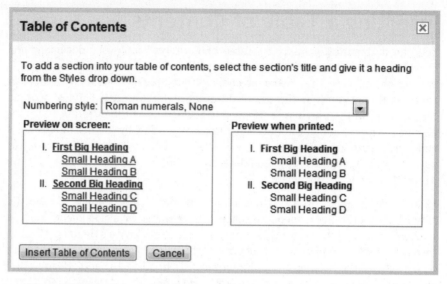

Figure 4-39: Inserting a table of contents dialog box

There are a number of options available for using numbers, bullets, Roman numerals and letters. For each of these options, you can choose to use the number type for the first level and nothing for the sub-levels, or use the numbering type for all levels. Experiment to find the format best suited to your document. In this example (see Figure 4-39) we have chosen Roman numerals with nothing for the sub-headings. When you make your selection for the numbering, click the "Insert Table of Contents" button on the bottom left of the dialog box. The table of contents will be inserted into the document (see Figure 4-40).

Table of Contents

Update now (clears edits) | Properties | Remove

Lorem ipsum dolor sit amet, consectetur adipiscing elit.

I. **Heading 1**
    Heading 1a
II. **Heading 2**
    Heading 2a
    Heading 2b
III. **Heading 3**
    Heading 3a
IV. **Heading 4**
    Heading 4a
    Heading 4b
    Heading 4c
V. **Heading 5**

Figure 4-40: Table of contents

When you click the table of contents (see Figure 4-40), three links appear just above it. To remove the entire table of contents, click the "Remove" link. Clicking the "Properties" link will load the table of contents dialog box (see Figure 4-39), where you can change the properties. The "Update" link will update the table of contents by scanning the document to see if any new headings have been added needing to be incorporated into the table of contents.

The actual table of contents will be generated when the document is printed or is viewed in print mode (see Figure 4-41). In this example, you placed the table of contents at the end of the document. In most cases you will want to place the table of contents at the beginning of the document, followed by a page break so the body of the document begins on a fresh page.

Table of Contents

The Document 0
II. **Heading 1** 2
Heading 1a 2
III. **Heading 2** 3
Heading 2a 3
Heading 2b 3
IV. **Heading 3** 4
Heading 3a 4
V. **Heading 4** 5
Heading 4a 6
Heading 4b 6
Heading 4c 7
VI. **Heading 5** 8

Figure 4-41: Generated table of contents

Working with Lists and Bullets

Working with lists and bullet points in Google Document is relatively easy. These can be used to enhance your document when some elements you want to emphasize may be better listed as a series of points and sub-points rather than woven into the flowing text of the document. Suppose there are five points you want to list in your document. Type them as five separate lines as shown below:

Point A

Point B

Point C

Point D

Point E

Use the mouse to select the five lines (see Figure 4-42a) and choose either the numbered list icon or the bullet point icon on the tool bar to format the five points as a numbered list, or a bullet point list (see Figure 4-42). In Figure 4-42b, the selected lines are formatted as a numbered list, while in Figure 4-42c they are formatted as bullet points. The numbered list icon and the bullet point icon are the first two icons in the "List & and bullet format" group. You can quickly switch between numbered list and bullet points while the text is selected by choosing the appropriate icon. The formatting also acts as a switch. If you select bullet point format, the selection is formatted as bullet points. If you select the bullet point formatting again to a selection already formatted as bullet points, it is turned off. The same is with numbered lists, thus it is easy to quickly change from one to the other.

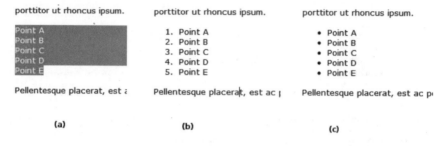

Figure 4-42: Numbered and bullet lists

You can easily add multilevel lists or bullet points to your documents. If you wanted to include three sub-points associated with Point A (see Figure 4-42), then after Point A type the three sub-points (see Figure 4-43a). Select the entire list and click the numbered list icon on the tool bar to produce the numbered list (see Figure 4-43b). Select the three lines containing the three new sub-points in the list and click the "Increase indent" icon in the tool bar. The three sub-points will now be demoted to sub-points and indented one level to the right under Point A (see Figure 4-43c). Notice that the numbering also changes to reflect the demotion. If the list were originally formatted as a bullet list, then demoting the three sub-points would result in a bullet list (see Figure 4-43d). Again, notice the shape of the bullets change to reflect the demoted points.

Point A	1. Point A	1. Point A	• Point A
Sub point 1	2. Sub point 1	1. Sub point 1	◦ Sub point 1
Sub point 2	3. Sub point 2	2. Sub point 2	◦ Sub point 2
Sub point 3	4. Sub point 3	3. Sub point 3	◦ Sub point 3
Point B	5. Point B	2. Point B	• Point B
Point C	6. Point C	3. Point C	• Point C
Point D	7. Point D	4. Point D	• Point D
Point E	8. Point E	5. Point E	• Point E
(a)	**(b)**	**(c)**	**(d)**

Figure 4-43: Multilevel lists

Using the "Increase indent" and the "Decrease indent" icons, you can select points in the list and demote or promote them as you wish. This enables you to create complex lists with multilevel points of interest in your document.

Tables

In most word processors, we have the ability to insert tables. Tables are useful when organizing a section of your document into precise rows and columns with or without borders. Tables can also be useful when allowing you to easily format a part of your document when it is difficult to work with margins. The text in the individual cells in a table can be formatted just the same as normal next using all methods covered so far. You can place text inside a table cell as well as images and other objects, which can also be placed in other parts of the document.

Although there is enough functionality in Google Document to create tables and manipulate the row and column formatting to achieve most purposes, one of the things you cannot do is manipulate them with cursor dragging. In other Office Suite word processors, you can manipulate the size of a table by placing your mouse cursor over the borders and dragging them to enlarge or shrink the borders. In Google Document, you can do this but only through a dialog box. However, the support of tables is still very applicable for a web-based word processor.

Creating Tables

To insert a table in your document, place your insertion point with the mouse at the point in the document where you want to place the table. This will typically be on a blank line as you cannot get text to wrap around a table as you can with an image. Click the "Table" option from the "Insert" menu. You will see the dialog box (see Figure 4-44). Fill out the elements of the dialog box to control the size and placement of the table to insert into your document.

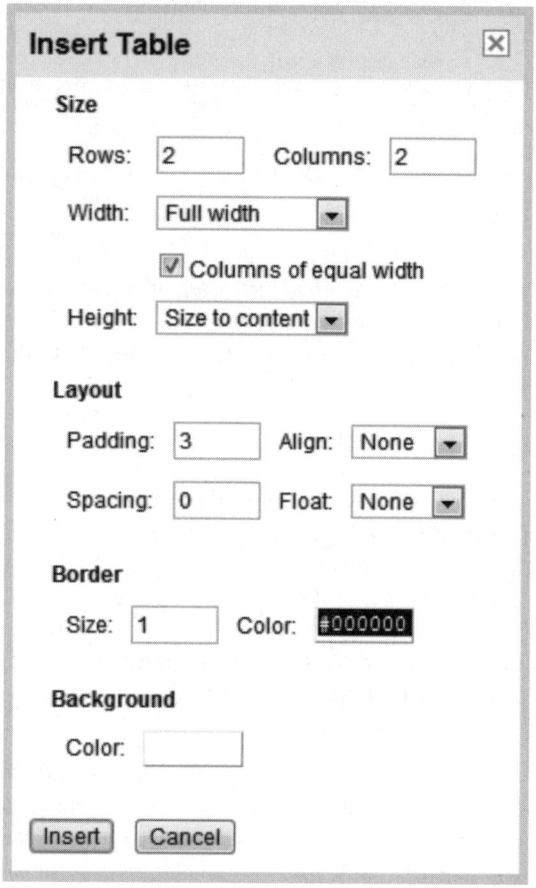

Figure 4-44: Insert table dialog

Size: Enter the number of rows and columns you want the table to initially have. You can add and delete from these at a later time. Use the drop-down width box to select the width of the table. You can select from a number of options including "Fill width," "Size to content," or "Pixels or Percent." With full width, the table will take up the width of a line of text. With pixels or percent, when you choose one of these options, a small box will appear just to the right where you type in the number of pixels or the percentage of the line width the table will occupy. The percentage option is much easier to work with as the pixels will depend on screen size and resolution. If you check the "Columns of equal width," the total width of the table will be divided as evenly as possible between all columns. There is a height drop-down list similar to the width, however this should typically be left on the option "Size to content" as changing the value will often not produce a result in the web environment.

Layout: The padding controls how much space is used for padding around the inside of the cell. The spacing controls how much space is placed between the table cells. If you modify this from standard zero, you may not notice a difference on some browsers. To the right of the padding is a small drop-down list for the align control. This will control where the table is placed within the line if the width of the table is less than that of the line. You can choose between none, left, center, and right. Underneath the align control is a similar control for the table floating property. Again, you can choose between none, left or right. At the time of writing there seems to be issues with this control and activity in blogs seems to indicate that Google is aware of the issue and will hopefully be fixed in a later version.

Border: This allows you to define the width of borderlines used in the table. This is a table property only and unlike other Office suite word processors, you cannot alter the borders of individual cells, rows, or columns. Using the border size, you can increase and decrease the thickness of the border or set it to zero. If you set it to zero, then while in edit mode you will see a light gray border around all cells in the table, but when it is viewed in "Print preview" mode or printed, no borders will be seen. This can often be used for effect in documents. You can also control the color of the borders. Clicking the color selector will cause a color chooser dialog to appear (see Figure 4-45). Select the color you want the borders to display with and the dialog will close.

Background: Similar to the border color, you can control the background color of the cells in the table. Click on the color selector and the drop-down color chooser dialog (see Figure 4-45) will appear. Choose the background for the table and the dialog will close.

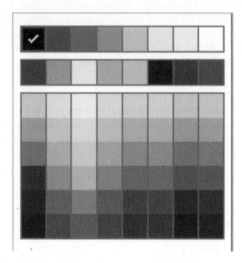

Figure 4-45: Color chooser dialog

When you have finished selecting the options for the table, click the "Insert" button in the bottom left of the dialog box, and the table will be inserted (see Figure 4-46).

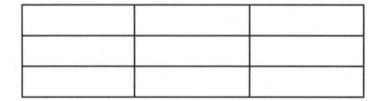

Figure 4-46: Inserted table

Changing Table Properties

You can change the properties of a table that were set when the table was inserted (as seen in the previous section) at any time. Use the mouse to click into a cell within the table. Choose "Modify table properties" from the "Table" menu from the menu bar. This will display the dialog box (see Figure 4-47). This dialog box is similar to the "Insert Table Properties" dialog box used when inserting a new table. The main difference is that the row and column size boxes are missing. Make any changes you need to the table properties and click the "Change" button in the bottom left corner of the dialog box.

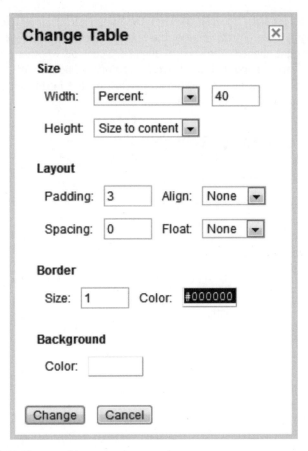

Figure 4-47: Change table properties

Resizing Rows and Columns

At any time, you can resize the rows and columns of your table. Click a cell within the table. Now you can select either "Modify row properties" or "Modify column properties" from the "Table" menu on the menu bar. If you choose to modify the row properties, the dialog box shown in Figure 4-48 will appear. In this dialog you can change the height of the row, the horizontal and vertical alignment, and the background color of the cells in the row. It is best to leave the row height set at "Size to content" unless you have a specific reason to increase the height of a particular row. If you want to change it, use the height drop-down box and choose pixels for the best result. A small input box will appear just to the right, and you can enter the size you want this row to be in pixels. You may need to experiment to get the correct size. You can then set the horizontal alignment to either left, center, or right. This controls whether the text in the cell of the row is left aligned, centered, or right aligned. The vertical alignment controls whether the text in the cells of the row are pushed to the top, center, or bottom of the cell. The background color is set as in the table properties, except in this option it controls the background color of all cells in the same row.

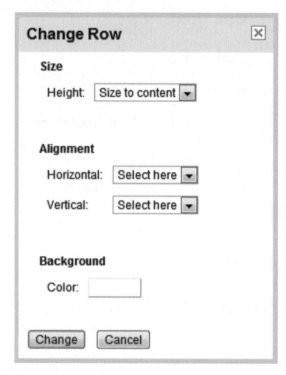

Figure 4-48: Change row properties

If you choose to modify the column properties, the dialog box shown in Figure 4-49 will be shown. In this dialog you can change the width of the column, the horizontal and vertical alignment, and the background color of the cells in the column. To change the width of the column, click the width drop-down box and choose an option. You can choose between full width, size to content, pixels, and percent. It is best not to use full width as this will allocate most of the space to the column being changed and little to the other columns. Choosing size to content will alter the column size depending on the width of the current content. Choosing pixels or percent will show a small box to the right where you type in the width of the column in either pixels or as a percentage of space of all columns combined. Using percent can help you even up all column sizes or make non-standard adjustments to a specific column. Using pixels can quickly adjust the size of one column without having to worry about the percentages of the other columns, but you may need to experiment a bit to get it how you would like. You can then set the horizontal alignment to either left, center, or right. This controls whether the text in the cell of the column is left aligned, centered, or right aligned. The vertical alignment controls whether the text in the cell of the column are pushed to the top, center, or bottom of the cells. The background color is set as in the table properties, except in this option it controls the background color of all cells in the same column.

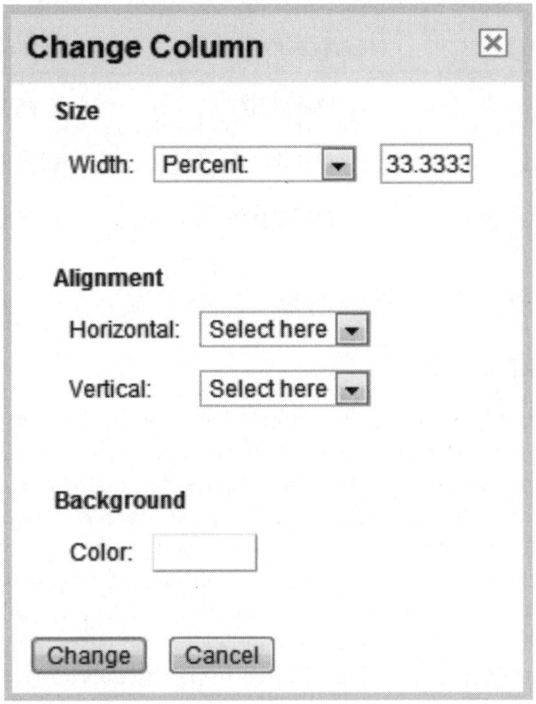

Change Column ☒

Size

Width: | Percent | ▼ | 33.3333

Alignment

Horizontal: | Select here | ▼

Vertical: | Select here | ▼

Background

Color:

[Change] [Cancel]

Figure 4-49: Change column properties

When you have made the changes to the row or column, click the "Change" button in the bottom left corner of the dialog box.

Borders

As discussed in the section "Creating Tables," using borders is a table property and cannot be changed for a particular cell, row, or column. We change the borders in the table properties and can change the color or the thickness. Turning the border off still displays a light gray border while in edit mode, but will not print when you print the document or view it in "Print preview" mode. You can set the background colors in rows or columns for effect, and if the first row of a table contains column headings, the text can be formatted differently to highlight this purpose (see Figure 4-50). In this example, although we can't control the borders on individual rows, we can achieve a similar effect by using multiple tables. Figure 4-50 uses two tables, the first single-row table to contain the borders and headings and the second is a multiple-row table with borders turned off to hold the data.

heading 1	heading 2	heading 3
data 1	datum 1	result 1
data 2	datum 2	result 2
data 3	datum 3	result 3

Figure 4-50: Formatted multiple tables

Formatting Cells

You can change the properties of an individual cell. Click into the cell in the table that you wish to modify. Select the "*Modify cell properties*" option from the "Table" menu on the menu bar. The change cell dialog box will appear (see Figure 4-51). There is not much you can alter here except the cell width, height, the text alignment, and the background color. Do not alter a cell's width or height through this dialog box. You cannot change the height of a single cell in a row, and similarly you cannot change the width of a single cell in a column. Thus altering the height or width will affect the entire row or column. It is best to perform this function using the appropriate change row or change column functionality.

ExplainED

Changing the width or height of an individual cell will change the width or height of an entire column or row.

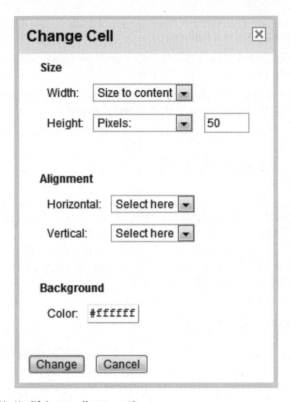

Figure 4-51: Modifying a cells properties

You can set the horizontal alignment of the cell to either left, center, or right. This controls whether the text in the cell is left aligned, centered, or right aligned. The vertical alignment controls whether the text in the cell is pushed to the top, center, or bottom of the cell. The background color is set as in the table properties, except in this option it controls the background color of a single cell.

Inserting and Deleting Rows and Columns

You can insert or delete rows and columns to increase or decrease the size of your table. You can even move entire rows either up or down. To do this, click a cell in the table you wish to modify. From the "Table" menu item on the menu bar, you can choose either:

Insert row above: This will insert a new, empty row above the row in the table containing the selected cell.

Insert row below: This will insert a new, empty row below the row in the table containing the selected cell.

Insert column left: This will insert a new, empty column to the left of the column in the table containing the selected cell.

Insert column right: This will insert a new, empty column to the right of the column in the table containing the selected cell.

Delete row: This will delete the entire row in the table containing the selected cell.

Delete column: This will delete the entire column in the table containing the selected cell.

Move row up: This will move the row containing the selected cell up one row effectively swapping the entire row above with the row containing the selected cell.

Move row down: This will move the row containing the selected cell down one row effectively swapping the entire row below with the row containing the selected cell.

Document Proofing

Google Document has a number of document proofing tools including spell check and word lookup to help you in your document writing. Currently, the selection is not extensive, but the Google apps are constantly being enhanced so it is worthwhile to check for these enhancements regularly. With Google Document, there are currently tools to spell check your document, look up words using the Internet, and a facility to translate your document.

Spell Checking

Spell checking in your document may be done at two levels depending on the browser you are using. If spell checking is built in to the browser, it will perform spell check as you type into your Google document within the browser's tab. Additionally, Google document has its own spell checking functionality. We have previously discussed the browser spell checking (Chrome), so we will only discuss the Google document spell checking in this section.

Once you have completed your document, or periodically if your document will be large, you can check for spelling problems. To do this, click the "abc" (or "Check Spelling") icon located on the right end of the tool bar. You can also choose the "Check spelling" option from the "Tools" menu on the menu bar. This may take a moment, but it will cause the spell checker to go through your document and check each word against its standard dictionary. All words not contained in the standard dictionary will be highlighted in yellow within the document (see Figure 4-52).

Prairie Dog

This paragrah is about the prairie dog and it's local habiat. A lot can be said about paririe dogs and their existance, not much wil be daid in this document. This is an exmple of more incorrectly spelled words. Aother example.

Figure 4-52: Spell-checked document

To correct a spelling mistake, click on a highlighted word and a small pop-up menu will appear (see Figure 4-53). A number of possible corrections to the word will be displayed in the pop-up menu. If one if these is correct, select it from the menu and the word will be corrected and the highlighting removed. Not all highlighted words will necessarily be misspelled. The word may be correct but not contained within the standard dictionary. You can add the word to the standard dictionary by choosing the "Add to dictionary" option in the pop-up menu. The word will be added to the dictionary and the highlighting of all instances of the word will be removed. If the word is poorly spelled, it may mean the spell checker may not be able to make a reasonable suggestion. You may need to correct the word yourself. You can then recheck the spelling by choosing the "Recheck spelling" option from the "Tools" menu, or you can choose to turn off the spell checker. To turn the spell checker off, click the spell check icon on the tool bar again, ultimately acting as a switch.

Before checking the spelling of your document for the first time, you should check that you are using the correct dictionary (or language for spelling). Click the "Select language (for spelling)" option from the "Tools" menu option on the tool bar. This will lead to a list of languages you can scroll in up and down. The current language being used will be checked with a tick character. Make sure this is correct and, if not, select the correct one to use.

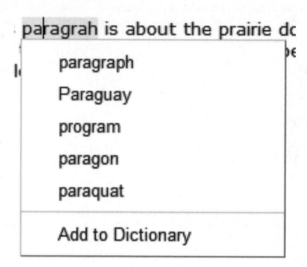

Figure 4-53: Correcting spelling mistakes

ExplainED

Make sure you are using the correct language for spelling before you use the spell checker.

Word Lookup

There is a word lookup facility in Google Document that acts like a dictionary, thesaurus, and encyclopedia all in one. To use this, first highlight the word you are checking by selecting all its characters. Then choose the "Look up word" option from the "Tools" menu on the menu bar. This further opens another pop-up menu (see Figure 4-54). Choose from the following options:

See definition: This will bring up a small window providing the definition of the word.

See synonyms: This will check the Merriam-Webster online thesaurus for a list of synonyms for the word, if any can be found. If found, they will be displayed in a small window. You will have the option of replacing the word in your document with one from the list.

See encyclopedia entries: This will look up encyclopedia entries in the Britannica.com online encyclopedia and display a list of clickable entries in a small window. Clicking one of the links will open a new tab and load the encyclopedia entry into the new tab.

Translate: This will bring up a small window and give you the option of translating the selected word from one language to another.

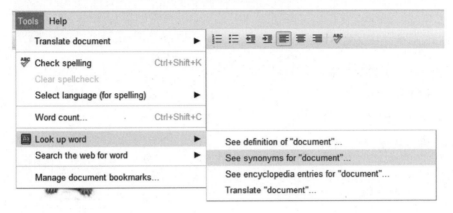

Figure 4-54: Word lookup

Translating Your Document

You have the ability to translate your document into another language. To do this, click the "Translate document" option in the "Tools" menu on the menu bar. This will open a scrollable list on the right (see Figure 4-55). Scroll up and down this list using the scroll bar on the right and choose the desired language to use for translating your document. When you select a language, a new tab will be opened in the browser and a translation of your document will appear in the new tab. This facility uses Google Translate to translate the document, so the reliability will depend on the accuracy of Google Translate. There seems to be no definitive answers by experts about the accuracy of Google Translate. Reading blogs on Google fan sites, instances are found where there are perfect translations and there are instances where there are poor translations. Google uses a statistical translation system instead of a rule-based approach, and much will depend on the languages involved and whether close language pairs are available.

If you send documents overseas, this facility may help by being able to provide the original and a way to quickly translate the document to the language of the destination.

197

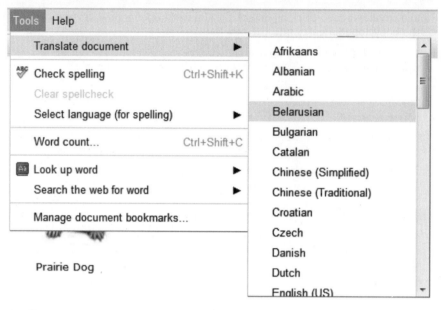

Figure 4-55: Translating a document

Footnotes

You have the ability to insert footnotes within a Google Document. Footnotes are used by the author to provide commentary on the main text within the document. These are typically indicated with a numeric superscript placeholder and the actual text of the footnote will appear at the bottom of the page when printed. To place a footnote with a document, click to the position in the text where you would like the footnote to appear. Choose "Footnote" from the "Insert" menu on the menu bar. A small breakout box will appear to the right of the line where the footnote was inserted. Click into this box and type the text of the footnote. The footnote will then appear (see Figure 4-56). Note that in Figure 4-56, the small placeholder for the footnote is marked with a circle and shown as a superscript hash (#) character. When the document is printed, these footnote markers will be converted to increasing numerical markers. The footnotes will also be printed at the bottom of the page where the footnote appears. To delete a footnote, click the small arrow in the upper right corner of the footnote text box at the right of the screen and click the "Delete Footnote" option when it appears.

This paragraph is about the prairie dog* and it's local habitat. A lot can be said about prairie dogs and their existence, not much Will be said in this document. |

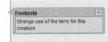

Footnote
Strange use of the term for this creature

Figure 4-56: Inserting a Footnote

As discussed in the section "Printer Settings," you can control the appearance of footnotes in the printing of the document. You can turn off the printing by checking the small check box next to the "Include footnotes" option, or you can control whether footnotes appear at the end of each page as footnotes or as endnotes at the end of the entire document. Footnotes and Endnotes are normally used to cite references or give credit to sources in the text. The main difference between them is the Footnotes appear in numerical order at the foot of the same page where the references are made, while Endnotes are placed at the end of the section or document where the references are made.

Working with Document Revisions

An important part of any word processing software is how well it will support collaborators and authors during the revision process. Most of the well-known word-processing software will allow authors and collaborators to insert comments, track changes made to documents by specific contributors, accept changes, and compare documents. These tools allow more than one person involved in the revision process to make modifications and have those modifications tracked. Currently, Google Document does not have the equivalent of OpenOffice or Microsoft Office "Track Changes." However, it does have a "Revision History" tool where you can keep track of various modifications and compare different revisions. In effect, it allows you to achieve something similar, but for those familiar with the track changes facilities of other word-processing software this will not be the same. In the following sections you will learn to use these tools for document revision.

Inserting Comments

Comments are generally used within documents for proofing purposes. When someone reads a document and wants to comment on the document for a correction, an appropriate way would be to insert comments. You can also insert comments for your own purposes if you believe something might need an internal explanation, but if this is to be displayed in the printing, you might consider a footnote instead. To insert a comment, click the position in the text where you would like the comment to be placed. Choose "Comment" from the "Insert" menu on the menu bar. A comment will be inserted and the insertion point will be at the beginning of the comment. Type the text of the comment and it will appear as a highlighted comment within the text tagged with the date and time it was inserted (see Figure 4-.57). The text of a comment should be kept as short as possible. If you click into the highlighted comment, a pop-up menu will appear giving you the option of deleting the comment, inserting the text of the comment into the document, or changing the shading color of the comment. If you are using comments for editing, you can use color-coded comments to indicate the status of the edit or as an indication of which editor made the comment.

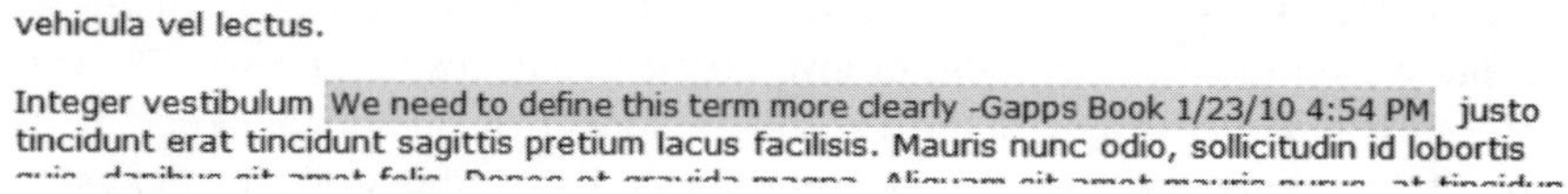

vehicula vel lectus.

Integer vestibulum We need to define this term more clearly -Gapps Book 1/23/10 4:54 PM justo tincidunt erat tincidunt sagittis pretium lacus facilisis. Mauris nunc odio, sollicitudin id lobortis

Figure 4-57: Inserting a comment

As discussed in the section "Printer Settings," you can control the appearance of comments in the printing of the document. You can turn off the printing by checking the small check box next to the "Include comments" option. As also indicated, there is currently a known problem with controlling comments. You cannot turn them off in printing, but Google is aware of the issue and is working on it at the time of this printing.

Document Revisions

As indicated at the beginning of this section, Google Document does not have a "Track changes" facility comparable to OpenOffice or Microsoft Office. You can still use the document revisions to see how the document has progressed over time. Due to the collaborative nature of Google Documents and the autosave facility, Google Document keeps a comprehensive list of all revisions as the document is altered over time, and you can review the revisions. If necessary, revert to the following: To review the document revisions of the current document, choose the "See revision history" option from the "File" menu on the menu bar. This will display the indexed revision history of the file (see Figure 4-58).

In the revision history interface (see Figure 4-58), if there are many revisions to a document (which happen over time), they will be grouped together in small groups roughly based on the time frame of the document saved. On the right side of the page, you will see the revision groupings appear as links (see Figure 4-58), much like you see groups of possible starting points to a DVD in the chapter menu. Each revision grouping will consist of a specific number of revisions indicated in the link (eg. Revisions 238-248).

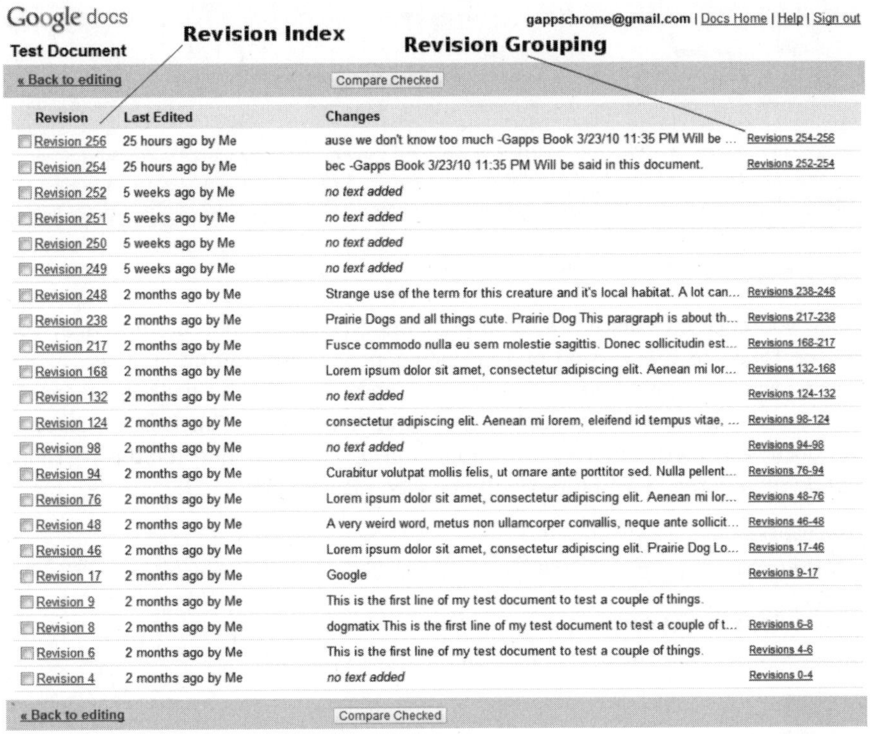

Figure 4-58: Document revisions interface

Associated with each of the revision groupings on the right side of the page will be a revision index link on the left side of the page. This revision index link will point to the latest revision in the revision grouping (the highest numbered revision). By clicking one of the revision grouping links in the right side of the page, you will be taken to a similar page but with the revisions in the revision group further subdivided into finer groups to allow for more choice within the range. For example, if you select the revision grouping containing revisions 238-248 on the right of the page (see Figure 4-58), you will see the page shown in Figure 4-59 displayed showing finer groupings for the original revision group. For a large group, you can continue this process by selecting another revision group, or you can click the "Back to Default View" link at the bottom right of the page to go back to the initial interface (see Figure 4-58).

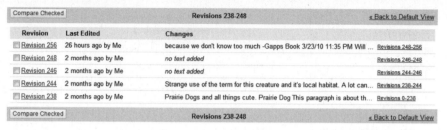

Figure 4-59: Revision grouping interface

When you click one of the revision numbers on the left side of the page, you will be taken to the version of the document you are editing as it was when that revision was saved. For instance, clicking revision 238 in the page shown in Figure 4-58 will show the document shown in Figure 4-60. This was the state of the document approximately two months prior. The timeline for the revisions can be seen in the "Last Edited" column (see Figure 4-58).

Test Document

Prairie Dogs and all things cute.

Prairie Dog

This paragraph is about the prairie dog and it's local habiat. A lot can be said about paririe dogs and their existance, not much Will be said in this document. This is an exmple of more incorrectly spelled words. Aother example.

« Back to Revision History   Showing revision #238   « Older | Newer » | Revert to this one

Figure 4-60: Viewing a specific revision

When viewing a document revision, quickly choose to view the next later revision or the previous earlier revision by clicking on the "Newer" or "Older" links shown in the top and bottom bar of the document (see Figure 4-60). In this way you can cycle backward or forward in time viewing the progression of changes to the document. If you find a revision of the document you wish to go back to and make the current version of the document, click the "Revert to this one" link in either the top or bottom bar of the document (see Figure 4-60). This revision will become the current state of the document, and any collaborators on the document will then see this version of the document when they edit it.

Comparing Revisions

Sometimes before reverting to an earlier revision, or when scrolling through document revisions, you may need to compare two revisions against each other to see the specific changes. When looking at document revisions, use the check boxes on the left of the screen to check two revisions to compare (see Figure 4-58 or Figure 4-59). You can only compare two revisions at a time. Click the "Compare Checked" link at the top or bottom of the page. A comparison document will then be created and you can compare the changes from one version to the next. For example, clicking revisions 248 and 238 (see Figure 4-58) will show the comparison document in Figure 4-61.

The comparison document (see Figure 4-61) shows deleted text from the old version of the document as green text formatted in strikethrough format, while newer text is shown in green highlighted format. Text which has not changed between revisions is shown in standard black on white text. By using the comparison feature, you can see the exact changes between different revisions.

While the two features of comments and document revisions is not exactly the same as a track changes facility, similar tasks can be achieved though it is more time consuming.

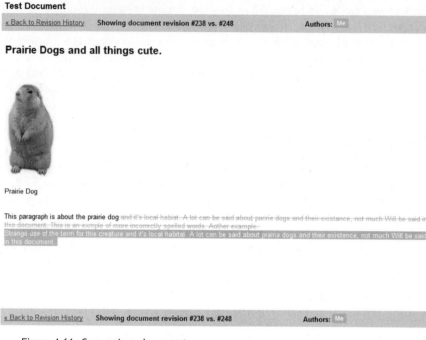

Test Document

« Back to Revision History   Showing document revision #238 vs. #248   Authors: Me

Prairie Dogs and all things cute.

Prairie Dog

This paragraph is about the prairie dog and it's local habitat. A lot can be said about prairie dogs and their existence, not much Will be said in this document. This is an example of more incorrectly spelled words. Aother example. Strange use of the term for this creature and it's local habitat. A lot can be said about prairie dogs and their existence, not much Will be said in this document.

« Back to Revision History   Showing document revision #238 vs. #248   Authors: Me

Figure 4-61: Comparison document

A Work Around

Some user blogs discussing the editing and revision process have mentioned a work around for the track changes issue, though it is not a consistent solution. If the document revisions and comments tools are not enough, it is recommended that collaborators use comments each using a different color of comment and that text changes again be done in different colors similar to the comments. As new text is added, the older text can be formatted with strikethrough to indicate its deletion. In this way a permanent record is maintained as the document progresses. One problem with this is that without the equivalent of an "Accept Changes" menu option, someone will have to go through the document manually and delete all strikethrough text, a process that could take quite a while on a large document.

Summary

In this chapter we have covered in detail using Google Document to create, edit, and enhance your text documents in this environment. First, we covered the very basics of entering and formatting text within your document. This process is similar to OpenOffice Writer and Microsoft Office Word. As we discussed, there are some limitations to formatting options in Google Document, notable in the number of font options, but these are improving on a continual basis. We then discussed incorporating images into your document to enhance it visually and add context to concepts, as well as further formatting using page breaks and footnotes. Incorporating a table of contents into a large document is helpful in providing the reader with a reference point, and we discussed this while working with bullet points and tables. Finally, we discussed document proofing with spell checking and word lookup as well as revision tools for helping during the revision process of large documents with collaborators.

Chapter 5

Google Docs – Spreadsheets

In this chapter, you will learn to create and build sophisticated spreadsheets in the Google Docs environment. This coverage of spreadsheets will be aimed at both the beginner and intermediate users, and it will provide sections on both basic and more advanced techniques of using spreadsheets. For example, you will learn about the basic manipulation and formatting of spreadsheets in Google Docs and how to use formulas. In the more advanced section, you will learn to use multiple sheets, data validation, sheet protection, and conditional formatting. A section on charts will show you how to use charts in the Google Docs environment and point out any limitations in the environment. You will also learn more advanced techniques for using formulas, such as the IF and VLOOKUP functions, as well as functions specific to Google Spreadsheets (Spreadsheets). Throughout the chapter, you will see hints and tips that point out features specific to the Google Docs environment.

The spreadsheet component of Google Docs offers a fully functional spreadsheet alternative to the major office suites, such as Microsoft Office and OpenOffice. One of the major advantages of Spreadsheets is that it lets you work online from any computer connected to the Internet; it also lets you share the spreadsheet without copying it to USB keys or e-mailing it to others, which can create versioning issues. This is a major benefit of an online tool like Spreadsheets. Notwithstanding the Internet advantage, Spreadsheets is a powerful, Web-based spreadsheet application that can read and save its spreadsheets in Excel, OpenOffice, and other standard text formats. By default, Spreadsheets saves its worksheets online, but it can also save them directly to your PC for local editing. However, leaving your files online gives you the versatility of *write once, edit anywhere*. If you share your files with others, Spreadsheets has the added advantage of ensuring that everyone is using the same software. This can be particularly useful in an office or classroom situation because it ensures that everyone uses the same software (and even the same version), eliminating minor inconsistencies.

You can either choose to upload and open an existing spreadsheet, or create a new one to work with. You do this through the Google Docs interface discussed in Chapter 3. Creating a new spreadsheet brings up a new, blank spreadsheet (see Figure 5-1).

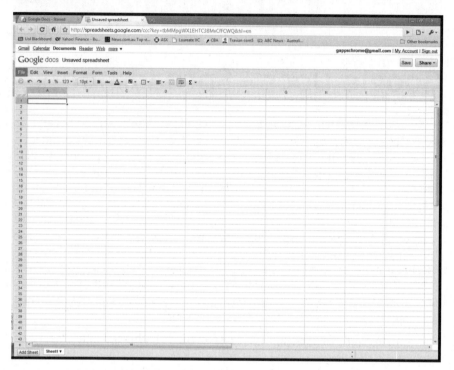

Figure 5-1: A new, blank spreadsheet in Spreadsheets

The new spreadsheet looks similar to those in spreadsheet applications from other office suites. The toolbar for Spreadsheets is less extensive, but significant additional functionality is provided through its toolbar and context-sensitive menus (which you access by right-clicking elements of the spreadsheet). One of the obvious differences is that the spreadsheet appears within the browser environment, so you still have access to your browser's functions and other tabs as you work on the spreadsheet.

Elements of the Spreadsheets Space

Now let's take a closer look at the major elements of the Spreadsheets. Figure 5-2 shows the major elements of the spreadsheet environment you will be working with.

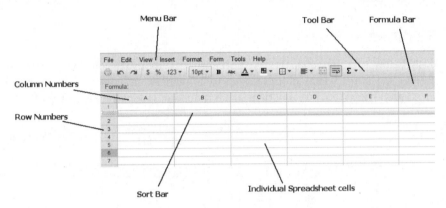

Figure 5-2: Annotated portion of the Spreadsheets environment

Apart from the various menubars and toolbars (which you will learn more about momentarily), the main working area for any spreadsheet is divided into cells. It is within the cells that you place the text, numeric data, and the formulas that give spreadsheets their calculating power. You can only see a small portion of the cells available to you on the screen at any given time; how much you can see depends on the size and resolution of your monitor. However, you can use the scroll bars at the right and bottom of the browser window to scroll to other areas of the spreadsheet. A new Spreadsheets document begins with 100 rows and 20 columns. This may seem limiting at first, but you can expand the size of the default spreadsheet at a later point, as required. Each cell is identified individually by its reference: the column number followed by the row number. Column numbers are numbered alphabetically from A to Z, AA to AZ, BA to BZ, and so on. Rows are numbered numerically from 1 to 100 (or however many rows you have). Thus, a cell reference might be D12, B23, or A1. You will learn more about cell references further later in this chapter.

Menubar

At the top of the spreadsheet area is the menubar, which lets you perform standard file functions, as well as perform editing functions, configure the view, specify formatting, and accomplish a range of toolbox-type tasks. As you learn about the various features of Spreadsheets throughout this chapter, you will constantly be referred to specific items on the menubar. Thus, you will learn to manipulate and edit a spreadsheet through these menu selections as you go. Additionally, some of the more common tasks associated with spreadsheet manipulation are also present on the toolbar for added convenience.

Toolbar

Just below the menubar is the Spreadsheets toolbar; you can click this toolbar's icons to gain quick access to a number of commonly performed functions. These tool box functions are arranged in groups (see Figure 5-3).

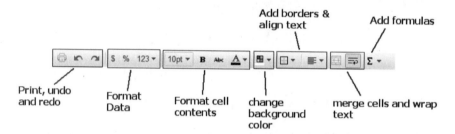

Figure 5-3: The expanded Spreadsheets toolbar with groupings

The first three icons allow you to print and undo or redo an operation. For instance, assume you want to undo something you have just done, such as some formatting. All you need to do is click the "Undo" button. If, after pressing the "Undo" button, you decide that it was OK after all, you can press the "Redo" button. The next three icons allow you to format the specific data type and its appearance in a spreadsheet's cell or cells. The next four icons allow you to change the appearance of the text appearing in a cell, such as its font size, bold face, and color. You can also change the background color of a cell or cells with the next icon. The next two icons allow you to format the borders and text alignment of a cell. You can merge horizontally adjacent cells, and invoke text wrap with the next group. The last icon lets you add formulas to the spreadsheet. We will discuss formulas in more detail later in this chapter.

Formula Bar

The formula bar is not shown on newly created spreadsheet documents, so you must turn it on explicitly. To turn the formula bar on, choose the "View" option from the menubar and click the "Show formula bar" option. This will turn the formula bar on and make it visible in the spreadsheet just below the toolbar. You don't need to have it turned on, but the formula bar will show you the contents of a cell when the cell is selected. This is invaluable for viewing the formulas within a cell without entering editing mode. When a cell is selected, then you will see only the result of a formula if the formula bar isn't visible. Other spreadsheet applications, such as Excel (Microsoft) and Calc (OpenOffice), have the formula bar turned on by default. If you're accustomed to using other spreadsheet software, then you will most likely want to turn the formula bar on to keep Spreadsheets as compatible as possible.

One major difference between the formula bar in Spreadsheets and other spreadsheet applications is that you cannot edit the contents of a cell directly through the formula bar. In Spreadsheets, the formula bar is a display-only element; instead, you edit a cell by entering edit mode for that cell. This difference seems inconvenient at first, but over time you will accept this behavior is merely a difference between Spreadsheets and other spreadsheet software.

The Sort Bar

The sort bar is an interesting feature of Spreadsheets. It helps you to sort your spreadsheet quickly according the data in one column. The Sort bar is shown in Figure 5-2, and it appears as a faint gray bar across the work area of the spreadsheet. When you create a new spreadsheet, the sort bar is located between rows one and two. This allows you to leave some data in the spreadsheet (such as column headings) unsorted when you sort the rest of the data. The sorting feature in Spreadsheets is fairly simplistic, allowing you to sort the spreadsheet on one column only, unlike the other Office Suites, which offer complex multi-column sorting. However, the needs of most spreadsheet users are not that complex, and the Spreadsheets' sorting feature is sufficient in most cases. Sorting the spreadsheet and using the sort bar is covered later in this chapter.

Getting Help

You can of course get help for Spreadsheets at any time by selecting the "Help" item on the menubar. This will show the drop-down "Help" menu (see Figure 5-4), and it provides you with a number of ways to get help when using Spreadsheets. Choosing the "Google Docs Help Center" item will load a Web page into another browser tab; this gives you a number of general links and some specific links on particular Google Spreadsheets topics. Some of these links can be quite helpful, but also it can be difficult to find something if you are having specific issues. If your problem is extremely specific, then you may be better off consulting with other Google Docs users. The "Learn from other Google users" option on the "Help" menu takes you to a forum where you can scan discussion threads on specific topics and even post your own questions. You can find some excellent tips on using Spreadsheets on this forum.

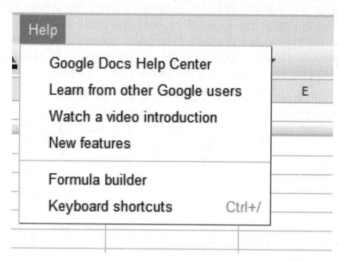

Figure 5-4: The drop-down "Help" menu

The "New Features" choosing from the "Help" menu item can help you keep abreast of new features in Spreadsheets; this option takes you to a Web page that lists all new features added. These new features are not just Spreadsheets features, but relate to Google Docs as a whole. However, it is not too difficult to scan down quickly and look for specific Spreadsheets items. If you are new to Google Docs, you might also want to check out an introduction to Google Docs video on You Tube. Selecting the "Watch a Video Introduction" option will load this into a new browser tab.

There are two more "Help" menu options. The "Formula builder" option helps you build and place formulas in cells. You will use this initially as you learn to use Spreadsheets and begin to create more complex spreadsheets requiring different formulas to achieve more complex documents. You can also access this function by selecting the "Add Formulas" icon from the toolbar. As you become more familiar with Spreadsheets and wish speed up your productivity, you can also access a list of keyboard shortcuts by choosing the "Keyboard shortcuts" menu option.

Document Functions

Before you begin to create your spreadsheets and delve into how to do all the complex things needed to create your perfect spreadsheet, you might find it worthwhile to perform a quick review of Spreadsheets' document functions. These are the functions that you use to load, save, and generally manipulate your spreadsheet documents. You access these functions through the "File" item on the menubar (see Figure 5-5). Some document functions are available from elsewhere in the spreadsheet, but all can be performed through this menu item. Some specific document functions such as renaming and exporting documents can also be performed through the Google Docs interface; however, you will learn how to access these functions from the menubar in this section.

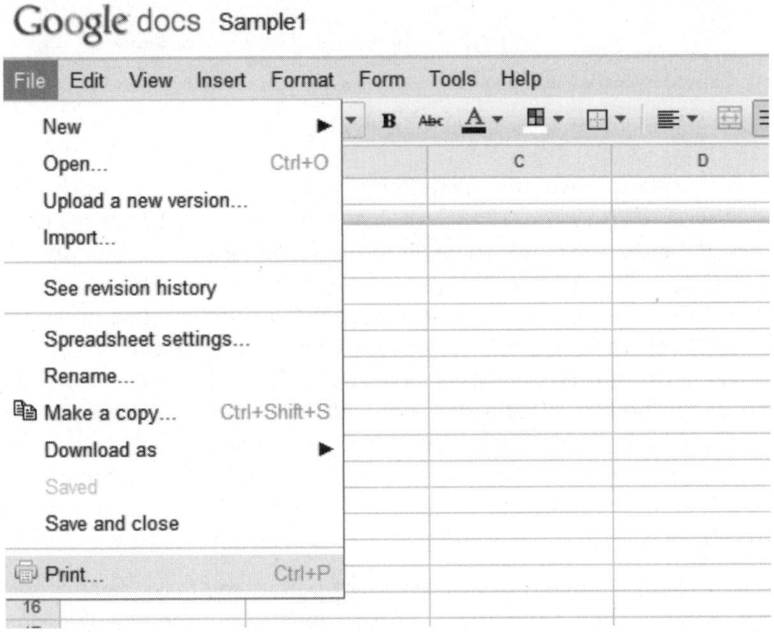

Figure 5-5: The drop-down "File" menu

Saving and Closing Documents

Two of the most common things you will need to do with your spreadsheet are to save it and close it when you finish with it. You can accomplish this by selecting the "Save and close" option from the "File" menu. If the spreadsheet is a new document and has not yet been saved, then the "Save spreadsheet as" dialog box will appear (see Figure 5-6). You just need to type in the name of your new spreadsheet and click the "OK" button. The spreadsheet will save your document using the new name supplied, and the spreadsheet document tab will close, taking you back to the Google Docs interface tab. You should see your new spreadsheet document from the Google Docs tab shortly thereafter. If the spreadsheet has been saved previously, then you will not see the "Save spreadsheet as" dialog box; instead, the spreadsheet will save and the Tab will close.

Figure 5-6: The "Save spreadsheet as" dialog box

You don't need to save the spreadsheet periodically as you work with it; rather, the spreadsheet is saved automatically. In fact, the spreadsheet is almost constantly saved as you edit it; when multiple people work on a document, they can see the changes almost immediately. The last time that the spreadsheet was auto-saved is displayed in a grayed-out box in the upper-right corner of the spreadsheet window. When you create a brand new spreadsheet, this grayed-out box appears as a "Save" button. When you click the button for the first time, it responds with the "Save spreadsheet as" dialog box, and you can choose a new name for the spreadsheet. Once you save a spreadsheet for the first time, and every time you open it thereafter, the button will be replaced by the grayed out "Autosave" box. You cannot click or otherwise configure this box; it exists only to provide information.

If you want to make a copy of a spreadsheet before you make some important changes, you can choose the "Make a copy" option from the "File" menu. You will then get a dialog box similar to the "Save spreadsheet as" dialog box. Here you type the name you want for the copy of the spreadsheet and click the "OK" button. This makes a copy of the current spreadsheet and changes the current tab to reflect the fact that you are now working on a new copy. Any changes you make now will be made to the new copy you have created. You can also rename the spreadsheet you are working on by choosing the "Rename" option from the "File" menu. Next, you type the desired new name of the spreadsheet and click the "OK" button. The new name will be reflected in the Google Docs interface tab, but this update can take a short while, depending on the speed of the Internet. You may need to reload the page to see the change reflected.

Opening Documents

You can open a Spreadsheets document in a number of ways. You can open one from the Google Docs interface tab as discussed in a previous chapter, or you can open another spreadsheet document when already working on a spreadsheet. To open another spreadsheet when working on one already, choose the "Open" option from the "File" menu; this brings up the "Open a spreadsheet" dialog box (see Figure 5-7). You can then choose from a list of available spreadsheets in the dialog box. Clicking one of the available spreadsheets opens it in a new tab and makes it the current spreadsheet. You can then switch back and forward between the spreadsheets by clicking the appropriate tab at the top of the browser window.

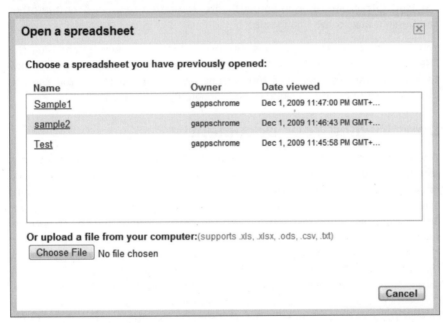

Figure 5-7: The "Open a spreadsheet" dialog box

In the "Open a spreadsheet" dialog box, you also have the option of loading an existing spreadsheet from your own computer. To do this, click the "Choose File" button located in the bottom-left of the dialog box (see Figure 5-7). This takes you to your computer's file selection window, where you can choose a

215

spreadsheet file to load. The types of spreadsheets you can import into Spreadsheets include older Excel (.xls) and newer Excel (.xlsx) spreadsheets, Open Office (.ods) spreadsheets, and comma delimited (.csv) and text (.txt) files. Once you select a file, it is transformed into Google Spreadsheets format. Next, an "Open now" link appears under the "Choose File" button. Click this link to complete the upload into a new tab. The newly uploaded spreadsheet now behaves as if you opened the spreadsheet from Google Docs. Also, you can now choose the "Save and close" option from the "File" menu for this imported file. At this point, you will see the spreadsheet with the Google Docs interface. You should be careful when uploading a spreadsheet from your local computer because, while Google Docs will do its best to translate the spreadsheet from its existing format to Google Spreadsheets format, the translation is not always perfect. This is true when translating any file from one format to another. Depending on the complexity of the document in one format, it may not translate perfectly into another. That said, the numbers and simple formulas are usually translated fine in Spreadsheets; formatted text cells, on the other hand, might have some small issues.

You can also open a new spreadsheet from the "File" menu by choosing the "New" ➤ "Spreadsheet" option from the "File" menu. This creates a new spreadsheet tab that becomes the current working spreadsheet. You can use this approach to create any kind of new Google Docs document.

Downloading Your Document

When you save your spreadsheet document, it is saved to your account on a secure Google online storage facility. However, there are times when you might wish to save your document locally, whether it's to your computer's hard drive, a USB key, or somewhere else. To do this, select the "Download as" option from the "File" menu. You can then choose from a number of options, such as what format you wish to use to download your spreadsheet. You can choose between comma delimited (.csv), HTML, text (.txt), Excel, OpenOffice, or PDF formats. The first three formats will only save the current sheets (see the "Working with Sheets" section later in this chapter). The Excel, OpenOffice, and PDF formats will download the entire spreadsheet. When you choose the comma delimited and text formats, the documents will be saved with the standard extensions of .csv and .txt respectively. These files can then be opened with any spreadsheet that supports these formats. When you choose the Excel option, the spreadsheet is saved in the older Excel (.xls) format, and it can be loaded into either Excel (old or new) or OpenOffice. You cannot currently save a Spreadsheets file in the newer Excel (.xlsx) format.

Choosing OpenOffice saves the spreadsheet in the standard OpenOffice Calc format (.ods).

If you choose HTML format, the current sheet will be converted to HTML format and then loaded into a new browser tab. The document will not be downloaded to your computer directly, unless you then choose to save this page from the browser's menu.

Choosing the PDF option works a little differently because the resulting PDF document is not a format that can be loaded back into a spreadsheet. You would choose this document format if you wanted to present the spreadsheet in a different manner. When you choose to save a spreadsheet as a PDF, Spreadsheets displays the "Export to PDF" dialog box (see Figure 5-8). You need to adjust the settings for the PDF export to suit your circumstances. The first setting indicates whether you want to export the entire spreadsheet or just the current sheet (see the "Working with Sheets" section). The second setting determines whether you want the PDF file to contain the spreadsheet at its actual size, or you want to scale it up so that it takes the entire page width in the PDF file (you might do this if the spreadsheet document is small). What you choose here will depend on the size and complexity of your spreadsheet. The third setting lets you choose between landscape or portrait mode. Due to their nature, spreadsheets may be better off exported in landscape mode; however, but you will need to experiment with this option to determine the style best suited to the current spreadsheet. The last setting is a drop-down menu that lets you dictate the paper size you wish to set the PDF file for.

When you finish adjusting the PDF settings, click the "Export" button located at the bottom-right of the dialog box. The resulting PDF file will be downloaded to your computer's default download area.

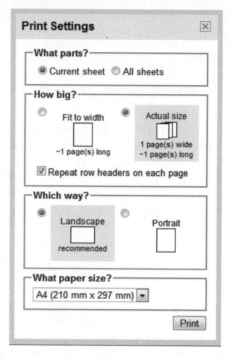

Figure 5-8: The "Export to PDF" dialog box

Printing Spreadsheets

You do not print your spreadsheet directly from Google Spreadsheets; instead, you do this using the export function described above. You can print the spreadsheet by selecting the "Print" option from the "File" menu or by clicking the "Print" icon on the toolbar, which brings up the "Export to PDF" dialog box described in the previous section. Select the settings you want, and then click the "Print" button located at the bottom right of the dialog box. This saves the spreadsheet in PDF format in your computer's default download area, as described previously. You can then print your document locally from your computer, just as you would any other file.

Alternatively, you can export the spreadsheet you wish to print to HTML format, and then use the browser's print functionality to print out the page in the newly created tab. In some ways, this may be a neater option because it does not involve saving the document on your local computer first. When you finish printing the document, you can close its tab.

Printing documents in this way may seem a little inconvenient; however, this is forced on Spreadsheets by the built-in limitations that enforce how a Web page can control elements on a local computer. Spreadsheets is an application that runs in a Web browser, so it is subject to the security limitations placed on all Web-based applications. These limitations are for our own protection.

Selecting Spreadsheet Settings

You can change some basic setting that the current spreadsheet will rely on in certain circumstances. You can access these settings by selecting the "Spreadsheet settings" option from the "File" menu. Currently, you can adjust only two settings:

Locale: This setting lets you use a drop-down box to select your country. This affects the formatting default for currency cells, which you will learn more about later in this chapter.

Time zone: This setting currently records the spreadsheet history in the selected time zone and affects some time-related functions.

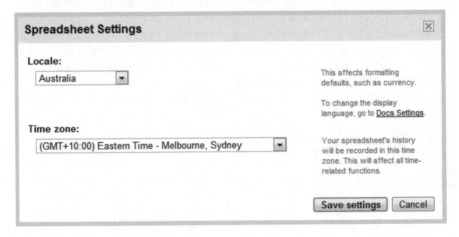

Figure 5-9: Spreadsheet settings

After making your desired changes, click the "Save settings" button in the bottom-right corner of the Spreadsheet Settings window.

Basic Spreadsheet Usage

In this section, we will look at how to use basic spreadsheet functionality, as well as examine some of the differences between Google Spreadsheets and

219

other spreadsheet applications. A spreadsheet is a numeric tool designed to increase the productivity of those who work with numbers. For examples, it helps people who need to enter numbers, sum columns and rows, calculate percentages, and perform other complex number manipulation. Of course, modern spreadsheets have evolved beyond simple numeric manipulation to more complex decision-support tools; as powerful as spreadsheets are, however, they remain a tool for manipulating numeric quantities. Thus, the operation of the spreadsheet revolves around the manipulation of numeric data. However, a spreadsheet must also let you enter textual information into spreadsheets to label the numeric data for clarification. For example, you might want to enter row and column headings, as well as data labels. Next, you can format the numbers and text for presentation purposes.

Types of Cells

The cells of a Spreadsheets document can be one of three basic types, and the type is determined by the kind of data that is entered into a cell. The cells can be any of three basic types: *text*, *number*, or *formula*. Essentially, if you enter a number (2, 456, 23.5, and so on), then the type of the cell is automatically determined by the spreadsheet to be a number cell, and the cell can take part in numeric calculations. If you enter any character data, then the cell is determined by the spreadsheet to be a text cell. Text cells normally won't take part in any numeric calculations; they are really there to *label* the data cells, so you know what type of data the number cells contain. A text cell might contain data such as "Tax Rate," "Customer Discount," "Name," and so on. If you begin by typing a number (34), but then continue to type characters (34 Fernwood Drive), then the cell becomes a text cell. Beginning the cell contents by typing an equal sign (=) means that Spreadsheets will regard that cell as a formula cell, and what follows the equal sign should be a valid cell formula. You will learn more about formulas later in this chapter. Classifying the types of cells by the content they contain is called auto-type detection, and it works well most of the time. Occasionally, however, you might want to type something such as a number or an equal sign, but have the cell interpreted as a text cell, rather than as a number or a formula cell.

ExplainED

Beginning the cell contents with a single apostrophe (') lets you force the cell type to be a text cell. When you finish entering the data into the cell, the apostrophe will not be displayed.

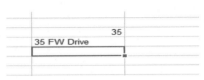

Figure 5-10: Default display of text and number cells

Spreadsheets will display number cells and text cells differently. By default, number cells are right justified, and text cells are left justified (see Figure 5-10). Of course, you can change the default display by formatting the cells. The similarity between text and number cells is that, once you enter the data or values, they do not change unless you specifically edit them. A formula cell, on the other hand, behaves quite differently. These cells contain formulas based on the content of (usually) number cells and possibly other formula cells. Their values change automatically when any of the cells that the formula uses change in value. In this way, you can create powerful spreadsheets that allow you to model anything from simple column calculations to complex sets of financial data. With a formula cell, you need to distinguish between the formula that the cell contains and the value that is displayed in the cell as a result of the formula. This is relatively easy to do with some practice.

Entering and Editing Data

To enter data into a spreadsheet cell, just click the cell and begin typing. The cell type is then determined by what you type. Once you start entering data by typing on the keyboard, the spreadsheet automatically enters *edit mode* for the cell, and what you type becomes the new contents of the cell (see Figure 5-11). If the cell already contains something, whether it's a value or a formula, clicking in the cell and typing replaces the existing content with the newly typed content. Sometimes you need to edit what is already in there. You have three approaches for editing a cell that already contains some data:

- Double-click the cell with the left mouse button
- Click the cell and then press the Return key
- Click the cell and press the F2 key

Each of these options causes the cell to enter edit mode, allowing you to edit the existing content.

221

Cell Selected   **Cell Edit Mode**

Figure 5-11: Entering edit mode for a cell

Sometimes you might enter edit mode for a cell and begin typing on the keyboard, but half-way through decide you don't want to complete the entry or make the current change. In this case, you can press the escape key (Esc) to take the cell out of edit mode and no changes will be saved.

Moving Between Cells

- As you develop your spreadsheet, you will need to move around the spreadsheet; that is, you will need to make different cells the current active cell to work on different parts of the spreadsheet. You have several choices for moving between cells in the spreadsheet:

- Click into a cell with the mouse cursor to make that cell the current active cell

- Use the arrow keys to move up, down, left, or right to move between cells

- Use the Tab key to move horizontally one cell to the right

- Use the combination Shift and Tab keys to move horizontally one cell to the left

- Use the scroll bars at the bottom and right of the spreadsheet to move the spreadsheet window to cells currently out of view or to center the window

Additionally, when you edit a cell, pressing the Return key causes the contents to be saved. It also causes the cell immediately beneath the saved cell to become the current cell. As you gain speed in using the Spreadsheets application, you will typically use a combination of the preceding methods to move around.

Cell References

You've learned a little about cell references so far; however it is worthwhile looking at these more closely because they form the basis of most formulas and are essential to building complex spreadsheets. The reference of a cell is the combination of its column number (a letter) and its row number (a number). The column and row numbers are displayed in the spreadsheet on a light-blue color bar across the top of the spreadsheet and down the left side of the spreadsheet (see Figure 5-2). As you move from cell to cell in the spreadsheet, the reference to the current cell changes; this process is indicated by the column and row numbers being grayed out within the column and row number bars (see Figure 5-12). To see the reference for a cell, click the cell you want, and then read the cell reference from the grayed-out column and row numbers. In Figure 5-12, "B2" is the cell reference of the selected cell.

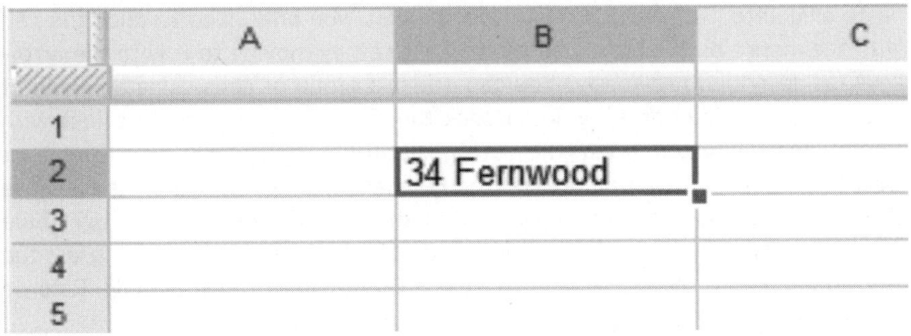

Figure 5-12: The cell references display

Cell Ranges

In some of the spreadsheets you use, some formulas will require a range of cells, as opposed to a single--cell reference. This is referred to as the *cell range*. Where a single-cell reference is given by its column and row numbers ("B2"), a cell range is defined by its top-left most cell and its bottom-right most cell. For example, the range of cells highlighted in Figure 5-13 has "A2" as its top-left most cell and "D4" as it bottom-right most cell. The cell range is referred to using a combination of these cell references. The cell range of the selected cells in Figure 5-13 is "A2:D4". You use a colon (:) to separate the upper-left cell from the bottom-right cell. As we discuss formulas in later sections, we will need to refer to cell ranges.

223

	A	B	C	D	E
1					
2	445	34 Fernwood	67A	Ref 12	
3	325	87 Logan	32B	Ref 67	
4	14	Waterloo	23S	Ref 34	
5					
6					

Figure 5-13: The cell range

Selecting Cells

When working with a spreadsheet, you will often need to select a specific cell or cell range, such as when selecting a cell range for a formula, selecting a group of cells for formatting, or even selecting a group of cells to cut-and-paste or delete. To select a single specific cell, you only need to click the cell with the mouse or make the cell the current cell by moving to it with the arrow keys, as described previously. You can select a group of cells using a couple of approaches. For example, you can click the first cell you want to select with the left mouse button; while the button is still depressed, you drag the cursor with the mouse until all of the desired cells are highlighted, and then release the left mouse button. This highlights all the selected cells with a light-blue color. Alternatively, you can click in the first cell you want to select, press the Shift key, and use the arrow keys to extend the selected range of cells. Release the shift key after you highlight the desired range of cells.

ExplainED

To select a cell range quickly without dragging, click in the top-left cell you want to select, hold down the Shift key, and then click the bottom-right cell you want to select.

Cutting and Pasting Cells

As in most office suite applications, you can use cut-and-paste functions to make copies of cells (or a range of cells) or to move a range of cells from one place in the spreadsheet to another. To achieve this, you can use either the standard keyboard short-cuts or do this through the "Edit" menu. To move a range of cells or a single cell from one place in the spreadsheet to another, first select the range of cells you want to move, as discussed previously. Next, use the Ctrl+X key combination. Alternatively, you can select the "Cut" option from the "Edit" menu. The selected text will now be highlighted with an orange dotted line that outlines the cells to be cut. Now choose the cell that will become the top-left most cell in the range at the new location and press the Ctrl+V keyboard key combination; alternatively, you can select the "Paste" option from the "Edit" menu. This moves the range of cells you *cut* to the new location; the new active cell you selected becomes the top-left most cell of the pasted cell range.

You can also copy a range of cells from one location to another without moving them. As in the previous paragraph, select the range of cells you wish to copy, and then press the Ctrl+C key combination or select the "Copy" option from the "Edit" menu. Then as before, select the cell in the spreadsheet that will become the new top-left most corner of the new cell range. Next, press the Ctrl+V keyboard combination or select the "Paste" option from the "Edit" menu. This makes a copy of the original cells and makes the new active cell you selected the top-left most cell.

Another option when pasting a range of cells you want to copy or move in a Spreadsheets document is to choose the "Paste values only" option from the "Edit" menu. You need to be careful when using this option because, if the original range selected contains formulas, only the *values* will be pasted. You will learn more about this in the section on formulas.

Text Display and Merging Cells

In many spreadsheet applications, typing a bit of text into a cell that is longer than the cell width causes the text to display over the top of the adjacent cells if they are empty. Most spreadsheet software does the same thing, so this has become accepted standard behavior in spreadsheets, and it is considered standard functionality. However, Spreadsheets does not share this accepted behavior. Instead, what you type into a cell remains in the confines of the cell, and it will not display outside the cell boundaries. For text that is longer than the width of the cell, the default option is for that text to wrap, with the height of the row changing so it can display the cell's complete text. For example, assume you type in the following string of text into a Spreadsheets' cell: "This is a very, very long piece of text for one individual spreadsheet cell." Entering this text causes the row height to change (see Figure 5-14).

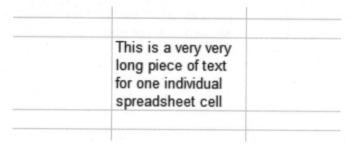

This is a very very
long piece of text
for one individual
spreadsheet cell

Figure 5-14: The auto-wrap feature for long text messages in a cell

NotED

In Spreadsheets, what you type into a cell remains in the confines of the cell, and it will not display outside the cell boundaries (in contrast to other spreadsheet software).

This may be acceptable in some circumstances, but you might prefer to display your headings horizontally across the row, rather than have the text auto-wrap. To do this, begin by turning off the wrap text feature for the cell. Select the cell with the wrapped text and click the "Wrap Text" icon on the spreadsheet toolbar (see Figure 5-3, second from the right). This turns off the wrap text feature, but now the text will be too long for the column width to display, and you will only see a portion of the text. You could alter the width of the column, but this would change the entire column width, which may not be acceptable depending on what else is placed in the column. To achieve the over-flow effect of other spreadsheet software, you can merge adjacent cells horizontally to make a bigger space for the text to display correctly. In the example in Figure 5-14, you turn off the wrap text feature as described, select the cell with the text and the three cells to the right of the cell, and then click the "Merge across" icon from the toolbar (see Figure 5-3, next to the "Wrap Text" icon). The three cells selected will now be merged, and the full text will be visible in the merged cell (see Figure 5-15).

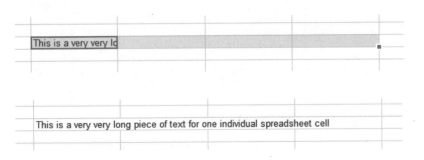

Figure 5-15: Merging cells

In Figure 5-15, the top image portion shows the cell containing the text that is truncated, as well as the four cells selected for merging. The bottom portion of the image shows the result of the merged cells. You can then format the cell containing the text as you please. Currently, Spreadsheets only supports merging adjacent cells horizontally across one row. Later, you can break apart the merged cells if you need to. To do this, you select the merged cell and click the same icon in the toolbar that you used to merge the cells initially. When you select a merged cell, this icon becomes the "Break apart" icon. The merged cells will then be restored to their individual status. If you have applied any formatting to the merged cell, breaking it apart causes all the individual cells to retain the same formatting.

ExplainED

If you merge adjacent cells that are not empty, the content of all cells except the left-most cell in the selection will be erased.

Deleting Cell Contents

Often you may need to delete (or erase) the contents of a cell or range of cells within the spreadsheet you are working on. You can achieve this in a variety of ways. For a single cell, click the desired cell; for a range of cells, select the range as previously described. You can then select the "Clear selection" option from the "Edit" menu, or right-click in the selection with the mouse and choose the "Clear selection" option. This clears the contents of the cells. If you have applied any formatting to the cells in the range to be cleared, this formatting will remain in place.

227

Inserting Rows and Columns

As indicated previously, a new spreadsheet begins with 100 rows and 20 columns by default. You can add rows or columns at any time as your spreadsheet grows, and Spreadsheets gives you a number of options for doing this.

To add a single row or column at a specific point in the spreadsheet, click a cell in the spreadsheet to make it the current active cell. Then from the "Insert" menu, choose one of the following options:

- Row above
- Row below
- Column left
- Column right

The first two options will insert a new blank row either above or below the currently selected cell, while the last two options will insert a new blank column either to the left or the right of the currently selected cell.

An alternative way to add columns to a spreadsheet is to right-click the column number bar (see Figure 5-2) on the specific number where you want to insert a new column. The entire column will then be selected, and a menu will appear (see Figure 5-16). You can then choose where to insert your column, such as "Insert 1 left" or "Insert 1 right" of the current column. If you select multiple columns by right-clicking a column number and dragging the mouse cursor over more columns in the column number bar before you release the right mouse button, then the menu will allow you to insert a number of columns before or after the selected columns. The number of columns you can insert depends on how many columns you have selected. This is a quick way to add multiple columns.

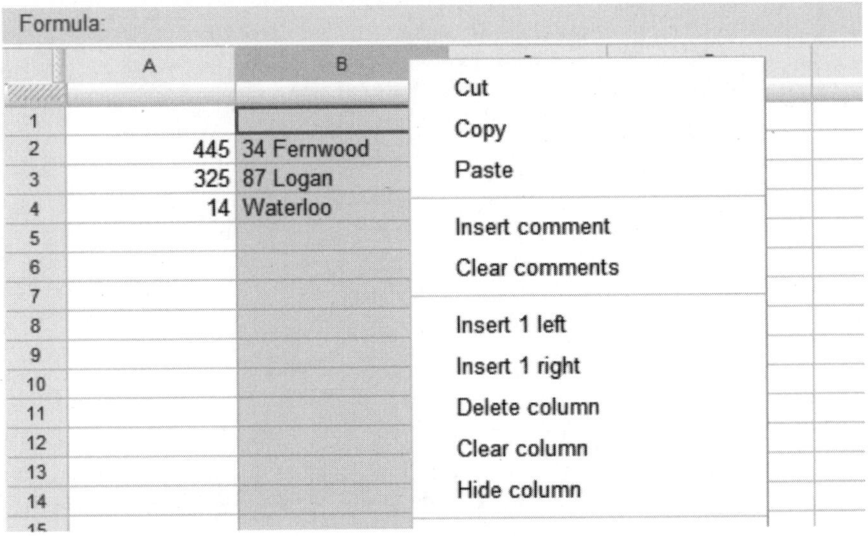

Figure 5-16: Inserting a column

Similarly, you can add a row to the spreadsheet by right-clicking the row number bar (see Figure 5-2) on the specific number where you want to insert a new row. This selects the entire row and brings up a menu (see Figure 5-17). You can then choose where to insert your row, such as "Insert 1 above" or "Insert 1 below" the current row. If you select multiple rows by right-clicking a row number and dragging the mouse cursor over more rows in the row number bar before you release the right mouse button, then the menu will allow you to insert a number of rows before or after the selected rows. The number of rows you can insert depends on how many rows you selected. This is a quick way to add multiple rows.

Spreadsheets also includes a method to add a large number of rows or columns to your spreadsheet quickly; you do this by adding new blank rows or columns to the beginning or end of the existing ones. First, you need to click the gray-box area in the column number bar to the left of the first column number and above the first row number (see Figure 5-18). This selects the entire spreadsheet. Next, click the "Insert" menu to bring up a drop-down menu (see Figure 5-18). You can add 100 rows above the first row or 100 rows below the last one. Alternatively, you can add 20 columns before the first column or 20 columns after the last one. This effectively lets you double the size of your existing rows or columns in one hit. If you don't need so many at once, you can use the former approach to add fewer rows or columns.

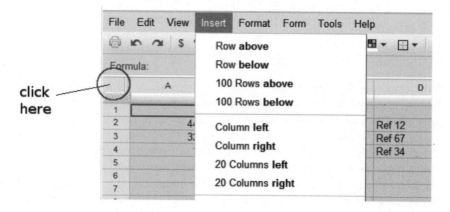

3		325	87 Logan		32B	
4		14	Waterloo		23S	
5	Cut					
6	Copy					
7						
8	Paste					
9						
10	Insert comment					
11	Clear comments					
12						
13	Insert 1 above					
14						
15	Insert 1 below					

Figure 5-17: Inserting a row

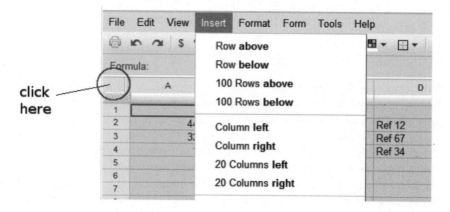

click here

Figure 5-18: Adding multiple rows or columns

Finally, you can add a number of rows to the bottom of the spreadsheet by clicking on the "Add Rows" icon, which is a small plus (+) symbol down at the bottom left of the browser window. Simply click the icon, type the number of rows to add, and click the "OK" button. This adds the appropriate number of rows to the bottom of the spreadsheet.

Deleting Rows and Columns

To delete an entire row or column, right-click the row number or column number in the row or column number bar to the left or top of the spreadsheet. In the context menu that appears, select the "Delete row" or "Delete column" option. This deletes that row or column from the spreadsheet. If you make a mistake and delete the wrong row or column, or if you decide that you did not want to delete it in the first place, you can click the "Undo" icon in the toolbar (see Figure 5-3). This puts back the row or column. Be careful because, if you decide to undo the delete, it is best that you make this your next step. Spreadsheets allows you only so many clicks that you can undo before it cannot perform any further undo requests.

You can delete multiple rows or columns by selecting multiple rows or columns in the row or column number bar. Do this by left-clicking a row or column number in the number bar and dragging the mouse cursor over a number of these rows or column numbers before releasing the left mouse button. This highlights all the cells in the selected rows or columns. Next, right-click the highlighted row or column numbers to bring up a context menu similar to that for deleting a single row or column. However instead of having a menu option to delete a single row or column; rather, it will let you delete the range of rows or columns selected. After selecting the rows or columns to be deleted, instead of right-clicking on the selected row or column numbers, you can select the "Edit" menu in the menu-bar and delete the rows or columns selected through the options in the drop-down menu.

ExplainED

If you use the right mouse button to select the rows or columns, releasing the button causes the context menu mentioned previously to be displayed automatically.

In the drop-down menus displayed in the preceding sections, you will notice that Spreadsheets includes options for clearing the selected rows and columns, as well as options for deleting the rows or columns. You can use these menu options to delete the contents of the selected cells. This achieves the same effect described in the "Deleting Cell Contents" section. Again, if formatting has been applied to the selected rows or columns, the formatting will remain; only the contents will be deleted.

Formatting Cells

As you build your spreadsheets, you might want to format different areas to make your spreadsheets suitable for presentation. Or, you might want to highlight different areas of the spreadsheet for viewing purposes. Spreadsheets provides a number of options for formatting elements of the spreadsheet to achieve this end. Its formatting options let you can change the size, font, and color of the text within a cell or for all types of cells (numeric, text, and formulas). You can control how the data appears, whether as bold, italic, or underline; you can also apply different background colors and fonts. One interesting thing you can do is to make text appear different based on rules you set up. Spreadsheets also includes extensive formatting that you can apply to numeric cells; you will learn about these in the following section.

NotED

Unlike some other spreadsheet software, Spreadsheets doesn't let you apply formatting to only part of the text in a cell; instead, Spreadsheets' formatting is applied to the entire cell.

You can choose to format a single cell or a range of cells. To format a single cell, select a cell to format and make it the current active cell. To format a range of cells, select the cell range to format, as discussed in the "Selecting Cells" section. You then apply the formatting options; this formatting will affect all selected cells.

Bold, Italic, and Underline

The simplest formatting that can be applied to a cell are the standard bold, italics, underline, or strikethrough formatting options. You can apply these by selecting the corresponding "Bold," "Italic," "Underline," or "Strikethrough" option from the "Format" menu. When you apply one of these options, a tick will appear against the appropriate menu option the next time you view it through the "Format" menu. To remove some particular formatting, select it again through the "Format" menu item when the cell or range of cells is selected.

You can access the bold and strikethrough formatting options quickly from icons on the Spreadsheets toolbar (see Figure 5-3).

Font

You can change the underlying font of the cell or range of cells by choosing the "Font" option from the "Format" menu. You cannot upload your own fonts at this stage of development; instead, you can only choose from the limited number of available fonts (see in Figure 5-19). The default spreadsheet font for all cells is "Normal." If you change fonts, the text content may no longer fit correctly in the cell due to the different display requirements of the font. In this case, you may need to resize the cell (see the "Resizing Cells" section later in this chapter).

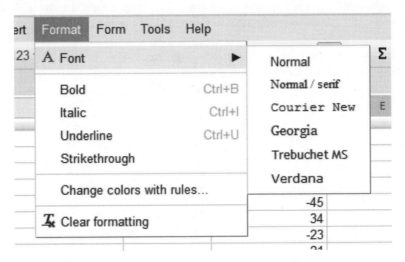

Figure 5-19: Available fonts

Size

You can resize the text in a cell to provide a heading, which helps improve the readability of your spreadsheet. You can do this for a spreadsheet heading or even perform a smaller resizing for some column headings. You can resize the text by selecting a cell or range of cells and adjusting the size by clicking the "Font Size" icon on the toolbar (see Figure 5-3). Clicking this icon gives you the option of changing the size of the text to one of the possibilities displayed in the drop-down selection (see Figure 5-20). Font size is usually measured in point size (pt) on a computer screen, where 1 point is 1/72 of an inch. The default point size for Spreadsheets is 10pt.

You need to be aware that resizing the text in a cell will most likely result in the text not displaying correctly. To fix this problem, you need to modify a couple of settings when you resize text; fortunately this doesn't take much time. If you start with some simple text such as "Balance Sheet" (see the left-most screen capture in Figure 5-21) and modify the size to say 18pt, then the text will be too large to fit across. In fact, Spreadsheets will probably default to wrapping the text as it tries to display it. You can then turn off the wrap text feature by clicking the "Wrap Text" icon on the toolbar, as discussed previously in "Text Display and Merging Cells" section). At this point, you will probably have a result similar to what is shown in the middle screen capture in

Figure 5-21. To display the text properly, you will then need to merge the cell (or cells) adjacent to the cell containing the text, as previously discussed (see the right-most screen capture in Figure 5-21). The height of the row will automatically adjust to accommodate the height of the resized text.

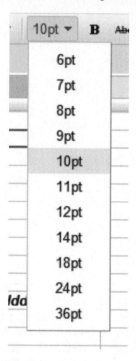

Figure 5-20: Changing the font size

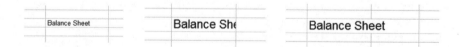

Figure 5-21: Font size change results.

Text Color and Cell Background

You can change the color of the text displayed in a cell or range of cells by selecting the cells you want to format, and then choosing the "Text color" icon from the toolbar. Doing so brings up the drop-down color chooser (see Figure 5-22). The current color will show a tick against it; the default color of a cell's text is black. Choose a new text color for the cell by clicking the color in the color chooser that you want. The text in the cell range will then be displayed with the new color.

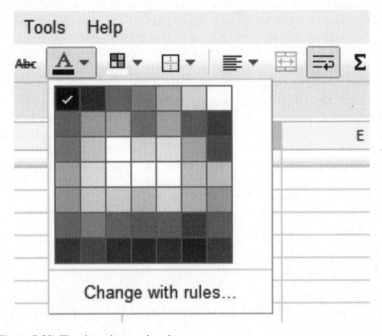

Figure 5-22: The drop-down color chooser.

You can also change the background color of a cell or cell range by selecting the cells, and then clicking the "Background Color" icon in the toolbar. Doing so displays a color chooser similar to the Text color chooser in Figure 5-22, with the current background color highlighted with a tick. The default background color is white. Choose the new background color to change the background color of the cells in the selection.

ExplainED

Use reasonable colors when choosing text and background colors. Anyone looking at the spreadsheet for a reasonable length of time can be affected by poor color combinations. Also, colors can look different, depending on the monitor, so choose color combinations that are easy to read.

Formatting Numeric and Date Types

One of the things you will find you do quite often in a spreadsheet is format number (numeric) cells for better visual display. Spreadsheets offers you a number of ways to format numeric cells so that they display their contents in a more readable format. You can control the number of digits after the decimal point, including whether a dollar ($) sign displays (used in business calculations). You can also use a percentage sign for percentage cells. This formatting is apart from the previously discussed standard textual formatting, which you can also apply. When you enter a number into a cell, you can enter a preceding dollar sign if the cell is to be a dollar amount, such as $56.54. You can also enter a trailing percent symbol (%) if the cell is to be a percentage, such as 5%. In this case, the cell will display the dollar or percentage symbols, but it remains a numeric cell that can be used in calculations. However, it is preferable that you don't do this and instead enter the numbers required, using the formatting options that follow to alter the way the cells are displayed.

ExplainED

Don't enter dollar signs or percent symbols directly into cells, even though you can for numeric quantities. Instead, use the formatting options to alter the way the cell is displayed.

Number (or numeric) cells form the backbone of any spreadsheet. The reason for using a spreadsheet is to automatically calculate and recalculate various formulas and complex calculations as the numbers in different cells change. This allows you to perform *what if* type scenarios. For example, you might wonder what happens if you change the interest percentage to 7%? Your spreadsheet can contain all sorts of numbers, so you need to format the numbers to suit your needs. To format a number cell or a range of number cells, select the cell you wish to format and make it the active cell, or select a range of cells (as previously shown), then click the "Number Format" icon in the toolbar (see Figure 5-3). The number format icon is labeled "123" in the toolbar. Clicking this icon displays the various number formats in a drop-down list (see Figure 5-23).

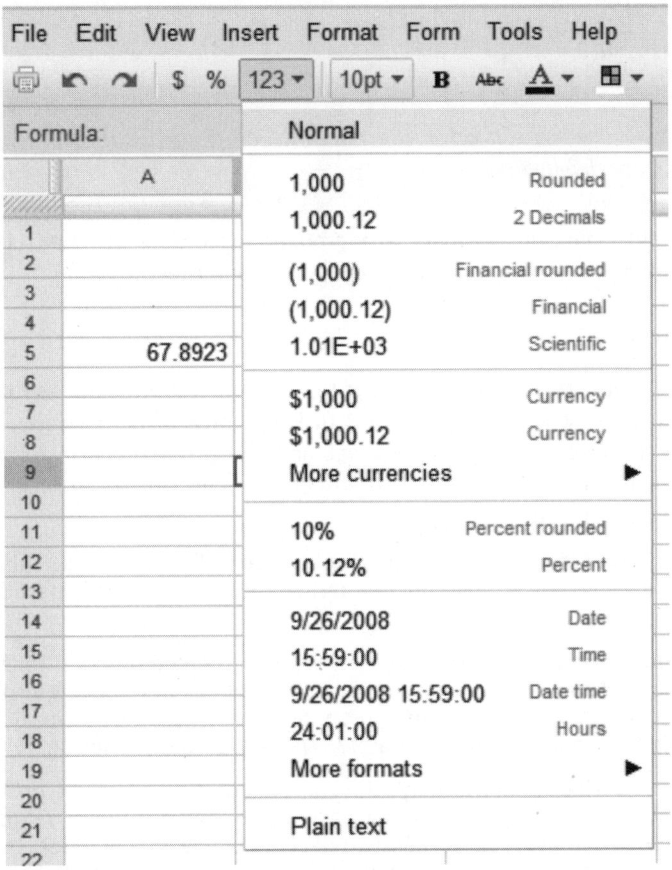

| File | Edit | View | Insert | Format | Form | Tools | Help |

Normal		
1,000	Rounded	
1,000.12	2 Decimals	
(1,000)	Financial rounded	
(1,000.12)	Financial	
1.01E+03	Scientific	
$1,000	Currency	
$1,000.12	Currency	
More currencies	▶	
10%	Percent rounded	
10.12%	Percent	
9/26/2008	Date	
15:59:00	Time	
9/26/2008 15:59:00	Date time	
24:01:00	Hours	
More formats	▶	
Plain text		

Cell A5 contains: 67.8923

Figure 5-23: The various number format options

When formatting a cell using the options that follow, it's important to remember that applying a format does not alter the contents of a cell, but only the way it is displayed on the screen. If you apply a rounding format or a format with two decimal places, then the cell will retain its original contents for any calculations; regardless of what you see when the cell is displayed on the screen. To see the contents of a cell, click the cell to make it the current active cell. This displays the result of the formatting within the cell; you can look at the formula bar to see the actual contents of the cell.

NotED

Formatting does not change the contents of a cell, but the way these contents are displayed.

The available numeric formats are grouped according to the subtypes of number, financial, currency, percentage, date, and time.

Numbers

Numbers are just the standard number types you enter with the keyboard, and they can represent anything you want to keep track of numerically. The only difference between the number format and the other numeric formatting is how the number is perceived. Spreadsheets allows you to format standard numbers in one of four ways:

Normal: This is the default format for number in Spreadsheets. This format displays the numbers in raw format, just as they are entered, including all decimal places.

Rounded: This format displays the contents of the cell rounded to the nearest whole amount. For example, a value of *46.4* in the cell displays in rounded format as *46* on the screen. Similarly, the value of *46.6* displays as *47* and *46.5* displays as *47*. The *0.5* always rounds up.

2 Decimals: This format displays the contents of the cell with two decimal places. Thus, *46.462* displays as *46.46*, and a value of *46* displays as *46.00*. If there are more than two decimal places in a number, then the contents display with the decimal component rounded to the first two decimal places when formatted with this option.

Scientific: This format displays numbers in scientific format. It uses standard scientific notation with a single digit before the decimal point, followed by the decimal component and the exponent of 10 required to preserve the absolute value of the number. For example, the value 46.321 displays as *4.63E+01*, which stands for 4.63×10^{1}.

Financial

Financial format allows you to format number cells in a format that is often seen on financial reports, such as company reports, balance sheets, and so on. The main difference is in how negative numbers are handled. There are two format options:

Financial rounded: This format behaves like the Rounded format, except that it displays negative numbers without the minus sign (-) in rounded brackets. Thus, *-46.321* displays as (*46*).

Financial: This format behaves like the 2 Decimals format, except that it displays negative numbers without the minus sign in rounded brackets. Thus, *-46.321* displays as (*46.32*).

Currency

You use currency format when you wish to display dollar amounts in cells. These cells are just number cells, but they do contain a currency symbol. You have three menu formatting options:

Currency rounded: This format behaves like the *Rounded* option, except that it displays numbers with a preceding currency symbol; the default is the dollar sign ($). It displays a negative number with the minus sign before the currency symbol. Thus, the value *46.321* displays as *$46*, and the value *-46.321* displays as *-$46*.

Currency: This format behaves like the 2 Decimals format, except that it displays numbers with a preceding currency symbol (the default is the dollar sign). It displays a negative number with the minus sign before the currency symbol. Thus, the value *46.321* displays as *$46.32*, and the value *-46.321* displays as *-$46.32*.

More currencies: The default currency symbol is the dollar sign. If you wish to use a different currency symbol, click this option to display a list of international currency symbols. Choose the one you want, and all cells in the range will use the new currency symbol when formatted with either of the two currency formats.

You can also implement this formatting using the "$" icon on the Spreadsheets toolbar. This is a quick way to format the selected cells with the Currency rounded format.

Percent

The percent format options are interesting. Everyone uses percentage calculations from time to time, but you must be careful how you enter the raw number into a cell. Recall that a percentage is a fraction of 100; in spreadsheets (including Google Spreadsheets), you enter a raw number representing a percentage as a fraction of one (1). Thus, you enter *5%* as *0.05*. You use the percent formatting options to display it how you think of it. You have two percent format options:

Percent rounded: This format displays the contents of the current numeric cell as a percentage, rounded to zero decimal places. You must be careful when using this option. Like other spreadsheets, Google Spreadsheets assumes that any cell you choose to format with this option contains a percentage value as a decimal fraction. Thus, it displays a value of *0.05* as 5%. Similarly, it displays a value *0.5* as *50%* and a value of *5* as *500%*.

Percent: This format is similar to the Percent rounded format, except that the percentage displays two decimal points in the display. Thus, it displays a cell contains the value of *0.052314* as 5.23%. Similarly, it displays a value of *0.52314* as *52.31%* and a value of *5.2314* as *523.14%*.

You can also use the "%" icon on the Spreadsheets toolbar. This icon lets you format the selected cells quickly with the percent format option.

Date and Time

Spreadsheets' Date and Time formatting options allow you to format a numeric cell into one of several different formats for displaying date and time quantities. People like to use a number of different methods to read dates and time, and it is difficult to cater to all preferences. Spreadsheets includes several of the more common display formats.

Regardless of how you wish to display your dates in Spreadsheets, you must first enter a date into a cell. How you enter a date depends on which country you selected in the "Locale" option in Spreadsheets' settings, as well as the default date format for your country. For example, if "United States" is your chosen locale, the date entry format is MM/DD/YYYY; if "Australia" is your chosen locale, the default date entry format is DD/MM/YYYY. Entering 05/07/2009 in a locale of "United Sates" enters the date of 7th May 2009, while entering the same text (05/07/2009) into a locale of "Australia" enters the date 5th July 2009. This can be a point of confusion, so you need to make sure you have your locale set correctly. Entering a date into a cell automatically tags that cell as being a "Date" cell. You can then choose the way you wish to format that date from the available formatting options. Note that you do not have to type the leading zeroes when entering a date that contains leading zeroes in the day or the month. Thus, you can type 5/7/2009 instead of 05/07/2009.

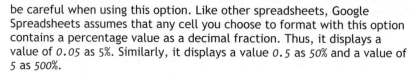

Before using dates, set the "Locale" option in the spreadsheet settings to your own country.

To enter a time into a cell, you type it in using the following template, HH:MM:SS. Again, you don't have to type in leading zeroes, but entering a time automatically tags a cell as a "Time" cell. By default, you enter a time in 24-hour format; for example, 5:26:21 is 5:26 AM, while 17:26:21 is 5:26 PM. Of course, you can enter the AM or PM suffix after the time to avoid any confusion, such as 5:26:21 PM. The default format for a "Time" cell is the HH:MM:SS 24-hour format, so entering 5:26:21 PM displays as 17:26:21 in a default "Time" formatted cell. Once you enter a time, you can choose from a number of formatting options to display the time.

A cell can also contain a combination of the date and time described previously. You achieve this by entering the date first, inserting a space, and then entering the time. For example, you might enter "5/7/2009 8:45:21 PM" as the value in a cell. You can enter the date and time in the formats described previously; the same rules for the date also apply. The date is determined by the default format of your current locale. The date must come first; otherwise, if you enter the time followed by the date, Spreadsheets won't understand what you are trying to do, and it will tag the cell as a normal "Text" cell.

Spreadsheets includes four standard format options for "Date" and "Time" cells, along with an additional sub-menu for more formats:

Date: This is the default format, and it displays the contents of the "Date" cell in the default format of your locale, usually either in dd/mm/yyyy or mm/dd/yyyy format.

Time: This format displays a "Time" cell in the default 24-hour format of hh:mm:ss.

Date time: A cell formatted with this option can contain a date and a time. There are no other formats that include date and time in a cell.

Hours: This format lets you enter a quantity that represents a number of hours, minutes, and seconds. You enter this the same way that you enter a "Time"; that is, you use the HH:MM:SS template. If you enter an amount of time less than 24 hours, Spreadsheets interprets the cell as a "Time" cell and tags it accordingly.

More formats: Once you enter a date or a time into a "Date" or "Time" cell, you can format the display of the cell further using a handful of Spreadsheets' additional formatting options for Date and Time (see Figure 5-24).

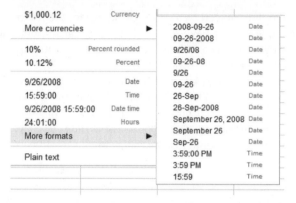

Figure 5-24: Additional formatting options for "Date" and "Time" cells

Date Picker

Once you enter a "Date" value into a cell and format it according to your preferences, you can easily change the date inside the cell. If you double-click a date cell with your mouse, Spreadsheets pops up a small calendar window. This allows you to choose another date quickly from the current month by clicking it or to scroll back and forward between the months to choose a new date (see Figure 5-25). Date picker doesn't work if the cell is blank; it only works if the cell contains a valid date value.

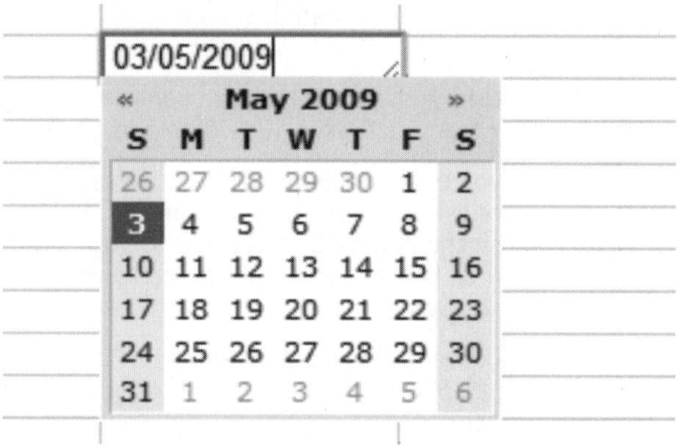

Figure 5-25: The date picker pop-up window

Resizing Cells

Sometimes you will want to resize some of the cells in the spreadsheet for formatting purposes. For example, if the spreadsheet contains rows of customer details, you may need an "Address" cell longer than the "Customer ID" cell. You can alter the size of some of your spreadsheet rows or columns. However, you cannot alter the size of a single cell; you must alter either an entire row or an entire column. When you type some text into a cell and use the formatting options already discussed to change the appearance of the text in the cell, Spreadsheets will usually auto-adjust the row height to make it fit. However, you can also manually adjust the row height to your needs. To do this, move your mouse pointer to the row number bar down the left-hand side of the spreadsheet window in the browser. Next, move your cursor into the small rectangle containing the row number, and then slowly move your cursor down to the boundary line between the bottom of the row that you want to adjust the size of and the top of the next row. For instance, if you wish to adjust the height of row 10, move your cursor down the row number bar to the border between row 10 and row 11. As the cursor passes over the border it will change to a vertical double-headed arrow (see Figure 5-26). Click the left-mouse cursor and drag the bottom of row 10 down to adjust the height of the row to something more suitable.

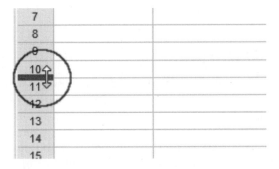

Figure 5-26: Adjusting the row height

You can use this same approach to adjust the column width of an entire column of cells. It is more common to adjust the column width because, while the row height auto-adjusts to accommodate changes in the text height, the column width does not. To alter the column width, move your mouse pointer to the column number bar in the top of the spreadsheet window in the browser. Move you cursor into the rectangle containing the column number, and then slowly move your cursor to the right, to the boundary line between the right-hand side of the column that you want to adjust the width of and the left-hand side of the next column. For instance, if you wish to adjust the width of column C, move your cursor across the row number bar to the border between column C and column D. As the cursor passes over the border, it will change to a horizontal double-headed arrow (see Figure 5-27). Click the left-mouse cursor and drag the right-hand side of column C across to adjust the width of the column to something that fits the contents of the cell.

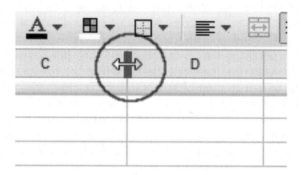

Figure 5-27: Adjusting the column width

Simple Formulas

In this section, we will look at the basics of using formulas in Google Spreadsheets. When it comes to formulas, Spreadsheets is no different than most other spreadsheet packages, such as Excel and Calc. It provides the ability to add the formulas to spreadsheets that give them their calculating power. A formula is a mathematical calculation that you place in a cell that relies on the contents of other cells. When the contents of these other cells change, then the formula is automatically recalculated; the result of the formula, which is displayed in the formula cell, changes as well. The best way to learn about formulas is to begin using simple ones, then build on these to create more complex formulas and spreadsheets.

Elements of a Formula

A formula is a calculation involving numbers (or values), cell references to cells containing numbers, mathematical operations (such as addition, subtraction, multiplication, and division), and built-in functions. You use the following symbols for the standard mathematical operations:

- Addition: +
- Subtraction: -
- Multiplication: *
- Division: /

You can also use the standard brackets—"(" and ")"—to group parts of mathematical calculations. A formula must begin with an equals sign (=). For example, perform the following steps in a blank spreadsheet

1. in cell A3enter: 37
2. in cell B3enter: 12
3. in cell C3enter: =A3+B3

The spreadsheet will now resemble the portion showed in Figure 5-28. If you look at the spreadsheet, you will see three numbers; the number displayed in cell C3 is the sum of cells A3 and B3. However, if you select cell C3 as the current active cell, the cell displays a number (49), which is the result of the formula. The Formula bar shows the content of the cell, which is the formula itself. You can see the major components of the formula to the right of Figure 5-28. The formula begins with the equal sign (=), followed by the addition of two cell references. You create all formulas along similar lines, albeit some formulas will be more complex than others, depending on what you are doing.

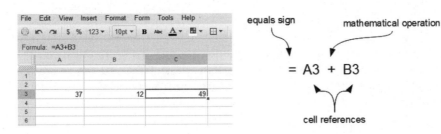

Figure 5-28: Elements of a formula

Creating and Copying Simple Formulas

You already created a simple formula in the previous section by adding together the contents of two spreadsheet cells. You can expand on this by looking at some other simple formulas, as well as some quick methods to duplicate them quickly. Let's look at some simple numbers in a portion of a spreadsheet designed to calculate some revenues and profits from the sale of different types of juices (see Figure 5-29). This table shows six products, each of which has a Product No., Description, Cost price, Sell price, and Quantity sold field. The spreadsheet has been formatted using some of the options previously discussed. You can now devise simple formulas to calculate the revenue and profit for each product. To calculate the revenue for the first product, you make the corresponding cell that will contain the Revenue calculation the active cell. You use this formula for the Revenue calculation:

(Sell price * Quantity sold)

Note the use of the asterisk symbol (*) for multiplication. This is standard in spreadsheets and computing in general. Translating the preceding calculation for use in the spreadsheet yields the following formula we type into the cell:

=D5 * E5

Formula: =D5*E5						
	A	B	C	D	E	F	G
1							
2	Product No.	Description	Cost	Sell	Quantity	Revenue	Profit
3			price	price	sold		
4							
5	2234	500 ml Orange Juice	$1.10	$2.50	457	$1142.5	$639.8
6	3912	1 Litre Orange Juice	$1.75	$3.75	712		
7	7854	750 ml Grape Drink	$1.45	$3.10	365		
8	4567	2 Litre Grape Juice	$2.64	$4.23	572		
9	6743	750 ml Apple Juice	$0.99	$2.99	984		
10	2141	350 ml Apple Juice Pack	$0.45	$1.50	1214		
11							

Figure 5-29: Simple revenue calculations

In Figure 5-29, the Revenue cell for the first product is selected, and you can see the formula for this cell in the formula bar. Similarly, you can create the formula for the Profit of the first product. You calculate the profit for a product like this:

Revenue – (Cost price * Quantity sold)

You translate the preceding formula for use in the spreadsheet like this:

=F5-(C5*E5)

Note the use of the brackets () to apply the correct calculations for the formula. The result of this formula is shown in cell G5 of the spreadsheet (see Figure 5-29). So far you have created the formulas for both the revenue and profit of the first product. Next, you can implement the same formulas for the remaining products. You can type these formulas in again in the appropriate remaining cells, remembering to adjust the cell references in the formula on each row to account for the different cells they reference. Alternatively, you can try a simpler, quicker approach. To create the Revenue formulas quickly for the remaining products, begin by selecting the Revenue cell for the formula you created in cell F5. Next, copy this cell by using the Ctrl+C keyboard shortcut or by choosing the "Copy" option from the "Edit" menu. Now use your mouse, to select the remaining Revenue cells (F6 through F10) that do not as yet contain a formula. At this point, you have the partial spreadsheet shown in Figure 5-30.

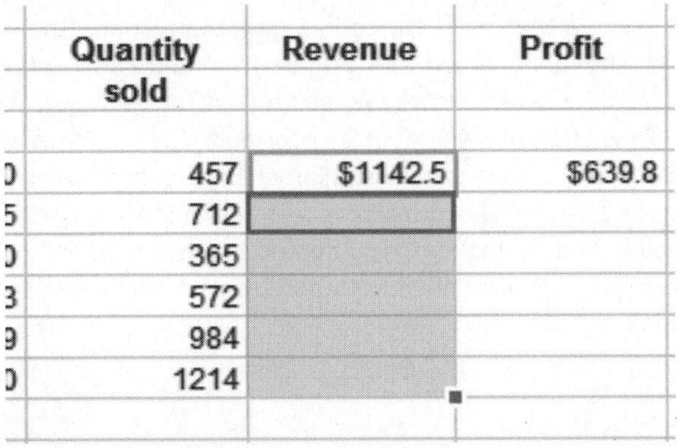

	Quantity sold	Revenue	Profit
)	457	$1142.5	$639.8
5	712		
)	365		
3	572		
9	984		
)	1214		

Figure 5-30: Selected cells ready a copy of the formula

Now click the first blank selected cell, which is F6 (see selected cell in Figure 5-30), and then paste the formula you have previously copied by using either the Ctrl+V keyboard shortcut or the "Paste" option from the "Edit" menu. This copies the Revenue formula for the first product to the remaining Revenue cells (see Figure 5-31).

Quantity sold	Revenue	Profit
457	$1142.5	$639.8
712	$2670	
365	$1131.5	
572	$2419.56	
984	$2942.16	
1214	$1821	

Formula: =D6*E6

Figure 5-31: Result of pasting the formula

Notice that although you copied-and-pasted the same formula into the remaining Revenue cells, the results are all different. You can see the reason for this in the formula bar result for cell F6 (see the formula shown to the right of Figure 5-31). When you copied the formula from cell F5 to cell F6 and all the remaining cells, the cell references were adjusted for each row you copied the formula into. Thus the references in the formula =D5 * E5 in row five were changed to =D5 * E5 in row six; a similar change occurred in the remaining rows, as well. Note that the column numbers remained the same, but the row numbers changed. That is because you copied down a column. If you copied a formula across a row, the row numbers would remain the same, but the column numbers would change.

NotED

When copying formulas, the cell references will change depending on whether you copy down a column, or across a row.

Now repeat the preceding steps for the Profit formula: select the formula, copy it, select the cells you want to copy the formula into, and paste the formula into the selected cell as described (see the result in Figure 5-32). Again, note that the cell references have changed in the copying process. You can see this by comparing the formula for calculating profit in selected cell (G10) in the formula bar (see Figure 5-32) to the formula for calculating profit developed for the first product.

Formula: =F10-(C10*E10)

	A	B	C	D	E	F	G
1							
2	Product No.	Description	Cost price	Sell price	Quantity sold	Revenue	Profit
3							
4							
5	2234	500 ml Orange Juice	$1.10	$2.50	457	$1142.5	$639.8
6	3912	1 Litre Orange Juice	$1.75	$3.75	712	$2670	$1424
7	7854	750 ml Grape Drink	$1.45	$3.10	365	$1131.5	$602.25
8	4567	2 Litre Grape Juice	$2.64	$4.23	572	$2419.56	$909.48
9	6743	750 ml Apple Juice	$0.99	$2.99	984	$2942.16	$1968
10	2141	350 ml Apple Juice Pack	$0.45	$1.50	1214	$1821	$1274.7
11							

Figure 5-32: Complete spreadsheet after copying the profit formula

You can save some time by using this Spreadsheets feature when developing a formula that needs to be repeated. In the preceding example, you had only six products, but it could have easily been more. You can use this technique for entering formulas to build useful functionality into your spreadsheets. The preceding approach uses the standard mathematical operations and references to cells instead of numbers; however, Spreadsheets also includes a wizard that provides a shorthand way to develop simple formulas quickly; you will learn how to use this wizard's built-in functions next.

Building Simple Formulas

Google Spreadsheets provides an easy-to-use tool for quickly developing formulas for most common tasks, as well as for providing easy access to its built-in mathematical functions. You do this by using the Formula button on the toolbar (see Figure 5-33). Clicking on the formula button gives you quick access to the most commonly used formulas in spreadsheets, such as Sum Average, Count, Max, and Min. The "More formulas" option gives you access to more than 250 mathematical and financial functions; you can leverage these to build complex spreadsheets.

For example, assume that you want to find the total revenue from all the sales in the spreadsheet shown in Figure 5-32. To do this, you add all the figures in the Revenue column, which you can accomplish by adding this formula to cell F11:

=F5 + F6 + F7 + F8 + F9 + F10

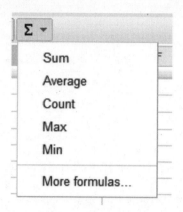

Figure 5-33: Accessing formulas through the formula button

A better option would be to use Spreadsheets' SUM function. You can access this function quickly through the formula button on the toolbar. First, you need to select the cells in the column you wish to SUM, as shown in the left-most column of Figure 5-34. Next, select the "Sum" option by clicking the "formula" button on the toolbar, and then clicking the "Sum" option. This places the SUM function in the cell immediately below the selected cells, as shown in the middle column in Figure 5-34). Notice that in the cell, the function, like any formula, begins with an equals sign (=). It is then followed by the cells to be summed in brackets. Next, press the Return key on the keyboard to enter the formula into the cell and display the result (see the right-most column in Figure 5-34).

Revenue		Revenue	Pr		Revenue
$1142.5		$1142.5			$1142.5
$2670		$2670			$2670
$1131.5		$1131.5	$		$1131.5
$2419.56		$2419.56	$		$2419.56
$2942.16		$2942.16			$2942.16
$1821		$1821	$		$1821
		=SUM(F5:F10)			$12126.72

Figure 5-34: Using the "Formula" button to SUM a column

This is a quick way to enter a simple formula for a built-in function like SUM. Note that when you select a range of cells and choose a function like SUM, Spreadsheets places the formula involving the range of cells in the cell immediately below the selected cells. If you choose a range of cells horizontally across a row, the formula is placed in the cell immediately to the right of the selected cells. This auto-placement usually suffices, but occasionally you might want to place the formula elsewhere. Just as you can quickly SUM a column or row of cells, you can also find the Average, Count, Maximum, and Minimum of a range of cells. You can place these functions as quickly and simply as the SUM function by selecting a column or row of cells you want to apply the function to, and then choosing the appropriate function from the "Formula" button on the toolbar.

Using Cell Ranges in Formulas

We discussed cell ranges in a previous section. Some functions in Spreadsheets use single-cell references, while others will use one- or two-dimensional ranges. You will see some examples of two-dimensional ranges later. In the previous section, the SUM function used a range to sum the cells in the Revenue and Profit column, such as SUM(F5:F10). In the previous example, you selected the range of cells to be used in the SUM function before you selected the SUM function from the "Formula" button's drop-down menu. This is because you used the auto-placement feature of this quick function selection. In some cases, you need to place a function that uses a range of cells somewhere else, rather than rely on the auto-placement. In such cases, you will need to select the range of cells the function requires during the placement of the formula, rather than before the function selection (as you did in the preceding example). For instance, if you want to place the formula with the SUM function in cell F12, but not directly underneath the range of cells to be summed, you need to do things a little differently. Select the cell where you want the formula located, click the "Formula" button in the toolbar, and select the "Sum" item. This creates a formula containing the SUM function in the selected cell, as shown in Figure 5-35 (a).

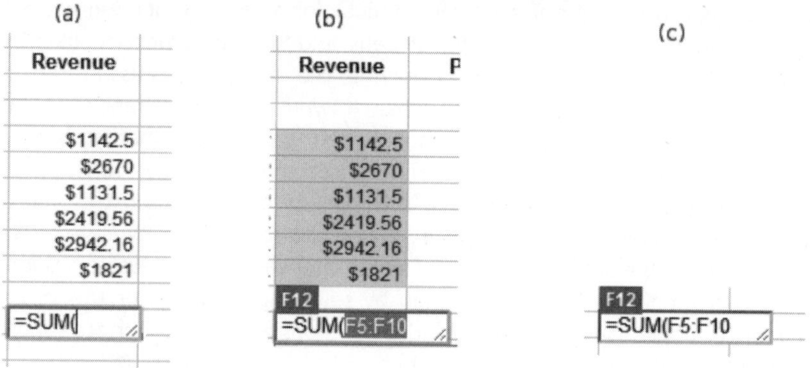

Figure 5-35: Selecting a range during function placement

Notice that no range has been placed in the SUM function; rather, it holds only the empty function itself at the stage. Use the mouse to select the cell range from F5 to F10. As you select this range, note that the selected cell range is added to the function in cell F12, as shown in Figure 5-35 (b). Instead of selecting the cell range with the mouse, you could also type in the range F5:F10 using you keyboard. The function is not quite complete yet, however; it is still missing the closing bracket—")"—at the end of the function, as shown in Figure 5-35 (c). Next, you can either type the closing right bracket yourself and press the Return key on the keyboard, or you can just press the Return key. Pressing the Return key completes the function and adds the closing right bracket if it is not there. Your formula is now complete.

You will encounter many functions that require you to select ranges as you place your formulas.

Quick Sum

Spreadsheets has a helpful bit of functionality called *Quick Sum* that you can use to see the results instantly for the application's most common functions (Sum, Average, Count, Minimum, and Maximum) for a specific range of numbers—all without placing any formulas. The same functionality in Excel is called *AutoCalculate*. If you have a range of numbers in a spreadsheet, and you wish to check for the results for any of the preceding functions, you can select the desired range of numbers with your mouse, as shown in Figure 5-36 (a). Now look at the bottom-right of the Spreadsheets' window, where you can see the Sum of these numbers located in the small cell in the bottom right corner, as shown in Figure 5-36 (b). If you click this cell with the left mouse button, a small window pops up that displays the results of the Quick Sum for the Sum,

Average, Count, Minimum, and Maximum of the selected cell range, as shown in Figure 5-36 (c).

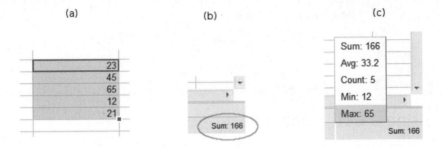

Figure 5-36: Using the Quick Sum feature

Using Percentages

People use percentages in spreadsheets frequently. You can use them to calculate interest on loans, bonus payments to sales staff, or yields on stock dividends. To enter a percentage, recall that you need to type it in as a fraction of one (1). Thus you type in 0.05 to enter 5% into a cell, and 0.12 to enter 12% into a cell. These examples represent the percentages as fractions. Once the raw percentage decimal is entered into a cell, it can be formatted using the formatting options described earlier. Using the percentage figure is a simple matter of multiplying a cell that contains a quantity you want to find a percentage of by the percentage cell. Let's use the percentages mentioned previously, 5% and 12%. If you type 0.05 and 0.12 into two cells and format them using the percent format described earlier, you can see the results in cells A2 and A3 of the spreadsheet (see Figure 5-37). To calculate the interest in column C of the amounts in column B, you just need to devise a simple formula. You can see the formula for the selected cell, C2, in the formula bar in Figure 5-37:

= A2 * B2

You get your result by just multiplying the cell that contains the percentage formatted amount (A2) by the cell that contains the amount (B2).

Formula: =A2*B2

	A	B	C
1	**Percentage**	**Amount**	**Interest**
2	5.00%	$213,523.00	$10676.15
3	12.00%	$345,627.00	$41475.24
4			

Figure 5-37: Using percentages

Editing a Cell's Formula

Sometimes you might need to edit a formula in a cell after it has been created. This may be for a number of reasons, such as to alter a cell range or to fix an incorrect calculation. To edit the formula in a cell, double-click the formula cell, just as you would to edit a value in a cell. This places the cell in edit mode, and you can then use the keyboard arrow keys (or even the mouse) to move around within the cell and delete or add parts of the formula. However, you must be careful when editing a formula. Unlike a cell that contains a value being edited, a cell that contains a formula will not exit edit mode if you click the spreadsheet outside the cell. Instead, it will place a cell reference within the cell you are editing at the point where the cursor currently is (the cell you just clicked).

ExplainED

When editing a cell that contains a formula, clicking outside the cell places a reference to that cell in the editing window.

This behavior can be useful if you want to build a long formula that contains cell references, but it can also cause unexpected results if you do this accidentally.

Using More Complex Functions

In previous sections, you created some simple formulas to add numbers. You also learned how to use of some of Spreadsheets' more common functions for basic column and row calculations: SUM, Average, Count, Minimum, and Maximum. You're now ready to look at some additional functions that are more complex, but still relatively easy to use. To see a list for function categories that you can use with a spreadsheet, click the "Formula" button and select the "More formulas" option. This opens the "Insert a function" dialog (see Figure 5-38). The functions are categorized into the following groups:

- Math
- Financial
- Logical
- Date
- Lookup
- Statistical
- Text
- Engineering
- Info
- Google

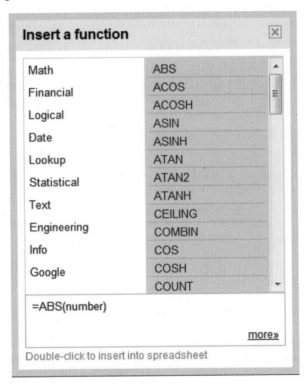

Figure 5-38: Insert a function dialog

These categories include more than 250 functions. Most spreadsheets for personal use or in business use the Financial, Logical, Lookup, and Statistical functions; however, those who use spreadsheets to analyze some scientific data can find many other extremely useful functions. The function list is always being revised and expanded; being a Web-based service, Spreadsheets will always be able to access the latest functions.

Now let's look at an example that uses a more complex function, the Future Value financial function. This function calculates the future value of an investment based on a constant interest and payments. This function requires some input data to perform its calculations. The function needs to know the following:

- The periodic interest rate
- The number of periods for the investment
- The amount of each regular payment into the investment
- The present cash value of the investment
- (Optional) Whether the payment is due at the beginning or end of each period

Next, set up a small portion of a spreadsheet, plugging these figures into appropriately labeled cells (see Figure 5-39, which includes some sample figures). Cell E5 contains either a one or zero, depending on whether the payment is made at the beginning or end of the period.

Formula:				
A	B	C	D	E
Interest rate	No. Periods (years)	Payment per period	Present Value	Payment due (1) begin, (0) end
4.00%	2	$750.00	$2,500.00	0
Future Value				

Figure 5-39: A spreadsheet that uses the Future Value function

To place the function in a formula in the spreadsheet, click cell B8. Next, click on the "Formula" button on the toolbar and select the "More formulas" option. In the dialog box that appears (see Figure 5-38), click the "Financial" category on the left-hand side and use the scroll-down slider bar on the right until you come to the FV function. Double-click the FV function in the dialog box on the right (the highlighted blue function name). This enters the following formula into cell B8 and opens the cell in edit mode:

=FV(rate, NPER, PMT, PV, type)

You now need to modify the cell and replace each of the function parameters with the cell reference to the cell that contains the required data. Replace the following cells as described:

rate: Replace with cell reference A5

NPER: Replace with cell reference B5

PMT: Replace with cell reference C5

PV: Replace with cell reference D5

Type: Replace with cell reference E5

You should now have this formula in the cell:

=FV(A5,B5,C5,D5,E5)

You can now press the Return key to complete the formula (see the completed spreadsheet in Figure 5-40). You can see the formula for the cell that contains the FV function in the formula bar. This formula calculates the future value of an amount with an annual interest rate of 4% per year, over a period of two years, contributing $750 per year to the investment, and with the payment made at the end of the year. The formula always returns a negative value with the future value amount. So the future value will be $4234.00. Given this spreadsheet, you can now play around with the figures in the cells and answer questions, such as: What would change if the interest were 5.5% per year? You can answer this by changing the value in the percentage cell to 5.5%. This is what gives spreadsheets their power, their ability to model various scenarios simply by changing some figures.

Formula: =FV(A5,B5,C5,D5,E5)

	A	B	C	D	E
1					
2	Interest rate	No. Periods	Payment	Present Value	Payment due
3		(years)	per period		(1) begin, (0) end
4					
5	4.00%	2	$750.00	$2,500.00	0
6					
7					
8	Future Value	-$4,234			
9					

Figure 5-40: Completed formula with the Future Value function

Of course, you can alter these formulas as your needs dictate. For instance, assume you wanted to find the future value after seven years, given an initial investment of $20,000, with an annual interest rate of 5%, but this time with *monthly* payments of $200 at the beginning of each month. This is not difficult, but it does require some careful thought. The payment is monthly, but over 7 years you need to modify the number of periods to 84 (7 x 12). You also need to change the interest rate to 5% the payment per period to 200, the present value to $20,000, and the payment due cell to one. The last change is in the formula. The interest rate is an annual rate, but the periods are not monthly, so you need to change the formula to this:

=FV(A5/12,B5,C5,D5,E5)

Note that you divide cell A5 by 12 in the formula to give a monthly interest rate equivalent. You can see the result for this calculation in Figure 5-41; you can see the new formula in the formula bar. You also now have a more flexible formula you can play with in the spreadsheet.

Formula: =FV(A5/12,B5,C5,D5,E5)				
	A	B	C	D	E
1					
2	Interest rate	No. Periods	Payment	Present Value	Payment due
3		(months)	per period		(1) begin, (0) end
4					
5	5.00%	84	$200.00	$20,000.00	1
6					
7					
8	Future Value	-$48,510.06			
9					

Figure 5-41: Modified Future Value function

As you have seen, it is not difficult to create formulas with more complex functions; you just need to think more about how you will implement the formula and display its results in the spreadsheet. Additionally, once you enter a formula, you can easily go back and edit it, as you did in the preceding example when you divided the interest rate by 12 to accommodate the change in the use of the function.

Auto Fill Spreadsheets includes an interesting tool that allows you to enter data into a spreadsheet quickly where a pattern is involved. You do this using the *Auto-Fill* feature, which you can use to repeat all types of data, provided Spreadsheets can discern a pattern. For example, assume you click a cell and enter the text "Tuesday" and make this the active cell. At this point, you will see the highlighted cell in Figure 5-42 (a) with the Auto-fill symbol circled. The Auto-fill symbol is a small, square element at the bottom right of a group of selected cells. Placing your mouse cursor over the Auto-fill symbol turns the cursor into the precision cross-hair cursor, as shown in Figure 5-42 (b). Click the symbol and drag it down, as shown in Figure 5-42 (c). When you release the mouse button, the highlighted section will be filled with the repeating pattern, as shown in Figure 5-42 (d). In this case, Spreadsheets discerned no pattern, so it filled the other cells with the original value.

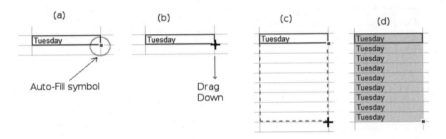

Figure 5-42: Using Auto-Fill

Now repeat this process, except this time with two cells that contain the first value, then the next value in the sequence in the cell below (or adjacent on the right), we can see the progression within Figures 5-43 (a), (b) and (c). The difference in this case is that Spreadsheets could detect a pattern between the two adjacent cells, so it built on the progression it recognized to fill the newly highlighted cells.

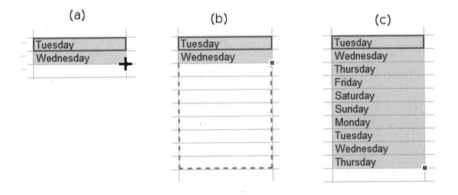

Figure 5-43: Auto-fill with a repeating pattern

You are not restricted to Auto-filling one column or row at a time, nor are you restricted to Auto-filling only one kind of value. Figure 5-44 (a) and (b) shows three columns being Auto-filled with month values, date values, and time values. If Auto-fill recognizes a pattern, the highlighted cells will be filled with increasing values of that pattern.

(a)

March	2 Mar 2009	9:30 AM
April	2 Apr 2009	10:30 AM

(b)

March	2 Mar 2009	9:30 AM
April	2 Apr 2009	10:30 AM
May	2 May 2009	11:30 AM
June	2 Jun 2009	12:30 PM
July	2 Jul 2009	1:30 PM
August	2 Aug 2009	2:30 PM
September	2 Sep 2009	3:30 PM
October	2 Oct 2009	4:30 PM
November	2 Nov 2009	5:30 PM
December	2 Dec 2009	6:30 PM
January	2 Jan 2010	7:30 PM

Figure 5-44: Auto-fill with multiple repeating patterns

NotED

If you drag the Auto-fill symbol in the opposite direction, the Auto-fill will fill in the cells in decreasing order of the detected pattern.

Building More Complex Spreadsheets

Apart from what you have learned already, there remain many small details to cover about Google Spreadsheets that will help you utilize the spreadsheets to their fullest extent. A lot of the smaller details bring together different things you have learned so far, enabling you to create even more complex elements. In this section, you'll learn how to use multiple-sheets within a spreadsheet; you'll also learn about cell referencing and ranges.

Working with Multiple Sheets

As with other office suite spreadsheet software, Google Spreadsheets lets you develop spreadsheets with multiple *sheets*, giving your spreadsheets the 3-D nature of a workbook with multiple pages. There are a number of reasons you may want to have multiple sheets within a single spreadsheet. This feature allows you to develop complex spreadsheets related to a specific topic, yet to reduce that complexity somewhat by placing parts of the spreadsheet into different sheets. It lets you break up the work into smaller chunks, yet keep it all together in the same spreadsheet. To see how many sheets are associated with a single spreadsheet, you can examine the bottom left of the spreadsheet window (see Figure 5-45). Each sheet is represented by a tab at the bottom of the window that contains the sheet's name. To add a new sheet to a spreadsheet, click the "Add Sheet" button at the bottom left of the spreadsheet window. This creates a new sheet with a new tab (with a default name), as shown in Figure 5-45.

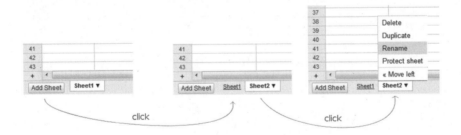

Figure 5-45: Adding and modifying sheets

If you create many sheets within a worksheet, it could become difficult to remember what is on each sheet. Fortunately, you can give each sheet a unique name. This name should reflect what each sheet contains, whether it's information about revenue, sales, profit, and so on. To name a sheet, click the sheet tab to bring up a small pop-up menu with a number of options (see Figure 5-45). In the pop-up menu, you can select options to delete, rename, protect, or duplicate the sheet. You can also change the order of the sheet tabs at the bottom by choosing either "Move left" or "Move right" in the pop-up menu for the sheet. Moving between sheets in a spreadsheet is simple; just click the tab at the bottom of the spreadsheet that is associated with a particular sheet, and that sheet becomes the active sheet. You can treat each sheet as a separate spreadsheet, but it is a good idea to use the sheets to store all related data in a single spreadsheet.

Data can be copied and moved between sheets by using the cut-and-past features you used for a single sheet. Additionally, formulas can be constructed that reference cells or cell ranges between different sheets.

Using Cell References between Worksheets

To see the how you can link sheets together by using formulas from one sheet referencing cells in another, you will extend to the earlier example where you looked at revenue and profit from the sales of different size juice containers in the section, "Creating and Copying Simple Formulas." Rather than using a simple sheet to hold everything, you can extend the example and have all the sales figures for a number of sales people contained on one "Sales" sheet (see Figure 5-46). The sales figures on the "Sales" sheet are broken down by sales person and product. The only formulas in the "Sales" sheet are the totals in the bottom row B11:H11. These formulas contain the simple SUM function (see Figure 5-46).

	A	B	C	D	E	F	G	H
1		Orange Jiuce	Orange Jiuce	Grape Juice	Grape Juice	Apple Juice	Apple Juice	Apple Juice
2	Sales Person	500 ml	1 Litre	750 ml	2 Litre	750 ml	350 ml	1 Litre
3								
4	Paul	4567	2391	4162	1272	3812	6234	2881
5	Mai-Ling	6543	3721	3518	4231	2172	4921	3241
6	Adam	3872	4123	4821	3821	3169	5174	2512
7	Sally	6152	2163	2381	2931	1931	3887	2779
8	Ahmed	3419	3129	5128	1211	3196	2191	3221
9	Ann Lee	6712	3271	2317	3341	2174	7119	1521
10								
11	Totals	31265	18798	22327	16807	16454	29526	16155
12								

'Sales' sheet =SUM(E4:E9)

Figure 5-46: The "Sales" sheet

On the "Income" sheet, you can include the totals for the each of the product lines in a simple sheet that calculates revenue and profit from the cost price and the total sales in the "Sales" sheet (see Figure 5-47). The Quantity Sold (column E) cells are populated with the total product sales figures from the

"Sales" sheet. The formula for the cell shown (for 750 ml Apple Juice) contains the reference to cell F11 from "Sales" sheet (see Figure 5-47). You can use this technique to separate the detailed sales figures from a higher level revenue statement in the "Income" sheet. However, all the sheets are related in as the sense that they keep different information about the same thing. To reference a cell from another sheet, you precede the cell with the desired sheet name, separated by an exclamation mark (!).

	A	B	C	D	E	F	G
1							
2	Product No.	Description	Cost price	Sell price	Quantity sold	Revenue	Profit
3							
4							
5	2234	500 ml Orange Juice	$1.10	$2.50	31265	$78,162.50	$43,771.00
6	3912	1 Litre Orange Juice	$1.75	$3.75	18798	$70,492.50	$37,596.00
7	7854	750 ml Grape Drink	$1.45	$3.10	22327	$69,213.70	$36,839.55
8	4567	2 Litre Grape Juice	$2.64	$4.23	16807	$71,093.61	$26,723.13
9	6743	750 ml Apple Juice	$0.99	$2.99	16454	$49,197.46	$32,908.00
10	2141	350 ml Apple Juice Pack	$0.45	$1.50	29526	$44,289.00	$31,002.30
11	2521	1 Litre Apple Juice	$1.05	$3.50	16155	$56,542.50	$39,579.75
12						$438,991.27	$248,419.73

'Income' sheet

=Sales!F11

Figure 5-47: Including references from "Sales" sheet on "Income" sheet

ExplainED

You can reference a cell from a different sheet by using the sheet name, an exclamation mark (!), and the cell reference in the sheet (e.g., Sales!F11).

Absolute Cell Referencing

You might recall this important piece of information you learned about in the section on cell references and copying formulas: when you copy a formula, the cell references in the formula change. If you copy down a column, the row number part of the cell reference changes. Thus, if you copy across a row, the column number part of the cell reference changes. This ability to have the cell references change when copying a formula is a feature, and it greatly simplifies creating complex spreadsheets that use a lot of the same formulas. However, there are times when a changing cell reference does not work correctly and causes invalid results. For example, assume you have a scenario where one cell has a fixed interest rate, and a number of customers have varying loan amounts (see Figure 5-48). The column labeled "Annual Interest" is used to calculate the annual interest owing for each customer. You could construct the formula in cell F4 like this:

=E4 * B2

Next, you could copy this cell formula for the other customers. However, if you do that, the cell references will change. This is fine for the cell references related to the different customers in the "Amount Owing" cell references. You need those references to change. However, the cell reference for the "Interest Rate" cell will also change, which you don't want to happen.

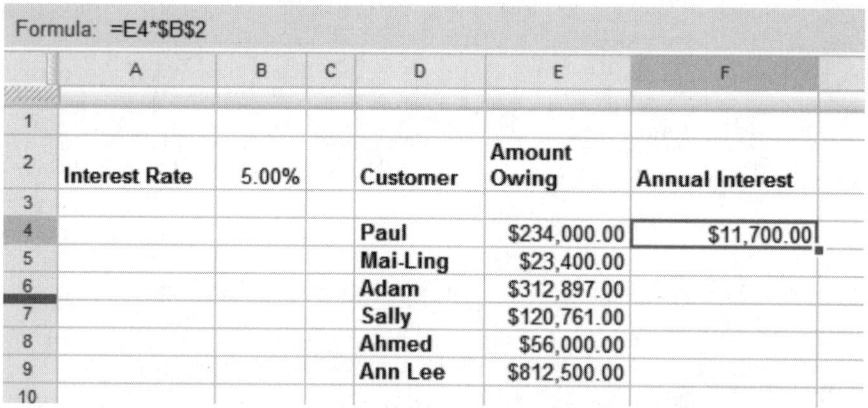

Formula: =E4*B2

	A	B	C	D	E	F	
1							
2	Interest Rate	5.00%		Customer	Amount Owing	Annual Interest	
3							
4				Paul	$234,000.00	$11,700.00	
5				Mai-Ling	$23,400.00		
6				Adam	$312,897.00		
7				Sally	$120,761.00		
8				Ahmed	$56,000.00		
9				Ann Lee	$812,500.00		
10							

Figure 5-48: Using absolute cell referencing to stop changing references

You can prevent the cell reference for the "Interest Rate" cell from changing by anchoring it. You do this by placing a dollar sign ($) before the column number and the row number. You can see this formula in the formula bar for cell F2 in Figure 5-48. You can anchor the "Interest Rate" cell reference with this formula:

=E4 * B2

This prevents the column number and the row number from changing as the formula is copied. Sometimes you might want the row number to change, but not the column number. You can do this by anchoring the column number (precede it with a dollar sign), but not anchoring the row number. You can also anchor the row number, but not the column number. Anchoring a cell's address is known as absolute cell referencing.

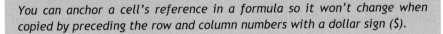

ExplainED

You can anchor a cell's reference in a formula so it won't change when copied by preceding the row and column numbers with a dollar sign ($).

Using Named Ranges

As you have seen, you often use cell ranges as opposed to individual cells when dealing with formulas and functions. As you get more formulas in your spreadsheet, remembering multiple cell references and ranges can become a problem. Fortunately, Spreadsheets includes a feature that addresses this by allowing the creation of named ranges. That is, you can assign a name to a range of cells, and use the name instead of a cell range when required. This can be helpful, especially when you're using large ranges in formulas. It also helps make the formulas more readable. For example, take another look at Figure 5-48. Instead of using the cell B2, which contains the interest rate, you can name the cell "Interest Rate" and use that in the calculation instead. To name a cell or a range of cells, begin by selecting the cell (or range of cells) to be named with the mouse. Next, choose the "Define new range" option from the "Named ranges" item on the "Edit" menu (see Figure 5-49).

When you select this option, the "Name" dialog window opens, and the range of cells you selected will appear in the field in the upper right of the dialog window (see Figure 5-50). If you didn't select a range of cells before opening the dialog, you can type the range of cells into this field or use the mouse to select the range from the spreadsheet; this causes the range to appear in the field. Now type in the *nickname* (the name you will use for this range). You can either click the "Done" button in the bottom right of the dialog or click the "Save" button underneath the nickname field. You need to click the "Save" button to save the new range name because clicking the "Done" button exits the dialog without making any changes. When you click the "Save" button to make the changes, the "Manage Ranges" dialog window appears with the list of all defined range names. You can also activate this dialog by clicking the "Manage ranges" menu option (see Figure 5-49). From this dialog, you can click the "Done" button to close the dialog or click the "Add another" link at the bottom left of the dialog to add another range name. You can also delete an existing range name by clicking the small cross symbol located to the right of each range name listed in this dialog window.

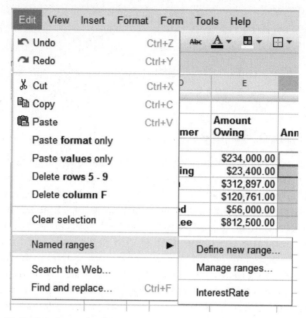

Figure 5-49: Defining a range name

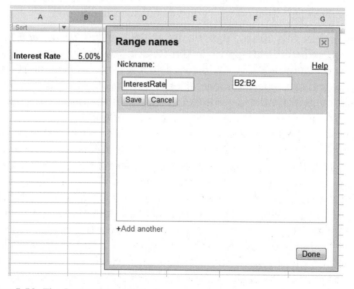

Figure 5-50: The Range names dialog

Once you define the range name for a cell or cell range, you can use it in a formula. For example, if you assign a range name of InterestRate to cell B2 in Figure 5-48, then the calculation in cell F4 becomes this:

```
=E4 * InterestRate
```

The interesting thing about this approach: you can now copy the formula without having to worry about cell references changing. Unlike cell references, range names do not change.

ExplainED

Use range names to prevent cell references from changing when copying a formula that relies on a fixed cell in its calculation.

Sheet Protection

When you collaborate with other users; that is, when you share your spreadsheet with invited collaborators (see Chapter 3), you might have elements of the spreadsheet you do not want everyone to be able to change. In this case, you can use the sheet protection to limit the write capability to a specific sheet. *Sheet protection* allows you to limit who among your collaborators on a spreadsheet has access to a specific sheet. If you use multiple sheets, you can further restrict access to one or more of those sheets. To use sheet protection, you must first select the sheet you wish to protect (see previous section on multiple sheets). Next, choose the "Protect sheet" option from the "Tools" menu. This opens the "Protect sheet" dialog (see Figure 5-51).

In this dialog, you can choose from one of three options for protecting a sheet by selecting the corresponding radio button for a given option (see Figure 5-51). The first option allows anyone who is a collaborator to edit the selected sheet, which offers no protection beyond what currently exists. The second option ("Only me") allows only the owner of the spreadsheet to edit the selected sheet. This is the strongest option. The third option ("Me and the collaborators selected below") allows you to select people from the current list of collaborators who can edit the current sheet. To select from the list of collaborators, use the check box shown to the right of each collaborator (see Figure 5-51). Click the "Done" button at the bottom of the dialog after you choose your desired level of protection. This change will then be applied to the current sheet. Thus, sheet protection lets you refine who has access to specifics parts of the spreadsheet. When a sheet has protection applied, a small padlock symbol appears in the sheet tab at the bottom of the spreadsheet window.

Figure 5-51: The "Protect sheet" dialog

NotED

Sheet protection is not as extensive as the protection mechanisms available in OpenOffice or Microsoft Office.

Spreadsheets does not offer the same level of sheet protection you can find in other major office suites such as OpenOffice or Microsoft Office. In Spreadsheets, you can only protect at the sheet level. At the time of writing, you cannot protect at the cell, row, or column level. However, this facility is currently on Google's radar for review. If you wish to protect several elements in a multiple sheet spreadsheet, you should endeavor to place all those elements on a single sheet, so that their modification can be restricted.

Data Validation

When creating a spreadsheet to perform quite complex tasks, you are often at the mercy of someone entering invalid data, no matter how sophisticated the spreadsheet. That is, if a series of calculations is arranged that relies on a few, or even a single cell, then invalid data in that cell can cause the calculations to be incorrect. This can be as simple as entering a number that is outside an expected range or accidentally pressing a character key instead of a number key. Indeed, any number of incidents can lead to an incorrect value being entered into a cell, which can then propagate into a series of errors due to the sophisticated chain of calculations related to cell references.

Spreadsheets lets you apply *data validation* criteria to cells (or ranges of cells) to ensure that input conforms to the criteria you specify. To apply data validation to cells, select the "Data validation" option from the "Tools" menu; this brings up the "Data validation" dialog (see Figure 5-52).

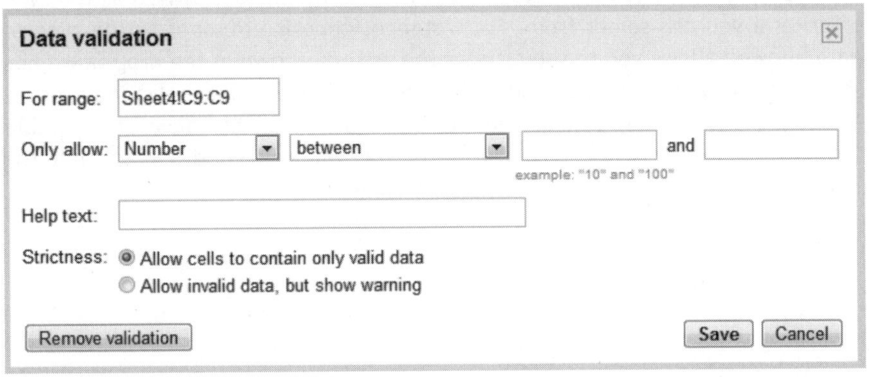

Figure 5-52: The "Data validation" dialog

This dialog lets you select the range of cells (or a single cell) you wish to apply the validation criteria to. The default is the currently selected cell. To apply validation to a different cell or range, either type the range directly into the

"For range" text box in the dialog or click the spreadsheet and use the cursor to select a cell or range of cells. When you click the spreadsheet, the dialog minimizes, and you see the cell selection dialog (see Figure 5-53). Select the cells you want to apply the validation criteria to and click the "OK" button at the bottom of the dialog when you're finished. The cell selection dialog disappears, and the data validation dialog reappears.

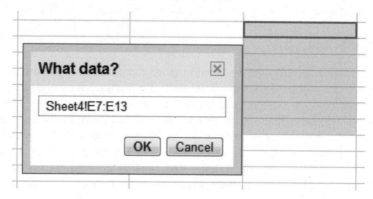

Figure 5-53: Cell selection

Once you select a range of cells to apply validation criteria to, you select the type of data you will restrict the cells can contain. Do this by choosing Number, Text, or Date from the "Only allow" drop-down box in the dialog. The type of data you allow dictates the fields that display in the dialog, as well as the type of criteria you can select from. For instance, choosing Number as the type of data allowed allows you to select from the criteria shown in the drop-down box shown in Figure 5-54. Choosing the "between" criteria displays two input boxes to the right that allow you to enter the boundaries of the range of allowable data values. For instance, you can enter the values 50 and 100 to limit the input in this range of cells to values between 50 and 100.

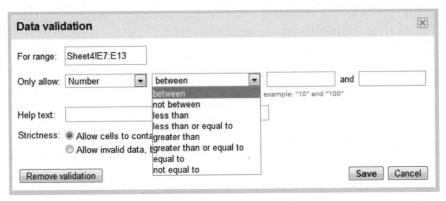

Figure 5-54: Selecting a criteria for numbers

Underneath the criteria specification, you can enter some help text. This text is displayed when someone hovers the mouse cursor over the input cell. You can also adjust the strictness level of the data validation by selecting either "Allow cells to contain only valid data" or "Allow invalid data, but show warning." If you choose to allow invalid data, the cell will display with a small orange symbol in the top-right corner; this symbol indicates that the cell contains invalid data, but the data will still be allowed. If you choose to allow only valid data, typing in something that violates the validation criteria causes the cell to be re-opened for editing; it also causes an error message to be displayed beside the cell. For example, take another look at Figure 5-54. If you were to choose a validation criteria of numbers between 50 and 100 for a cell, and then enter the value 45, Spreadsheets would display an error message next to the cell, with the contents in edit mode (see Figure 5-55). To save the data validation criteria you specified in the dialog, click the "Save" button on the bottom right of the dialog. To exit without saving any of the criteria, click the "Cancel" button.

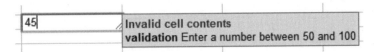

Figure 5-55: Invalid contents in a cell

When a cell is in edit mode after data validation detects a problem, pressing the Return key or clicking out of the cell causes the contents of the cell to revert to their state before the invalid data was entered. To remove data validation on a cell or range of cells, you need to choose the "Data validation" option from the "Tools" menu, and then click the "Remove validation" button

271

at the bottom left of the dialog when the data validation dialog box appears. This removes the validation criteria for those cells.

There has been a lot of criticism over Spreadsheets' data validation options. Specifying the validation criteria is limited, and you cannot use cell references in the criteria fields. This means you cannot parameterize any data validation, and the application of the data validation criteria to cells can take a small amount of time to activate. This amount of delay depends on Internet loads and the complexity of the spreadsheet. This is because the changes are being applied over the Internet to a sheet that other collaborators may be editing simultaneously.

Conditional Formatting

It is possible to apply conditional formatting to cells in a spreadsheet. This will basically allows you to change the appearance of data in a cell based on some criteria you establish. For instance, you might color values in a cell red if they are negative. This ability allows users to see areas of poor performance quickly in a financial document. However, the conditional formatting available in Spreadsheets, referred to as "Change color by rules," is extremely limited. This feature only lets you set up simple rules to change either a cell's text or background color based on its contents. To apply conditional formatting to a cell, select the cell or range of cells that you wish to apply the formatting to; note that you cannot select them during the process of applying these rules. Next, choose the "Change colors with rules" option from the "Format" menu on the menubar to bring up "Change colors based on rules" dialog (see Figure 5-56).

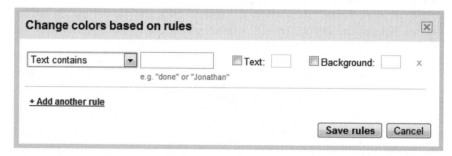

Figure 5-56: The "Change colors based on rules" dialog

You can select your criteria for the rule by clicking the first text box in the dialog, which displays the drop-down list of criteria (see Figure 5-57). You can choose from rules based on cells containing text, dates or numbers, and each of the categories has several possible rules you can select from (see Figure 5-57). The type of rule you choose also determines the input boxes associated with the rule. For example, Figure 5-57 shows the "is between" rule and two input boxes to the right of the rule; you use these input boxes to set the lower and upper boundaries. For each rule, there are "Text" and "Background" check boxes you can select. When you select one (or both) of these check boxes a color chooser palette will appear; from here, you just select the color of the text or background of the cell you want to use if the rule is satisfied. For example, assume that you enter the boundaries as 50 and 100 for Figure 5-57; also, assume that you   choose the text to be colored red. At this point, the cell will display any number entered between 50 and 100 in red.

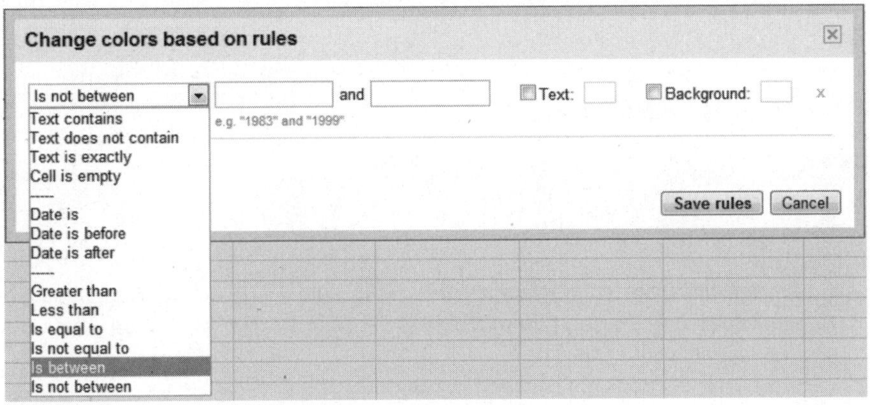

Figure 5-57: A drop-down list of selectable criteria

When you finish specifying the rule for the color, click the "Save rules" button or click the "Cancel" button to exit without saving. Sometimes you will need more complex rules. For example, you might want to create rules that display values of various ranges in different colors. You can add more rules for the cell by clicking the "Add another rule" link shown at the bottom of the dialog (see Figure 5-56). For example, Figure 5-58 shows three rules set to change the color of a cell based on the three intervals: greater than 50, less than 100, and less than 0. If you use multiple rules, then you need to be aware that they may not be applied correctly if you specify them in the wrong order. Spreadsheets begins by applying the rules for conditional formatting, but stops at the first rule that is applicable, using that corresponding color. If you wish to delete an existing rule, you can do so by clicking the small cross symbol (x) to the right of the rule (see Figure 5-58).

273

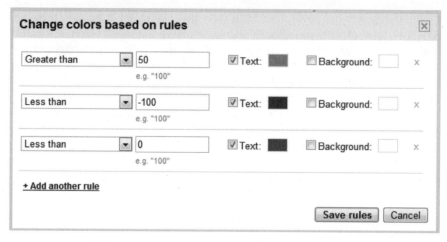

Figure 5-58: Using multiple rules

ExplainED

If you use multiple color-change rules, the rules will be applied in the order you specify them; Spreadsheets will stop at the first rule that is applicable and apply that color.

These rules are fairly simplistic. Again, one of the biggest disadvantages of these rules is that you cannot parameterize them. That means that you cannot use cell references or formulas within the rules, which severely limits their usefulness. However, there are workarounds for some common problems. For example, assume you wish to set up a specific cell (A1) with a number, and then enter numbers in other cells, such as cells A2 to A5. Now assume you want to color code these cells, depending on their relationship to cell A1, For instance, you may wish to color cells green if their value is equal to or greater than cell A1, yellow if their value is between the value of cell A1 and 50% of A1, or red if their value is less than 50% of the value of A1. You cannot do this directly because you cannot use formulas within the rules; however, you can insert a small thin column to the right of these cells, and place a formula in each cell to divide the cells value by the value in cell A1. You can then set up color change rules for the adjacent cells in the column that contains the formulas, and then set both the background and text colors to the same value. This would have the effect of placing a corresponding color bar to the right of each of the cells containing values, based on a cell's relationship to cell A1. This is not an ideal solution, but it is a workaround.

Freezing Rows and Columns

When dealing with large spreadsheets that contain a lot of data, you will often find yourself in a situation where you need to scroll either vertically or horizontally to access a different part of the spreadsheet. When you do this, any headings in the first row will scroll off the top of the window, and any columns you may need to remain visible will scroll off to the left of the spreadsheet. You can eliminate this problem by *freezing* rows or columns, fixing them in place so they do not scroll. For example, consider the small sheet shown in Figure 5-59.

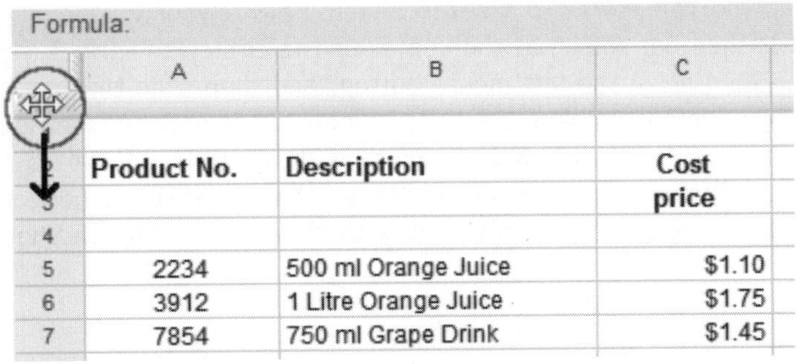

Figure 5-59: A spreadsheet with column headings and an important first row

When you use the vertical scroll bar on the right of the spreadsheet window, the spreadsheet will scroll up, including the column headings shown in Figure 5-59. You can freeze the column headings by manipulating the sort-bar. You can move the sort bar by placing your cursor on the hashed bar, which is shown at the center of the circle in Figure 5-59. Click and hold down the left mouse button, then slide the sort bar either up or down, between rows 1 and 11. When you release the mouse button, the sort bar will be placed at that point. Anything above the sort bar will be frozen; that is, when you use the vertical scroll bar at the right of the page, the rows above the sort bar will not scroll (see Figure 5-60).

Formula:						
	A	B	C	D	E	F	G
1							
2	Product No.	Description	Cost	Sell	Quantity	Revenue	Profit
3			price	price	sold		
9	6743	750 ml Apple Juice	$0.99	$2.99	16454	$49,197.46	$32,908.00
10	2141	350 ml Apple Juice Pack	$0.45	$1.50	29526	$44,289.00	$31,002.30
11	2521	1 Litre Apple Juice	$1.05	$3.50	16155	$56,542.50	$39,579.75
12						$438,991.27	$248,419.73
13							
14							

Figure 5-60: Frozen rows above the sort bar

Similarly, if you have a lot of rows in the spreadsheet, then scrolling horizontally will scroll the first rows off the left of the screen. Often these rows can contain a Part Number or ID Number that you need to remain in place as you examine columns further out. You can freeze columns in much the same way that you can rows. To freeze columns, place your cursor on the small vertical hashed bar shown at the center of the circle in Figure 5-61(a). Next, click and hold down the left mouse button, and then slide the sort bar either left or right, between columns 1 and 6. When you release the mouse button, a vertical bar will be placed at that point, as shown in Figure 5-61(b). Anything to the left of the vertical bar will be frozen; that is, when the horizontal scroll bar is used, these columns won't scroll with the rest of the spreadsheet.

(a)

Formula:			
		B	C
1			
2	Product No.	Description	Cost
3			price
4			
5	2234	500 ml Orange Juice	$1.10
6	3912	1 Litre Orange Juice	$1.75
7	7854	750 ml Grape Drink	$1.45

(b)

Formula:				
	A		D	E
1				
2	Product No.		Sell	Quantity
3			price	sold
4				
5	2234	$1.10	$2.50	31265
6	3912	$1.75	$3.75	18798
7	7854	$1.45	$3.10	22327

Figure 5-61: Freezing columns

You can also freeze rows and columns using the "Tools" menu on the menubar. You can access these menu options by selecting the "Freeze rows" or "Freeze columns" options from the "Tools" menu. Under each of these options, you can choose to freeze up to the first ten rows of a spreadsheet or the first five columns. These same limitations apply when dragging the bars to freeze rows or columns. You cannot drag the sort bar past row 10, nor can you drag the vertical bar past column 5.

NotED

Currently you can only freeze a maximum of 10 rows and 5 columns.

Using the "Solve" Tool Spreadsheets includes a tool that helps you solve particular types of maximization and minimization problems. These are called optimization problems, and you can encounter them in a variety of situations, including the Finance, business, and scientific fields. Spreadsheets' "Solve" tool provides functionality similar to the "Solver" feature in both OpenOffice Calc and Microsoft Excel. This tool basically allows you to allocate different resources to maximize some variable, such as profit within a business-type problem.

The best way to see how the "Solve" tool works is to study an example. Consider this simple example, where you have a bakery that makes and sells three products (see Figure 5-62).

Formula:

	A	B	C	D	
1		Ovens		10	
2		Baking Sheet Capacity per oven		140	
3		Fixed Cost per month		$4,000	
4					
5		White Bread	Muffins	Bagels	
6	Dough Capacity	8000	10000	6000	
7	Baking Sheets Capacity	10	30	20	
8	Profit	0.1	0.05	0.08	
9					
10					
11		White Bread	Muffins	Bagels	
12		1	1	1	
13					
14			Constraints		
15	Bread		<=	8,000	
16	Muffins		<=	10,000	
17	Bagels		<=	6,000	
18	Baking Sheet Usage	0.18333333333333	<=	1400	
19					
20	Profit	-$133.103333333333			
21					

Figure 5-62: A spreadsheet with baking problem data

In the baking problem, you have three products: white bread, muffins, and bagels. Now assume that the bakery has the capacity to produce the dough for 8000 white breads, 10,000 muffins and 6000 bagels per day. Each baking sheet can hold 10 white breads, 30 muffins, 20 bagels. Each pan can also hold a mixture of each: three muffins are equivalent to one white bread, as are two bagels. The profit for each of the three products on a per item basis is 10 cents for white bread, 5 cents for a muffin, and 8 cents for a bagel.

There are some fixed quantities that represent assumptions in the problem: The bakery has 10 ovens, each oven has a capacity of 140 baking sheets per day, and the cost of running the bakery is $4,000 per month, regardless of what it bakes. Also assume that each month has 30 days.

These elements of the problem are represented in rows 1-8 of the spreadsheet (see Figure 5-62).

In this scenario, you can use the "Solve" tool to help maximize the profit per day by deciding what mix of white bread, muffins and bagels to bake each day.

In row 12, you set up the figures that represent the number of white breads, muffins and bagels to be baked each day. These are currently set to one (1) each. The "Solve" tool will change these to maximize the profit shown in cell B20.

The current profit is calculated using this formula, which is calculated from the profits of each of the different items in row 8 and the number of items baked in row 12:

=(B8*B12 +C8*C12 +D8*D12) − (D3/30)

The problem also has the following constraints:

- Total white breads cannot exceed 8,000
- Total muffins cannot exceed 10,000
- Total bagels cannot exceed 6,000
- The baking sheet usage—which is calculated (=B12/B7 +C12/C7 +D12/D7) using the number of white bread, muffin and bagel items baked at row 12, divided by their respective baking sheet capacities in row 7, and then added together—cannot be more than the total number of baking sheets per day, which is 1,400 (10 ovens x 140 sheets per day)

You can now use the "Solve" tool to maximize the profit by changing the number of each of the items to bake, based on the constraints. Select the

"Solve" option from the "Tools" menu on the menubar to bring up the "Solve" dialog (see Figure 5-63).

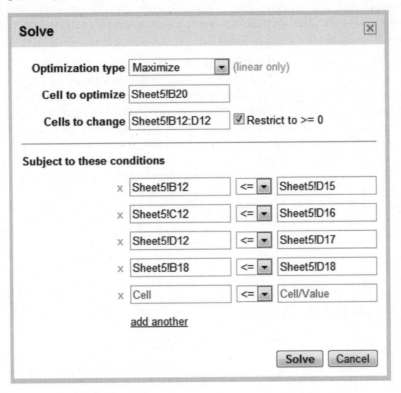

Figure 5-63: The "Solve" dialog

All the constraints have been entered in the solve dialog shown in Figure 5-63. Begin by using the top drop-down box to state whether you want to maximize or minimize something. In this case, you will maximize the profit, so you select *Maximize*. Next, choose the cell to maximize by clicking the "Cell to optimize" box and then clicking the cell in the spreadsheet that contains the profit calculation. You do this the same way you select cells you want to change. The cells to change will be the three cells in row 12, which contains the number of each of the items to bake. The "Solve" utility will calculate the optimum number of each item to bake to maximize the profit. To enter the constraints, you need to select a cell that contains a value you want to constrain. The first three values are the numbers of each of the items in row 12, and their constraints are the maximum number of each of these items that can be baked. For example, you can see the number of white breads to be manipulated in cell

B12 and its constraint in cell D15 (the value 8,000). You can select the constraint symbol between the two fields from a drop-down box. You can use either <= (less than or equal to), =, or >= (greater than or equal to). The last constraint is that the total baking sheet usage given by the equation in B18 must be less than the value in D18.

You can add as many constraints as you want; however, adding too many constraints will slow the calculation down. When you finish setting up the problem, click the "Solve" button at the bottom right of the dialog or click "Cancel" button to exit. Clicking "Solve" in the dialog in Figure 5-63 prompts the utility to manipulate the number of items in an effort to maximize the daily profit, which will also be shown in the spreadsheet (see Figure 5-64). You can see the number of each of the items you should make to maximize your profits in row 12, as well as the projected, maximized profit in cell B20.

10				
11		White Bread	Muffins	Bagels
12		7,667	10000	6000
13				
14			Constraints	
15	Bread		<=	8,000
16	Muffins		<=	10,000
17	Bagels		<=	6,000
18	Baking Sheet Usage	1400	<=	1400
19				
20	Profit	$1,613.33		

Figure 5-64: Results of the "Solve" utility's calculations displayed in a spreadsheet

The "Solve" utility is an interesting feature, and it can be a powerful tool in the right circumstances. The utility's most significant limitation at this time is that the underlying equations it solves must be linear. However, this constraint is similar to those you see in the solving utilities of other spreadsheet software.

Using Gadgets

The last feature we will discuss in this section is the use of Google Gadgets, which are objects that can be incorporated into your spreadsheet. Gadgets provide some visual representation of data in some of the cells of the spreadsheet. There are quite a number of gadgets you can incorporate into your sheets, and the list continues to grow. While we cannot discuss them all, they are all essentially similar in how you incorporate them and then configure them to represent some cells in the sheet. The example in this section we will demonstrate is called the Timeline gadget.

To place a gadget in your spreadsheet, choose the "Gadget" option from the "Insert" menu to bring up the "Gadget Selection" dialog (see Figure 5-65). You can use this dialog to select an appropriate gadget to include in your spreadsheet. The gadgets are divided into categories that you can select from the links shown on the left in Figure 5-65.

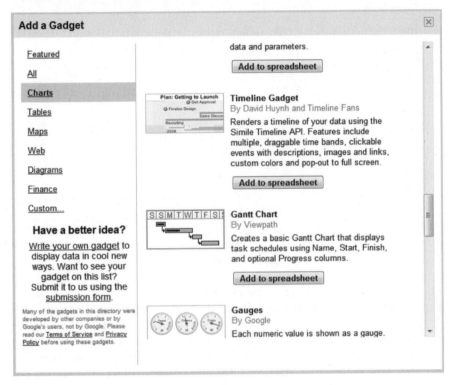

Figure 5-65: The gadget selection dialog

In this example, you select the "Timeline gadget" option from the "Chart" category on the left. Once you locate the gadget you want to include, click the "Add to spreadsheet" button associated with the gadget; this incorporates the gadget into your spreadsheet. When you add the Timeline gadget, you will see the gadget in edit mode (see Figure 5-66). In edit mode, you configure the parameters of the gadget as required. To find out more about each gadget, click the "Help" link shown in the upper left corner of the gadget (see Figure 5-66).

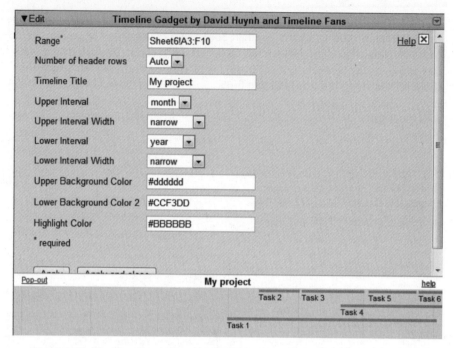

Figure 5-66: The Timeline gadget in edit mode

The Timeline gadget displays a timeline chart with clickable timelines based on task names, start dates, and end dates within the spreadsheet. To work, the Timeline gadget requires data similar to what you see in Figure 5-67. This gadget requires a number of tasks listed with start and end dates, and possibly a longer description that will be shown if a timeline is clicked. The gadget also needs images and links to be displayed in certain circumstances; these are not necessary for minimal functioning. In this example, only the headers were included. While editing the gadget in edit mode (see Figure 5-66), you specify the ranges for the spreadsheet data (see Figure 5-67), and then enter a Title for the timelines and other configuration data. All of these affect what the gadget will display. This data will be different for each gadget selected.

	A	B	C	D	E	F
1						
2						
3	title	start	end	description	image	link
4	Task 1	01/01/2010	03/04/2010	a longer description for task 1		
5	Task 2	15/01/2010	02/02/2010	a longer description for task 2		
6	Task 3	03/02/2010	02/03/2010	a longer description for task 3		
7	Task 4	20/02/2010	25/04/2010	a longer description for task 4		
8	Task 5	04/03/2010	25/03/2010	a longer description for task 5		
9	Task 6	26/03/2010	04/05/2010	a longer description for task 6		
10						

Figure 5-67: The Timeline gadget input cells

Once you finish editing the gadget and filling out all required fields with range data from the spreadsheet, click the "Apply and close" button at the bottom of the edit window. Your gadget will then be displayed in the spreadsheet (see Figure 5-68). Clicking one of the task lines brings up a bubble that shows additional task details, as entered in the spreadsheet (see Figure 5-68).

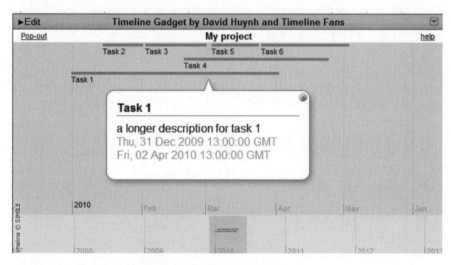

Figure 5-68: The final display of the Timeline gadget

Gadgets provide a method for further enhancing the visual representation of data within a spreadsheet. Many of the gadgets are based on the Google Spreadsheets' Chart API, which means you can also find them in Spreadsheets' "Charts" menu selection.

Inserting a Chart

One of the things that makes spreadsheets so powerful, apart from their ability to model different scenarios by plugging in new numbers to see what happens, is that they let you quickly produce charts from the data within a range of cells. Being able to produce visual data quickly from rows of numbers helps us as humans to consolidate the information contained within a spreadsheet. Indeed, for complex spreadsheets, visual data is necessary for an understanding of the relationships that may exist between elements of the spreadsheet. Spreadsheets lets you insert charts within spreadsheets, just as other spreadsheet software does. There are some limitations with Spreadsheets' charting features. For example, the range of charts is not as extensive the range of charts you can find in other office suite software, and the formatting and data selection options are limited. However, it must be pointed out that, for a Web-based office suite, Spreadsheets is extremely sophisticated. Also, Google is improving Spreadsheets' features all the time.

To insert a chart within a sheet, choose the "Chart" option from the "Insert" menu item on the toolbar; this displays the "Create" chart dialog window (see Figure 5-69).

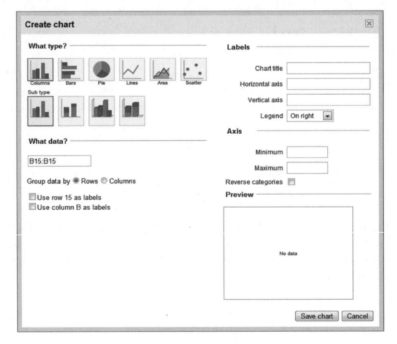

Figure 5-69: Create chart dialog window

Chart Elements

This dialog includes several options for setting up your charts. The dialog window is divided into a number of areas, and each area contains fields or drop-down boxes with options that control the way the data is grouped for display, as well as the look-and-feel of the charts. You will learn more about these in the sections that follow; you will also see some practical examples that show you how to insert and use two different types of charts.

Chart Types

There are six basic types of charts to choose from in the "What Type" area of the "Create chart" dialog (see Figure 5-69). These are located at the top left area of the dialog window, and each chart type is represented by a small icon. Each chart type also includes several subtypes. The chart types are:

Columns: Standard column chart types, including clustered and stacked

Bars: Charts that display their bars displayed horizontally, offering an alternative to the vertical column-charts

Pie: Standard pie charts with pull-apart capability

Lines: Line charts for a variety of different charting requirements

Area: Standard area charts

Scatter: Scatter charts that are useful for plotting data between two variables

Each of the chart types allows you select from one of a several possible subtypes. For example, the Column chart type has four subtypes. The first displays a standard column chart if one column of data is selected, but displays a clustered column chart if more than one column is selected. The third option is just a 3-D rendering of the first subtype. The second subtype displays a standard column chart if one column is selected, but a stacked column chart if more than one column is selected. The fourth subtype is a 3-D rendering of the second subtype. The Bar chart type has similar options.

You select a chart type by clicking one of the icons that represent the different chart types. Once you select a chart type, you need to select which subtype you want to use. If you don't select one, your chart will default to the first subtype.

NotED

The chart type you choose will depend on the data ranges you wish to chart. It does not always make sense to choose a particular type of chart for some data ranges.

3-D Charts

Some chart types will have 3-D rendered versions among their subtypes. This is to provide a more visually appealing alternative in some circumstances. For example, the Column, Bar, and Pie chart types provide 3-D versions. Sometimes these types of charts can look good in a spreadsheet, but other times they can distract. You will need to experiment with your own data to see which version works best for a given set of data.

Data Range

You can see a section labeled "What data?" under the selection for chart type. This is where you select the data range you want to include in the chart. You can select the desired range of cells before you click the menu item to insert a chart, but you don't have to. In this case, the selected data range is displayed in the field in this section. If you did not select a data range prior to inserting a chart, you can do so now. If you click the spreadsheet, the "Insert chart" dialog window shrinks, letting you see more of the spreadsheet window. Select your data range and click the "OK" button in the smaller dialog window to restore the dialog window to its full size, (see Figure 5-69). Note that you must include the cells that contain the column and row headings that describe your data when you select a data range; these are used to determine how to label the chart.

Grouping

You now need to decide how you want to group the data. You can choose to group data by rows or columns. Generally speaking, if you select only one column of data to chart, you should select the "Group by Columns" option. If you select one row of data to chart, you should select the "Group by Rows" option. If you select multiple rows and columns, then the grouping you should choose will depend on how you want the chart to display. You will need to experiment.

As mentioned previously, you need to select the Row and Column headings as part of the data range. You can find two check boxes beneath the "Group data by" selection. You use these to decide which of the rows or columns in the data range will be used as labels. You will only have the option of choosing the first row or the first column in the selection as labels. This is one of Spreadsheets' basic charting limitations; you don't have the flexibility of choosing different rows or columns as labels.

Labels

In the top-right section of the "Create chart" dialog, you can now assign labels to elements on the chart, including the Chart Title and labels on the horizontal and vertical axes. The chart title should be entered, but the options for the horizontal and vertical axes may not always be available, depending on the chart type you have chosen to insert. For example, a pie chart has no vertical or horizontal axis. If the chart contains a "Legend," you can choose where to place it (or even not to place it) using the drop-down box beneath the Chart and axis titles.

Axis

You can decide how the numeric scaling on the axis should be shown by filling out the fields in the "Axis" section underneath the "Labels" section. This option will only be available if the chart type selected has an axis consisting of numeric quantities. For example, you won't see this option in a pie chart. By default, the scaling on the axis is determined by the minimum and maximum values in the data range. If the minimum value in the data range is 2000, then the axis will begin at the value 2000. You can change this. If you want the axis to begin on zero, type this value in as the minimum. Similarly you can specify the maximum you want to use.

Preview

As you change the options in the "Create chart" dialog, the preview section will display an updated scaled version of the spreadsheet. You can watch this section as you make changes to determine quickly whether you have chosen the correct options. In any case, you can always edit a chart and return to this dialog after you create a chart.

Limitations to Spreadsheets' Charting

As mentioned previously, Spreadsheets' charting features have some limitations. For example, there is a limit to the number to chart types and subtypes available. There is also a limit to the flexibility you have when specifying the columns and rows you want to use as labels at the point you create your charts. You can see this in action when you need to do to produce a chart from a spreadsheet that has been formatted for visual appeal, so it includes blank lines and columns to produce an uncluttered the spreadsheet. For example, the spreadsheet shown in Figure 5-46 has a blank row of cells in row 3 to separate the headings from the data. Additionally, the headings have been spread over two rows for formatting purposes. Both of these points will affect the charting feature's ability to produce graphs from the data without modification. The examples in the next two sections reveal strategies for overcoming this limitation.

Inserting a Pie Chart

In this example, you will produce a pie chart from the Revenue column in Figure 5-47 for the different juice pack containers in column B. A limitation of the pie charts in Spreadsheets is that the Label column (B) must be adjacent to the data column (F). You can address this by either altering the spreadsheet or making a copy of the relevant columns, and then building a chart from those. The easiest way to address this is to place a copy of the two columns in a separate sheet and then create the chart. The Overall revenue data is located in the "Income" sheet, so first create a new sheet and label it ("ChartData"). You could copy the range B5:B11 to B5:B11 in the "ChartData" sheet and do the same for range F5:F11, except copy the values only to C5:C11 in the "ChartData" sheet. However, this would only copy the values; if the original values in the "Income" sheet changed due to changes in the "Sales" sheet, the pie chart would not change because it would be based on the "ChartData" sheet's static data. Instead, you can duplicate the dynamic content of the two columns from the "Income" sheet in the "ChartData" sheet.

Note that the first cell to include in the pie chart from the "Income" sheet is B2, and the first cell from the Revenue column is F2. Move to the new "ChartData" sheet and type the following entries into the specified cells:

B2: =Income!B2

B3: =Income!B3

C2: =Income!F2

C3: =Income!F3

Now you can use Auto-Fill feature to finish. Select the cell range B2:C3, click the Auto-fill symbol, and drag it down another five rows, and release. This will fill the two columns with the appropriate data from the B and F columns from the "Income" sheet (see Figure 5-70). By using only cell references in the formulas (such as =Income!B2), you can ensure that if the data in the "Income" sheet changes, the data in the "ChartData" sheet will update, as well. Thus, the chart produced from the specified cell range will be dynamic. Now turn your attention back to the "Income" sheet.

	A	B	C
1			
2		500 ml Orange Juice	$78162.5
3		1 Litre Orange Juice	$70492.5
4		750 ml Grape Drink	$69213.7
5		2 Litre Grape Juice	$71093.61
6		750 ml Apple Juice	$49197.46
7		350 ml Apple Juice Pack	$44289
8		1 Litre Apple Juice	$56542.5

Figure 5-70: Auto-filled sheet

You can now insert the new pie chart in the ("Income") sheet, even though you are using the cell range in the "ChartData" sheet to generate it. Select the "Chart" option from the "Insert" menu to bring up the "Create chart" dialog (see Figure 5-69). Click the spreadsheet to make the dialog window shrink. Next, click the "ChartData" tab to move to the "ChartData" sheet, and then select the range, B2:C8. Now move back to the "Income" sheet and click the "OK" button in the minimized dialog window. The "Create chart" dialog will restore to its previous size, and you can see the cell range displayed in the "What data?" field:

    ChartData!B2:C8

Select the Pie chart type, and then the second subtype, which represents a 3-D pie chart. Next, select the "Group by Columns" and the "Use Column B as labels" check boxes. In the "Labels" section, type in "Revenue Chart" for the chart title (see Figure 5-71).

289

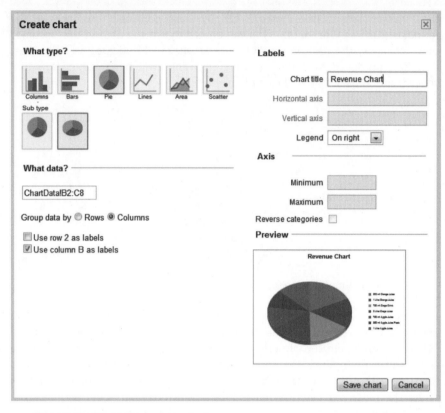

Figure 5-71: Creating a new pie chart

Now click the "Save chart" button to generate the chart (see Figure 5-72). If you click the chart, it will become active, and a small menu bar will appear at the top. However, if you click one of the colored icons in the legend to the right of the pie chart, the corresponding segment in the pie chart will explode outwards a small amount. Also, clicking a segment will display its label, numeric value, and the overall percentage of the pie chart the segment represents (again, see Figure 5-72).

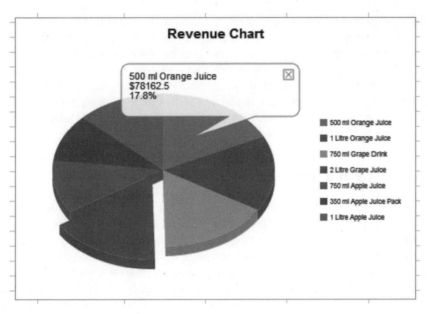

Figure 5-72: A pie chart showing the exploded feature

Positioning, Resizing and Editing a Chart

Once a chart has been place into a sheet, it can be positioned and resized relatively easily. If you click the chart, it will become active, and a small menu bar will appear at the top. You can click and hold the mouse key over this menu bar and drag the chart to any location in the sheet that you want. If you place your cursor on the border (edge) of the chart window, the cursor will change to either a horizontally or vertically resizing cursor. Just click and hold, and then drag the window edge to resize the chart. To resize both horizontally and vertically in proportion to each other, place the cursor on the bottom right or left corner; this causes the cursor to change to an angled resize cursor. Click and drag until you reach the desired window size.

In the menu bar located at the top of a selected chart window, there is one menu item: "Chart." Clicking this gives you a number of menu options. You can delete or edit the chart. If you choose to edit the chart, a dialog window identical to the "Create chart" dialog will open, and you can edit the chart as you did when you initially created it. You can also choose the "Save image" option. This option converts the chart to a graphic image, and you can download it to your computer's default download folder. You can then retrieve the file from there. This is a useful option for importing charts of your spreadsheets into a word processor for publishing.

The final option in the "Chart" menu is to move the chart to its own sheet. If you choose this option, the chart will be removed from the current sheet, a new sheet will be created, and the chart will be placed in this new sheet as a full window chart, occupying the entire sheet window. Once you move a chart to its own sheet, you cannot move it back, so be careful when using this option. The use of charts such as the one shown here is highly recommended when presenting spreadsheets with a lot of raw data. Charts add a visual dimension to the data that enhances the usability of spreadsheets.

Sorting a Column

Sometimes you would like to sort the rows in your spreadsheet to make a quick visual lookup a little easier. This is especially so when you have a few rows of data with multiple columns that need to be visually scanned to find specific values. For example, you might want to create a student list to look up a specific grade, a customer list to find a discount value, or even a competitor list in a sport event to find someone's average track time. If the data is sorted according to some criteria, finding the values becomes easier. You can easily sort the data in your spreadsheet by using the sort bar. When you use the sort bar to sort the spreadsheet, anything above the sort bar remains unsorted. Thus, you can move the sort bar up and down the rows; however, you still have that limitation insofar that you cannot currently move the sort bar down below row 10. You can move the sort bar to above row 1 if you want everything to be sorted. You begin the process of moving the sort bar by placing your cursor on the hashed bar shown at the center of the circle in Figure 5-73. Click and hold the left mouse, and then slide the sort bar either up or down, between rows 1 and 11. When you release the mouse button, the sort bar will be placed at that point.

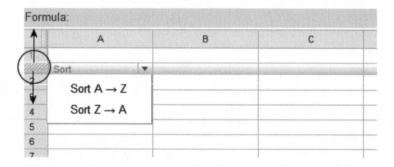

Figure 5-73: Manipulating and using the sort bar

To sort the data in your spreadsheet, decide which column you wish to sort on, and move the cursor over the sort bar in that column. The sort bar in that column will turn orange, and a small drop-down menu icon will appear on the sort bar in the right-hand side of the column (see Figure 5-73). In the drop-down menu, you can choose to sort in either ascending or descending order. If the column contains numbers, they will be sorted numerically; if the column contains text, the data will be sorted alphabetically (either ascending or descending). All the rows in the spreadsheet will be re-arranged according to the sorted values in the column you have selected.

	A	B	C	D	E	F
1	Customer No.	Last Name	First Name	Account Number	Sales Volume	Discount Value
2	21349	Mehra	Fulki	34764532	$6,789.00	2.50%
3	23345	Jones	Vernon	98275671	$3,441.00	2.50%
4	43561	Sung	Mai-Ling	80986445	$7,895.00	2.50%
5	56167	Darbyshire	Paul	23055672	$7,890.00	2.50%
6	65643	Wong	David	76896774	$34,212.00	10.00%
7	67832	McKilroy	Adam	34128765	$9,087.00	2.50%
8	87231	Habib	Amir	76845112	$564.00	1.00%
9	98127	Wienberg	Sally	68796775	$19,711.00	10.00%
10	98723	Schmidt	Eric	67098312	$421.00	1.00%
11						
12						

Figure 5-74: Unsorted spreadsheet rows

For example, if you have the rows in a spreadsheet similar to what is shown in Figure 5-74, then trying to find the Account Number of a customer whose name you have can be time consuming if the list is long. Sorting the spreadsheet by the Last Name column sorts all the rows in the column in alphabetical order (see Figure 5-75). You can now quickly scan the list alphabetically and find desired customer name, which is now across from the account number. You can re-sort the spreadsheet at any time on any column, depending on how you want to view and read the spreadsheet.

	A	B	C	D	E	F
1	Customer No.	Last Name	First Name	Account Number	Sales Volume	Discount Value
2	56167	Darbyshire	Paul	23055672	$7,890.00	2.50%
3	87231	Habib	Amir	76845112	$564.00	1.00%
4	23345	Jones	Vernon	98275671	$3,441.00	2.50%
5	67832	McKilroy	Adam	34128765	$9,087.00	2.50%
6	21349	Mehra	Fulki	34764532	$6,789.00	2.50%
7	98723	Schmidt	Eric	67098312	$421.00	1.00%
8	43561	Sung	Mai-Ling	80986445	$7,895.00	2.50%
9	98127	Wienberg	Sally	68796775	$19,711.00	10.00%
10	65643	Wong	David	76896774	$34,212.00	10.00%
11						
12						

Figure 5-75: Spreadsheet rows sorted on Last Name column

One limitation that is often leveled against Google Spreadsheets is that you can only sort on one column, whereas other spreadsheet packages allow you to sort on multiple columns. This is a limitation, but the single column sort feature will suit most circumstances, and you can work around it somewhat.

ExplainED

You can achieve a two column sort by first sorting on the secondary column in the desired order, then sorting on the primary column in the order required. This small work around currently works due to the nature of the sort algorithm, but it's possible this could change in future.

Using More Advanced Formulas

So far you have learned how to use simple formulas in Spreadsheets. You also learned how to use other formulas with moderately more complexity, such as the Future Value financial function. There are many other functions that that can add complexity to your spreadsheets. And while these functions do increase the complexity of the spreadsheet, they also add to its flexibility and increase your ability to model situations for reporting and other financial-decision making. In the last sections, you will look at some additional examples that rely on more complex formulas and functions from some of the categories you have learned about.

Using the IF Function for Conditional Calculations

The logical functions are always worth examining because they provide some interesting functions that enable some conditional processing in a spreadsheet. Consider the example shown in Figure 5-46 and Figure 5-47, where revenue and profit are calculated from sales data generated from the sale of a number of different juice packs by different sales people. If you want to offer bonuses to your sales people based on their total revenue to the company, first you need to calculate the total revenue per sales person, based on each person's sales of the different products and the selling price of those products. You can do this in a separate sheet called (name it "Bonus") by setting up the columns as shown in figure 5-76. Calculating each of the sales revenue figures for each sales person requires a long but simple formula. Place this calculation in the B2 cell:

```
=(Sales!B4*Income!D$5)+(Sales!C4*Income!D$6)+(Sales!D4*Income!D$7)+
(Sales!E4*Income!D$8)+(Sales!F4*Income!D$9)+(Sales!G4*Income!D$10)+
```

(Sales!H4*Income!D$11)

In this case, the formula is longer than it would otherwise be because the cells you are using are spread across different sheets, and you need to include the sheet names. All the formula consists of is the addition of all the sales numbers, multiplied by the selling price for each product. Note that this formula uses absolute cell referencing to anchor the row number from the "Income" sheet; otherwise, those row numbers would change when you copied the formula down the column. That would result in incorrect calculations.

Formula: =IF(B2>BonusThreshold,B2*BonusRate, 0)

	A	B	C	D
1		Total Sales Revenue	Bonus	
2	Paul	$69,498.89	$0.00	
3	Mai-Ling	$84,333.46	$2,530.00	
4	Adam	$82,277.49	$2,468.32	
5	Sally	$64,601.17	$0.00	
6	Ahmed	$65,416.62	$0.00	
7	Ann Lee	$72,863.64	$2,185.91	
8				
9				
10	Bonus threshold	$70,000.00		
11	Bonus Rate	3.00%		
12				

Figure 5-76: Using the IF function to calculate bonuses

Once you have the sales revenue for all sales people, you can calculate their bonuses. A bonus percentage rate was entered in cell B11, and a bonus threshold was set in B10. The reason for the bonus threshold is you only want to pay bonuses to sales people who sold more than $70,000 worth of goods. This example sets up two range names, *BonusThreshold* and *BonusRate*, to represent these respective quantities. You only want to allocate a bonus if the sales revenue was higher than $70,000 in the Bonus threshold cell. To implement this, you need to use the *IF* function, which is located in the Logical category of functions. The *IF* function looks like this:

IF(test, then_first_value, otherwise_second_value)

This is a conditional function. The test is evaluated first, and if it is true, the value in the cell becomes the first_value; otherwise, it becomes the second_value. You can make a quick test to see whether the value of the

295

revenue of a sales person is greater than the value of the bonus threshold. You can see the formula for cell C2 in the formula bar in Figure 5-76:

```
=IF (B2 > BonusThreshold, B2 * BonusRate, 0)
```

You can see from this formula that the test is B2 > BonusThreshold. If the value of the sales revenue in B2 is greater than the value in the cell referenced by the BonusThreshold range name, then the value of the cell becomes (B2 * BonusRate), which is the value of the sales revenue multiplied by the value of the percentage cell referenced by the BonusRate range name. If the test is not true; that is, if the value of the revenue is less that the bonus threshold, then the value of the cell becomes 0.

To place this formula in cell C2, select C2 and click the formula button. Select the "More formulas" option; next, in the "Insert a function" window, click the Logical function category on the left-hand side. Now double-click the IF function on the right-hand side within the Logical function category. Close the "Insert a function" window, and the IF formula will be placed in the cell C2, with the cell in edit mode. You now need to modify the formula, so it looks like the one shown in the formula bar in Figure 5-76. Press the Return key to enter the formula. You can now copy this formula and paste it to cells C3:C7. The references won't change when you copy this range because the formula uses range names to represent the bonus threshold and the bonus rate.

Using VLOOKUP

As an alternative to using the IF function, you can choose to allocate a bonus based on a sliding scale with a much lower cut-off point. You can accomplish this using the VLOOKUP function, which essentially allows you to look up a value in one column of a table, and then return the value from another column.

For example, consider the spreadsheet shown in Figure 5-77. This spreadsheet somewhat extends the example shown in Figure 5-76. The bonuses are allocated on a sliding scale according to the table in the slightly shaded cells in the range, F2:G6. This range represents a table where the first column is used as a lookup for the sales revenue. The second column is the value of the bonus percentage associated with the lookup in the first column. For instance, if the sales revenue was $17,500, you look down the first column (F) of the table until you come to the largest value, which is less than the value you are using to look up the table. In the case of $17,000, this would be the value $15,000 in cell F3. You then use the value of the percentage in the second column on the same row as the $15,000, which is 2%. So $17,000 worth of sales earns a 2%

bonus. You can then use this value to calculate the dollar value of the bonus for this person. The VLOOKUP function does this for you automatically. The format of the function looks like this:

```
VLOOKUP( Search, Array, index)
```

In the function description, the "Search" item is the value you are looking up. So, for the "Paul" sales person, the value you are looking up is in cell B2. The Array item is the range of cells that represent the table you are looking up. In this example, the range of cells F1:G6 is the table, but this has been given a range name of BonusTable. So you use BonusTable in the formula. The Index item represents the column number from which you will return the value associated on the same row with the lookup value you find in the table. In this example, column G represents the value to be returned, which is the table's second column. Thus, the value is 2. The VLOOKUP formula for cell C2 (see Figure 5-77) looks like this:

```
=VLOOKUP( B2, BonusTable, 2)
```

Formula: =VLOOKUP(B2, BonusTable, 2)

	A	B	C	D	E	F	G
	Sort						
1		Sales Revenue	Bonus percent	Bonus value		Bonus Table	
2	Paul	$12,395.00	0%	$0.00		$0.00	0%
3	Mai-Ling	$15,976.00	2%	$319.52		$15,000.00	2%
4	Adam	$19,456.00	2%	$389.12		$20,000.00	5%
5	Sally	$21,276.00	5%	$1,063.80		$25,000.00	7%
6	Ahmed	$25,678.00	7%	$1,797.46		$30,000.00	8%
7	Ann Lee	$30,100.00	8%	$2,408.00			
8	Samuel	$70,000.00	8%	$5,600.00			
9							
10							

Figure 5-77: Using the VLOOKUP function to calculate bonuses

You can copy this formula to the remaining cells as the range name BonusTable, so cell references won't change. You then simply use the returned percentage from the VLOOKUP in a simple calculation in column D to multiply the sales revenue by the percentage of the bonus earned.

The use of VLOOKUP can greatly enhance the flexibility of spreadsheets when some sort of sliding scale needs to be applied to the value of some quantity. You can find the VLOOKUP function in the Lookup category of functions.

Using Google Functions

For the last example of using more complex formulas in spreadsheets, you will look at Google functions. These are interesting, and they make it easy to perform some tasks in a Spreadsheets document that are otherwise difficult (but not impossible) to accomplish in other spreadsheet software. The reason this is easier in Google Docs is that you use this spreadsheet software from the Internet, which is serviced by a Google server. You are already online, and this functionality is offered through the Google server.

One Google function is the ability to look up stock quotes online and return various attributes of a specific company listed on the stock exchange to a spreadsheet. These functions are located in the Google category of functions that you see when inserting a function through the formula button on the toolbar. The function to look up listed companies and return attributes is called *GoogleFinance*. You access it using this formula:

```
=GoogleFinance( symbol, attribute )
```

In this formula, the symbol item represents the stock exchange code for a company to lookup. This can reside in a different cell, and you can use the cell reference in the formula. The attribute item is the attribute you want to return to the spreadsheet. A partial list of attribute items includes:

price: the current market price of the stock

high: highest price for the day

low: lowest price for the day

volume: the number of shares traded for the day

datadelay: the delay of the data stream for the stock in minutes

pe: the current Price to Earnings ratio

eps: earnings per share

change: the change in price since yesterday's close

changepct: percentage change since yesterday's close

closeyest: previous day's closing price

You must enclose the symbol and the attribute used in the formula in double quotes (e.g., "volume") unless you use a cell reference. Figure 5-78 shows you how to use this function in a formula. This example shows a number of attributes and illustrates how to use several different formulas for leveraging separate GoogleFinance functions. For example, the formula bar shows how to use the GoogleFinance function in the formula; which is located in cell I20 and shown at the top of Figure 5-78. The attribute name is used, but the ticker symbol comes from cell I18. This makes it easy for someone using the spreadsheet to type in the ticker symbol to look up any stock.

Formula: =GoogleFinance(I18, "Price")

Exchange Code	BAC values
Latest Price	$15.63
Earnings Per Share	$0.03
PE	553.86
Percentage change	2.76
Data Delay (mins)	0

Figure 5-78: Using the GoogleFinance function

You can use the GoogleFinance functions to increase the flexibility of a spreadsheet that might be calculating financial performance based on a stock portfolio. GoogleFinance functions enable you to incorporate some (almost) real-time data in your spreadsheet. You can then build complex calculations around the current stock Prices, Volume, Eps, and so on.

The stock ticker symbols refer to the various stock symbols used on the different exchanges. Primarily, the symbols used are taken from the NYSE (New York Stock Exchange), unless you precede the ticker symbol with an exchange code and a colon (:). For example, the symbol BAC will be taken from the NYSE. To look up a symbol on the ASX (Australian Stock Exchange), you would need to precede the stock you want to look up with the ASX symbol. For example, you might use the symbol, ASX:CBA.

There are limitations when using a GoogleFinance function use in a spreadsheet. Currently, you can have no more than 250 GoogleFinance functions in formulas in one spreadsheet. If you include two GoogleFinance functions in one formula, that counts as two functions. Also, the stock quotes are provided by external financial exchanges, so there is a disclaimer about the reliability of the data provided. As always when leveraging such data, you should use the data returned with caution.

Summary

In this chapter, we have covered in detail many of the basic and advanced features of Google Spreadsheets. The chapter began by covering the basic document functions, although you can find a full treatment of dealing with these spreadsheet document functions in the Google Docs chapter, which serves as the interface for all Google Docs. This chapter provided a full treatment of basic spreadsheet usage and walked you through how to format cells in a spreadsheet. This pair of topics gives a beginner the necessary information to start leveraging spreadsheets for the first time. However, for those readers more familiar with spreadsheets from other office suites, this chapter also provided hints and tips to help smooth transition to Google Spreadsheets. This chapter also covered how to use formulas and the difference between editing and placing formulas within the Google Docs environment. More advanced features covered in this chapter walked intermediate users through working with multiple sheets, sheet protection, data validation, and conditional formatting. It also covered the use of charts in Google Spreadsheets, explaining how to leverage them and touching on their limitations in the Spreadsheets environment. The chapter ended by looking at some of advanced formula usage, including specific functions only available in the Google Docs environment.

Readers new to the Google Docs environment will find the Spreadsheets component a robust and extensive tool that provides all the capabilities of other spreadsheet software, along with all of the advantages of the cloud-computing environment. Google Spreadsheets is an excellent example of the versatility of the Web environment and what can be achieved in responsive, Web-based, user-oriented applications.

Chapter 6

Google Docs - Presentations

Presentation-type software is used everywhere by people who want to make presentations to others, whether in person or over the Internet. Academics use presentation software for lectures; business leaders use presentation software for display of company results at shareholder meetings; and you can use presentation software, too. You can use presentation software for putting together either a professional-looking presentation for school or work, or even for a meeting at your local sporting club. Traditionally, presentation software is used to put together a series of slides that are projected onto a large screen; this software includes the ability to flick backwards and forwards between the slides. More recently, people have begun using presentations in a web-based setting. The advantages remain the same, whether you deliver the presentation in person or not. The ability to quickly add pictures; text in point form, whether bulleted or numbered; and other graphics, including the ability to set up templates for your logo; has helped such software become the tool of choice for anyone who delivers either oral or web-based presentations. In this chapter, we will cover how to create presentations in Google Presentations (Presentations). We will begin with the basics of Presentations, and then cover how to make the most of its features. At the end of the chapter, we will also provide some tips for creating good presentations.

Google includes Presentations in Google Docs. This suite enables you to create professional looking presentations similar to those in other major office suites, such as Microsoft Office or OpenOffice. By creating your presentations in an online environment, you have access to them from anywhere; you can also share these presentations with collaborators. You can upload existing presentations, or you can create new presentations online. This is usually done using the Google Docs interface discussed in Chapter 3, although it can also be initiated while editing an existing document. When a new presentation is created, you will see the blank presentation in your browser tab (see Figure 6-1).

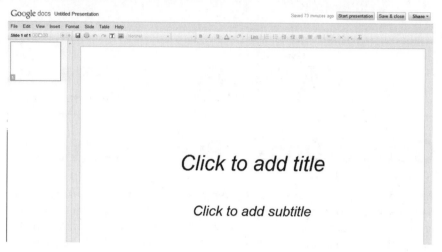

Figure 6-1: A blank Google Presentations document

Only part of the window is visible in Figure 6-1; for example, the bottom part of the opening screen does not contain any features other than the remaining half of the blank document. This screen does appear in one of your browser's tabs, which means you are operating in a browser environment, instead of a local window.

Elements of the Presentations Workspace

If we examine the Presentations working window a little closer, we can see the major elements of the Presentations environment that we will be working with throughout this chapter. Figure 6-2 shows an annotated, expanded view of the Presentations environment.

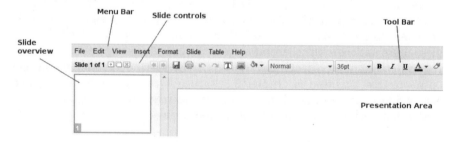

Figure 6-2: An annotated view of the Presentations environment

You can see that, as in other Google Apps, the menubar gives you access to Presentations' various functions and formatting options. The toolbar gives you quick access to a lot of functionality. Some of this functionality can be accessed by going through the menus, but the toolbar provides a shortcut to access many of the more commonly used features. To the left of the presentation area, you can see a smaller vertical area that contains a scrollable, visual list of all the slides in the presentation. This is a slide overview list, and you can use this to quickly scan down the list using the scroll bar to the left to select a slide for viewing in the presentation area. Just above the slide overview list, you can see a set of slide controls. These allow you to quickly insert and delete slides, as well as scroll through the overview list without the scroll bar. The presentation area is the main slide area, where you can add text, graphics, and other objects to build your slide presentation.

Menubar

At the top of the Presentations area, you can see the menubar, which provides a number of pull-down menus that enable you to perform many of the common functions associated with building your presentation. Here's a quick overview of the menu options:

- *File*: Lets you perform standard file functions and print your slide.
- *Edit*: Includes standard edit functions, such as redo, undo, copy paste, and so on.
- *View*: Allows you to begin viewing the presentation, show notes, and zoom in and out.
- *Insert*: Lets you insert objects, including drawings, shapes, text, images, and so on.
- *Format*: Lets you apply various format and alignment settings to text and objects.
- *Slide*: Allows you to insert new slides, copy slides, and delete slides.
- *Table*: Lets you insert and manipulate tables in your presentation.
- *Help*: Gets help on various aspects of Google Docs documents.

As we go through the various features of Presentations throughout this chapter, we will constantly refer to specific items on the menubar. We will use these items to manipulate and edit our Presentations as we progress. Additionally, this toolbar contains some of the more commonly used menu items, giving us a shortcut to features that can help us improve productivity. We will refer to these options as much as possible.

Toolbar

Just below the menubar is the Presentations toolbar, which gives you quick access to a number of commonly performed functions by clicking icons on the toolbar. Some of the toolbar icons are grouped according to common functionality (see Figure 6-3).

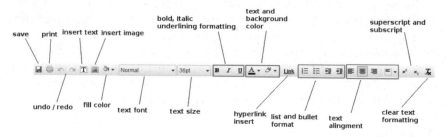

Figure 6-3: An expanded Presentations toolbar

The first two icons are the Save and Print icons, followed by the "Undo" and "Redo" icons. These allow you to undo an operation you have just performed, such as a formatting operation, or even a deletion or insertion. You click the "Undo" icon to reverse the last operation. If, after clicking the "Undo" option, you realize that the operation was all right after all, you can click the "Redo" icon to automatically restore the operation. The next two icons are the "Insert text" and "Insert image" icons. These are two of the most common operations you will perform when creating a slide presentation. There is also a fill color icon that allows you to quickly fill in large areas of the presentation with a specific color. The next two icons allow you to format text, specifically the font and size. The next grouping of three icons allows you to apply standard bold, italic, and underline formatting to text, while the following group lets you control the text and text background colors. The "Link" icon/link lets you insert hyperlinks in your document; it also allows you to control the appearance of the hyperlink. The list and bullet formatting group of icons allows you to format text as either bullet points or lists, as well as control the demotion or promotion of sub-points. The next group of icons allows you to control the alignment of selected text. There are two icons following this group that allow you to apply subscripting and superscripting formatting to text elements, while the final icon on the toolbar lets you clear any formatting applied to selected text or objects.

As we work through this chapter, we will refer back to these toolbar icons, as well as cover in detail the operations they perform and how they are applied.

Getting Help

You can get help for Presentations at any time by selecting the "Help" item on the menubar. This will display the drop-down "Help" menu in Figure 6-4, providing you with various ways to get help when using Presentations. Choosing the "Google Docs Help Center" item will load a web page into another browser tab, giving you a number of general links, as well as some specific links on particular Presentations topics. Some of these links are extremely helpful, but finding help on specific issues or features in Presentations can be difficult. You may sometimes need to persist and use the search facility located at the top of the Google Docs Help screen when looking for specific issues. If your problem is specific, then you may be better off consulting with other Google Docs users. The "Learn from Other Google Users" option on the "Help" menu takes you to a forum where you can scan discussion threads on specific topics and even post your own questions. There are some excellent tips on using the Presentation features of Google Docs in here.

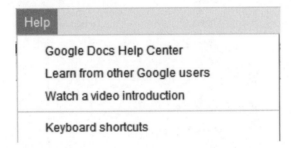

Figure 6-4: The drop-down "Help" menu

If you are new to Google Docs in general, you can find an introduction to Google Docs video on YouTube here. Selecting the "Watch a Video Introduction" option will load this video into a new browser tab. This introductory video is not specifically on Presentations, but Google Docs as a whole. As with Google Documents and Google Spreadsheets, becoming more familiar with Presentations can speed up your productivity; you can access a list of keyboard shortcuts by choosing the "Keyboard shortcuts" menu option. When you choose this option, a web page will be loaded into another browser tab, giving you a list of keyboard shortcuts that are commonly used in Google Docs applications.

Understanding Basic Presentation Functions

As with the other Google apps we have discussed, such as Documents and Spreadsheets, it is worthwhile to quickly review Presentations' standard document functions before you try using the program to create professional-looking slide presentations. These are the functions that you will need to be familiar with to load, save, and manipulate your presentations. These functions are accessed through the "File" menu item from the menubar (see Figure 6-5). Some presentation functions are available from elsewhere within Presentations, as well as from the Google Docs main interface, but all of them can be accessed through this menu item. We will briefly discuss these options here.

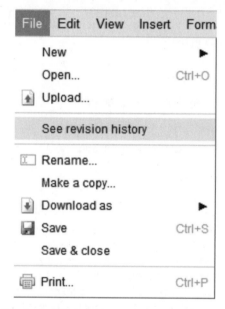

Figure 6-5: The drop-down "File" menu

Saving and Closing Presentations

One of the most common things you will need to do with your Presentations documents (as with the other Google Docs documents we have discussed) is to save it and close it when you are finished. This can be accomplished by selecting the "Save and close" option from the "File" menu. If the document is a new document and has not been saved yet, then choosing the "Save and close" option automatically gives the new document a name based on the first few words you typed in the first text area in the document. Thus, if "My slide show" was the first sentence you typed in the document, then this phrase would become the name of your new document. However, you can change the name of the document at any time (see the next section for information on how to do this). Once the document has been saved, the document tab will close, taking you back to the Google Docs interface tab. You should be able to see your new document from the Google Docs tab shortly afterward, though this may take a little while, depending on the server use at the time; some circumstances may require you to reload the tab.

If you wish to save the document, but not exit the application and continue editing, then you can either select the "Save" menu option from the "File" menu, or you can click the "Save" icon on the toolbar (see Figure 6-3). This will save the current document, and then you can continue editing. However, if the file is new and has not been saved previously, it will be automatically assigned a name from the first few words in the first text area in the document, as happens with the "Save and close" menu option. There is no need to periodically save the document as you work; it is automatically saved as you work on it. In fact, the document is saved approximately once every minute if changes are being made. This is necessary, so that when multiple people are working on the presentation at the same time, they can see any changes as soon as possible. The last time that the presentation was auto-saved is displayed in grayed-out lettering in the upper-right corner of the Presentations window. The auto-save feature is currently not able to be configured.

If you want to make a copy of a document before you make some important changes, you can choose the "Make a copy" option from the "File" menu, which will bring up the dialog box shown in Figure 6-6. You need to click the "OK" button to go ahead and make a copy of the document. If your document has collaborators, and you wish them to also have the copy available to them, check the "Also copy document collaborators" box before pressing the "OK" button. The new document will be given the same name as the existing document, except it will be preceded by the words, "Copy of." If your document name is "Test," the new document will be called "Copy of Test." You can change the name at a later time (see next section for more information). A copy of the current document will be made and loaded into a new browser tab. The tab name will reflect the name of the new copy. Any changes you make will then be made to the new copy you have created.

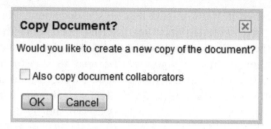

Figure 6-6: The "Copy Document" dialog box

Renaming a Presentation

While editing a presentation, you can change the name at any time by choosing the "Rename" menu option from the "File" menu. Choosing this option causes a dialog box to appear (see Figure 6-7), and the current name of the presentation will highlighted. You can then type the new name of the presentation and click the "OK" button; the new name will be reflected in the current browser tab. When you exit from editing the presentation, the new name should be reflected in the Google Docs interface tab, but this change take a short while to take effect, depending in the speed of the Internet and load on the server. You may need to reload the page.

Figure 6-7: The "Rename" dialog box

Opening Presentations

You can open a Presentations file from a number of places. You can open one from the Google Docs interface tab (as discussed in a previous chapter), or you can open another slide presentation while working on an already open presentation. When working on a presentation, you can choose the "Open" option from the "File" menu item, rather than closing it and then opening a different presentation. A new tab will be opened in the browser, and the Google Docs interface will be loaded, showing only the list of presentation files you have access to (see Figure 6-8). Choose the new presentation you wish to open from the list available. When you click one of the available presentations, it will be opened in a new tab, and then that will become the current presentation. You can then switch back and forth between the different presentations by clicking the appropriate tab at the top of the browser window.

Figure 6-8: Opening a presentation from the Google Docs interface tab

You can also open a new presentation by switching tabs to the Google Docs interface tab, which should still be available after you open your first presentation, unless you specifically close it. From this tab, choose the new presentation to open, and it will be opened in a new tab and become the current presentation. One thing to be aware of is that, when you open a new presentation while already editing another, this process will always create a new tab, with the Google Docs interface showing the presentation files first. Unless you first change to the Google Docs interface tab and choose a new presentation to open, you will end up with multiple interface tabs in the browser window. You will need to manually close the ones you don't want.

You can also create a new presentation from the "File" menu; just choose the "New ~TRA Presentation" option from the "File" menu, and this will create a new document tab that will become the current working presentation. When you create a new presentation in this way, it will be initially untitled. When you save it, it will be given a name based on the first few words of the first test area in the document; you can simply rename this document at a later time. In addition to creating a new slide presentation while editing an existing one, you can also create any new Google Docs document from this menu option.

Uploading Existing Presentations

You can upload existing slide presentations into Google Docs, so you can work with them online and collaborate together with multiple authors. To upload a presentation file from your local computer, select the "Upload" menu option from the "File" menu (see Figure 6-5) to open the Upload Files utility in a new browser tab (see Figure 6-9). To begin uploading existing files, select the "Select files to upload" link shown in Figure 6-9. This will take you to your computer's file-selection window, where you can choose a slide presentation file to load. The types of slide presentations currently supported are limited to Office PowerPoint (.ppt and .pps) files. OpenOffice slide presentations are currently not supported; however, you can save OpenOffice presentations in PowerPoint (.ppt) format, which you can then upload into Google Docs.

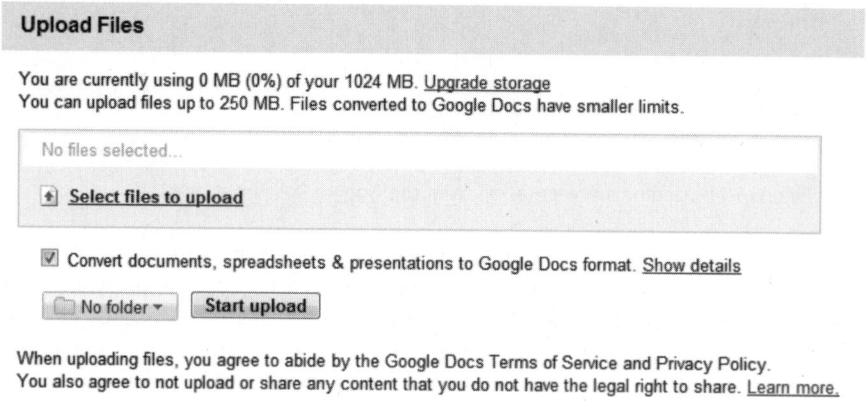

Upload Files

You are currently using 0 MB (0%) of your 1024 MB. Upgrade storage
You can upload files up to 250 MB. Files converted to Google Docs have smaller limits.

No files selected...

⬆ **Select files to upload**

☑ Convert documents, spreadsheets & presentations to Google Docs format. Show details

📁 No folder ▾   **Start upload**

When uploading files, you agree to abide by the Google Docs Terms of Service and Privacy Policy.
You also agree to not upload or share any content that you do not have the legal right to share. Learn more.

Figure 6-9: The "Presentation upload" option

After you select a file for uploading, you will be taken back to the Upload Files utility, where you can select more files to upload by clicking the "Select more files" link (see Figure 6-10). This allows you to select multiple files and batch upload them in one hit. When you are ready to upload, click the "Start Upload" button at the bottom of the list of files (again, see Figure 6-10). Each file will be uploaded in turn and converted to a Presentations document. When the process finishes, each file you have chosen to upload will have a green tick symbol displayed just to the left of the file name.

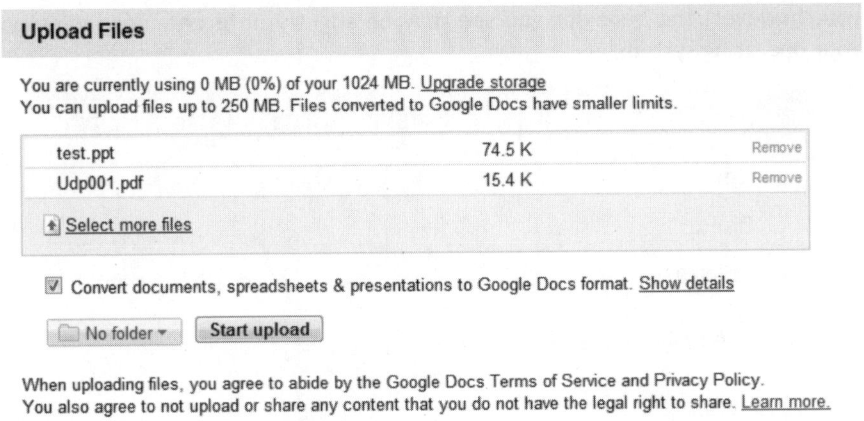

Upload Files

You are currently using 0 MB (0%) of your 1024 MB. Upgrade storage
You can upload files up to 250 MB. Files converted to Google Docs have smaller limits.

test.ppt	74.5 K	Remove
Udp001.pdf	15.4 K	Remove

[+] Select more files

☑ Convert documents, spreadsheets & presentations to Google Docs format. Show details

[📁 No folder ▾] [Start upload]

When uploading files, you agree to abide by the Google Docs Terms of Service and Privacy Policy.
You also agree to not upload or share any content that you do not have the legal right to share. Learn more.

Figure 6-10: Uploading multiple files

The newly uploaded slide presentations are not automatically opened in a browser tab, but they will be visible from the Google Docs interface tab (you may need to reload the page to access them). Depending on the complexity of the formatting in the uploaded document, it may not translate perfectly. In particular, there may be minor formatting problems if the uploaded presentation uses complex features from the slide-presentation software that you imported the document from. For example, some translation will occur if your presentation uses of some of the more exotic fonts or complex slide transitions.

Downloading Your Presentation to Your Computer

When you save your presentation, it is saved to your account at a secure Google online storage facility. However, there are times when you might wish to save your presentation locally, using one of your own computer's local storage options, whether that's a hard drive, a USB key, or something else. To do this, you need to select the "Download as" option from the "File" menu. This gives you a handful of format options that you can choose from to save your presentation as (see Figure 6-11). For Presentations, your choices are limited; you can choose between PowerPoint (.ppt), PDF (.pdf), or Text (.txt) formats. Choosing PDF, PowerPoint, or Text will create a new local document of the type chosen and download it to your local computer's default file-download area. Once the file is downloaded, you can then retrieve the file from your download area, as you would any other file. The default download area will be automatically chosen without any input from you; however, the behavior you see may be slightly different, depending on your operating system.

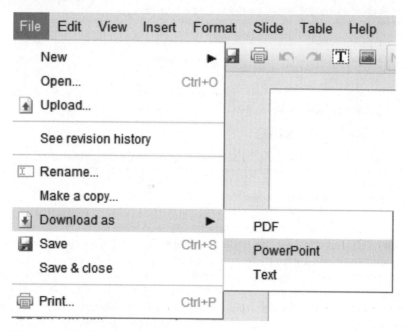

Figure 6-11: The "Download as" option

When you download your presentation as a PowerPoint file, you cannot save in .pptx format at this time, but only in the standard (.ppt) format. A good, portable format to utilize when downloading your presentation is the Adobe PDF format. Slide presentations translated to the Adobe format are able to be displayed using Adobe Presenter. All you need is the latest Adobe reader to be able to view the presentations in PDF format.

When you download your presentation, you must remember that your presentation is being translated into the specific file type you have specified. As with any translation, a best effort is made, but in some instances the format may not end up exactly the same as in the original. This will usually be caused by the complexity surrounding embedded objects; in the case of presentations, this can include things like different fonts, slide transitions, and so on. This is not a Google Docs-only problem. The same is true for any translation from one document format to another.

Printing Presentations

Although slide presentations are meant to be shown through a projector onto a large screen or viewed as a web-based presentation, often speakers will print a copy of their slides. This is so they can refer to the main points during a presentation without having to specifically stop and refer to the presentation displayed on a larger screen. Additionally, presentation slides can be annotated with speaker notes that may be printed out, but not displayed on the presentation itself, as the slides are viewed by an audience.

Printing your presentation is not done directly from Presentations, but is instead achieved by first transforming the document to PDF format, similar to the process of exporting the presentation in the "Downloading as" option (as described in the preceding section). You can print the spreadsheet by selecting the "Print" option from the "File" menu, or by clicking the "Print" icon on the toolbar. When you do, a "Print Preview" dialog box will appear (see Figure 6-12). You can use this dialog box to decide how the slides will be printed by using the drop-down "Layout" button in the left side of the dialog. You can choose to print from 1 to 12 slides per page. In the example in Figure 6-12, six slides per page is chosen, and the viewing area to the left shows you approximately what your printed page would look like. When printing slides, there is usually no need to print only one per page. This is because slides are usually in a large font size in a point-based form (bulleted or numbered), and printing six per page can be enough to help you quickly refer to the print-out and refresh your memory. There are two check boxes you can click, depending on whether you want to show the background image (if any) when printing, and whether you want the speaker notes to be printed, as well. If you want to print the speaker notes, you might need to restrict the layout to two slides per page. You will need to experiment to see which layout is best suited to the task at hand.

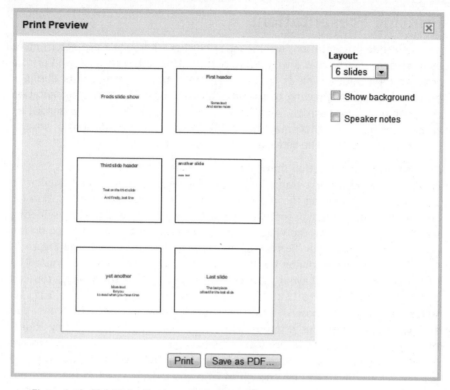

Figure 6-12: The "Print Presentation" dialog box

When you have chosen the desired layout for printing, you can print the presentation by clicking the "Print" button at the bottom of the dialog box. The presentation is then saved in PDF format in your computer's default download area. You then need to print this file locally on your computer, as you would any other file.

The reason the printing is handled in this way is due to the security restrictions placed on web pages that control browser access to elements of the local computer. Presentations is an application running in a web browser, so it is subject to the security limitations placed on all web-based applications. These limitations are for our own protection.

Creating Your First Presentation

To create your first presentation, you need to start a new presentation from the Google Docs interface (see Chapter 3) or create a new presentation from the "New" option in "File" menu, as described earlier in this chapter. When you open your new presentation initially, you will see the default first slide in the presentation area (see Figure 6-13). When you create a new presentation, the first slide is created with a layout consisting of two text areas: one for the title and one for the subtitle, as indicated by the "Click to add title" and "Click to add subtitle" elements on the screen, respectively. When a blank text area is created in a slide, default text such as "Click to add content" is displayed in the area until some text is entered into the area.

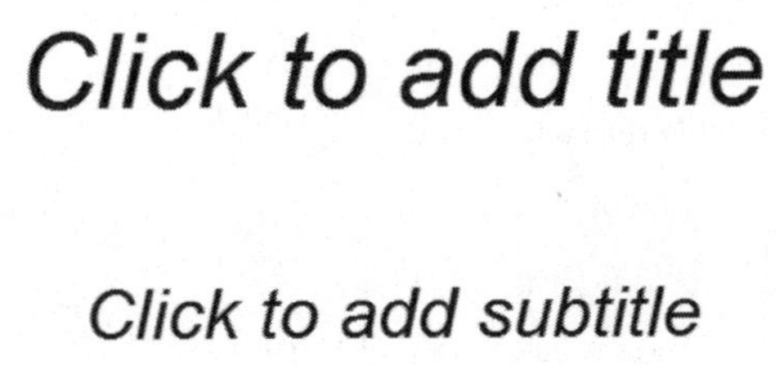

Click to add title

Click to add subtitle

Figure 6-13: Presentation's default opening slide

To add a title to the slide presentation, click the "Click to add title" area and enter the desired title of the presentation. To add a subtitle, click the "Click to add subtitle" area and enter a subtitle (see sample text entered in Figure 6-14). When you click a text area for the first time, the default text disappears, and your cursor flashes while waiting for you to enter some text. Here you enter the text you want and press the Return (or Enter) key to start a new line. If you keep typing, the text will wrap around to the beginning when it reaches the edge of the text area. When you click the text area, it will be outlined with a gray box that indicates its dimensions. To stop entering text in the text area, click out of the text area box to see the result.

One thing you should be aware of when creating presentations is that you should usually use point form (bulleted or numbered) in a presentation to write brief text sentences. The purpose of a presentation is to list points the speaker will expand on when giving an oral presentation using a slide show. The slides are as much for the speaker as they are for the audience, to prompt for the points that will be discussed at length throughout the talk. You also add graphics and other objects to the presentation slides to give additional information and enhance the points made, but the text should be kept to a minimum.

Cats or Dogs

which makes the better pet?

Paul Darbyshire

Figure 6-14: Entering a title and subtitle

ExplainED

People new at creating slide shows often make the mistake of putting too much text in a slide; keep text to a minimum and use large font sizes.

When you create a slide show, you should also consider the audience. The audience will usually be sitting far from the projected slide show, and thus the font sizes used should be large enough for people in the back to see. Many people who are new to creating slide shows often make the mistake of putting too much information in a slide and resort to using small text fonts. You need to put less text in the slide and use fonts large enough that everyone can read them. Notice the size of the fonts in the default text areas for the default first slide. You can change the fonts, of course, but you do need to consider the audience.

Inserting and Deleting Slides

You can easily insert new slides and delete existing ones using the slide controls just above the slide overview area (see Figure 6-15). The first slide control icon allows you to insert a new slide after the current slide; the last slide control icon allows you to delete the current slide. The middle icon allows you to create a duplicate copy of the current slide and insert it just after the current one. This is an extremely useful option because the slide layout options are limited. If you spend a lot of time creating a new slide with a custom layout, then, instead of duplicating that effort, you can use this option to create a copy of the slide and just modify the text in the new copy.

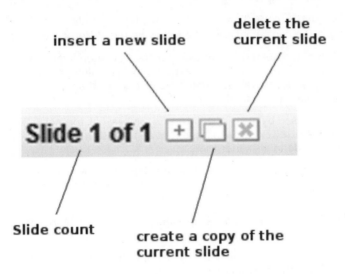

insert a new slide

delete the
current slide

Slide count

create a copy of the
current slide

Figure 6-15: The slide controls

You can also use the options in the "Slide" menu from the menubar. This drop-down menu has three options, each corresponding to one of the icons in the slide control bar shown in Figure 6-15. You can use icons or menu options to achieve exactly the same effects. In some instances it is much easier to use the icon bar. Additionally, as you are working on a slide, the corresponding slide in the overview will be highlighted in a light yellow color. This is the indication of the current slide. Thus when you insert a new slide, it will always be after the current slide. And when you delete the current slide, it will be the highlighted one in the overview list.

ExplainED

Be careful when you delete the current slide; you will be given no warning before the slide is deleted. However, you can always retrieve it by clicking the undo icon on the toolbar.

Using Layouts

When you insert a new slide, you need to choose a layout option for the slide before it is inserted. Click the "Insert slide" icon in the slide control bar, and you will see the "Choose slide layout" dialog box (see Figure 6-16). This dialog box gives you the choice between the following five different layouts:

Title: This is the default layout used for the first slide in all new presentations. This consists of a text area in the middle of the page that uses a large font, as well as a text area just below that area to place the subtitle or author in a smaller font.

Text: This is used by many presenters as their layout for most slides. It consists of a title text area in large font and a text area that takes up the rest of the slide in a smaller font.

Two Columns: Similar to the Text layout, but with the main text area split into two columns, this option is good for a slide that compares two things.

Caption: This is a blank slide with a small text area at the bottom for a page caption.

Blank: This is a blank layout (i.e., there is nothing on the slide); use this if none of the other layouts are suitable.

The layouts act like small templates that help you with the formatting of your slide presentations. Other office-suite slide presentation software also uses templates, but other apps usually have a few more layouts at their disposal. However, the layouts in Presentations cover the most commonly used approaches, and there is a blank template that you can customize as needed for any form. Choose the most suitable layout and click it. The new slide will be inserted based on the layout you chose. Each of the text areas on the page will be blank and contain default text, such as "Click to add title," or "Click to add content," or something else appropriate to the content it will contain. You can now enter text in the text areas. If you chose a blank layout, you can add your own text areas or title areas, format them, and add text to them as you wish.

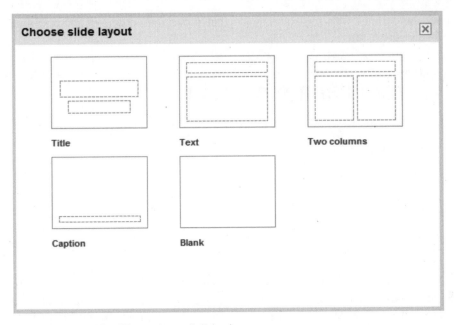

Figure 6-16: The "Choose layout" dialog box

The text areas in the layouts are in predefined positions, but you can change anything you need to about a slide, including one created with predefined layouts. You can also alter the size and position of any text area. We will discuss this in the next section.

Adding Text to a Presentation

As previously discussed, if a slide contains a text area with nothing added, it will be displayed with a default message, such as "Click to add content" (see Figure 6-17).

Click to add content

Figure 6-17: A blank text area with the default message

To add text to a text area, click the default message shown in Figure 6-17. The default message will disappear and your cursor will be placed in the text area, waiting for you to type text. As you type text into the text area, the text area will be outlined with a gray rectangle that shows the borders of the text area (see Figure 6-18).

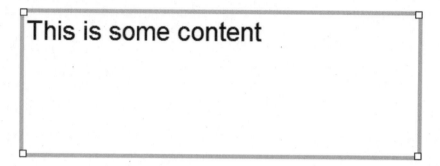

This is some content

Figure 6-18: Entering text into a text area

Type in the text you need to, bearing in mind that you should keep the text to small bullet points or short sentences in point form. If you're typing in text and reach the right border of the text area, the text will automatically wrap within the text area. That is, it will automatically continue on the next line, just as it does when you type text into a word processor. Use the Return key to begin new lines within the text area. As you add new lines of text, the cursor will continually move towards the bottom border of the text area. If you are at the bottom of the text area and press the Return key, you won't run out of space; rather, the text area will grow downwards as you add new lines at the bottom. However, this is not a word processor, so you must be careful that the text area does not expand beyond the bottom of the slide. If it does, then the text that goes below the slide will not be seen during the presentation.

ExplainED

All text must appear within the page boundaries, or it will not be seen during a presentation.

If you chose a blank layout when you inserted the current slide, you can add your own text area to the current slide. To do this, click the "Insert text" icon on the toolbar (see Figure 6-3). Alternatively, you can choose the "Text" option on the "Insert" menu on the menubar. When you do this, a new text area will be added to the current page. If there is already a text area on the current page, the new text area may overlap this one. You will need to adjust the size and location of the new text area to suit your slide (see the next section for more information). Once the new text area is added, it will be initially blank and displayed with the default message shown previously. You are now free to add your text to it.

Manipulating the Text Area

Once you place a text area in a slide, you will most likely need to alter its size and position within the current slide. To alter the size of a text area in a slide, click the text area. When you click the text area, the outline of the text area is shown in gray; however, the outline also shows four small *drag points* at each corner of the text area (see Figure 6-18). To alter the size of the text area, left-click one of these drag points, and with the mouse button depressed, drag the point so that the text area expands (or shrinks). As you drag this area, the new shape of the text area is shown by a small dotted (broken) outline that changes shape as you drag the point (see Figure 6-19).

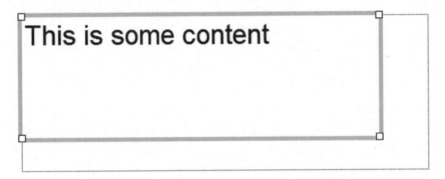

This is some content

Figure 6-19: Altering a text area's size

When you change the *drag point* of the text area so that the new desired size is outlined correctly by the broken outline, release the mouse button. The text area will be resized according the new size determined by the broken outline. You can change the size as much as you need to and as often as you want. Just be careful that the entire boundary stays within the slide's boundaries.

It's relatively easy to move a text area from one place in the slide to another, without changing its shape. Click the text area so that its outline is displayed. Move the mouse cursor over one of the gray border lines; as the cursor moves over one of the borders, it will change its shape to a *Move Cursor* shape. This shape will depend on the operating system on your computer; on Windows, this shape is usually a double-ended vertical arrow overlaid with a double-ended horizontal arrow. When the cursor changes shape, left-click the mouse button and keep it depressed. Now drag the text area with the mouse. As you drag the area, a broken outline border will appear and move; this indicates the new position of the text area (see Figure 6-20). Keep dragging this until the broken border is in the new position desired for the text area, and then release the mouse button. The text area will be moved to the new location.

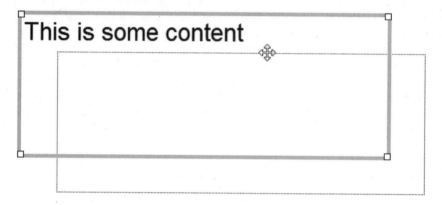

Figure 6-20: Moving a text area

Often, you will find you need to resize an area after moving it. Just repeat the steps described previously, making sure the text area remains within the slide's boundaries.

Manipulating Text

Now you are able to create presentations and add text areas to your slides. The most common task is now to add the text of your presentation to the slides, and then format it to get your slides to look consistent and professional. Adding the text is easy (as you have seen); as in word processing, the challenge often lies in manipulating the text and formatting it until you are happy with the results. In this section, we will look at manipulating the text and formatting options. Much of this section is similar to how we manipulate and format text in Google Documents. However, there are a few differences because the text areas we deal with have small predefined sizes. Thus, when viewing the presentation, we must be aware at all times of the sizes we use for the text and headings. Nonetheless, the mechanics for manipulating and formatting text is similar.

Selecting Text

Quite often, we need to deal with a selected portion of the text, whether to move it from one place in the slide to another; to move it between slides; or to delete it, edit it, or to apply formatting to it. To select a portion of the text within a text area, click left-click at the point in the text area just before the first character of the text you wish to select, and while the button is still depressed, drag the cursor with the mouse until all of the desired text is highlighted; finally, release the left mouse button. All the selected text within the text area will be highlighted with a light-blue color. Alternatively, you can left-click just before the first character you want to select, press and hold down the Shift key, click just after the last character you want to select, and then release the Shift key. All the text in between will be selected. Alternatively, you could just hold down the shift key and use the arrow keys to move from the current position to your desired endpoint. Additionally, double-clicking a word will select that word and triple clicking will select that paragraph. This last feature is the same as the one provided in Google Documents; it is also similar to a feature provided in Microsoft Office applications.

ExplainED

You can quickly select text by double-clicking a word to select that word or by triple-clicking within a paragraph to select that paragraph.

Cutting and Pasting Text

As with Google Documents, you can use cut-and-paste functions to make copies of selected text or to move a selection of text from one place in a text area to another. To achieve this, you can either use the standard keyboard shortcuts or do this through the "Edit" Menu. To move a selection of text from one place in a text area to another, first select the text to be moved, as discussed in the previous section, and then use the Ctrl+X key combination. Alternatively, you can select the "Cut" option from the "Edit" menu. The selected text will then be removed from the text area. Now choose the point in the text area where you want the selected text to be moved to, and press the Ctrl+V key combination; alternatively, you can select the "Paste" option from the "Edit" menu. The selected text that was cut will now be inserted at the new location in the text area.

You can also copy a selection of text from one location to another without moving it. As described in the previous paragraph, select the text you wish to copy, and then use the Ctrl+C key combination to copy it; alternatively, you can select the "Copy" option from the "Edit" menu. Then, as before, select the point in the text area where a copy of the text is to be inserted and press the keyboard Ctrl+V combination; alternatively, you can select the "Paste" option from the "Edit" menu. A copy of the original text selection will be inserted at this point.

You are not limited to cutting, copying, and pasting within the same text area or even in the same slide. You can cut-and-paste text from any text area into another on the same slide; or, you can choose a different slide from the slide overview list, and then select a text area in that slide to paste the text into. If you have a document or presentation open in another tab, you can copy or cut the text from one document or presentation, select the tab with the other document or presentation, and paste the selected text into the new document. The only limitation with Presentations is that selected text must be pasted into a text area within a presentation. If a slide does not contain a text area, you can add one before pasting the text.

Cutting-and-Pasting Text Areas

You can cut-and-paste entire text areas within your presentation from one slide to another. To do this, click the text area that you want to copy or cut, so that its outline is displayed. Move the mouse cursor over one of the gray border lines. As the cursor moves over one of the borders, it will change to a Move Cursor shape. Left-click while the mouse cursor is hovering over the border with the move shape displayed. You can now use the "Edit" menu or the appropriate key combination described previously to cut or copy the entire text area. Now use the slide overview list and/or the slide controls to move to a new slide in the presentation. When you have selected a new slide, click a point in the slide that is not within an existing text area and does not contain an object. Next, either from the menu, or using the key combination as above, paste the text area into the new slide. The text area will appear in the new slide in the same position where it was cut or copied from the old slide.

Formatting Text

To format the text within a text area, you first need to select the text you wish to apply the formatting. You can change the font face of the selected text by using the drop-down "Text font" icon button on the toolbar (see Figure 6-3). There are a limited number of fonts that you can select, which are shown in Figure 6-21. The current font is indicated by a check mark (tick symbol) in the list. You cannot add new fonts to the list at this stage; the Normal font is the one used if all formatting options on the selected text have been removed,

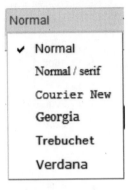

Figure 6-21: Changing a text font

You can also change the size of the selected text by clicking the "Text size" icon button on the toolbar (see Figure 6-3). A drop-down list of predefined text sizes will appear, with the current size indicated with a check mark (tick symbol) in the list (see Figure 6-22). Font size is usually measured in Point size (pt) on a computer screen, where 1 point is 1/72 of an inch.

To change the size of the text, choose a new size from the list or click the "Add" option at the end of the list. If you click the "Add" option, a small dialog box will appear, as shown in Figure 6-23. Enter the custom size you need for the selected text and click the "OK" button at the bottom of the dialog box. The text will then be resized according to the new custom size. If you remove all the formatting options from selected text, the size of the text will revert to the default size for the text area (see the next section).

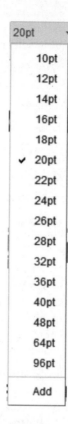

Figure 6-22: Changing text size

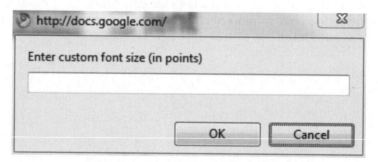

Figure 6-23: A custom-sized dialog

> ## NotED
>
> *Removing formatting from selected text means that the size and font of the text will default to the size and font of the current text area.*

You can also apply standard bold, italic, and underline formatting to the selected text by clicking the "Bold," "Italic", or "Underline" icons on the toolbar (see Figure 6-3). These formatting options act like switches; click an icon once to turn a formatting option on; click the same icon a second time to turn that option off.

Superscript and subscript formatting often comes in handy for annotating some points in a slide; sometimes they can be augmented with slide notes at the end of a slide or group of slides. To use superscripting and subscripting, select the text to be formatted and click either the superscript or subscript icons on the toolbar (see Figure 6-3). The results can be seen in Figure 6-24.

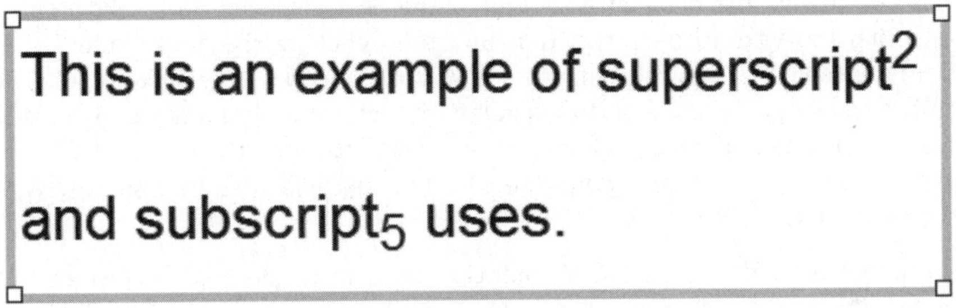

This is an example of superscript^2

and subscript$_5$ uses.

Figure 6-24: Superscript and subscript text

You can remove all formatting from the selected text by clicking the "Clear formatting" icon on the toolbar (see Figure 6-3). When you do this, the selected text will be displayed according to the text area format defaults.

Text Alignment

You can alter the alignment of the text in a paragraph within a text area. This is a paragraph style type formatting option, thus any change you make affects the whole paragraph. To alter the alignment of a paragraph, just place the cursor somewhere in the paragraph to be aligned by clicking it with the mouse left button. You can choose either the "Left Justify," "Center Justify," or "Right Justify" text alignment icons from the toolbar (shown in Figure 6-3) to left, center or right justify the text in the current paragraph. These icons are displayed in expanded form in Figure 6-25 and are the first three icons shown.

Figure 6-25: The "Text alignment" icons

The last icon in Figure 6-23 is the "Vertical text alignment" icon, and this will align all text within a text area vertically. Pressing this icon causes a small drop down toolbar to appear, giving you the choice if Top, Center, or Bottom alignment of the text within the text area. This applies to the entire text area, regardless of where you place your mouse cursor in the text area.

Text Color

You can change the color of a section of the text displayed in a text area by selecting the text to be formatted, and then clicking the "Text color" icon from the toolbar. You will get a drop-down color chooser (see Figure 6-26). The current color will show a tick against it, and the default color of the presentation text is black. Choose a new text color for the selected text by clicking the color that you want. The selected text will then be displayed with the new color.

In the bottom left of Figure 6-26, you can see a small plus sign (+), which I've circled to highlight it. If you click this, a small dialog box opens (see Figure 6-27) that allows you to define a custom color for the text display. You can enter the custom color in either hexadecimal color format or RGB color format. In RGB color format, you enter three digits separated by commas; these numbers representing the red, green and blue color mix combination. For example, (0,0,0) is black, and (255,255,255) is white. You can learn more about color specification in either hexadecimal format or RGB format from a variety of online sources. An excellent source of information that includes color charts in both RGB and hexadecimal format is the W3schools.com web site (www.w3schools.com/); see this page for information specifically on colors: www.w3schools.com/html/html_colors.asp.

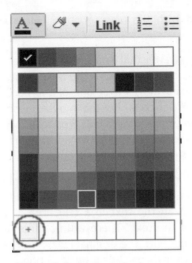

Figure 6-26: The "Color chooser" drop-down box

Figure 6-27: The "Custom color" dialog box

You can also change the background color of a section of text in the text area by selecting the text and then clicking the "Text Background Color" icon on the toolbar. A color chooser similar to the Text color chooser in Figure 6-26 will open, displaying the current background color highlighted with a tick. The default background color is white. Click a new background color to change the background color of the text selection; alternatively, you can define you own custom color.

Formatting a Text Area

When you insert a new text area, the text inside will have this default formatting: Normal font, 20pt-font size, and left-aligned. You can change the default formatting for a text area, which will mean that all text in the text area will be displayed with the new settings, unless you specifically change some selected text.

To do this, click the text area that you want to change the formatting options of, so that its outline is displayed. Move the mouse cursor over one of the gray border lines. As the cursor moves over one of the borders, it will change to a Move Cursor shape. Left-click while the mouse cursor is hovering over the border with the move shape displayed. You can now use the any of the formatting options discussed in the previous sections, and any changes will apply to all the text in the text area.

There is also a "Fill color" icon in the toolbar that applies to text areas, which can be used for filling in the color of a text area. For instance, you can use this feature when you select all the text in a text area and change the text color and background color of the text. There will be large areas, or areas between lines, that will still appear with the original color. You can fill in all the color in a text area by selecting this icon. Begin by selecting the text area to be filled in, and then click the "Fill color" icon in the toolbar to bring up a color chooser (see Figure 6-28). Select the color to be the fill color, just as you would select a text color. You can even define a custom color, if needed. The text area will then be back-filled with the new selected color. The "Fill color" icon also includes an option for selecting no fill color; this option is in the top left of the color chooser (see Figure 6-28). Choosing the no fill option for a text area that already has a fill color will turn the existing fill color off.

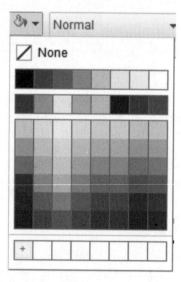

Figure 6-28: The "Fill color" dialog box

Using Bullets and Number Points

You can use bullet and number points on text in a text area the same way you did for text in Google Documents (see Chapter 4). These can be used to enhance the point form of text in a text area; they are especially useful in a presentation because text is most often written as a series of bullet or numbered points. For example, suppose there are five points you want to list in your text area; you type them as five separate lines, as follows:

- Point A
- Point B
- Point C
- Point D
- Point E

Next, use the mouse to select the five lines, as in Figure 6-29(a), and then choose either the numbered list icon or the bullet point icon on the toolbar to format the five points as a numbered list or a bullet point list (see Figure 6-29). In Figure 6-29(b), the selected lines are formatted as a numbered list; in Figure 6-29(c), they are formatted as bullet points. The "Numbered list" icon and the "Bullet point" icon are the first two icons in the "list & bullet format" group shown in Figure 6-3. You can quickly switch between numbered list and bullet points while the text is selected by clicking the appropriate icon. The formatting also acts as a switch. If you select bullet-point formatting, the selection is formatted as bullet points. If you select bullet-point formatting for a selection already formatted as bullet points, it is turned off. Numbered lists work similarly, making it easy to quickly change from one to the other.

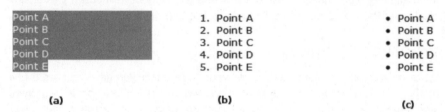

(a)　　　　　　　　　　(b)　　　　　　　　　　(c)

Figure 6-29: The Numbered and Bullet lists

You can easily add multilevel lists or bullet points to your text area. For instance, if you wanted to include three sub-points associated with Point A in Figure 6-29, then type the three sub-points after Point A, as shown in Figure 6-30(a). Now select the entire list and click the numbered list icon on the toolbar, to produce the numbered list shown in Figure 6-30(b). Now select the three lines containing the three new sub-points in the list, and click the "Increase indent" icon in the toolbar, as discussed previously. The three sub-points will now be demoted to subordinate points and indented one level to the right under Point A, as shown in Figure 6-30(c). Notice that the numbering also changes to reflect the demotion. If the list were originally formatted as a bullet list, then demoting the three sub-points would result in the bullet list shown in Figure 6-30(d). Again, notice the shape of the bullets changes to reflect the demoted points.

Point A	1. Point A	1. Point A	• Point A
Sub point 1	2. Sub point 1	1. Sub point 1	◦ Sub point 1
Sub point 2	3. Sub point 2	2. Sub point 2	◦ Sub point 2
Sub point 3	4. Sub point 3	3. Sub point 3	◦ Sub point 3
Point B	5. Point B	2. Point B	• Point B
Point C	6. Point C	3. Point C	• Point C
Point D	7. Point D	4. Point D	• Point D
Point E	8. Point E	5. Point E	• Point E
(a)	**(b)**	**(c)**	**(d)**

Figure 6-30: Multilevel lists

Using the "Increase indent" and the "Decrease indent" icons, you can select points in the list and demote or promote them as you wish. This enables you to create complex lists with multilevel points of interest in your document.

You can also select an entire text area, as previously discussed, and click either the "Numbered list" icon or the "Bullet list" icon. When you do this, every paragraph in the text area will become a bullet point or numbered point, including any blank lines. These blank lines can easily be turned off by clicking the line in the text area, and then clicking the appropriate icon.

Re-ordering Slides

Quite often, you will want to re-order your slides after you have created a few of them. This is natural because, when you write the text for slides or indeed any other type of document, you often think of a better arrangement after some material has already been added. You can create new slides, and cut-and-paste entire text areas if needed; however, if all you need is to rearrange the slides, Presentations provides an easy way to do this.

You can rearrange the order of your slides by using the slide overview area on the left of the browser window. To move a slide in the current order, left-click one of the small squares representing a slide, keep the left mouse button depressed, and begin to drag the slide. As you do this, the cursor will change shape to a moving shape cursor, and you can drag the slide up or down in the order until you find the place where it needs to go (see Figure 6-31). Release the left mouse button, and the slide will be moved to the new place in the order. You can do this with any number of slides. You can also select a number of slides to move by left-clicking on the first slide in the group to move, holding down the Shift key, and then left-clicking the last slide in the group to move. All the slides in between the first and second slide clicked will be selected. Now left-click this group, keep the left mouse button depressed, drag the entire group to the new place in the list, and release the mouse button.

Figure 6-31: Moving a slide by dragging

Alternatively, you can select a slide (or group of slides) to move in the overview list (as described previously), and then right-click somewhere in the group. You will see a pop-up menu displayed (see Figure 6-32). Choose either the "Move slide up" or "Move slide down" option to move the entire group up or down one slide. Using this method, you can only move up or down one slot in the order of slides at a time.

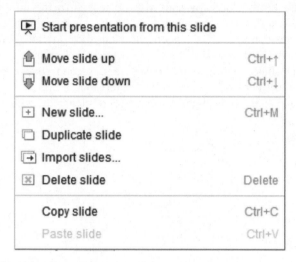

Figure 6-32: Using the menu to move slides

Using Advanced Features

What we have concentrated on so far in this chapter is the placement and arrangement of text within the presentation. While text will form the backbone of any presentation, it is often Presentations' more advanced features that will enhance a presentation and help us deliver our points more clearly. In particular, the use of images and clip art, as well as video and sound, can enhance a presentation greatly. In this section, we will look at utilizing more of the available objects we can insert into a presentation for this purpose.

Using Images

Images can be inserted into presentations for two reasons: to aesthetically enhance the presentation; or to become part of the presentation you are creating by providing visual backup for your points. The use of images in a presentation is often necessary. For example, you might use graphs and charts for financial presentations, or even medical images in a presentation to a health-based conference.

You can include images from two sources in your slide: your computer or the Web. In the first case, you will need to have an image already located on your personal computer; in the second, you will need the URL (web address) of the image to include. Select the slide you wish to add the image to, and then choose the "Image" option from the "Insert" menu on the menubar to bring up the "Insert image" dialog (see Figure 6-33).

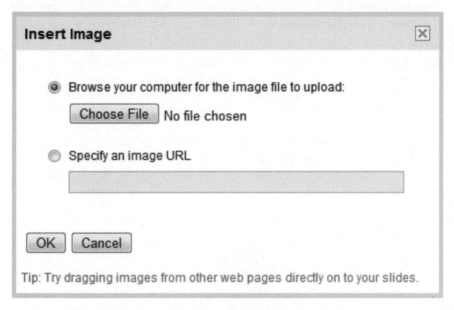

Figure 6-33: Inserting an image

From the dialog box in Figure 6-33, you can choose to insert an image from your computer or from the Web by clicking the appropriate radio button for the corresponding choice in the dialog box. If you choose to load an image from your computer, click the "Choose File" button. You will then be presented with your operating system's file selection utility. Navigate to the place on your computer where the image file you want to use resides, and then select the image. You will then be taken back to the dialog box shown in Figure 6-33, and the name of the chosen image will be shown just to the right of the "Choose file" button. If you wish to select another image, click the button again and select the new file to load. If you want to load your image from the Web, you need to know the URL of the image. Select the radio button's "Specify an image URL" option. The text box underneath the radio button will become active, and you can type in the URL of the image you wish to insert into your slide. Click the "OK" button to insert the image, or click the "Cancel" button to exit without inserting. If you click the "OK" button, the image will then be inserted into the current slide.

If you decide to use images from the Web, the right to use and distribute the image usually belongs to the owner of the Web site and/or the image's owner. You should obtain permission from the owner of an image to use it before you include it for public viewing in a presentation or web site. There may be penalties associated with using images without authorization. One source of free images is the Freeimages site in the UK: (www.freeimages.co.uk).

When you insert your image, it will most likely not be in the correct place in the slide. Moving an image from one place in the slide to another without changing its shape is relatively easy. Click the image so that its outline is displayed, and you will see the cursor change to a Move Cursor shape. With the cursor in the move shape, left-click and keep the left mouse button depressed. Now drag the image with the mouse. As you drag the image, a broken outline border will appear and move, indicating the new position of the image (see Figure 6-34). Keep dragging this until the broken border is in the desired new position and release the mouse button. The image will be moved to the new location.

Figure 6-34: Moving an image

Resizing Images

You will often need to resize an image once it is inserted into a slide, usually to make it fit within the slide dimensions. To do this, click the image; this shows the outline of the image in gray, but the outline also shows four small drag points at each corner of the image (see Figure 6-35). To alter the size of the image, left-click one of these drag points, keep the mouse button depressed, and drag the point so that the image expands or shrinks. As you drag it, the new shape of the image is shown by a small dotted (broken) outline that changes shape as you drag the point (see Figure 6-35).

Figure 6-35: Resizing an image

When you have moved the drag point of the image so that the new size desired is outlined correctly by the broken outline, release the mouse button. The image will be resized according to the new size determined by the broken outline, and then redrawn so it fills the new shape. One problem is that, if you don't resize the image correctly (i.e., according to scale), the image will be distorted either horizontally or vertically. You can resize the image according to scale by pressing and holding down the Shift key before you click and drag one of the drag points on the image. This will ensure that, no matter how much you move the mouse cursor, the dimensions of the image will stay in scale (i.e., proportional to each other).

ExplainED

You can keep an image in scale when resizing by pressing and holding the Shift key down before dragging one of the corner drag points.

Re-ordering Objects

As you insert objects in the slide and drag them around, some objects will end up overlaid on the top of others. This can work to good effect, but occasionally you might need to re-order the objects in relation to each other. You should consider the objects as items that can be stacked one on top of one another. If the one on top gets in the way of the one underneath, you can swap their positions. For example, when you inserted an image in the previous section and moved it, it may have been placed on top of some text (see Figure 6-36).

Figure 6-36: Objects overlaying each other

If we want to change the order, we can select the object on top and move it either down one in the stack, or to the back of the stack of objects. Similarly, we can select the one underneath and move it to the top. In this case, we can right-click the image. When you do this, a pop-up menu will appear, and you can select the "Order" option to display a further sub-menu (see Figure 6-37).

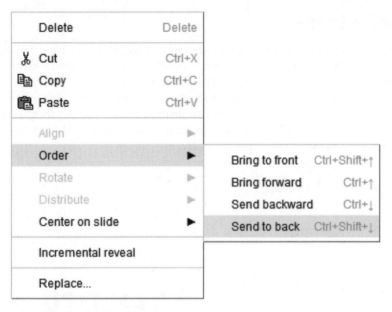

Figure 6-37: The "Order objects" menu

You can choose from the options in the menu to bring an object to the front, bring it forward one layer, send it backwards one layer, or send it to the back of the stack. Choose the "Send to back" option to send the image to the back of the stack, behind the text area (see Figure 6-38).

Figure 6-38: Re-ordered objects

You can re-order the position of any object in the stack on a slide using this method.

Adding Shapes

There are some predefined shapes that you can add to your slides. These can be accessed by choosing the "Shapes" option from the "Insert" menu (see Figure 6-39). Click one of the shapes, and it will be inserted into your slide. You can then move it around and resize it, as you did with images in previous sections. It is also possible to rotate the shapes by right-clicking them to bring up a pop-up menu; from here, you can select the "Rotate" option, which lets you flip the shape horizontally or vertically.

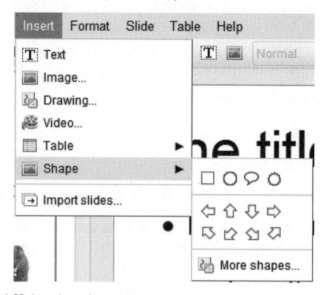

Figure 6-39: Inserting a shape

At the bottom of the "Insert Shape" pop-up menu shown in Figure 6-39, you can see the "More Shapes" option. If you click this option, it will open the Insert Drawing window, just as if you had clicked the "Drawing" option in the "Insert" menu on the menubar (see the next section for more information).

Drawing Objects

You can use the drawing facility in Presentations to put together a small drawing to insert into your slide. This facility offers you a scribble tool for drawing freehand, as well as a variety of predefined shapes and line-drawing tools you can use. You can insert a drawing by selecting the "Drawing" option from the "Insert" menu, which will display the Insert Drawing window (see Figure 6-40).

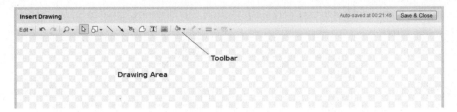

Figure 6-40: An annotated Insert Drawing window

With the Insert Drawing window, you have access to a full-featured drawing tool that will let you make sketches or create line art using predefined shapes that can be inserted back into your slide when finished. You can add text and images, as well as shapes, lines, lines with arrows, and other termination symbols and freehand drawings. When you create lines, you can change their color, thickness, or even style using the "Dashes" icon. It is beyond the scope of this section to provide a complete treatment of the Drawing facility, but the interface if fairly intuitive and user friendly. An expanded view of the Drawing toolbar is shown in Figure 6-41.

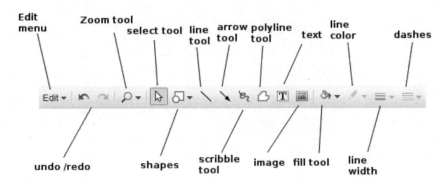

Figure 6-41: The "Drawing" toolbar

Along with all the options for creating your own line-art, a number of predefined shapes are also provided. These options are always a good starting point for someone wishing to create their own images. To insert one of the shapes, click the "Shapes" icon in the toolbar. This will display a drop-down list of predefined shapes you can choose from (see Figure 6-42). To insert one of these shapes, just click one. When the drop-down menu disappears, left-click the drawing area of the Drawing window; then, while keeping the left mouse button depressed, drag the cursor to insert the new shape and size it at the same time. Or you can simply click the drawing area to insert a pre-sized shape.

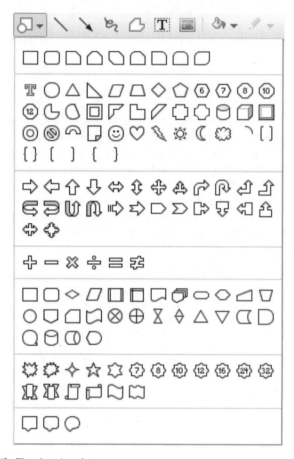

Figure 6-42: The drawing shapes

You can click an inserted shape at any time and re-size it by clicking a drag point and dragging the mouse as the shape resizes, just as you resized the images in previous sections. To keep the shape in proportion, depress the Shift key as you drag the mouse.

When you have finished creating your drawing, click the "Save & Close" button in the top-right corner of the drawing window (see Figure 6-40). The new drawing object will be inserted into the slide. Like any other object, you can move it, resize it, and delete it.

Using Tables

You can add a table into your slide by clicking the "Table" option of the "Insert" menu. When you do, a small drop-down window will open by the "Insert" menu. This window will contain a small grid of squares that will become colored light blue as you move your cursor to the right and down. This is used to determine the size of the table that you want to insert (see Figure 6-43). As you move your cursor over the grid and the squares change colors (and then back again while you resize), the size of the table (the colored grid you are creating) is displayed in the bottom of the window. In the example in Figure 6-43, the size is 3 x 3. Click the grid when you have it sized to the size of the table you want to insert. The menu will disappear, and a table of that size will be inserted into the slide.

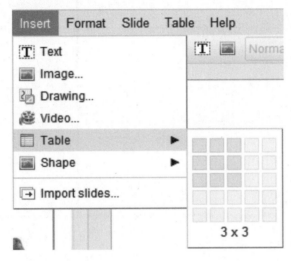

Figure 6-43: Inserting a table

Once the table has been inserted, you can then add text to the table cells. Each cell in the table acts like a text area. You can click the cell and add text. As you add text, it will be wrapped within the boundaries of the column; however, if you keep adding text, the bottom of the cell will be automatically pushed down to accommodate more lines.

You can adjust the table at any time by adjusting the width of a column or the height of a row. Do this by clicking anywhere inside the table. When you do this, you will see the outside of the table highlighted with a gray border (see Figure 6-44). Now you can move your cursor over the column and row lines inside the table. As your cursor crosses a row grid line or a column grid line, it will change shape. When it does, left-click and keep the left mouse button pressed down. If you clicked on a row grid line, with the left mouse button depressed you can drag the line up or down to increase or decrease the height of the table row. If you clicked a column grid line, with the left mouse button depressed you can drag the line left or right to increase or decrease the width of the table column. In this way, you can adjust the width of a column or all columns, as well as the height of a row or all rows.

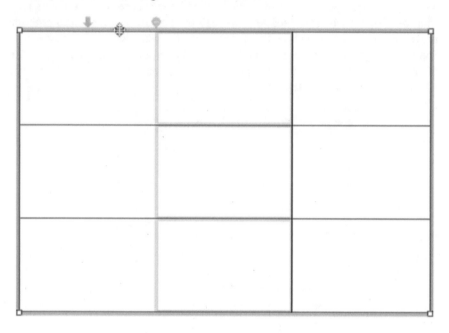

Figure 6-44: Adjusting a table

You can select an entire row or an entire column. To select a column, move your mouse cursor to the top of the gray table border (see Figure 6-44). When your cursor is over the outside border, it will change shape to a *move shape* cursor. Click and hold the left mouse button down, then drag the table to a new position. However, if you keep moving the mouse cursor along the top border, you will see a gray-arrow shape appear above the middle of the column as it approaches the middle of that column (see Figure 6-44). If you click this, the entire column will be selected. Similarly, if you move your cursor down the left- or right-table border, you will be able to select an entire column. You can select the entire table by clicking somewhere outside the border of the table.

You can format the contents of a cell by selecting it, and then choosing any of the formatting options previously discussed. Similarly, you can format the text in a row or column of the table (or the whole table itself) by first selecting the desired row, column, or table, and then applying the formatting.

You can also insert columns or rows by clicking a cell of the table, and then clicking the "Table" menu on the menubar; this will bring up the following options:

Insert row above: This will insert a new empty row above the row in the table containing the selected cell.

Insert row below: This will insert a new empty row below the row in the table containing the selected cell.

Insert column left: This will insert a new empty column to the left of the column in the table containing the selected cell.

Insert column right: This will insert a new empty column to the right of the column in the table containing the selected cell.

Delete row: This will delete the entire row in the table containing the selected cell.

Delete column: This will delete the entire column in the table containing the selected cell.

Delete Table: This will delete the entire table you clicked.

Move row up: This will move the row containing the selected cell up one row, effectively swapping the entire row above with the row containing the selected cell.

Move row down: This will move the row containing the selected cell down one row, effectively swapping the entire row below with the row containing the selected cell.

You can use these options to add and delete rows, columns, or the entire table (see Figure 6-45).

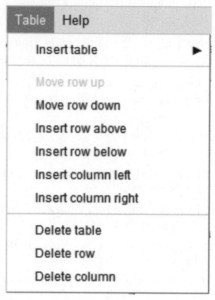

Figure 6-45: Adding or deleting rows, columns, and tables

Adding Video

Additionally, there is a facility in Presentations to add video clips to your slides. These video clips are sourced from YouTube. To insert a video into your presentation, choose the "Video" option from the "Insert" menu. This will bring up the "Select Video" dialog (see Figure 6-46). A selection of recent videos will be shown in the small dialog. Use the scroll bar on the right to scroll down the list and find a video to insert. If you are looking for videos on a particular topic, type in the search term in the "Search videos" text box shown at the top if the dialog box (see Figure 6-46). A new list of videos will be shown that is relevant to the search term used.

Figure 6-46: Selecting a video

Once you find a video you want to insert into your slide, click the video entry, and then click the "Select video" button at the bottom left of the dialog box. The video will now be inserted into the slide (see Figure 6-47). The video will act like an image in some respects; click it to see the border and drag points of the inserted video. Next, drag it to where you want it in the slide, and then drag one of the drag points to resize the video (if necessary).

347

Figure 6-47: Insert a video

Once you are ready to play the video within the slide, double-click it and the video will activate as it would in a normal YouTube video (see Figure 6-48). You will see the Play controls, the volume control and full-screen mode icons on the bottom of the video clip. You use these as you would when viewing any YouTube-style video on the web.

Figure 6-48: Activating a video

Using Speaker Notes

Sometimes you might need to write some speaker notes to help prompt you on certain points of the presentation as you are giving it. Or perhaps there are certain points that need elaboration or references that need a citation. You can add speaker notes to a presentation to help you in this regard. To turn on speaker notes, select "Show speaker notes" from the "View" menu on the menubar. Alternatively, you can click the "Speaker notes" icon located in the bottom-left corner of the slide (see Figure 6-49).

Figure 6-49: The Speaker notes icon

Once you choose to have the speaker notes shown, they will appear in a special section down the right side of the current browser window (see Figure 6-50). You can type in the speaker notes that you wish to add to the current slide; the speaker notes will change as you cycle through the slides in the presentation.

Figure 6-50: The Speaker notes window

349

When you are presenting the slides, you can view the speaker notes by selecting the "View speaker notes" option. You also have the option of printing any associated speaker notes when you print the slides (see the "Printing Presentations" section later in this chapter for more information).

Backgrounds and Themes

To enhance the visual appearance of the presentation, you can choose themes for your slides, or you can choose to use an image as a background. This can be an effective tool when delivering a presentation, but it should be used carefully. Choosing the wrong image as a background can detract from the presentation, making it too *busy*, and thus difficult to see. The background must not do anything to make the text more difficult to read. The background and themes are changed through the "Presentation settings" option, which can be accessed from the "Format" menu on the menubar. "Presentation settings" gives you two options: change the theme or change the background.

Choose "Change theme" to change the slides current theme, if any. When you choose this option, a dialog box will be displayed showing a number of slide themes you can choose from (see Figure 6-51). Use the scroll bar on the right to scroll up and down to find a theme you wish to use. Click a theme, and it will be applied to all slides in your presentation. The first theme is a blank one; if you wish to turn off a theme you have chosen, just apply a different one or a blank one.

To choose a background image to be applied to a slide, select "Change background" from the "Presentation settings" option on the "Format" menu. You will see the dialog box shown in Figure 6-52. In the dialog box, you can either choose to load a background image from your own computer, or you can use the "change background paint fill" icon to give the slide a different background color. This "Paint fill" icon behaves exactly like the "Fill color" icon on the toolbar. Click the icon to bring up a color chooser, then choose a color or create your own by typing a color code, and the new color will become the background color of the slide. To load an image you want to become the background of the slide, click the "Insert image" link in the dialog box. This will display a "Choose file" button.

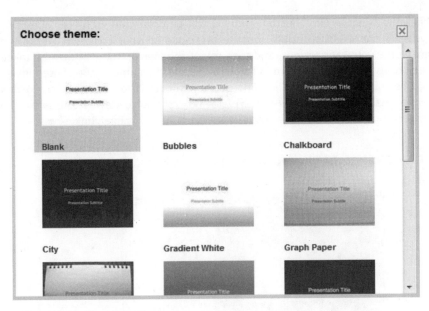

Figure 6-51: Choosing a theme

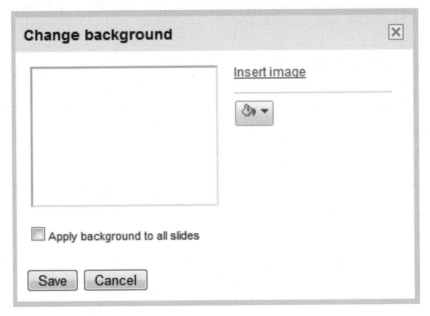

Figure 6-52: Change the background dialog box

Click the "Choose File" button, and you will be presented with your operating system's file selection utility. Choose the place on your computer where the image file you want resides, and then select the image. You will then be taken back to the dialog box shown in Figure 6-53, and the name of the chosen image will be shown in place of the "Choose file" button. The image will be loaded into a small viewing window in the dialog box for you to view. If this is not the correct image, select another by clicking the "Change image" link.

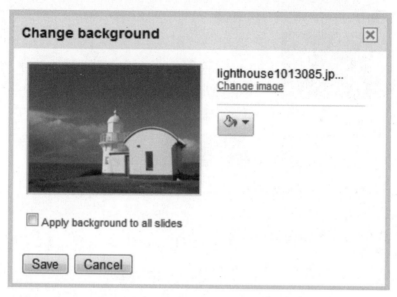

Figure 6-53: The selected image (image source: www.freeimages.co.uk)

If the image is correct, you can click the "Save" button on the bottom left of the dialog box. The image will become the background image of the current slide. If you select the small "Apply background to all slides" check box before you click the "Save" button, then the new image will become the background image of all slides in the presentation. Figure 6-54 shows this image applied to one of the slides in the presentation.

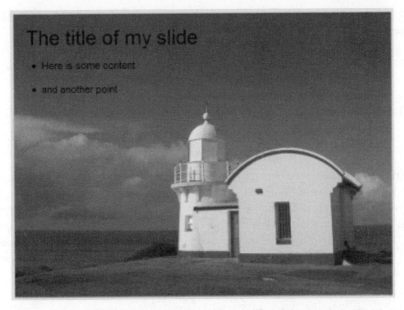

The title of my slide

• Here is some content

• and another point

Figure 6-54: A slide with a background image (image source: www.freeimages.co.uk).

Delivering Your Presentation

The last thing you need to do after you have created your presentation is to present it somewhere. This could be at a conference, at your local club, or even to an audience of online viewers. With Presentations, you will need access to the Internet to show the presentation; however, this also means you won't arrive in a different country without your slides because you have access to them wherever there is an Internet connection.

Presenting Your Slide Show

To begin your presentation, select the "Start Presentation" option from the "View" menu on the menubar. Alternatively, you could click the "Start presentation" button in the upper-right corner of the Presentation browser window. A new window will open, and the Presentations will display the first slide. To move to the next slide, click somewhere in the slide window. Keep clicking in the window to cycle through the slides until they are finished. When you are finished, a link will appear on the right, enabling you to go back to the first slide. If you are finished, you can simply shut the window using the window control icons in the top-right corner of the window.

As you are going through the slides, sometimes you will need to skip through slides or move back to a previous slide. You can do this in a number of ways:

- Use the mouse to click the slide window to move forward.
- Press the N key or the right-arrow key to move to the next slide.
- Press the P key or the left-arrow key to move to the previous slide.
- Move your mouse cursor down the bottom left of the slide window and click the "Back" or "Forward" button.
- Press the escape (Esc) key to finish the presentation.

In the presentation window, there will be a small black bar at the bottom of the window. On the bar will be a figure indicating what slide number you are viewing. Additionally, the bar will have an "Actions" drop-down menu called, that gives you access to some of the functionality you have already learned about. This menu lets you print the slides, download as a .pdf, download as a .ppt file, and show the speaker notes. However, at this stage most people will be using this window to cycle through the slides in the presentation.

Best Practices for Creating Slides

While there is no strict rule book for creating presentations, there are a number of steps you can follow to try and make as a good a presentation as possible. After more than 23 years giving lectures and conference presentations, we have seen the best and the worst. Of course, the nature of your slides will vary, depending on whether you are presenting in person or sending your presentation to somebody to view in his own time. For the moment, we will assume you are presenting in person.

One of the common mistakes that new presentation users make is to clutter their slides too much. Slide elements should be kept to a minimum, with only a handful of key points per slide. These points are often better made in bullet point form, rather than wordy sentences. The purpose of a slide is to prompt discussion from the audience and jog the presenter's memory of the points she is trying to make. New presenters tend to put too much in a slide, worried that they will be nervous and forget everything. We have all been there, but this is a big mistake because, if you are nervous, too much information on a slide can confuse you. Additionally, people can read much faster than you can talk; if there is too much information, they will not hear what you are saying— so keep it simple.

You should also use large fonts because not everybody in the room is as close to the slides as you are. The minimum font size needed will depend on the size of the room and the size of projector screen (this determines how much the slides will be enlarged). Some people recommend no smaller than 30-point size in Arial font. While 30-point size may be a little large for some people's liking, the font should really be no smaller than 20-point size (remember not to clutter the slide!). Arial is a good font to use in a slide, whichever size you go with; it is crisp and clean, but not distracting. Other fonts might seem to look good, but their use in a bit of text can distract the reader. Additionally, you should be careful choosing colors. Remember that colors won't look the same on different devices. While you may have a passion for a sporting team's colors, your readers probably won't share that passion; also, such colors, while looking good on a team uniform, are designed to standout, and they might distract in a presentation. Use colors sparingly, limit the number of them per slide, and choose colors that have mutual contrast (e.g., blue and white). Also remember that some people are color blind and will not see the colors as you see them.

Additionally, you should be careful when choosing themes for your slide. Don't choose a theme that is too *busy*; that is, don't select a theme with so much detail that it will distract your audience or make the writing hard to read. A good theme will use soft colors and be slightly transparent, giving it a washed-out look.

Another thing to keep in mind is that a presentation is (or can be) a highly visual experience. The use of images is recommended. The images should be relevant to the discussion and not there for padding. In many cases, a relevant image with a few words will be all you need for a slide. We have seen presenters talk for 20 minutes using one presentation slide with a good image. While this may be the extreme, it does highlight the point. A picture *can* be worth a thousand words, sometimes more for a presentation.

Limit your presentation to a few well-designed slides. A recommended number often suggested is you should have between 10 to 12 slides for a 20 minute presentation. Most people will come away remembering only a couple of ideas from the presentation; too much clutter and slide overkill will further limit how much they remember.

To sum it all up, you should do the following in your presentation:

- Keep the presentation to a small number of well-designed slides (around 10-12 slides).
- Do not clutter the slide with text.
- Use bullet points for a few key points per page.

- Use a large font, from 20 to 30 points in size. Your font should be bold and simple; Arial is a good choice.

- Use colors sparingly, and use mutually contrasting colors for the text and background.

- Use simple, not overly busy backgrounds.

- Keep your background images simple and faded (washed-out or slightly transparent).

- Use relevant images (with a small amount of text or no text at all).

Summary

In this chapter, we discussed in detail how to create presentations in Google Presentations. First we covered the basics of building presentations, which are fairly similar, no matter what presentation software you are using. (Of course, Google Docs uses the cloud-computing paradigm.) We looked at Presentations' features, such as creating and manipulating text boxes and formatting the text, including some of the current limitations to the formatting options. As we discussed, these limitations are mainly in the number of available fonts and sizes; that said, Google is updating its applications constantly with new features and options. We then walked through some of Presentations' more advanced features, such as using images, adding shapes, and ordering objects within a presentation. We also looked at utilizing the drawing features for drawing objects and incorporating tables, video, and themes into your presentation. Finally, we discussed a few rules for building good presentations.

Chapter 7

Forms

The forms feature is a very interesting and exciting addition to the Google Docs stable. It is basically a data collection tool which works in conjunction with Spreadsheet (See Chapter 5). You create a Google Form that comes with a URL (web address). Users access the form, answer the questions you have written, and the results are automatically collated in a spreadsheet. Alternatively, you can create a custom spreadsheet, then create the form from the spreadsheet, where the results will be collated. For anyone who has ever tried to collect data either from an online survey, or from a distributed group of people, you will recognize the usefulness of this application. There are a number of other online tools for achieving this same end such as Survey Monkey. Some of these are free and some require subscription for a service, but Google Forms is free as part of Google Docs, and integrates very nicely with Spreadsheet. The forms feature also comes with some basic built-in reporting. However, you also get the power of having your results directly inputted into a spreadsheet so you can perform advanced mathematical functions on your data easily.

Why do I need Forms?

Forms allow you to easily automate many different tasks involving collection of data from users such as surveys. Managing surveys can be a long and daunting task with a lot of work; an example of this would be a survey for a community group.

A community group may want a survey which contains various elements such as multiple choice questions, numerical scale questions and feedback in either short or long answer format. Handled manually a small survey of 10 different types of questions will generate a lot of work not only in preparing the survey questions but also creating the appropriate number of copies, distributing the survey, collecting the survey and then finally processing the survey. Each step of this process can be very time consuming and critical sections such as processing the surveys can be fraught with human error in data entry.

Forms allow you to simply automate many different aspects of surveying a large group of people. With an electronic form, you don't need to photocopy or print 100 copies. An electronic form also makes distributing your survey easy; you can notify groups of over 1000 people simply by sending an email. Electronic forms also prevent you from chasing people down; users can simply fill in the form in their own time.

The biggest advantage of forms is that there is no human error in the processing of data. If a user enters a number, there is no chance it will me incorrectly entered, this is of immense value when the survey is designed for large groups. Using forms to survey groups especially large ones can save countless hours of work and provide error free data allowing you to continue with more important issues.

Creating a form

There are two ways to create a new form. If you already have a spreadsheet to collect the data, you can create a form from within the spreadsheet. However, if you want to create the data collection interface first (which is the approach we will take in this chapter), begin by clicking on the "Form" option in the "Create new" drop-down list in the Google Docs Interface (see Chapter 3) shown in Figure 7-1.

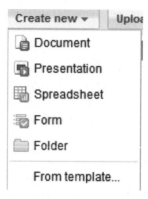

Figure 7-1: Creating a new form

After clicking Form, a new blank form appears, shown in Figure 7-2. The form shown in Figure 7-2 is annotated to highlight the major elements of a new form.

Menu

Form Title

Form
Information

Questions

Duplicate

Published Address

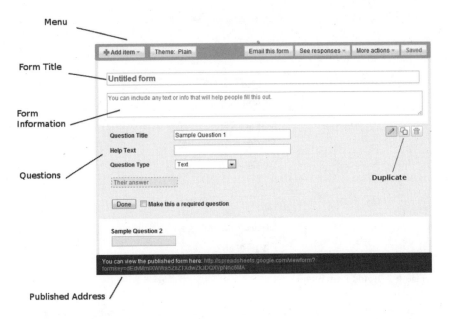

Figure 7-2: An annotated new form

The page displayed in Figure 7-2 is a blank form that you can manipulate freely. The first thing you should do is give your form a name. You can do this by clicking the "Form Title" and typing out a name. Next, fill in the "Form Information." This will help people to understand the form's purpose and the reason for you collecting the data.

Types of questions

You can ask several types of questions. Each type will allow you to get a different set of information. The answers are saved into a spreadsheet format which will allow you to perform mathematical and charting functions on your results. You can add new questions by two methods. The first method is to use the menu and clicking on the "Add item" button. This will bring down a menu that asks what type of question you want displayed in Figure 7-3.

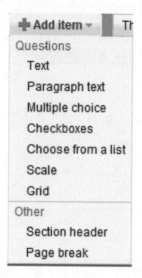

Figure 7-3: Add item menu

Alternatively, you can click on the "Duplicate" button to create a copy of an existing question. This is handy for some of the more complex questions type such as a Grid question. The "Duplicate" button is located at the top of each question. The button is located between "Edit" and "Delete" shown in Figure 7-4.

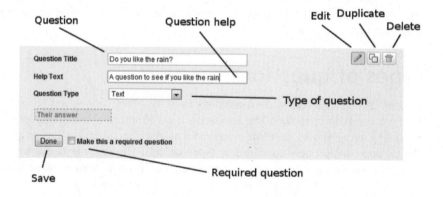

Figure 7-4: A sample text question

Figure 7-4 shows a constructed question ready to be published. There are many types of questions, each with individual options that allow you to customize the data you are collecting. You can edit existing questions by clicking the "Edit" button at the top of the question and making a copy of your question by clicking the "Duplicate" button. You can also delete a question by clicking the "Delete" button.

ExplainED

Use the duplicate button to create copies of complex questions to save time rather than copy them manually.

When you create a new question, you should ensure that your questions are easy to understand. Then you should enter and description of the question in the "Help Text" field. If you check the "Required Question"" check box this will force the person who is filling out the form to answer the question if they wish to submit the form.

Once you have finished editing your question, click the *"Done"* button and this will save your question. If you have made a mistake in the question you can simply click the *"Edit"* button on the question you wish to modify which is shown in Figure 7-4.

If you wish to delete a question, simply click on the *"Delete"* button and then *"OK"* on the confirmation window when it opens.

NotED

People filling in your form are generally doing you a favor; always make it easy as possible for the person filling in the form. Do this by using simple to understand language and refraining from required questions where possible.

There are a number of different questions you can construct in Forms. These are covered in the following sections.

Text

The first Type of question you can ask is text. This is a basic question designed for responses of no more than a few words. Figure 7-4 is an example of a text question. When the question shown in Figure 7-4 is published, the user will see the question as shown in Figure 7-5.

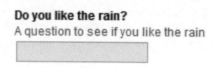

Do you like the rain?
A question to see if you like the rain

Figure 7-5: Published text question

Paragraph text

Paragraph text works in exactly the same way as a regular text question, with a larger response area to encourage a more detailed response to your question. An example of constructing a paragraph text question is shown in Figure 7-6

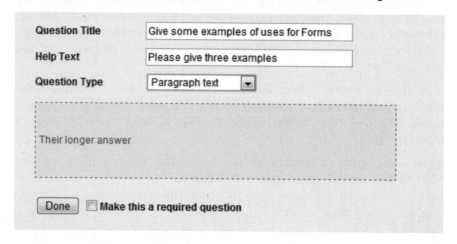

Figure 7-6: A sample paragraph text question

Once the question is published, the user will see the question as shown in Figure 7-7.

Figure 7-7: Published paragraph text question

Multiple Choice

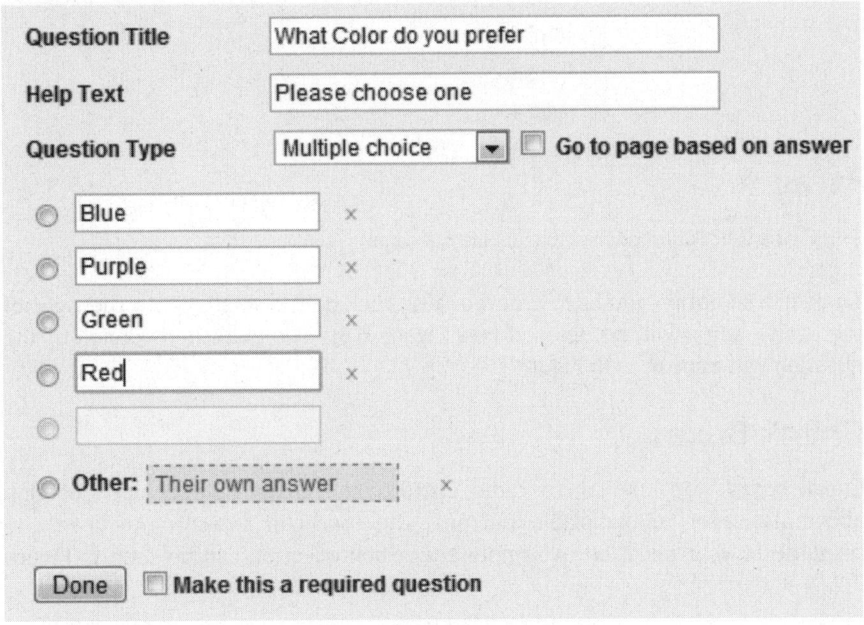

Question Title	What Color do you prefer
Help Text	Please choose one
Question Type	Multiple choice ▾ ☐ **Go to page based on answer**

○ Blue   ✕

○ Purple   ✕

○ Green   ✕

○ Red   ✕

○

○ **Other:** Their own answer   ✕

[Done] ☐ **Make this a required question**

Figure 7-8: A sample multiple choice question construction

A multiple choice question allows you to present users with a set of answers with radio buttons. Radio buttons allow you to specify a number of options while only allowing the user to select one of. To create the answers, all you have to do is to type text over the default "*Option*" text which appears in a new alternative. To create extra options, all you have to do is click on the grayed out empty box next to "or" add "Other." Clicking here will create a new box for answers. You can also create an "*Other*" field which allows the person to enter their own text response. This field acts like a simple text question. You can see the construction of a sample multiple choice question in Figure 7-8.

What color do you prefer
Please choose one

- ⊙ Blue
- ⊙ Purple
- ⊙ Green
- ⊙ Red

Figure 7-9: Published multiple choice question

To delete an option you have created, just click on the small "x" to the right of the option and it will be deleted (see Figure 7-8). The published version of the question will appear as in Figure 7-9.

Check Boxes

Check boxes work similar to radio buttons in the multiple choice question above. However, unlike radio buttons, the user can select more than one response to your question. A sample check box question can be seen in Figure 7-7.

Figure 7-10: A sample check box question construction

The check-box style question is useful when a number of options may be true in a question. You can use these questions in a test situation to see if the person is aware of all options. Also, the form may be used in a commercial situation when you are trying to find answers to questions with multiple answers. The published version of the question is shown in Figure 7-11.

What do you want on your sandwich
Please choose

☐ Cheese

☐ Chicken

☐ Lettuce

☐ Vegemite

Figure 7-11: Published check box question

List

A list-style question works in a similar method to a radio-button style question, and achieves a similar result to a multiple-choice style question. It requires the user to pick a single answer. However, the choices are presented in the form of a drop-down list and the different answers are hidden.

This can be used to save space and make your form look cleaner. You can create extra answers for the list the same way you create extra options for both multiple choice and check boxes. Unlike the multiple-choice style question and the check-box style question you cannot allow the users to provide their own answers in a text box. An example of the construction of a List question is shown in Figure 7-12. The published version can be seen in Figure 7-13.

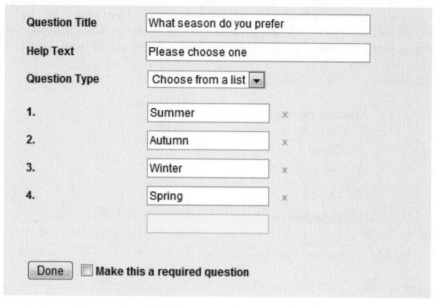

Figure 7-12: A sample list question

Figure 7-13: Published list question

Scale

Scale-style questions allow you to set a scale between any two numbers. This type of question can be used to gauge a user's feelings about a particular topic. You can only create two options for a scale-style question. To change the number of items that appear in the scale, all you have to do is click on the drop-down list next to the word "Scale" and set how many items you wish to display. A sample scale question is shown in Figure 7-14.

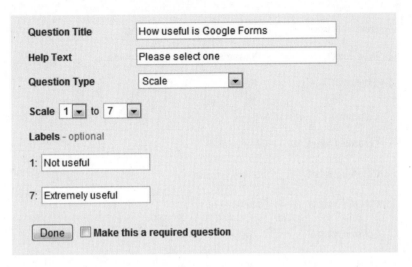

Figure 7-14: A sample scale question

Scale-style questions allow you to create questionnaires with Likert-type questions. This allows the user to choose along a discrete scale. Likert -type questions are commonly used in questionnaires and also allow the survey maker to retrieve some quantitative data. The published version of the scaled question in Figure 7-14 can be seen in Figure 7-14.

Figure 7-15: Published scale question

Grid

A grid-style question works like a scale-style question, except that it allows you to expand the question. Much like the scale-style question, it can be used to gather psychometric responses showing how a user feels about a topic on a discrete range. However, with a grid, you can gauge the user's feelings about multiple topics in the same question.

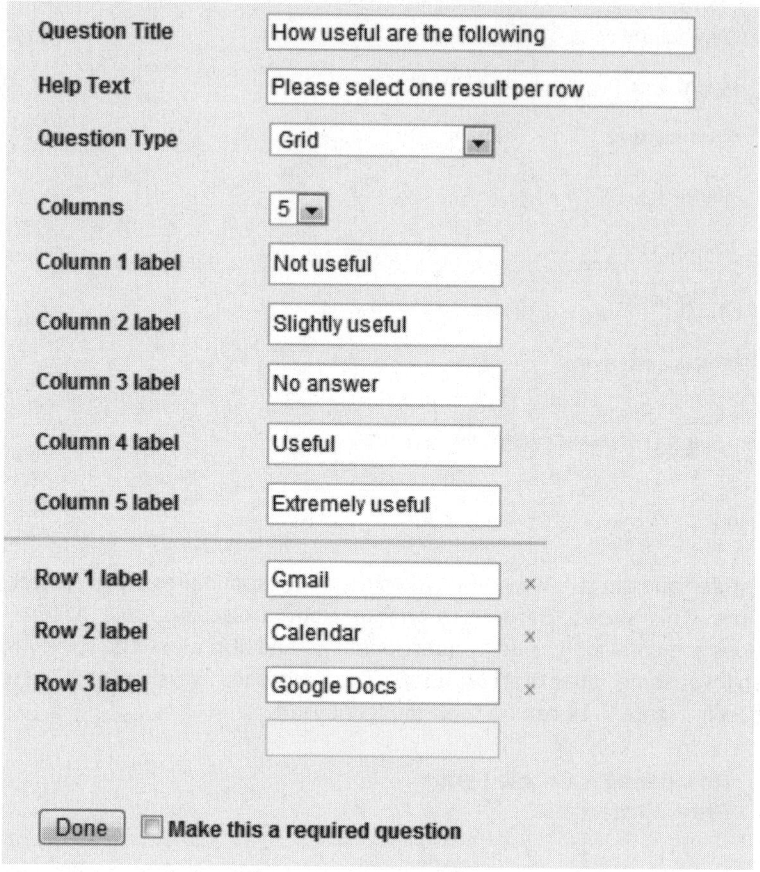

Question Title	How useful are the following
Help Text	Please select one result per row
Question Type	Grid ▾
Columns	5 ▾
Column 1 label	Not useful
Column 2 label	Slightly useful
Column 3 label	No answer
Column 4 label	Useful
Column 5 label	Extremely useful
Row 1 label	Gmail ✕
Row 2 label	Calendar ✕
Row 3 label	Google Docs ✕

[Done] ☐ **Make this a required question**

Figure 7-16: A sample grid question

In this question, you can name each individual column by clicking next to the label you wish to use and entering the column name. You can also create extra rows by clicking on the grayed out "Row Label" to create an extra row. You can create grid-style questions with up to five columns for scales. You can name each row of the scale by replacing the "Item" name. A sample grid question can be seen in Figure 7-16. The published version of the grid question can be seen in Figure 7-17.

How useful are the following

	not very	slightly	moderately	useful	extremely useful
GMail	○	○	○	○	○
Calendar	○	○	○	○	○
Google Docs	○	○	○	○	○
My cat	○	○	○	○	○

Figure 7-17: Published grid-style question

NotED

A grid question can only have a maximum scale (number of columns) of five.

Adding Questions

When you first create a form, it will be created with one default question. After you choose the question type and build the question as discussed in the previous sections, you click on the "Done" button at the bottom of the current question to complete it. See Figure 7-4. This will save the question and take you out of the editing mode for that question. To add another question, select the question type from the "Add Item" drop-down list on the menu bar shown in Figure 7-2. Choose from the questions types discussed previously. A new question of this type will be added to the end of the existing questions. You can change the type by selecting the new type of the question from the drop-down *"Question Type"* list shown in Figure 7-4.

Adding questions allows you to build lengthy questionnaires or even multiple choice tests for a teaching environment.

Adding Sections and Page Breaks

You can divide your questionnaire or test into pages and sections to provide a logical order. For example, if you are teaching history, you might have a section on medieval times followed by a question about the renaissance era. Or, if you are selling products, you might have a section about collecting product information and a section collecting payment details. The layout is up to you. To add a different section to your form, choose the "Section Header" option from the "Add Item" drop-down list on the menu. This will add a section header to the form after the existing last item. See Figure 7-18

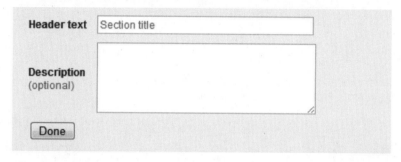

Figure 7-18: Section Header

You then provide a Section Header text and an optional description is the space provided in Figure 7-18, and click the "Done" button when finished. The header text and description will be displayed before any new questions are added.

Similarly, you can add a page break to divide questions between pages. This will be useful for advanced use of multiple choice questions discussed in the next section. To add a page break, choose the "Page Break" option from the "Add Item" drop-down list on the menu. This will add a page break to the form after the existing last item.

Each page break is a different page that will be displayed to the user. You can force users to go to certain pages based on certain answers. For example you can create a form that targets professionals and students. In this form you can create two pages—one which you can direct students or professionals to based on the answer to a multiple choice question which could be 'Are you a professional or a student?'.

Editing the page break is exactly like editing the section header shown in Figure 7-18. You provide a page title text and an optional description is the space provided. The page title and description will be displayed before any new questions that are added. By using pages and structuring your questions carefully, you can design a questionnaire or test that allows you to skip pages based on specific answers to multiple-choice questions.

Advanced Use of Multiple Choice Questions

When designing multiple choice questions, as discussed in a previous section, there is an advanced feature we can make use of to design more complex questionnaires or tests. In Figure 7-8, you check the check-box labeled "Go to page based on answer," you activate the more advanced design feature. You will see the edit form for the multiple choice question change slightly as shown in Figure 7-19.

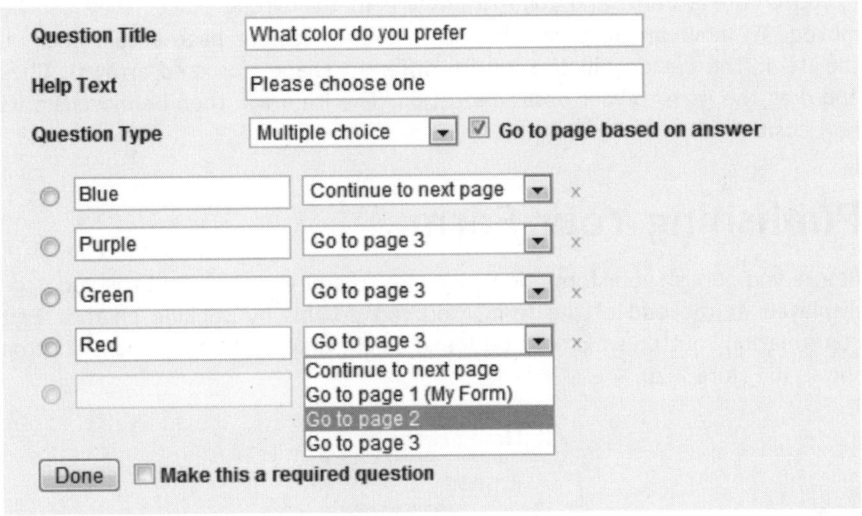

Figure 7-19: Advanced use of Multiple choice questions

For each of the question's options, you can control what the user is asked next. As can be seen from the drop-down list in Figure 7-19, for each possible option in the multiple choice question you can allow the questionnaire or test to continue to the next page naturally, or you can re-direct the questionnaire or test to a specific page based on the option. At the end of each page in the questionnaire or test, two buttons will be displayed "Back" and "Continue". "Back" won't be shown on the first page and "Continue" won't be shown on the final page. When the user clicks "Continue", they will be taken to the page you chose.

By careful planning and the use of multiple pages, you can construct complex questionnaires or tests that are based on the user's response to multiple choice questions. Only with the use of multiple choice questions can you achieve this.

ExplainED

You can create adaptive questionnaires or tests with the use of multiple choice questions and pages.

Moving Items

If you create a Form and some items are in the wrong place, they can be moved. To move an item, including a section header or page break, click on the item. The cursor will turn into a different shape, (crossed arrows). Click and drag the item to your desired location. The item will then be moved to its new position.

Publishing Your Form

Before you publish your form, you may wish to edit the default thank you page displayed at the end of the form. You can do this by clicking on the "Edit confirmation" button which can be found by clicking the "More actions" button shown in Figure 7-20.

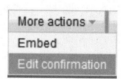

Figure 7-20: More actions menu

Once you have clicked on the "Edit confirmation" link, you will be presented with a page shown in Figure 7-21. From here, you can edit the text that users will see when they complete the form. You can also allow people to view the summary of the form by clicking on the check box labeled "Let everyone see the response summary." This will allow everyone to see the summary which will be discussed later in this chapter.

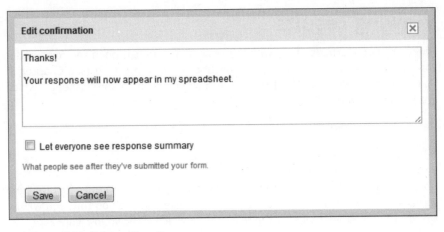

Figure 7-21: Edit confirmation

There are a few ways you can distribute your form to people. The first method is to copy the link from the bottom of the form page and send it to someone using Google Talk or another form of social networking. The second method is to click "E-mail this form" This will open up a window displayed in Figure 7-22.

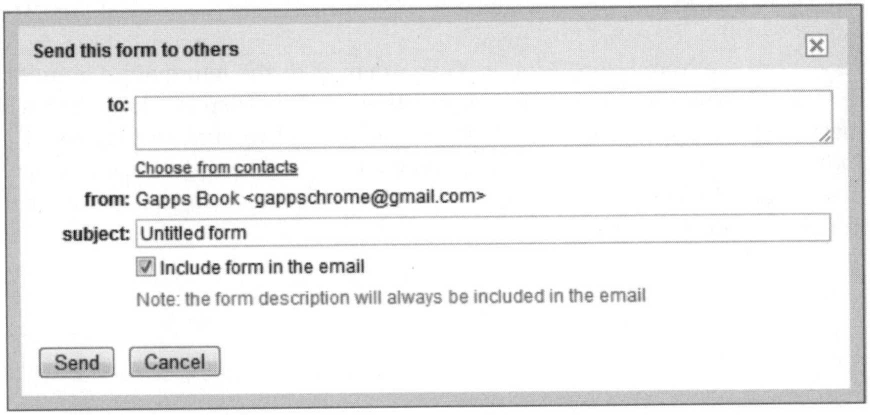

Figure 7-22: Email form

From here, all you have to do is enter the e-mail addresses of the people you want to receive the form. The subject line is automatically set to the name of the form. You can change this if you wish, however you should keep the subject descriptive. You also have the ability to include the form inside the e-mail.

The final method of sharing your form is to include it on your website. For more information on this feature please refer to Chapter 3.

Viewing results

There are two methods of viewing the results. The first is open the form under spreadsheet view. To do this, go to the Google Docs interface (see Chapter 3) and look for your form. The forms have a similar icon to spreadsheets, which are shown in Figure 7-23.

Figure 7-23: Form in Google Docs interface

Note the icon for the form. The tick in the corner of the icon indicates that the spreadsheet has been generated from a form. Once you click on this, you will be taken to a spreadsheet view of the results data which is shown in Figure 7-24.

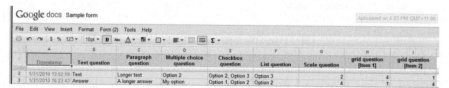

Figure 7-24: Results of a form

As you can see from Figure 7-24, you can examine all the information from the questions submitted. You can then manipulate the data from this form with the methods discussed in Chapter 5. The second method to view the results of a form is to go to summary mode. You can go here by selecting "Show summary of responses" from the "Form(x)" drop-down menu item on the spreadsheet menu, shown in Figure 7-25.

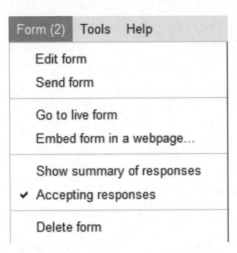

Figure 7-25: Form menu

ExplainED

You can see how many people have responded to your form by looking at the number inside the brackets at the top of the form menu.

Once you click on the "Summary" button, you will be sent to the summary page. This is partly shown in Figure 7-26.

The summary page depicted in Figure 7-26 gives you a brief overview of the responses to the form. From this page, we can see there have been two responses to the form and we can see the summary of three questions. Note that the questions with fixed answers can be graphed.

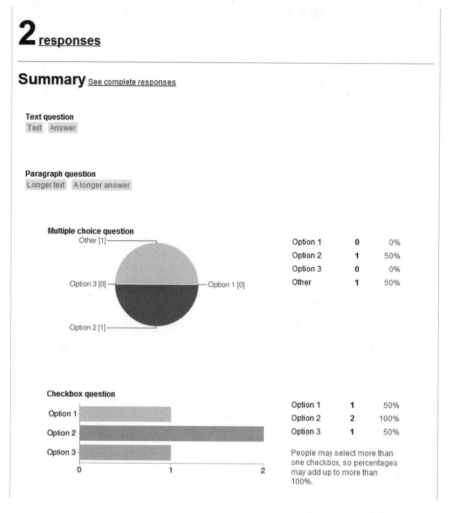

2 responses

Summary See complete responses

Text question
Text   Answer

Paragraph question
Longer text   A longer answer

Multiple choice question
Other [1]
Option 3 [0]
Option 1 [0]
Option 2 [1]

Option 1	0	0%
Option 2	1	50%
Option 3	0	0%
Other	1	50%

Checkbox question
Option 1
Option 2
Option 3
0   1   2

Option 1	1	50%
Option 2	2	100%
Option 3	1	50%

People may select more than one checkbox, so percentages may add up to more than 100%.

Figure 7-26: Summary

Editing forms

To edit your form, you have to go to the spreadsheet view of the form. Once there, you have to go to the forms menu that was shown in Figure 7-25, by selecting "Edit form" from the "Form(x)" drop-down menu item on the spreadsheet menu. This will open a new Web browser page where you can edit the form as we have already covered. This page looks like the one in

Figure 7-2. Once you have finished making your changes, simply click the "Save" button this will update your publicly available form.

NotED

If you edit your form, it will also edit what is required in the answers spreadsheet. Only edit to correct minor mistakes, otherwise you may invalidate any data already collected.

Deleting forms from Spreadsheets

You can delete your form from the Spreadsheet results view by clicking on the "Delete" under the "Form" menu that was shown in Figure 7-25. Once you click on "Delete," you will be presented with a confirmation dialog box where you must click "OK".

Themes

Like many other Google products, you can change the theme of the form. You can do this by clicking on the "Theme" button located in the Forms menu while you are editing. This will take you to a page depicted in Figure 7-27. From there, all you have to do is find a theme that you like. This will automatically preview the theme in the window. Click "Apply" to set the theme in the publicly visible form, otherwise you can click "Cancel".

ExplainED

Always make sure that your form is easy-to-read with the theme you have chosen and consider people with eyesight worse than yours.

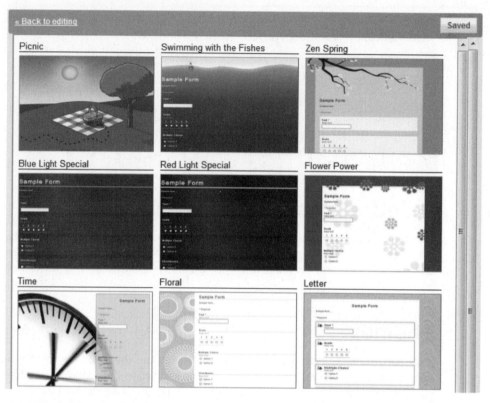

Figure 7-27: Selecting a theme

Summary

In this chapter we covered how to use Google Docs Forms. We began by creating a new form. Then we covered the different types of questions for users. We continued by covering various ways to edit and format your forms. Next, we examined moving items, publishing a form and viewing the results. We finished with editing, deleting and changing the theme of a form.

Readers who are new to the idea of using survey tools will find Google Docs Forms to be an invaluable tool for creating a survey and analyzing the results. Google Docs Forms is a fitting example of how different items can be integrated to provide you with an advanced platform.

Chapter 8

Calendar

Desktop calendar applications can be very useful for people who are always at their desk, and most of these can be synchronized with smaller applications for your cell phone or Smart Phone. Calendar applications are proficient time management and productivity tools. Google Applications offer Google Calendar as an alternative to many commercially available calendar applications including Microsoft Outlook and Lotus Notes. Google Calendar is a robust and reliable online calendar. One of the advantages to Google Calendar is that it is a web-based application. Wherever you go, as long as you have an Internet connection, you have access to your Google Calendar. You don't need to sync if your device has access to the Internet through a browser, though Google Calendar can be synched with a number of devices and calendar applications on these devices. As the data for Google Calendar is stored in the cloud, your data is in one place so you are protected from faults, therefore your calendar is always accessible.

If you have already registered for a Gmail account, you already have access to Google Calendar. To access Google Calendar, register for a Gmail account (as outlined in Chapter 2).

Creating a New Calendar

You can access Google Calendar in a variety of ways. From the Google home page (google.com), sign in to your Gmail account and choose the "Calendar" menu option from the "More" drop-down menu in the GoogleApps tool bar. Alternatively, if you are in Gmail, select the "Calendar" link in the GoogleApps tool bar. You can also type the appropriate URL [google.com/calendar] into the Chrome address bar. The first time you go to Google Calendar, create your calendar and a screen will be displayed (see Figure 8-1).

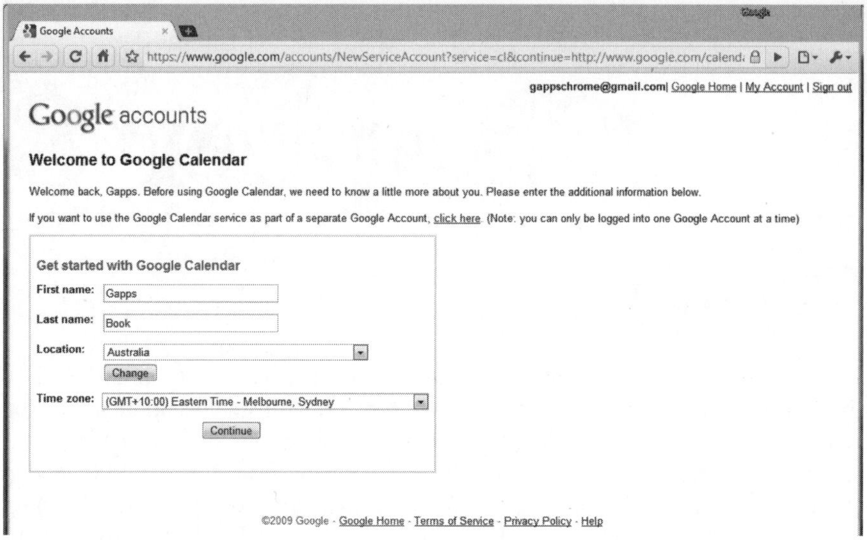

Figure 8-1: Create new calendar

At this screen, you will need to configure the details of your calendar. If the information on the screen is correct, click the "Continue" button at the bottom of the input area finalizing your calendar and taking you to the opening screen. Otherwise, if there are errors you can correct them. If, for example, part of your name is spelled incorrectly, you can click the field with the incorrect data and using your keyboard you can type the correct information. If your time zone or country is incorrect, click the field that contains the incorrect information and two drop-down lists will appear providing you a number of options (see Figure 8-2).

When you are presented with the drop-down lists for the location or time zone, scroll through the list, find the right value, and select it. If you change the location field, click the "Change" button below the location to register the change. This will update the drop-down list with the appropriate time zones for the location. Once this is complete, click the "Continue" button at the bottom of the input area taking you to the main calendar screen.

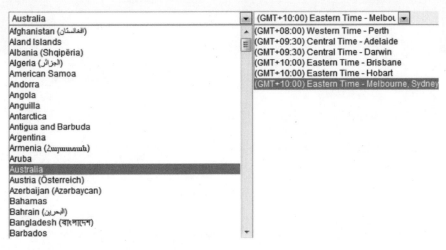

Figure 8-2: Country and time zone drop-down lists

Once you have successfully created a new calendar (or if you are returning to your existing calendar), you will be directed to the main calendar screen (see Figure 8-3). Your calendar will be displayed in a weekly view format. In this format, your calendar for the rest of the week will be shown with one column for each day and the current day column will be highlighted with a pale yellow background (see Figure 8-3).

Elements of the Screen

The default (opening) view of your calendar is displayed with a quick overview of your week's schedule and the ability to change the information the calendar displays. You can also add events and modify the event details of existing events. The weekly view format provides a quick at-a-glance overview of your entire schedule for the week, broken down into half-hourly time slots. Figure 8-3 shows an annotated view of the default Google Calendar view.

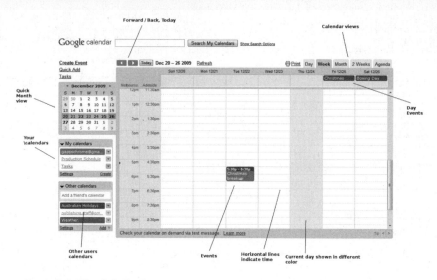

Figure 8-3: The default view

The most important elements of the screen are the events displayed in the calendar. Each event is displayed in a shaded box with the times of the event and a brief description of the event. The size of the shaded box indicates the length of the events in "Day," "Week," and "4 Days" views as seen in "Viewing Options." In the weekly view format, the calendar is ruled by horizontal lines indicating time, with the time increments shown on the left side of the calendar. An event beginning at 4 p.m. and ending at 8 p.m. will have a shaded box that starts at the timeline of 4 p.m. and ends at the timeline for 8 p.m. (see Figure 8-4).

On the lower left side of Google Calendar are a series of displays and links called "My calendars" and "Other calendars." These provide access to more advanced features (discussed later in this chapter). When you initially create your calendar, it will automatically add "Public holidays" from a special calendar containing the public holidays based on the selected country location (see Figure 8-1). This will vary depending on the location you are using and whether Google has a public holiday calendar for your location. You can import public holidays from these special calendars at any time.

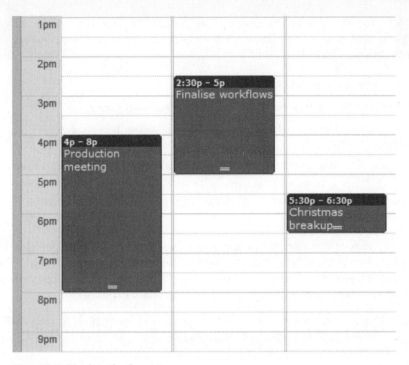

Figure 8-4: The length of events

Also on the left side of calendars is the "Month quick view." This allows you to get a basic, quick overview of the month regardless of the view you are using in the main part of the calendar screen. In the "Month quick view," the current date is shown by a background color that is dark blue by default. Days that have tasks on them are shown with bold numbers for the day in the "Month quick view."

Figure 8-3 also displays two "Day events," which are events scheduled to run the entire day including birthdays, anniversaries, and public holidays. The indicators for these day events are located on the top portion of the calendar just under the date for the particular day and are always a fixed size.

Calendar Views

With Google Calendar, you can choose how to view your calendar. The "Week" view is the default when you open Google Calendar. This will show the current week with the current day highlighted in yellow (see Figure 8-3). However, there may be occasions when you need to take a different view, including a more detailed view of a particular day or more of an overview of the entire month. You can choose the desired view by selecting the appropriate link at the top right of the calendar (see Figure 8-3). The calendars are presented to you in "views," including:

Day: See the entire day in detail.

Week: Default view, where you can see a week at a glance.

Month: Monthly view where you can see the days with overviews of appointments.

4 Days: This is a four-day view allowing detailed planning four days ahead by default.

Agenda: Displays the agents of upcoming appointments and scheduled events.

The day view of the calendar is useful when you have a busy schedule that you need to keep track of meetings and events. You can leave this open at all times and continually add and refer to it (see Figure 8-5). In this mode, appointments can be seen with finer granularity with more detailed explanations.

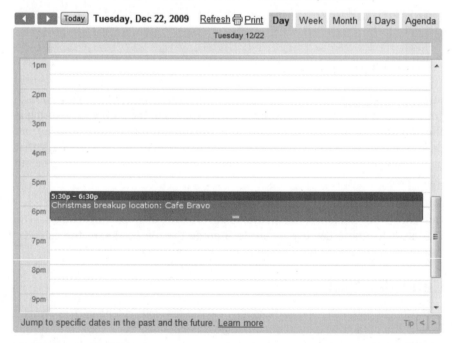

Figure 8-5: The day view

This can be seen by comparing the "Christmas break-up" event (see Figure 8-3) and the event depicted in Figure 8-5. These events have the same details; however the "Day" view provides more space to show the event text. The next calendar view is "Month" view. Access this view by clicking the "Month" link in the "Calendar Views" links on the top right corner of the calendar (see Figure 8-6).

◀ ▶ Today **December 2009** Refresh	🖨Print	Day	Week	**Month**	4 Days	Agenda

Sun	Mon	Tue	Wed	Thu	Fri	Sat
29	30	Dec 1	2	3	4	5
6	7	8	9	10	11	12
13	14	15	16	17	18	19
20 4p Production m	21 2:30p Finalise w	22 5:30p Christmas	23	24	25 Christmas	26 Boxing Day
27 Public Holiday	28	29	30	31	Jan 1 New Year	2

See the weather forecast in your calendar. Learn more   Tip < >

Figure 8-6: The month view

"All day" events including Christmas and Boxing Day are surrounded by a colored box, and the normal events are displayed in a condensed text version. Another downfall of "Month" view is that it can only display a limited number of events on each day. Figure 8-7 shows a day with more items in it than can be displayed in "Month" view.

ExplainED

Use "Month" view to get a quick overview of your schedule when deciding when to hold events.

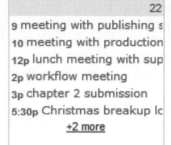

Figure 8-7: A busy day

The month view can only show a limited number of items based on the size of the day (see Figure 8-7). The number of items shown in the day is limited to the size of the calendar inside your browser. If you increase or decrease the size of your browser window, the calendar inside the browser will also resize. At the base of the overcrowded day, you will see a link labeled "+2 more" telling you how many more events there are on the days not displayed (see Figure 8-7). The number will change depending on the number of events hidden due to the size of the day. This also allows you to view the rest of the events on that day in an external window (see Figure 8-8).

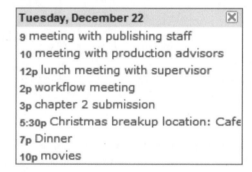

Figure 8-8: Extended view of a day

Figure 8-8 shows the window created when you click the "More items" link (see Figure 8-7). The pop-up window is also limited with space, so it will only show a brief overview of the items. To close the window, click the "x" in the upper right corner of the pop-up window. The next view is the "4 Day" view (see Figure 8-9).

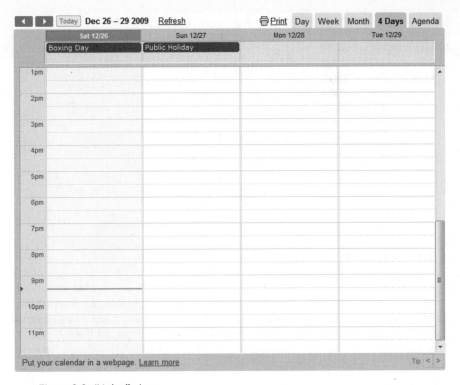

Figure 8-9: "4 day" view

The "4 Day" view is similar to the "Week" view and is useful for giving you a more detailed look at the next few days' events. The "4 Day" view is a custom view, meaning it is configurable in "Settings" to "5 Day," "6 Day," "2 Weeks," etc. The final view is the "Agenda" view. This view doesn't show days, but only events on your calendar (see Figure 8-10).

Figure 8-10: Agenda view

Creating Events

There are two ways to create events in your calendar. We discuss the more detailed method first, and then present the short-cut, as this can lead to the details discussed in this first section depending on what you need to add to the event. To create an event for your calendar, click the "Create Event" link at the top left of the calendar screen (see Figure 8-3) bringing you to a display screen (see Figure 8-11). "Guests" and "invitations" will be covered later in this chapter.

Once on the "Create event" page, you can enter the details of the event you wish to create. Begin by entering the details including what the event is in the "What" field. The information entered here should be a short description of the event such as "Meeting with production team" or "Lunch with the family." After you have entered the details of the event, select when the event is scheduled. Click on the first field next to "When." Clicking on this will bring up a date picker window (see Figure 8-12).

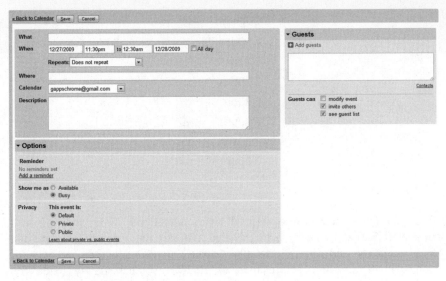

Figure 8-11: Create event

12/28/2009   6:00pm

« **December 2009** »

S	M	T	W	T	F	S
22	23	24	25	26	27	28
29	30	1	2	3	4	5
6	7	8	9	10	11	12
13	14	15	16	17	18	19
20	21	22	23	24	25	26
27	28	29	30	31	1	2
3	4	5	6	7	8	9

Figure 8-12: Date picker

The date picker allows you to quickly pick a date from the list. To select a date, scroll to the correct year and month by using the arrows at the top of the picker. Once you have selected the appropriate month and year, click the date you wish to select and this will automatically update the field next to "When."

Once you have selected the date, select the start time. Click the next field over from the date. This will bring up a drop-down list for you to select what time the event starts (see Figure 8-13). The list is organized in half-hour time slots. You can select from the drop-down list or type the time into the field if it begins outside of a half-hour time slot.

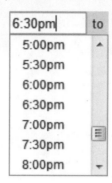

Figure 8-13: Time chooser

Once you have located the desired time, select the time and this will automatically update the time field. After selecting the desired start date and time, select the end time. By default, Google Calendar allocates one hour for each event. If the event requires more or less time, you can specify the desired end time by using the same process as setting the start time. Following event times are the repeating events. With these options, you can set events to repeat on your calendar. If you click the "Repeats" field, a drop-down list will be displayed of possible repeat options. Event repetition will be covered in depth later in this chapter.

After "Repeats," you get the option of entering a location. This can be a note to yourself such as "Café down the road" or a full address such as "Melissa Cakes, 22 Pier Street, Altona."

ExplainED

If you enter the full address of the event location in the "Where" field, you and people you invite will be able to see a link showing the location on Google Maps.

Below "Where" is a field called "Calendar and clicking this will bring up a drop-down box containing all of your calendars. At this stage of the chapter, you should only have one calendar to choose from in this box. We will cover creating more calendars and how they are useful to you later in this chapter. The next part of creating an event is the description. This field is not mandatory but can be quite helpful in jogging your memory on the details of the events or items to bring.

Below "Description," you can set reminders alerting you when an event is approaching. By clicking the "Add a reminder" link under options (see Figure 8-11), you will see a new line appear in the "Create event" window (see Figure 8-14).

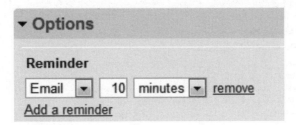

Figure 8-14: Reminders

The reminders allow you to have messages sent to you in a variety of ways reminding you of an upcoming event. The default method is to e-mail you, however you can click the drop-down box with "E-mail" in it to present you with a drop-down list of different methods that can be used to remind you of an event (see Figure 8-15).

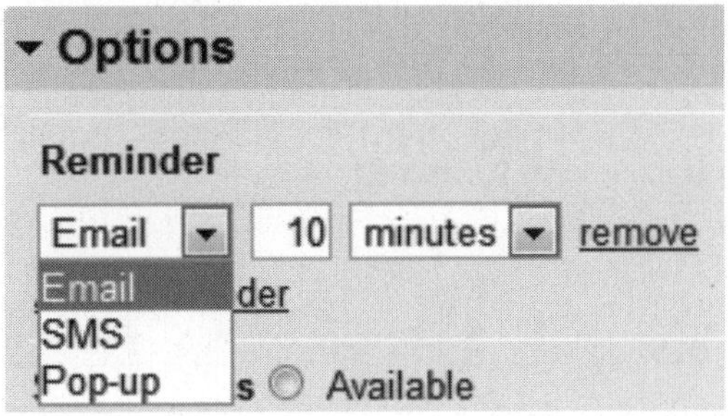

Figure 8-15: Reminder types

As the default method of reminding you of an event is by e-mail, the e-mail will provide details of the event including the time of the event, location, the calendar that the event is in, and any extra details you have included (see Figure 8-16). E-mail reminders are useful if you regularly monitor your e-mail or have a mobile phone checking your e-mail account.

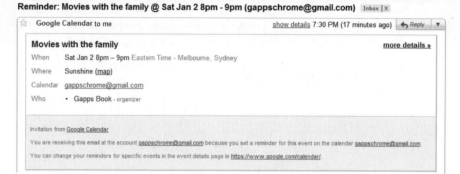

Figure 8-16 E-mail reminder

The next notification type is "Pop-up." This displays a message inside the Google Calendar window reminding you of an event. This method is not recommended unless you spend a significant amount of time on your computer as you need to have Google Calendar open to receive the reminder. A "Pop-up" notification will appear (see Figure 8-17).

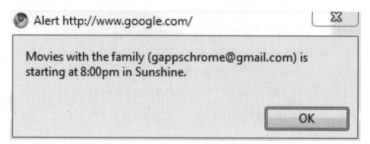

Figure 8-17: Pop-up reminder

The final option for reminders is to send a Text Message to your mobile phone. This method sends a short message to your mobile phone and contains the basic details of the event (see Figure 8-18). We will cover the steps to be taken to setup Text notifications later in this chapter.

Figure 8-18: Text reminder

After setting the type of reminder to be sent, you can specify when the reminder will be sent by setting how long before an event you would like the notification. Type a number inside the box next to the type of reminder and select whether the number refers to minutes, hours, days, or weeks before the event.

The next set of options explains how to set your availability during appointments. This feature is used in calendar programs that can use the information in Google Calendar. For example, you could use this feature to show an allotted time when you are available for other people to make appointments with you. Click the "Available" radio button next to "Show me as."

The final set of options labeled "Privacy" allows you to set whether or not the details of the event can be viewed by people. These options are only activated if you are sharing your calendar. The default setting will always be private unless you have set your calendar to public. If you set the event to public, anyone with viewing access to your calendar will see all of the details of the event. Otherwise, if the event is set to private, people with viewing access to your calendar will only see that you are busy. This is dependent on how much access a person has. Sharing calendars and privacy settings will be discussed later in this chapter.

Clicking to Add Events

A faster method for creating an event at the desired time is clicking the time slot you wish to allocate. If there are already no events scheduled in the slot, a dialog box will be displayed (see Figure 8-19).

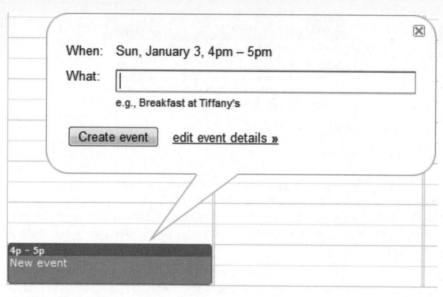

Figure 8-19: Clicking an empty location

By clicking on a free space at 4 p.m., a blank event in that time slot will be created (see Figure 8-19). You can type a name into the "What" field and click the "Create event" button, and the event would be finalized. You can also click the "Edit event details" link and the "Create dialog box" will be displayed.

Quick Add

Near the top left side of the calendar window (see Figure 8-3), there is a link called "Quick Add." This allows you to quickly enter events into your calendar using natural language. This is a useful feature and can help you quickly add events to your calendar. If you click the link, a dialog box will appear (see Figure 8-20).

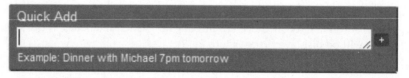

Figure 8-20: Quick add

To add an event by "Quick add," type the details of the event such as "Dinner with the family tomorrow 7 p.m." and press enter. This will create an event between 7 and 8 p.m. on the next day with the name "Dinner with the family" (see Figure 8-21). Google Calendar will interpret your statement trying to make sense of what you entered. This usually works well as long as you are clear and concise.

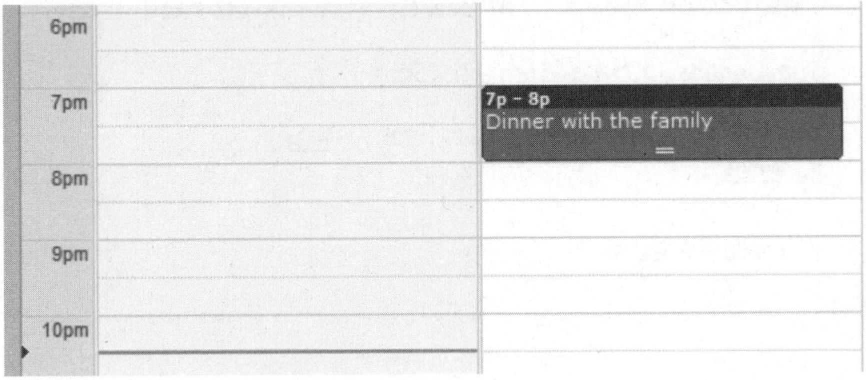

Figure 8-21: Results of quick add

This process is easier than the previous two methods of adding events. "Quick add" is not limited to creating simple events. It can be used to create more complex events including ones scheduled in different time zones. Scheduling events over different time zones makes the "Quick Add" function more efficient than the regular add. Another more complex example of the "Quick add" would be to enter "Business meeting Monday 9 a.m. to 11 a.m. at Conference Room B." Placing that into the "Quick add" will create an event on the closest 9 a.m. Monday time slot. If it is currently 8 a.m. on a Monday, it would create the event at 9 a.m. on the same day, however if it was 9:01 a.m., the event would be created the following Monday.

The "Quick add" function works by reading keywords from text you enter and matching words against internal keywords including "at," "on," "in," "with," "next," and "for." The "on" or "at" keywords can be used to specify the time of an event such as "on Tuesday" or "at 3:15 p.m." A "Quick add" using the "at" and "on" keywords would be "Production meeting on Tuesday at 12:45 p.m."

The next keywords are "in" and "at" and can be used in different situations where it is followed by an address such as "In Conference Room B" or "At 276 Brunswick Street, Fitzroy." An example of a "Quick add" task with the keywords described so far would be "Production meeting on Tuesday at 12:45 p.m. at 276 Brunswick Street, Fitzroy." That "Quick add" would create an event on Tuesday at 12:45 p.m. for one hour, which will have the "Where" field with "276 Brunswick Street, Fitzroy" with the name "Production meeting."

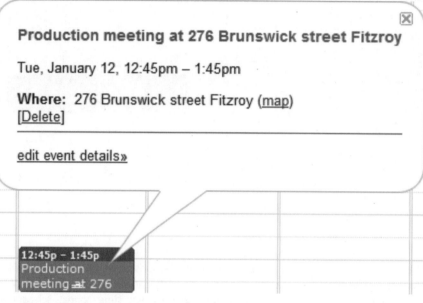

Figure 8-22: Results of a more complex quick add

As seen in the event details, the "Quick add" has placed all information inputted into the appropriate place in the event. The next keyword in "Quick add" is "with." The "with" keyword can be used to invite people to events and will be covered later in this chapter. The final keyword is "for." Using this keyword allows you to set repetition on events (again to be covered later in this chapter).

As well as the keywords, "Quick add" has the ability to add events that are in different time zones. You can be based in Australia and quickly schedule a phone call to an office in New York. Additionally, you can use "Quick add" and append the three-digit time code after the time. For example "Call head office at 9 a.m. EDT." You can use any three-digit time code, however the options are limited and time zones from all countries are not implemented.

Finding, Viewing and Modifying Events

Once you have created your events, locate and view the details for events. To locate events, use the "Search" function located on the top of every page in Google Calendar. The search function will check the contents of every event and return a list of events that match. To search for events, enter the term you are looking for in the search field seen at the top of Figure 8-3 (see Figure 8-23).

Figure 8-23: Search results

As seen in Figure 8-23, all events in the calendar have been located with the word "meeting" in them. You can further limit the number of results by entering a more precise term. For example, if there was an upcoming meeting located off site where the only information you had was the name of the suburb, you could enter the name such as "Fitzroy" as a search term and click the button next to the field named "Search My Calendars." This will perform the search and return all events with the word "Fitzroy" in them. You can use the search to check more than one word such as "Meeting" and "Fitzroy" returning results with both of the terms in the event.

You can perform more complex searches by clicking the "Show Search Options" link next to the "Search My Calendars" button. This will present you with a set of options (see Figure 8-24).

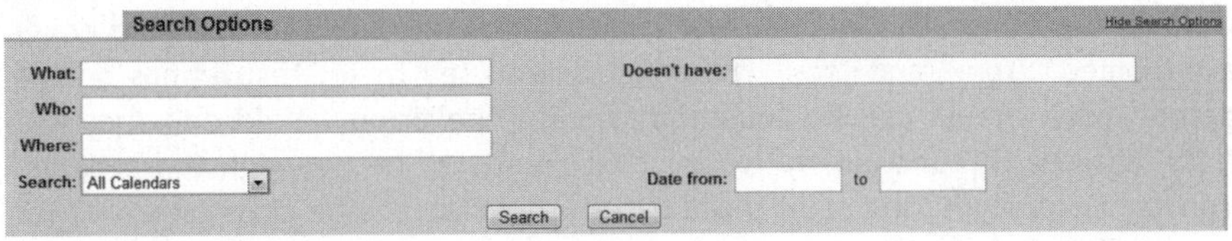

Figure 8-24: Advanced search

The fields shown in Figure 8-24 allow you to search various parts of the event information for keywords. You can search the "What" field for various terms such as "Family" in the "What" field and "Mum" in the "Where" field, and the search will find any events containing both terms in the appropriate fields. With the advanced search, you can also search in your own or other people's calendars (who have access to yours). Select the calendar you wish to search from the drop-down list (see Figure 8-25). This list displays two other options of search only within your calendars by using "All My Calendars," or only in other people's calendars ("All Other Calendars").

NotED

You can only select one option to search.

Figure 8-25: Searching calendars

As well as being able to search what text exists in the events, you can further exclude results by entering data in the "Doesn't have" field. The search function will exclude any events containing words entered into that field. For example, you could search for the word "meeting" in the "What" field and exclude "status meeting" by entering "status" into the "Doesn't have" field. Entering those options will instruct the search to locate any event containing the word "meeting" in the "What" field, but will remove events with the word "status" in them.

The last set of fields that can be used to restrict your results are the two fields next to "Date" located in the lower right side of the search box. These boxes are labeled "from" and "to." These fields are used to set restrictions on the dates where events can be found. If you set the "from" field and the "to" field, the search function will restrict all results to be between those dates. You can also only fill in one of those dates to instruct the function to search for events after or before a certain date depending on what field you enter.

ExplainED

Always enter as much information as possible when creating an event to make it easier to find with a search.

If you can see the event in your calendar, you can click part of the event's colored background to get a speech bubble to appear with the event's details excluding the "Description" field (see Figure 8-26).

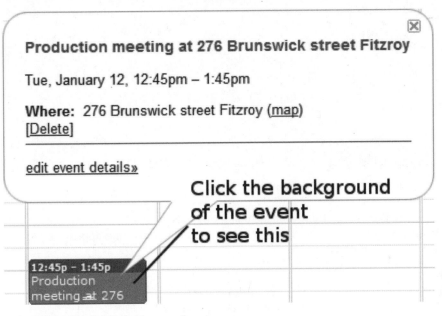

Figure 8-26: Quick viewing events

This method will provide a quick overview of the event. Next to the data in the "Where" field (see Figure 8-26), a link will appear looking like "(map)." If you have entered a street address in the field, you will be able to click the link to Chrome, which will create a new tab and you can then see a map of the local area in Google Maps (see Figure 8-27). This was displayed by clicking the "(map)" link in Figure 8-26.

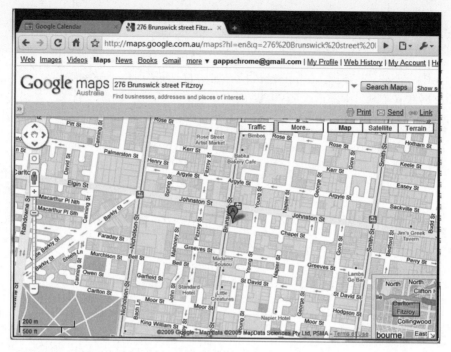

Figure 8-27: Map of the event's location

To see all details of the event including the "description," click the text in the event. As your mouse goes over the text, you will see a line appear under the text (see Figure 8-28).

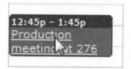

Figure 8-28: Underlined text on an event

Once you have clicked the event's text, you will be taken to a page where you can edit events. This page (shown in Figure 8-29) looks and acts like the "Create Event" page with a few differences. The only notable difference for this section is the addition of the map below the "Where" field after you have entered a suitable address in the "Where" field (Figure 8-29). To return to your calendar, click "Cancel."

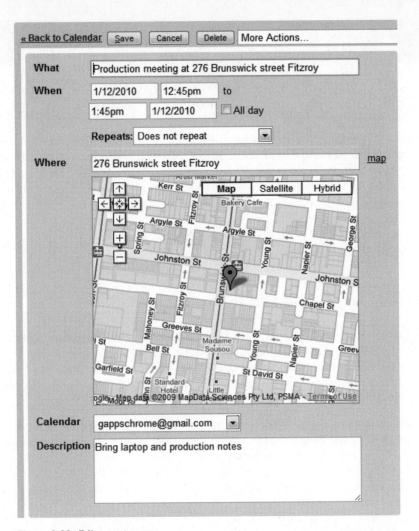

« Back to Calendar [Save] [Cancel] [Delete] | More Actions...

What   Production meeting at 276 Brunswick street Fitzroy

When   1/12/2010   12:45pm   to

             1:45pm   1/12/2010   ☐ All day

             Repeats: Does not repeat   ▾

Where   276 Brunswick street Fitzroy   map

Calendar gappschrome@gmail.com   ▾

Description Bring laptop and production notes

Figure 8-29: Edit event page

There are various methods for editing events that can be used depending on what screen you are looking at and what you intend to do. If you wish to move an appointment to a different time or day, click the event object and drag it to where ever you wish. This will move the single event to the desired time slot.

Rather than editing the details of an event to change the time, you can also increase or decrease the time allotted to an event by moving your mouse over the top or bottom of the event. The mouse icon will change (see Figure 8-30). Click and drag the top or bottom of the event object to change the starting and finishing time of the event. This will also change the length of the event.

Figure 8-30: Editing event times

To edit the details of the event, click the text in the event. As your mouse goes over the text, you will see a line appear under the text (see Figure 8-28). Once you have clicked the event's text, you will be taken to a page shown in Figure 8-29. From here you can make the changes you wish to an event and then click the 'Save' button.

To delete an event you simply have to click the 'delete' link that is shown in Figure 8-26 or the delete button that is shown in Figure 8-29. After you delete an event, in case you have made an error, a small message will appear at the top of the screen stating "Event deleted Undo." Click the "Undo" link to restore the event. You will only have a short period of time to activate this link.

The final way to view events is by both "agenda" and "search" view. Both agenda and search show events in a similar way so the same method works on both. Viewing the basic details of the event is a simple process. Locate the event by search or in the agenda view and click either the times or the title of the event (see Figure 8-31). When you are in month view, click on the event in the day in order to display the speech bubble (see Figure 8-26). To view the full event in the month view, click on the "Edit event details" link contained within the speech bubble.

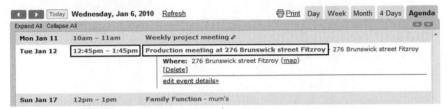

Figure 8-31: Agenda and search events

The details presented are the same as in Figure 8-26. To view the full details of the event including the "Description" field, click the "Edit event details" link.

Recurring Events

Having repeating events in your calendar saves you from manually and continually entering events. To organize repeating events, click the "Create Event" link, and you will be returned to the "Create" page (see Figure 8-11). When you are in the "Create event" page, locate the repetition options shown in Figure 8-32.

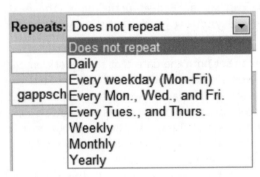

Figure 8-32: Repeat options

The repeat options (see Figure 8-32) allow you to set how often the event repeats in your calendar. Setting this option to "Daily" will present you with a list of options (see Figure 8-33).

Figure 8-33: Daily options

When you select "Daily," you are presented with the option to repeat after a set number of days. You can also set the option to specify an end date by clicking the "Until" radio button. Once you click the radio button, a date chooser will be displayed where you can select the date the repetition will end. You can also manually enter the date in the "Until" field in the format "month/day/year" in number format such as 12/28/2009.

The next three repeat formats allow you to set events to repeat on either weekdays: Monday, Wednesday, and Friday, or Tuesday and Thursday. Like daily events, you can set a "Repeat until" date. The next repeat style is weekly. With the weekly setting you can set the days of the week in which the event will repeat (see Figure 8-34).

Like "Daily," you can set both the date that the repetition ends and how many weeks apart the events repeat. Unlike the "Daily" option, you can set a more advanced combination of the days in which the events repeat. You can see in Figure 8-34 that there are seven check boxes with letters next to them. These letters symbolize the days of the week. The check box next to "M" is selected indicating the event will only be placed in Monday's schedule. If you click a check box next to a day such as Wednesday, the event will be added to Wednesday at the set time. You can select all days if you wish and the event will appear in your calendar on every day.

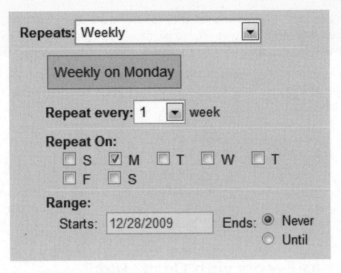

Figure 8-34: Weekly options

The next repetition style is "Monthly," and this type allows you to have events that repeat once a month such as monthly status reports (see Figure 8-35).

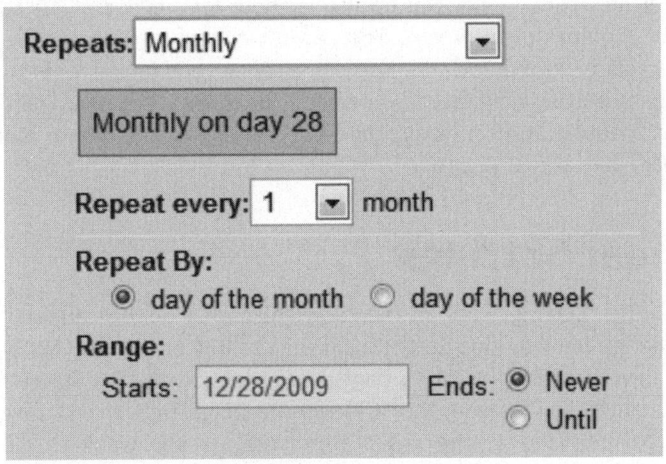

Figure 8-35: Monthly repeat options

Again, like the "Daily" option, you can set the events repetition and end date, however, you can also determine how the event is to repeat every month. With "Monthly," you get the option to repeat an event based on the date in the month like the 30th of the month or the day of the week. If you create an event

405

on December 29, 2009, you can set it to repeat on January 29 or the same day of the week that the event was set. In this case, setting it to repeat on a day of the week would place the event on the last Tuesday of each month.

The final type of repeat option is "Yearly." This behaves like the daily repeat option in that you can only set the number of years between repetitions and the end date.

ExplainED

You can use the "Day of the week" function in monthly reminders to schedule an event that runs on a set day of the month like a progress meeting that occurs on the last Friday of the month.

Repeating Events with Quick Add

You can also create repeating events with the quick add by using the "for" keyword (mentioned above in "Creating Events"). You can add the keyword for after a date or time. You can enter "Weekly project meeting Monday at 10 a.m. for eight weeks." This will create an hour-long event at 10 a.m. every Monday for the next eight weeks. You can set events to repeat daily, weekly, monthly or yearly with quick add. You can also set repeating events that do not have limits by stating how often you want it to repeat. For example, "Monthly production meeting at 10 a.m. on the first Tuesday of the month monthly" or "Anniversary January 26 yearly".

Calendar Settings

By clicking the "Settings" link in the top right corner of the calendar window, you can change the way Google Calendar acts to better suit the way you work. Once you have clicked the link, a page will be displayed (see Figure 8-36). To save any changes you make in the "Calendar Settings," click the "Save" button at the bottom or top of the page. Otherwise, if you want to discard the changes, click the "Cancel" button located at the bottom or top of the "Calendar Settings" window.

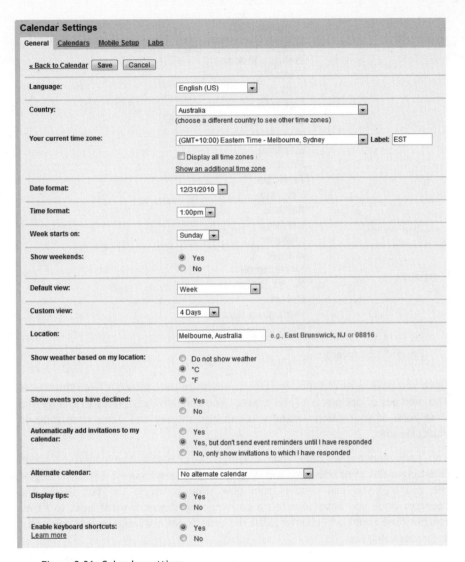

Figure 8-36: Calendar settings

Some of the settings you already have set before while creating your calendar. The first setting you can change is language. If you wish to change the language that Google Calendar is presented in, click the box and select from a list of languages (see Figure 8-37).

407

Figure 8-37: Languages

Once you have selected the language you wish to use, select it from the menu. The next set of options is "Time zones." You can use the options to change the time zone of your calendar and you can also display one extra time zone on your calendar.

You can change the time zone settings by changing the country through selecting a different one from the drop-down list (see Figure 8-38). By changing the country, you can choose from new time zones in the box below the country. Once you have selected a country, the drop-down list next to "Your current time zone" will change to all the time zones available in your country.

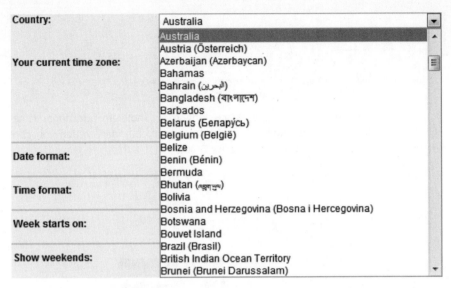

Figure 8-38: Country selection

To edit your local time zone, click the drop-down list next to "Your current time zone" and select the appropriate one. If your desired time zone is not in the list, you can either change the country selected above or click the check box next to "Display all time zones." Selecting this check box will display all time zones in the drop down list regardless of the country.

Next to the time zone drop-down list is a box named "Label." Entering a word into this field will place it above the "Time axis" in the calendar (see Figure 8-39).

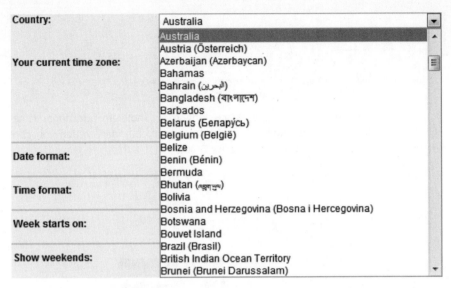

Figure 8-39: Time zone label

NotED

The time zone label can display at most 10 characters.

You can add one extra time zone by clicking the "Show an additional time zone" link. This will create another column on your calendar, which you can set to be any desired time zone (see Figure 8-40).

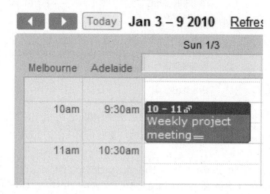

Figure 8-40: Extra time zone

The extra time zone allows you to show two different time zones next to each other so you can gauge the time difference in events. This can be useful when dealing with scheduling events in different cities. The next set of options relates to date and time formats. These allow you to change the way dates and times are displayed on your calendar. The first option "Date format" allows you to adjust how dates are displayed between the three major formats being "day/month/year," "month/day/year," and "year/month/day" (see Figure 8-41). Below "Date format" is the "Time format" drop-down list. With this list you can choose between 12-hour and 24-hour time by selecting the appropriate option (see Figure 8-41).

Figure 8-41: Date and time format

The next set of options can adjust how the calendar handles weekends. The first option is the "Week starts on." You can use this to set the first day of the week according to your preference. Change this by selecting the appropriate day from the drop-down list (see Figure 8-42).

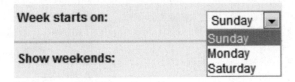

Figure 8-42: Day of the week

The next option below "Week starts on" is "Show weekends." This is on by default if you disable it. Saturday and Sunday will not be displayed on your calendar. This is useful for businesses using Google Calendar.

The next option named "Default view" allows you to set the displayed view when you login to Google Calendar. You can choose between the default setting of "Week" or other options (see Figure 8-43). This is usually preset to "Week."

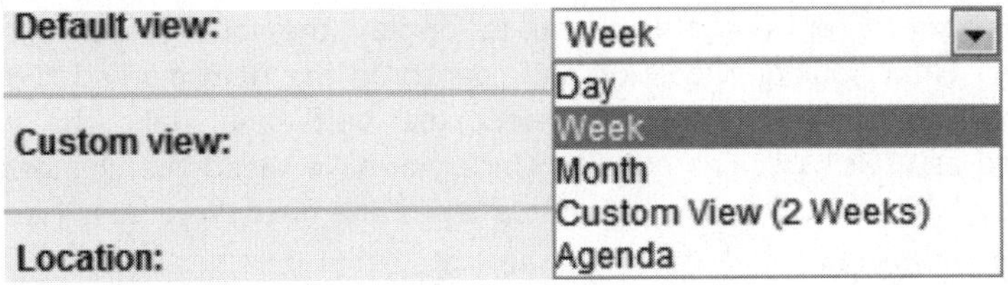

Figure 8-43: Default view

"Custom view" allows you to change "4 day view", in the drop-down list. You can choose to change the "4 day view" to multiple styles from two days to four weeks (see Figure 8-44).

411

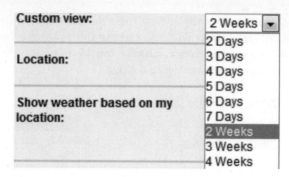

Figure 8-44: Custom view

Once you change the "Custom view," the "4 day view" will be renamed to the appropriate setting. Changing the "4 days" to "2 weeks" will change the "4 day view" to "2 week view" where you select the view (see Figure 8-45).

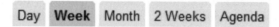

Figure 8-45: Custom view

The next set of options allows you to display the local weather on your calendar. Enter your city location and country in the field marked "Location" such as "Melbourne, Australia." Select the units you want the weather displayed as (Celsius or Fahrenheit). Once you have saved the changes, other small icons will appear above today's date and the next three days (see Figure 8-46).

Figure 8-46: Weather

The weather icons give you a quick look at what the weather on the given day will be. If you click the weather icon, a box will be displayed that shows you more details about the weather over the next four days and the current local temperature (see Figure 8-47).

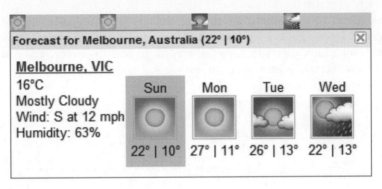

Figure 8-47: Detailed weather

Inviting Other People

When creating or editing events, you can invite people to add to the event to their calendar. Enter their e-mail or their name if you have added them as a contact in Gmail. When you type out the first few letters of a contact name, a box will appear below the "Guests" area (see Figure 8-48).

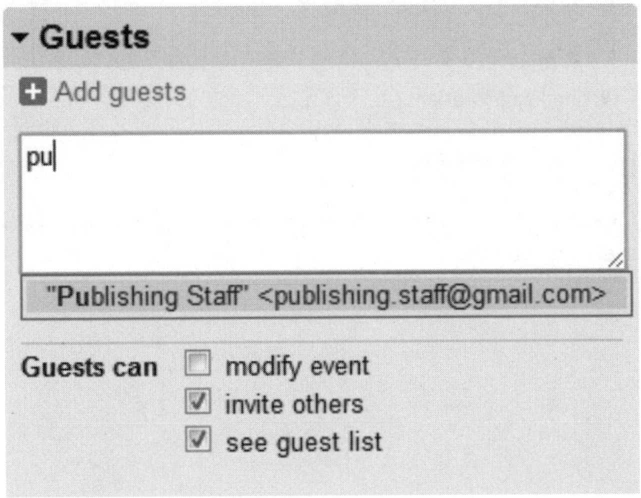

Figure 8-48: Invitations

When you see this box appear, click the correct person's name. Otherwise you can keep typing the e-mail address. If you wish to invite multiple people to an event, separate their e-mail addresses with a comma (for example "example@example.com, example2@example.com"). Once you have added all

413

of the guests to the event, set the permissions for the guests. By default, guests can see who else is invited and invite other people to events. The final access level allows guests to have full control to edit the event. You can also change the access guests have to events by checking or unchecking the appropriate text boxes.

Always avoid allowing guests to modify the event unless it's necessary.

Once you have entered the details of the event and save it, an option will be displayed to send invitations out to the event guests (see Figure 8-49).

Figure 8-49: Sending invitations

Receiving Invitations

If you are invited to an event, you will receive an e-mail containing the invitation (see Figure 8-50).

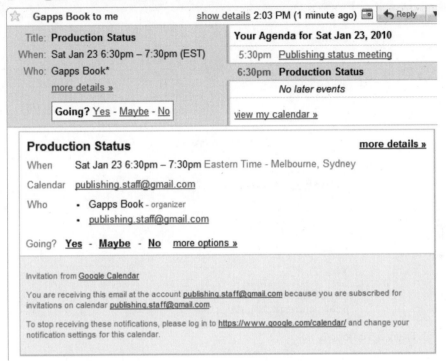

Invitation: Production Status @ Sat Jan 23 6:30pm - 7:30pm (publishin g.staff@gmail.com) Inbox | X

Figure 8-50: E-mail invitations

The e-mail in Figure 8-50 is designed to give you a quick overview of the event, as well as an easy way to respond to the invite. On the top right section of the e-mail, you can see the events near the scheduled time for the event you are invited to. The lower part of the e-mail contains the details of the event.

You can quickly respond to the event by clicking either the "yes," "no," or "maybe" links at both the top and bottom of the e-mail. By clicking the response, you will notify the event's creator if you are coming.

If you click the "More information" link, you will be taken to the event page and a set of options will be displayed allowing you to view who has been invited to the event, and if they have responded, and sending e-mails to the event's creator and participants (see Figure 8-51).

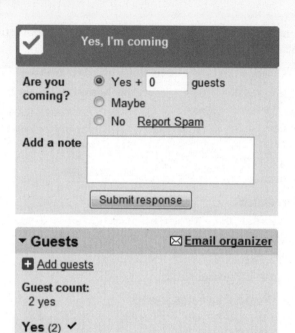

Figure 8-51: Options

From the options, you can leave a message for the event's creator by filling in the "Add a note" box and clicking "Submit response." You can also specify that you are coming with a number of guests by entering a number in the field next to the "Yes" radio button. If you have permission to invite guests to an event, you will see a link named "Add guests." If you click the link, an "Add guests" dialog will be displayed that looks like and acts the same way as the one shown in Figure 8-48. You can also e-mail other people who have been invited to the event by clicking the "E-mail organizer" Link (see Figure 8-52).

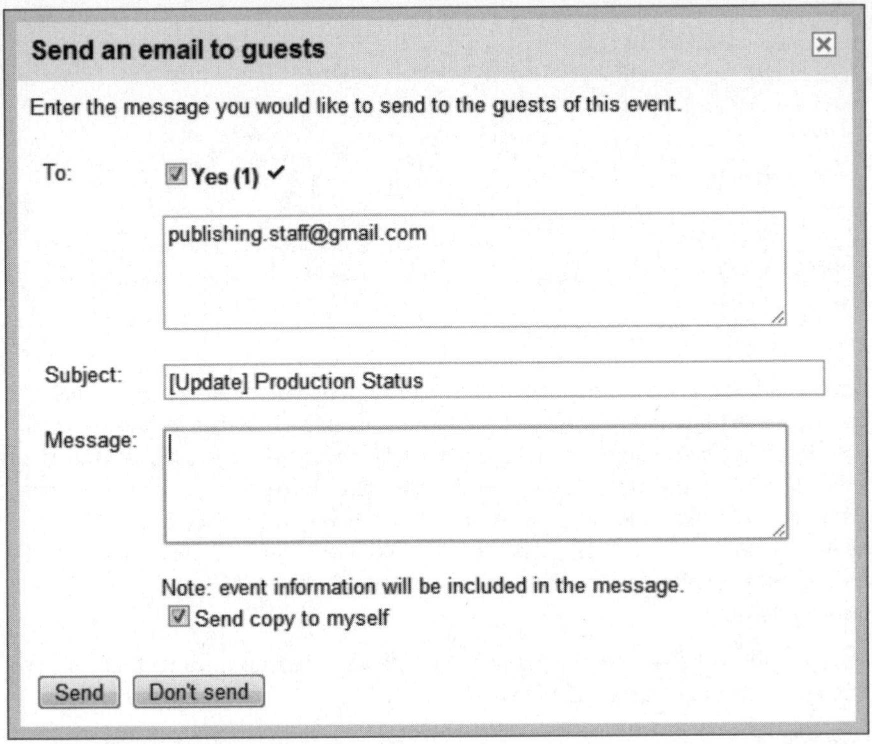

Send an email to guests ☒

Enter the message you would like to send to the guests of this event.

To: ☑ **Yes (1)** ✔

```
publishing.staff@gmail.com
```

Subject: [Update] Production Status

Message:

Note: event information will be included in the message.
☑ Send copy to myself

[Send] [Don't send]

Figure 8-52: Options

From this dialog box, you can send an e-mail to everyone who is invited to the event based on their attending status. If you wish to send an e-mail to people who are coming to the event, check the box next to "yes" and the same for "no" and "maybe." You can enter the subject of the e-mail and message and click "Send" or "Don't send."

Creating and Deleting Calendars

You can have more than one calendar in which you can store your events. You can use this to create both public and private calendars. This can be useful to people who manage sporting or social calendars. You can create a second calendar you can share with the public (covered later in this chapter). To create a new calendar, go to the settings menu and select "Calendars" located on the top menu (see Figure 8-53).

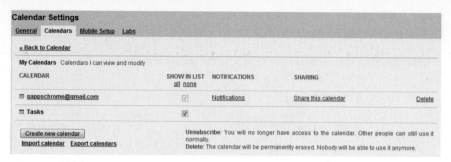

Figure 8-53: Calendar settings

Once you are on this screen, click the "Create new calendar" button. This will open a new page (see Figure 8-54). From this page you can enter the basic details of the new calendar including a name, description locations, and time zone. For all of the fields except time zone you, have to type your response, although the time zone fields work in the same way as in Figure 8-2. You also have the ability to set calendar sharing (covered later in this chapter). To create a new calendar, click "Create Calendar" after you have filled in the information.

You can delete calendars by clicking the "Delete" button next to them on the "Calendar settings" page (see Figure 8-53).

NotED

You cannot delete your primary calendar, however by using the delete function on your primary calendar you will clear all of the information and settings from it.

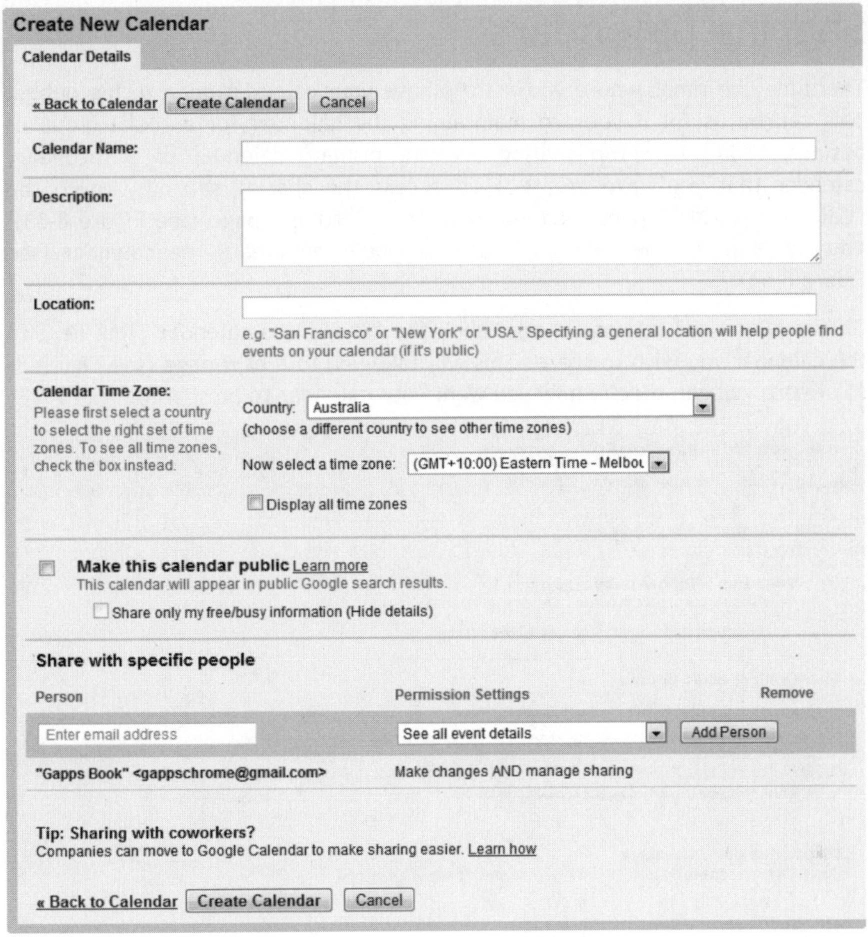

Create New Calendar

Calendar Details

« Back to Calendar | Create Calendar | Cancel

Calendar Name: [   ]

Description: [   ]

Location: [   ]

e.g. "San Francisco" or "New York" or "USA." Specifying a general location will help people find events on your calendar (if it's public)

Calendar Time Zone:
Please first select a country to select the right set of time zones. To see all time zones, check the box instead.

Country: [Australia ▼]
(choose a different country to see other time zones)

Now select a time zone: [(GMT+10:00) Eastern Time - Melbou ▼]

☐ Display all time zones

☐ **Make this calendar public** Learn more
This calendar will appear in public Google search results.

☐ Share only my free/busy information (Hide details)

Share with specific people

Person	Permission Settings	Remove
[Enter email address]	[See all event details ▼]	[Add Person]
"Gapps Book" <gappschrome@gmail.com>	Make changes AND manage sharing	

Tip: Sharing with coworkers?
Companies can move to Google Calendar to make sharing easier. Learn how

« Back to Calendar | Create Calendar | Cancel

Figure 8-54: New calendar

Why Use Multiple Calendars?

Using multiple calendars allows you to easily manage different aspects of your life. You can create a calendar to manage your social events, one to keep track of your meetings at work, and one to keep track of your family outings. Each calendar is displayed in a different color so you can easily keep track of your entire schedule and easily locate free times. You can also share different calendars with different people. You can share a calendar of business trips with your family so they know when you will be away or a list of sporting events so your friends and family know when you will be playing.

Sharing Calendars

There may be times where you wish to have your calendar open to the public. This can be useful if you are maintaining the calendar for a social group or business. You can setup sharing on your primary calendar or a secondary calendar that you have created. To access the sharing settings, go to the "Calendar settings" page located under the "Settings" page (see Figure 8-53). You can also set the "Sharing" settings when you create the calendar (see Figure 8-54).

On the "Calendar settings" page, click the "Share this calendar" link next to the calendar you wish to share. This will take you to a new page (see Figure 8-55) where you can specify how you want your calendar to be shared.

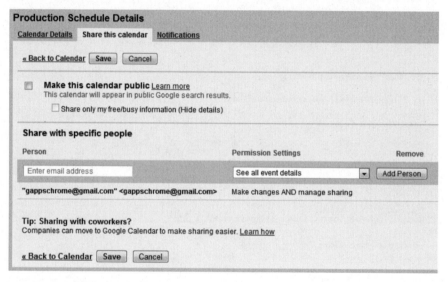

Figure 8-55: Sharing settings

On this page, you can first set whether or not you want the calendar to be publicly viewable. If you check the check box next to "Make this calendar public," this will make the calendar you have selected visible to anyone and will make the calendar searchable on Google. Below is an option to hide the details of an event on the calendar. If you check that check box, people will be able to view that you have an event at that time, however they will not be able to see any details including names or places.

ExplainED

Always ensure that you have selected the right calendar before saving any sharing options.

Below these options, you can then share the calendar with people you select with Google accounts. You can give people different levels of access from viewing the calendar to controlling who else can manage the calendar (see Figure 8-56).

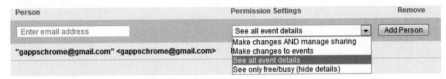

Figure 8-56: Sharing with individuals

To assign someone permission to access your calendar, enter their e-mail address in the field, select their level of access, and click "Add person" (see Figure 8-56). Once you have changed the permissions, save your changes by clicking the "Save" button. Otherwise you can click the "Cancel" button.

Once you save the changes, you will be taken back to the "Calendar settings" page. If you made your calendar public, you will need to get the address of the calendar to give to people. Click the name of the calendar and you will be taken to that calendar's settings page (see Figure 8-57).

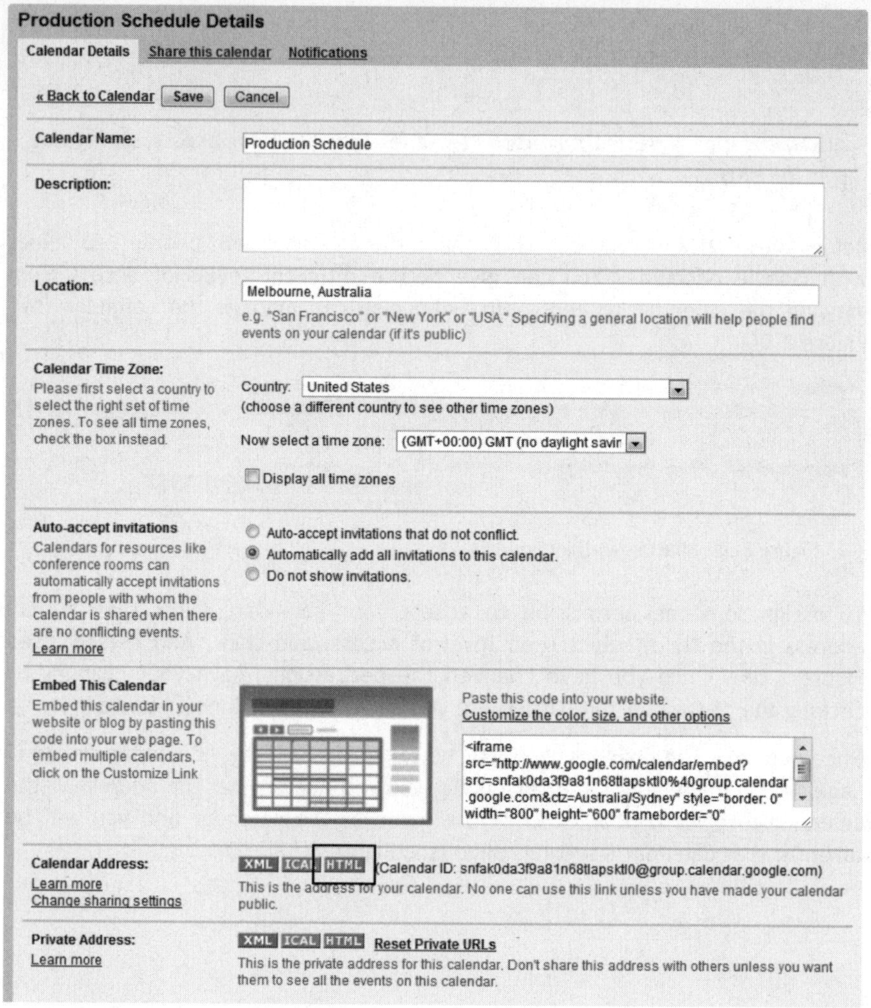

Production Schedule Details

Calendar Details   Share this calendar   Notifications

« Back to Calendar   [Save]   [Cancel]

Calendar Name:	Production Schedule

Description:

Location: Melbourne, Australia

e.g. "San Francisco" or "New York" or "USA." Specifying a general location will help people find events on your calendar (if it's public)

Calendar Time Zone:
Please first select a country to select the right set of time zones. To see all time zones, check the box instead.

Country: United States
(choose a different country to see other time zones)

Now select a time zone: (GMT+00:00) GMT (no daylight savir ▼)

☐ Display all time zones

Auto-accept invitations
Calendars for resources like conference rooms can automatically accept invitations from people with whom the calendar is shared when there are no conflicting events. Learn more

○ Auto-accept invitations that do not conflict.
◉ Automatically add all invitations to this calendar.
○ Do not show invitations.

Embed This Calendar
Embed this calendar in your website or blog by pasting this code into your web page. To embed multiple calendars, click on the Customize Link

Paste this code into your website.
Customize the color, size, and other options

```
<iframe
src="http://www.google.com/calendar/embed?
src=snfak0da3f9a81n68tlapsktl0%40group.calendar
.google.com&ctz=Australia/Sydney" style="border: 0"
width="800" height="600" frameborder="0"
```

Calendar Address:
Learn more
Change sharing settings

XML ICAL **HTML** (Calendar ID: snfak0da3f9a81n68tlapsktl0@group.calendar.google.com)
This is the address for your calendar. No one can use this link unless you have made your calendar public.

Private Address:
Learn more

XML ICAL HTML Reset Private URLs
This is the private address for this calendar. Don't share this address with others unless you want them to see all the events on this calendar.

Figure 8-57: Calendar settings

On the page shown in Figure 8-57, go to the bottom of the page and click the "HTML" button next to "Calendar Address" highlighted in the figure. Once you click this link, you will be taken to an external view of the calendar. Copy the URL in the address bar and send it to the people you would like to view your calendar, or store it on a website for people to click on.

Accessing Your Calendar from Outlook and Other Applications

You can access your Google calendar from Microsoft Outlook. This allows you to continue using the Outlook interface. This can be useful if you need to use Outlook for work or if you are already using Outlook to access e-mail off your Gmail account.

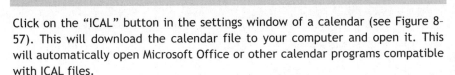

NotED

You will need Microsoft Outlook or an equivalent calendar program installed to do this.

Click on the "ICAL" button in the settings window of a calendar (see Figure 8-57). This will download the calendar file to your computer and open it. This will automatically open Microsoft Office or other calendar programs compatible with ICAL files.

Receiving Notifications on Your Mobile Phone

As mentioned earlier, you can have event notifications sent to your mobile phone. You can register your phone by going to the "Settings" menu then and going to "Mobile set-up" (see Figure 8-58).

ExplainED

Your mobile phone provider may charge you for using this service. Confirm with your carrier before you setup mobile notifications.

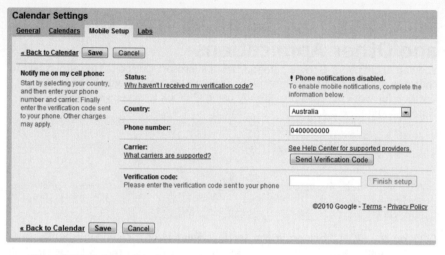

Figure 8-58: Mobile settings

Once you are on this page, ensure your country is correct and enter your mobile number in the box. Click "Send verification code." After sending the code, you will receive an Text message (see Figure 8–59).Text Once you have received the Text message code, enter the value into the verification code box at the bottom right of the "Mobile set-up" screen (see Figure 8-58) and click *"Finish setup"* and *"Save"*. This will allow you to use Text notifications (addressed earlier in this chapter).

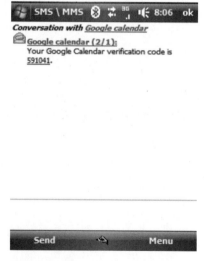

Figure 8-59: Text verification code

Synchronizing Google Calendar with Your Mobile Phone

NotED

People who own a Google Android-based phone do not need to follow this step, Refer to your user guide on how to display your calendar.

You can install a program on an iPhone, Blackberry, Windows Mobile, or Nokia S60 mobile phone to automatically synchronize your calendar and contacts using the Google Sync program for your mobile.

ExplainED

This procedure uses mobile Internet. Check with your carrier to see if you have mobile Internet active and it is reasonably priced. Google Sync can use up to 50 megabytes of mobile traffic a month for a normal user.

To see the installation instructions for your mobile phone, visit google.com/mobile/sync and follow the instructions for your phone.

Summary

In this chapter we have covered many aspects of Google Calendar in detail. We began by covering the basics of how to create and navigate calendars. We then covered in detail how to create events including reminders. Next we covered different and quicker methods for adding events including creating events by clicking the time slot using the "Quick add" box and reoccurring events. We then learned how to change the settings of calendar to customize it to for your needs. We covered editing events and invitations in depth. In the final sections, we discussed editing individual calendars, synchronizing with Outlook, the Google Sync application for mobile phones, and setting up Text notifications.

Readers new to the concept of an electronic calendar can find Google Calendar a significantly useful productivity tool that can provide the advantage of an advanced platform. This platform has different aspects and features coupled with the advantage of the cloud computing paradigm and the versatility of accessing it anywhere. Google Calendar is a fitting example of how advanced technology and concepts can be integrated seamlessly into our busy lives.

Chapter 9

Google Sites

Google Sites helps you to build good looking web sites easily, and with very little effort. You can also host your web site free of charge on Google Sites servers. Building a web site used to be difficult work, and was restricted to those that knew HTML scripting, perhaps some ASP and PHP, knew how to organize menu links, include images, and of course, had access to a server to host the web site. These days, it can still be difficult to build a web site unless you have the right tools, and there is still the question of hosting the site. But as we become more connected, many people are building and maintaining web sites for various reasons from keeping in touch with family, displaying family memorabilia and success, supplementing income with small business sites, creating information in a personal field of expertise, or even building their own family small business web sites. The web site has become the 21st century business card.

There are many web sites that allow you build and host your site for free, but many of these will have restrictions. Google Sites is a structured wiki offered by Google as a way for people to make information easily accessible in the form of a web site. You can add videos, include your Google Docs documents, Calendar information and incorporate Google Maps. You can even use Google AdWords and AdSense to advertise your web site to potential customers and earn advertising money. Additionally, Google Sites is free, and their storage limits are large, at approximately 100 megabytes per site at the time of writing, and very few restrictions on page size.

To start Google sites, click on the "Sites" option from the "more" menu on the Google Apps toolbar in your browser (See Figure 9-1). You will need to be logged into your Google account. If you do not have one, see Chapter 2.

Figure 9-1: Accessing Google sites

If you have not already created web page in Google Sites, you will see the screen appear as shown in Figure 9-2. To go ahead and create you Google Site, click the "Create site" blue button toward the right side of the screen (See Figure 9-2).

Figure 9-2: Initial sites web page

Creating a Site

When setting up your site for the first time, the screen shown in Figure 9-3 appears. Using this screen, you will be prompted to set up the initial elements of your web site. You need to choose a template to use for your site. A template gives you a blueprint for your site and the pages will be arranged around this blueprint. The information on each page will be arranged within the text areas that have been set up based on your template. To choose a template, select from the "Blank" template or one of the others on the screen.

Figure 9-3: Initial setup

There is also a link to the right called "Browse the gallery for more." Click this link to bring up a small dialog box with a set of categorized templates (See Figure 9-4.) When you choose a category, a list of associated templates for this category is shown on the right. Use the scroll bar to scroll up and down. When you find one, click the template. A small overview of this template will be shown in the dialog box. You can click the "Select" button to choose this template, or click the "*Cancel*" button to go back to browsing templates in the dialog box. If you wish to see a preview of the template, you can click the link "Preview template." This will open a new browser tab, and you will be taken to a web site containing a set of pages created with the template for viewing. Close the browser tab when finished.

Figure 9-4: Template gallery

When you have chosen your template with the "Select" button, the dialog box will be closed and an icon representing the theme you have chosen will be displayed in the set-up screen. As an example for this chapter, a theme called "Training" from the "Business collaboration" category was chosen.

Choosing a Theme

You can now choose a theme for the site. A theme is a color combination and background pattern that will be applied to the template. Choose a theme by clocking the small plus (+) sign next the "Choose a theme" under the section you entered the web site name. A list of themes with sample patterns will be displayed below. Choose one of these by clicking the associated button underneath the particular theme. Under the theme selection, you can choose to select more options for the site, but these can be modified at any time.

Site Name and URL

You now need to choose a name for your site. Enter this in the "Name your site" text box shown below the theme selection. You can only use the characters (a-z, A-Z and 0-9). As you enter the name for your site, the URL will be shown in the text box below. For example, if we enter the site name, "ABCTraining" the URL shown will be "http://sites.google.com/ site/abctraining". You can place your cursor in the URL box and change the last part of the URL. For this example, we will leave the URL default to the site name.

To create the site, you will need to type the code shown at the bottom of the screen in Figure 9-3 into the box provided. The purpose of this is to stop automated scripts from utilizing this facility. The code will be slightly distorted so it cannot be read by a letter recognition program. Type the code into the box provided and click the "Create site" blue button at the bottom of the page, otherwise click the "Cancel" button to exit without creating the site. If you accidently type in the wrong code, which is not uncommon as it is difficult to read, another will be displayed. Just re-enter the new code until you get it correct. If you take too long to set up the information, it may time out, giving you an incorrect code when you type it in.

Additionally, if the site name has already been used by someone else, or the URL has been used, the page will be re-displayed with your options still selected but with some expanded information in the "site name" section (See Figure 9-5).The name or URL will be highlighted, depending on which has already been used. Just choose a different name or URL, or both, and try again. A list of possible unused alternatives similar to the one you have chosen will be displayed. If you don't want to keep trying for a different name yourself, or you don't really care about the name and URL, you can choose from the alternatives by just clicking the appropriate button next to your choice and then clicking the "Create site" blue button again.

 In this example, we will select from the alternatives "abctrainingproject." The site name and URL will be adjusted accordingly. You may need to enter a new code before the site will be created.

Once you have created the initial site successfully, a complete "shell" will be created for you. That is, a set of pages conforming to the template you chose, containing some sample information. Once this shell is created, the new web site will then exist, and you will then be able to edit the site at any time.

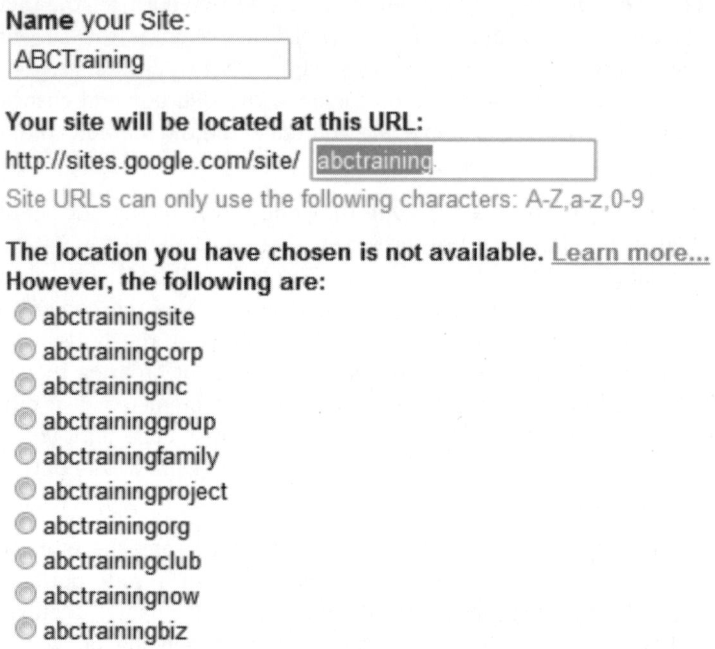

Name your Site:

ABCTraining

Your site will be located at this URL:

http://sites.google.com/site/ abctraining

Site URLs can only use the following characters: A-Z,a-z,0-9

The location you have chosen is not available. Learn more...
However, the following are:

- abctrainingsite
- abctrainingcorp
- abctraininginc
- abctraininggroup
- abctrainingfamily
- abctrainingproject
- abctrainingorg
- abctrainingclub
- abctrainingnow
- abctrainingbiz

Figure 9-5: Site name / URL correction

Editing a Site

Once a web site has been created, it will be available for editing. When you sign into Google and select the "Sites" from the drop-down menu in Figure 9-1, you will be taken to the "Sites" initial screen. You can set up many web sites using Google Sites, and the initial screen allows you to choose which of your web sites to edit. Click on the site you wish to edit.

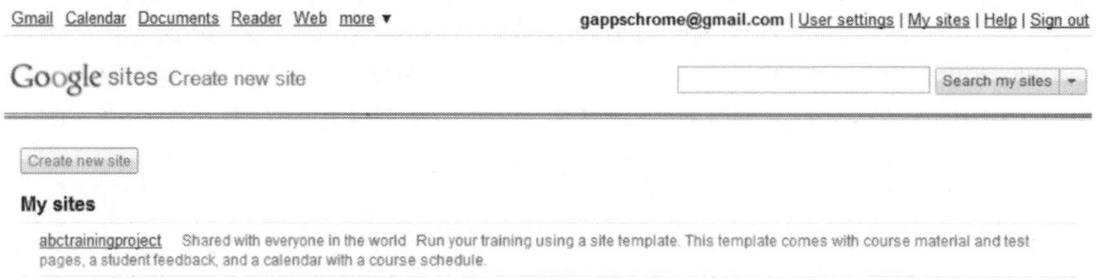

Gmail Calendar Documents Reader Web more ▼   gappschrome@gmail.com | User settings | My sites | Help | Sign out

Google sites Create new site   [   ] Search my sites ▼

Create new site

My sites

abctrainingproject   Shared with everyone in the world Run your training using a site template. This template comes with course material and test pages, a student feedback, and a calendar with a course schedule.

Figure 9-6 Selecting your site

The site you choose to edit will then be opened at the "Home" page and you can proceed to edit the site. If you choose the ABC Training site we initially created, you will see the initial opening screen of the project as shown in Figure 9-7. What you see on the page is what the Web users will see, except for the links on the page allowing you to edit aspects of the web site. Underneath the Google Apps toolbar from the Web browser shown at the top of Figure 9-7, you will see three buttons "Create a page," "Edit page" and "More actions." It is through these buttons that we will add and delete pages to the web site and edit the existing ones. We will cover the functionality provided in the following sections.

Figure 9-7: Web site project opening screen

It is worth noting that, in the following sections, we will cover the details of editing and formatting the initial shell site. However, some of the layout aspects of the site are dependent on the initial template chosen. Most of the aspects and techniques will be general in nature and will be relevant to any template. But each template is slightly different in layout, and you will need to be aware of this when working on a different template.

NotED

The following sections deal with editing and formatting the initial site, built from a specific template.

Getting Help

You can get help for Google Sites at any time by selecting the "Help" link on the web browser Google Apps toolbar (on the top right of the screen, see Figure 9-7). Clicking this link will load a web page into another browser tab, giving you a number of general links and some specific links on particular Google Sites topics (See Figure 9-8). Some of these links are very useful, but finding help on specific issues or features in Sites may be difficult to find. You may sometimes need to persist and use the search facility located at the top of the Help screen (not shown) when looking for specific issues. If your problem is very specific, then you may be better off consulting with other Google Docs users. The "Google Sites Help Forum" link on the Help Page is located at the bottom right of the page shown in Figure 9-8, and takes you to a forum where you can scan discussion threads on specific topics and even post your own questions. There are some excellent tips on using Google Site features in here.

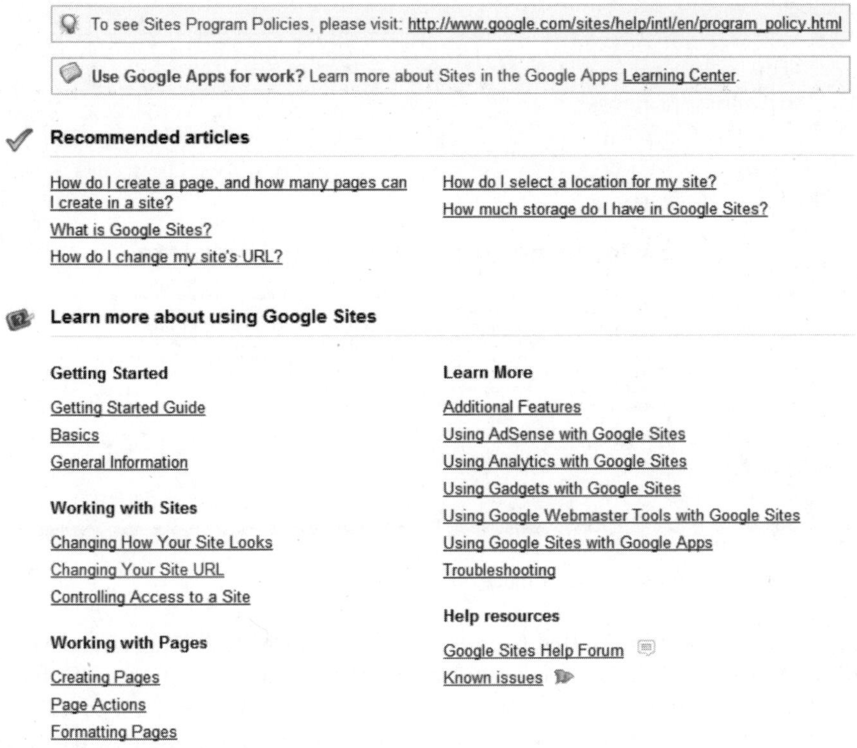

💡 To see Sites Program Policies, please visit: http://www.google.com/sites/help/intl/en/program_policy.html

📋 **Use Google Apps for work?** Learn more about Sites in the Google Apps Learning Center.

✓ **Recommended articles**

How do I create a page, and how many pages can I create in a site?

What is Google Sites?

How do I change my site's URL?

How do I select a location for my site?

How much storage do I have in Google Sites?

📖 **Learn more about using Google Sites**

Getting Started

Getting Started Guide

Basics

General Information

Working with Sites

Changing How Your Site Looks

Changing Your Site URL

Controlling Access to a Site

Working with Pages

Creating Pages

Page Actions

Formatting Pages

Learn More

Additional Features

Using AdSense with Google Sites

Using Analytics with Google Sites

Using Gadgets with Google Sites

Using Google Webmaster Tools with Google Sites

Using Google Sites with Google Apps

Troubleshooting

Help resources

Google Sites Help Forum

Known issues

Figure 9-8: Google sites help

Editing a Page

We can edit any page in the web site by first making that page our current page. We do this by navigating to the page through the existing links on the web site. For example, in the shell web site created at the beginning of this chapter, the first page displayed when we choose to edit our site is shown in Figure 9-7. This template contains a list of links in a small sidebar on the left side of the page which provides links to the other default pages set up in the web site shell. Click on one of those to navigate to any of the pages and make it the current page. For this example we will stay on the home page first loaded when we chose to edit the site. To edit this page, select the "Edit page" button located at the top right of the page, under the Google Apps toolbar. This will then place the current page into edit mode and the page will appear as in Figure 9-9.

Figure 9-9: Web page in edit mode

An annotated version of this page is shown in Figure 9-10. The web page is divided into sections, and you can format different aspects of the web page from different menus. The sidebar shown on the left of the diagram contains a series of quick links to other web pages in the site. When we add new pages to the site, we can also add references to them in the sidebar. In some sites, you may use the sidebar to add quick links to subsets of pages, but how you decide to do this is up to you. Currently, all pages can be accessed from here. You cannot edit the sidebar from a normal page edit mode. You need to click the "Edit sidebar" link below just below the sidebar. This will not be visible to the world when they view the web page, and we will discuss editing the sidebar later.

Figure 9-10: Annotated web page mode

The **site header** is seen at the top left of each page in the site. This can be altered through general settings discussed later. Additionally, the size and text color of the site header can be modified. A logo can also be included if needed.

The attachments and comments sections at the bottom of the page are configurable, and you can turn these off for each page in the site. The attachments section allows you to attach files which can be accessed from the page, while the comments allow people to add comments.

The content title (or page title) is related to the current link pointing to this page in the sidebar. In the diagram shown in Figure 9-10, the current page is the Home page, and the content title is set to Home, to reflect the content of the page, reached by clicking the "Home" link in the sidebar. In edit mode, you can place your cursor in this area and change the text. If you do, when you save the changes, the corresponding link text in the sidebar will also be changed to reflect the new contents title. You cannot change the format of the content title here, just the text. The format can be changed elsewhere.

The content text can also be changed. This is the text associated with the web page, the content of the web page. To change this text, just place you cursor in this area by clicking into it with the left mouse button. This will position the insertion point of the text. You change the text in the same way as discussed when changing text in a Google document. The insertion point is indicated in your content area by a flashing vertical bar. You can locate the insertion point anywhere in the document by just clicking at a new point with the mouse cursor. To insert new text, just begin typing. Use the same keys as we discussed in the Google Document chapter to move around and edit or delete text, the arrow keys, page up and page down keys for large content areas, the delete and backspace key and the return key to create new lines. Also use the home and end keys to move to the beginning and end of the current line.

Changing Text

Once you click into a text area after entering edit mode, you can then change and format the text in that area. Changing the text is done in much the same way as discussed in Chapter 4 Google Docs Document and in Chapter 6 Google Presentation. While with Google Sites, although the pages are essentially HTML pages (or web pages), the mechanics of changing and formatting the text areas is similar. Thus in the following sections we will not discuss the mechanics of manipulating and formatting text in as much detail as previous chapters, as it has already been covered.

Selecting Text

As with Document and Presentation, we can select text to either move it from one place to another, or to move text between site pages, to delete, edit or to apply formatting. To select a portion of the text within a text area, left-click and drag the cursor over the text you wish to select. All the selected text within the text area will be highlighted with a light-blue color, indicating the selected text. Alternatively, you can click with the mouse just before the first character to be selected, depress the Shift key and the click with the mouse just after the last character to be selected, then release the Shift key. All the text in between will then be selected.

ExplainED

To quickly select, double mouse clicking on a word will select that word, triple mouse clicking within a paragraph will select that paragraph.

Cutting and Pasting Text

As with Google Document and Presentation, you can use cut-and-paste functions to make copies of selected text, or to move a selection of text from one place in a text area to another. To do so, you need to use the standard keyboard short-cuts. To move a selection of text from one place in a text area to another, first select the text to be moved as discussed in the previous section. Then click the control and x-key at the same time. The selected text will then be removed from the text area. Now choose the point in the text area where you want the selected text to be moved to, and press control and z at the same time. The selected text that was cut will now be inserted at the new location within the text area. You can copy a selection of text from one location to another as well without moving it. Select the text you wish to copy, and then use the key combination Ctrl-C, to make a copy of the text. Then as before, use the keyboard combination Ctrl-V, to paste a copy of the original text at some point in the text area.

Formatting Text

We can format the text within a text area in much the same way as we did in Document or Presentation. Most of the formatting options are accessed from the menu and toolbar. When you enter edit mode for a web page, the screen changes as shown in Figure 9-9. A menu and toolbar appear and an expanded version of these are shown in Figure 9-11. The toolbar shown in Figure 9-11 has much of the same formatting options as the similar toolbar in Document and Presentation. Because of the complexity of HTML coding, there are fewer options than in the traditional word-processor like in Document or Microsoft Word.

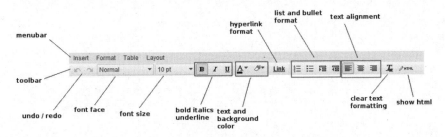

Figure 9-11: Edit mode menu and toolbars

The undo and redo options are present in the toolbar. Use the undo option when you realize you have made a mistake. The undo option will undo the last operation you preformed. If after using the undo, you realize it was correct in the first place, use the redo to reapply the operation.

The styles of the text are limited, which is in line with HTML styles. Some styles are used for formatting other areas of the site, but in the context text area to select a style, choose "Format" from the menu and you will see the drop-down list of options shown in Figure 9-12. You can choose the styles from the "Heading Styles": heading (H2), sub-heading (H3), minor heading (H4) and normal paragraph text. These are paragraph styles, so when you select one of these styles, the entire paragraph in which your cursor is positioned will be changed to this style. These styles are usually intended only for headings, which can then be used to insert a table of contents as in the Chapter Google Docs Document.

NotED

The first line of the content text shown in Figure 9-10 (in large bold font) is using a style that is not available from the "Format" menu or from the toolbar. If you change it, you may not be able to reproduce it exactly at a later stage from the menu and toolbar options.

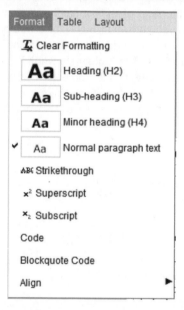

Figure 9-12: Content text styles

You can change the font for a selection of text in the content area. First, select the text you wish to modify, then choose the "Font face" drop-down list from the toolbar (see Figure 9-11). You will see a limited selection of fonts you can choose from (See Figure 9-13). Choose one of these fonts, and the selected texts font will change to this selection. Note that the "Normal" font is set up in the page settings (discussed later) and will be the font used if no other selections have been applied.

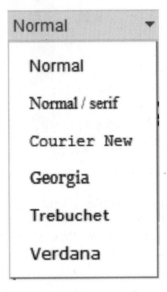

Figure 9-13 : Content text font selection

Text can be re-sized in the content area, or only a portion of the text can be re-sized to suit your purposes. You can do this by selecting the portion of text in the content area to be re-sized, then adjusting the size by clicking the "font size icon on the tool bar. When you click this icon a drop-down list will appear, and you will have the option of changing the size of the selected text to one of the options displayed in the a drop-down list (See Figure 9-14). Font size is usually measured in point size (pt) on a computer screen, where 1 point is 1/72 of an inch.

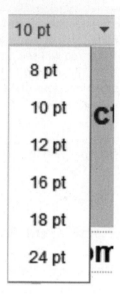

Figure 9-14: Content text font size

You can apply the standard formatting of bold, italics and underlining, to the selected text by choosing the bold, italics or underline icons from the toolbar. These formatting options act like switches, select them once to turn the formation option. Choose the same format option to the selected text a second time to turn them off.

The color of section of the text displayed in a context area can be changed by selecting the text to be formatted then choosing the "text color" icon from the toolbar. You will then get the drop-down color chooser shown in Figure 9-15. The current color will show a tick against it, and the default color of the text will depend on the site template and the color theme you have chosen. Choose a new text color for the selected text by clicking on the color in the color chooser that you want. The selected text will then be displayed with the new color. You can change this at any time by re-selecting the text and applying a new color, or by removing the formatting from the selected text.

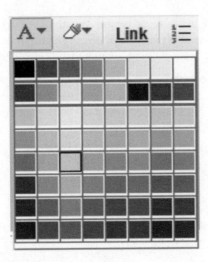

Figure 9-15: Changing text color

You can also change the background color of section of text in the text area by selecting the text and then clicking on the "Text Background Color" icon in the toolbar. A color chooser similar to the text color chooser in Figure 9-15 will be displayed with the current background color highlighted with a tick (if any). The default background color of the text will depend on the site template and the color theme you have chosen. You can change this at any time by re-selecting the text and applying a new background color, or by removing the formatting from the selected text.

Numbered and bullet lists can be set up within you text area. The use of numbered and bullet lists have been covered extensively in previous chapters, Google Docs Document and Google Presentation. They work exactly the same in Google Sites. Type in and enter a number of points in separate paragraphs (usually single line paragraphs). Select them and click the numbered list or bullet list icons on the toolbar to turn the respective lists on and off, (the icons on the toolbar act as a switch). You can create sub-lists with bullet points or numbered points by selecting a subset of the points in the list then using the right line indent icon to demote points to sub-points, or the left line indent to promote sub-points to a higher level. As you do this, the numbering will change for numbered lists, and the shape of the bullet will change for bullet lists. The line indent icons are just to the right of the number list and bullet list icons on the toolbar.

The text alignment icons on the toolbar can be used to align the text within a paragraph (this is a paragraph style tool). You can align the text to either the left margin, the right margin, or center the text. Text centering is normally used for heading styles and figure captions in some circumstances. You cannot use justification (left and right text alignment) in Google Sites.

You can remove all formatting from the selected text by clicking the "Remove formatting" icon from the toolbar (see Figure 9-11). When you do this, the selected text will be displayed according to the defaults either on the page, or dictated by the template and color theme.

ExplainED

Using Remove Formatting if a number of formatting options have been applied to a selection will remove all formatting options. You might need to re-apply some options afterward.

There are some other formatting options available. These can be accessed from the "Format" menu item on the menu (See Figure 9-12). After the style formats, the remaining formats able to be chosen are strikethrough, superscript, subscript, code and blockquote code. The code format is often used to format a section of text that contains computer programming or scripting code. It displays better in this format. The blockquote format is used when quoting large sections of text from another source. The font used is similar to code, but is displayed with a grayed background. The text alignment options also found on the toolbar can be accessed from this menu as well.

To save any changes you have made to the formatting, click on the "Save" button at the top right of the screen. This will save all current changes you have made to the web page while in edit mode. To exit without saving any of the changes, click on the "Cancel" button. Either option will result in you leaving edit mode and return to viewing mode.

Adding Links

One of the things you often need to do within web pages is incorporate links to other web pages. Google Sites templates will, in most circumstances, include a sidebar with links to other pages in your sites which you can modify, or add to, any time you wish. However, you may want to direct your page to another web address (URL). Google Sites provides an extremely easy way for you to do this using the "Link" option on the toolbar (See Figure 9-11). To add a link into your web page text, when in edit mode, select a portion of the text, or a word that will be used as the link. Then click the "Link" icon on the toolbar. A dialog box will be opened as shown in Figure 9-16.

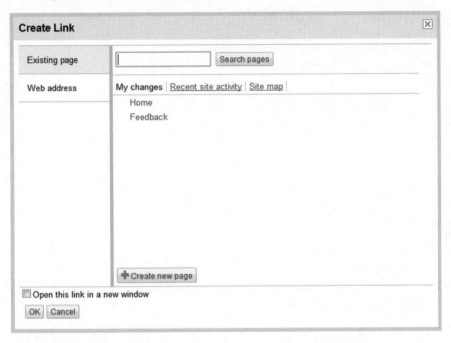

Figure 9-16: Add link dialog box

From the dialog box, you can choose to link to an existing page from the current site. To find the correct page, you can use the search facility, or display a site map and choose from there. You can even select to create a new page in the current site and use that page in the link. However, to link to a URL somewhere else in the web, select the "Web address" link toward the top left of the dialog box (See Figure 9-16). This will then display another dialog as shown in Figure 9-17.

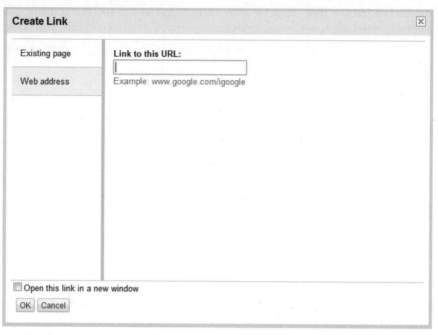

Figure 9-17: Link to Web URL

Type in the URL of the page to link to in the text box labeled "Link to this URL." If you want the new page to be opened in a new browser Tab when the link is clicked, check the "open this link in a new window" check box. If you don't check this box, then when the link is clicked, the current page within your web-site will be reloaded with the new web page pointed to by the URL you have just entered. If you want your web site to remain loaded at all times, then you should check this box. When you have finished, click the "OK" button to save these changes, otherwise click the "Cancel" button to exit without saving. You will then be taken back to edit mode for the current page. When you are back in edit mode, you will see the selected text you used to add the link to now appear as a clickable link. When in edit mode, if you click a link, you will see the URL of the link appear in a shaded box just below the link, with the option to delete the link or to edit it (See Figure 9-18). Clicking the "Change" link will take you to the dialog box in Figure 9-17 where you can edit or replace the URL. Clicking on the "Remove" link will remove the link placed in your text. You will not be given a warning; the link will be removed without further dialog. However, you can always use the undo icon in the toolbar.

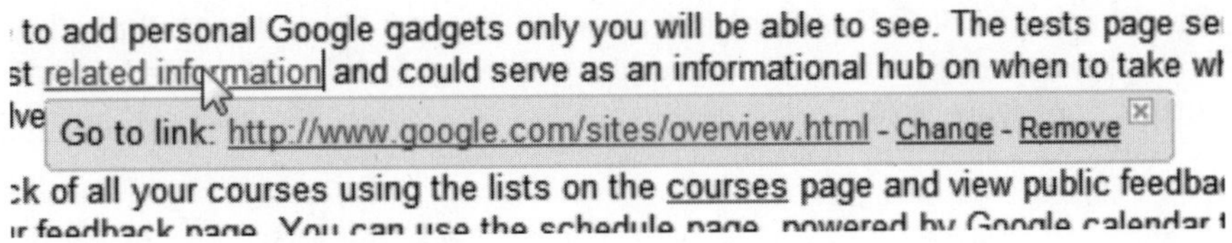

to add personal Google gadgets only you will be able to see. The tests page se
st related information and could serve as an informational hub on when to take wh
lve

Go to link: http://www.google.com/sites/overview.html - Change - Remove ☒

k of all your courses using the lists on the courses page and view public feedba
r feedback page. You can use the schedule page, powered by Google calendar t

Figure 9-18: Edit mode link

To save any changes, click on the "Save" button at the top right of the screen. This will save all current changes you have made to the web page while in edit mode. When in viewing mode, if you click on the link you have just added to your page, the link will be activated and the new page loaded.

Adding Images

There are a number of ways to include images into your content area. You can include images from either your computer or from the web. You will need to have the image already located on your personal computer, or you will need the URL of the image to include. Select where in the content area you wish to add the image to by clicking there with your mouse and then choose the "Image" option from the "Insert" menu on the menu. You will then see the small dialog as shown in Figure 9-19.

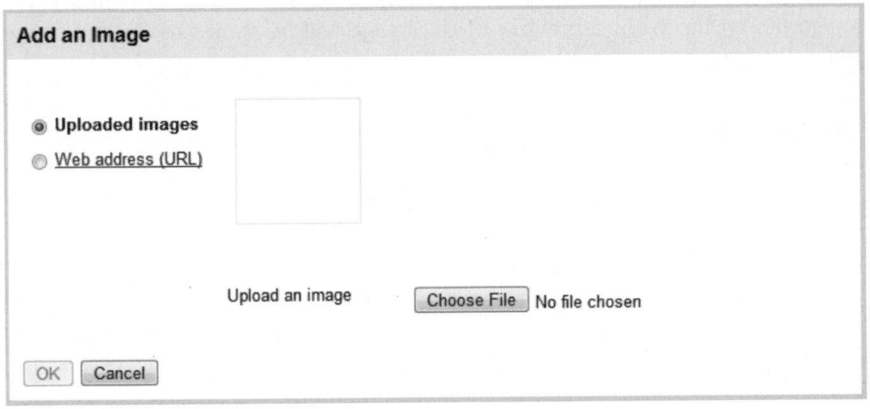

Add an Image

⦿ **Uploaded images**
○ Web address (URL)

Upload an image   [Choose File] No file chosen

[OK] [Cancel]

Figure 9-19: Inserting an image

From the dialog box in Figure 9-19, you can choose to insert an image from your computer (uploaded images) or from the web by clicking the appropriate button for the corresponding choice dialog. If you choose to load an image from your computer, click the "Choose File" button. You will then be presented with your operating system's file selection utility. Select the file you want. You will then be taken back to the dialog box shown in Figure 9-19, and a small preview of the chosen image will be displayed just to the right of the "Uploaded Image" button. See Figure 9-20).

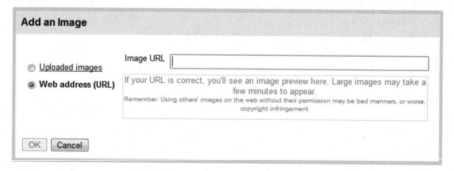

Figure 9-20: Image preview

If you wish to select another image, click the "Choose File" button again and select the new file to load. If you want to load your image from the web, you need to know the URL of the image. Select the button "Web address (URL)." You will then see the dialog box shown in Figure 9-21. You can then type in the URL of the image you wish to insert. If the URL is correct and points to an image file on the Web, a preview of the image will be shown below the image URL you typed.

Figure 9-21: Inserting an image from the Web

In either case, to insert the image, click the "OK" button, or "Cancel" button to exit without inserting. The image will then be inserted into the current position in the content area (See Figure 9-22). Once an image is inserted into the content area, you can configure its options. When in edit mode, click on the image. You will see the image and the configurable options appear below the image in a small shaded box. See Figure 9-22. There are not many options, and they appear as small links in the shaded area beneath the image. You can configure the alignment by clicking on either the L, C or R option (for left, center and right). Choose the size of the image by clicking either S, M, L, or *Original* (small, medium, Large, original size). Choose to turn word wrap for the image either On or Off by clicking the appropriate option. In the example in Figure 9-22, the image is left aligned, small, with word wrap on. The current option is highlighted in bold and is not able to be clicked. Word wrapping images will allow your text to flow around the images rather than writing only above and below the image.

Welcome to the Training T

This Google sites template will help you get started on organizing your
You can use this page to add personal Google gadgets only you will be
as a summary of all test related information and could serve as an infor
tests. The tests themselves are sub pages of the test page and are cre

You can keep track of all your courses using the li
public feedback from your students from your feedl
page, powered by Google calendar to keep your cl
clearly visible to all. Lastly you can use the contac
Google form to privately interface with your instruct

This is another paragraph of the welcome page of t
purpose of this paragraph is to demonstrate the wr

Align: L C R - Size: S M L Original - Wrap: **on** off - Remove ⊠

Figure 9-22: Configuring an image

These are all the options available. You can also choose to delete the image from the content area by clicking the remove option. This will remove the image without further dialog. You can click the undo on the toolbar to retrieve it if you made a mistake.

Using Tables

You can insert and change tables into your content area as well. The use of tables in HTML is limited, but the options in Google Sites does allow for easy changes. Inserting a table is much the same as inserting a table in Google Presentation. You add a table by clicking on the "Insert" option of the "Table" menu. When you do, a small drop-down window will open by the "Insert table" menu item. This will contain a small grid of squares that will become colored light blue as you move your cursor to the right and down. This is used to determine the size of the table that you want to insert (See Figure 9-23). As you move your cursor over the grid and the squares turn colored, then back again while you re-size, the size of the table is displayed in the bottom of the window. In the example in Figure 9-23, the size is 3 x 3. When you have the grid sized according to the size of the table you want to insert, click the grid. The menu will disappear, and a table of that size will be inserted into the content area.

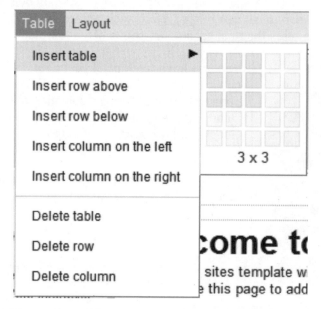

Figure 9-23: Inserting a table

Once the table has been inserted, you can then add text to the table cells. Each cell in the table acts like a text area. You can click into the cell and add text. As you add text, it will be wrapped within the boundaries of the column, but if you keep adding text, the bottom of the cell will be automatically pushed down to accommodate more lines.

You can adjust the table at any time by adjusting the width of a column or the height of a row. To do this, click inside any cell of the table. When you do this, you will see the cell become highlighted and drag points appear around the outside of the cell (See Figure 9-24). To adjust the size of a cell, left-click on one of the drag points and drag the point to adjust the size of the cell. If you clicked on a drag point in the middle of the top or bottom of the cell, you can adjust the height of the cell. If you click on a drag point in the middle of the left or right side of the cell, you can adjust the width. Clicking and dragging on one of the corner drag points allows you to adjust the height and width of a cell. One thing to keep in mind, though, is that you cannot adjust the height or width of an individual cell. Adjusting the height of a cell adjusts the height of the entire row. Adjusting the width of a cell adjusts the width of the entire column.

NotED

You cannot adjust the height or width of a single cell. Only the height of the row, or width of a column.

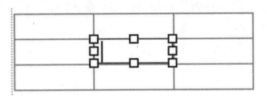

Figure 9-24: Adjusting a table

You can also insert columns or rows by clicking into a cell of the table. Then from the "Table" menu on the menu, you will see options to:

Insert row above: This will insert a new empty row above the row in the table containing the selected cell.

Insert row below: This will insert a new empty row below the row in the table containing the selected cell.

Insert column left: This will insert a new empty column to the left of the column in the table containing the selected cell.

Insert column right: This will insert a new empty column to the right of the column in the table containing the selected cell.

Delete row: This will delete the entire row in the table containing the selected cell.

Delete column: This will delete the entire column in the table containing the selected cell.

Delete Table: This will delete the entire table you clicked into.

Use these options to add and delete rows, or columns, or the table (See Figure 9-25).

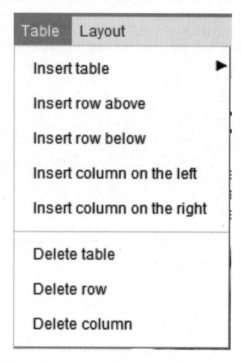

Figure 9-25: Adding or deleting rows and columns

Using Layouts

The current layout of your page is already determined by the initial template you chose to set up your web site with. For this example, we chose the theme called "Training" from the "Business collaboration" category. The layout of the home page was shown in Figure 9-10. This consisted of a sidebar on the left side of the page with the main content of the page having a small content title area at the top and the main content area below that, with attachments and comments below. In edit mode, we can alter the layout of an existing area easily using the "Layout" menu. To alter the layout of the home page, make sure the home page is the current page, then click the "Edit Page" button to place the page in edit mode. You can only change the layout of the main content o a page. Other areas will be for specialized purposes, for example the content tile area of the home page, and these cannot be changed.

Click on the "Layout" menu on the menu. You will see the drop-down menu shown in Figure 9-26. From this menu, you can choose from a number of options to adjust the layout. The current layout style has a check mark against it on the left side. In this example, the current layout of the home page is a single column.

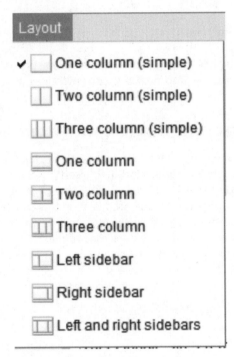

Figure 9-26: Layout menu

To choose a new layout, simply click on one of the options. In this example, we will choose the simple two column layout. The menu will then close and the layout of the content area on the page will be adjusted accordingly. You can now click into either of the two areas in the content area add text and images and utilize the formatting options we have previously discussed (See Figure 9-27).

453

Figure 9-27: Adjusted layout

The use of layouts has been made as simple as possible for non HTML programmers to utilize. It also makes it extremely easy to change layouts as your web site evolves.

Inserting Different Objects into Your Web Pages

There are a number of other elements or objects we can insert into our web pages. These can be found by clicking the "Insert" menu option of the menu when a page is in edit mode (See Figure 9-28). Some of these we have discussed already and some of these will be discussed later in this chapter. While we won't cover all of these types of objects in this chapter, it is worth spending a little time on some of the more interesting ones. One of the most exciting things about Google Sites is the ability to integrate Google Apps. For instance, the Documents, Spreadsheets and Presentations we have discussed in previous chapters, and of course Spreadsheet forms that will be discussed later.

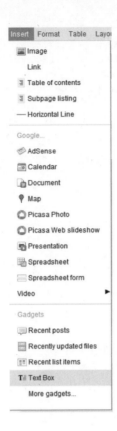

Figure 9-28: Insert menu

Inserting a Calendar

We can insert a calendar into our page by choosing the "Calendar" option from the menu in Figure 9-28. This will give us access to any of the Calendars we have created under the account your account. When you choose this option, a list of your current calendars is displayed and you can select from the list. Once you have made your selection, an insert calendar dialog box will be shown (See Figure 9-29).

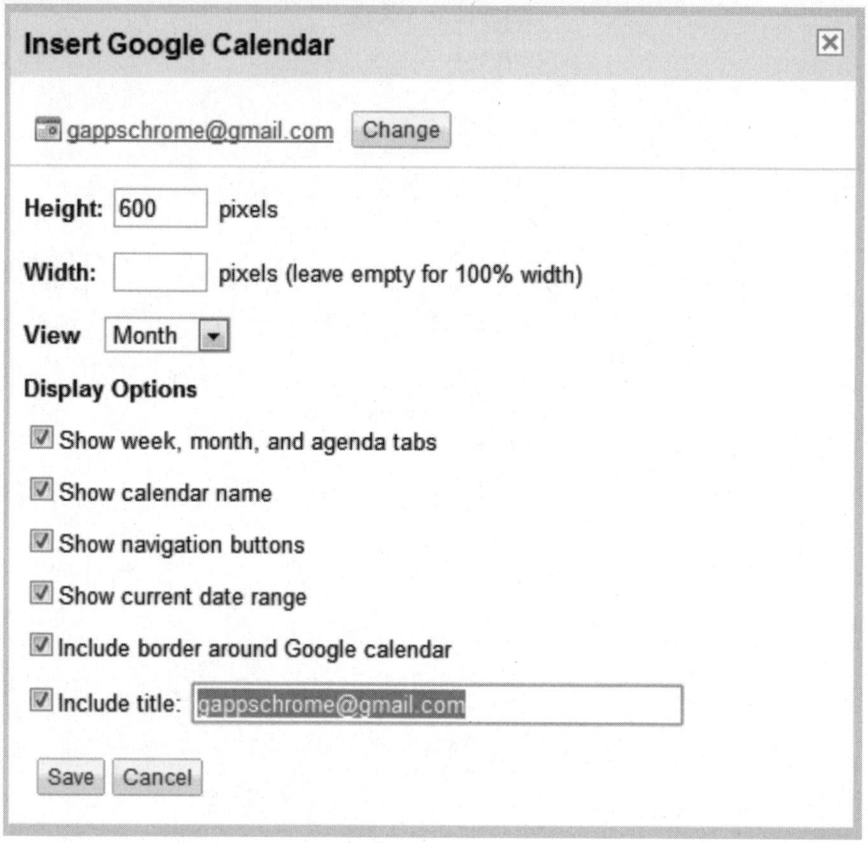

Insert Google Calendar ☒

🖅 gappschrome@gmail.com [Change]

Height: [600] pixels

Width: [   ] pixels (leave empty for 100% width)

View [Month ▾]

Display Options

☑ Show week, month, and agenda tabs

☑ Show calendar name

☑ Show navigation buttons

☑ Show current date range

☑ Include border around Google calendar

☑ Include title: [gappschrome@gmail.com]

[Save] [Cancel]

Figure 9-29: Insert calendar dialog

Using the dialog box, you can configure the appearance of the calendar, including the height and width of the calendar on the screen, the view (monthly, weekly etc.), what navigation buttons will be available and any tabs and other options which you want to make available to the user. Once you have chosen the options you want, click the "Save" button at the bottom of the dialog to save the options and include the calendar in the web page, or click the "Cancel" button to abandon the insert. When in edit mode, the calendar will be displayed as simply an object with the name Calendar (See Figure 9-30).

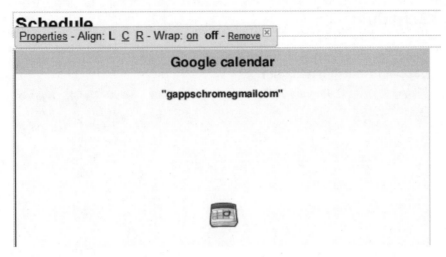

Figure 9-30: Calendar object and options

Clicking on the calendar object in edit mode will display the configurable options in a small shaded box (See Figure 9-30). There are not many options and they appear as small links in the shaded area beneath or above the calendar object. You can configure the alignment by clicking on the L, C or R option. Choose to turn word wrap for the calendar either On or Off by clicking the appropriate option. Clicking on the "Properties" link will show the same dialog as in Figure 9-29, where you can modify the calendar properties, including choosing a different calendar. You can choose to delete the calendar by choosing the "Remove" link. When the page is saved and returned to viewing mode, the calendar will be seen as in Figure 9-31.

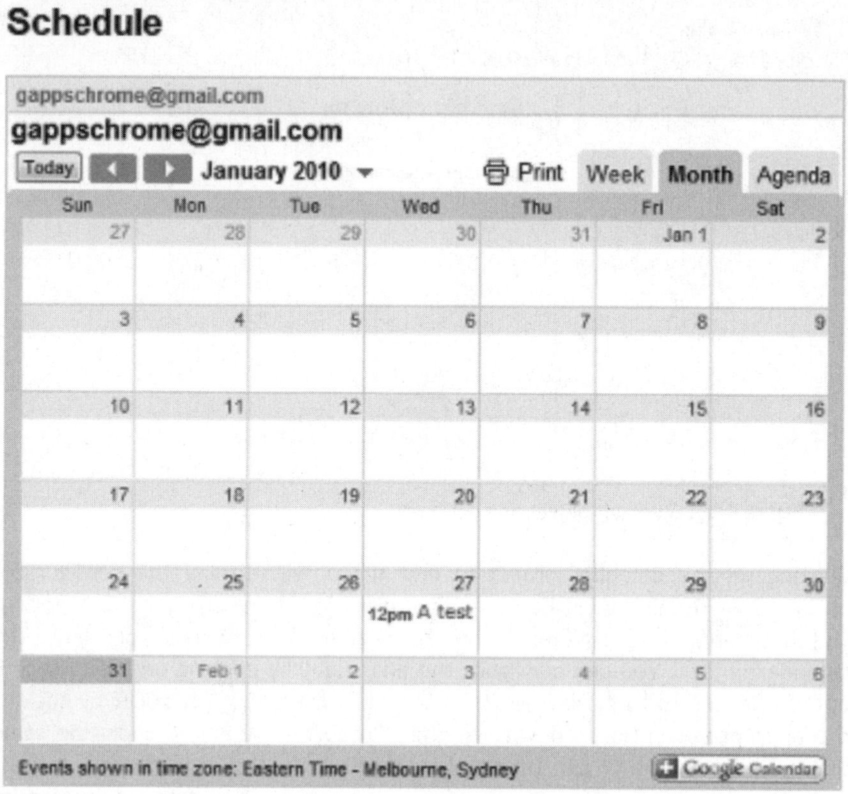

Schedule

Figure 9-31: Calendar final display

Inserting Documents, Spreadsheets, Presentations and Forms

In exactly the same way we inserted a Calendar, we can insert a Document, Spreadsheet, Presentation and Spreadsheet Form. In each case, we choose the element we want to insert form the "Insert" menu. A list of the appropriate elements created in the current Google account will be listed on the screen. We choose the one we want and press a "Select" button. We will then be presented with a dialog box, similar to the one displayed in Figure 9-29. The options in each dialog box will be slightly different, depending on the type of element we will be inserting, but in each instance we can control the height and width of the element in pixels, as well as other display options. When the element is inserted in edit mode, it will just display as a blank object. When you click it, you will see a small shaded box at the top or bottom giving you options to format the object. You will be able to format the alignment of the object and whether word wrapping around the object is turned off or on. Additionally, you will be able to edit the objects properties and remove the object. In viewing mode, you will see the object and be able to utilize scroll bars if necessary top scroll up and down the object.

With an embedded presentation object, you will be able to scroll through the slides in the presentation or initiate a presentation display by selecting the appropriate buttons associated with the presentation object (See Figure 9-32 for an embedded presentation object).

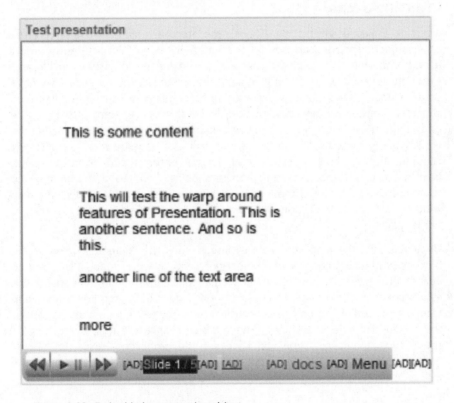

Figure 9-32: Embedded presentation object

The interesting and useful thing about inserting Documents, Spreadsheets, Presentations and Forms from Google Apps into our Google site, is that if the original document, spreadsheet or presentation is changed, the changes will be reflected on our web site after reloading. This highlights an extremely useful aspect of using Google Apps for maintaining your web sites and other documents. You can include a document to be shown in your web site, and yet the contents of the document could be shared with someone whose job is to maintain the document. While they may know nothing about maintaining a web site (despite the ease with which Google Sites makes this), the contents of the document they maintain will automatically be updated in the web page.

This makes it easy to delegate work to people spread all over the world to maintain and update various forms of documents which can be integrated together into a Google Site.

Inserting a Map

Inserting a Map is interesting. Though the steps are similar to inserting the other objects discussed previously, the Map behaves a little differently. Insert a map into your web page by choosing the "Map" option from the "Insert" menu on the toolbar. This will give us access to any of the Calendars we have created under the account we are using to create the web site. When you choose this option, a new dialog will open loading Google Maps into a window on the right (See Figure 9-33). You can pan around the Google World Map in the window using the cursor to drag the map to a position and then progressively zoom-in. Also, as shown in Figure 9-33, you can enter an address in the search box and quickly relocate the map to that point. You can then zoom-in and zoom-out using the plus and minus (+, -) buttons in the upper right of the map window (See Figure 9-33) until you have the map as you would like to embed it in the page.

Once you have the map you want to insert, click the "Select" button at the bottom of the dialog to save the options, or click the "Cancel" button to abandon the insert. A dialog box will then appear allowing you to configure the Map properties to be embedded in the web page. The dialog box is shown in Figure 9-34, and allows you to select the size of the embedded map, as well as the border and title of the map. You can also change the map by clicking on the "Change" button. When you have set the properties, click the "Save" button at the bottom of the dialog box, or choose "Cancel" to abandon the insert. The Map will then be inserted into the page.

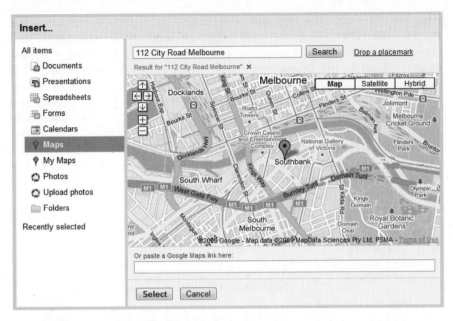

Figure 9-33: Selecting a Map to insert

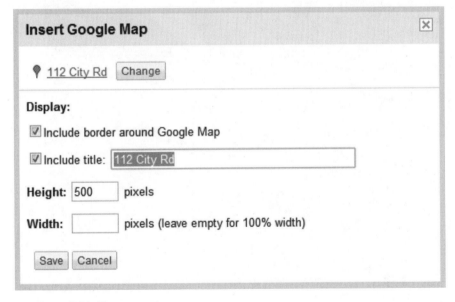

Figure 9-34: Map properties

When in edit mode, the map will be displayed as an object with the name Google Map. Clicking on the map object in edit mode will display the configurable options in a small shaded area beneath or above the map object, similar to the calendar object in Figure 9-30. You can configure the alignment by clicking on either the L, C or R option (for Left, Center, Right). Choose to turn word wrap for the calendar either on or off by clicking the appropriate option. Clicking on the Properties link will show the same dialog as in Figure 9-34, where you can modify the map properties, including choosing a different map. You can choose to delete the map by choosing the "Remove" link. When the page is saved and returned to viewing mode, the map will be seen as in Figure 9-35.

Schedule

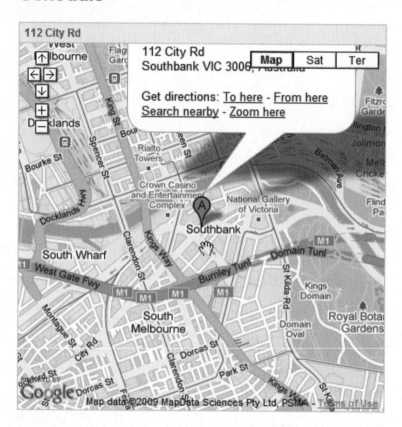

Figure 9-35: Map final display

When viewing the map, you can click on the map shown and with the left mouse button depressed drag or pan the map to a different location. This is not a permanent change, and when the page is reloaded, the map will be re-displayed with the original zoom factor chosen and coordinates.

Viewing and Editing the HTML Source

When in edit mode, clicking on the "HTML" icon on the toolbar (the last icon on the right), will display the HTML source of the current content area. If you are not familiar with HTML code, or have not used a scripting language previously, then it is suggested that you do not use this utility. However, if you are familiar with HTML scripting, this can be a good way to fine-tune the appearance of the web site. The options available for formatting in Google Sites are limited due to the extensive automated nature of the interface. Using the HTML code does allow you to add other HTML markup that might not be automatically generated by options in Google Sites.

Editing the Side Bar

At some time you will need to add r modify some of the navigation links in the sidebar. As you add pages to your site, or delete old pages, you will need to modify the sidebar to reflect these changes. You can do this from either edit mode or view mode. Click the "Edit sidebar" link that appears just underneath the sidebar (See Figures 9-7 and 9-9). This will display the Manage Site page shown in Figure 9-36. The default option selected when you enter this page is the "Site Layout." This is indicated by the highlighted blue link towards the bottom left of the page (See Figure 9-36). The page shown to the right of the links displays the general layout of your pages, with the header area across the top, the sidebar area to the left and the page content on the right taking up most of the space.

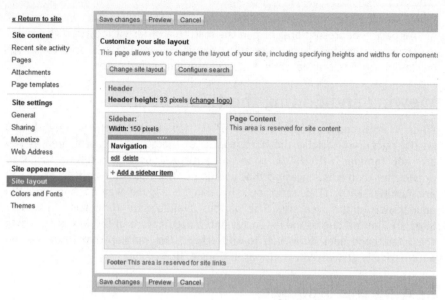

Figure 9-36: Manage site page

Within the sidebar area is a small box area labeled "Navigation," (See Figure 9-36). Underneath this are two (2) links: "*Edit*" and "*Delete*." Choosing the "Delete" link will delete the entire sidebar from your site. However choosing the "Edit" link will allow you to edit the links in the sidebar. This will display the Configure Navigation dialog as shown in Figure 9-37. In this dialog, you can configure many aspects about the sidebar. If you check the box called "Display title," you can include the text in the text box above that as the title of the sidebar. Beneath that is a list of all the links that appear in the sidebar, except the "Sitemap" link. That is a standard link; however you can choose not to include it by unchecking the check-box labeled "Sitemap." Additionally, located at the bottom of the sidebar area is a link called "Add a sidebar item." Using this link, you can add different elements to the sidebar that will be displayed in the web site. You can choose to place an "AdSense" item in the sidebar (discussed later in this chapter) and if you have previously deleted the navigation links from the sidebar, you can add them by adding "Navigation." Other items you can add to the sidebar are "Text", a list of "Recent Activity" on the site and a "Countdown." With the countdown, you can set a timer that displays the number of days remaining to so a specific date. This is useful if you are a company hosting a special event or just any organization with an upcoming event you want to notify people about.

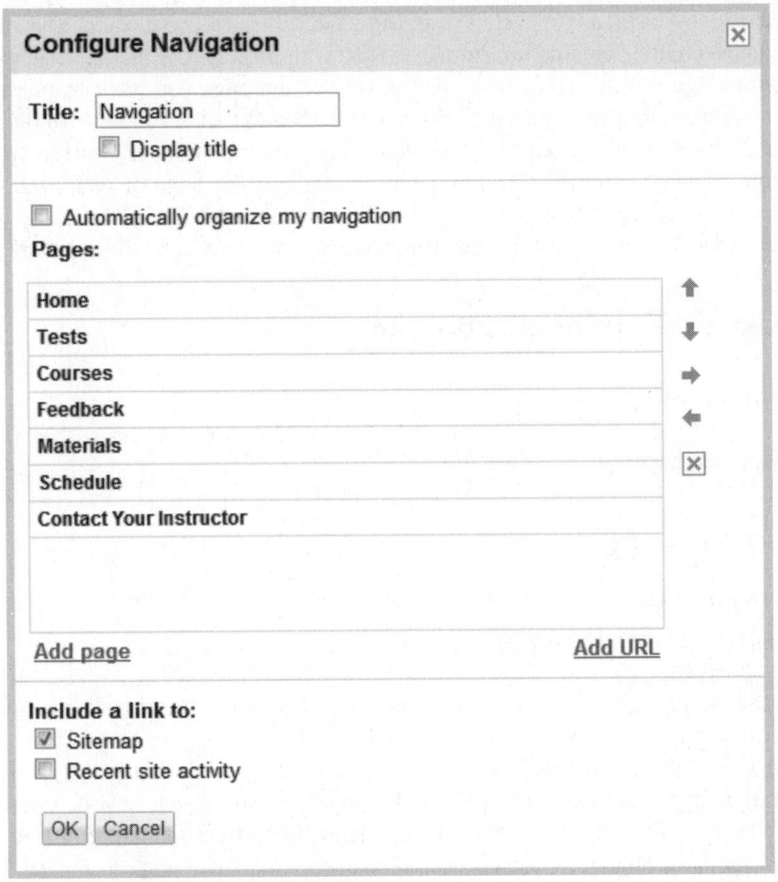

Configure Navigation   ☒

Title: Navigation

☐ Display title

☐ Automatically organize my navigation

Pages:

Home	⬆
Tests	⬇
Courses	➡
Feedback	⬅
Materials	☒
Schedule	
Contact Your Instructor	

Add page   Add URL

Include a link to:
☑ Sitemap
☐ Recent site activity

OK   Cancel

Figure 9-37: Configure navigation dialog

You can modify the order of the links in the sidebar by clicking on one of the sidebar entries in the list in Figure 9-37 and using the small up and down arrows on the right to move the entry up or down the list. You can also use the left and right arrows to indent and unindent the entries to create hierarchical relationship between the links. Use the small cross icon on the right to delete the current entry. You cannot modify the URL of a particular entry, but you can very quickly delete it and add a new link. If you select the check-box "Automatically organize my navigation," Google Sites will use a built-in navigation system that controls how the links in the sidebar are shown. It has a basic expandable and collapsible hierarchical link display.

To add a new sidebar link, click the "Add URL" link to the right of the dialog box underneath the sidebar entries. This will display the small dialog box shown in Figure 9-38. You can enter the URL of the page you want to link to or you can enter an e-mail address. Then, enter the text that you wish to display. Click the "OK" button to add the sidebar entry, or the "Cancel" button to exit without adding the entry. To add a link for an existing page of your web site, click the "Add page" link instead of the "Add URL" link. This will display a list of your existing pages; just choose the one you want to add to the sidebar.

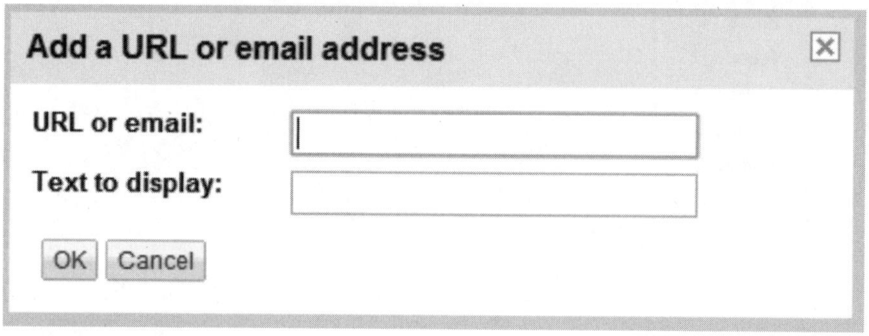

Figure 9-38: Add URL to sidebar

You cannot change the text of the sidebar entry in this Configure Navigation page. However, it can e changed by modifying the text of the "Page Title" area when viewing the corresponding page in edit mode (See Figure 9-10). This will alter the corresponding text in the sidebar when the page is saved. Click the "OK" button to save the navigation configuration when you are finished and then the "Save changes" button on the bottom left of the page in Figure 9-36. You can then return to the site by clicking the "Return to site" link at the top left of the page.

Creating New Pages

To create a new page in your site, when in viewing mode, click the "Create page" button in the top right of the page (Figure 9-39). From this page, you can then select the type of page you will be adding to the web site. You can currently choose from four (4) types: "web page," "Announcements," "File Cabinet" and "List." Each type of page serves a specific purpose. The "Announcement" template will set up a page which is able to quickly add announcements to a page. Similarly, the "File Cabinet" template will set up a page that can quickly add files to a page for uploading and downloading. The "List" template is to be used when you wish to create a page with lists of items. There are various configurable options you can choose from. The most common pages in your site will use the "Web Page" template.

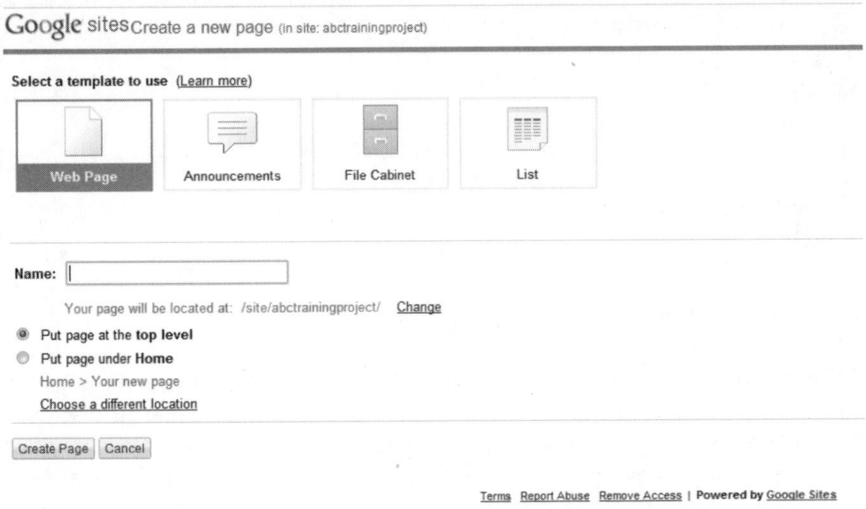

Figure 9-39: Adding a new page

Adding a Standard Web Page

Click on the "Web Page" template icon to highlight it, and then enter the name of the page, for example "Products." The URL to the new page will be shown underneath the Name you just typed in. There is no need to remember this, as you can easily locate it when you need to link to it at a later stage. You can now choose to put your new page at the top level in the site. This will make it equal to the other pages created by default that all have links into the sidebar. Also, you can choose to rank this page as subordinate to another page. You can click the "Put page under Home" button to place it directly under the home page, or click the "Choose a different location" link tom place it under another page. Making your page a subordinate to another page will just place a "breadcrumb" trail at the top of the page (a link trail such as "Home > List >" at the top of the page). You can always move this page at a later stage to be subordinate to a specific page. For the moment, leave the page at the top level and click the "Create Page" button at the bottom of the page or the "Cancel" button to exit without creating the new page.

You will then have a new page with a page title of "Products," and placed in edit mode, as shown in Figure 9-40.

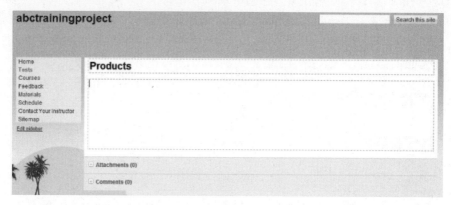

Figure 9-40: Newly added page in edit mode

Once a new page is added, as in Figure 9-40, you can add new text to the content area or you can add the page as a new link in the sidebar as discussed in a previous section, and format it as we have already covered. Once you add a link to your new page using the methods discussed, either in the sidebar or in the content area using the "Link" icon, users will be able to view you page when they navigate to it.

Adding a File Cabinet Page

A "File Cabinet" page is used as a storage area for files that can be downloaded from your web site. This is extremely useful for a site that makes files available to users. While similar functionality can be incorporated into a normal web page (Figure 9-39), it would require adding some specialized HTML code to the web page, but a File Cabinet page will automatically incorporate this functionality. To create a "File Cabinet" page, click on the "File Cabinet" icon shown in Figure 9-39 to highlight it, and then enter the name of the page. For example, "FilingCabinet." The URL to the new page will be shown underneath the name you just typed in. There is no need to remember this, as you can easily locate it when you need to link to it at a later stage. As with adding a new "Standard Web Page." you can choose where to locate the page. Once you have done that, click the "Create Page" button at the bottom of the page, or the "Cancel" button to exit without creating the new page. You will then have a new "Filing Cabinet" page with a page title of "FilingCabinet" and placed in edit mode, as shown in Figure 9-41.

Figure 9-41: Newly added Cabinet Page

This new page is created with the built-in functionality to upload files and link them to the page, making it easy for people visiting your site to download these files. This is done by using the "Add file," "Move to", "Delete" and "Subscribe to" buttons located at the top of the page. To add a file to your page, click the "Add file" button and you will see the "Add file" dialog box shown in Figure 9-42. You can choose to either add a file from your computer or to add a URL to the cabinet page by selecting the appropriate button shown in Figure 9-42. Adding a URL will just add a link to that address from your own cabinet page.

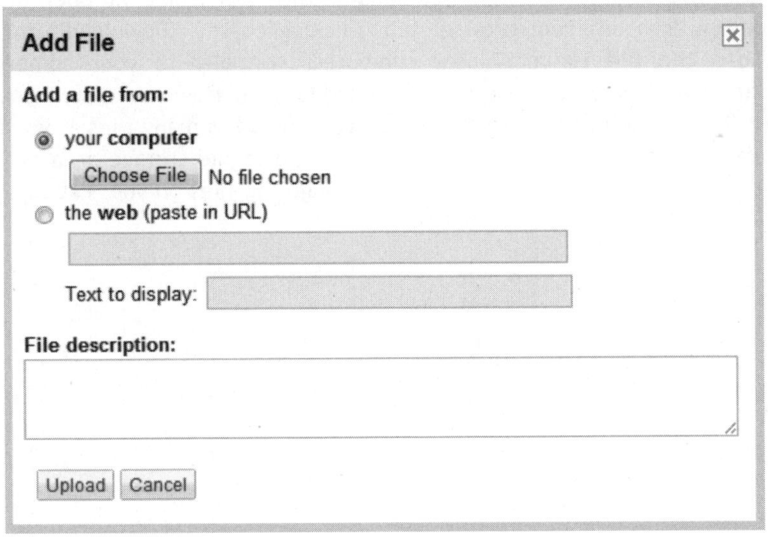

Figure 9-42: Add File dialog box

To add a file to your cabinet pa select the "your computer" button and then click the "Choose File" button located just below the radio selection. This will display your own computer's file selection window. Use this to navigate around your directories and select the file you wish to upload. When you select the file to upload, the file name will be displayed next to the "Choose File" button. To upload the file, click the "Upload" button located at the bottom of the dialog box in Figure 9-42. The file will then be uploaded and a link to it placed on your cabinet page (See Figure 9-43).

Figure 9-43: Uploaded file on the cabinet page

If the upload file can be viewed by a standard Google application, such as one of the Google Docs applications, it will contain a "View" link just underneath the file name, and a "Download" link as well,(See Figure 9-43). Otherwise, it will just have a "Download" link. Clicking on the "view" link will open the file for viewing in a different browser tab. Clicking on the "Download" link will download the file to your local computer, normally to your computer's specified download area. Once it is downloaded to your own computer, you can access it as you would any other file. You can upload as many files as you need to a cabinet page and this type of page becomes a file storage area for your web site (See Figure 9-44). You can also arrange the files on your cabinet page into folders as they are in Figure 9-44.

Figure 9-44: Cabinet page with many files arranged in folders

To create a folder, click on the "Move to" button at the top of the cabinet page, and this will show the drop down menu shown in Figure 9-45. To create a new folder, click on the "New folder" option, enter the name of the folder in the dialog box that appears and click the "Save" button. You can then move your files on the cabinet page into the folders you create. To do this, select the check-box for the files you wish to move, located to the left of the files name on the cabinet page. Then, from the "Move to" drop down menu shown in Figure 9-45, select the existing folder they will be moved to. The cabinet will then be re-displayed with the files arranged under their new folders. This arrangement will look something like Figure 9-44.

Figure 9-45: Drop-down "Move to" options

Adding files through a "Cabinet Page" is different than inserting a Google Document. When you insert a Google Document, you are displaying the contents of an existing Google Document within the web page, allowing people browsing the page to view the contents. However, by inserting a file in a

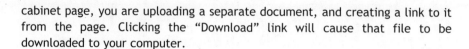

cabinet page, you are uploading a separate document, and creating a link to it from the page. Clicking the "Download" link will cause that file to be downloaded to your computer.

Adding a List Page

A "List" page is used to help you keep track of lists of information. Quite often we will need to track lists of data in different formats, and using a "List" page will allow you to choose from a number of different list formats. To create a "List" page, click on the "List" icon shown in Figure 9-39 to highlight it, and then enter the name of the page, for example "ListPage." The URL to the new page will be shown underneath the name you just typed in. Similar to adding a new "Standard Web Page" or a "File Cabinet Page," you can choose where to locate the page. Once you have done that, click the "Create Page" button at the bottom of the page, or the "Cancel" button to exit without creating the new page. You will then have a new "List" page with a page title of "ListPage," and placed in edit mode, as shown in Figure 9-46.

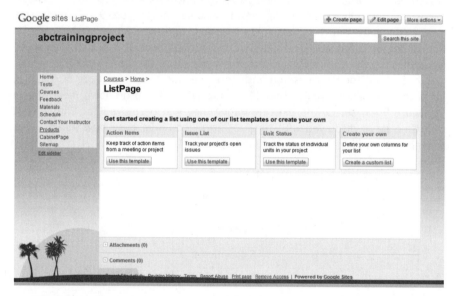

Figure 9-46: New List page

In the new "List" page created, you will see a number of list templates for you to use, including a *"Create your own"* template. As an example, if you choose the "Action Items" list format in Figure 9-46, the "List" page will be formatted as an page, where you can add actions to be undertaken, give each action an owner, a description, a resolution and indicate when it is completed(See Figure 9-47 for the blank *action list* page).

Figure 9-47: Blank action list page

To add an action to the list, click the "Add Item" button and fill out the dialog box shown in Figure 9-48. For example, in Figure 9-48, Paul is the owner of the action. The action is to book a rental car for vacation, and the resolution is that the action is currently "in progress." When this action has been completed, this action can be re-edited and the complete check-box can be selected.

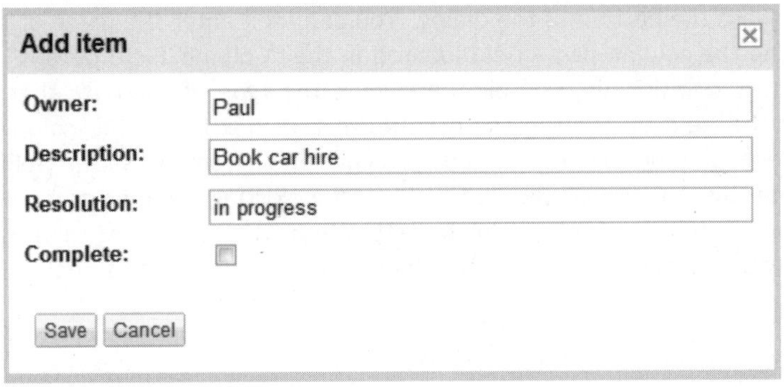

Figure 9-48 : Add Item dialog box

Click on the "Save" button when you have finished filling out the form. The action will then be displayed in the list with the appropriate information, (See Figure 9-49). In this figure, four actions have been added in various stages of completion pertaining to a holiday being arranged.

Courses > Home >

ListPage

Add item | Customize this list

Showing **4** items

Owner	Description	Resolution	Complete
Sort ▼	Sort ▼	Sort ▼	Sort ▼
Stacey	Pack suit cases		
Paul	Book car hire	in progress	
Adam	Book Hotel room	waiting for confirmation	
Cathy	Book flights	booked	✓

Showing **4** items

Figure 9-49: Action list with 4 items

When some progress on a particular action has been made, you can click on the action in the list in Figure 9-49, and the "Edit Item" dialog box will appear where you can modify the action's status and save the results. The "Edit Item" dialog is the same as the "Add Item" dialog shown in Figure 9-48. Sometimes you may need to add more columns for information concerning the actions. In this case, you can customize the standard action list format by clicking on the "Customize this list" link, next to the "Add Item" button. This will show the "Customize your list" dialog box shown in Figure 9-50. Using this dialog box, you can add a new column to the action list by clicking the "Add a column" "link toward the bottom of the dialog. You can then enter the name of the new column in the column name field located in the "Column/Field Details" part of the dialog. Additionally, you can determine the type of the data that can be kept in the field by clicking the drop-down text box below the column name and selecting an option. The options you can select from are shown in Figure 9-50. Using this dialog, you can also rename the existing columns or modify their order by clicking on a column in the left side of the dialog and then using the up-and-down arrow icons that appear beside the column name selected.

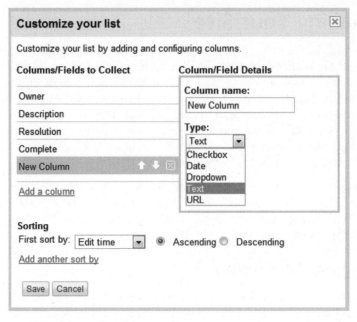

Figure 9-50: Customize you list dialog box

If when you first inserted the new list page, you selected the "Create your own" list option in Figure 9-46, the you would see the "Customize your list" dialog box shown in Figure 9-50 appear, except there would not be any pre-defined columns. You create your own list from scratch, adding new columns, naming them, selecting their type, and ordering them as needed. The other list types in Figure 9-46 are variations of these.

Deleting Pages

You can easily delete an existing page by choosing the "Delete page" option from the "More actions" drop-down list button shown at the top right of the page. This will then give you the option of deleting the current page you are viewing or canceling the delete. If you choose to delete a page from your site, you need to make sure your site remains consistent. Thus, you need to delete any links in your site which may cause a user to navigate to a deleted page. This includes changes to the sidebar and any other page in the site that may have linked to it.

There is nothing more annoying than visiting a web site and clicking links that no longer exist. This can drive people away from your web site.

Managing Your Site

There are a number of options available to you for managing your Google Site. Some of these we have already seen, but in this section we will touch on a few more of the available options. One of the things you cannot change is the template you initially use to create the site. As mentioned earlier, the initial template becomes the blueprint for all pages in the site. It is possible with individual page changes for text and font changes that you could massage your site to look like something else over time. But it is easier to take your time in the beginning and choose the correct template.

To manage and edit many of the parameters that define the site, from viewing mode, select the "Manage Site" option from the "More actions" drop-down list at the top right of the web page. This will take you to the Google Sites configuration page shown in Figure 9-36.

Changing the Theme

One of the things we did at the beginning when setting up the Site was to choose a Theme. This was basically a color theme with images to be used in conjunction with the chosen template. You can change the theme at any time through the site manager. From the site configuration page, click the "Theme" link at the bottom left of the page, among the Site Appearance links. This will display a page of possible themes to select, exactly as we did in the beginning after setting the template. Browse the themes and select one by clicking the button located just beneath each theme. When you have selected a theme, click the "Save changes" button to select the theme, or click "Cancel" to exit without selecting a new theme.

Note that when you change Themes, you are basically re-painting your web site with a new face color. The underlying template remains the same.

Customizing the Site Layout

We covered part of the Site layout previously, specifically editing and positioning the elements of the sidebar. However, when you click the "Site layout" link on the left side of the screen of the site configuration page, you can also customize other aspects of the layout. Click on the "Change site layout" button at the top of the customize site layout screen. You will see the dialog box appear as shown in Figure 9-51. Using this dialog box, you can specify the site width by either using the theme's default value or by clicking the button next to the small text box underneath and specifying a width value.

You can specify the width as either a percentage of the screen width or as a specific pixel value by entering the unit after the value.

You can also adjust the height of the Site Header (See Figure 9-10). You can use the default theme value or specify the height in pixels of one of a number of standard values. It is also possible to remove the Site Header by clicking the "No header" button.

Additionally, you can also specify the height and placement of the sidebar. It is possible to also remove the sidebar by clicking the "No sidebar" button.

When you have made changes to the site layout, click the "Save changes" button to select set these changes, or click "Cancel" to exit without changing.

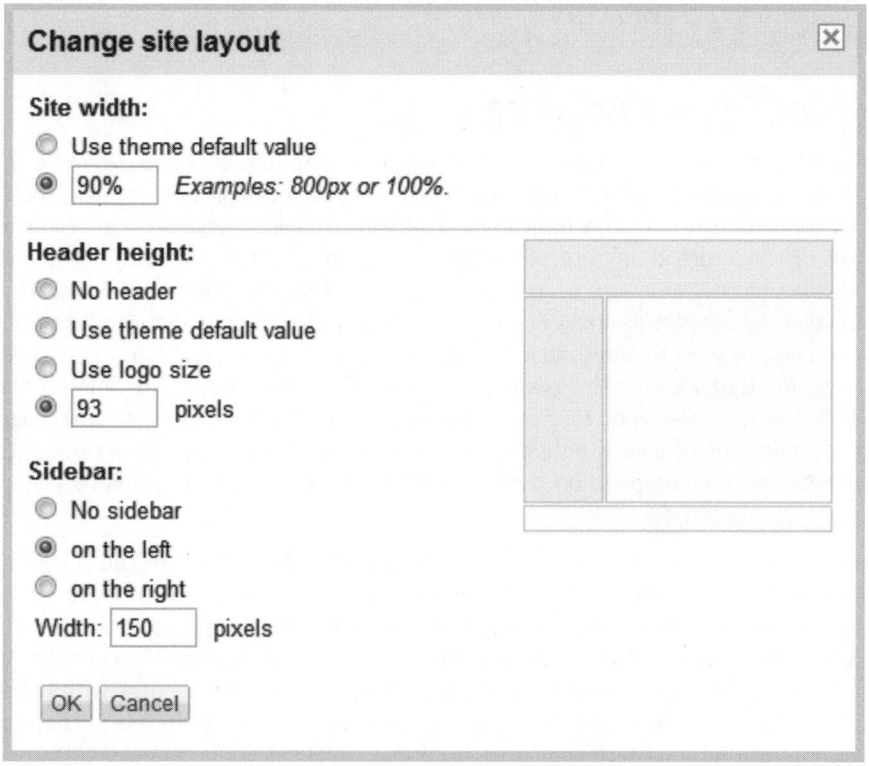

Figure 9-51: Change Site Layout dialog

Displaying the Site on Your Own Domain

If you own a custom domain name, for example, a www.yourname.com, or www.yourname.net, then you can display your Google site on your custom domain. To do this, you click the "Web Address" link on the left of the manage site screen. From there you can add your own URL where the Google site will be hosted. You will need write access to your custom domain CNAME records.

ExplainED

Modifying domain records is a delicate process. Please consult a technical professional to assist you with this.

Using Google AdSense

If you plan to develop web sites which you intend to maintain and expand over time, it may be possible to earn income from your project by utilizing Google AdSense. Google AdSense basically places advertising on your web pages. Yet AdSense is more than just advertising; it is an electronic form of targeted advertising to your users, based on the content of your web site. The advertising appears as small boxes within your Google Sites sidebar. Currently, you can place up to three AdSense units per page. You get paid on a per-click basis for the adverts. The customers do not have to purchase anything, only click the advertisement for you to receive the commission for that particular advertisement. Google won't disclose how much you earn per advertisement, because this will depend on the type of ad and how much Google is receiving from the advertisers.

Before you incorporate Google AdSense into your web site, you should read the Google AdSense Program Policy. There are policies in place governing the use of AdSense on a web site. You can't automatically just add Google Add Sense advertisements as Google must maintain its reputation and good standing with advertisers and can't display their ads on poorly designed web sites with little or no original content. You must register and apply to Google for permission to incorporate AdSense into your sites.

You can incorporate Google AdSense advertisements into your page you can click the "AdSense" option in the "Insert" menu while in edit mode. However, you first have to enable AdSense for your web site. From the Site configuration page shown in Figure 9-36, click on the "Monetize" link on the left. This will take you to the page shown in Figure 9-52. From here, you can read the Google

AdSense program policy and other information on using AdSense by following the links shown on the right.

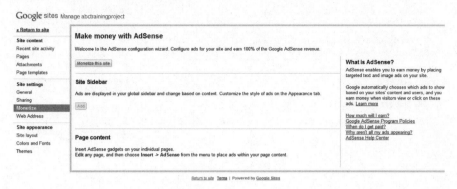

Figure 9-52: Monetize Site web page

To Enable AdSense and configure your site, click on the "Monetize this site" button shown at the top of the page. This will display the screen shown in Figure 9-53. AdSense will now be enabled, but you must complete the sign-up process by clicking on the link shown in the shaded area to complete the account information form (not displayed). This will involve gaining final approval for your site to incorporate AdSense, which may be rejected. You need to read the Google AdSense program policy before applying to make sure your site will conform to the standards expected by Google.

Once your site has been enabled for AdSense, you can then click on the "Add" button in the "Display Ads" section of the page shown in Figure 9-53. Not long after that, contextual ads should start appearing in the sidebar on the pages. Your site needs to be enabled for public access before ads will appear. This is usually the default unless you change it.

Figure 9-53: Enabling AdSense

Sharing

The final thing we need to discuss is that of sharing on your web site. Under Google Sites, the web site is open to anyone in the world for viewing. You can make a web site private by blocking access to the outside world. Additionally, you can also invite people to be owners or collaborators of the web site. To manage this sharing of your site, you need to click on the "Sharing" link from the site settings page, or from viewing mode select the "Share this site" option from the "More actions" drop-down list button. This will take you to the sharing options page shown in Figure 9-54. The left side of the page allows you to choose the sharing options and which levels. The right side of the page shows a list of people in the different categories.

NotED

You can only share access to people who have Google accounts.

480

Invite people to your site

○ as owners ● as collaborators ○ as viewers

```
"Publishing Staff"
<publishing.staff@gmail.com>
```

Separate email addresses with commas

Choose from contacts

[Invite these people]

Advanced permissions

☑ Anyone in the world may view this site (make it public)

Sharing with coworkers?

Companies can securely manage multiple sites. Learn more

People with access

Owners (1)

gappschrome@gmail.com - Remove

Collaborators (0)

Viewers (0)

Figure 9-54: Sharing options

You can make the web site private by blocking access to the outside work. This is done by unchecking the box labeled "Anyone in the world may view this site," toward the bottom of the page. Once you uncheck this box and save the changes, the web site will no longer be available to be viewed by the outside world. You will need to invite people specifically to be viewers.

There are three types of people we can specifically invite to our web site. The three types represent different capability sets. These are:

Owners: Can invite other people to the web site within the three categories, including other owners. Owners can change site themes, layout and the site name. They can also, delete the site and do everything a collaborator can do.

Collaborators: Can delete, edit and create other web pages for the site. They can also add attachments and comments and modify the sidebar.

Viewers: Can view pages.

To invite a user to be either a viewer, collaborator or owner, first click the appropriate button for the type of user you want, then click the small link "Choose from contacts" link underneath the e-mail address text box. This will display a list of your Google contacts and their e-mail address. Click the users you want to invite into the category you have chosen. You can click more than one, which places a green check mark besides the contact. Click it again to unselect it. Once you click the button to choose these contacts, the e-mail addresses will be added to the text box as shown in Figure 9-54. Now, click the "Invite these people" button below the email text box. This will display the dialog box shown in Figure 9-55. You can type in a message that will be sent to the e-mail addresses with the notice that they have been added in the chosen category. The people will then be listed on the right hand side of the sharing options page shown in Figure 9-54.

Tell these people about the site?

To: publishing.staff@gmail.com

Subject: abctrainingproject

Message:

I have given you access to the ABC Training Project Google Site.

Note: a link to the site will be included in the message

Send | Skip sending invitation | Cancel | ☐ CC me

Figure 9-55: Inviting contacts to join the web site

Revision History

Google Sites' revision history allows you to quickly compare and restore older versions of your sites. This feature is extremely useful to allow users to quickly revert to an earlier version of the website in the case of inaccuracy or emergency. You can access the revision history by two methods.

The first method is to go to "Pages" in site management shown in Figure 9-36. Here, you will be presented with a page such as the one displayed in Figure 9-56

List | Tree — ‹Prev 1-18 of 18 Next›

Item	Created by	Last updated by	Revisions
calendar	Gapps Book (31 Mar 2010 03:02)	Gapps Book (31 Mar 2010 03:16)	2
Contact Your Instructor	Eric Seaton (3 Oct 2009 04:10)	Mandy Sladden (31 Oct 2009 04:36)	1
Courses	Eric Seaton (3 Oct 2009 03:47)	Eric Seaton (3 Oct 2009 03:53)	1
Doctest	Gapps Book (29 Mar 2010 22:47)	Gapps Book (30 Mar 2010 01:52)	8
Feedback	Eric Seaton (3 Oct 2009 04:06)	Gapps Book (29 Jan 2010 03:56)	2
form	Gapps Book (31 Mar 2010 03:35)	Gapps Book (31 Mar 2010 04:00)	3
Home	Anil Sabharwal (15 Sep 2009 14:15)	Gapps Book (29 Mar 2010 22:44)	23
map	Gapps Book (31 Mar 2010 03:02)	Gapps Book (31 Mar 2010 03:07)	2
Materials	Eric Seaton (3 Oct 2009 04:06)	Gapps Book (1 Feb 2010 01:34)	5
present	Gapps Book (30 Mar 2010 21:42)	Gapps Book (30 Mar 2010 21:44)	2
Products	Gapps Book (1 Feb 2010 02:20)	Gapps Book (1 Feb 2010 02:26)	2
Sample Presentation	Eric Seaton (3 Oct 2009 08:22)	Mandy Sladden (31 Oct 2009 04:35)	1
Sample Test 1	Eric Seaton (3 Oct 2009 09:04)	Sample User (24 Oct 2009 06:55)	1
Sample Video	Eric Seaton (3 Oct 2009 08:42)	Eric Seaton (3 Oct 2009 09:02)	1
Schedule	Eric Seaton (3 Oct 2009 04:02)	Gapps Book (31 Jan 2010 22:56)	8
SpreadsheetTest	Gapps Book (30 Mar 2010 00:05)	Gapps Book (31 Mar 2010 03:36)	13
Spreadsheettest2	Gapps Book (30 Mar 2010 00:18)	Gapps Book (30 Mar 2010 02:07)	17
Tests	Eric Seaton (3 Oct 2009 09:03)	Mandy Sladden (31 Oct 2009 04:35)	1

List | Tree — ‹Prev 1-18 of 18 Next›

Figure 9-56: Page Management

From this page, you can access the revision history by locating the page you wish to edit and then clicking on the number on the right side of the page under the heading "Revisions." This will take you to the revision history for the page you have selected (See Figure 9-57).

Version history for Home « view page listing — ‹Prev 14-23 of 23 Next›

Version	Last edited	Edited by	
Version 23 (current)	29 Mar 2010 22:44	Gapps Book	
Version 22	2 Feb 2010 19:09	Gapps Book	(Revert to this version)
Version 21	1 Feb 2010 01:57	Gapps Book	(Revert to this version)
Version 20	31 Jan 2010 04:30	Gapps Book	(Revert to this version)
Version 19	31 Jan 2010 04:12	Gapps Book	(Revert to this version)
Version 18	31 Jan 2010 03:52	Gapps Book	(Revert to this version)
Version 17	31 Jan 2010 02:48	Gapps Book	(Revert to this version)
Version 16	31 Jan 2010 02:47	Gapps Book	(Revert to this version)
Version 15	31 Jan 2010 02:42	Gapps Book	(Revert to this version)
Version 14	31 Jan 2010 01:54	Gapps Book	(Revert to this version)

Version history for Home « view page listing — ‹Prev 14-23 of 23 Next›

Figure 9-57: Revision history

Figure 9-57 shows the version history of the page "Home." From this page, you can see which users edited each revision of the page and what time the changes were made. . You can view a revision by clicking on the version number link located on the left side of the page. Clicking on a version shows the contents of the page (See Figure 9-58). The second method of getting to the revision history for a page is to go to the page you wish to examine the revisions for, and then select the "More actions" button and then select "Revision History" which is the first item from the drop-down list. Selecting this will take you to the page shown in Figure 9-57.

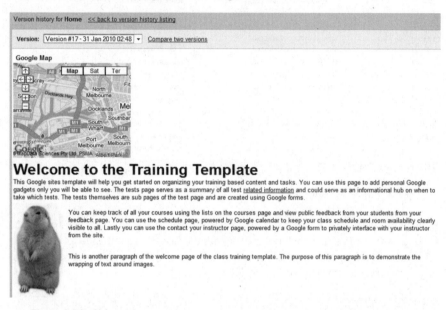

Figure 9-58: Old revision

On this page, we can see the older version of the home page, and users can easily switch between versions by selecting a version number from the drop-down list at the top of the screen labeled "Version." You can also compare two versions of the page next to each other by clicking on the "*Compare two versions*" link at the top of the page. Clicking on this will take you to a new page where you can compare the differences between two versions of the page (See Figure 9-59).

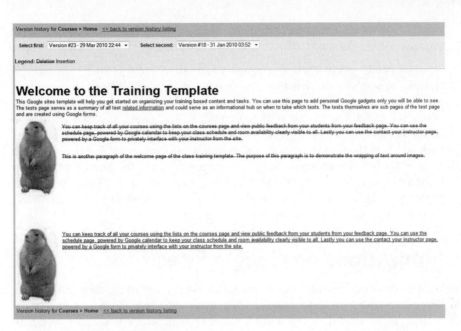

Figure 9-59: Comparing two versions

From Figure 9-59, we can see the entire site was deleted and re-written. Any text which has a line through it has been deleted. You can also easily spot text that has been inserted by the underline. Any text which is underlined has been added in the changes between the versions. You can compare the different versions of the page by selecting which versions of the site you wish to compare in the drop down lists shown at the top of Figure 9-59.

Once you have finished examining previous versions or comparing versions, simply click the "Back to version history listing" link at the top of the page.

Once you have found the version you wish to revert to, you simply have to click the "Revert to this version" link located next to the version number of the page to which you wish to revert. This will take the version you have selected and insert it into a new revision of the page.

Backing up your site

As your web site is stored in the cloud, it is automatically backed up by Google, removing the need for you to worry about backups of your site. However, if you wish to have backup copy of your web site that you can store on your computer and browse locally, there are third-party tools available to help in doing this. One such tool you can use is called *google-sites-liberation*. At the time of writing, this tool could be located at http://code.google.com/ p/google-sites-liberation/.

Another point which is often discussed is that of moving your web site. In traditional web site construction, this may need to be considered from time-to-time. However, with Google Sites, there is no need to consider this option. When you build a web site with Google Sites, the pages are located at web addresses on the Google servers, and you become the owner and are provided with a link to them to share with the world. If, at some point in time, you wish to give the site to someone else, you only have to share the site with the other person before transferring ownership of the site, similar to Google Docs. This person then becomes the new owner, but the actual web site is not physically moved, only a transfer of ownership takes place.

Limitations on Google Sites

Google Sites provides a great way to quickly create a set of professional looking web pages with a lot of functionality. Being a productivity tool, there are some limitations to what you can do as well as some limitations on your free user accounts. Currently there is a 100 megabyte limit on file and page storage for your site, with a maximum of 500 files per site. Additionally, the maximum file upload limit is 10 megabytes, which places a limitation on the size of any attachment to 10 Megabytes.

There seems to be a page view limit that puts a limit on the number of pages from your site that can be viewed each month. This is difficult to pinpoint as it is now advertised widely. Google mentions 5 million pageviews a month in Google Analytics, but some users have reported reaching pageview limits at around 1.3 or 1.5 million pageviews per month. These limits are still very generous, and if you do experience problems, Google can be approached on the topic.

Some other limitations that may be experienced are mainly design restrictions based on the Google Sites Page Creator tool and security limitations. For instance, there is no general Wiki tool to create a Wiki site. This would be difficult at best anyway given security restrictions on who can and cannot edit pages. However, it would be possible to create a restricted Wiki (perhaps a project based site), by assigning as collaborators to the site a group of Google accounts.

Web Site Tips

We would like to conclude this chapter by mentioning a few tips on creating web sites. It is always difficult to provide general tips as everybody has an idea of what does and does not make a good web site. Additionally, tips will be different depending on the type of web site you are constructing. However, there are some general tips that can be applied to most sites regardless of the contents. Some of these we have gained through experience, and many more can be found in pages on the web itself.

- Use Appropriate Colors: Make sure you do not overwhelm visitors with bad color combinations. Some people are color blind and will not perceive colors the same. Yet, inappropriate colors will discourage anyone. Use soft colors for the background, or a neutral color such as white. Make sure the text contrasts with the background strongly enough so that it is easily visible without having to strain to read it.

- Don't use a font too small. You may want to fit a lot on your page, but if the font is too small, people will not read it. Yes, browsers can be adjusted so the font appears bigger, but that can upset the format of the original page and it won't display the same. It is better to do it properly at the source.

- Use images and graphics appropriately. It is true that a picture (or diagram) is worth a thousand. Use these to help explain your point; if you are trying to convey information on a web page.

- Don't clutter the page. One of the traps novice web designers often fall into is using a lot of interesting looking gadgets, animated images and gadgets on the same page. This will make the page too distracting.

- Don't make pages too long. You may have a lot to say, but there are many studies which have documented web users' behavior. Many visitors will not scroll down a page if your text runs off the end of the screen. This may be an extreme case, but consider breaking your text into multiple pages. Put the important information in the immediately visible area when the page loads.

- Use a consistent format for all of your pages. This gives your site a more professional appearance. Use a good template for your pages to help you achieve this.

- Use a consistent approach with links to your pages so a user will not get confused. In the example template in this chapter, the sidebar contained links to all the top level pages. If you create sub-pages underneath these, make sure the top level pages contain links to the direct sub-pages. The visitor needs to understand the navigation rules of your site, and this can be achieved through a consistent use of links.

- Always keep your pages relevant to a topic. Try not to have too many topics on one page.

- If you are using AdSense, use it appropriately. Don't overload your visitors with too many adverts.

- Always conform to the standards and legal requirements of the country where the site is hosted, and where you live.

Summary

In this chapter you have learned how to build and manage web sites with Google Sites. We initially learned how to create a web site and choose an appropriate theme for your web site. We also discussed the site name and the URL. We then provided a detailed section on how to edit your new site, including editing a page, changing text and inserting links and images. We also covered using tables, layouts and incorporating other Google objects into your site, such as Google Documents, Spreadsheets, Presentations, Calendars and Maps. Then, we discussed inserting new pages, including standard web pages, or file storage and list pages which provided useful functionality for attaching documents or maintaining lists. We then covered how to manage your site, including changing themes, customizing the layout, displaying your site in your own domain and utilizing Google AdSense to generate income from the page. Finally, we looked at using Google Sites revision history to track changes to the pages and restore previous versions.

Chapter 10

Google Maps

Maps have always been important to people; from navigational charts to GPS devices, different kinds of maps have been around for thousands of years and have always played an important role in society. Recently Google took the unprecedented step of releasing maps of the planet for free, accessible to anyone, anywhere.

Google Maps has made an amazing difference in how people use and interact with maps. For example, home buyers may use Google Maps to examine an area to buy a house. Other examples abound: TV news services use Google Maps to show their viewers the location of incidents; investigators use Google Maps to plan surveillance, and many people use Google Maps to get directions.

Panning and Zooming Maps

Once you have opened Google Maps by going to [maps.google.com] or clicking "*Map*" in the Google toolbar, you will be presented with the screen shown in Figure 10-1. This is the default opening screen, and it presents you with a map of the United States of America.

We will begin by learning how to move around these maps. If you hold your cursor over the map, you will notice that the cursor changes to a hand. This indicates that you can drag the map around to view different areas. You do this by clicking the map area and moving your mouse. You will notice that when you move your mouse around, the map follows your mouse. This process is known as panning.

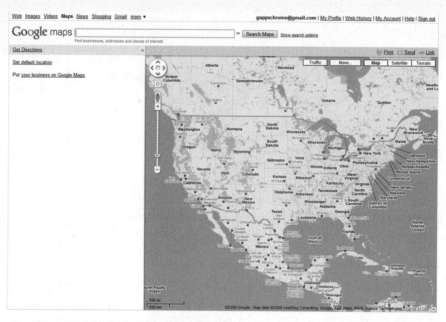

Figure 10-1: The Google Maps default view

Another important feature is *zooming*. You can easily zoom in on an area by holding your mouse over the location you want to zoom in on and double-clicking with your left mouse button. This will zoom your map in one level. You can zoom out by double-clicking with your right mouse button when you do this, and it will zoom out one level.

On the left side of the map window you will notice a set of controls (see Figure 10-2) that also allows you to pan and zoom. The four arrows at the top of the image allow you to pan by clicking the arrow pointing in the direction you want to pan. Clicking the hand inside the four arrows will return you to your previous search result. Both methods of panning and zooming yield the same results however zooming using the slider is significantly faster than double clicking. However, by using double click to zoom you re-center the map where you zoom into.

Figure 10-2: The navigation controls

The lower part of the navigation controls is a zoom slider that you can drag either up or down to zoom in and out. The final part of the navigation controls is an icon that looks like a person; this is used to activate street view, which will be discussed later in the chapter.

You can zoom in close enough to view a city street or zoom out far enough to see the entire planet.

ExplainED

You can zoom in and out with your mouse wheel

You can also right-click a section of a map to bring up the menu shown in Figure 10-3; you can use this menu to perform various actions.

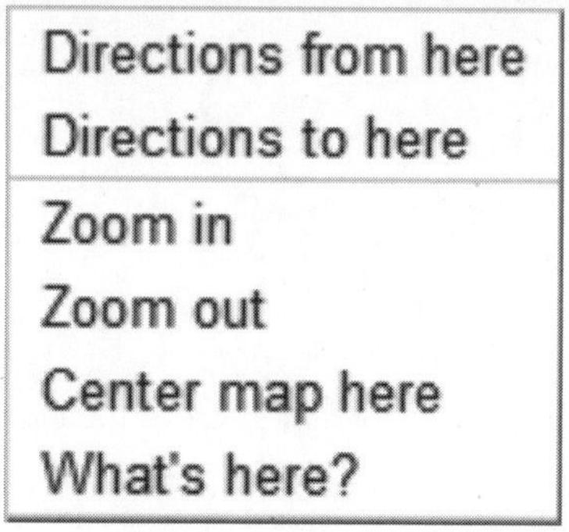

Directions from here

Directions to here

Zoom in

Zoom out

Center map here

What's here?

Figure 10-3: The right-click menu

This menu lets you zoom in and out by clicking the appropriate menu item. You can also center the map here by clicking the "Center map here" menu item. This will move wherever you right-clicked the map to the middle of your screen. For example, if you right-clicked the corner of the map and clicked the "Center map here" option, you see the map pan in that direction. You can also perform more advanced functions, such as using the location for directions, which will be covered later.

Changing the Default location

By default Google Maps will always show you maps for the country where you are located. For example maps.google.com will center Google Maps on the United States of America, using maps.google.com.au will center Google Maps on Australia; however, you can change this to anywhere you desire by clicking the "Set default location" link on the left side of the screen. This will open a dialog box where you can type in your preferred location. For example, you could enter "Melbourne, Australia" and then click the "Save" button. You can also enter a street address or a landmark/feature as a default starting location, such as "Carlton Gardens, Melbourne"

Change default location

carlton gardens, melbourne

Save   Cancel   Remove

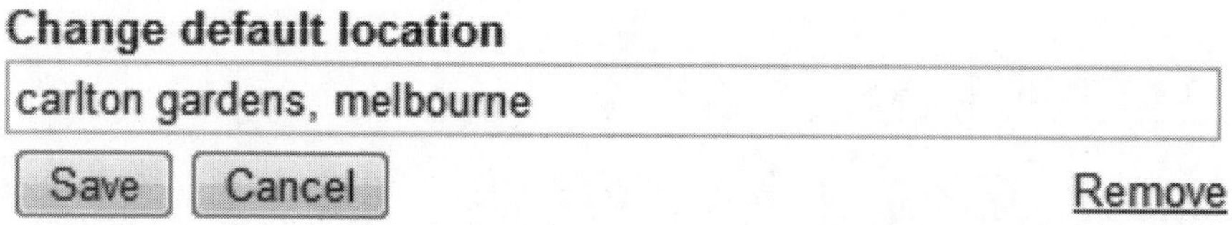

Figure 10-4: Setting the default location

Once you set the location, you will be shown that location by default every time you load Google Maps.

Searching for a Business or Location

If you want to search for a business or location, you can easily do so by using the search field that is located at the top of the screen. You can search for addresses, streets, landmarks, businesses, cities, and countries. This gives you a lot of freedom when composing searches. For example, you can search for "Cafes in Altona, Victoria" to locate cafes in Victoria (see Figure 10-5).

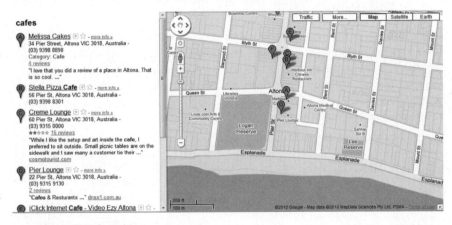

Figure 10-5: Searching

As you can see, a number of markers have appeared with letters in them. There are two types of markers that you will see when using searches. First, you will see the large markers with a letter inside them. These large markers indicate that this marked location can be found in the list of results on the left side of the screen. Second, you will see small markers. These are small dots that you can see at the base of larger markers and by themselves. Small markers that are by themselves indicate that the location of a result from your search is not shown in the search results on the left. You can see examples of large and small markers in Figure 10-5.

You can find out more information about a marker by clicking the marker or the title of a location in the results list. The area you can click is surrounded by black squares in Figure 10-6; this figure also shows the information box that opens when you click a section.

Figure 10-6: Examining the results

As you can see in Figure 10-6, the information box that opened up has given us some information about the business and presented us with some things we can do. The first thing we can do is see more information about the business. We can do this by clicking the "more info" link that is near the top of the information box. This will take us to another page that contains more information on the result the page (see Figure 10-7).

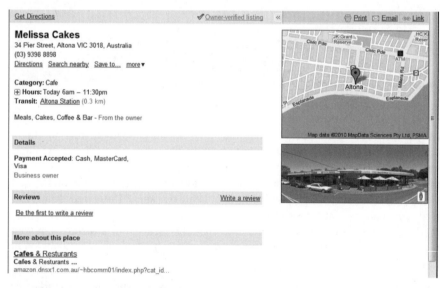

Figure 10-7: More information

As you can see, this page provides you with information about the business. Figure 10-7 is broken up into sections. The first section, at the top, contains some basic information about the business, including the address of the closest public transport and some assorted information. Below this section is the "Details" section, which provides information set by the owner of the business. Next is the "Reviews" section, which allows you to see other people's experiences with the business. The final section on the page allows you to see what other web sites have referenced this business.

The first information to take note of is in the middle of the screen, at the top. There is a tick with "Owner-verified listing" next to it. This indicates that the business owner has entered the details of the business, so that the details are correct.

The first section contains the basic information about the business. It also gives you a number of options, including the ability to use the location for directions or search nearby, topics that are covered later.

NotED

Business listings can differ from each other; some information available for one business may not be available for the next business you search for.

In the information box, you can also see today's business hours. To see the hours for the rest of the week, click the "+" icon next to the hours for the day you wish. Immediately beneath the opening hours, you can see the closest public transport; the store in Figure 10-7 has a train station that is 300 meters (330 yards) away.

The "Details" section contains information that has been entered by the business owner directly; this information can't be edited. This section usually contains more details about the business.

Searching Near a Location

The "Search nearby" option was previously mentioned, and it allows you to search near the location, which can be useful in many situations. For example, you can search for a friend's house and then search nearby for a cafe. Alternatively, if you are going to a restaurant, you can search nearby for ATMs. Clicking the "search nearby" link shown in Figure 10-6 will open a search box, which is depicted in Figure 10-8.

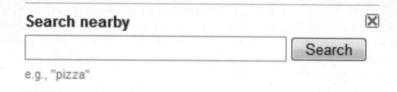

Figure 10-8: More information

If you search for "ATM" in the "Search nearby" text box, you will see that the results depicted in Figure 10-9 are limited to what is near the location you searched from.

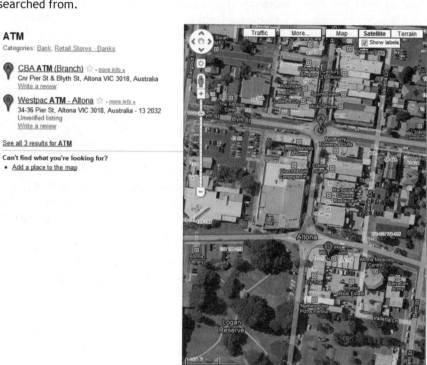

Figure 10-9: Local results

Reviewing Businesses

Reviews allow you to see what other people thought about a business and to leave your own opinions about the business. Google has integrated the ability to review businesses listed in Google Maps. This allows users to quickly gauge how good a business is before you deal with them. You can see existing reviews and create your own from the reviews section of the business listing shown in Figure 10-7.

To create a review, you simply have to click the "Write a review" link; this will open the form that is shown in Figure 10-10.

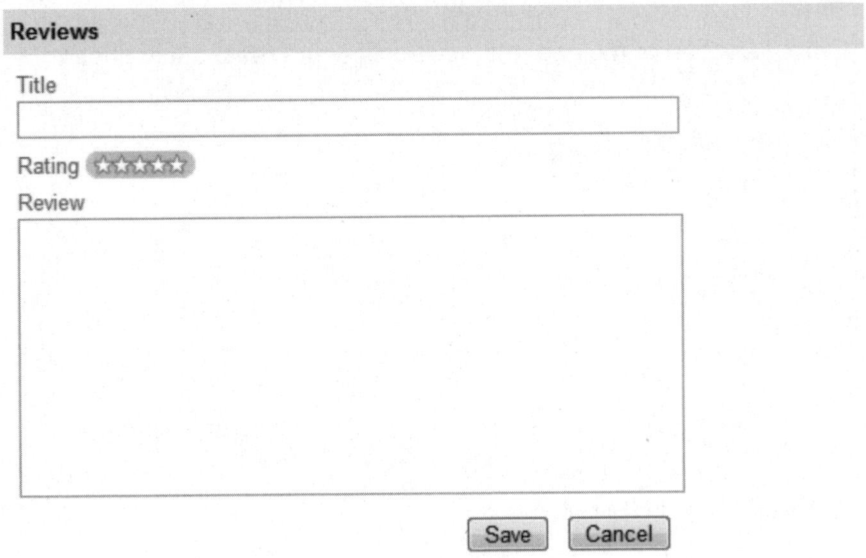

Reviews

Title

Rating ⭐⭐⭐⭐⭐

Review

Save   Cancel

Figure 10-10 Writing a review

Once you have opened the form, all you have to do is enter a title, write some review text, and then click the number of stars you believe the place deserves in the rating. Finally, click the "Save" button (see Figure 10-11).

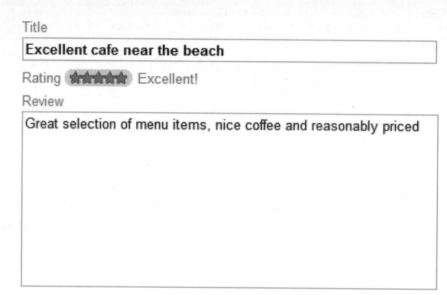

Figure 10-11: Writing a review

Once you have submitted your review, it will instantly be placed online for everyone to see. You will be able to edit or delete your review at any time by clicking the appropriate links that are displayed on the review (see Figure 10-12).

Your review
★★★★★ **Excellent cafe near the beach** - - Today
Great selection of menu items, nice coffee and reasonably priced
Edit - Delete

Figure 10-12: A completed review

ExplainED

Do not post vexatious reviews and always ensure that your reviews are an accurate reflection of your experience.

Filtering Search results

Sometimes when you search, you get too many results that are not relevant to what you want. You can see an example of this in Figure 8-13; the results in this example were gathered by typing "Cafe, Melbourne" into a search.

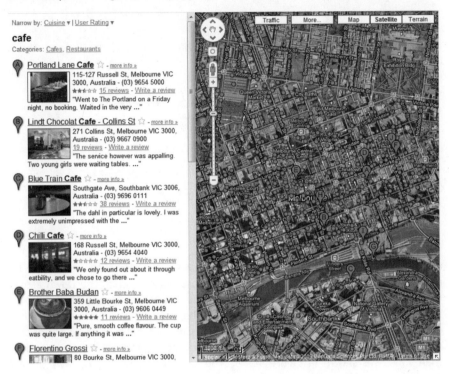

Figure 10-13: A crowded search

As you can see, there are too many results from that search, so we must narrow down the results to provide us with more useful information. The first way to narrow down the results is to search again using a more precise search question. For example, you could re-perform the search with "cafes in South Melbourne." This search will limit the results returned that are in South Melbourne.

The next method of narrowing down search results is to zoom in on an area. If you zoom in, the search is automatically re-performed, returning only results that you can see within the map window. You can use this to provide more precise results. You might use this approach to search for restaurants near the beach and then zoom in closer; this will remove results that are more inland.

The next method of narrowing a search is to use the category system that Google provides. Above the search results for cafes, there are two drop-down lists that you can access. Both lists are pictured in Figure 10-14.

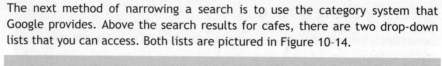

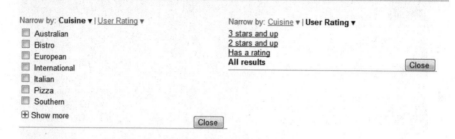

Narrow by: **Cuisine** ▼ | User Rating ▼

- Australian
- Bistro
- European
- International
- Italian
- Pizza
- Southern

⊞ Show more

[Close]

Narrow by: Cuisine ▼ | **User Rating** ▼

3 stars and up
2 stars and up
Has a rating
All results

[Close]

Figure 10-14: The search categories

As you can see, searching for cafes provides two categories that we can use to narrow with the search. To access the category options, click the Down arrow next to the category that you wish to use. This will present you with the list of items you can use to narrow the results. In the Melbourne cafes example, you can tick the "European" option under the "Cuisine" category to narrow the number of results to less than ten; this result is significantly more valuable than what was shown in Figure 10-13. You can then view the reviews of the cafes that have been found in the search, which will assist you in locating a place.

Search by Pointing to a Location

Figure 10-3 showed the menu that appears when you right-click a map. This menu includes a "What's here?" option. If you use this function, Google Maps will automatically take the location of your mouse pointer on the map and convert that to a street address that can be searched.

You can see an example of this by locating the Sydney Opera House, which is shown in Figure 10-15.

Figure 10-15: The Sydney Opera House

Once you have located the Sydney Opera House, simply right-click it and select the "What's here?" option. This will find the address at the location and tell you what is there. However, this can never be completely accurate, so at times you may be reading information about the premises next door. An example of this is the Sydney Opera House. By right clicking on the Sydney Opera House and selecting "What's here?" we are presented with Figure 10-16.

Sydney Harbour Tunnel ☆ - more info »
Dawes Point NSW 2000, Australia

Directions Search nearby Save to... more ▼

Explore this area »

Photos

Places
Sydney Opera House

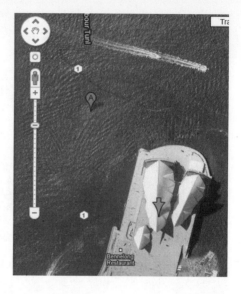

Figure 10-16: What's here

In Figure 10-16, Google Maps has selected the closest road to place where the map was right-clicked. In the lower part of the search result, you can see that it has the Sydney Opera House listed under "Places" that could also be at this address.

Checking Traffic Conditions

The first advanced feature we'll cover is called Traffic. This feature allows you to see a quick overview of the traffic in your city. Traffic can be seen by clicking the button marked "Traffic" that is located at the top right of the map window. This will draw colored lines over the existing roads on your screen to indicate traffic movement.

NotED

The traffic feature may not be available in your local area, or it may be restricted based on the cooperation between your local government and Google.

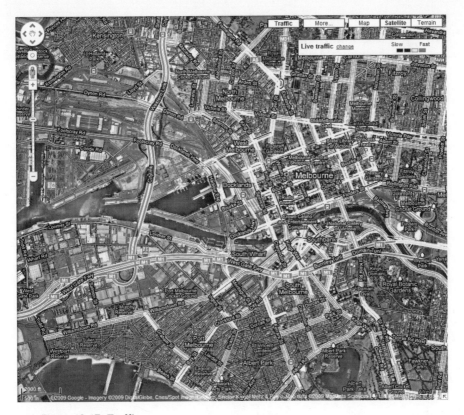

Figure 10-17: Traffic

In Figure 10-17, the major roads have been covered with traffic indicators. The colors of the traffic indicate the speed; red and black show congested traffic in the area, while green indicates free-flowing traffic.

In some cities, such as New York, you are presented with extra information, such as planned road works and accidents (see Figure 10-18).

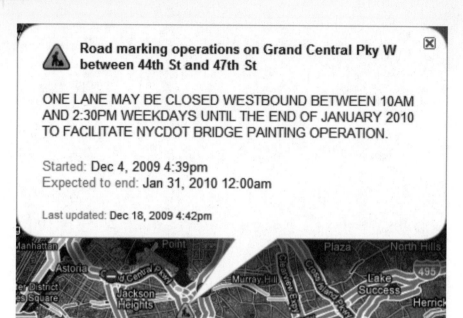

Figure 10-18: Road warnings

There are two different warnings shown in this example. First, a little workman icon shows scheduled road works. Second, the red warning icons show important notices about road conditions.

Getting Directions

The directions feature allows you to plot the most effective ways of travelling between locations. To begin, click the "Get Directions" option, which is located on the top-left corner of maps. This will open a new box (see Figure 10-19).

ExplainED

You should always thoroughly examine any route which you are presented. Mapping technology is not perfect, and routes can have mistakes.

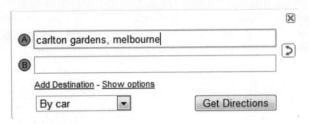

Figure 10-19: Getting directions

If you wish to get directions, all you have to do is enter where you are in text box A, where you want to go in text box B, and then click the "Get Directions" button. This will provide you a map and directions to your destination (see Figure 10-20).

ExplainED

You can set your destination by right-clicking where you want to go on the map and clicking the "directions to here" option; select the "Directions from here" option to set where you are leaving from.

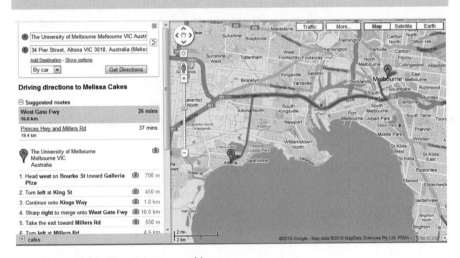

Figure 10-20: Directions to an address

Figure 10-20 shows the suggested route from Carlton Gardens to 34 Pier Street in Altona. On the left side of the screen, just below the directions box, there is a section called "Suggested routes"; this area allows you to examine the alternate routes that Google has calculated by clicking that the link. Suggested routes can be useful if you there are major road works along your route, in which case you can switch to an alternate route to avoid them.

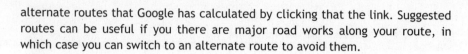
ExplainED

Combine your route planning with the "Traffic" feature to assist you in locating the fastest route.

You can plan more advanced routes by adding extra destinations to travel to. You do this by clicking the "Add destination" link. This will add an extra destination box with the label "C". If you fill in all the boxes, Google Maps will then give you directions from A to C by B. You can use the "add destination" feature to add as many stops as you require. To remove destinations from the list, you simply have to click the small "x" on the right side of the direction box you wish to remove.

By clicking the "Show Options" link, you can set a few options for Google Maps to avoid tolls and highways, and to change the units that distances are shown in.

The final set of options for directions is in a drop-down box at the base of the directions box. By clicking this, you can specify whether you wish to make the trip by car, by walking, or by public transport.

NotED

The public transport option may not be available in your local city.

Viewing the details of a route

You can view the route that Google Maps presents you by clicking any of the directions on the right-hand side. This will take you to a photo of the turn in question, as shown in Figure 10-21.

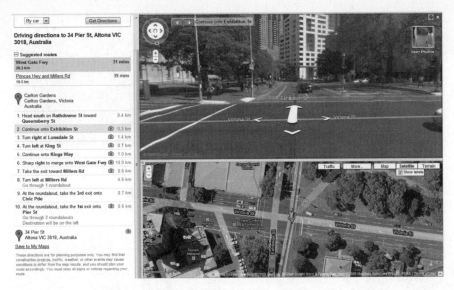

Figure 10-21: Viewing an intersection

Figure 10-21 depicts the directions that Google has provided. You can use the arrows at the top middle of the screen to view the next intersection that you need to take. To exit this screen, click the "x" located in the upper-right corner.

Using Overlays to Show Extra Information

Google Maps allows you to overlay the maps with items such as photos, videos, and even real estate information. To add or remove layers, begin by hovering your mouse over the "More..." button that is located at the top of the window (see Figure 10-22).

Figure 10-22: The "More..." button

Turning on one of the items in the "More..." menu will place markers at various places on the map. For example, turning on the "Photos" option will place links to photos on the map (see Figure 22-23).

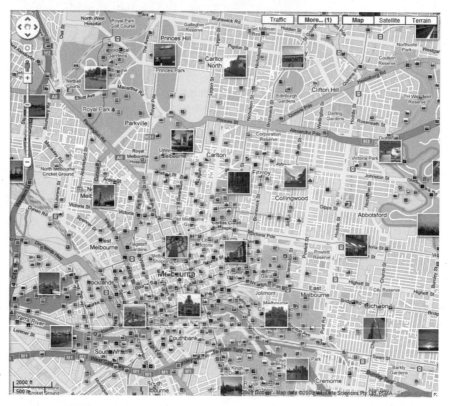

Figure 10-23: Photos

As shown in Figure 10-23, Google Maps places the photos based on where they were taken. You can see a larger version of the picture by clicking it (see Figure 10-24).

Figure 10-24: An enlarged photo

This option shows the photo in a larger format; it will also allow you to view the full photo or video by clicking the icon in the lower left corner. Note this icon will change depending upon where the photo or video is located on the Internet.

Using Different Views

Google Maps gives you three different views that you can use to see different information: Maps, Satellite, and Terrain view.

- The Map view allows you to see the roads and plan your journey easily; this is the default view.

- The Satellite view allows you to see the ground as actual photos taken from space that are composited together.

- The terrain view allows you to view the terrain; it's useful for planning hikes and other outdoor activities.

To change between the views, simply click the button for Map, Satellite, or Terrain view. These buttons are located at the top of the map area (see Figure 10-22). You can see an image of Satellite view in Figure 10-25 and Terrain view in 10-26.

Figure 10-25: The Satellite view

As you can see, Satellite view allows you to zoom in and see aerial shots of actual buildings. This can be quite useful for a number of purposes.

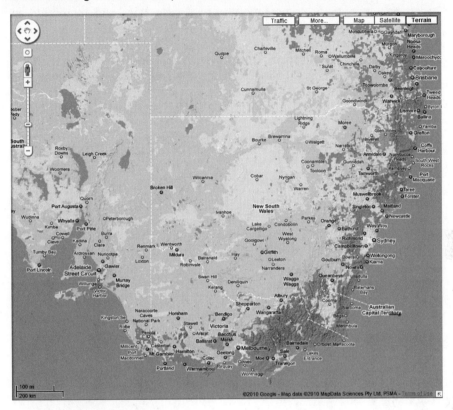

Figure 10-26: The Terrain view

The Terrain view allows you to see what the physical terrain of an area looks like. Terrain view allows you to quickly see if an area has significant amounts of vegetation and to roughly judge its elevation. Figure 10-26 shows a map of Australia in Terrain view. Although we can not see it in this print book, Terrain view shows that a significant part of Australia is a deep yellow, which signifies desert. Terrain mode also shows us that there are significant levels of vegetation along the east side of the country. We can also determine that, because the green patches in the east are dark, Australia has a lot of mountains along the coast. Finally, Terrain view also shows patches of gray near the major population centers of Melbourne (South) and Sydney (East); gray signifies a population center. White signifies snow.

Exploring with Street View

Street view is a fairly recent addition to Google Maps and represents an amazing effort by Google to literally drive down every street in cities of many countries and photograph the views. This gives us the ability to select a location, and then choose Street view to get a panoramic view of the location; we can use our mouse or keyboard to follow the path of the vehicle that took the pictures.

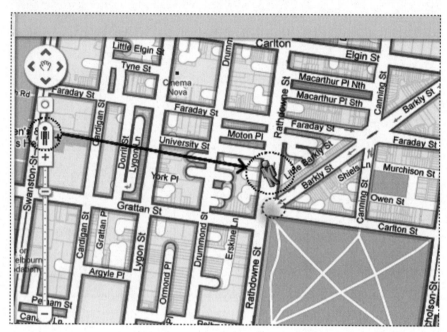

Figure 10-27: Dragging the person icon to enter Street view

You can enter Street view in two ways. First, when viewing a map (such as the one shown in Figure 10-27), click the small person icon in the upper left of the map and drag it to a position on the map that you would like to view at street level (see Figure 10-27). When you drop the icon on that position, the map window will change, and you will be in Street view mode. Second, you can search for a specific address in Google Maps. When the map is displayed, a small marker will be shown at the address specified (see Figure 10-28). Clicking this marker will show a number of options (again, see Figure 10-28), and selecting the "Street view" link just underneath the small picture will enter Street view mode at that approximate address.

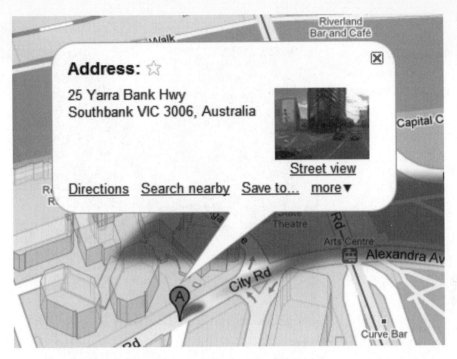

Figure 10-28: Selecting the map marker to enter Street view

When you enter Street view, you will be shown an image similar to that shown in Figure 10-29, depending on the location you have chosen to enter. Street view represents a snapshot of that particular location at the time the Google vehicle was driving through that area. Street routes are shown by a transparent yellow line that shows directions; when the location is at an intersection, branching yellow lines will show the directions of these, as well. You can use the mouse to click the image and drag the view either left or right, or you can use the keyboard's left and right arrow keys. This will rotate the view either left or right, mimicking the effect of standing at that location and turning around to get a panoramic view.

Figure 10-29: A Street view

You can click the arrow keys on the yellow route lines (see Figure 10-29) to move in that direction. This will have the effect of moving slightly down the road in the direction of the arrow. You can stop and turn in all directions again or continue moving in another direction. In this way, you can walk down the road from the comfort of your own home. This feature allows you to do a walkthrough of a location you intend to visit before you leave. Thus you can familiarize yourself with the location first, rather than becoming confused and looking for a specific landmark while driving.

For a business, it is also a great tool to advertise not only your location on a map, but also to give potential customers a first-hand look at the actual location where you are situated. This adds to the customer experience when visiting your web site.

NotED

Street view is not available in all countries and areas.

Summary

In this chapter, we have looked closely at Google Maps to perform a variety of functions. We first looked at using and navigating through maps, and then at searching for specific locations. Next, we looked at other users' reviews and how to filter the results of searches. Under the advanced topics, we found out how we could use Google Maps to find out about current traffic conditions (where available), as well as how to use Google Maps to get from one location to another. We could then view that route. Finally, we looked at different views we could enter in Google Maps, including Terrain, Satellite, and Map views. With Street view, we learned how to place ourselves at a specific location and get a panoramic view of that location; in fact, we could virtually walk down a road or street from the safety of our own computer.

Chapter 11

Google Talk

Google Talk allows you to communicate instantly anywhere in the world by text or voice. Google Talk is Google's instant messaging system for use on either fixed or mobile devices. Beginning in the 1960's, Instant Messaging (IM) has changed significantly from its humble beginnings being used to notify other users when various computing resources were busy. Currently, Instant Messaging, in one of its many forms, serves as a valuable tool for business communication and a tool for friends to communicate. It is used in many online classrooms, news forums and social networking sites all over the world. There are many IM systems in the world today which work differently, rely on different technology and are built for specific purposes. An example of an instant messaging technology most people have used is a SMS message (text message) on a mobile phone. However, Google Talk allows you to chat, transfer files, send voice mail and even talk with others not using Google Talk.

NotED

To work through the examples of this chapter, you will need a friend on a separate computer or someone who already uses Google Talk and is willing to help you.

Getting Talk

We did mention in the introduction that all you needed to run the Google Apps an Internet connection and a web browser. Google Talk is tightly integrated with Gmail (see Chapter 2), and you can use Google Talk by invoking a Chat session in Gmail. However, Google Talk can also be downloaded independently as a client application on your computer. For the remainder of this chapter, we will discuss the Google Talk App from the perspective of having it installed on your local machine. However, most of what we discuss can be duplicated through the Gmail interface.

To get Google Talk, you must go to http://www.google.com/talk/install.html in your browser. This will take you to an automatic download of Google Talk. Once this has been downloaded, load the program and follow the steps to setup the program. The first stage of the setup is to agree to the licensing agreement.

ExplainED

Always read and understand the user agreements before you agree.

If you agree to the terms of the license, click "I Agree" to continue installation, otherwise click "Cancel" to cancel the installation. If you click "I Agree" the installer will automatically install Google Talk.

Getting Started

The first time you start Google Talk you will be presented with a logon prompt, displayed in Figure 11-1.

Figure 11-1: First run

When you are at the window displayed in Figure 11-1, you simply have to enter your Gmail username and password and click "Sign I". In the future, you will automatically be logged in to Google Talk.

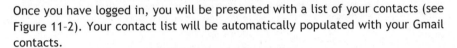

If you are on a public computer uncheck "Remember Password."

Once you have logged in, you will be presented with a list of your contacts (see Figure 11-2). Your contact list will be automatically populated with your Gmail contacts.

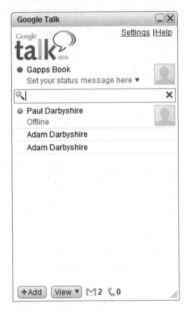

Figure 11-2: Contact List

Adding Contacts

To communicate with someone, they need to be in your contact list. You can add new people to your contact list by clicking on the Add button located in the lower left corner of the main window shown in Figure 11-2. This will bring up the window displayed in Figure 11-3.

To add a new contact, you must enter their e-mail address in the field. This will send them an e-mail which will provide them with instructions on how to get and use Google Talk. Also, you can click the "Choose from my contacts..." button, which will allow you to select your Gmail contacts displayed in Figure 11-4.

Figure 11-3: Add a contact

Figure 11-4: Gmail contacts

In this window you simply have to select which contacts you wish to add to Gmail and click the "OK" button in the lower right corner.

You should never give out private information in Google Talk or any other online instant messaging tool for your own security.

Responding to a Friend request

If someone adds you as a contact, you will receive a notification inside Google Talk (see Figure 11-5). You can either accept or deny the request by clicking "yes" to add them to your contact list or "no" to deny them.

Figure 11-5: Request notification

Warnings

The Internet is a wonderful place where you can find information about almost any topic; however the Internet can also be dangerous if you are not careful. Instant Messaging can be particularly dangerous.

When using any form of IM, you should always remember the following:

1. Always have a current virus scanner.

2. People on the Internet may not be who they say they are.

3. Never give out personal details to strangers.

4. Never give out passwords or credit card information to anyone, even if you know them.

5. Always be careful about accepting files.

6. Never accept any files with an .exe or .msi extension.

Communicating with Contacts via IM

To communicate with a contact, you need to double click on the desired contact. This will open a chat window that can be seen in Figure 11-6.

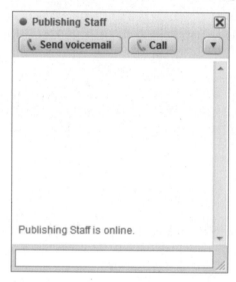

Figure 11-6: Chat window

Once the window is open, all you have to do is type your message and press Enter. You can see a chat window in use in Figure 11-7.

Figure 11-7: Used chat window

When someone sends you a message, a small window will appear at in the lower right corner of your monitor (see Figure 11-8). To switch to the chat window, click on the notification window.

Figure 11-8: Notification window

Personalizing Google Talk with Display Pictures

You can set a picture that will be displayed next to your messages (see Figure 11-9).

Figure 11-9: Display Picture

You can change your display picture by clicking on it under the Help button on the main window shown in Figure 10-10.

Once you click on the window, you will be shown a list of display pictures you can choose (see Figure 11-10). To select the display picture from the list, simply click on the picture you want. Otherwise, you can select a picture stored on your computer by clicking "More pictures". This will open a window that will allow you to select the image you want.

Figure 11-10: Display Picture

Further Interaction with your Contacts

Google Talk also allows you to do more than just send text messages. You can send files from your computer and communicate using voice. The easiest way to access these features is to right click on your user in the user list. This will bring up a menu of available tasks (see Figure 11-11).

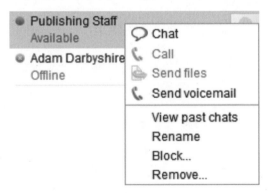

Figure 11-11: Right click menu

You can also interact with your contacts from the Chat window, using the same menu controls as the right click menu (see Figure 11-12).

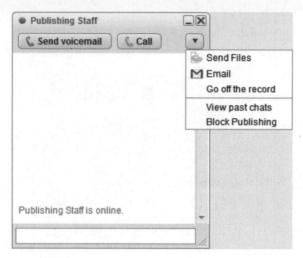

Figure 11-12: Chat menu items

Sending Files

You can also send files to other users. You can do this by right clicking on the user in the contact list and clicking on "Send file." This will allow you to select the file you want to send. After you select the file, a notification will be sent to the recipient giving them the option of downloading the file.

Receiving Files

If someone tries to send you a file, you will receive a notification (see Figure 11-13).

Figure 11-13: Notification of a file request

Figure 11-13 shows the notification you receive after a file transfer request. You should always know what is being sent to you before you accept. You can either accept or deny the request.

Never accept any file that ends in .exe or .msi because they may contain viruses.

Once the file has been successfully downloaded, you will be able to find the file in your "My Documents" directory in "Google Talk."

Communicating with Contacts via Voice

You can chat with another person using Google Talk by clicking on the phone icon in the contact list highlighted in Figure 11-14 or the "Call" button located within the chat window.

527

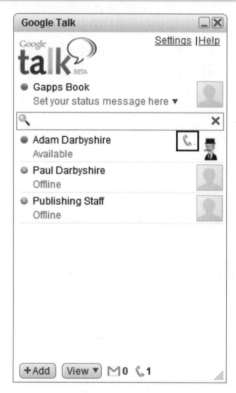

Figure 11-14: Call button

This will notify the other party of the chat that you want to speak to them. If you are called by someone, you will see a small notification above the clock in your Start bar (see Figure 11-15). This notification is also accompanied by a ringing sound.

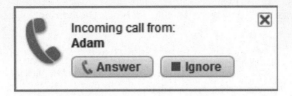

Figure 11-15: Call notification

If you choose to click on "Ignore" the person calling you will have the option of leaving you a voice mail that is delivered to your e-mail inbox. If you accept the call by clicking on "Answer" a chat window will open to the person calling you (see Figure 11-16).

Figure 11-16: Call

From this window you can still communicate with your chat partner using text; however at the top of the window is an extra row of information. There are two sets of bars; these indicate the volume coming from the source. They will allow you to see your speaking volume. You can also mute chat by clicking on the "Mute" button. When you have finished talking to the person, simply click "End Call" to end the voice chat.

Blocking contacts

Occasionally, you will have a contact you don't want to communicate with for some reason or another. To block a contact, you have to click on the "Block" button from the right click menu or from the Chat menu. This will bring up a confirmation dialog (see Figure 11-17). To block the contact, simply click "OK" on the dialog.

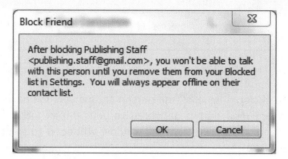

Figure 11-17: Confirmation dialog

Once you have blocked the contact, it will be removed from your contact list and added to a block list.

Unblocking Contacts

To unblock a contact, you have to click on the Settings menu located in the top right corner of Talk. This will take you to the settings window where you need to click on the "Blocked" menu item that is highlighted in Figure 11-18.

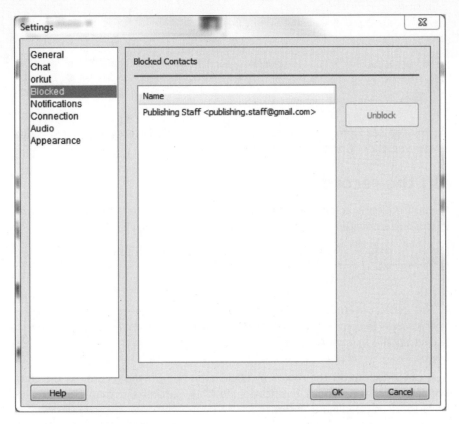

Figure 11-18: Blocked menu

Once you are in the "Blocked menu", you have to click on the contact that you want to unblock then click the "Unblock" button. This will remove the contact from the blocked list and return them to your normal contact list.

Viewing your Chat History

You can view your chat history with a contact by simply right clicking on a contact and clicking on "View past chats". This will open your web browser and take you to the "Chats" label of Gmail. Each individual chat is saved as an e-mail you can view in Gmail (see Figure 11-19).

Figure 11-19: Gmail chat history

As you can see from Figure 11-19, you can view all your previous chat sessions unless you click "Go off the record."

Off the record

If you frequently communicate with people, there may be times when you are discussing a private issue you do not want to be stored in chat history.

ExplainED

This can be useful when discussing sensitive issues when another person has access to your Gmail account, or you are unsure of the privacy of your chat partners Gmail account.

You can switch to off the record by clicking on "Go off the record" in the chat window. This will send a notification to both parties and then stop logging conversations (see Figure 11-20).

ExplainED

If the person you are talking to does not use the Google Talk client, they may still be saving the conversation history.

You are now off the record (from now on, chats with Publishing will not be saved in Publishing's Gmail account or yours) Learn more Cancel

Figure 11-20: Turning on "Off the record"

Figure 11-20 shows the notification that you see when switching "Off the record" on. You can learn more about this feature by clicking the "Learn More" link, you can also leave off-the-record mode by clicking "Cancel" You can also leave "Off the record" by clicking "Stop chatting off the record" in the drop-down menu in your chat window. When the person you are chatting with enables "Off the record" you will see a notification that looks like the one shown in Figure 11-21.

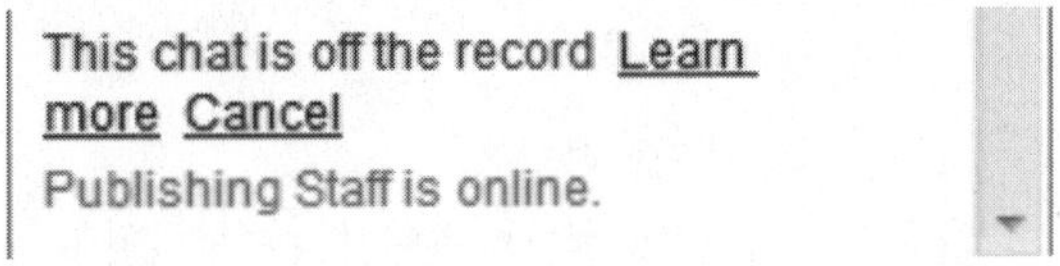

This chat is off the record Learn more Cancel

Publishing Staff is online.

Figure 11-21: Conversation partner turning on "Off the record"

Once "On the record" is switched off, you will see a notification that reads "This chat is no longer off the record."

Setting your Preferences

The Settings menu allows you to adjust how Google Talk behaves. You can access the Settings menu by clicking on the "Settings" link at the top of the window (see Figure 11-12). From here, you can make general changes to the program.

Start Automatically When Starting Windows: If you select this option, Google Talk will automatically load when you start your computer.

Open Gmail when I click on e-mail links: By selecting this option, every e-mail address you click on in Google Talk will open a web browser and take you to the e-mail composition screen in Gmail.

Sort by Name: By checking this option, your contact list will be sorted in alphabetical order.

Hide Offline Friends: Checking this option will hide your contacts not currently online in Google Talk.

Hide Google address book contacts not on my Google Talk Friends List: Selecting this option will hide your contacts unless you have added them as a friend in Google Talk.

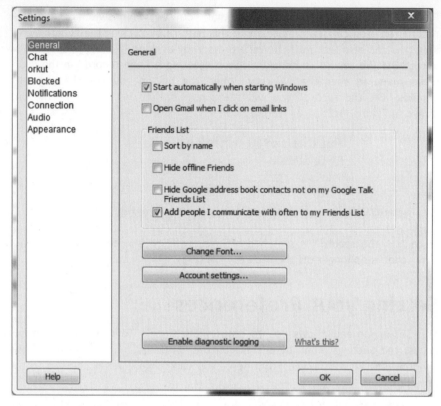

Figure 11-22: Settings window

Add people I communicate with often to my Friends List: This option will automatically add the people you frequently communicate with on Gmail to your Google Talk contact list. You can hide these contacts by selecting "Hide Google address book contacts not on my Google Talk Friends List."

Clicking the "Account settings" button will open your web browser and take you to the account settings page of your Google Account.

You can change your font by clicking on the "Change Font" button. This will bring up a dialog box (see Figure 11-23).

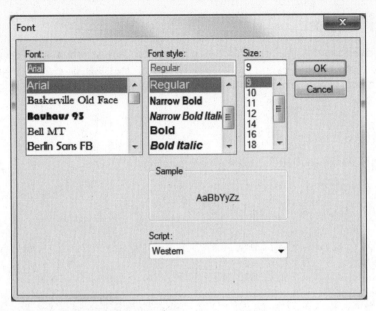

Figure 11-23: Fonts window

Clicking on the "Enable diagnostic logging" button instructs Google Talk to create log files that contain information that can be helped to solve a technological problem. This function is for advanced users and it is not recommended that you use it.

Logging

The next part of the Settings window is the Chat settings which can be located by going to the "Chat" item on the left side of the Settings window. This window allows you to specify if Google Talk logs chat history in Gmail (see Figure 11-24). In this window, there are two radio buttons that will allow you to set logging. Logging is enabled by default.

Orkut

By clicking on the "orkut" button, you will be taken to the settings page for Google orkut. This is a social networking service offered by Google. Orkut allows you to communicate with your friends, post pictures and leave messages. Using orkut is not covered in this book.

Notification

By clicking on the "Notification" menu, you can adjust when you are given notifications of new events such as a new chat message or e-mail. You can enable and disable event notification by checking or unchecking the relevant check box.

Audio

You can change your audio settings here (see Figure 11-24).

ExplainED

If you are having problems with voice calls, try adjusting the audio settings.

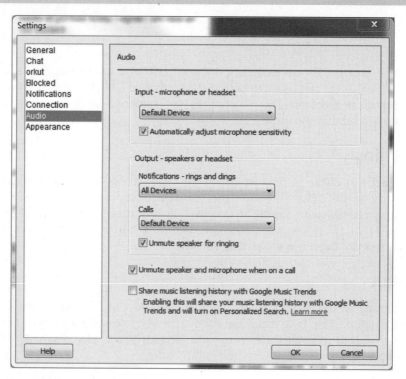

Figure 11-24: Audio settings

The options in this window allow you to adjust your speakers and microphone hardware. If you have more than one sound card or microphone, you will have the ability to change the drop-down lists (see Figure 11-25).

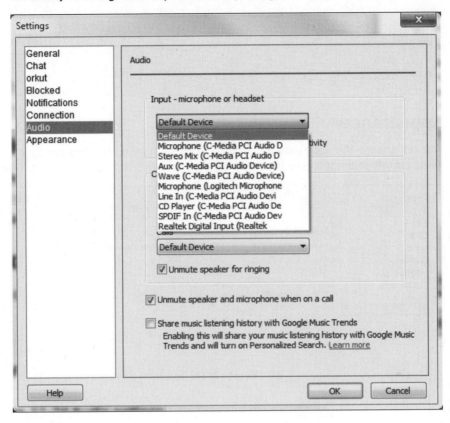

Figure 11-25: Audio devices

Each item in the list shown in Figure 11-25 is recognized as a microphone by Google Talk, while your computer may not have as many items as in this list, you can still switch the items around if your audio is not working properly.

- If you cannot hear the other person, but they can hear you, adjust the "Calls" drop-down list under output.

- If you can year the other person but they cannot hear you, adjust the "Input" settings.

You can try each individual item systematically until you find a working combination. If you are unable to get Voice calls to work properly, you may need to consult a computer technician.

ExplainED

Do not adjust these settings if voice calls work.

Appearance

You can change the appearance of your chat by clicking on the "Appearance" menu button on the left (see Figure 11-26).

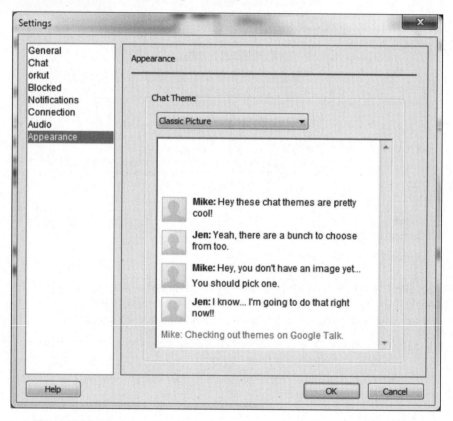

Figure 11-26: Themes

There is a drop-down list in the middle of the page that allows you to pick a different theme to use in Google Talk. The theme change adjusts how the text is displayed. In the middle of the window is a location allowing you to preview the theme which you have selected. Once you have chosen a theme you like, simply click the "OK" button to apply it. The changes you make to the appearance will only be reflected in your chat windows. There are many themes you can choose from. The "Classic Picture" theme is shown in Figure 12-26. The "Ping Pong Picture" theme is shown in Figure 11-27.

Figure 11-27" "Ping Pong Picture" theme

Summary

In this chapter we have thoroughly covered the use of Google Talk. We started by covering contacts and friend requests. We then discussed best practices for communicating on the Internet. Next, we covered how to communicate with contacts on the Internet by IM. We then covered how to send and receive files from contacts, followed by voice communication. Next, we examined how to block contacts, look at chat history and off-the-record mode. Finally, we covered the settings of Google Talk including logging, notifications, audio and appearance.

Users new to the concept of Instant Messaging will learn how to use Google Talk to effectively communicate with contacts in real time. Users will understand the advantages of using instant messaging as well as having a basic understanding of how to protect their personal information and their computer against viruses.

Chapter 12

Blogger

Blogging (indeed social networking) has recently become a powerful force in the media; however blogging in some form has existed prior to 1990 when people used to post on Usenet news services. Blogging, in its current form, began emerging as a phenomenon in the mid-90s with online journals. Online blogging started as a way for people to share details of their lives, but expanded to people using blogs to post reviews of items, political commentary, and many other topics. The web site Blogger.com was created in 1999 and bought by Google in 2003. The term "blog" came about by combining the words "web log""and is used to describe both the web sites and the action of creating content on these web sites. After 2004, several blogs have been created by people wishing to get their views on an issue accessible to the public ultimately providing an unprecedented amount of connectivity for the general public. In an example, a government minister can easily look for blogs relating to an issue and discern the public's view. Previously this type of communication (usually letters to the editor, which were extremely restricted because they could always be censored) was largely ignored by newspapers or other media, while a blog allows a user to express what they want to say in their own words uncensored for everyone to see. However, as with all communication methods, there are inherent risks. If a blogger posts something that can be determined as defamatory, they can be subject to a defamation lawsuit. Additionally, a blogger who anonymously releases private company information via a blog may have their details ordered released by the courts so they can face civil action (as seen in an increasing number of cases). A police officer named Richard Horton, who was posting his experiences on a blog, was forced by the courts to remove his anonymity and was disciplined for his blog.

In this chapter we will discuss in detail the use of Blogger.com (also referred to as just Blogger) and work through the main components of utilizing this application. We will cover how to create a blog and how to create and send posts, and to create and edit a profile. We will also look at utilizing images and video within blog messages. You will find how to update the Blogger.com settings and be shown how to manage blogs, customize your blog, interface it with Gmail, and use the blog on your mobile phone. Readers new to the idea of blogging or Blogger itself will find this chapter an invaluable tool into the workings of Blogger. Readers will quickly understand how Google's Blogger can be used as a tool to get their ideas and opinions out into the public domain.

Creating a Blog

To create your blog, go to blogger.com (see Figure 12-1).

Figure 12-1: Blogger start page

In the upper corner of the page, enter your Google account username and password and click the check box labeled "Remember me." This will remember your login details so you won't need to login on the same computer again.

ExplainED

Don't use "Remember me" on a public computer. If you do, everyone else who uses that computer can access your account.

Once you have logged into your account for the first time, create details for your account (see Figure 12-2). Enter the name you want to publicly appear on your blog when creating posts. Enter a name you want in the text box in the middle of the screen. You can also elect to receive emails from Blogger by clicking the check box below the name field. Check the check box at the bottom of the page indicating that you have read the terms and conditions of using Blogger. You can see the terms of service by clicking the "Terms of service" link next to the check box. If you accept the terms of service, click the continue arrow at the bottom of the page.

Figure 12-2: Blogger account

NotED

You should always read any terms of service before you sign up for a service.

After finalizing your account setup, you will then be taken to a page where you can create your individual blog (see Figure 12-3). On this page, specify the details of your blog. Begin by entering the title of your blog, such as "My Blog." In the next field down, choose where your blog is accessible. The text box lets you set the sub domain. For example, if you were to enter gappschrome in the text box when you create the blog, then the blog will be publicly accessible from gappschrome.blogspot.com.

Once you have entered an address where you would like your blog to appear, click the "Check Availability" link. This well let you see if anyone else has the address you wish to register. If the address is taken, you will see "Sorry, this blog address is not available" appear in red writing below the "Check availability" link. If you can use the address, you will see green writing stating "This blog address is available." Once you have found an address that is available, enter the verification. These are designed to be difficult so a program can't read the address. If you have trouble reading the words, click on the wheelchair icon which will read the text out loud to you, or refresh the page to generate a new image.

Figure 12-3: Creating a blog

Once you have entered all the details and the verification, click "Continue." This will take you to the page allowing you to choose the template and the theme of your blog. Once you are on the "Theme select" page (see Figure 12-4), scroll through the list of themes available and click the radio button below the color scheme and style you wish to use. Once you have selected the theme, click "Continue" at the bottom of the page.

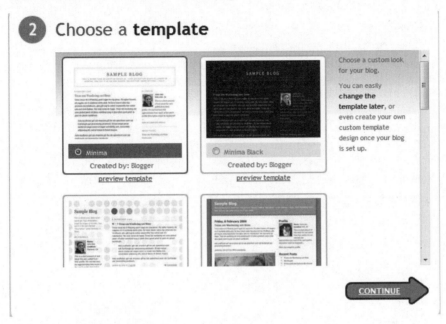

Figure 12-4: Theme selection

Once you click "Continue" from the "Themes" page, you will be taken to the confirmation page. From here, click "Continue" at the bottom of the page (the advanced features will be covered later in this chapter). Clicking continue will take you to your "Dashboard" providing an overview of your account. The "Dashboard" is the page you will be taken to when you sign in.

NotED

You may need to change your time zone settings as Blogger will not automatically set them. This can be done in the "Formatting" settings page (discussed later in this chapter).

545

Dashboard

The Dashboard is the center point for your account showing you an overview of your account (see Figure 12-5).

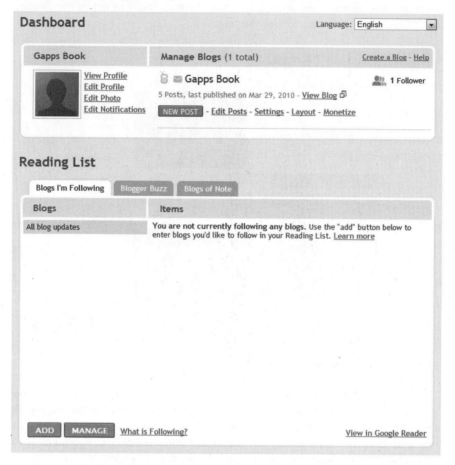

Figure 12-5: The Dashboard

The dashboard is broken up into two main sections, then broken down further into multiple sections. The top section is an overview of your account. On the left side you can see an overview of your Blogger profile and you can also edit your profile there. On the right side of the top section is a list of your blogs and a small set of functions you can perform on each blog.

ExplainED

You can return to your Dashboard at any time by clicking the Blogger logo in the top left corner.

Editing Your Profile

Your Blogger account has a publicly accessible profile allowing your readers the ability to know more about you. To edit your profile, click "Edit Profile." This will take you to a page broken into several sections with each section containing settings relating to each other. Due to the size of this section and the fact that most of the information is your own choice, we will only cover the beginning of creating a profile (see Figure 12-6).

ExplainED

Do not provide too much personal information in your profile as it may make you vulnerable to identity theft.

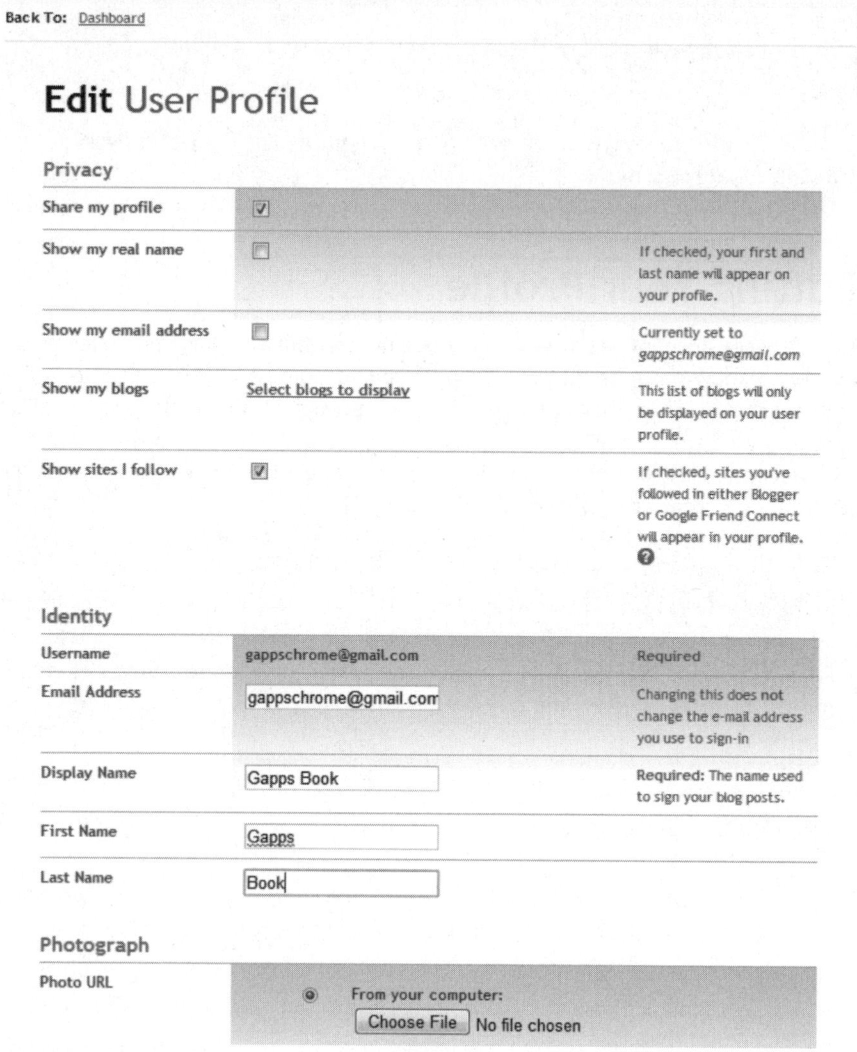

Back To: Dashboard

Edit User Profile

Privacy

Share my profile	☑	
Show my real name	☐	If checked, your first and last name will appear on your profile.
Show my email address	☐	Currently set to *gappschrome@gmail.com*
Show my blogs	Select blogs to display	This list of blogs will only be displayed on your user profile.
Show sites I follow	☑	If checked, sites you've followed in either Blogger or Google Friend Connect will appear in your profile. ❓

Identity

Username	gappschrome@gmail.com	Required
Email Address	gappschrome@gmail.com	Changing this does not change the e-mail address you use to sign-in
Display Name	Gapps Book	Required: The name used to sign your blog posts.
First Name	Gapps	
Last Name	Book	

Photograph

Photo URL	⦿ From your computer: [Choose File] No file chosen	

Figure 12-6: Your profile

Privacy

The first group of settings relates to your privacy (see Figure 12-6). The first option under privacy is the ability to allow the public to see your profile. Unchecking this option will prevent everyone from viewing your profile. You can also show either your real name or email address by clicking the appropriate check boxes. You can choose to hide what blogs you are following by unchecking the box next to "Show sites I follow."

Identity

The "Identity" section contains your personal information. Only the "Display name" is required and shown publicly unless you have changed your privacy options. You can change your email address and real name by changing the text boxes here.

Creating a New Post

To create a new post, click the "New Post" button. This will take you to the new post page (see Figure 12-7). First enter a title for your blog entry.

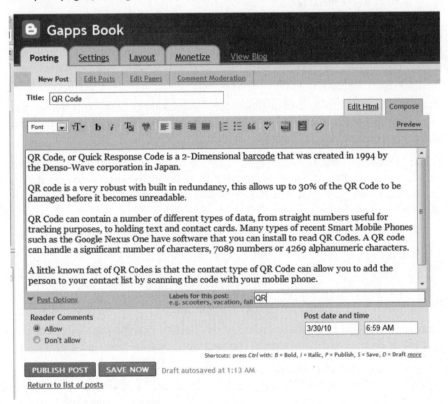

Figure 12-7: Creating a new post

Below the title box is the tool bar where you can change the style of your text (see Figure 12-8).

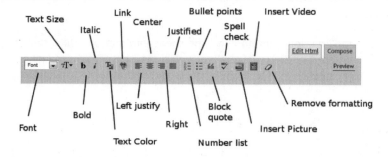

Figure 12-8: The menu bar

As you type your blog post, you may wish to change colors and styles by selecting the option you want from the menu bar. You can change the settings, and can do this as you type to affect any text you type or you can select text and select the style you wish to change.

When you have completed your blog post, assign a label to it. This allows you to quickly sort through all of your blog posts to find relevant posts and to allow visitors to see blog posts of a similar topic.

If you click the "Post Options" link, a set of extra options will be displayed allowing you to allow or deny comments on that single post. A comment is a response to your post that another person with a Google Blogger account can leave for everyone else to view.

NotED

You can change how blogger handles comments in settings.

You can also adjust the date and time of the post by changing the values of the text boxes on the right-hand side of the post options area (see Figure 12-7).

Once you have finished working on your post, you can either publish or save it as a draft by clicking the "Publish Post" or "Save now" buttons. Once you have published your post, you will be taken to a page where you can view the post (see Figure 12-9).

QR

QR Code, or Quick Response Code is a 2-Dimensional barcode that was created in 1994 by the Denso-Wave corporation in Japan.

QR code is a very robust with built in redundancy, this allows up to 30% of the QR Code to be damaged before it becomes unreadable.

QR Code can contain a number of different types of data, from straight numbers useful for tracking purposes, to holding text and contact cards. Many types of recent Smart Mobile Phones such as the Google Nexus One have software that you can install to read QR Codes. A QR code can handle a significant number of characters, 7089 numbers or 4269 alphanumeric characters.

A little known fact of QR Codes is that the contact type of QR Code can allow you to add the person to your contact list by scanning the code with your mobile phone.

POSTED BY GAPPS BOOK AT 2:17 AM
LABELS: QR

o COMMENTS:

POST A COMMENT

Comment as: Gapps Book (Google) ▼ Sign out

[Post Comment] [Preview]   Subscribe by email

Figure 12-9: A published post

Placing Images in Your Blog Posts

You can place images inside your blog posts by clicking the "Inset Image" icon (see Figure 12-8). You will be presented with a popup window (see Figure 12-10).

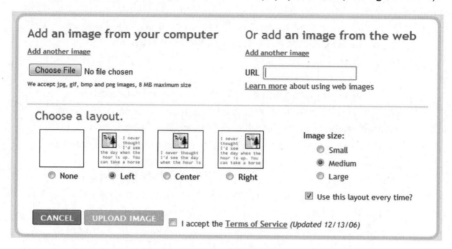

Figure 12-10: Insert image popup window

The insert image popup will allow you to upload images from your computer or add them from another existing web site. To upload an image from your local computer, click the "Choose File" button and select the file you wish to add to your blog. You can also enter the URL of the image you wish to use in the URL box. You can add extra boxes by clicking the "Add another image" link above the file selection boxes.

ExplainED

Always ensure that you have permission to repost the image. You can find images that do not have copyright protection on web sites such as openphoto.net or creativecommons.org.

When you enter a URL for a photo, you are pointing to the image that is on another web site which may cost the owner for the extra traffic that loading the image takes. You should always save a copy of the image on your computer and upload it so you do not add to someone's costs.

The second set of options on the page allows you to choose the layout of the image and the text on the page. The first option "None" will place the image where the cursor is on the page. The left or right layout will place the image to the left or right side of the page and allow you to write normally next to each image. The center layout will prevent you from writing any other text on the same lines as the image. At the bottom of the popup window are two check boxes on your first image upload. The first check box is the "Remember layout" check box. By clicking this, the layout you choose when uploading this image will automatically be set for the next time you try to upload a new image. The final check box (located on the bottom of the window) is an agreement of the "Terms of service." You must check the box to upload your image and this check box will not appear when you upload subsequent images (see Figure 12-11).

QR Code

QR Code, or Quick Response Code is a 2-Dimensional barcode that was created in 1994 by the Denso-Wave corporation in Japan.

QR code is a very robust with built in redundancy, this allows up to 30% of the QR Code to be damaged before it becomes unreadable.

QR Code can contain a number of different types of data, from straight numbers useful for tracking purposes, to holding text and contact cards. Many types of recent Smart Mobile Phones such as the Google Nexus One have software that you can install to read QR Codes. A QR code can handle a significant number of characters, 7089 numbers or 4269 alphanumeric characters.

A little known fact of QR Codes is that the contact type of QR Code can allow you to add the person to your contact list by scanning the code with your mobile phone.

Try scanning the QR Code above with your mobile phone.

Figure 12-11: A completed post with an image

Placing Videos in Your Blog Posts

You can also add videos to posts and the videos are uploaded to the Google Video website (which is not covered in this book). To add a video to a post, click the "Insert video" button located in the menu bar (see Figure 12-8). When you click the button, a window will be displayed (see Figure 12-12).

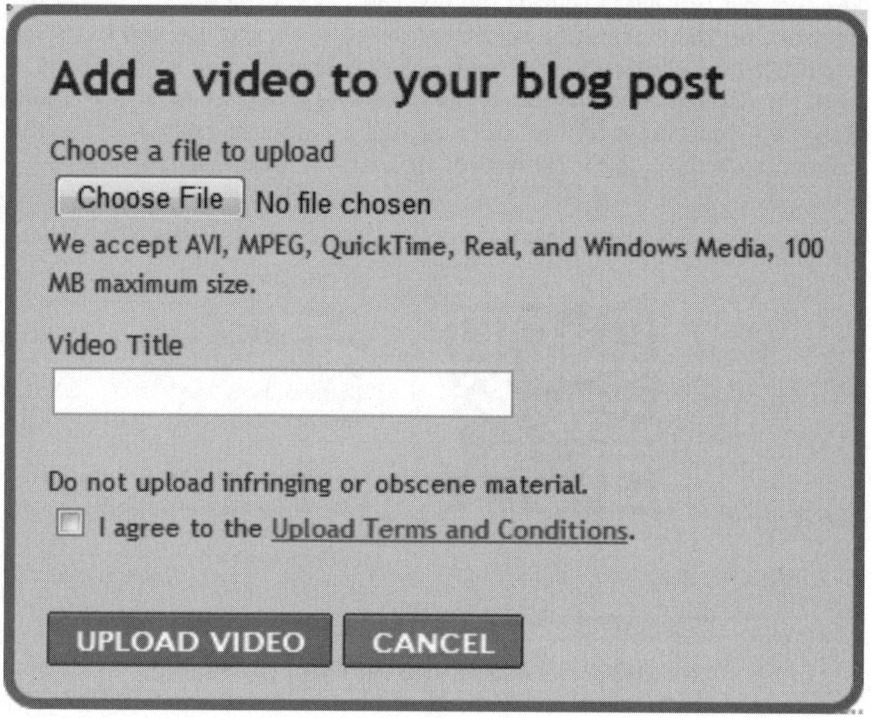

Add a video to your blog post

Choose a file to upload

| Choose File | No file chosen

We accept AVI, MPEG, QuickTime, Real, and Windows Media, 100 MB maximum size.

Video Title

Do not upload infringing or obscene material.
☐ I agree to the Upload Terms and Conditions.

UPLOAD VIDEO **CANCEL**

Figure 12-12: Insert video popup window

This window allows you to choose the file on your local computer under 100 megabytes in size. Once you have selected your video, enter a title for the video. The first time you upload a video, agree to the terms of service for Google Video. Once you read and agree, click the check box next to "I agree" and click "Upload Video."

Always ensure that you have permission to repost a video.

Inserting Links into Your Posts

If you wish to include a link to a web site in one of your posts, use the "Link" button in the menu bar. Type the text you want to use for the link, which can also be the link itself. For example, if I were to insert a link to google.com, I would first type "Google," select the text, and click the "Link" button. This will open a new window that will require me to type the link I wish for the text to point to. This will create a link in the blog post with the selected text (see Figure 12-13).

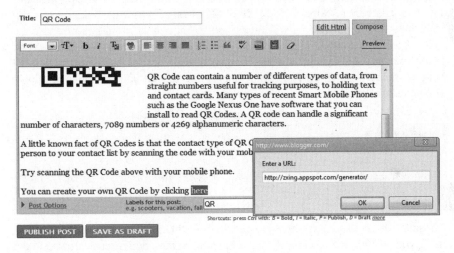

Figure 12-13: Inserting a hyperlink

Editing Existing and Draft Posts

You can access your posts to edit or edit and post your drafts by going to the "Edit posts" link from your Dashboard (see Figure 12-5). When you click the link, a list of all of your posts and draft posts will be displayed (see Figure 12-14).

Figure 12-14: Edit post list

You can search through your existing posts using the search field at top. Enter a part of the title of the post you wish to edit and click "Search." This will return a list of all posts with the words you searched for in the title.

Draft posts can be easily spotted by the word draft on the right-hand side of the window near the date of the post. You can quickly filter through different types of posts by clicking the "Drafts," "Published," or "All" links on the top right side of the page. This will allow you to show only messages of a certain type. Clicking the drafts link will display only draft messages. The final way to filter your posts is by clicking the label you want to look at on the left-hand side of the screen. When you select one of the labels, you will only be shown the posts in that label.

ExplainED

You can also edit your blog posts when viewing them by clicking the pencil icon while viewing the posts.

To edit the content of a message, click the Edit button next to the post or draft you wish to edit. This will take you to the same page as post creation (see Figure 12-7). From here you can edit the contents and date of your blog post and republish.

NotED

Never edit the details of a post later to hide your mistakes. It can be considered unprofessional and dishonest.

Adding Web Pages to Your Blog

You can create up to 10 normal web pages that you can link on your blog in addition to blog posts. You can use these pages to display information about you or something related to yourself.

To create a page, go to the "Edit posts" link from the Dashboard (see Figure 12-5). This will take you to the "Edit posts" page, and from there you can click "Edit Pages" in the top menu of the screen. This will take you to the "Page management" screen (see Figure 12-15).

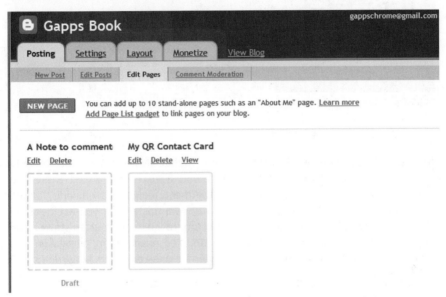

Figure 12-15: Page management

You can create new pages for your blog, edit, or delete existing pages you have created (see Figure 12-15). To create a new page for your blog, click the "New Page" button. This will take you to a "Page creation tool" (see Figure 12-16).

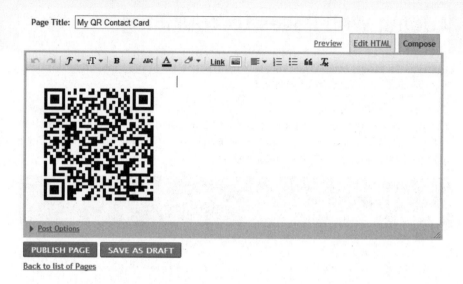

Figure 12-16: New page composer

The page creation page works in the same way that "New post" does. The only difference is some of the items in the menu have changed and there are different post options. The differences in the menu include now having "Undo" and "Redo" buttons allowing you to quickly undo a mistake. If you accidentally delete a paragraph, click the "Undo" button to correct your mistake. The "Redo" button allows you to undo an undo. For example, a paragraph you deleted and brought back with undo can again be deleted by clicking redo.

The font drop-down list now acts like the text size button, so click the button to bring down a selection of usable fonts. The alignments have also been converted to a single button. You must click this to select a justification.

Other minor changes include the inability to post videos in pages and having the ability to change the background color of text (much the same as when you use the text color).

In the "Post" options (like blog posts), you can allow or disallow comments that are disabled by default. Other "Post" options relate to advanced topics not covered in this chapter. Once you have finished editing the page, click "Publish Page."

When you publish your first page, Blogger will automatically install the "Pages" gadget on your blog (see Figure 12-17). The "Pages" gadget -presents readers with a list of the pages on your blog. Without a gadget installed, you will need to manually create links to each page.

How would you like the Pages Gadget to appear?

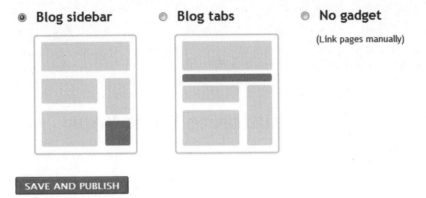

◉ **Blog sidebar**   ◉ **Blog tabs**   ◉ **No gadget**

(Link pages manually)

Figure 12-17: Page gadget install

There are two locations you can choose from: the default location is on the right side of the blog and you can also choose to have the Page Gadget displayed as a list of tabs along the top of your web site. If you choose "No Gadget," you will have to link to your pages within your blog posts.

Editing, Viewing, and Deleting Your Pages

Your pages can be edited, viewed, and deleted from the page management screen (see Figure 12-15). To edit a page, locate the page to be edited and click the "Edit" button. This takes you to the page creation tool allowing you to edit the page. If you wish to view published pages, select "View" and this will allow you to view the page on your blog.

ExplainED

You can find published pages based on their color. Blue pages are published and gray pages are drafts.

To delete pages, locate the page to be deleted and click the "Delete" link. This will request a confirmation that you wish to delete the page by clicking "Delete it."

ExplainED

You can also edit your blog posts when viewing them by clicking the pencil icon when you read your posts.

Blogging with Caution to Limit Your Liability

Whenever you post a blog online, you own whatever you post in turn making you liable. Use common sense when posting on the Internet. Keep the following tips in mind when posting to your blog for your own protection:

1. Do not post legally privileged information.

2. Do not post confidential information.

3. Do not defame an individual or company online.

4. Do not post links to illegal material in your country.

Commenting on Blogs

The comment system on a blog allows you to leave messages for anyone to read. This allows you to interact with your readers in a way that is not possible with all web sites. Like all things on the Internet, etiquette must be followed. Otherwise there can be no value in the feedback it generates.

Making Comments on Other People's Blogs

Creating a comment on a blog is a simple process. Go to the blog post you want to comment on, enter your comment in the box below the post, and click "Post comment." This will leave a comment on the blog that instantly appears unless the comment moderation is on. Comment moderation allows blog owners to examine comments before they are immediately posted. This process can be useful if people have started posting inappropriate comments (see Figure 12-9).

NotED

You may need to do a CAPTCHA word verification when you post a comment if it has been requested by the blog owner.

Some blog owners will have comment moderation. When you post on a blog that has comment moderation enabled, your message will be sent to the owner of the blog to reject or approve the comments.

Comments on Your Blog

Commenting on your own blog is much like commenting on another person's blog. However, you also have the ability to delete inappropriate comments. You can delete a comment by clicking the "Trash can" icon next to the comment you wish to delete (see Figure 12-18).

1 COMMENTS:

 Adam Darbyshire said...

You should always remember above all else. 'If it seems too good to be true, it is.'

MARCH 31, 2010 2:41 AM 🗑

Figure 12-18: Comment deletion

If you decide to remove a post, there are two ways to delete them. The first option shows visitors that there was a comment there but was removed. Visitors will see "This post has been removed by a blog administrator" where the comment was. Locate the comment to delete, click the "Trash can" icon next to the comment, and click "Delete Comment."

You can remove the comment entirely so visitors do not know it existed by clicking the icon next to the comment you wish to delete and clicking the "Remove forever" check box and then the "Delete Comment" button.

ExplainED

You can permanently remove a deleted comment by clicking on the "Trash icon" next to a deleted comment.

Moderating Comments on Your Blog

Comment moderation allows you to view any comments someone wishes to put on your blog before they are visible to all users. This can be a useful feature to activate if you have found people posting inappropriate material on your blog. When someone comments on your moderated blog, you will see a link appear on your Dashboard (see Figure 12-19) and you will receive an e-mail if you have made the appropriate settings.

Figure 12-19: Comment notification

When you click the link shown in Figure 12-19, you will be taken to a new page where you can see all of the pending comments needing moderation (see Figure 12-20). The first thing to note on the moderation page is that posts are showing only part of the text. To view the full comment, click each comment. When you click a comment, it will be expanded so you can read the full text.

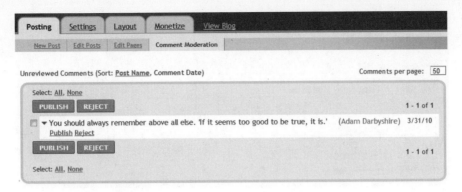

Figure 12-20: Comment moderation

Comments are sorted by the creation date and this allows you to see when the major activity was on your blog. It may be difficult to find out where your comments are going. You can display comments by the post they are attached to by clicking "Post name" at the top of the page. The comments will be displayed in groupings based on the post they are attached to. This makes it easy to see which posts belong where.

You can individually reject or publish comments by clicking the "Publish" or "Reject" links at the bottom of the comments when you click them. You can publish or reject multiple posts at the same time by selecting the check boxes next to the comments and clicking either the "Publish" or "Reject" buttons.

Viewing the Reading List

The reading list allows you to easily view blogs you are following, including the official Blogger blog and blogs that have been deemed noteworthy.

Following Other Blogs

You can follow other blogs' updates using the reading list. You can follow other blogs by going to the blog and copying the URL from the address bar. Go back to your Dashboard and in the area below "Blogs I'm following," click the "Add" button. This will open a new window (see Figure 12-21).

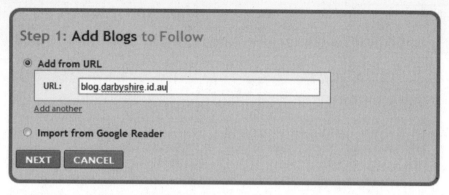

Figure 12-21: Following another blog

The window shown in Figure 12-21 allows you to add blogs in two ways, first by putting the URL for the blog in the "Add from URL" box. The second method is to use Google Reader. When you have entered the URL for the blog you wish to follow, click the "Next" button. This will take you to an options screen (see Figure 12-22).

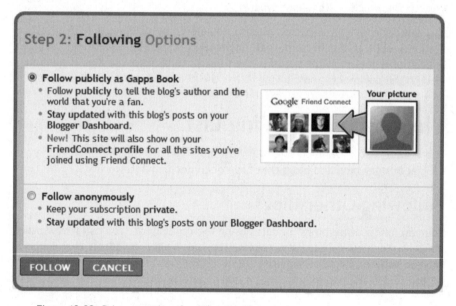

Figure 12-22: Privacy settings for following blogs

The window shown in Figure 12-22 allows you to choose how you wish to follow the blog. You can publicly follow the blogs telling the blog's author that you are a fan allowing everyone to see that you have followed this blog. It also allows you to show the blog on "Friend connect" (not covered in this book). You can privately follow blogs which will not show the blog in your "Friend connect" profile. Regardless of what you choose, the blog will be placed in your reading list. New posts on the blogs you follow will automatically be shown in the "Items" list.

NotED

Sometimes it can take up to 12 hours for items to appear in the "Items" list.

Blogger Buzz

By clicking the "Blogger buzz" tab, you will see bloggers' official blog and here you can see the latest updates from Blogger. You can use this to see what features are going to be added, tips and tricks, and what features will be removed from Blogger.

Blogs of Note

"Blogs of note" are a collection of blogs that have been deemed noteworthy by the owners of Blogger. When you go to "Blogs of note," you can see a list of blogs and the list shows the name of the blog and the URL so you can easily add it to your reading list. To visit one of the blogs in "Blogs of note," click the name of the blog.

Setting Your Preferences

The blog settings allow you to modify how your blog behaves, and the settings are broken up into various categories based on the settings control. The following settings apply to an individual blog, and you can have more than one blog per blogger account (discussed later). It is worth noting that some setting's categories are large and will require you to scroll down. We have included a picture of the basic settings requiring you to scroll down. Most of the options in the menu must be changed by clicking the drop-down box next to the option you wish to change and choosing a new option. To save the settings you change, click the "Save Changes" button at the bottom of each page you change. Some of the settings tabs are not discussed as they contain advanced topics outside the scope of this book.

Basic Settings

The basic settings control the behavior of the blog, from the name and details to privacy settings and adult content (see Figure 12-23).

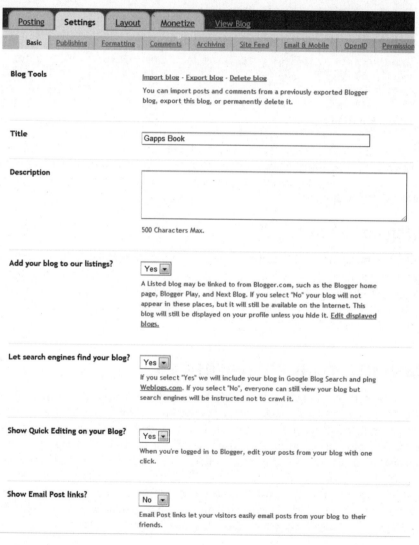

Figure 12-23: Basic settings

The first setting's "import blog" and "export blog" allow you to transplant your blog to or from another blogging service. To export your blog, click the "Export blog" link and click the "Download blog" button. This will download a full copy of your blog to your local computer in XML (extensible markup language designed to transmit data in easy-to-manipulate form). You can also import an exported copy of your blog by clicking the "Import blog" link from the basic settings page. This will take you to a page where you can select an XML file and answer the CAPTCHA. Once this is done, you can either select to publish the imported posts or leave them as draft posts. On the first line is the "Delete blog" link. If you wish to delete your blog, click the link and you will be taken to a confirmation page where you will need to click "Delete this blog."

The next two options allow you to change the title and description of your blog. These change what people can see about your blog. The first setting "Add your blog to our listings?" will allow your blog to be found randomly by users. This option is enabled by default.

The next option gives you the ability to allow search engines such as Google from finding your blog. This is enabled by default. If you disable this option and the listings option above, you can hide your blog from being found by people unless you invite them.

NotED

A user can still guess the URL of your blog and visit.

The option "Show quick editing" on your blog places the pencil icon on your blog posts so that you can edit them (see the "Editing your posts" section). If you disable this option, the pencil icon, used to edit your blog posts while viewing them, will disappear.

The "E-mail posts" option allows readers of your blog to e-mail the posts to them by clicking the button. This option is disabled by default. The next option labeled "Adult Content" allows you to warn visitors if you have any material on your blog that is deemed unsuitable for children.

Global Settings

The "Global Settings" allow you to change settings for all blogs in your blogger account (see Figure 12-24). "Global Settings" are located at the bottom of "Basic settings," regardless of which of your blogs you are looking at.

Global Settings   (Applies to all of your blogs.)

Select post editor

○ Updated editor - *Check out the latest features!*
◉ Old editor
○ Hide compose mode - *Select only if you typically do HTML editing instead of WYSIWYG text editing.*

Enable transliteration?

Disable ▾ in Hindi - हिन्दी ▾   Learn more

Adds a button to the toolbar for converting words from English to the selected language. (You may later change the language in the Post Editor). Your transliteration corrections will be saved to help Google improve this tool. See Privacy Policy for details.

SAVE SETTINGS

Figure 12-24: Global Settings

The first setting in Global Settings is for changing the "Post editor," By default, use the "Old editor." You can choose the "Updated editor" which acts like the "Pages editor." You can view the features added to the updated editor by clicking on the "Latest features" link. You can also select "Hide compose mode" disabling the simple editors so you can enter your text directly. However, this mode requires knowing how to create web pages in the HTML programming language. This method is not advised for beginners.

NotED

The features of the updated editor can frequently change, so frequently check the "Latest features" link to see what's new.

The final setting of "Global Settings" allows you to enable a button in the "Post editor" that will allow you to change the language in your post automatically. This option may be useful if you intend to write to an audience in a language you are not completely familiar with.

Changing the Location of Your Blog

The publishing settings allow you to change the location of your blog. The first option allows you to switch to custom domain (not covered in this book). The second option allows you to change your blog spot address. Note that if you change the address of your blog, you will need to fill in the CAPTCHA.

Changing the Formatting Settings

The formatting settings will adjust how your blog is viewed by other people and how you interact with your blog while creating new posts.

Show at most: This allows you to select how many posts appear on your blog's front page. You can set this to a fixed number of posts by changing the value in the box. You can also get this to show a number of days by changing the "Posts" drop-down list to "Days." Note that a limit of 500 posts can be shown in your blog's front page.

Date header format: This allows you to select how the date is displayed to your users. If you click the drop-down list next to the question, a list of other styles you can use for the date on your posts will be displayed.

Archive index date format: With this you can select how your archived posts are listed on the side bar. This option acts like "Date header format" and only changes what text is displayed there and does not modify how archiving is done.

Timestamp format: This setting lets you choose how you want the time to be displayed on your posts and comments. You can use this option to switch between 12- and 24-hour time formats.

Time zone: This setting lets you set the blog's time to your local time. You should ensure this is set correctly as it is not set to your Google account's time zone by default.

Language: With this setting, you can change the language of the interface you are presented with, and your readers will not be affected.

Convert line breaks: This changes how the new post window interprets blank lines. If you change this setting, each time you press enter in a blog post it will insert a blank line in your posts by HTML. It is recommended that you do not change this setting.

Show title field: This option (enabled by default) shows a field where you can enter a title with your blog posts. If you disable this option, you will not be able to give your blog posts titles.

Show link fields: This option (disabled by default) allows you to submit a URL following each post.

Enable float alignment: This allows users to input manual code to align images and text, and it is recommended that you do not touch this setting.

Post template: The text you enter here will automatically be inserted into your blog post editor when you create a new post.

Changing Your Blog's Comment Settings

Comments: The first option allows you to hide all existing comments and prevent anyone from creating new comments (select "Hide"). You can show all of the existing comments again by setting your comments to "Show."

Who can comment: This option allows you to specify who can leave comments on your blog. You have the ability to allow anyone to leave comments on your blog regardless of whether they have an account or not. The next option allows you to specify that users must have an OpenID to post comments. An OpenID is a system where different types of popular blogs can share their user base with each other. The next option requires anyone wishing to comment on your blog to have a Google account. The final option for controlling the comments requires that you provide a person with permission to write comments on your blog. Permissions are covered later in this section.

Comment form placement: This option allows you to specify how people can make comments. By default, a response window is shown below the comments on a post. You can change this so that anyone who wishes to respond will be presented with a pop up window with the reply box in it by selecting "Pop-up window." They may also be taken to another page to respond by selecting "Full page."

Comments default for posts: With this option, you can choose whether comments are allowed on your blog by default by changing the "Comments default for posts." If you change this setting, you will need to turn on comments manually for posts if you want viewers to comment.

Backlinks: Backlinks allow you to track links other blogger users are posting to your posts. If you turn links back on, you will see a new link appear next to each of your blog posts when viewing your blog named "Links to this post." If you click this link, you will be taken to the bottom of your post allowing you to see who on Blogger has linked to your post.

Backlinks default for posts: The option "Backlinks default for posts" works in the same way "Comments default for posts" if you set this to not require backlinks by default. You will need to turn on back links in every post.

Comments timestamp format: This allows you to adjust how the time appears on comments.

Comment form message: This allows you to leave a message above the comment window. This can be used to ask the commenter to include information, avoid topics, etc.

Comment moderation: The "Comment moderation" option allows you to specify if all comments, some comments, or no comments on your blog have to be moderated by you.

ExplainED

This feature can help you stop inappropriate comments. Turn this feature on if you are having issues with some of your commenters.

By default, this is turned off. To enable Comment moderation for all comments, select the "Always" button. You can enable Comment moderation for your posts that have been posted for a certain amount of time. You could require approval of all comments older than 30 days. The e-mail field can be used to send notifications to your email address when there are new comments to be examined.

ExplainED

If you have a popular blog, this could generate a lot of e-mails.

Show word verification for comments: Enabled by default, this allows you to force commenters to answer a CAPTCHA question each time they make a post. If you disable this, anyone with an account can post without answering the CAPTCHA question.

ExplainED

If you disable the CAPTCHA, you may find that your blog will get spammed. Turn this feature off if you have limited the access to your blog with permissions.

Show profile images on comments: This option will display posters' profile images with their comments. This is activated by default.

Comment notification email: This allows you to specify which e-mail addresses are sent messages when someone posts a message on your blog. You can enter multiple e-mail addresses by separating them with semicolons (mail@example.com; mail@example2.com).

Automatically Archiving Your Older Posts

Archiving allows you to specify when your older posts are removed from your front page and placed in the archives section of the site. You can choose to archive your older blog posts monthly, weekly, or daily by selecting the option from the drop-down list. You can also disable archiving from the list.

Granting Permissions to Your Blog

The final settings discussed here allow you to assign permissions to users and restrict who can access your web site. To invite someone to be an author, click the "Add authors" button. This will open a box where you can enter the e-mail addresses of the people you wish to add. You can also click "Choose from contacts," which will bring up a window from which you can select e-mail addresses. Locate the contacts you wish to use, click them, and click the "Done" button.

When you are satisfied with the people you wish to add, click "Invite" and Blogger will send out instruction e-mails for those you have invited. You can remove authors at any time by clicking the "Remove" link next to the author you want removed.

Always be sure you can trust the person you are assigning author permission to. When a user is granted author permission, they have full control over all content on the blog.

As well as inviting people to be authors, you can also invite people to read your blog. After doing this, the only people allowed to read your blog will be on this list. To enable this feature, click "Only people I choose" opening an e-mail box similar to the one for inviting authors. You can have up to 100 people with permission to read your blog. The final option "Only blog authors" restricts access to your blog even further by requiring that anyone who can read your blog must be an author of your blog.

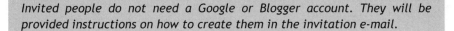

Invited people do not need a Google or Blogger account. They will be provided instructions on how to create them in the invitation e-mail.

Changing the Layout of Your Blog

The layout and feel of your blog can be changed in the "Layout" tab. You can change the position of gadgets in your blog, and the color scheme is independent of the theme. You can also change the theme you are using and advanced users can change the code of the web site.

Customizing Page Elements

There are multiple elements of your blog and each can be customized. The "Page Elements" screen allows you to edit these elements (see Figure 12-25).

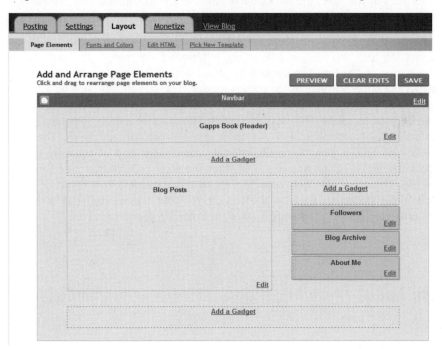

Figure 12-25: Elements of your blog

Note that all of the "Edit" links are shown in the blog. The edit links allow you to edit various parts of your blog. Some of these edit links allow you to edit the settings available in the "Settings" area of your blog previously discussed. In this window, you can move gadgets to different locations. You can also add, edit, and remove gadgets.

To move a gadget, click it and drag it. When you start dragging a gadget around the screen, you will see different colored patches appearing. These correlate to where you can move the gadget. To add a gadget, click the "Add a Gadget" link opening a gadget selector. This works in the same way as the gadget selector on Google Sites. You can also edit a Gadgets setting by clicking the "Edit" link next to the gadget you wish to edit. When you are happy with your gadget placement, preview the changes by clicking the "Preview" button opening a popup window. Save your changes by clicking the "Save" button or cancel your changes by clicking the "Clear Edits" button.

Customizing Fonts and Colors

You can edit the colors of the individual items in your blog, and you can change the colors of the text, the background, links, etc. You can also edit the fonts of your text. To edit the colors, go to "Fonts and Colors" under "Layout." From there, a page will be displayed (see Figure 12-26).

Select the item you wish to edit on the left side of the screen. In the middle of the screen at the top, the options for that item will be displayed. Figure 12-32 shows the options available for editing a color. The screen is broken up into four sections. The first section "Colors from your blog" gives a list of colors already in use by your template. The second section "Colors that match your blog" show colors designers think match the color scheme you already have. The third section of your screen "More Colors" give you a large grid of colors to choose from. The final section allows you to enter the color code of the color you want to use. There are also two links "Revert to template default," reverting all of your template colors back to the default for your theme. You can also click "Shuffle blog colors" randomizing all of the colors on your blog.

Figure 12-26: Customizing your blog

ExplainED

Any changes you make can be automatically previewed below the settings.

Choosing a New Template for Your Blog

Going to "Pick a new template" in the "Layout" section takes you to a page similar to the one in Figure 12-4. You can choose what template you wish to use for your blog. Select the theme you want and click "Save Template."

NotED

If you change your template, your "Page elements" layout will remain the same.

Making Money from Your Blog

If your blog is popular, you may wish to attempt to generate income from your traffic. Discussed in Chapter 9, Google AdSense can generate a small income stream from your blog. To begin using AdSense on Blogger, go to your Dashboard and click "Monetize" on the blog for which you wish to set up AdSense. When you click "Monetize," you will be taken to the AdSense setup page (see Figure 12-28).

| Posting | Settings | Layout | Monetize | View Blog |

AdSense Overview | AdSense For Feeds | Amazon Associates

Make Money with AdSense

Earn money by configuring Google AdSense for your blog.

○ [AD] **Display ads in my sidebar and posts**
Recommended. Ads will be displayed in your sidebar and below each post.

○ [AD] **Display ads in my sidebar**
Ads will be displayed in your sidebar.

○ [AD] **Display ads below my posts**
Ads will be displayed below each post.

○ [AD] **Don't add new ads. Just enable AdSense reporting.**
If you already manually enabled ads on your blog, choose this option to start seeing AdSense reports on the Monetize tab.

NEXT

Figure 12-27: AdSense set up

From here you are able to choose where you wish to place ads in your blog. The recommended setting is placement in the side bar of your screen and between blog posts. To continue, click "Next." On the next screen you can choose to create a new AdSense account or login to an existing one. To create a new AdSense account, click "Next." Otherwise, you will need to sign in to your existing account. After clicking "Next," you will be taken to an AdSense site where you need to follow the provided instructions.

ExplainED

Ensure that you read and understand all terms and conditions.

Controlling your ads

You can control how AdSense ads are displayed on your blog by going to the AdSense for feeds" tab under "Monetize," (see Figure 12-28).

Start by choosing ads to be presented to your users or readers. The defaults are both text and image ads. You can change your feeds to show only image or text ads.

You can adjust the frequency of the ads, and the default setting is an ad below every blog post. From the drop-down menu, select whether you want the ads to appear below every item or up to every fourth item. You can also choose the minimum post length for an ad to be displayed, and you can set this to have an ad for every post regardless of its length. You can also require that posts be up to 500 words in length before ads start appearing.

You can select where the ads appear with respect to each post. By default, ads appear below your posts; however you can set them to appear above. Once you have changed the settings, click "Next."

AdSense for Feeds: Setup

Please configure how you would like ads to begin displaying on your feed.

Ad type
- ● Text/image ads
- ○ Text ads only
- ○ Image ads only

Frequency   [Each feed item   ▼]

Post length   [Posts of any length   ▼]

Position
- ● At the bottom of the feed item
- ○ At the top of the feed item

[NEXT]

Figure 12-28: AdSense feeds

ExplainED

Generally, you should aim to please your readers. Do not overload them with ads. If you overload your readers with ads, they may not come back potentially losing your extra revenue source.

Amazon Associates

Much like Google AdSense, Amazon Associates allows you to earn money from your blog posts. This method is a sales-based rewards program allowing you to insert text and image ads directly into your blog posts. The difference between Google AdSense and Amazon Associates is that to earn money through the

Amazon rewards program, your readers have to click your links and purchase an item. For more information on the Amazon Associates program, visit (affiliateprogram.amazon.com/gp/associates/blogger).

Blogging with E-mail

You can set Blogger to post updates when you e-mail. Click the mail envelope icon next to the name of the blog in which you wish to enable e-mail posting (see Figure 12-29).

Figure 12-29: E-mail Blogging set up

In this window all, enter a secret word to be attached to an e-mail address at Blogger.com. Any email that is sent to that address will be automatically posted from your account.

ExplainED

Do not hand out this e-mail address. People could pose as you on your blog.

Blogging with Your Mobile Phone

You can also create new blog posts with your mobile phone. Click the mobile phone icon next to the blog in which you wish to enable SMS message posting (see Figure 12-30).

Figure 12-30: Mobile Blogging set up

SMS the code presented in the window to the phone number that you have been given. You may need to refer to your mobile phone's instruction manual.

Once you have verified your code, any SMS message you send to the Blogger number will automatically be posted on your blog.

Fees from your mobile carrier may apply. Please check with your provider.

Creating Multiple Blogs

If you wish to create another blog, click the "Create a Blog" link at the top of your Dashboard taking you to a page (see Figure 12-3). Follow the instructions provided in the section on "Creating a blog." Once you have created your new blog, you will have two independent blogs that you can control from your Dashboard. Changing the settings of a blog will not affect other blogs unless you change one of the global settings. A Blogger account with two blogs on it is shown in Figure 12-31.

Figure 12-31: Multiple blogs

Using Your Google Account with OpenID

Open ID is an agreed standard between companies allowing you to login to various web sites using one set of credentials. For example, you can use your Google account to post comments on a Live Journal account, post a message on Yahoo forums, and any number of other activities. To read more information about how OpenID works and see a current list of providers who use OpenID, visit openid.net.

Marketing Your Blog

There are a large number of blogs on the Internet (over 100 million by some estimates). Each blog is trying to attract readers, which can make blogging a very cut-throat environment. There are many people who claim to know the secrets to having a successful blog, however creating a successful blog comes down to the following common-sense tips:

- Have interesting and intelligent posts.

- Ensure that your site is easy for your readers to follow.

- Build a reputation for yourself online by commenting on other related blogs and web sites.

- Do not alienate your commenters. Be sure to respond to people who leave comments on your blog.

- Include a link to your blog in your e-mail signature.

- Make new posts on your blog regularly.

- Know your intended audience and write for them.

- If you are posting about a select area, find the top bloggers in your area and think of ways you can be more like them.

Most of all, do not pay for someone to advertise your blog. Much like business, word of mouth is the best form of advertising. This method may be slower, but if you treat your readers with courtesy and respect, they will tell others about your blog.

Summary

In this chapter we have discussed Google Blogger in great detail. We started off with creating a Blogger account and a blog. We then covered how to create blog posts including how to use a rich content editor, and inserting images and video. Next we explored how to edit a blog entry and manage pages in a blog. We then covered comments in depth including how to manage and moderate comments on your own blog. We looked into following other blogs and blog settings. We moved on to controlling the layout of your blog and also looked at how to integrate ads into your blog. We covered blogging by e-mail and SMS and creating more blogs on your account. Finally, we covered OpenID and how to market blogs.

Chapter 13

Integrating Google Apps

In previous chapters of this book we discussed extensively and learned about some of the available Google Apps. The Google Apps list is continually being added to by Google, but we have discussed the main apps in this book, particularly Google Docs. We have concentrated in each previous chapter on one particular app, and briefly discussing how one particular Google App may be used with another. In this chapter, we will concentrate on the integration of the apps. Google Apps have a high degree of integration due to their design, and in some cases different apps are integrated or can be directly integrated with other apps. In this chapter, we will discuss which of the Google Apps can be integrated and show examples of the each working together where possible. We will also briefly discuss how some of the Google Apps can be integrated into other software, for example, using maps in standard web pages and opening documents via Google Document from browsers other than Chrome.

While there is generally a high degree of integration among many of the Google Apps, there are two focal points of integration: Google Sites and iGoogle (see Figure 13-1). We have discussed Google Sites in Chapter 9, but we will cover sites in the following section, focusing on integration aspects. iGoogle is a personalized and customizable home page associated with your Google account. You can add any number of gadgets to your iGoogle page and many of these will allow you to interface with some of the Google Apps we have discussed in this book.

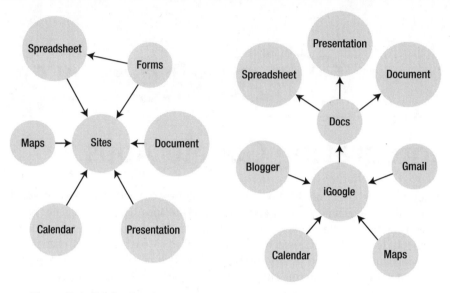

Figure 13-1: Focal points for integration

Additionally, some Google Apps will also utilize others within their operation including the ability to attach Google Documents to an event in Google Calendar, or putting Gmail messages in calendar as well. We will look at the possibilities of cross Integration Google Apps.

Using Sites to Integrate Google Apps

Google Sites is a major focal point for the integration of many Google Apps. We discussed many of these in Chapter 9, but we should now concentrate on the integration aspects. Different people will find different aspects of sites" integration useful, but from a web site management perspective, one of the most useful integration features is the ability to integrate Google Documents directly into a web page in Google Sites.

Google Document

When you are positioned on any page in the site you are editing, you can choose to insert a Google Document. When you select "Document" from the "Insert" menu on the menu bar, you will be given a list of Google Documents to choose from. Choose one of these from the available list and click the "Select" button. You can then apply a small amount of formatting before the document is embedded within the web page. This is controlled by a dialog (see Figure 13-2).

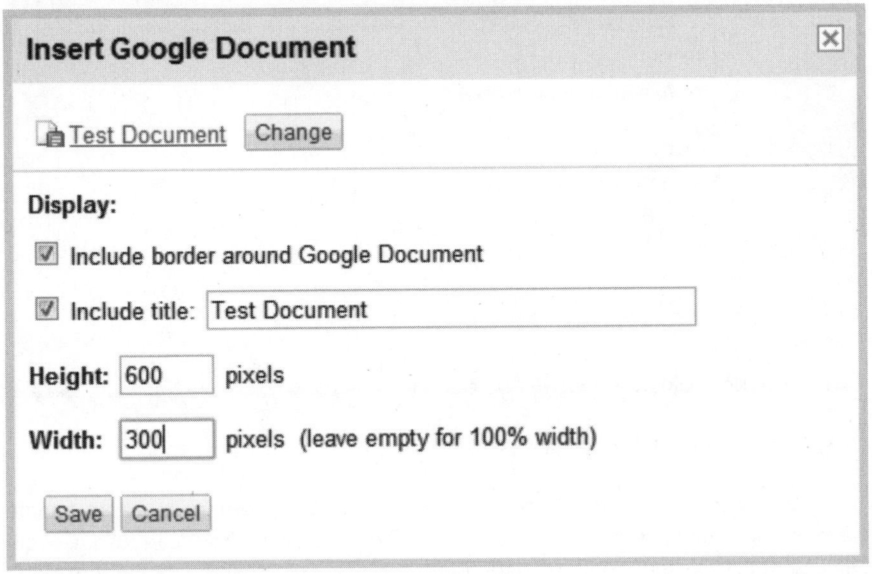

Figure 13-2: Insert Google Document dialog

You can enter the height of the embedded document and the length, whether you're including a border around the document and optionally whether to include the title of the document. Using the border and title formatting options are a matter of personal preference, but by not using them and defaulting the width of the embedded document to the width of the sites' web page, you can make it appear that the information in the sites' web page has been directly entered into the page. This will not be the result of an embedded document (see Figure 13-3).

The example in Figure 13-3 uses the example site from Chapter 9 and embeds an example Google Document from Chapter 4. By removing the border, title, and setting the width to the page width default, it appears that the information in the sites' web page has been entered and directly formatted.

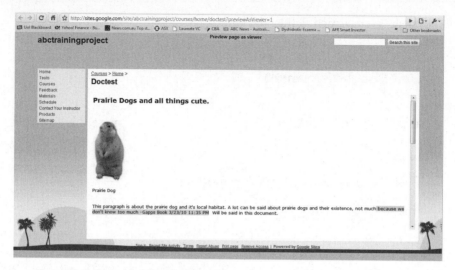

Figure 13-3: Embedded Google Document

Using this technique, you can maintain a sites' web site where multiple people have responsibility for various parts of the web site. You can use Google Documents as a document management tool by creating the documents and sharing various documents (as previously described) with people responsible for their content. In this way, you can embed documents within Sites web pages without sharing access to the web site. This allows you to maintain tighter control of the web site formatting while people maintaining the document have access to the content. Any change made to a shared document embedded in a Sites page will be shown within the web page when the page is reloaded. This allows document collaborators to control the content of the pages. This is an excellent way to collaborate and maintain control at the same time.

As a final important point, after you embed the document into a web page for viewing, it needs to be published as a web page through the Google Docs interface or through using the "Share" button while editing the document itself in Google Document. Check the option to automatically republish when the document is modified. Once this is done, the embedded document will be readily visible from the web page.

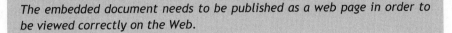

NotED

The embedded document needs to be published as a web page in order to be viewed correctly on the Web.

Google Spreadsheets

Similar to using embedded Google Documents within a Google Sites web page, you can also use an embedded Google Spreadsheet. When you are positioned on any page in the site you are editing, you can choose to insert a Google Spreadsheet by selecting "Spreadsheet" from the "Insert" menu on the menu bar. You will be given a list of Google Spreadsheets to choose from. Choose one of these from the available list and click the "Select" button. Formatting is similar to that of a Google Document with one exception (see Figure 13-4). When embedding a spreadsheet, you can choose from the "View as" drop-down list; either the *"Spreadsheet"* option or the "List" option. These two options will determine what you can do with the embedded spreadsheet and the appearance.

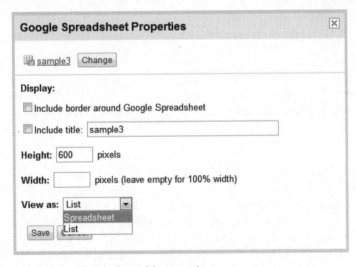

Figure 13-4: Insert Google Spreadsheet settings

If you choose the "Spreadsheet" option from the "View as" drop-down box (see Figure 13-4), you can embed a spreadsheet the same as you would a document (see Figure 13-5). The benefits of embedding a spreadsheet are similar to a document. If a web page in the Google Site is created from the information in a spreadsheet, you can embed the spreadsheet in the site and share the spreadsheet document with a collaborator who is to maintain the pertinent data. Any changes made to the spreadsheet will be reflected in the web page when it is loaded or reloaded. The responsibility for maintenance of the data in the sheet is kept separate from the responsibility of the site maintenance and appearance.

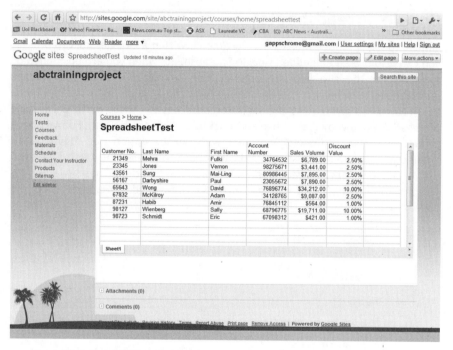

Figure 13-5: Embedded spreadsheet

If the embedded spreadsheet has multiple tabs, these can be selected below the spreadsheet similar to a normal spreadsheet viewing. After embedding a spreadsheet into a web page for viewing, it needs to be published as a web page through the Google Docs interface or through using the "Share" button while editing the spreadsheet itself in Google Spreadsheet. Check the option to automatically republish when the spreadsheet is modified. Once this is done, the embedded spreadsheet will be readily visible from the web page.

NotED

Protecting a sheet in a spreadsheet will not stop it from being viewed when the spreadsheet is viewable to everyone in a web page.

If your spreadsheet has multiple sheets and you want people to only view a particular one, use the publishing options when publishing the spreadsheet as a web page. From the "Sheets to publish" drop-down list when publishing the document as a web page, choose either "All sheets" or the sheet you want to publish. If you publish only one sheet, only that sheet will be displayed to users through the embedded spreadsheet.

If you choose the "List" option (see Figure 13-4), the spreadsheet will be embedded as an editable list in the web page (see Figure 13-6). Using this option, the contents of the spreadsheet can be edited by anyone who has access to the web page.

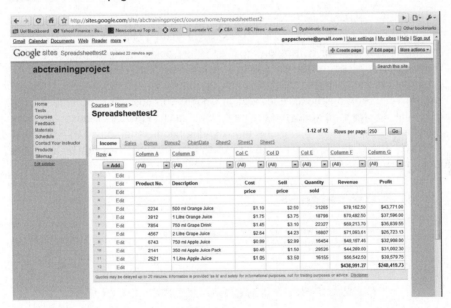

Figure 13-6: Embedded spreadsheet as a list

Clicking on the "Edit" option in the first column of any row will place that row in "Edit" mode and the web page viewer can replace the values as desired. Clicking the "Add" button in the upper left of the spreadsheet will allow the viewer to add a new row. While this option may be useful in a particular set of circumstances, it is not possible to control if the spreadsheet was open to the entire web community. Anyone loading the web page would be capable of changing any value in the list. Changes made to an embedded spreadsheet in "List view" will also be reflected in the underlying spreadsheet. Please use this option with caution.

> **Caution:** Unless specific circumstances warrant it, do not embed a spreadsheet in "List view" for anyone to view or edit, as you cannot control the editing process.

Figure 13-7: Editing a row of an embedded list

If you are embedding a spreadsheet using "List View," publishing the spreadsheet as a web page (as in "Spreadsheet View") will not be adequate for making it available for editing on the Web. The Google Site web page will need more security access to the document to enable editing. To enable this page to properly function, choose "Get the link to share" when clicking the, "Share" button while editing the spreadsheet in Google Spreadsheet. You will see the "Get link to share" dialog (see Figure 13-8). Check both check boxes allowing anyone to view or edit. If the check box giving people the ability to edit is not selected, the "Edit" links for each row of the spreadsheet will not be available (see Figure 13-6).

Figure 13-8: Get the link to share dialog

Once you the set these options, the web page with the embedded spreadsheet will correctly display and the elements of the spreadsheet will be editable. Using this option, if you have multiple sheets in the spreadsheet, you cannot stop anyone from viewing all sheets in the embedded spreadsheet. However, you can set sheet protection providing only you the ability to edit the spreadsheet. In this case, anyone on the web page changing to a protected sheet will be able to view the spreadsheet, but the "Edit" buttons will not be displayed allowing for the protected sheets to not be edited.

NotED

Using sheet protection for embedded spreadsheets in "List view" will disable those sheets from being editable.

Google Forms

As discussed in Chapter 7, a Google Form is associated with a spreadsheet and is used to collect information from users over the Web, with results automatically collated in an associated spreadsheet. When you create a Google Form, you can cut and paste the provided URL of the form and send it via email, blog or other such methods as posting in a web page to select people. In some cases, you may want to open the form to the global community, especially if you are conducting a web survey and want as many people as possible to respond. In Google Sites, you can embed your form within a Sites web page allowing it to be accessed by the global community on the Web.

To embed an existing form within a Sites page while you are positioned on any page in the site you are editing, choose to insert a Google Form by selecting "Spreadsheet form" from the "Insert" menu on the menu bar. You will be given a list of Google Spreadsheet Forms from which to choose. Choose one from the available list and click the "Select" button. Formatting is the same as that of a Google Document (see Figure 13-2). By choosing not to include a title or border around the embedded form, you can give your web page the appearance of a custom-designed page custom, not that of an embedded form. Using one of the forms created in Chapter 7, the embedded form in a Sites web page will appear (see Figure 13-9).

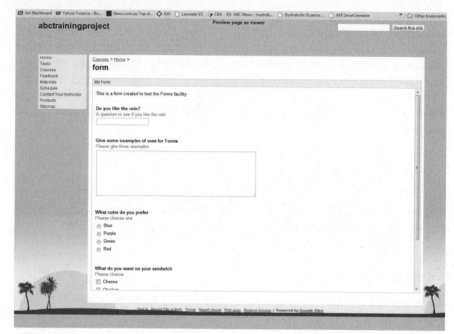

Figure 13-9: Embedded Google Form

As a Google Form is designed to be used as a web page to collect information from users, it does not need to be specifically published and will appear correctly in a web page as soon as it is embedded. However, the associated spreadsheet is not public, and if you wish to also include that on the sites to share the collected information with participants, as is often done, you will need to share the spreadsheet as outlined in the previous section.

Google Presentations

In Chapter 9, we discussed in detail how to embed a presentation within a Google Sites web page. The advantages are similar to those for documents and spreadsheets in so much as the management of the content can be delegated through the sharing of the document while the Sites management can be kept separate. When a presentation is embedded (if the original presentation is modified), the change can be viewed within the embedded presentation as soon as the page is reloaded or loaded again after modification. This can be a useful feature, particularly for those creating a series of academic presentations that may be updated from time to time. This gives the ability to upgrade the content without affecting the presentation in the web site.

As with document and spreadsheet embedding, in order for the pages to display the embedded presentation you will need to publish it by selecting the "Publish / embed" option from the "Share" drop-down button while editing. You can also do this from the Google Docs interface. The "Publish this presentation" dialog is shown below (see Figure 13-10).

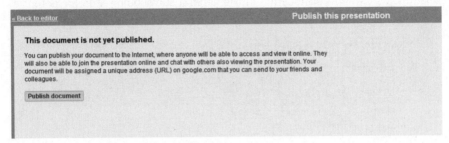

Figure 13-10: Publishing a presentation

To publish the document, click the "Publish document" button (see Figure 13-10). A further dialog will be displayed (see Figure 13-11) that will give you further display options. You can choose the size of the player and the time to transition to the next slide once the slide show is initiated. However, these can be ignored as the options can be set in Google Sites when first embedding the presentation. HTML code will be displayed (see Figure 13-11) that you can cut and paste if you are designing a web site using other software instead of Google Sites. This will allow you to embed the presentation in a non-Sites web page. However, if you are using Google Sites, you do not need this code.

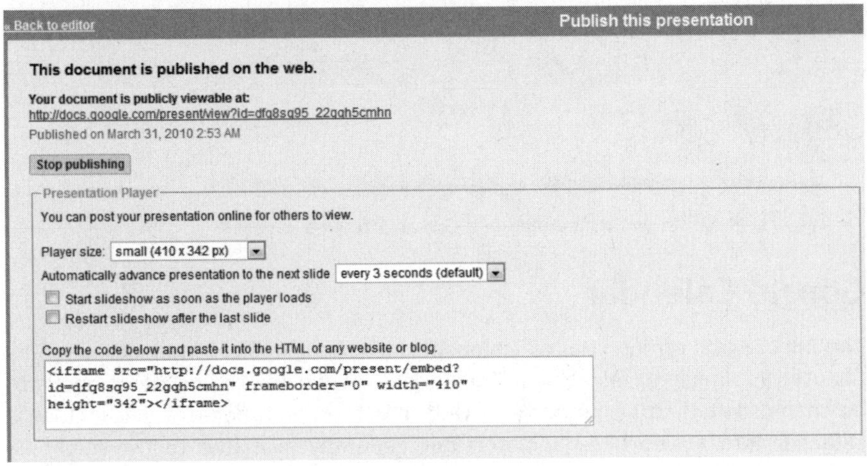

Figure 13-11: Further presentation publishing options

Google Maps

Inserting a map was covered in detail in Chapter 9. The web page will automatically have access to the maps as these are not created by a specific user, but are owned and made available by Google. Many businesses will use a small map showing their location in the general surrounding area for potential customers (see Figure 13-12).

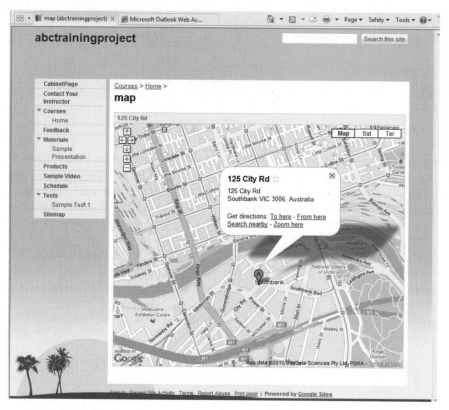

Figure 13-12: An embedded map in a Google Site web page

Google Calendar

The mechanics of inserting a calendar into Google Sites was discussed in Chapter 9, similar to inserting a Google Map. However, the calendar needs to be shared if it is to be properly viewed in a Sites web page. If you include a calendar into a web page and it is not generally available to the public, a calendar will show in the page when viewed over the Web. However, the events belonging to the specific calendar you embed will not be shown. To make the events available within the embedded calendar, share this calendar. Sharing calendars was discussed in Chapter 8. When you click the drop-down menu associated with the calendar you wish to share, choose the "Share this calendar" option and you will see a dialog box (see Figure 13-13).

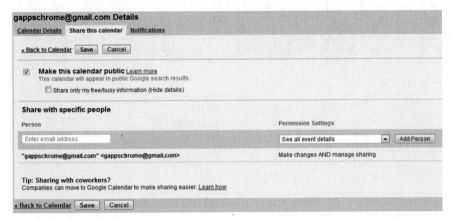

Figure 13-13: Sharing calendar dialog

To share the calendar, check the "Make calendar public" dialog box and click the "Save" button either at the top or bottom of the dialog. This will make the calendar events public and the embedded calendar in the Sites web page will correctly display these events.

Use caution before embedding a personal calendar into a web site viewable by the global web community; however, for a business, sharing a calendar can be a good business decision. For instance, a training company, advertising a calendar of training events, or a local club or theater company publishing their meeting or performance dates, could be beneficial.

When you view a calendar through a Google Sites page, the calendar will be displayed (see Figure 13-14). You will have limited interaction with the calendar when viewing it this way. You can scroll through the calendar dates (months and years) and you can change the view from month to week or to "Agenda view." You can also print the calendar. Additionally, you can click an appointment within the calendar to see it expanded (see Figure 13-14). You cannot modify or add appointments to the calendar. Once a calendar is made public, you cannot control who has access. Not being able to modify anything can be a sensible precaution.

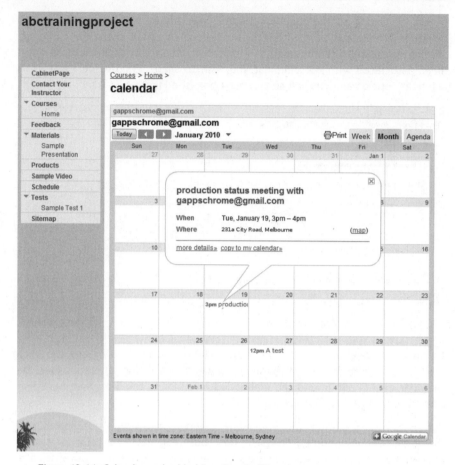

Figure 13-14: Calendar embedded in a Google Sites page

Using iGoogle to Integrate Google Apps

Another general focal point for integrating Google Apps is iGoogle. iGoogle is a highly customizable home page offered within your Google account. You can choose your iGoogle page as your home page from within any browser. First ensure you are logged into your Google account, and from your Google home page, select the "iGoogle" link shown in the upper right corner of the page.

When you select the "iGoogle" link, your iGoogle home page will become your default home page unless you revert back to the previous page. Select the "Classic home" link that will appear in place of the iGoogle link when you choose iGoogle. Your iGoogle home page will come with a default configuration when first used (see Figure 13-15). The iGoogle home page is populated with gadgets, and you can add as many gadgets as you like to the page.

Figure 13-15: iGoogle default home page

The page is highly customizable and gadgets can be deleted or moved around to suit your purposes. To move the date and time gadget (see Figure 13-15) from the lower center of the page to the upper center, move your mouse cursor to the title bar at the top of the gadget and the mouse cursor will change shape to the crossed arrows shape (see Figure 13-16). Click with the left mouse key, and while the key is pressed, drag the gadget where you would like. As the gadget is dragged, it will become transparent and the outline of the gadget will move in discrete steps as it is dragged into a new position. As the gadget is moved, other gadgets will be moved out of the way, either down or up to make way for the new position of the gadget being dragged (see Figure 13-16). You can move all gadgets around until you have them in the desired positions.

Figure 13-16: Moving gadgets

Adding and Deleting Gadgets

To add a new gadget, click the "Add stuff" link displayed in the bar above all the gadgets to the right side of the iGoogle page (see Figure 13-15). When you click this link, you will be taken to a page displaying a list of gadgets (see Figure 13-17).

Each page will contain a list of approximately seven gadgets with a small description beside each gadget. At the bottom of the page (not shown in Figure 13-17) are a "Next" link and a "Previous" link, allowing you to scroll backward and forward between the pages of gadgets. There are hundreds of these, so you may wish to use the "Search for gadgets" box in the top right corner of the screen (see Figure 13-17). In this way, you can somewhat narrow a search. To add a gadget, click the "Add it now" button beneath the small image of the gadget (see 13-17). This will add the gadget to your page and you can continue scrolling through the gadget list. To exit back to the iGoogle home page, click the "Back to iGoogle home" link located in the upper right corner of the web page.

Figure 13-17: Inserting a new gadget

To delete a gadget from your iGoogle page, select the small down arrow icon in the gadgets title bar on the right-hand side. This will open a small drop-down list of options (see Figure 13-18). One of these is "Delete this gadget." Selecting this will delete the gadget from your iGoogle page causing others to possibly move around to fill the vacant spot. There are options you can select from this drop-down menu including options to edit settings where applicable, minimize the gadget, and sharing the gadget.

Figure 13-18: Deleting a gadget

Most of the available gadgets are from third-party sources, but some are provided by Google, and in particular, some Google gadgets provide access to some Google Apps already discussed. This allows you to integrate these (to some degree) in your iGoogle home page. These gadgets will be described in the following sections.

Docs Gadget

If you use the gadget search facility to search for "Docs," you will find the Google Docs gadget. This can integrate the Google Docs interface (discussed in Chapter 3) into a gadget on the iGoogle home page. When you add this gadget to your iGoogle page, the gadget will be displayed (see Figure 13-19). The gadget will by default display the first five files (when sorted by "Last viewed") displayed in the Google Docs file list. If you edit the gadget settings (discussed in the previous section), you can display up to nine items in the gadget list. Clicking one of the displayed Google Docs files in the gadget will cause it to be opened in a new browser tab making it the current tab.

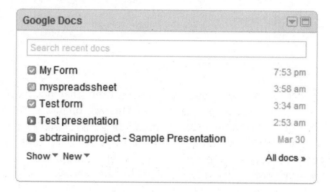

Figure 13-19: Google Docs gadget

There are three small links at the bottom of the file list in the gadget window. The "Show" link allows you to filter files listed in the gadget. You can choose either "Opened by me," "Owned by me," and "Starred." Since the number of files listed is small and you only want specific files to be shown in the gadget for quick access, set the "Star" flag against those you want shown (see Chapter 3). Through the "Show" link, choose only "Starred" files. The "New" link allows you to create a new Google Docs file and provides a small drop-down menu allowing you to choose the type of new file. Clicking the "All Docs" link will open a new browser tab and load the Google Docs interface into this tab. The new tab will become the current browser tab.

By integrating the Google Docs interface, this gadget provides quick and easy access to a limited number of files in Google Docs and also gives you access to some of the most common functionality you would use in Google Docs.

Gmail Gadget

Similar to the Google Docs gadget, you can integrate Gmail into your iGoogle page. Search for "Gmail" in the gadget search facility when adding a gadget to the page. There will be a number of gadgets available to integrate Gmail for you, but choose the one posted by Google.com. When you add this gadget to your iGoogle home page, you will see a familiar gadget display (see Figure 13-20). By default, the latest five emails in your Gmail inbox will be displayed in the gadget sorted by the received data.

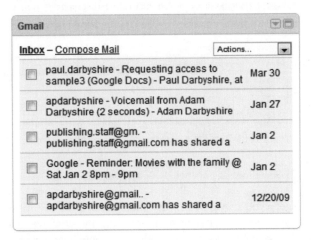

Figure 13-20: Gmail gadget

Click one of these emails to open it in the current window. For example, click the third message to have it open. You will see the Gmail message opened in the current window (see Figure 13-21). When the message is opened, you can perform most of the usual Gmail actions including reading, archiving, responding, and forwarding the message (see Figure 13-21). To return to your iGoogle home page, click the "Home" link on the left side of the browser window.

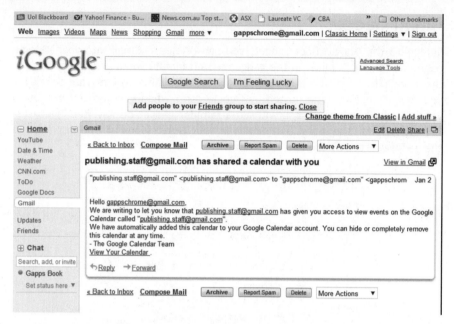

Figure 13-21: Gmail message opened by Gmail gadget

Within the gadget, you can perform common actions on the messages. Check the messages you wish to perform actions on by clicking the check box associated with the messages in the gadget window (see Figure 13-20), and choose the action from the drop-down "Action" list in the upper right corner of the gadget. These are the same actions available in the standard Gmail window (see Chapter 2). Additionally, the "Inbox" link will load your Gmail inbox into the current tab, and the "Compose Mail" link will allow you to compose and send a new message in the current tab. If you edit the settings of the gadget, you can choose how many messages are displayed in the gadget (up to a maximum of nine), and additionally you can check a small check box named "Open emails in full Gmail." By checking this option, you can click a message and it won't be opened in the current browser tab, but in a new browser tab after the full Gmail interface is loaded.

Finally, the Gmail gadget does not use the HTTPS protocol. If you have set your general Gmail settings to "Always use https" for browser connections, you will need to change this option to "Don't always use https" in the Gmail settings if you want to use this gadget (see Chapter 2).

ExplainED

This gadget does not use HTTPS. To use this, you may need to change your Gmail settings.

Calendar Gadget

By searching for "Calendar" in the gadget search facility when adding a gadget to the page, you will find the *"Official Google Calendar gadget"* allowing you to integrate Google Calendar into your iGoogle page. You will then see the gadget (see Figure 13-22). The calendar displays in the gadget with a mini calendar in month view in the top part of the gadget, while the agenda displays in the lower half of the gadget.

Figure 13-22: Google Calendar gadget

You can scroll backward and forward between the months using the small arrow links on the left and right side of the month name in the mini calendar. Days with events will be bolded in the mini calendar, and clicking a day will show the events for that day in the agenda. Clicking one of the events will display the details of the event in the agenda area below the mini calendar including any links to associated maps. Once you view the details of an agenda item, click the "Back" link displayed in the bottom left of the agenda to return to normal agenda viewing.

At the bottom of the agenda area are several links. The "Today" link will return the mini calendar to the current month and day in the top part of the gadget. The "Add" link allows you to add an event for the current day or a future date. The "Options" link allows you to turn off the display of the mini calendar or the agenda areas.

If you edit the settings of the calendar gadget, you will see a small dialog area above the mini calendar with changeable options (see Figure 13-23). You can change when the week starts, the date format, the time format, and whether to display the mini calendar or hide the agenda. Click the "Save" button to save any modified settings.

Figure 13-23: Google Calendar gadget edit settings

Clicking the "Google Calendar" link in the title bar of the gadget opens the full calendar in a new browser Tab.

Maps Gadget

By searching for "Google Map Search" in the gadget search facility when adding a gadget to the page, you will find the "Google Map Search" gadget so you can integrate Google Maps into your iGoogle page. When you add this gadget, you will see a similar gadget appearance (see Figure 13-24). The Google Map integration in this gadget is fairly simple. The map displays in the gadget, and you can click the map and drag it around to a different location (described in Chapter 10). You can use the arrow buttons and the zoom in and zoom out buttons in the upper left of the map (see Figure 13-24) to move the map. Use the "Search" field at the bottom of the gadget to do a standard Google Map search (described in Chapter 10).

Figure 13-24: Google Map gadget

If you edit the settings of the Google Map gadget, you will see a small dialog area above the map with changeable options (see Figure 13-25). With these options, you can set the default location. Although you can move the map around, when you reload the iGoogle page the map will always return to this default location. You can also change the default size of the Google Map gadget by checking the "Large Map" check box. The default for this is being currently checked. Click the "Save" button to save your setting for this gadget.

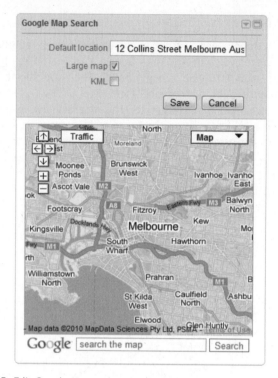

Figure 13-25: Edit Google Map gadget settings

Blogger Gadget

If you search for "Blogger" in the gadget search facility when adding a gadget to the page, you will find it published by http://www.blogger.com/blogger.com, allowing you to integrate Google Blogger into your iGoogle page. When adding this gadget, a similar gadget will appear (see Figure 13-26). The Blogger gadget allows you to quickly post new entries on your blog. Much like the new post-composing tool (see Chapter 12), you have the ability to set the title of your blog entry. Enter the text of your blog entry and enter any labels you would like to use. If you have multiple blogs on your Blogger account, you can post in any of them by clicking the drop-down list in the upper right-hand corner of the gadget and selecting the blog in wish you wish to post. Clicking the link on the top of the Blogger gadget will open a new browser tab and load the Blogger Dashboard for your blogs.

Figure 13-26: Blogger gadget

To modify any settings in the Blogger gadget, don't select the "Edit Settings" from the same location as done in previous gadgets. To edit available options in the Blogger gadget, click the small icon in the Blogger gadget title bar among the group of three icons in the right of the bar. This will be the left icon of the three (see Figure 13-27). The only currently available and modifiable settings allow the gadget to know who you are and give you access to your friends group. It also allows you the ability to post any activity to your blog's updates. Click the "*Save*" button to save any option changes.

Figure 13-27: Blogger gadget options

Cross Integration of Google Apps

Aside from the two major focal points discussed for integrating the Google Apps (Google Sites and iGoogle), there is a small degree of cross integration between some of the Google Apps covered in this book. This cross integration centers on the three Google Apps: Gmail, Google Calendar, and Google Maps. We have already covered much of these applications in their respective chapters, but it is worth pointing out the integration between them to provide a more complete picture (see Figure 13-28). While this is not a complete picture of Google Apps, it shows the major integration points currently available in the applications discussed.

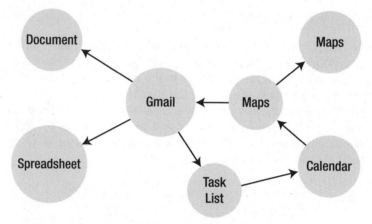

Figure 13-28: Cross integration of Google Apps

Gmail has had built-in integration with the Google Docs for some time. Whenever you receive a mail message with either a Microsoft Word or Excel spreadsheet attachment, Gmail will provide the option to open these as Google Documents. If you choose the "Open as a Google Document" link for these attachments, they will be uploaded to your Google account and converted to either a Google Document or a Google Spreadsheet, then will also be opened for editing in the appropriate Google App. The documents are then available for sharing or personal editing.

Gmail is integrated with Google Calendar through the "Task List" available in both of these apps. The same "Task list" is used and in Gmail you can choose to add a Gmail message to the task list through the "Add to Tasks" option from the "More Actions" drop-down list button. If you edit the task and add a due date, the task will appear as data in your calendar. In this way, the task list becomes a bridge from your inbox to your calendar. Additionally, you can set up reminders that will be emailed to your Gmail account using calendar events (or any other email account), or can be sent via SMS to your cell phone. Additionally, if an event in a calendar requires a meeting, a place can be designated utilizing Google Maps. This map can be associated with an event, and all parties having access to the event will have the ability to find the exact location by the embedded map.

These cross integration aspects of Google Maps make the Google Apps a powerful desktop tool to help get you organized and to manage your documents. Google continually improves the various applications and we look forward to more integration between the applications as time goes on.

The Google Dashboard

While not strictly an integration tool for Google Apps, Google Dashboard brings together into one place a summary of what information you have stored and configured for each application. It also provides a central access point for configuring and managing the applications. To bring up the Dashboard, login to your Google account and from the Google home page select the "Google account settings" link from the "Settings" drop-down list in the upper right of the home page (see Figure 13-29).

Figure 13-29: Accessing the Dashboard

This will open the Google accounts page and underneath the "Personal settings" heading, you will see a link to the Dashboard. Click this link and Google will ask you to reaffirm your password for this account. You will see the Google sign-in box with your e-mail already entered shown in the right side of the browser window. Enter your password for this account and click the "Sign-in" button. You will be taken to the Google Dashboard for your account (see Figure 13-30). The Google Dashboard will show a listing for each of the apps you use and have configuration data stored.

Figure 13-30: Dashboard view

For each of the apps, the listing on the left side of the browser screen contains information including the name of the application and summary information specific to that application. Figure 13-31 shows an expanded image of the Dashboard listing for the Google Docs and Gmail Dashboard entries. The docs summary information includes the number of documents owned, the number opened, how many are sitting in the trash folders, and the number of starred documents. The data listed in the Gmail entry includes the number of conversations in the inbox and the overall number including the number of conversations in the "Sent mail" folder, chat history conversations, and the number of spam conversations.

Docs

Owned by me **13 documents**
Most recent: Introduction on Apr 16, 2010

Opened by me **21 documents**
Most recent: Reddit's Favorite Android Apps and Games at 10:13 AM

Trashed **3 documents**
Most recent: Introduction on Apr 16, 2010

Starred **1 document**
Most recent: Cats or Dogs on Jan 23, 2010

Manage documents

Sharing documents

Gmail

Inbox **10 conversations**
Most recent: Android at 3:02 AM

All mail **25 conversations**
Most recent: Android at 3:02 AM

Sent mail **6 conversations**
Most recent: another test on Apr 1, 2010

Chat history **6 conversations**
Most recent: Chat with Adam Darbyshire on Mar 30, 2010

Spam **1 conversation**
Most recent: Delivery Status Notification (Failure) on Mar 18, 2010

Manage chat history

Manage HTTPS settings

Manage all Gmail settings

Gmail privacy policy

Privacy and security help

Figure 13-31: Closer look at Dashboard entries

On the right-hand side of the browser window for each of the Google Apps listed in the Dashboard, you will see links leading to different browser pages allowing you to manage applications and edit various settings of the applications or information pages. For example, for docs in Figure 13-31, there are two links: "Manage documents" which opens the Google Docs main interface page allowing you to manage all aspects of your different documents, and "Sharing documents" taking you to the information page for sharing and publishing documents. There are five links associated with Gmail. Three of these will take you to different settings pages, and the last two links will load information pages on the Gmail privacy policy and privacy and security help.

The dashboard can become an important focal point for managing settings for you applications and to quickly glean important information about some of the data stored.

Google Apps and Non-Google Software

Some third-party applications now provide add-ons or plug-ins to enable access to some of the Google Apps leading to some limited integration with the apps. In other cases, software vendors may not directly supply these plug-ins, but they are made available by individuals and are accessible from the Web. In this section, we will provide a brief description of the purpose and features of some of these plug-ins, without providing detailed "how to" guides. There are many of these and we will not cover them all, but we have chosen a cross-section of important applications as examples.

Google Apps Sync for Microsoft Outlook

Google Apps Sync is a plug-in available for Microsoft Outlook users or enterprises that have made the switch from exchange to Google Apps but still want to keep using the Outlook interface. Exchange is Microsoft's messaging and collaboration platform. When you switch from one service to another, the transition can be simpler if you can access your data with the old interface. Google Apps Sync will let you export your data from an exchange-hosted service to Google Apps, and you can keep your Google Apps (Gmail and calendar) synched with Outlook. You can then access your document from the cloud using Outlook, and this can also be accessed from your Google account as you have learned in previous chapters.

You can import your Outlook Mail into Gmail and Outlook Calendar to Google Calendar and Contacts. You can also import Outlook Notes, Tasks, and Journal items into your Google Apps profile (these will not be available via Google Apps). They will only be available from your Outlook interface. Some features in Outlook do not translate over to Google Apps, and a full list comparison is available from Google in their document "Google Apps Sync for Microsoft Outlook."[1]

Google Apps Widgets for Mac, Vista, and Windows 7

With Windows Vista, Windows 7, and Mac OS X operating systems, you can download and install widgets that can be quickly accessed from the operating system's interface. In this context, a widget is a small application providing specific information. In these operating systems, you can download widgets and install them on the desktop providing quick access to their functionality, and in some cases providing continual updated information by connecting to the Web. For example, a widget that displays the current temperature in your location can be installed on the desktop to give you a continual picture of the outside weather as you work in your office.

---

[1] http://www.postini.com/webdocs/gapps_sync/google_apps_sync_chart_v1.7.pdf (available at the time of writing)

There are several Google widgets available for Mac OS X, Vista, and Windows 7 allowing you to interface to the Google Apps. In Windows 7, the widget is installed on the desktop; in Vista it can be installed in the sidebar; and in Mac OS X, the widgets are normally installed into the Mac OS Dashboard. These widgets offer similar functionality to the gadgets installed on the iGoogle home page discussed earlier. Each of the operating systems has widgets for Gmail and Google Calendar with other widgets for Blogger, Talk, and Maps also available in one or more of the operating systems. The downloading and installation of the widgets are different for each of these operating systems, and the *"Help"* system should be viewed. However, the process is not difficult. Figure 13-32 shows a Gmail widget installed on a Windows 7 desktop. The widget continually checks Gmail for new messages and displays the number of new messages including a small portion of the header and the sender in the widget. Clicking one of the Gmail headers will open Gmail in your operating system's browser. The Gmail account information is configurable within the widget.

Figure 13-32: Gmail widget on Windows 7 desktop

Google Apps and Microsoft Office

Microsoft Office has been the standard Office Suite installed on many PCs for quite some time. Microsoft provides no direct way to integrate to the Google Apps, but OffiSynch[2] provide a Microsoft extension adding a new tool bar to Microsoft Office and allows users of Office share documents over the Web by integrating Microsoft Office with Google Docs and other Google Apps. There are both free and premium versions of this extension available. This extension is a

---

[2] http://www.offisync.com/ (available at the time of writing)

third-party product; however Google is working toward integrating with Microsoft Office products.

Google has acquired DocVerse, a startup company, in March 2010 (reported in Digital Trends[3]) in an effort to develop a fully functional Google solution to integrating Google Apps and Microsoft Office. DocVerse is a product that extended Microsoft Office by allowing real-time editing and sharing by plugging in and synching in the cloud. At the time of writing, the acquisition has taken place, but the plans are to first integrate DocVerse with the Google Apps as a first step to integrating Microsoft Office with Google Apps.

Google Apps and WS02

WS02 is representative of applications providing the user with single sign-on functionality for an enterprise or even individuals owning domains that might need it. One of the problems we find as we move to a cloud-based environment is that of identity. This is seen when you need to identify yourself in places in the cloud in order to access various applications and services in which you have registered. Identity management applications can centralize identity management for companies and users to a single point, and one sign-in will allow access to all entitled applications and services.

WS02 is an identity management application able to integrate with Google allowing a single sign-in for Google and all cloud-based services. You must own a Google Apps domain, and once setup, a key pair is generated for becoming your "Cloud Identity." When you try accessing Google Apps, you will be automatically redirected to your WS02 cloud identity requiring you to authenticate access. You then have to access to your Google Apps and any other cloud-based application or service which you have registered with the WS02 cloud identity management system.

Chrome Extensions

It may seem unrelated to be discussing Chrome extensions to integrate with the Google Apps, as we have discussed Google Chrome in the first chapter of this book. But Chrome is first and foremost a web browser. We have used it extensively while discussing all Google Apps, but it is still a browser used for needs other than Google Apps. You can install extensions to Google Chrome that interface to some Google Apps. Some of these extensions are provided by

---

[3] http://www.digitaltrends.com/computing/google-buys-docverse-to-bring-microsoft-office-to-google-apps/

Google, and many are third-party extensions. For example, Google provides a "My Shortcuts" extension integrating a series of short cuts into the Chrome tool bar ultimately saving the user potentially long series of clicks to perform a variety of functions (see Figure 13-33).

Figure 13-33: My Shortcuts Chrome extension

Some third party-extensions to Chrome include a Gmail checker available at chromeextensions.org placing an icon on the Chrome tool bar, along with an indication of the number of unread mail messages. This extension checks the inbox for new mail and adjusts the icon in the tool bar accordingly. Additionally, Google Alerter (available at chromeplugins.org) shows unread messages in Gmail, Google Reader, and Google Wave.

Backup utilities

The last tool we will discuss in this chapter is a backup utility. Google performs its own backups and maintains redundancy in the cloud to provide users with a robust and effective service. However, many users feel the need to maintain their own backups and retain some control in this area. One such utility integrating with Google Docs is GdocBackup. This is a small utility allowing you to enter your Google account information, (a backup folder on your local machine) and provides you with an "Execute" button. All your Google Docs files will be downloaded to the backup folder. Once you run the backup for the first time, any subsequent backup will be a partial backup, as it will only backup files changed since the last execution.

Summary

In this chapter, we learned of the integration aspects of the Google applications that we have concentrated on throughout the book. We discussed the two main focal points of integration for the Google Apps, including Google Sites and Google's customizable home page iGoogle. We learned how to add gadgets to an iGoogle page and how to modify existing gadgets. In particular, we looked at the gadgets allowing us to integrate Google Apps into our home page providing quick and easy access. We also covered some of the cross integration aspects of Google Apps we have discussed in previous chapters. Finally, we took a brief look at the Google Dashboard and how some non-Google applications are integrated with the Google Apps.

Index

A

Account settings button, 534
Accounts and Import tab, 94
Add a reminder link, 391
Add another image link, 552
Add File dialog box, 469
Add new task button, 85
Add stuff link, 598
Add without sending link, 117
Adobe Flash plug-in, installing, 36
Adobe Presenter, 312
AdSense, setting up and using, 576
Agenda view, 387
Amazon Associates program, 578
Apply changes button, 125
Apply this theme button, 35
Archive button, 70
Auto-Fill feature, 14, 258
autosave feature, 145
auto-type detection, 220
Avast, 43

B

Blank template, 429
Blogger
    Add another image link, 552
    adding a gadget, 574
    adding web pages to a blog, 557
    AdSense, setting up and using, 576
    Amazon Associates program, 578
    archiving old posts automatically, 572
    assigning a label to a blog post, 550

assigning permissions to users, 572
Basic settings, changing, 566
Blogs of note, viewing, 565
CAPTCHA question, requiring, 571
changing a blog's layout, 573
changing the location of your blog, 568
Check Availability link, 544
Choose File button, 552
choosing a new template, 575
choosing a template and theme, 545
comment moderation, 562
Comment settings, changing, 570
commenting on your own blog, 561
comments, allowing or disallowing, 558
creating a blog, 544
creating a comment on a blog, 560
creating a new post, 549
creating a successful blog, 582
creating blog posts with a mobile phone, 580
creating multiple blogs, 581
customizing fonts and colors, 574
customizing page elements, 573
Dashboard, contents of, 546
Delete link, 560
deleting a post, 561
displaying comments by the post to which they are attached, 563
Edit button, 559

Edit posts link, 555
Edit Profile link, 547
editing drafts and existing posts, 555
editing your profile, 547
editing, viewing, and deleting pages, 559
electing to receive e-mails from Blogger, 543
E-mail posts option, 567
example profile, illustration of, 547
exporting a blog, 567
filtering through different types of posts, 556
following updates from other blogs, 563
fonts, selecting, 558
Formatting settings, changing, 569
generating income from your blog, 576
Global settings, changing, 567
Google Video website, 554
Identity section, 549
image layout, choosing, 553
importing a blog, 567
Insert Image popup window, 552
Insert Video popup window, 554
inserting images in blog posts, 552
inserting links into posts, 555
inserting videos in blog posts, 554
inviting people to be authors, 572
legal implications of blogging, 560
Link button, 555
moving gadgets to different locations, 574
New Page button, 557
New Post button, 549
OpenID, 581
origins of blogging, 541
Page creation tool, 557
Page Elements window, 573
Page management window, 557

Pages gadget, 558
pencil icon, 567
Post Options link, 550
posting updates when you e-mail, 579
privacy settings, 548, 564
publishing a post, 550
reading list, viewing, 563
Redo button, 558
rejecting or publishing comments individually, 563
restricting access to your web site, 572
saving a draft version of a post, 550
searching for posts, 556
setting the sub domain, 544
setting up an account, 542
setting your preferences, 565
SMS message posting, enabling, 580
start page, illustration of, 542
Terms of service link, 543
text layout, choosing, 553
Theme select page, 545
tool bar, illustration of, 550
transplanting a blog to or from another blogging service, 567
Undo button, 558
uploading images from a computer or web site, 552
Blogs of note, viewing, 565
bookmarks
Bookmark bar, 6
Bookmark Manager, using, 31–33
controlling whether the bookmarks toolbar is displayed or hidden, 24
creating a new bookmark, 26
creating a new bookmark folder, 28
managing, 26
Other Bookmarks folder, 6
selecting a bookmark, 29
See also Chrome

C

Calendar
accessing, 379
accessing a calendar from Microsoft Outlook, 423
Add a note box, 416
Add a reminder link, 391
Add guests link, 416
advantages of, 379
Agenda view, 387
assigning permissions to access a calendar, 421
automatically synchronizing your calendar with your mobile phone, 425
Calendar Settings, Calendar tab, 417
Calendar Settings, General tab, 406
Calendar Settings, Mobile Setup tab, 423
changing date and time formats, 410
changing the 4 day view setting, 411
choosing a daily, weekly, or monthly view, 383
choosing the type of event reminder, 391
clicking an empty time slot to add an event, 393
configuring calendar details, 380
Create event button, 394
Create Event link, 388
Create new calendar button, 418
creating public and private calendars, 417
custom (configurable) views, 387
date picker, 389
default country, changing, 408
default language, changing, 407
default time zone, changing, 408

displaying local weather, options for, 412
displaying two different time zones next to each other, 410
dragging an event to a different time slot, 401
Edit event details link, 403
editing the details of an event, 402
E-mail organizer link, 416
events, creating, 388
events, display of, 382
events, editing and deleting, 401
events, finding and viewing, 397
events, repeating, 390, 403
getting the URL of a calendar, 422
handling weekends, options for, 411
hiding the event details on a public calendar, 420
ICAL button, 423
increasing or decreasing the time allotted for an event, 402
inviting people to add an event to their calendars, 413
main calendar view, illustration of, 381
making a calendar public, 420
making a calendar searchable on Google, 420
Month quick view, 383
More items link, 386
multiple calendars, benefits of, 419
My calendars, 382
opening view, illustration of, 379
Other calendars, 382
performing an advanced search for events, 397
Pop-up notifications, using, 392
privacy settings for shared calendars, 393
Quick add feature, 394

619

receiving event notifications on a mobile phone, 423

resizing, 386

responding to an event invitation, 415

restoring a deleted event, 402

scheduling events over different time zones, 395

search function, using, 397

searching other people's calendars, 398

selecting from the country and time zone drop-down lists, 380

sending an e-mail to those coming to an event, 417

sending out invitations to event guests, 414

setting a Repeat until date, 404

setting appointment availability, 393

setting calendar sharing, 418

setting reminders, 391

setting the permissions for invited guests, 414

Settings link, 406

Share this calendar link, 420

Show an additional time zone link, 410

Show Search Options link, 397

three-digit time code, using, 396

time chooser, 389

using keywords with the Quick add feature, 395

using natural language to quickly enter events, 394

using text notifications, 424

viewing all details of an event, 400

viewing who has been invited to an event, 415

weekly view format, 381

See also events

Call button, 527

call notification, 528

CAPTCHA question, requiring, 571

cell ranges, 223

cell references, 223

Change colors based on rules dialog box, 272

Change owner button, 130

Chart API, 283

Chat window
opening, 522
switching to, 523
See also Talk

Check Availability link, 544

Check availability! button, 48

Check spelling link, 55

Chrome
accepting the default import options, 2

Adobe Flash plug-in, installing, 36

Apply this theme button, 35

Auto-Fill, disabling, 14

backward and forward buttons, 5

Bookmark bar, 6

Bookmark Manager, using, 31–33

bookmarks, managing, 26

browser screen, illustration of, 4

ChromeSetup.exe, running, 2

clicking the Reload button in the Google toolbar, 6

configuring, 9

controlling how Chrome handles passwords, 12

cookie settings, changing, 16

creating a new bookmark, 26

creating a new bookmark folder, 28

Customize button, 6

Customize Menu drop-down list, 6

Customize Your Settings dialog box, 3

default encoding, changing, 19

description of, 1

DNS pre-fetching, 14

downloading and installing, 2

downloading materials to a local computer, 39

drop-down search field,
    activating, 25
font settings, changing, 20
Fonts and Encoding dialog
    window, 21
Get themes button, 34
Google Chrome Options dialog
    window, 9
Home button, 5, 9
Install plug-in button, 36
Internet security, best
    practices, 40
language setting, changing, 22
loading web pages in windows
    or tabs, 6
Make Google Chrome the
    default browser option, 3
malware sites, 42
New incognito window,
    selecting, 8
opening a new tab, 7
opening the Javascript console,
    24
Operating Systems window list,
    7
Other Bookmarks folder, 6
password option bar, 11
Passwords and Exceptions
    dialog window, 12
passwords, saving and not
    saving, 11
phishing and malware
    protection, 15
phishing, definition of, 42
placing the browser in full-
    screen mode, 25
plug-ins, 35
privacy settings, controlling, 14
reloading the current Web
    page, 6
reordering multiple tabs in a
    window, 8
right-clicking a link to open a
    new tab or window, 7
running Google Apps in, 1
running web pages in protected
    environments (sandboxes), 1
security certificates, 41

security guidelines, 43
security in, 10
selecting a bookmark, 29
setting the home page, 5, 9
Show cookies button, 17
surfing in stealth mode, 8
surfing the web with, 4
text size, controlling, 18
Themes gallery, 34
themes, accessing, 33
trusted and untrusted web
    sites, 41
using tabs instead of windows
    to save system resources,
    7
viewing the current web page
    source, 23
working with multiple browser
    windows, 6
YouTube and, 36
Zoom menu, 18
Classic home link, 596
cloud computing, 110
color chooser, 166
comment moderation, 562
Compose Mail link, 50, 602
Compose mail toolbar, illustration
    of, 52
Configure Navigation dialog box, 464
Contacts link, 79
conversation view, 62
cookies, 16
Create an account button, 46
Create chart dialog box, 284
Create Event link, 388
Create new button, 114
Create new calendar button, 418
Create Page button, 467
Create site button, 428, 431
Customize button, 6
Customize Menu drop-down list, 6
Customize Your Settings dialog
    box, 3

D

Data validation dialog box, 269
date picker, 389

Day events, 383
Delete button, 127
DNS pre-fetching, 14
.doc and .docx formats, 150
Document
    accessing functions from the
        context-sensitive right-
        click menus, 140
    adding a word to the standard
        dictionary, 195
    adding multilevel lists or bullet
        points to documents, 184
    Align option, 168
    annotations, setting, 154
    applying formatting to
        characters or paragraphs,
        162
    assigning each collaborator a
        different color for
        comments, 204
    automatically generating a
        table of contents, 181
    autosave feature, 145
    batch uploading of documents,
        148
    changing a document's
        background color, 166
    changing table borders, 191
    changing table properties, 188
    changing the color of text, 165
    changing the location and size
        of an image, 175
    choosing the Google Docs Help
        Center, 142
    Clear formatting option, 165
    Close preview button, 157
    closing documents, 144
    color chooser, 166
    comparing two document
        revisions, 203
    controlling the appearance of
        an inserted image, 175
    Copy image option, 174
    correcting a spelling mistake,
        195
    creating and inserting tables,
        185

cutting, copying, and pasting
    text, 161
default font, setting, 164
default point size for text, 165
deleting a header or footer,
    180
deleting page breaks, 179
.doc and .docx formats, 150
document formats supported,
    147
document proofing tools, 194
Document settings dialog box,
    167
Download as option, 149
downloading documents as
    HTML, 149
downloading documents as PDF
    files, 139
downloading documents to a
    local computer, 149
Edit menu, 141
editing existing text, 160
endnotes, inserting, 198
entering text, 157
File menu, 141, 143
finding synonyms, 196
fixed-width page, 158
fonts, changing, 164
footnotes, inserting, 198
footnotes, showing, 159
Format menu, 141
formatting lines as a numbered
    list or bullet point list,
    184
formatting table cells, 192
formatting text, 162
Free images UK, 172
giving collaborators access to a
    document, 145
Google Docs interface tab,
    switching to, 147
Google Translate, 197
Help menu, 141
hiding all the control elements
    in the current tab, 159
image formats, 171
images, working with, 171
inability to show pagination, 178

Insert image dialog box, 172
Insert menu, 141
inserting a page break at the
    insertion point, 178
inserting comments, 199
inserting headers and footers,
    179
inserting images, 172
Keyboard shortcuts menu
    option, 143
Learn From Other Google Users
    option, 142
line spacing, setting, 169
lists and bullet points, 183
loading an image from the web,
    173
Look up word option, 196
looking up encyclopedia
    entries, 196
major elements of the working
    screen, illustration of, 140
Make a copy option, 145
margin width, setting, 170
margins, setting, 154
menu bar, list of menu options,
    141
Microsoft Word format, 139,
    150
moving around a document, 159
moving text with drag and
    drop, 162
new blank document,
    illustration of, 139
New Document option, 147
obtaining images, 171
opening documents, 146
OpenOffice format, 139
paper size options, 154
PDF print dialog box, 151
predefined styles, 163
preview mode control buttons,
    illustration of, 156
previewing documents, 155
Print as webpage option, 151
Print preview option, 155
Print Settings dialog box, 153
printing the PDF version of a
    document, 151

Properties link, 183
Recheck spelling option, 195
removing text styles, 163
renaming documents, 146
resizing text, 165
reverting to an earlier
    document revision, 203
revision history interface, 200
revision index link, 201
ruler-guides, lack of, 140
Save and close option, 144
Save icon, 145
saving documents, 144
See revision history option, 200
Select files to upload link, 147
selecting text, 160
selecting the Help item on the
    menu bar, 142
setting the default settings for
    an entire document, 167
setting the horizontal or
    vertical alignment of a
    table cell, 193
spell checking, 194
Table menu, 141
Table of contents option, 181
table rows and columns,
    inserting and deleting,
    193
table rows and columns,
    modifying, 189
tables, working with, 185
text alignment, setting, 168
text area, 157
Text Background Color icon,
    166
Text color icon, 165
Text font icon, 164
text indent, setting, 170
Text Style icon, 163
tool bar, illustration of, 141
tools for document revision,
    199
Tools menu, 141
translating documents into
    another language, 197
turning an image into a link,
    177

Upload Files utility, 147
uploading documents, 147
using styles Heading 1 to
    Heading 5, 181
View menu, 141, 158
viewing a comprehensive list of
    all document revisions,
    200
viewing a formatted page as it
    will be printed, 140
Web page preview, 159
WinRar, 149
WinZip, 149
word lookup feature, 196
wrapping text around an image,
    177
Zip files, 149
Documents link, 113
DocVerse, 614
Download as option, 216
Download button, 132
draft messages, 67
drag points, 321
Duplicate button, 360

E

Edit Item dialog box, 474
Edit posts link, 555
Empty trash button, 128
encoding, changing Chrome's
    default setting, 19
End Call button, 529
events
    clicking an empty time slot to
        add an event, 393
    creating, 388
    Day events, 383
    dragging an event to a different
        time slot, 401
    duration and display of, 382
    Edit event details link, 403
    editing and deleting, 401
    editing the details of an event,
        402
    finding and viewing, 397
    hidden, 386

increasing or decreasing the
    time allotted for an
    event, 402
performing an advanced search
    for events, 397
public holidays, automatic
    adding of, 382
receiving event notifications on
    a mobile phone, 423
repeating, 390, 403
responding to an event
    invitation, 415
restoring a deleted event, 402
scheduling events over
    different time zones, 395
search function, using, 397
sending an e-mail to those
    coming to an event, 417
sending out invitations to event
    guests, 414
using natural language to
    quickly enter events, 394
viewing all details of an event,
    400
viewing who has been invited
    to an event, 415
See also Calendar
Excel format, 216
Export to PDF dialog box, 217-218

F

File menu, 306
Filters tab, 102
Firefox, 5
folders
    adding a file to a folder, 125
    assigning multiple folders to
        files, 123
    color-coding, 124
    creating a new folder, 123
    creating a new folder within an
        existing folder, 124
    deleting folders and subfolders,
        127
    Folders button, 125
    My Folders option, 123

options for manipulating folders, 126
sharing, 126
Trash folder, using, 127
working with, 123
See also Google Docs
font settings, changing, 20
Fonts and Encoding dialog window, 21
Forms
  Add item drop-down list, 359, 369
  adding a page break to a form, 370
  adding a section header to a form, 370
  allowing users to view the form summary, 372
  annotated blank form, illustration of, 358
  automating the collection of survey data from users, 357
  Back button, 371
  changing a form's theme, 377
  choosing the type of survey question, 359
  Continue button, 371
  creating a copy of an existing question, 360
  creating a form from a spreadsheet, 358
  creating a new form, 358
  deleting a question, 361
  dividing a questionnaire into sections and pages, 369
  Done button, 361, 369
  Duplicate button, 360
  Edit confirmation link, 372
  editing a form in spreadsheet view, 376
  editing existing questions, 361
  editing the default thank you page, 372
  Go to page based on answer check box, 371
  Google Talk, 373

grid-style question, creating, 367
Help Text field, 361
integration with Spreadsheet, 357
Likert-type question, creating, 367
list-style question, creating, 365
methods for adding new questions, 359
methods for distributing a form, 373
moving form items, 372
multiple choice question, creating, 363, 371
Page Break option, 370
paragraph text question, creating, 362
publishing a form, 372
Question Type drop-down list, 369
redirecting users to certain pages based on their answers, 370
Required Question check box, 361
sample text question ready to be published, illustration of, 360
scale-style question, creating, 366
Section Header option, 370
setting a scale between any two numbers, 366
specifying options with check boxes, 364
specifying options with radio buttons, 363
summary page, example of, 375
text question, creating, 361
viewing results data in spreadsheet view, 374
viewing results data in summary mode, 374
ways of viewing form results, 374
formula bar, turning on, 210

Formula button, 249
formula cells, 221
formula, definition of, 245
Forwarding and POP/IMAP tab, 100
Free images UK, 172
Future Value function, 256

G

Gadget Selection dialog box, 281
GdocBackup, 616
Gears, offline viewing and editing
    of Google Docs, 110
Get Directions button, 504
Get link to share option, 120
Get themes button, 34
Gmail
    accessing actions for the
      current e-mail, 58
    Accounts and Import tab, 94
    Add new task button, 85
    adding a contact to a group, 84
    adding a new contact, 79
    adding another e-mail address,
      98
    adding notes to a task, 89
    Archive button, 70
    archiving messages, 68
    assigning a due date to a task,
      88
    basic e-mail functions, using,
      49
    browser connection setting, 93
    Check availability! button, 48
    Check spelling link, 55
    choosing a security question, 48
    choosing text-formatting
      options, 52-54
    Compose Mail link, 50
    Compose mail toolbar,
      illustration of, 52
    Contacts link, 79
    contacts list, managing, 78
    conversation group, viewing, 63
    conversation view, 62
    Create an account button, 46
    creating a contact group, 79,
      84

    creating a custom label, 73
    creating a first task, 85
    creating a new filter, 102-105
    creating a password, 48
    creating a signature, 93
    creating an account, 46
    default contact group, 81
    default Gmail view, 49
    deleting a contact, 83
    deleting messages, 68
    draft messages, 67
    editing a contact, 83
    editing a task, 87
    e-mail toolbar, 58
    e-mail, composing and sending,
      50
    e-mail, displaying and reading,
      57
    e-mail, replying to, 60
    filtering the flow of new e-
      mails, 102
    Filters tab, 102
    Forwarding and POP/IMAP tab,
      100
    forwarding e-mails to another
      e-mail address, 101
    General Settings tab, 92
    Gmail home page, 46
    Google Sync program, 106
    grouping contacts into
      categories, 83
    importing e-mails and contacts
      from another e-mail
      account, 94
    inbox, 49
    indenting (demoting) a task, 87
    Insert Emoticon option, 53
    integration with Google Talk,
      517
    Internet Message Access
      Protocol (IMAP) access,
      102
    Labels menu, 74
    labels, using, 72
    message lists in folder view, 75
    New Contact icon, 79
    New Group icon, 79
    Not Spam button, 78

origin of, 45
parent and child tasks, 87
Plain text link, 54
Post Office Protocol (POP)
     access, 101
preferences, setting, 91
removing a task within a list,
     90
Reply button, 59
reviewing sent messages, 65
selecting a different font, 52
selecting a theme, 105
selecting groups of e-mails, 65
Sender Policy Framework (SPF)
     rules, 99
sending e-mails from a Gmail
     server or SMTP server, 99
sending e-mails that appear to
     come from a different e-
     mail address, 97
Sent Mail folder, 65
Settings link, 91
Settings window, illustration
     of, 91
spam filtration system, 45, 77
spam folder, 78
spell checker, 55
Starred folder, 71
starred messages, 65, 70
storage capacity of, 45
Switch list drop-down menu, 90
synchronizing Gmail with a
     mobile phone, 106
system labels, list of, 73
task list, creating, 84
Themes tab, 105
Trash folder, 68
unstarred messages, 65
user labels, 73
using Outlook and other e-mail
     programs, 100
vacation responder, creating,
     93
Google AdSense, incorporating into
     a web site, 478
Google Analytics, 486
Google Apps
  accessing the Dashboard, 609
Chrome extensions, 614
displaying application-specific
     summary information in
     the Dashboard, 610
DocVerse, 614
GdocBackup, 616
Google Apps Sync for Microsoft
     Outlook, 612
Google Apps widgets for Mac OS
     X, Vista, and Windows 7,
     612
importing Outlook Mail into
     Gmail, 612
integrating Microsoft Office, 613
integrating with non-Google
     software, 611
integration of Gmail with Docs
     and Calendar, 608
major points of cross
     integration, 608
Manage documents link, 611
Sharing documents link, 611
using Sites to integrate Google
     Apps, 584
WS02 cloud identity
     management system, 614
Google Chrome Options dialog
     window
  Basics tab, 9
  Personal Stuff tab, 10
  Under the Hood tab, 14
  See also Chrome
Google Docs
  Add without sending link, 117
  adding a file to a folder, 125
  Apply changes button, 125
  assigning file ownership, 118
  assigning multiple folders to
     files, 123
  assigning ownership of a
     document, 137
  benefits of using, 109
  Change owner button, 130
  checking who has access to a
     file, 117
  color-coding folders, 124
  concurrent editing and conflict
     resolution, 122

concurrent editing and performance delays, 121
Create new button, 114
creating a new folder, 123
creating a new folder within an existing folder, 124
creating documents, 114
data security, aspects of, 111
data security, physical and logical, 110
Delete button, 127
deleting a file, 127
deleting a shared file, 129
deleting folders and subfolders, 127
Document, 109
document export options, 131
Documents link, 113
Download button, 132
embracing the cloud computing model, 110
Empty trash button, 128
exporting (downloading) a document, 130
exporting more than one document at a time, 132
exporting to HTML, 132
file listing options, 113
file sharing options, 116
file upload options, 134
Folders button, 125
Forms, 109
Gears, 110
generating a new revision after each document save, 122
Get link to share option, 120
hiding (archiving) a document, 136
integration with Google Sites and iGoogle, 110
interface, 113
inviting others to share a document, 116
launching, 112
main screen, illustration of, 113
modifying a collaborator's file access, 118
moving between documents, 115

My Folders option, 123
offline viewing and editing, 110
opening several documents at once, 115
options for manipulating folders, 126
Presentation, 109
Publish document button, 135
publishing documents on the web, 135
removing all collaborators, 118
Rename button, 127
renaming a file, 127
Select files to upload link, 133
sending out invitations to collaborators, 116
setting permissions, 119
Share button, 116
Share with others dialog box, 116
sharing a folder, 126
sharing documents and collaborating online, 110
sharing documents with web users, 115
sharing via a link, 120
Spreadsheet, 109
synchronizing document editing with collaborators, 121
tool bar, 113
Trash folder, using, 127
Trash for everyone button, 129
Undelete button, 128
Upload button, 133
uploading documents, 133
uploading documents without converting, 135
working with folders to store documents, 123
Google Docs Help Center, 142, 211, 305
Google Sites Help Forum link, 434
Google Sync program, 106
Google Translate, 197
GoogleApps toolbar, 46
GoogleFinance function, 298

H

Help menu, 305
Help Text field, 361
hexadecimal color format, 328
Home button, 5, 9

I

ICAL button, 423
Identity section, 549
IF function, 294
iGoogle
    Add stuff link, 598
    adding a gadget, 598
    All Docs link, 600
    Blogger gadget, 606
    Calendar gadget, 603
    changing the default size of the
        Map gadget, 605
    choosing as your home page,
        596
    Classic home link, 596
    Compose Mail link, 602
    default home page, illustration
        of, 597
    deleting a gadget, 599
    Docs gadget, 600
    editing options in the Blogger
        gadget, 607
    editing the settings of the
        Calendar gadget, 604
    editing the settings of the Map
        gadget, 605
    Gmail gadget, 601
    Gmail gadget and HTTPS
        protocol use, 602
    Inbox link, 602
    loading the Blogger Dashboard
        for your blogs, 606
    Maps gadget, 605
    moving gadgets to a new
        location, 597
    New link, 600
    Show link, 600
    Today link, 604
    viewing available gadgets, 598
Inbox link, 602
information box, 493

Insert Emoticon option, 53
Insert image icon, 304
Insert Image popup window, 552
Insert text icon, 304
Insert Video popup window, 554
Install plug-in button, 36
Instant Messaging (IM)
    guidelines for using safely, 521
    origin of, 517
    See also Talk
Internet Explorer, 5
Internet Message Access Protocol
    (IMAP) access, 102

K

keywords, using with the Quick add
    feature, 395

L

Labels menu, 74
labels, using, 72
language setting, changing, 22
Learn From Other Google Users
    option, 212

M

malware sites, 42
Maps
    centering the map, 492
    changing the default location,
        492
    checking a city's traffic
        conditions, 502
    default opening screen, 489
    dragging the map around to
        view different areas, 489
    examining alternate routes to a
        destination, 506
    Get Directions button, 504
    information box, 493
    Map view, 510
    markers, large and small, 493
    More info link, 494
    navigation controls, 490
    panning, 489
    Photos option, 508

plotting directions to an address, 504
reviewing a business, 496
right-click menu, 491
road warnings, 504
Satellite view, 510
search categories, 500
search information, using, 494
Search nearby link, 495
search results, filtering, 499
searching by right-clicking a map location, 500
searching for a business or location, 493
selecting the map marker to enter Street view, 512
Set default location link, 492
Show Options link, 506
Street view, 512, 514
Suggested routes area, 505
Terrain view, 510
Traffic button, 502
uses for, 489
using overlays to display additional information, 507
viewing the details of a route, 506
viewing the next intersection, 507
What's here? option, 500
Write a review link, 497
zooming in and zooming out, 490
markers, large and small, 493
Microsoft Word format, 139, 150
Monetize this site button, 479
Month quick view, 383
My calendars, 382
My Folders option, 123

N

New Contact icon, 79
New Group icon, 79
New Page button, 557
New Post button, 549
Not Spam button, 78

Notification window, 523
number cells, 221
Number Format icon, 236

O

OpenID, 581
OpenOffice format, 139, 216
Operating Systems window list, 7
Other Bookmarks folder, 6
Other calendars, 382

P

Page creation tool, 557
Pages gadget, 558
panning, 489
password option bar, 11
Passwords and Exceptions dialog window, 12
PDF format, 216, 312
phishing, definition of, 42
Plain text link, 54
Post Office Protocol (POP) access, 101
Post Options link, 550
presentation area, 303
Presentations
    accessing a list of keyboard shortcuts, 305
    adding a title to a presentation, 315
    adding multilevel lists or bullet points to a text area, 331
    adding predefined shapes, 340
    adding speaker notes to a presentation, 349
    adding text to table cells, 343
    adding YouTube video clips to slides, 346
    adjusting a table's column width or row height, 343
    Adobe Presenter, 312
    altering the size of a text area, 321
    applying a different background color to a slide, 350
    Bullet point icon, 331

changing a text font and its size, 324
changing the background color of a section of text, 329
changing the default text formatting, 329
changing the layered order of objects, 338
changing the text alignment, 327
changing the text color, 328
Choose file button, 352
Choose slide layout dialog box, 318
choosing a background image for a slide, 350
choosing a theme, 350
Click to add title element, 315
closing a presentation, 306
converting downloaded presentations, 312
creating a first presentation, 314
creating a new presentation, 309
creating slides, best practices, 354-356
customizing a blank template, 318
default download area, 311
default opening slide's text areas, 315
Download as option, 311
downloading a presentation to a local computer, 311
Drawing toolbar, annotated illustration of, 341
duplicating a slide, 316
Edit menu, 303
entering a custom font size, 325
entering text into a text area, 319
file formats currently supported, 310-311
File menu, 303, 306
Fill color icon, 330
Format menu, 303

formatting text, 324
formatting the contents of a table cell, 345
getting online help for, 305
Google Docs Help Center, 305
Help menu, 303, 305
hexadecimal color format, 328
Insert image icon, 304
Insert menu, 303
Insert Shape menu, 340
Insert text icon, 304
inserting a freehand sketch or line art, 340
inserting a table into a slide, 343
inserting and deleting slides, 316
inserting images into a presentation, 334
keeping an image in scale when resizing, 337
Learn From Other Google Users option, 305
Link icon, 304
making a copy of a presentation before changing it, 307
menubar, list of pull-down menus, 303
Move slide down option, 333
Move slide up option, 333
moving a text area, 321
moving an image within a slide, 336
Numbered list icon, 331
Open option, 308
opening a presentation, 308
Order option, 338
overview of, 301
predefined shapes, inserting, 341
presentation area, 303
Presentations workspace, annotated illustration of, 302
Print icon, 304
Print Preview dialog box, 313

printing a presentation in PDF format, 313

rearranging the order of your slides, 332

Redo icon, 304

removing all formatting from the selected text, 325

renaming a presentation, 308

resizing a text area after moving, 322

resizing images, 336

restricting text within the page boundaries, 320

RGB color format, 328

Save and close option, 306

Save icon, 304, 307

saving a presentation, 306

Select video button, 347

Select Video dialog box, 346

selecting a layout for slides, 317

selecting a table column, 344

selecting multiple files for batch uploading, 310

selecting text, 323

Shapes option, 340

slide controls, 303, 316

Slide menu, 303, 317

slide overview list, 303

Speaker notes icon, 349

Start Presentation option, 353

superscript and subscript formatting, 327

Table menu, 303

Table option, 343

text area's drag points, 321

tips for presenting a slide show, 353

toolbar, annotated illustration of, 304

Undo icon, 304

Upload Files utility, 310

uploading a presentation, 309

uses for presentation software, 301

using large font sizes for slide visibility, 316

using numbered or bulleted points in a presentation, 315, 331

using the cut-and-paste functions to copy text, 323

using the PDF format for downloading a presentation, 312

View menu, 303

yellow highlighting of the current slide, 317

Preview template link, 429

public holidays, 382

Publish document button, 135

Publish Post button, 550

Q

Quick Sum, 252

R

Redo button, 210

Reload button, 6

Rename button, 127

Reply button, 59

RGB color format, 328

road warnings, 504

S

sandboxes and Chrome's protected environments, 1

Satellite view, 510

Save and close option, 213

Save now button, 550

search categories, 500

Search nearby link, 495

security certificates, 41

Select files to upload link, 133

Sender Policy Framework (SPF), 99

Sent Mail folder, 65

Set default location link, 492

Settings link, 91, 406

Share button, 116

Share this calendar link, 420

Share with others dialog box, 116

Sharing link, 480

sheet protection, 267
Show an additional time zone link, 410
Show cookies button, 17
Show formula bar option, 210
Show Search Options link, 397
site header, 437
Sitemap link, 464
Sites
    Add File dialog box, 469
    adding an action to a list, 473
    adding files through a Cabinet Page, 471
    adding links, 444
    adding text to table cells, 450
    adjusting a table's row height and column width, 451
    aligning images, 449
    annotated web page, illustration of, 436
    Automatically organize my navigation check box, 465
    Blank template, 429
    changing the background color of text, 443
    changing the current layout, 452
    changing the font selection and size, 441
    changing the site's theme, 476
    changing the text color, 442
    Choose File button, 447
    choosing a site name and URL, 430
    choosing a theme, 430
    Compare two versions link, 484
    comparing and restoring older versions of a site, 482
    Configure Navigation dialog box, 464
    configuring a calendar's appearance, 456
    configuring map properties, 460
    content text, changing, 437
    content title, 437
    Create Page button, 467
    Create site button, 428, 431
    creating a folder, 471
    creating a new web page, 466
    creating a site, 429
    customizing the site's layout, 476
    customizing the standard action list format, 474
    deleting an existing page, 475
    displaying a site on your own domain, 478
    Edit Item dialog box, 474
    edit mode menu and toolbars, illustration of, 439
    Edit page button, 435
    Edit sidebar link, 436, 463
    editing a site, 432
    editing the current page, 435
    embedded presentation objects, 459
    embedding a Google Document in a web page, 584
    embedding a Google Form in a web page, 591
    embedding a Google Map in a web page, 594
    embedding a Google Presentation in a web page, 592
    embedding a Google Spreadsheet as an editable list in a web page, 589
    embedding a Google Spreadsheet in a web page, 587
    embedding a shared Google Calendar in a web page, 594
    File Cabinet page, adding, 468
    formatting text in a content area, 439
    Get link to share dialog box, 590
    getting help for, 434
    Google Analytics, 486
    Google Sites Help Forum link, 434
    Google Spreadsheet Properties dialog box, 587

heading styles, 440
Help link, 434
Home page, 433
HTML code for embedding a
    Google Presentation in a
    non-Sites web page, 593
HTML markup, adding, 463
HTML source code, viewing and
    editing, 463
incorporating Google AdSense
    into your web site, 478
initial setup screen, illustration
    of, 429
Insert Google Document dialog
    box, 584
Insert menu, 454
inserting a calendar, 455
inserting a map, 460
inserting an image into a
    content area, 447
inserting documents,
    spreadsheets,
    presentations and forms,
    458
inserting table columns or
    rows, 451
inserting tables, 450
inserting various elements and
    objects, 454
launching, 427
Layout menu, 453
limitations on free user
    accounts, 486
Link icon, 445
Link to this URL text box, 446
List page, adding, 472
loading an image from the web,
    448
Make calendar public dialog
    box, 595
making a web site private, 480
managing your web site, 476
Monetize this site button, 479
options for sharing your web
    site, 480
overview of, 427
owners, collaborators, and
    viewers, 481

page templates, using, 466
Preview template link, 429
Publish this presentation dialog
    box, 593
publishing a Google Document
    as a web page, 586
publishing a single worksheet in
    a spreadsheet, 589
ranking a page as subordinate
    to another page, 467
removing all text formatting,
    444
Revert to this version link, 485
revision history, 482
Save button, 444
saving a backup copy of your
    web site on a local
    computer, 485
saving all current editing
    changes, 444
setting up numbered and
    bulleted lists, 443
Share this calendar option, 595
sharing a spreadsheet with a
    collaborator, 588
Sharing link, 480
sidebar link, adding, 466
sidebar, adding items to, 464
sidebar, editing, 436, 463
sidebar, removing, 464
site header, 437
Sitemap link, 464
template gallery, using, 429
template, choosing, 429
tips for creating good web
    sites, 487
transferring ownership of a
    site, 486
typing the CAPTCHA code, 431
undo and redo options, 439
Upload button, 470
using Google Documents as a
    document management
    tool, 586
using sheet protection on
    embedded spreadsheets,
    591

using to integrate Google Apps, 584

word-wrapping images, 449

slide controls, 303, 316

slide overview list, 303

SMS (text) messages, 517

Solve tool, 277

sort bar, 211, 275, 292

spam filtration system, 45, 77

speaker notes, 349

spell checker, 55

Spreadsheets

3-D charts, 286

absolute cell references, 263

adding multiple rows or columns, 229

adding rows or columns, 228

advanced formulas, using, 294

annotated illustration of the Spreadsheets environment, 209

applying conditional formatting to cells, 272

applying data validation criteria to cells, 269

assigning labels to chart elements, 287

Auto-Fill feature, 258

auto-saving of documents, 214

auto-type detection, 220

auto-wrapping text in a cell, 225

Bar chart type, 285

basic types of cells, 220

building formulas using mathematical and financial functions, 249

cell ranges, 223

cell references, 223

Change colors based on rules dialog box, 272

changing basic settings, 219

changing the background color of a cell or cell range, 235

changing the date inside a cell, 242

changing the font of a cell or cell range, 232

changing the text color, 234

Chart API, 283

chart types, selecting, 285

closing documents, 213

column and row numbers, 209

Column chart type, 285

copying and pasting formulas, 247

Create chart dialog box, 284

creating simple formulas, 246

currency format, 239

cutting and pasting cells, 224

Data validation dialog box, 269

date and time formats, 240

Define new range option, 265

deleting cell contents, 227

deleting rows or columns, 230

document functions, overview of, 213

Download as option, 216

edit mode, 221

editing a cell's formula, 254

entering and editing data in cells, 221

Excel format, 216

Export to PDF dialog box, 217–218

File menu, 213

financial format, 238

formatting cells, 231

formatting number (numeric) cells, 236

formatting standard numbers, 238

formula bar, turning on, 210

formula basics, 244

Formula button, 249

formula cells, 221

formula, definition of, 245

freezing rows or columns, 275

Future Value function, 256

Gadget Selection dialog box, 281

getting online help, 211

Google Docs Help Center, 211

GoogleFinance function, 298

grouping chart data, 286

grouping parts of mathematical calculations, 245
HTML format, 217
IF function, 294
import formats, 216
importing a spreadsheet saved on your computer, 215
Insert a function dialog box, 255
inserting a chart, 284
inserting a pie chart, 288
inserting gadgets into a spreadsheet, 280
Learn From Other Google Users option, 212
learning about chart elements, 285
list of functions by category, 255
looking up stock quotes online, 298
major elements of, 209
making a copy of a spreadsheet before changing, 214
menubar, 209
merging adjacent cells horizontally, 226
moving between cells, 222
named ranges, 265
number cells, 221
Number Format icon, 236
Open a spreadsheet dialog box, 215
Open option, 215
opening documents, 215
OpenOffice format, 216
overview of, 207
PDF format, 216
percent format, 239
positioning, resizing and editing charts, 291
previewing a chart, 287
printing spreadsheets by exporting to PDF, 218
Protect sheet dialog box, 267
Quick Sum feature, 252
Range names dialog box, 265
Redo button, 210

resizing cells for formatting purposes, 243
resizing the text in a cell, 233
restricting access to a worksheet, 267
Save and close option, 213
Save spreadsheet as dialog box, 214
saving a document locally, 216
saving documents, 213
scrolling within a spreadsheet, 209
selecting a cell or cell range, 224
selecting a cell range without dragging, 224
selecting a chart's data range, 286
selecting criteria for data validation, 270
setting the numeric scaling for a chart axis, 287
sheet protection options, 267
Show formula bar option, 210
Solve tool, using, 277
sort bar, 211, 275, 292
sorting a column, 292
Spreadsheet settings option, 219
SUM function, 250
symbols used for the standard mathematical operations, 245
text cells, 220
Timeline gadget, adding, 281
toolbar with groupings, illustration of, 210
Undo button, 210
using basic spreadsheet functionality, 219
using brackets in formulas, 247
using cell ranges in formulas, 251
using cell references between worksheets, 262
using percentages, 253
using the equal sign in formula, 245

VLOOKUP function, 296
working with multiple
    worksheets, 261
standard dictionary, adding a word
    to, 195
Starred folder, 71
Street view, 512, 514
SUM function, 250
system labels, list of, 73

T

Talk
    Account settings button, 534
    Add button, 519
    adding contacts, 519
    Appearance button, 538
    audio settings, changing, 536
    audio, troubleshooting, 537
    blocking contacts, 529
    Call button, 527
    call notification, 528
    Change Font button, 534
    Chat settings, 535
    Chat window, opening, 522
    Chat window, switching to, 523
    Choose from my contacts...
        button, 520
    communicating with contacts
        by voice, 527
    contact list and Gmail contacts,
        519
    creating log files, 535
    default font, changing, 534
    downloading and installing, 518
    Enable diagnostic logging
        button, 535
    End Call button, 529
    going off the record, 532
    Instant Messaging (IM),
        guidelines for using safely,
        521
    Instant Messaging (IM), origin
        of, 517
    integration with Gmail, 517
    interacting with contacts from
        the Chat window, 526

    logging chat history in Gmail,
        535
    logon prompt, 518
    microphone and speakers,
        adjusting, 537
    muting chat, 529
    Notification window, 523
    personalizing with a display
        picture, 524
    preferences, settings, 533
    receiving a file transfer
        request, 527
    responding to a friend request,
        521
    right-click menu, 525
    sending files, 526
    Settings menu, list of options,
        533
    SMS (text) messages, 517
    themes, changing, 539
    unblocking contacts, 530
    viewing your chat history with a
        contact, 531
Terrain view, 510
text cells, 220
Theme select page, 545
themes, accessing, 33
Themes tab, 105
three-digit time codes, using, 396
time chooser, 389
Timeline gadget, 281
Today link, 604
Traffic button, 502
Trash folder, 68
    Empty trash button, 128
    emptying, 127
    Trash for everyone button, 129
    Undelete button, 128
    undeleting a file, 128

U

Undelete button, 128
Undo button, 210
Upload button, 133
user labels, 73

V

vacation responder, creating, 93
VLOOKUP function, 296

W

WinRar, 149
WinZip, 149
WS02 cloud identity management
    system, 614

Y

YouTube, 36, 143

Z

Zip files, 149
Zoom menu, 18
zooming, 490

You Need the Companion eBook